D1479067

Nasser

A Political Biography

Robert Stephens

SIMON AND SCHUSTER   NEW YORK

Acknowledgements

Many people in the Middle East and elsewhere – political leaders, ministers, officials, soldiers, scholars, colleagues and friends, including the late President Nasser – gave me valuable help directly or indirectly in the writing of this book. I am deeply grateful to all of them, but I would particularly like to thank Mohammed Hassanein Heykal, editor-in-chief of *Al Ahram*, for his generous help, advice and information; Ahmed Baha' ed-din, editor-in-chief of *Al Mussawar* and *Dar el Hilal* publications, for general good advice; the UAR Information Department in Cairo and the London embassies of the UAR, Jordan and Israel; King Hussein of Jordan, Salah ed-din el Bitar, Abdullah Mohammed Nomaan, Khaled Mohieddin, Yigal Allon, Lord Robertson of Oakridge, Sir Ralph Stevenson and General Rikhye for their help in clarifying various points; and Walid el Khalidi, Abdul Rahman Bushnaq, Albert Hourani, Tom Little and my colleagues on the *Observer*, Patrick Seale, Gavin Young and Colin Legum, for their friendly enlightenment on Middle Eastern affairs over many years. Needless to say, except where otherwise stated, those named above are not responsible for the opinions and conclusions expressed in the following pages, which are my own.

Contents

Contents

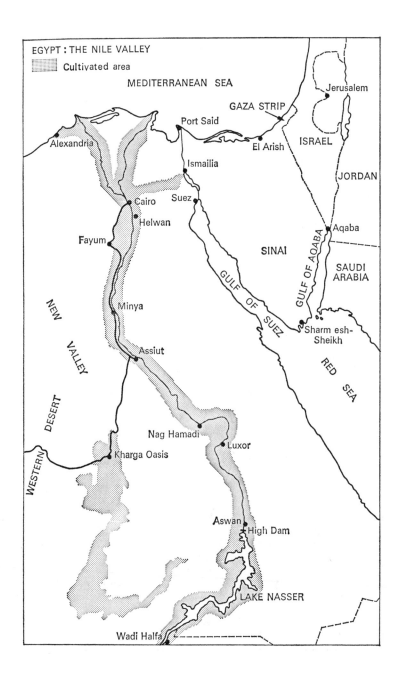

EGYPT : THE NILE VALLEY

Cultivated area

MEDITERRANEAN SEA

Jerusalem

GAZA STRIP

Port Said

ISRAEL

Alexandria

El Arish

Ismailia

JORDAN

Cairo   Suez

Helwan

Aqaba

Fayum

SINAI

GULF OF AQABA

SAUDI
ARABIA

NEW

Minya

GULF OF SUEZ

Assiut

VALLEY

Sharm esh-
Sheikh

RED   SEA

DESERT

Nag Hamadi

WESTERN

Luxor

Kharga Oasis

Aswan

High Dam

LAKE NASSER

Wadi Halfa

PALESTINE AND ISRAEL

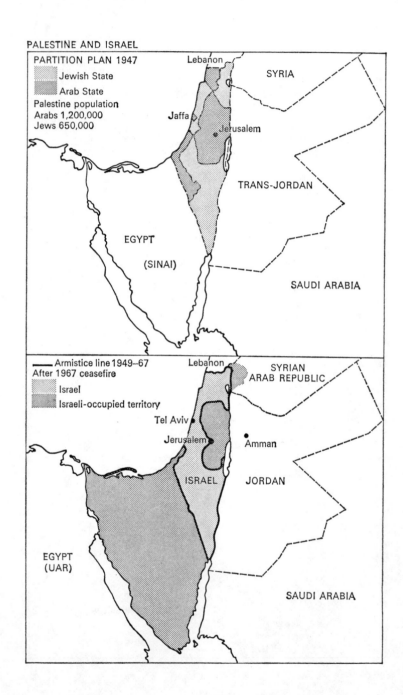

PARTITION PLAN 1947
  Jewish State
  Arab State
Palestine population
Arabs 1,200,000
Jews 650,000

Lebanon
SYRIA
Jaffa
Jerusalem
TRANS-JORDAN
EGYPT
(SINAI)
SAUDI ARABIA

—— Armistice line 1949–67
After 1967 ceasefire
  Israel
  Israeli-occupied territory

Lebanon
SYRIAN ARAB REPUBLIC
Tel Aviv
Jerusalem
Amman
ISRAEL
JORDAN
EGYPT
(UAR)
SAUDI ARABIA

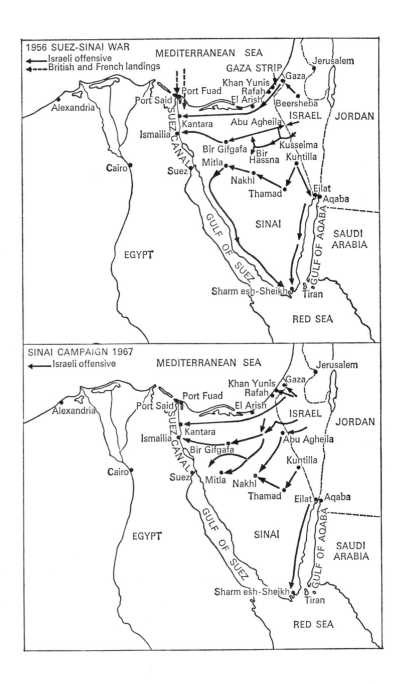

1956 SUEZ-SINAI WAR
← Israeli offensive
←--- British and French landings

MEDITERRANEAN SEA

Jerusalem

GAZA STRIP
Gaza
Khan Yunis
Rafah
El Arish
Beersheba
Port Fuad
Port Said
Alexandria
Kantara
Abu Agheila
ISRAEL
JORDAN
Ismailia
Bir Gifgafa
Bir Hassna
Kusseima
Kuntilla
Mitla
Suez
Nakhl
Thamad
Eilat
Aqaba
SINAI
SAUDI ARABIA
EGYPT
Cairo
SUEZ CANAL
GULF OF SUEZ
GULF OF AQABA
Sharm esh-Sheikh
Tiran
RED SEA

SINAI CAMPAIGN 1967
← Israeli offensive

MEDITERRANEAN SEA

Jerusalem

Khan Yunis
Gaza
Rafah
Port Fuad
El Arish
Port Said
Alexandria
ISRAEL
JORDAN
Kantara
Ismailia
Abu Agheila
Bir Gifgafa
Kuntilla
Cairo
Suez
Mitla
Nakhl
Thamad
Eilat
Aqaba
SINAI
SAUDI ARABIA
EGYPT
SUEZ CANAL
GULF OF SUEZ
GULF OF AQABA
Sharm esh-Sheikh
Tiran
RED SEA

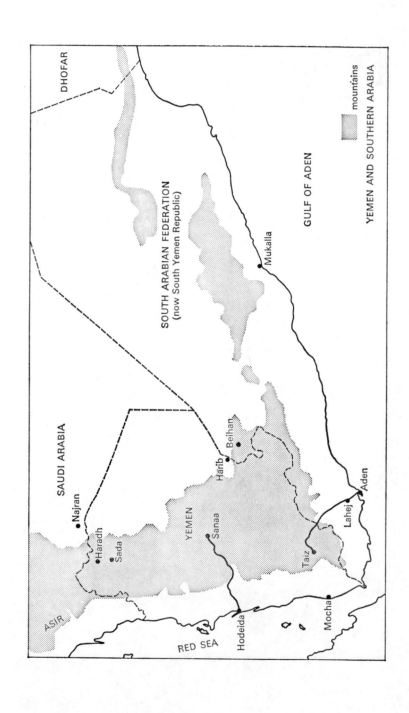

DHOFAR

SOUTH ARABIAN FEDERATION
(now South Yemen Republic)

GULF OF ADEN

Mukalla

SAUDI ARABIA

Najran

Beihan

Härib

Haradh
Sada

YEMEN

Sanaa

Aden

Lahej

Taiz

ASIR

Mocha

Hodeida

RED SEA

mountains

YEMEN AND SOUTHERN ARABIA

Nasser

A Political Biography

Prologue

President Nasser's sudden death in September 1970 at the age of fifty-two had an international impact the scale of which reflected both his own political stature and the critical state of affairs in the Middle East and the Arab world, which he had dominated for eighteen years.

The aim of this book is to give a coherent account of Nasser's life and career for the general reader and to describe the historical circumstances which helped to form his political character and ideas. It will also try to distinguish what, if anything, was his own distinctive contribution to political thought or practice. Because it deals with such recent history, it obviously cannot be more than an interim study.

In January 1967 when Nasser had just entered his fiftieth year and had already been ruling Egypt for thirteen years, I went to see him in Cairo. It was my third meeting with him, the previous occasions being in 1955 and 1964 (I saw him for the last time in July 1969, the year before he died). Like the earlier meetings this one took place at his house at Manshiet el Bakr on the outskirts of the Egyptian capital, an expanded version of the suburban villa he occupied as a lieutenant-colonel. He received me without fuss in the small formal drawing room where he usually saw journalists. Its Louis XV-type furniture and chandeliers – conventional official style and the norm of aspiring Egyptian bourgeois taste – and signed photographs of other statesmen, with Nehru and Tito in pride of place, were described in many newspaper interviews.

As usual, Nasser gave the impression of self-contained energy and considerable stature, not only in physique but also in personality. His tall, heavy body with its deep chest and wide shoulders was thickening with middle-age but not ponderously so. His black crinkly hair was greying slightly at the temples. His habit of crouching in his seat and pushing his head well forward from his powerful neck gave an extra thrust to his broad jutting jaw. His large, pale and dark-rimmed brown eyes stared widely open, cool and curious, observant rather than penetrating, and with a hint of melancholy and irony. He was courteous but reserved, listened intently to questions and answered succinctly. He had the switch-on-and-off attention of the busy leader, conserving his energies and caring less than in previous years about charming his listener, hardened to the buffets of hostile opinion and absorbed with an endless round of practical business. He seemed more relaxed, more subdued and more formidable.

My mind went back to our first meeting in 1955. Then he received me in a white, open-necked shirt and sandals, in his study. The table by his desk was piled high with foreign newspapers and magazines. Reading them was always a habit with him, a hobby, almost an obsession. On top of the pile was the British *New Statesman*. He had been working until three that morning but seemed fresh and eager to talk. He usually worked long hours, in intense bursts of energy and then, nearing exhaustion, would break off and relax completely.

In the 1967 meeting we talked for an hour or so, together with the editor of the Cairo newspaper *Al Ahram*, Mohammed Hassanein Heykal, his close friend and confidant. The main subject of my questions at that time was the situation in South Arabia, Aden and the Yemen, which had once more envenomed Anglo-Egyptian relations. But when I asked him what was his most pressing problem of the moment he replied at once: 'The fact that another 175,000 people will be born in this country this month and have to be fed.' The Arab dispute with Israel was touched on only briefly: it did not at that time appear to cause Nasser much concern. Either my impression was false or he was mistaken.

Five months later, on the evening of 9 June 1967, in a broadcast from Cairo to the Egyptian people, Nasser announced his decision to resign from all his official and political functions. He was ready, he said, to assume 'entire responsibility' for the disastrous defeat (which he called 'the setback') that Egypt's armed forces had just suffered at the hands of Israel. But by the next day, Nasser produced one of those dramatic turn-abouts, such as his overthrow of General Neguib in 1954, that marked his career. He was re-established in power by a wave of deep and spontaneous mass emotion that produced popular demonstrations not only throughout Egypt but over most of the Arab world. Just over three years later, as this book was being completed, he died but Egypt and Israel were not yet at peace.

Nasser, who had a sense of humour, might have been wrily amused at the fulsomeness of some of the tributes paid to him after his death, especially in Western countries. For in his lifetime, as he himself knew, he was a man who evoked strong and conflicting feelings. Attitudes towards him varied between eulogy and execration. To some he was a nationalist hero: to others he was an inflated, war-mongering dictator.

While Nasser was first of all himself, a complex and perhaps tragic human being with a subtle political mind, he was deeply influenced by the historical and cultural framework within which he operated. An Egyptian, a Muslim and a self-proclaimed Arab, he was also essentially a revolutionary of the Third World. He was a product and animator of the same anti-colonial and anti-imperialist revolution that produced Nehru and Mao Tse-tung, Sukarno and Nkrumah, Castro and Ho Chi Minh.

To be born an Egyptian is to be the heir to sixty centuries of glory and of pain. To be a Muslim in the twentieth century is to be a member of a still living faith and of a society which is passing through a deep spiritual crisis. To consider oneself an Arab is to feel part of a world civilization, like that of China or India, which is struggling to reassert its identity and restore a legendary unity and vigour. To grow up a man of spirit and ambition in an Afro-Asian country in the first half of this century was to suffer from the humiliation of poverty, backwardness and political dependence and to experience an irresistible urge to try to overcome it.

The convulsions caused by the Afro-Asian anti-imperialist revolution have been severe and prolonged in the Middle East because they coincided there with two other powerful conflicts: the confrontation of the United States and Russia in strategically important areas where European empires once dominated and a unique and tragic clash between two re-emerging cultures, the Arab and the Jewish national revivals. In the Middle East since the Second World War a dozen new Arab nations and Israel have emerged as independent states. Their relations with one another, and with the Great Powers competing for influence among them, have produced a succession of international crises and continuous minor upheavals which have filled the newspaper headlines. Within these new states there have also been more fundamental social and economic changes which have been rarely or only perfunctorily reported.

These often violent developments have taken place against a background broader in space and time than the modern Middle East. They have been part of the tense interaction which began at the end of the eighteenth century between Western military power and industrial society on the one hand and the ancient but technically underdeveloped civilizations of Islam and the Afro-Asian world on the other. Because of their geographical position linking Europe, Asia and Africa and their close historical and cultural ties with Europe, the Middle East countries have been deeply and continuously involved in this process. Egypt above all was early and profoundly affected.

Egypt's evolution has been important to others besides herself, because she is the centre of Muslim orthodoxy, the largest Arabic-speaking country and an influence in Africa. Her modern history is a classic example of the virtues and vices of Western military and economic imperialism.

*

As an Egyptian, Nasser was a citizen of the oldest continuously organized and unified state in the world. He was the latest in a line of rulers which included many great names and stretched back to the first Pharaohs 3,500 years before the Christian era.

Among the inhuman miseries in which many Egyptians have had to live in modern times, it is easy to forget Egypt's amazing past. Yet how extraordinary it was. Of the Egyptian Old Kingdom, Breasted wrote,

To us it has left the imposing line of temples, tombs and pyramids, stretching for many miles along the margin of the western desert, the most eloquent witnesses of the fine intelligence and titanic energies of the men who made the Old Kingdom what it was; not alone in achieving these wonders of mechanics and internal organization, but building the earliest known sea-going ships and exploring unknown waters or pushing their commercial enterprises far up the Nile into inner Africa. In plastic art they had reached the highest achievement; in architecture their tireless genius had created the column and originated the colonnade; in government they had elaborated an enlightened and highly developed state, with a large body of law; in religion they were already dimly conscious of a judgment in the hereafter, and they were thus the first men whose ethical intuitions made happiness in the future life dependent upon character. Everywhere their unspent energies unfolded in a rich and manifold culture which left the world such a priceless heritage as no nation had yet bequeathed it.[1]

Nasser was the first native ruler of an independent Egypt since the Persian invaders destroyed the twenty-sixth and last Pharaonic dynasty in 525 B.C. In the intervening twenty-five centuries Nasser's predecessors were Persians, Macedonian Greeks, Romans, Byzantines, Arabs, Turks, Mamelukes (slave soldiers, usually Circassian), French, Turco-Albanian and British. Little that influences modern Egypt's culture or political thought has survived directly from the Greco-Roman period. Nor, except for the traditions of the three-million-strong Coptic minority, have Egypt's centuries of Christianity left much mark. But from Pharaonic times there has persisted a necessary tradition of a strongly organized central government and bureaucracy capable of ensuring the maintenance of the Nile irrigation works without which Egypt could not live. The compactness of the long narrow Nile valley and its isolation from the outside world by deserts and seas make rebellion difficult to sustain and thus facilitated the autocratic rule of a unified country. It also made it easy for foreign conquerors to dominate the whole country once they had broken through its natural frontiers.

The conquerors who left the most lasting imprint were the proselytizing Muslim Arabs of the seventh century. They brought not only the Islamic religion and Arabic language, which have been the dominant elements in Egyptian culture ever since, but also a political philosophy and social system which held un-challenged sway as an ideal, if not always applied in practice, until Napoleon violently threw open the gates of Egypt to Euro-pean civilization at the end of the eighteenth century. Napoleon and his train of French scholars found an Egypt impoverished, debased and enslaved by five centuries of Mameluke rule. The Mamelukes, a military slave caste who seized power from their masters and themselves later acknowledged Turkish suzerainty, had followed the glittering medieval Arab empires of Saladin and the Fatimids. These empires had represented the high noon of Islamic civilization in Egypt when Cairo became not only the chief Egyptian city but also a great imperial capital casting, like Constantinople or Vienna, a glow far beyond its immediate national frontiers. Cairo has never entirely lost this imperial character. Even today if one stands, for example, on the roof of the ninth-century Ibn Tulun mosque, lifts one's eyes from the silent, massive cloisters below to the surrounding minarets, palaces and towers and looks across the vast, murmuring city to the Gizeh pyramids as solid as geometry on the desert horizon, this sense of past empire is almost palpable.

*

Napoleon's arrival brought to Egypt both an awakening and a resistance to the Western world. For his expedition was not an altruistic civilizing mission but an act of conquest: it marked the recognition by a European military genius of Egypt's strategic importance in the unfolding pattern of European empire in India and the Far East. From Napoleon onwards Egypt was preoccu-pied with what is still her central dilemma and the dilemma of most of the 'Third World' of Asian and African countries. They all have to determine how to modernize their societies without losing either their political independence or their own cultural character. They have to find means of benefiting from Western scientific and industrial civilization without being disrupted, swamped or ruled by it.

During the nineteenth century and the beginning of the twen-tieth, Muslim Egypt's reaction to the increasing impact of Western ideas produced three different schools of thought. Between those who would swallow European civilization whole and those who recoiled into a lost golden age of medieval Islam, the third school believed it must be possible to reform the social practices of Islam, so that the benefits of European civilization could be adopted while preserving Muslim moral and ethical principles. The middle way was developed most influentially by Sheikh Mohammed Abdu who began as one of the disciples of the pan-Islamic revolutionary, Jamal ed-din al Afghani, and became 'the most important thinker produced by modern Egypt'.[2] The thought of Mohammed Abdu was the spiritual source of the mainstream of Egyptian nationalism, which flowed from the unsuccessful revolt against the Khedive and his European advisers led by Colonel Arabi in 1881-2 (though Abdu disapproved of Arabi's action) through the partially successful campaigns of the Wafd, Egypt's main modern nationalist party, between the two world wars, and eventually to the army revolution of 1952 onwards led by Nasser.

In this part of Nasser's intellectual and political heritage as an Egyptian and Muslim leader, the Islamic elements were matters both of principle and of tone. Mohammed Abdu and his followers had specially singled out from the mass of traditional customs and beliefs which formed the surface of Islam, the ideal of social responsibility, of the just ruler in tune with the moral consensus of the community. The tone of their ideas was egalitarian and puritan, but tolerant and pragmatic.

The two ideals of national freedom and social reform or modernization which the impact of Westernism had inspired did not always go easily hand in hand. The technical modernization of Egypt had begun under Mohammed Ali. An Albanian soldier-adventurer who stood only for the independence of his personal fief from his nominal overlord, the Turkish Sultan, he was, for the Egyptians, a foreign ruler. The frantic and extravagant attempt of the Khedive Ismail to accelerate the modernization of Egypt led to the reimposition of foreign control, this time not from Constantinople but from Egypt's European creditors acting through Britain. It was the British army, sent by Gladstone, which intervened to crush the revolt led by Arabi against the Khedive and his European supervisors.

The failure of the Arabi revolt and the unexpectedly prolonged British occupation of Egypt to which it led, switched the emphasis in the Egyptian national movement back for a time to modernization rather than freedom. But beneath the surface the national revolution was gathering strength for a new outbreak.

New revolutionary national forces were also emerging in other Muslim countries and in other parts of the East. The Young Turks had seized control of the Ottoman empire; in Iran another old empire faced the challenge of constitutional reform; in China the most ancient empire of all had been overthrown by revolution; while Japan had shown in her war with Russia that an Eastern country could learn the secrets of European power well enough to defeat a great European state.

All these trends at home and abroad were accelerated by the First World War. In Egypt there were some specific material reasons (conscription, requisitioning and the rising cost of living) for discontent. Above all, the war created a new political climate. It speeded up the collapse of empires and the reawakening of the East. The fearful mass slaughter by Europeans of each other and the destruction of the Austro-Hungarian and Russian empires showed that European civilization, so long regarded as a paragon of wisdom and power, was also capable of the utmost cruelty, folly and weakness. But the advent in the world arena of the United States and the Wilsonian philosophy of national self-determination seemed to bring a new hope of sanity and freedom. Britain and France had already promised independence to the Arabs in revolt against the Turks and foreshadowed the creation of new Balkan states. By the end of the war the Middle East was thick with promises – some of them conflicting and laden with future tragedy, such as the promise in the Balfour Declaration of 1917 to the Zionists of a Jewish National Home in Palestine and the pledges to the Arabs which were reconcilable only by the most subtle diplomatic casuistry. It soon became clear that in other ways, too, the promises were not quite what they seemed. France and Britain were discovering new political formulae for extending their empires. The imperial compromise of the age was to be a system of shadow empire: mandates, treaties, protectorates, instead of outright colonies or imperial dependencies.

But the treatment of Egypt was at first in sharp contrast with that of the rest of the Middle East. While others were at least promised independence, Egypt's political status became more primitively subservient. The Khedive had been brusquely dismissed and replaced, and Egypt became a British Protectorate in name as well as fact. Her spokesmen, whether official or unofficial, were denied the right to present her case to the Versailles Peace Conference or even to the British government in London.

This political disillusion and social and economic discontent produced a ferment which needed only a leader to give it revolutionary force. The leader who arose was Saad Zaghloul Pasha, founder of the Wafd, the great national party of pre-Nasserite Egypt, the equivalent of the Indian National Congress. He was in 1918 a fifty-eight-year-old former judge and minister. After imprisonment in his youth as an Arabi supporter, he had for long been a moderate reformer, a disciple of Abdu and a protégé of the great British pro-consul, Lord Cromer. Zaghloul led the post-war movement to obtain recognition of Egypt's claims to national independence. The British rejection of these claims led to the explosion in 1919 of a revolution in Egypt – a resumption of Arabi's national revolt – which continued sporadically until, after Nasser's *coup* in 1952, national independence from Britain was finally completed in 1956.

*

The 1919 revolution was a purely Egyptian affair, but it was a symptom of the state of the whole Muslim world and coincided with a wider national movement in other Arab countries. 'Arabism', the sense of Arab cultural unity and the political consequences that flow from it, has never been a negligible part of Egypt's national consciousness, though it has become an active element of her national policy only in recent years. Apart from Egypt's use of the Arabic language, there is the Arab tradition interwoven with the history of Islam, since Arabic is the language of the Koran and of the Prophet and the Arabs were the instruments for the spread of Islam. The medieval Arab empires briefly centred in Cairo, under the Fatimids and the great Saladin, have left the legend not only of the final repulse of the Crusades but also the visible monuments of the second Golden Age of Egypt's history after the Pharoahs and before the dark centuries of the Mamelukes.

Mohammed Ali's campaigns in Syria and Arabia in the early nineteenth century might be claimed as showing some recognition of a nascent Arab nationalism and of its possible importance to Egypt. Soon afterwards an Arab cultural revival began with a link between its two main centres of Beirut and Cairo. But it was only in the early twentieth century that this movement began to crystallize into an assertion of Arab nationhood and a demand for political independence.

Arab nationalism in its modern form first emerged as an anti-Turkish movement of the Asian Arab provinces of the Ottoman empire. Its first aim was an independent Arab state built round historical Syria (which included not only present-day Syria but also what became known as Palestine, Lebanon and Trans-jordan) together with Iraq and the Hejaz. The inner deserts of Arabia were to be left, as they had always been, to their local sultans and Bedouin chieftains. The idea of a wider Arab unity, embracing all the Arab-speaking countries including Egypt and North Africa, which Nasser came to symbolize, was a later development.

Despite their cultural links, the Egyptian and Arab national movements remained at first politically distinct. It was not until the 1930s, with the growth of the Arab–Jewish conflict in Palestine and the Italian colonial repression in Libya, that Egyptian nationalists or Egyptian government policy began to take a closer interest in Arab affairs. It was not for another ten years, during the last years of the Second World War, when more Arab states had attained independence, that Egypt began to think of herself seriously as politically part of a larger Arab grouping.

*

The First World War brought European domination of the Arab and Muslim worlds to its highest point. Paradoxically it also marked the beginning of the breakdown of European imperialism. With the collapse of the Ottoman empire, the chief bastion of Islam, since the fall of the Moguls in India, European control was extended over Muslim countries from Morocco to Indonesia. At first it seemed as if only Kemalist Turkey in a desperate rally, Reza Shah in Iran, and Ibn Saud sallying out of the Arabian desert were able to stem this spreading European tide. But it was an illusion. The seeds of decay of this vast European empire were already germinating, planted not only by a greedy overstretching of European Powers weakened by the world war, but also by Europe's virtues, the spread of ideas and knowledge which were the basis of its ephemerally superior power. The Egyptian revolution of 1919 was something of a harbinger and a model for the anti-colonial revolution that was eventually to sweep through India, Burma, Ceylon, Indonesia, Indochina and later Africa.

Nasser's own life and political career thus spanned years of tremendous revolutionary change in his own country, in the Middle East and the world as a whole. The Egypt into which he was born was on the eve of a national explosion which within a year or two forced from the British at least a nominal recognition of Egyptian statehood. But it was not until thirty-eight years later that the last British troops withdrew from Egypt and Nasser became president of a country which Egyptians felt for the first time to be really independent. This was, of course, not the solution of Egypt's other pressing problems of poverty and political and social progress, or even of her external problems. It was only the beginning of an opportunity for her to try to solve them in her own way.

Part One

The Egyptian Revolution

Chapter 1

A Troubled Youth, 1918–36

Gamal Abdul Nasser* was born on 15 January 1918 in Alexandria, Egypt's second city, chief port and commercial centre, where his father worked as a post office clerk. He was the first child of a family which was eventually to number eleven children (ten of them sons) from two successive wives.

For most of his life Nasser lived and was educated in big cities, Alexandria and Cairo, but his family was from the country and, like many Egyptian town families, maintained close rural connexions. He lived for some years until he was eight in a small township in the Nile Delta, and spent holidays in his father's native village in Upper Egypt. His father, Abdul Nasser Hussein, had been born thirty years before into a modest but, by Egyptian rural standards, comparatively well-off peasant (fellah) family in the village of Beni Murr, near the west bank of the Nile, some three miles from the large town of Assiut.

From Alexandria to Beni Murr is a distance of some 500 miles down the Nile Valley, that long green streak between vast expanses of naked brown desert and rock that is the miraculous human heart of Egypt. After the agricultural slum of the Delta with Cairo and its pyramids, imperial minarets and factory chimneys at its apex, the train rolls slowly for 250 miles down to Assiut through the narrow valley, between the Nile itself and the Ismail Pasha Canal, the longest canal in the world. The landscape rarely changes but is full of movement and life. In Egypt 'man saturates Nature'[1] as nowhere else in the world. Across the flat valley stretches a patchwork of closely cultivated small fields, like market garden allotments, interspersed with palm trees, thick plantations of sharp green sugar cane or tall rustling maize. Villages of brown mud houses lie as close as single farmsteads in a European landscape and many of them crowd the population of a small market town into an area less than that of an English hamlet.

Brown-skinned peasants in the dull grey or blue gallebyah or

*'Abdul Nasser' means 'servant of the victorious one'.

robe are bent laboriously over mattock or hoe in the fierce sun or rest in the shade squatting on their heels. Sometimes on one side of the valley a long range of granite cliffs or low crumbling sandstone hills and on the other, beyond the green, a clean edge of desert sand.

The landscape begins to vary slightly as you travel farther south. There are more rich orchards and orange groves and along the raised canal bank a classic frieze of Egyptian country life. Turbanned men and black-robed women pass briskly on donkeys. Camels, with only their necks peering forward wildly out of great bundles of dried sugar cane stalks on their backs, lurch along like huge thatched tortoises. Boys with shepherds' pipes and flocks of sheep and goats step in single file delicately and nimbly along the canal and river banks, and the strange and precious gamoose or water buffalo, grey and hairless like a giant wood louse, lifts it obstinate head. The evening is magical: calm silver canal, dark trees and people, deep pearl and pink haze on the horizon.

Apart from its fresh water, electricity pylons and telephone, and the nearby primary school and social welfare centre serving the district as a whole, Beni Murr probably does not look much different today from what it did when Nasser spent holidays there as a child. The rough road approaching it runs beside a small canal, through palm groves, and past high fences of brown dried maize stalks. The unpaved dusty streets, full of children playing, twist between large two-storey houses of reddish mudbrick with tall carved wooden doors. At the beginning of the century some 2,000 people lived there, but today its population is about 6,000, including some Coptic Christians as well as the Muslim majority, who have to support themselves off little more than 2,000 acres of land.

According to local tradition the village got its name from the Beni Murr tribe which came from Hejaz in Arabia and settled there, presumably during the Arab conquest of Egypt in the seventh century. The old tribal motto is said to be 'We never attack unless attacked'. But Nasser's family, one of the big family groups or clans which traditionally dominate Egyptian villages, each long-established in its own quarter, came to Beni Murr about 200 years ago. Nasser's grandfather, Hussein Khalil, was a lusty peasant who lived to be 107, married his third wife when he was sixty-five and had his third child by her when he was ninety. This uncle of Nasser's, Taha Hussein, a gentle, handsome man, probably younger than was Nasser himself, still works as a farmer in Beni Murr, as does another older uncle, Atiah. They each own about seven acres. Nasser's father (who died in 1968) was one of seven children, six sons and a daughter. He was born in 1888 and after a year learning to read and write at the new Koranic school in the village, set up in a room next door to the mosque provided by the private initiative of the village families, he was sent at the age of thirteen to a Coptic school in nearby Assiut. The pressure on increasingly scarce land meant that even families like Nasser's with more than average land holdings had to find jobs elsewhere for some of their sons. To become a government official or a religious teacher were the most prized ways to both economic security and higher status, in a traditionally bureaucratic and theocratic society. Armed with a 'diploma', the precious certificate of elementary studies, Abdul Nasser Hussein was able to secure a job in the postal service. At the outbreak of the First World War he was sent to Alexandria to be sub-postmaster in a suburban district. It was a lucky first assignment. The big, cosmopolitan city was full of novelty and excitement for a young man, but it was also the home of relatives from Upper Egypt who could provide some security and a sense of continuity. Throughout the nineteenth century, as it grew from an almost derelict township of 8,000 to a flourishing modern city of half a million, Alexandria's expanding industries and business activities had attracted not only thousands of European and Levantine merchants who dominated its commerce and trade, but also a stream of migrant workers from the Egyptian peasantry, including a substantial community from Upper Egypt.

It was from among this community that Nasser's father found a wife. He was married in 1917 to the daughter of a successful contractor and coal merchant, Mohammed Hammad, originally from Mellawi in the Upper Egyptian province of Miniah, and a family friend. Nasser's mother, who seems to have had a stronger influence on him than his father, perhaps transmitted to him some of her family's shrewd business acumen. Brought up in

Alexandria, she may have had a more lively and sophisticated personality than his village-bred father. The Upper Egyptians or Saidis, as their compatriots call them, have a reputation for manliness, hard work, shrewdness and a stubborn down-to-earth quality which has caused them to be described as the Yorkshiremen or Texans of Egypt. Perhaps a more apt comparison might be with Sicilians, for the Saidis are also distinguished by a Southern warmth and by their pride and puritanical concern for personal honour, especially in respect of their women, which lead them easily into vendettas and crimes of passion. Their poverty is extreme, their hospitality prodigal and their religion intense. Strong feelings lie beneath the austere and dignified demeanour expected of a Saidi man. In business and family affairs the Saidis display a Mafia-like solidarity. Bandits, too, had their place in the life of the countryside and often provided the bravos of great local land-owners. A modern Egyptian writer has given a vivid description of the harsh feudal village life and uncompromising moral code of Upper Egypt where 'women who spent the day among the high maize stalks are found in the evening with their bellies slit open'.[2] These traditions of pride and revenge combined with the war-time grievances of the peasantry and the political emotions of the middle classes to produce the occasional savagery of the peasant risings in the revolution that broke upon Egypt in 1919 and simmered and erupted at intervals throughout Nasser's childhood and youth.

The Egypt into which Nasser was born was still a British Protectorate. All real power was in the hands of the British army and of the British government's representative, the High Commissioner. British officers commanded the Egyptian army and police; British officials controlled all key government departments either directly or indirectly as 'advisers'. Their number and powers had increased rather than decreased since Cromer's time. Below the British came the nominal ruler of Egypt, the Khedive or Sultan, at this time Fuad, great-grandson of the great Mohammed Ali. He had been brought up in Italy, lived in Geneva and Vienna and spoke Italian and French more easily than either Arabic or English. Plump and dignified – he would get up at 5 A.M. to do exercises to keep his figure[3] – his discreet pursuit of good works, such as the founding of the new Egyptian University and the patronage of the war-time Red Cross, had concealed an authoritarian political ambition until he was chosen for the throne by the British in 1917.

Around and below the Sultan, social and economic, if not political power, was controlled by an upper class of big landowners and high officials, often of Turkish ancestry. They were sometimes rivals, and sometimes partners of the powerful foreign business communities who, with the help of Levantine middlemen, controlled most of Egypt's finance, trade and industry. Then came a growing but still relatively small Egyptian intelligentsia of professional men, lawyers, doctors, engineers, teachers, journalists, and a less Westernized class of middle peasants, village headmen, traditional religious leaders and minor officials who had formed the backbone of support for the earlier national revolt of Arabi Pasha and from which Nasser's family came. Finally there were the masses of city workers, poor peasants and landless labourers.

The new feature of the 1919 revolution was the way in which Egyptians from all these classes had fused together, at least temporarily, in the first genuinely nation-wide movement for independence symbolized in the leadership of Saad Zaghloul and the Wafd. The sufferings of the peasantry from requisitioning and conscription and of the city workers from rising living costs and the sweated labour conditions in the new industries that had sprung up during the war fed the discontent, but they were not the main cause of it.

In Alexandria, traditionally a city of high tension, all these classes mingled. In great houses along the seashore and among gardens along the north bank of the canal which linked the city with the Nile lived the English merchants who dominated the cotton market, and the other rich, mostly foreign, families. Out of a population of 447,000 some 46,000 were foreign, mostly Greek and Italian, many of whom were artisans and skilled workers. At the other extreme were the poor Muslim quarters in the old Turkish city and the migrant workers living in slums like the villages they had just left. The Bacos quarter where Nasser was born was a quiet lower-middle-class area. His parents lived in a simple mudbrick house of three or four rooms with a small garden and trees around it. His father may have been helped financially by his mother's family who were comfortably off. Nasser's father's brother, Khalil, who had come to school in Alexandria, was living with them. Nasser's father did not take an active interest in politics. But there is a story that Nasser's uncle Khalil was arrested for political reasons and sent to prison for some time – perhaps as a result of student demonstrations or the more serious riots in Alexandria of 1921.[4]

Nasser grew up during troubled years for his country and his own early life was as unsettled as the times. His family moved frequently as his father was posted to different parts of the country. He lived in many different places and houses, often away from his family, and went to many different schools. These were also years of recurrent economic crises and hardship as cotton prices, the lynchpin of Egypt's livelihood, rose and fell with the booms and depressions of world trade between the wars.

The family's first move from Alexandria, when Nasser was three, was back to Assiut, but in 1923 Abdul Nasser Hussein was sent to run the post office at Khatatba, a small township north-east of Cairo on the edge of the Delta and the desert. Thus Nasser first went to school in the primary school for railway employees at Khatatba, but in 1924 he was sent to Cairo to stay with his uncle Khalil Hussein and the following year began primary school there. Khalil was working with the Ministry of Waqfs (Religious Properties) and also running a small business in his spare time.

The first chapter of the post-war Egyptian national revolution was then drawing to a close in tragic circumstances and with only partial achievement. On 28 February 1922 the British government, under threat of resignation from Lord Allenby, the High Commissioner in Cairo, had authorized a unilateral declaration ending the Protectorate and recognizing Egypt as a sovereign independent state under a constitutional monarch. But the declaration of independence was subject to the reservation of four points which were left to be negotiated in a treaty between Britain and Egypt.

These four points were the protection of British imperial communications (primarily the Suez Canal), the defence of Egypt against external attack, the protection of foreign interests and minorities, and the status of the Sudan. The Sultan was proclaimed King Fuad I and work was begun on drafting a parliamentary constitution which was enacted on 19 April 1923.

On the surface, at least, the political history of Egypt for the next thirteen years, as Nasser grew to adolescence and political consciousness, turned on the interpretation and implementation of these two documents, the British declaration and the Egyptian constitution. In the attempt to work the Constitution there was a see-saw struggle between the king and the most powerful political party, the National Wafd, with the British throwing their weight first one way and then another. The king wanted to retain strong autocratic powers even to the extent of suspending the constitution and ruling by decree. The Wafd, which asserted the supremacy of parliament, won massive victories in every election not rigged by the palace, but was itself not averse to the dictatorial use of its parliamentary majorities against its political opponents.

The conflicts of interest and shifting alliances between the British, the king, and the Wafd led Egypt into a political maze from which there seemed no escape. The frustrations thus created led each of the three to try, at one time or another, to settle the question by brute force: the British by traditional gunboat diplomacy, the presentation of ultimatums backed up by the despatch of warships to Egyptian ports; the king by what were virtually royal *coups d'état*; and the Wafd by semi-revolutionary mass agitation leading to riots and occasional terrorism.

The heart of the problem was that the British sought to keep the Wafd out of power so long as the Wafdist terms for independence and for a treaty were unacceptable to Britain, but at the same time the Wafd was the only power in Egypt with which a durable treaty acceptable to a freely elected parliament could be negotiated. The king and the governments he formed from minority parties or from courtiers might be willing to compromise on the Wafd's demand for complete British withdrawal from Egypt and the Sudan, in order to retain British support for their domestic position, but they could not impose such agreements on Egypt against the revolutionary will of the Wafd.

However, Britain at that time, though she might not have had the strength or the political will to impose a new settlement on Egypt, still seemed strong enough to maintain the *status quo* and protect what she considered her vital interests.

These intervening years provided a turbulent background to Nasser's schooldays. In Cairo he lived for three years with his uncle Khalil in one of the old and picturesque parts of Cairo near the Al Azhar mosque and the great bazaars of the Khan el Khalil. He was left a good deal to his own devices while his uncle was out at work. Together with an older boy who was lodging with his uncle he explored the animated life of the district with its many small shops, skilled craftsmen, popular cafés, splendid mosques and decayed palaces. At school he learned to read and write Arabic, some arithmetic and Muslim religious teaching. Learning was then still mostly by rote.

With his uncle's help, he would frequently exchange letters with his mother. He loved her intensely but saw her only on holiday visits to the family home in Khatatba where three younger brothers were already competing for her attention. But from the end of April 1926 he had no more letters from his mother. She had died, but Nasser was not told the news until months later when he returned home. Until then his family had kept up the pretence that his mother was ill or away on a visit to her parents in Alexandria. The shock of discovery accentuated a natural grief and left a deep and lasting impression on a boy already marked by an appearance of seriousness and reserve.[5] Nasser himself described it as 'a cruel blow that was imprinted indelibly on my mind' and said that for years afterwards he had kept himself apart from his family.[6] Some have said it gave him a horror of death which led him to avoid bloodshed whenever possible when he came to power. It may also have been a cause of his later persistent fears and suspicions of conspiracies against him. The extent of Nasser's humanity as a statesman may be left for later discussion, but at least his mother's early death must have added another element of insecurity to a disturbed childhood in which he was constantly parted from his family and never had the feeling of a real home. The experience of life away from his family in early years may have helped to produce that combination of restlessness, suspicion, tension and passion with patience and ability to conceal his real feelings, which was among his later characteristics as a private conspirator and public figure. One of his early official biographies describes him during his early school-days as 'robust and tall for his age, thoughtful, lonely and absent-minded, neglecting meals and absorbed in reading'.

The memory of another death soon after may have left a passing impression on him. On 23 August 1927 Saad Zaghloul died. For the funeral of the national hero so many people poured into the streets of Cairo that the whole centre of the city had to be closed. Nasser was then only nine but may have seen the funeral and heard political talk from his uncle, a nationalist but no longer politically active. He himself recalled

... when I was a little child every time I saw aeroplanes flying overhead, I used to shout:

> O God Almighty, may
> A calamity overtake the English.

Nasser tried, he says, for some time to find out what this meant and discovered afterwards that 'we had inherited this invocation from our forefathers living under the Mamelukes'. It had originally been:

> O God All-Glorious
> Destroy the Ottomans.[7]

In 1928 Nasser's father remarried and a fourth son, Shawky, was born. Nasser seems not to have got on with his step-mother from the start and consequently also became estranged from his father.

Nasser later described his father as 'a quiet man' who did not drink or smoke or go to the café, and never spoke about politics. His only diversion from work was to go shooting. He loved his family and wanted his children to be educated and independent.[8]

After his father's second marriage, Nasser was sent to Alexandria to stay with his maternal grandparents and spent some time at the El Attarin secondary school there. But he did not do well and was then sent as a boarder to a school at Helwan on the outskirts of Cairo. In 1929 his father was transferred to Alexandria where Nasser rejoined the family and went to the Ras el Tin secondary school. It was here that he had his first contact with the political fervour, expressed in strikes and demonstrations, that were a constant feature of Egyptian school and university student life until Nasser himself brought them almost to an end. Students and schoolboys then thought of themselves, with encouragement from the rival political parties, as the vanguard of an oppressed and backward nation. It was their duty to protest if their elders were too frightened or too closely controlled to do so. At the same time the students felt an extra responsibility as the potential educated *élite* who would not only bring Egypt independence but also modernize her social and cultural life. They were conscious of a wide gulf in this respect between themselves and their parents and elders.

For, parallel with Egypt's political conflicts over independence and foreign occupation and between king and parliament, there were also clashes of culture and manners. The rise of Kemalism in Turkey and the abolition of the Caliphate had roused controversy over the relation of religion and politics. The conservative Muslim divines of the ancient Al Azhar university in Cairo had begun to react fiercely against the challenge of new ideas introduced by Egyptian writers and thinkers who had been influenced by Western liberalism and rationalism.[9]

More superficial but of more immediate concern to the ordinary Egyptian were the changes in clothes and customs to a more European style and the controversies over the status of women, polygamy and divorce.

Nasser himself wrote later of the 'astounding confusion and bewildering complexity that torments our minds' in the Egyptian society in which he grew up.

I sometimes consider [he wrote], the state of an average Egyptian family – one of the thousands of families which live in the capital of the country. The father, for example, is a turbanned fellah – a thoroughbred country fellow. The mother is a lady of Turkish descent. The sons and daughters attend schools respectively following the English and French educational systems. All this is in an atmosphere where the thirteenth-century spirit and twentieth-century manifestations intermingle and interact. ... We live in a society not yet crystallized. It is still in a state of ferment and agitation. It is not yet stabilized in its gradual development compared with other people who passed before on the same road.[10]

When Nasser took part in his first political demonstration he was still only a young schoolboy. It was in Alexandria. He stumbled into it by accident, and did no more than follow the lead of slogan-chanting elders. He was hit in the face by a police baton and spent the night in jail before his father rescued him. He asked his cell-mates about the reasons for the demonstrations. They told him it was a clash between the police and the 'Misr el Fatat', the 'Young Egypt' party. He was moved to another school, perhaps to try to keep him out of further trouble, for during the next three years to demonstrate, even as a schoolboy, became a more serious and dangerous matter. Egypt was under the virtual dictatorship of the king and the government of the iron-fisted Ismail Sidky Pasha. Sidky had been one of the original leaders of the Wafd but had broken with Zaghloul. He was an intelligent, cynical politician of strong character with a high reputation as a financial expert. He showed a readiness to use force and fraud ruthlessly to suppress popular opposition. During his rule there were hundreds of dead and wounded in clashes between demonstrators and the police and army. Opposition political meetings were prevented, and a new constitution was introduced which limited both suffrage and the powers of parliament.

In 1933 Nasser's father was posted to Cairo to run a post office at Khoronfish in the old quarter of Bab Sharkieh or the East Gate. Nasser went on with his secondary school studies at the El Nahda al Misria (Egyptian Renaissance) school. The three-storey building which housed both the post office and Nasser's family was in a *cul-de-sac* called Khamis el Ads (Lentils Thursday) between a small synagogue of the Karaite Jewish sect and a Jewish chemist's shop. Nasser's family rented a second-floor four-room flat for three or four pounds a month from a Jewish landlord named Samuel who lived next door. Nasser himself had a room at the back of the flat overlooking a courtyard. This was his home for the next four years. With his father's growing family, he can have found little peace at home and he would sometimes go to the quiet courtyard of a nearby old mosque to read.

El Nahda school had a reputation for playing a leading part in schoolboy and student demonstrations. Towards the end of his time there Nasser was in the forefront of the demonstrations and was chairman of the executive committee of Cairo secondary school students. During his last full school year between 1935 and 1936 Nasser was so involved in politics that he spent only forty-five days actually in school. But he seems to have found time nevertheless for a good deal of reading during these years, mostly history, politics and biographies of famous men by Arab and Muslim nationalist authors. They included works on Mohammed and on the great pioneers of Egyptian nationalism, Jamil ed-din al-Afghani and Mohammed Abdu; and especially the writings of Mustafa Kamil, the brilliant young demagogue who founded the Egyptian National Party. Apart from Mohammed and Gandhi, Mustafa Kamil was perhaps Nasser's chief hero of the East. He also read the works of one of the most influential of the early Islamic reformers and anti-imperialists, Abdul Rahman el Kawakibi, a Syrian nationalist who had fled to Egypt to escape Turkish persecution. In his two most famous books, *Umm el Qura* (*Mother of Villages* – the name given to Mecca) and *Taba'a al Istibdad* (the *Characteristics of Tyranny*), el Kawakibi dealt with two themes which were to become central in Nasser's future political ideas.[11] The first was a discussion of how the East can overcome its backwardness and rid itself of foreign domination and it emphasizes the central role the Arabs should play in the regeneration of Islamic society. The second argues that when a Western power occupies an Eastern country it does not bring liberty to the people but combines with local despots and a minority of politicians and religious leaders to exploit them. Nasser also read and was impressed by a famous Egyptian novel entitled *Resurrection*, by Tewfik el Hakim. *Resurrection* describes the life of a young boy of fifteen, Mohsen, who lives with his uncles in Cairo and goes home to his parent's country estate in the holidays. It gives a sensitive picture of the awakening of a shy but passionate adolescent to love, to social conscience and to patriotic self-sacrifice. The background of country and city life is drawn with sensitivity, humour and a feeling for nature that reminds one of Turgenev. Nasser could easily have identified himself with the character and circumstances of Mohsen who lived claustrophobically in an overcrowded Cairo flat, felt the widening gap of culture and generation between himself and his parents, and plunged feverishly into the demonstrations of the 1919 revolution with which the novel ends.

Nasser also read in Arabic translation Victor Hugo's *Les Misérables* and Dickens's *Tale of Two Cities*, as well as biographies of Alexander, Caesar, Gandhi and of famous Frenchmen, including Napoleon, Rousseau and Voltaire. He was especially interested by the French Revolution. In an article in his school magazine on 'Voltaire, Man of Liberty', he singled out for approval Voltaire's opposition to the abuse of power and to the Church. He also admired Voltaire because 'he was a calm man, not cruel'.

Dickens's novel of the French Revolution is said to have come to his mind when in the future Council of his own revolution he opposed shedding the blood of political enemies, since the book had left him with the lesson that violence breeds violence.[12]

Perhaps more undeniably prophetic was Nasser's performance of the role of Caesar when Shakespeare's *Julius Caesar* was presented as the school play in January 1935. When Gamal–Caesar was stabbed on the stage, his father got up from his seat in the audience in a fright until he was reassured that his son was still alive and moving.

By the beginning of 1935 the royal dictatorship was coming to an end and the Wafd was pressing for a return to the 1923 constitution. Nasser and his school friends began to make contact with the political parties which were now emerging into a slightly freer atmosphere after Sidky Pasha's regime. They decided to form a committee to represent secondary school pupils, of which Nasser became chairman. Nasser tried out most of the main nationalist parties of the day including the Wafd and beginning with the Misr el Fatat or 'Young Egypt' party of Ahmed Hussein, a right-wing radical and Islamic group encouraged by the palace and financed by secret Italian subsidies. In the continued clash

between the king and the Wafd and between modernists and Islamic reactionaries, new methods of political organization and
violence were being imported from Europe. The Misr el Fatat
developed a fascist-type 'Green Shirt' youth movement to which
the Wafd later replied by creating 'Blue Shirts' of its own.
Socialists and Communists who had begun to form small groups
in the early 1920s had been driven underground by repressive
measures. The Muslim Brotherhood, a movement combining
extreme nationalism with Islamic fundamentalism founded in
1928 by Hassan el Banna, a devout teacher of calligraphy from
Ismailia, had begun its conspiratorial organization on a secret
cell basis. The influence of the Muslim Brothers was strong
among schoolboys and students especially in Cairo after 1934
when Hassan el Banna moved to the capital. Nasser did not join
the Brotherhood but worked for a time with both the Wafdist
youth and the Misr el Fatat, without becoming firmly attached to
either for long. His sentiments appear to have been closest to
those of the old National Party founded by Mustafa Kamil. The
followers of Kamil had dwindled to a tiny group more uncompromising than the Wafd in their attitude to the British: they
demanded complete and immediate British withdrawal without
negotiations. Nasser maintained a close connexion with the Vice-
President of the National Party, Fathi Radwan, who was associated in those days with the Misr el Fatat. Later, Radwan became
Minister of National Guidance for a time in Nasser's revolutionary government.

Above all what still moved Egyptians, including students and
schoolboys, was the straightforward national cause – independence from foreign rule. The most popular party was the one
which seemed most likely to bring this aim about. Something of
the earnest and exalted state of Nasser's feelings on this subject
can be sensed, below the adolescent rhetoric and exaggeration, in
a letter he wrote to his closest school friend Hassan el Nashaar
in September 1935.

Today the situation is critical and Egypt is in an impasse. It seems to
me that the country is dying. Despair is great. Who can end it? ...
Where are the men ready to give their lives for the independence of the
country? Where is the man who can rebuild the country so that the

weak and humiliated Egyptian can stand up again and live free and independent? Where is dignity? Where is nationalism? Where is the so-called activity of our youth? . . . They say the Egyptian is a coward, that he is afraid of the slightest sound. He needs a leader to lead him in the struggle for his country. By this means this same Egyptian would become a thunder-clap which would make the walls of tyranny tremble. Mustafa Kamil said: 'If my heart moves from right to left, if the Pyramids move, if the Nile changes its course, I shall not change my principles.'

We have said several times that we are going to work together to wake the nation from its sleep, to bring surging forth the forces hidden within individuals. But, alas, so far nothing has been carried out.

My dear fellow, I expect you at my place to discuss these matters on 4 September 1935 at four in the afternoon. I hope you won't fail to come.[13]

Within a few weeks of this letter Nasser's demand for action was to be temporarily satisfied, though with eventual results that did not please him.

The desire to regain power through a return to parliamentary government, combined with the threat posed to Egypt by Italian expansion in Africa, especially the Italo-Abyssinian war, drove the Wafd and the British towards compromise. The Wafd let it be known that it would be prepared to negotiate a new treaty if parliamentary government were restored on the basis of the old 1923 constitution. It took a year to bring this condition about: the king was reluctant to concede it and the British, while agreeing that the 1930 constitution of Sidky Pasha should be liberalized, intimated that they considered the 1923 constitution undesirable because it was unworkable. The unwise repetition of this opinion in a public speech by the British Foreign Secretary, Sir Samuel Hoare, led to accusations from the Wafd of British interference in Egyptian domestic affairs and to a series of student and school-boy riots.

For three days in succession after Sir Samuel Hoare's speech, Nasser organized secondary school student demonstrations in Cairo in conjunction with the university students. The police opened fire and two students were killed and many arrested. A bullet from a British police officer's revolver scored Nasser's forehead, leaving a permanent scar.

On 12 December 1935 King Fuad restored the 1923 constitution. The same day a National Front of the Wafd and other party leaders called on the British to open negotiations for a new treaty. There was some delay because of the death on 25 April of King Fuad, who was succeeded by his son Farouk, still a minor at school in England. But in May the Wafd was returned to power in a general election and the new prime minister, Mustafa Nahas Pasha, opened formal treaty negotiations with Britain in July. The treaty was quickly completed and signed on 26 August 1936.

The treaty replaced the British occupation with a military alliance which gave Britain the right to station up to 10,000 troops in Egypt in peace time in a defined zone along the Suez Canal, with the right to use facilities throughout the country in time of war. Britain was also to sponsor Egypt's entry into the League of Nations. Egypt agreed to the provisional continuation of the condominium over the Sudan. Britain accepted the abolition of the old and hated system of Capitulations under which foreign citizens enjoyed special legal privileges which were often abused. The treaty was approved by the Egyptian parliament and by all political parties, except the National Party.

Nasser himself later summed up his political activities at that time and his hostile reaction to the Treaty. No two Egyptians, he said, differed on the aim of a strong, liberated Egypt, but they had different ideas about the way to liberation and strength. He had decided early on that 'positive action' was needed but his ideas about what kind of action changed.

At first,

at a certain phase of my life, 'positive action' meant enthusiasm. But I later came to realize that I ought not to be alone in that enthusiasm. To be effective, it had to be communicated to others.

I was then a student at the Nahda school, leading many demonstrations in those days, shouting myself hoarse, followed by other fellow-students, in our insistent demand for complete independence. But it was to no avail – our cries died into faint echoes that moved no mountains and blasted no rocks. Then I came to believe that 'positive action' could be found in the solidarity and agreement of all leaders of the nation. So our rebellious, roaring ranks went round visiting these leaders in their homes, calling on them, in the name of Egypt's youth, to agree on concerted action. They did actually agree but it was on a calamitous decision which destroyed my conviction – they agreed to conclude the 1936 Treaty.[14]

Although the Treaty may have completed Nasser's disillusion because it still left British forces in a commanding position in Egypt, he had already been obliged to curtail his political activities in a last-minute rush to complete his secondary school studies. His headmaster would not at first let him come back to school: he was forced to readmit him by a strike of the school pupils who even insisted that Nasser return as a hero riding in a carriage by the headmaster's side. In the summer examinations Nasser scraped through his baccalaureat and so ended the first part of a sketchy and constantly interrupted education. Now, at the age of eighteen, he had to begin thinking seriously not only about his political feelings but about his future career. A new phase was about to open in Egypt's life and in his own.

Chapter 2

The Army and Politics:
Egypt in the Second World War, 1936–46

Nasser was always attracted to the military life.[1] His first foreign
hero, he once told a British interviewer, was Nelson. When a
young boy he had read about Nelson and admired his self-
sacrifice in volunteering for a dangerous task. (Perhaps the
example was skilfully chosen to suit the nationality of the interviewer, though in the same interview Nasser had already mentioned the prophet Mohammed and Gandhi as men whose lives
had most impressed him.)[2]

But the army was not Nasser's first thought for a career. He
wanted to go to university and study law. He decided to try to
enter the Military Academy as the only way to escape from
difficulties at home: he did not get on with his father after his
father's second marriage.[3] He could not, however, afford to live
away from home as a university student.

His first application to enter the Military Academy was rejected, probably for lack of family influence or the social status
required at that time to become an army officer. As a second best
he then applied to enter the Police School. He tried the police
against his will, to please his family who were urging him in that
direction. The Cairo police, still under a British commander, the
legendary Russell Pasha, were then considered a *corps d'élite*.
Only Nasser's grandfather at Beni Murr supported him against
the family pressure, predicting higher things for the young man.[4]

He was again rejected. Ironically it appears to have been
Nasser's own police dossier of student agitation which barred
him from the police school. Meanwhile he was able at least
temporarily to pursue his original ambition by beginning to
study law at Cairo university. His law studies lasted only a few
months but long enough for him to experience the restless excitement, hopes and frustrations of student life in a big city university
where an increasing number of the students were drawn from less
well-off homes and faced meagre prospects of employment after
their graduation. In March 1937 he applied again for the Military

Academy and was accepted. Two new developments helped his application this time. Following the signature of the 1936 Treaty with Britain, the Egyptian army was being expanded. More officers were needed quickly and, under the more egalitarian influence of the Wafdist government of the day, they were being recruited from a broader social class. Nasser had also succeeded, through his uncle Khalil and influential friends in Assiut, in contacting privately the general newly appointed in charge of the selection board and had made a good impression on him.

Nasser entered the Military Academy in Cairo on 17 March 1937 and after five months' probation was formally accepted as a student. He quickly made his mark and was among a small group specially selected for a one-year crash course in place of the usual three years, in view of the urgent need for new officers. Seven other members of the future revolutionary leadership of the Free Officers who made the 1952 revolution entered the Military Academy at or about the same time as Nasser. They were Abdul Hakim Amer, Abdul Latif Baghdadi, Anwar es-Sadat, Hussein esh-Shafei, Zacharia Mohieddin and the brothers Gamal Salem and Salah Salem. Another leading Free Officer, Kamal eddin Hussein, entered a year later and graduated in 1939, and Khaled Mohieddin, cousin of Zacharia, graduated in 1940.[5]*

Two of the closest of Nasser's future revolutionary associates, Zacharia Mohieddin, for long his chief instrument in internal security matters and briefly prime minister, and Abdul Hakim Amer, who was to become his most intimate friend and his chief link with the army, were not among his friends at the Academy. Their friendship did not begin until they met later in Alexandria. But Nasser met at this time the wild and colourful Anwar es-Sadat who at first was disagreeably disconcerted by Nasser's rather gloomy silences. Later, impressed by the force of Nasser's

* Of these nine only two still held high official positions by 1970 when Nasser died: Hussein esh-Shafei and Anwar es-Sadat, both Vice-Presidents and the latter Nasser's successor. Salah Salem died from cancer in 1961, Gamal Salem died in 1968 after a long illness, and Amer committed suicide after an abortive *coup* in 1967. Khaled Mohieddin was still politically active in the Arab Socialist Union and as a journalist. Baghdadi, Zacharia Mohieddin and Kamal ed-din Hussein had been dropped from office and were living in obscure retirement.

character, he became a faithful admirer. Anwar es-Sadat has described the austere celebration of Nasser's twentieth birthday at the Military Academy with a meal of lentils, sugar cane and chestnuts. This sparse fare was washed down with some earnest rhetoric from Nasser calling on all present to remain united and to build the future together.[6] Nasser was already both physically strong and mentally mature for his age. He read a great deal, in English as well as Arabic, especially military and political history and biographies, including five books on Napoleon, three by Winston Churchill, others on Ataturk, T. E. Lawrence, Garibaldi, Bismarck, Foch and Gordon.[7] A common love of reading was later to be one of his links with Amer, whose gentle, warm and impulsive nature was otherwise in sharp contrast with Nasser's sombre reserve.

Nasser passed his final examinations at the Military Academy with distinction on 1 July 1938. He was commissioned as a second lieutenant in the infantry and sent to barracks at Mankabad, one of the main garrisons of the Egyptian army only a few miles from his father's native village of Beni Murr in Upper Egypt.

The profession of arms has been a channel for ambition throughout the ages. Yet in spite of Nasser's obvious driving ambition, both personal and political, and his avowed predilection for the military life, there is perhaps something unexpected about the choice – even a second choice – by a fiery young radical agitator, of a career in the military establishment, particularly in an army still subject to foreign control. In spite of the 1936 Treaty, the Egyptian army and the defence of Egypt were then still largely controlled by Britain. The army provided, it is true, one of the easier roads to financial security and social status in a poor country, especially at a time of economic depression when many educated young men and university graduates were unemployed.

Since the Egyptian army revolution in 1952 and other military *coups* in the Middle East a good deal has been written – almost a new political theory – about the special role of the army in Eastern politics.[8] To the extent that it rests on the fact that Nasser was a soldier and used the army as a political instrument, the theory needs to be treated with some caution. For Nasser was, on his own evidence, not so much a soldier who went into politics as a politician who went into the army. He would have been politically active in any profession. Nevertheless, the theory has force and there are clearly some special social and historical features of the army in Egypt which need explaining if Nasser's choice of career and subsequent political role are to be fully understood.

In 'developing countries', it has been pointed out, the army has frequently formed part of the revolutionary vanguard because it has been not only the most coherent, organized force in politically chaotic situations, but also historically provided an early and influential part of the Westernized technical élite. Nasser himself said that 'in countries like Egypt the army is a force of education'.[9] In his *The Philosophy of the Revolution* he argued that the army was the only truly *national* and classless force which could lead Egypt out of the dilemma posed by two simultaneous and conflicting revolutions, the movement for national independence which required unity and the social revolution which entailed inevitable class conflict and thus national disunity: only the army could open the way to the necessary execution of both revolutions together.[10]

Since, in the Ottoman Empire, for example, the modernization of the army was intended in the first place to resist Western military and political encroachment, it had bred within it a nationalist spirit which in times of foreign domination was bound to become revolutionary in character. In the Arab and Ottoman East, all government has until recent times been most frequently military in character and the army the career most open to talent. In Egypt, the situation was complicated by the racial gulf between the Turkish–Circassian military ruling class, which until the middle of the last century dominated the officer corps, and the native Egyptians who were brutally conscripted into the ranks. So that it was against these officers, linked with the Khedive, as well as against European influence, that Colonel Arabi Pasha, an Egyptian officer of peasant origin, led the first unsuccessful nationalist revolt in Egypt in 1882 which ended in the British occupation.

From the crushing of Arabi onwards the Egyptian army became subservient to the British occupiers and to the Khedive, only showing some signs of political effervescence in the Sudan in 1924. It appears not to have stirred politically during the 1919 revolution. British policy wavered between making the Egyptian army efficient enough for limited purposes, such as internal security and the reconquest of the Sudan under British command, and preventing it from becoming strong enough to be a serious independent threat to Britain's position in Egypt.

With the 1936 Treaty the Egyptian army came at last under Egyptian command, but the Treaty stipulated that its training and arms should be British. A British military mission was sent out to Egypt in January 1937. Its first report was brisk and candid.[11] The army for which Britain had been largely responsible for fifty years and which Nasser had just chosen for his career was in a deplorable state. Its eleven battalions of infantry possessed neither heavy nor light machine-guns nor any form of support or anti-tank weapons. The artillery was inadequate and ill-equipped. The army had no tanks, wireless or anti-aircraft weapons. The Egyptian army air force was small but well-trained with thirty-eight aircraft, though these were not armed and the pilots had had no bombing practice. Army training, said the British Mission's first report, was based 'on tactical ideas of almost proto-dynastic antiquity'.

The method by which the army was recruited also burdened it with internal weaknesses which reflected and magnified those of Egyptian society. At one extreme were mostly upper-class officers commissioned through influence and at the other were unwilling conscripts, usually illiterate peasants who could not afford to buy exemption and who regarded their enforced five years' service in the army as a disaster for their families and themselves. At the top, the Egyptian High Command and Staff was 'perhaps the weakest component in the whole of their military fabric'.

Into this archaic and politically torpid force the expansion programme after the 1936 Treaty injected a new wave of young men like Nasser and his friends. They came from the middle and lower middle classes, and they were ambitious, energetic and politically indoctrinated products of the student revolution, itself resulting from the expansion of secondary education in Egypt between the wars.

In a letter to his school friend, Hassan el Nashaar, soon after arriving at Mankabad, Nasser wrote of the place and his feelings in his characteristically intense way:

It is a beautiful place, the atmosphere is poetic and stirs the imagination. It is a landscape of desert, cultivation, pools and canal. To the north sown fields and to the south a range of mountains which stretches from east to west, surrounded by the desert as if by strong hands.

I am glad to tell you that my character has remained unshaken. Gamal at Mankabad is the same Gamal that you have known for a long time, who seeks in his imagination reasons for hope but whose hopes evaporate like clouds.[12]

Mankabad itself was a village round which there was an army garrison of 3,000 men. There was not much to do there in free hours except talk and read or at week-ends to visit Nasser's relatives at Beni Murr. In camp or round the camp-fire out on manoeuvres Nasser and his young officer friends talked mostly professional shop and politics, partly because some of them were politically minded and, as young men in developing countries, felt a special political responsibility, partly because young Muslims especially, lacking feminine society and other entertainment, often have little else but politics to talk about. Outside the immediate family circle such social life as there was in Muslim Egypt tended to be all-male and hierarchic in character. Except among the cosmopolitan upper class, sport and the social amusements of a mixed society were rare. Apart from their careers, there were few other outlets except politics for the energy, idealism and romanticism of adolescents: religion was in doubt, sexual life restricted, good works of a social welfare kind scarcely developed, and literature also highly political in content. Egyptian youth of this generation was uncertain of its identity, surrounded by a bewildering confusion of cultures and even of different languages. Their country seemed to them to be ruled half by foreigners and for the rest by a sham king and a sham parliament: a veneer of constitutionalism concealed a police state and a revolutionary opposition.

Thus Nasser and his friends found plenty to criticize in the army they served, in their relations with their own senior officers and the British instructors, and also in the state of their country and of the world at large. Like their contemporaries in Europe in the 1930s they were stirred by visions of social justice, by hopes of changing society and by opposition to militaristic imperialism. But the context of these feelings and the focus of these aspirations were quite different.

The political outlook of young men growing up in Europe or America in the 1930s and coming to maturity in the immediate pre-war years – an experience which usually left a mark for life – would have been mostly profoundly influenced by such developments as the great economic depression and the growth of socialism, Communism and Fascism; by the Spanish Civil War and Munich; by the choice between pacifism and rearmament; by the persecution of the Jews and the struggle to preserve democratic freedoms. But just as for Europeans the contemporary struggle of China against Japanese invasion and of India for her freedom took second place to their own problems, so young Egyptians like Nasser saw their most important problems closer at hand. In these formative years the most immediate political impact on their minds was made by the continued foreign occupation of their country, despite the fig-leaf of the 1936 Treaty, in close collaboration, when needful, with a royal dictatorship; by Egypt's lack of political freedom, and its crushing poverty.

Egypt had also suffered from the world economic depression, because of its effect on cotton exports. But she had not yet reached the stage where a crisis in the capitalist system would have such a wrecking effect as in the United States and Europe. Most of her population was so near sheer subsistence level that they could hardly sink lower: even the conditions of the unemployed in the industrial cities of the west would have seemed almost luxurious to the average Egyptian peasant. Living in a mud hut with their animals and owning perhaps an acre of land or none at all, a peasant family might earn about 50 p a week. Up to half of the revenue from rented land went to the landlord, often an absentee. Six per cent of the land-owners held forty per cent of the land between them. Farm labourers earned 2½-3 piastres (2½-3 p) a day or about £E15 a year. As a citizen, the peasant hardly existed. He was alternately bullied by the police and dragooned to vote by his landlord or by the government through the officially appointed omdeh or headman, and occasionally wooed by political parties where there were rivalries in the village. Nor was the growing class of urban industrial workers much better off. Ghastly slums were proliferating in the cities as the surplus unemployed population poured in from the countryside in search of work. Working conditions were not unlike those in early nineteenth-century Britain before the Factory Acts. Boys and girls under ten were employed on work that should have been done only by youths and adults; women worked fourteen to sixteen hours a day; there was no weekly rest; wages were miserably low and there was no compulsory accident insurance of any unemployment or sickness benefit. The few trades unions were weak and hamstrung by official restrictions. Unions were neither recognized nor forbidden, but they were prohibited from forming a union federation. Governments, mostly representing the propertied classes, were only too ready to help crush strikes by using the police or the army. There was some public discussion of social problems but it was limited by the preoccupation with national liberation and by censorship and severe repression of socialist and Marxist writings and activities. The main revolutionary currents in the Middle East still sprang from an earlier source, from the French Revolution and the nineteenth-century European movements of nationalism and constitutional reform. The impact of the Russian Revolution had hardly yet been felt, except in a few small and isolated left-wing groups. Culturally and socially Egypt was still grappling with problems of religion, free thought and freedom of manners that had been controversial in the Europe of the Enlightenment.

At the top of Egyptian society, as in eighteenth-century France or nineteenth-century Russia, was a glittering brittle crust formed largely from a culture alien to the mass of the people below. For those at the top the 1930s were gay and luxurious years.[13]

The new King Farouk ascended the throne on 19 July 1937

at the age of eighteen, after a brief Regency. He seemed charming and innocent, and his advisers, such as the Sheikh of Al Azhar, Mohammed el Moraghi, made sure that he also appeared pious. His popularity was at first immense. It was even greater when he married the attractive Farida, daughter of an Egyptian aristocrat. But the atmosphere of the court, seething with intrigue, and the pandering of menial favourites, had begun the corruption of a prince perhaps already doomed by a trivial mind, an insatiable greed and a disastrous education.

Beyond the court stretched the 'society' of Cairo and Alexandria: the big Turco-Egyptian and Egyptian land-owning Pashas and the few new Egyptian industrialists and bankers who had succeeded in breaking into what had for long been the preserve of foreigners, Europeans and Levantines, the more wealthy of whom, reinforced by the embassies and by foreign visitors escaping the European winter, formed the most effervescent part of the social round. This champagne froth of balls, cocktail parties, sports, receptions, varied sometimes by the opera or cultural lectures, swirled around key points such as Shepheards and other big hotels; the Mohammed Aly Club, the haunt of the older politicians; the Gezira sporting club, a large British oasis of cricket, polo and pink gin beside the broad, brown Nile; the British and French embassies and the sumptuous villas of the great Pashas. But right in the heart of Cairo, the sound of bugles from the Kasr el Nil barracks, where British troops were still stationed, was a daily reminder of the ultimate power that helped to keep this glamorous crust in place.

Beneath this sumptuous surface there were not only the ragged, illiterate peasants and workers, but also the growing new middle class of engineers, lawyers, doctors, journalists, teachers, small businessmen, with new expectations and new capacities, but no power. Sometimes they had received European educations and had even gone abroad as students, but once back at home they had little or no contact with the foreign *élite* which held much of Egypt in its grip. Moreover, though they also found it hard to communicate with the older generation brought up in the traditional Muslim culture, many of this new middle class, like Nasser and his colleagues, were in touch with the peasantry of the villages through their own families. The gap between the country and the town was narrowing.

Some had seen and admired democracy at work in Western Europe and wanted more freedom in Egypt. Others were impressed by the apparent discipline and mobilization of national energies under Hitler and Mussolini. Most of them found it difficult to feel deeply engaged in the struggle between the British and French democracies against Italo-German fascism in Europe. True, Italy had behaved abominably in colonizing Arab Libya, as she had in conquering Abyssinia. Her presence on the borders of Egypt and near the sources of the Nile with powerful and growing armies was a dangerous threat. But, they might argue, the British military presence in Egypt was as much a provocation of Italian covetousness as it was a protection against it. This was really a quarrel between rival Great Powers in which Egypt would much prefer to remain neutral if she could. And then, looking round the Middle East and the Arab and Muslim world, were the democracies behaving so much better? They might preach liberal democracy but where outside their own countries did they practise it? To many Egyptians it seemed as if the British were always prepared to sacrifice democratic principles and support unrepresentative governments even if they were brutal and corrupt, if this were necessary to preserve Britain's imperial interests and prolong her military presence.

In all the neighbouring Arab lands tied to Egyptians by language and religion, young Egyptians saw a similar picture. In Iraq, they saw revolution and repression and the same kind of pseudo-independence under British occupation as in Egypt, with oil rather than the Suez Canal as the motive. In Transjordan, there was a puppet emir with a British-controlled army. In the Sudan, the British ruled under a so-called condominium from which Egypt, the other power on paper, had been squeezed out in practice. In North Africa, the French were in control, and Algeria, in particular, was subjected to French colonization, economic domination and virtual annexation to France. Above all, there was Palestine. There the Egyptians saw an Arab majority being held down by force by the British in order to protect the influx of Zionist immigrants aiming to build their own state and in order to provide Britain with a military base. The Palestine Arabs had been engaged in a large-scale popular rebellion for self-government and independence since 1936. If there was any-thing outside their own country which had an effect on the mind of idealistic young Egyptians comparable with the impact of the Spanish civil war on the youth of Britain and France, it was the Palestine Arab revolt. They saw there a small people with few resources fighting on for three years against powerful British forces. Among those who volunteered to help the Palestinian guerrillas the Muslim Brothers in Egypt were in the forefront.

The only Middle East states which had remained free – and hoped to stay neutral – were Kemalist Turkey which had earlier defied and fought the Western Allies; Reza Shah's Iran, per-forming a balancing act between Britain and Russia which was to fail when these two Powers unexpectedly became allies; Saudi Arabia, still independent because the extent of its oil treasure was not yet fully known and because its oil partner was America which had not yet developed imperial habits in the Middle East; and the Yemen, because it was remote, backward and commerci-ally unattractive. In the wider Muslim world, the 150 million Muslims of India, Indonesia and Malaya were part of the British and Dutch empires, the millions of Muslims in Africa were ruled from London and Paris. In Central Asia, ancient Islamic states had been crushed by the Russians, by Tsars and Bolsheviks alike, and were now being Communized by force. Nowhere in 1938 or 1939 did the world prospect look bright, but the priorities of injustice and woe were different depending on whether they were seen from London, Paris or Cairo, from the Cambridge of John Cornford or the Mankabad camp-fire of Gamal Abdul Nasser.

According to Anwar es-Sadat, who was at Mankabad at that time, if the young officers in their midnight talks showed signs of straying off into light-hearted gossip, 'it was invariably Gamal Abdul Nasser who interrupted to bring us back to graver topics'. Nasser was

reserved and serious in manner and his convictions were deep-rooted. He was a true son of the Said. He was passionately attached to the land of his origin and his conversation was sown with proverbs and sayings from his native province.[14]

Sadat's account of these days – written nearly twenty years later, perhaps with some hindsight, after the revolution – quotes Nasser as already advocating a revolution to overthrow 'imperialism, monarchy and feudalism' and rescue Egypt from chaos. It was then, says Sadat, that 'at the beginning of 1939, the officers of Mankabad founded a secret revolutionary society dedicated to the task of liberation'.[15] Other evidence suggests, however, that the 'Free Officers', the secret organization inside the army which eventually carried out the 1952 *coup*, was not formed until much later. It began in embryo form in 1942, held its first organized meetings in 1944 and became more seriously organized after 1949.[16] At Mankabad a group of idealistic and intelligent young officers found they had a common concern and discontent about which they continued to keep in touch during the years to come, though they were scattered to different posts and duties and their own political allegiances and activities diverged.

Early in 1939 Nasser was posted from Mankabad to an Egyptian infantry battalion in the Sudan. Sadat says that Nasser volunteered for service in what was then regarded as a place of exile for army malcontents, because he believed he was already in the bad books of his army seniors for his outspoken views.[17] Before going to Khartoum, Nasser went to Alexandria where he became better acquainted with Amer and Zacharia Mohieddin, who were both in his battalion. A letter from Nasser to his friend Hassan el Nashaar describing his encounter on the train down to Khartoum with a loud-voiced, talkative senator showed that behind his outward seriousness there was a streak of sharply observant humour. In later years it was to show in a sardonic, half-mocking, sometimes mischievous counter-point to the darker and heavier side of his personality. His comrades in the Sudan noted that he rarely laughed, but he often smiled. He liked animals and kept a big pet monkey in his room.[18]

Nasser spent nearly three years in the Sudan, much of the time out at the Jebel Aulia dam on the White Nile. It was there that he developed his close friendship with Amer. The outbreak of the Second World War thus found Nasser in a situation which must have aroused mixed feelings of frustration and relief. He was serving 1,000 miles from home in an army which was incapable through lack of equipment, training and experience of making a serious contribution to the defence of its own country. Yet this army was called upon to be involved indirectly in a war which it did not really feel to be its own. Even in the Sudan, the Egyptian army remained on static guard duties while the Sudanese Defence Force under British command made ready for active operations against a possible Italian attack. A soldier and a patriot must have felt a double humiliation, professional and political, and yet also a feeling of relief that Egypt was not actually committed to fight beside the British occupier.

Nasser's own view of the war was that Egypt should remain neutral: if she could not avoid being involved in the war then she should take advantage of the Axis operations to help get rid of the British. There is no evidence that he was pro-German in the sense of being Nazi-minded: his attitude was like that of Irishmen such as Sir Roger Casement in the First World War, or of the Finns in the Second World War who called for German help to fight the Russians. During a large part of the war, especially when the Middle East was an active theatre of operations, Nasser was outside Egypt in the Sudan. The war was not in any case the formative experience for him that it was for young men of other nationalities.

It is possible that if Britain had been able to treat the Egyptian army as potentially a serious ally, to train and equip it for a more active role, she might have been able to gain its goodwill, at least on the professional level. But Britain herself was short of equipment and still lacked confidence in either the military usefulness or political reliability of the Egyptian army. Nor was the attitude of the Egyptian government and of the Egyptian army's chief of staff reassuring. King Farouk had dismissed the elected Wafd government at the end of 1937 and a palace government of minority parties, put in place by rigged elections, was now headed by Aly Maher, former chief of the Royal Cabinet. Aly Maher gave an assurance that Egypt would fulfil all her obligations to Britain under the 1936 Treaty, but Egypt did not declare war on Germany and was more concerned about Italy. The king and Aly Maher kept out feelers to Rome for a possible agreement by which Italy would refrain from attacking Egyptian territory in return for Egyptian neutrality. Egyptian public opinion favoured neutrality and especially after the German victories in Europe and the fall of France there seemed nothing to be gained for Egyptian interests from entry into a war which Britain, left alone, seemed certain to lose.

The Franco-German armistice and Italy's entry into the war transformed the situation in the Mediterranean. At one stroke it robbed the British in the Middle East of the powerful support of the French army in Syria and the French Mediterranean fleet, while bringing large Italian forces into action against them. When Italy declared war on 10 June 1940 she had some 215,000 troops in Libya with a powerful air force. 80,000 Italians were massed on the Egyptian frontier at the end of the 1,000-mile-long Libyan desert road. Facing them were some 50,000 British, Indian, Australian and New Zealand troops under General Wavell. The Egyptian army had three battalions with some artillery in the Mersa Matruh sector. The Aly Maher government, in an effort to avert involvement in war with Italy, had ordered Egyptian forces to withdraw from the immediate frontier areas and to take no offensive action unless Italy invaded Egyptian territory or bombed Egyptian cities.

Under the pressures of war, the velvet glove of Egyptian political independence put over the British military presence in Egypt by the 1936 Treaty was beginning to wear thin. On 22 June 1940 Aly Maher was dismissed by the king under British pressure because of his reluctance to take security measures against Italian nationals in Egypt. The Egyptian chief of staff, General Aziz al Misry, a pan-Arab nationalist of Turco-Circassian origin, who had been early put on indefinite 'sick leave', was finally dismissed in August 1940 at the request of the British who suspected him of pro-Axis sympathies.[19]

As the Italian offensive in September 1940 penetrated to Sidi Barrani, sixty-five miles inside Egypt, some of the nationalist officers, chiefly Anwar es-Sadat, began secret contacts with the Italians. Their aim was to plan a *coup* in Cairo to coincide with a possible expulsion of the British by the advancing Italians. For this purpose Sadat, acting, so he says, on the instructions of his 'Revolutionary Committee', got in touch with the leader of the Muslim Brotherhood, Sheikh Hassan el Banna, and General Aziz al Misry.[20]

These plans led to no serious action, and by December 1940 Wavell had driven the Italians out of Egypt and back to Tripolitania. But Sadat's contacts bore later fruit. They established between the Muslim Brothers and Nasser's group of army officers a long, important and finally violent relationship of fluctuating intensity: Sadat became one of the principal links between the two groups, though he was not a member of the Brotherhood, and many other influential officers were either members or sympathizers. By that time the Muslim Brotherhood had ceased to be merely a religious or moral revivalist movement. It had begun to see itself as a political force with a large mass influence and had formed a secret paramilitary organization. Sadat found el Banna 'at once fanatical and clear-thinking', with a 'surprising intuitive grasp of the problems facing Egypt'. He saw in the Brotherhood at that time a potentially useful mass support for a future army insurrection.[21] Nasser himself had already met Hassan el Banna in Alexandria but had never become a member of the Brotherhood.[22]

Sadat does not identify the 'Revolutionary Committee' on whose orders he made these contacts but it seems likely to have been one of several fluid groups of nationalist malcontents in the army. Its contacts with Nasser, then far away in Khartoum, were probably extremely tenuous.

By the spring of 1941 the Axis forces in Libya, now reinforced by the Germans and commanded by Rommel, had driven the British back again and besieged Tobruk. Sadat's nationalist group were then in touch with Rommel's agents to seek help for an Egyptian *coup* to link up with the revolt of Rashid Ali al-Ghailani in Iraq.[23] Aziz al Misry, who had earlier been contacted by the Germans, was sceptical about the Iraqi rebels but decided himself to go to Beirut, then under Vichy French control, to contact the German armistice commission there. He tried unsuccessfully to leave Egypt by submarine and then on a plane piloted by nationalist air force officers who were later prominent in the revolutionary regime. But the plane crashed soon after take-off and al Misry was arrested. He claimed to have taken this initiative only after having offered the British cooperation in return for a pro-Arab settlement of the Palestine question, an offer which the British rejected.[24] He was later sentenced to a mild prison term for conspiring to endanger the security of the state.

After the Aziz al Misry fiasco, the Egyptian army conspirators seemed at a dead end. Nasser wrote dolefully from Khartoum to his friend Hassan el Nashaar in August 1941 about his failure to make any headway with his Egyptian colleagues there:

> My fault is to be frank. I know nothing about flattery or deviousness. I don't run after my superiors. . . . Being the only one, in this milieu, who believes in conscience and fidelity, I am persecuted. . . . Do you remember our plans of reform which were to be carried out in ten years? Now I think they will need a thousand years.

Nasser and his friends dreamed and planned reform and revolution for Egypt as other young men dream of fame, fortune, writing novels, making a million dollars, marrying a beautiful girl.

Nasser returned to Egypt at the end of 1941. He was again nearer the centre of events and able to be in closer touch with the other nationalist officers. He was stationed at first at Al Alamein, then a boring desert post sixty miles west of Alexandria and still far behind the battle line. But when Rommel launched his new offensive at the beginning of 1942, there was growing unrest in Egypt encouraged not by the young officers but by a pro-Axis clique inside the palace. Axis propaganda was intense and there was considerable economic discontent; food and other goods were in short supply, owing partly to lack of shipping for imports. Students of Al Azhar university, encouraged by the Muslim Brothers and the palace group, demonstrated in favour of Rommel and called for the return of Aly Maher. The stage was set for another and more dramatic British political intervention which was to have unexpected, far-reaching effects on the future of Egypt, on Anglo-Egyptian relations and on Nasser's career.

In January 1942 the Egyptian government under Hussein Sirry Pasha broke off relations with Vichy France at British insistence. King Farouk was away from Cairo when the decision was taken. He objected that he had not been consulted and demanded the resignation of the Foreign Minister. The Hussein Sirry government resigned on 2 February and a political crisis developed. The British feared the king was planning to bring back Aly Maher to head a more pro-Axis or neutralist government or to control it from behind the scenes. The British ambassador, Sir Miles Lampson, urged the king on 3 February instead to form a new government headed by Nahas Pasha, the Wafdist leader. The British believed the Wafd, the party with the strongest popular following, to be the only Egyptian group able and ready to hold the country in alliance with the British and to control popular unrest in the face of the growing Axis military threat.

To enforce his demand, the British ambassador sent an ultimatum to the palace at midday on 4 February stating, 'Unless I hear by 6 p.m. that Nahas Pasha has been asked to form a cabinet, his Majesty King Farouk must expect the consequences'. A meeting of party leaders and elder statesmen called by Farouk at the Abdin Palace in Cairo at 3 p.m. that afternoon agreed to form a coalition under Nahas but also signed a protest note to be sent in reply to the British ultimatum. The message, in the name of the President of the Chamber of Deputies, protested at 'this aggression against the independence of Egypt'. This move may have been intended to provide a more dignified and face-saving preparation for eventual acceptance of the British demand. But Lampson, an overbearing and impatient man, decided on immediate and drastic action, since technically his ultimatum had not been complied with. A battalion of British troops with a section of armoured cars surrounded the Abdin Palace. Then at 9 p.m. Lampson accompanied by General R. G. W. H. Stone, the goc British troops Egypt, and escorted by a specially selected platoon of officer cadets in light armoured vehicles, drove up to the palace through the main entrance. There was no resistance from the palace guards and the ambassador's party were taken first to a waiting room and then to the king's study. But, according to one version, the gates had to be forced open by the

armoured vehicles and the officers of the guard disarmed, after
which Lampson rushed quickly up to the king's study, flanked by
two South African ADCs with drawn revolvers, brushing the
palace attendants aside. Farouk is said to have stationed three
Albanian guards with pistols behind the curtain of his study
door.[25]

In the event, the violence of the scene was only mental and
moral. The ambassador told the king he must appoint Nahas
prime minister with a free hand to choose his own cabinet or he
must himself abdicate. After a moment's hesitation the king
agreed to the British terms.

The Wafd was indeed still the most popular party in Egypt
and it proved an effective ally for the British war effort during
the next critical period of the war when the Axis armies under
Rommel penetrated to Al Alamein, when the British were considering evacuating their headquarters from Cairo and the Allied
cause was at a low ebb all round the world. But the method by
which the British ambassador put Nahas into power and thus
secured this vital short-term gain (whether the method was
necessary is still a matter of controversy) was to have the long-
term effect of destroying almost the whole of the established
political structure of Egypt and its relations with Britain. It
opened the way for the next wave of revolutionary nationalism
which was to overthrow the king, the Wafd and the British
alliance. It undermined the nationalist reputation of the Wafd
because Nahas had accepted office with British backing; it
destroyed both the king's own morale and his popular influence
and showed that the 1936 Treaty was built on force not friendship.

The 'Abdin Palace *coup*' is a striking example of how differently nations see the significance of the same event. Most English
people have probably never even heard of it: for those who have,
it is simply a footnote to a long imperial history, and one minor
incident in a great war for national survival. But to the Egyptians
at the time this was a national humiliation and disaster, and
4 February 1942 has since become a cardinal date in their modern
history.

Nasser, like other army officers, reacted with fury to the

Abdin Palace *coup*, not because of any love for the king but because he saw it as an insult to the whole country. General Mohammed Neguib, later the public leader of the 1952 *coup* and then a lieutenant-colonel of infantry, sent a letter of resignation to Farouk, which the king refused to accept.[26]

Some of the revolutionary officers met in Cairo to discuss possible retaliation against the British but more cautious counsels prevailed. Nothing serious could be done. The revolutionary movement in the army was nevertheless given a new impetus. 'Abdul Nasser and Adbul Hakim Amer determined that Egypt must never again suffer such a humiliation. The real revolutionary conspiracy dates back to this time. The movement had now passed from the theoretic to the militant phase.'[27]

Nasser's first reaction was a feeling of shame that the army had not acted at once against the *coup*. Ten days later, after he had heard more details about it, he wrote to his friend Hassan el Nashaar:

I have received your letter and what it tells me makes me boil with anger. But what is to be done in the face of the *fait accompli*? We have accepted everything with resignation. In fact I believe the English were playing with only one trump card in their hands. They only wanted to threaten us. If they had felt there were some Egyptians who intended to shed their blood and to oppose force to force, they would have withdrawn like prostitutes. It is their way of acting, it is their habit. As for us, as for the army, this event has been a deep shock; hitherto the officers talked only of enjoyment and pleasure. Now they talk of sacrifice and of defending dignity at the cost of their lives. . . . You see them repenting of not having intervened in spite of their obvious weakness to restore the country's dignity and cleanse its honour in blood. But the future is ours.

The *coup*, added Nasser, was 'a severe lesson' which taught the army that 'there is something which is called dignity that one must be ready to defend'.[28]

Many of Nasser's characteristics can be seen in this angry letter – his passionate pride and attachment to the idea of national dignity; his coupling of angry emotion with a calculation of the power situation; and his readiness to wait and plan patiently for a more favourable moment to react, as was shown in his subsequent activities.

Nasser concentrated on quietly recruiting officers for the underground revolutionary movement, but for a few months it looked as though a chance for quick action might have come. In the summer of 1942 Rommel's advance into Egypt and the German sweep into the Caucasus seemed to threaten an early Allied defeat and the loss of the whole Middle East. The revolutionary group in the Egyptian army worked out a plan to profit from this situation. They would carry out a military *coup* in Cairo to replace Nahas Pasha by Aly Maher and join up with the advancing Axis forces to drive the British out of Egypt. The plan depended partly on internal support from the Muslim Brothers and external liaison with the Germans. Anwar es-Sadat was the leading spirit in making both these contacts and neither was successful. The Supreme Guide of the Brotherhood, Hassan el Banna, was friendly but non-committal. He ended by suggesting that the army officers join the Brotherhood – a proposal Sadat rejected because 'the ideology of the Brotherhood was essentially different from ours and [that] the merger would be virtual suicide for our party'.[29]

With the Germans, Sadat was even more unlucky. Rommel sent two agents to Cairo in June 1942 who contacted Sadat through another army officer, Major Hassan Ezzat. One of the agents, Hans Appler, alias Hussein Gaafar, was the son of a German mother and an Egyptian stepfather, who had been educated in Egypt and spoke perfect Arabic. He and his companion drove through the British desert lines via the Siwa oasis, dressed in British uniform and in a British vehicle, bringing with them a radio transmitter and £40,000 in false banknotes. But in other respects they seem to have been an ill-equipped and amateur pair of spies. They set up headquarters in a houseboat next to that of one of Cairo's most famous belly-dancers and began to spend their money in high living. They soon attracted attention and were quickly arrested by British Intelligence. According to Sadat's story, the two German spies talked after Winston Churchill, then in Cairo in August 1942 on his way to the Moscow conference, had personally interviewed them and promised to spare their lives.[30] Sadat was then arrested, tried before a special court composed of two British Intelligence officers and one Egyptian police officer and on 8 October 1942 sentenced to be cashiered and imprisoned in a detention camp at Minah. Sadat had managed to conceal his connexions with the army revolutionary group.

Nasser himself was no longer in Egypt while Sadat's adventure with the two German spies was taking place. He had been promoted captain and posted back to the Sudan on 9 September 1942. By the time he returned to Cairo on 7 February 1943, on appointment as an instructor at the Military Academy, the war situation had been radically transformed and with it the immediate prospects of the army revolutionaries. By May 1943 the Germans and Italians had been driven completely out of Africa and the Caucasus. In the course of that year it became clear that the Allies would eventually win the war. Though heavy fighting still lay ahead in Europe and the Far East, the Axis threat to the Middle East was over.

This prospect led the nationalists in Egypt and elsewhere in the Arab world to two conclusions. First, the more extreme gave up hope of getting rid of the old conquerors, the British and French, with the help of their enemies. They believed they had now to rely on themselves, though some already saw in the Americans and even the Russians possible future instruments of pressure on Britain and France. Secondly, it was time to start staking out political claims for the post-war period. For, apart from those, such as Rashid Ali in Iraq, the Mufti of Jerusalem, and a small group of young officers in Egypt, who had gambled on an Axis victory, the majority of Arab leaders and Arab public opinion had backed the Allies or remained at least benevolently neutral, partly in the hope that this cooperation would not only ensure survival but also bring eventual post-war political recognition. The rewards they sought were full post-war independence for those Arab states still under mandate or restrictive treaties and above all an assurance that the British policy for Palestine drawn up in the White Paper of 1939 would not be abandoned under Zionist pressure. The full Arab claim in Palestine was for the immediate creation of an independent state with an Arab majority. Their minimum demand was for the fulfilment of the White Paper. This would have made Jewish immigration eventually subject to Arab consent. It would thus have ensured that, unless the Arabs improbably agreed, Palestine would never have a Jewish majority and so never become a Jewish state. It was partly on the assumption that the White Paper would be carried out – and partly from exhaustion in their struggle – that the Palestine Arab rebels had accepted a tacit truce at the outbreak of the war.

To compete with Axis propaganda, to ensure Arab cooperation and so to free the all-too-few Allied troops from local security worries, and to facilitate the seizure of Syria and the Lebanon from Vichy French control, British policy had shown sympathy with Arab national aims in general terms while seeking to avoid specific commitments. The most generous British promises were made – and, more surprisingly, carried out – to those Arab people who were under the control of others – to the Senussi of Libya who were promised freedom from Italian colonization and future independence: to Syria and the Lebanon, promised an independence which was achieved on paper by 1943 but not in practice until the departure of French and British troops in 1946. But attempts by Egyptian moderate nationalist leaders to secure promises of British withdrawal after the war as a *quid pro quo* for the present fulfilment of the 1936 Treaty had brought no concessions or promises from the British. Egypt, the British appeared to think, should be grateful enough for having secured British military protection and the war had shown the value of the Treaty to both countries. The British government had also evaded attempts by Arab leaders, especially Nuri es-Said of Iraq, to pin them down to a firm pledge about the fulfilment of the Palestine White Paper. Churchill did not approve of the White Paper. He had always been a keen Zionist, seeing a Jewish state in Palestine not only as good for the Jews but also as a valuable British imperial stronghold and ally in the Middle East. Moreover, while the White Paper, in spite of Churchill's views, remained official British policy in Palestine, it was becoming increasingly difficult for the British government to apply it. Reports were gradually leaking out of the terrible massacres of Jews by the Germans in Europe. The political and moral pressure on the

British government to open the doors of Palestine to greater Jewish immigration was fast increasing. It was backed both by American Jewry and by the development of a powerful Jewish underground military organization in Palestine which was encouraging illegal immigration and preparing itself for armed revolt if necessary against the White Paper policy.

As early as 1942, a crucial year for Allied fortunes in the Middle East and for the future of Egyptian nationalism, the Zionist movement also reached a historic turning point. At the conference held at the Biltmore Hotel in New York on 9–11 May 1942, a meeting of international Zionist leaders adopted the programme advocated by David Ben Gurion, then chairman of the Jewish Agency for Palestine, of working for the immediate establishment of a Jewish state in Palestine and unlimited immigration under Jewish Agency control. This was a reversal of the earlier Fabian tactics of Dr Chaim Weizmann whose policy had been to let a Jewish state gradually evolve *de facto* by building up a Jewish majority through immigration while Britain remained the governing mandatory power. Ben Gurion's policy sprang not merely from the new urgency created by the Jewish holocaust in Europe. It was also based on the assumption that the Zionists could no longer count on British protection to enable them to build a majority gradually by immigration. For the White Paper had put British power behind a policy of restricting immigration and preserving an Arab majority. Logically therefore a Jewish majority and a Jewish state would now have to be built in defiance of the British as well as the Arabs. Already in the later years of the war, the Jewish authorities had begun to develop and strengthen their underground military arm, Haganah, originally set up to protect Jews from Arab attack. From 1943 onwards two more extreme military organizations also developed their activities – the Irgun Zvai Leumi, an offshoot of the Revisionist Party, an extreme right-wing Zionist group, and the Stern Group, a strange little band of fanatical nationalists, left-wingers and religious mystics. By 1944 these two organizations had begun terrorist attacks, firing the first shots in what was to develop into a general Jewish revolt.

One placatory British gesture towards the Arabs was to encourage moves for Arab unity for which Anthony Eden, as Foreign Secretary, had formally expressed British sympathy in a declaration in May 1941. It was with British blessing that the Egyptian premier, Nahas Pasha, took the initiative in July 1943 in calling for a meeting of Arab states in Alexandria to discuss the formation of an Arab League. The protocol agreeing to establish the League was signed on 8 October 1944. (The League and its Charter were not effectively established until 22 March 1945, following a meeting at Yenbo between King Farouk and King Ibn Saud.) But the very next day the Nahas government was dismissed by King Farouk. The British, who had intervened before to prop up Nahas, now let him fall. The worst of the war was over and the Wafd government had become increasingly unpopular.

There was a despondent lull in the activities of the army revolutionaries. In November 1944 Sadat escaped from jail and went underground with the police on his tracks. This was also a time of preparation for Nasser, for both his career and his private life. At the Military Academy Nasser was instructing in small arms and tactics and studying to prepare for his own entry into the Staff College. His friend, Amer, was an instructor in the Army School of Administration. They both used their contacts with the cadets to recruit promising young men to the secret movement. Khaled Mohieddin was one of Nasser's recruits at this time. He has described his meeting with Nasser – 'a proud man, conscious of his dignity and respectful of that of others'.[31]

Nasser and Amer used to visit the house of a friend, Abdul Hamid Kazem, owner of a small rug factory, who lived near Abbassia in the same district as the Military Academy. Kazem was the son of a successful tea merchant of Iranian nationality and a friend of Nasser's uncle, Khalil Hussein. His mother and one sister were dead but another sister, Tahia, was living with him. She was pretty, dark-haired, quiet and comfortably off, for her father had left her about £800 a year ($200 a month) income from stocks and shares. Nasser married Tahia about a year after their first meeting, when she was twenty-two and he was twenty-six. She was an educated girl but from a conservative middle-class family. She was to provide a calm and stable family background for Nasser's hectic conspiratorial activities and later for his open political life.

According to Nasser she had discovered within three months of their marriage that 'something fishy was going on'.[32] But she was discreet, did not gossip or ask questions; on occasion she would help by carrying messages for the conspirators. Her main preoccupation was with her home and her children of whom there were eventually to be five. Even when Nasser had emerged into public life and fame, she remained quietly in the background in the traditional Muslim manner, and was scarcely known to the Egyptian public.

Chapter 3

Disillusion, Defeat and Conspiracy, 1946–9

When the Second World War ended, Nasser was aged twenty-seven, married and beginning to found a family. He was well advanced in his profession, a captain on the threshold of the Staff College, a conscientious and able officer with a strong personality and a studious turn of mind, but no combat experience. In the greatest war of modern times in which his own country had been one of the key objectives and battlefields, he had been only a spectator. His sympathies had not been seriously engaged on either side, but politically he, or at least some of his group, had seen a chance of national liberation through the defeat or weakening of the British whom they regarded as their dominators rather than protectors. Like others more eminent and better informed, they had miscalculated the world forces involved. The world which Nasser and his friends saw round them after the war was not one of hopes fulfilled and dreams of the future. It was a world of disillusion with a hangover of old ills and injustices which they seemed powerless to remedy – at least for years to come.

Outwardly Nasser was a quiet, reserved professional soldier. He lived in a small house near the Military Academy in a Cairo suburb and spent his spare time reading, studying, going to the cinema and meeting his fellow-officers and friends. Inwardly he was seething with well-concealed political passions. Secretly he was beginning to plan a revolutionary organization to give these feelings eventual public expression. It is doubtful whether he had then a clear long-term plan in his mind, or any definite objective, except to get the British out of Egypt, but his angry resentment and frustration at what he saw as the continued subjugation of Egypt at the end of a war supposedly for freedom was echoed in the country round him and throughout the Middle East.

For Egypt was once more in revolutionary ferment. The national revolution, which had begun in 1919 and then subsided as a result of the 1936 Treaty and the war, had begun its second wave which was to break with the army *coup* in July 1952.

Egypt had emerged from the Second World War in a strange

position. She was neither victor nor vanquished nor neutral. Like Turkey, she had belatedly declared war on Germany and Japan in January 1945 to secure a seat at the United Nations. The declaration had cost the life of her prime minister, Aly Maher, assassinated as he came out of parliament by a young nationalist lawyer. Egypt's war record as a reluctant ally had been a mixture of double-dealing and of courageous cooperation with the British at the worst time of crisis. Superficially her situation in 1945 was very different from that of 1919. She was at least nominally an independent sovereign state with a king and a parliament. So that on paper at least the two main aims of the 1919 revolution – independence and constitutional government – had been achieved. But in other ways she seemed to have regressed to the 1919 situation. British troops were still all over Egypt in large numbers – not merely in the Canal Zone and limited to 10,000 as the 1936 Treaty stipulated.

There was the inevitable friction between foreign troops and local inhabitants, magnified by the fact that the Allied troops usually saw only the seamiest side of a very poor country. To most British soldiers the Egyptians were simply 'wogs', despicable, dirty, treacherous – a mental legacy which, when these troops returned home, continued to bedevil Anglo-Egyptian relations for years after.

The Abdin Palace affair of February 1942 was only the chief of many incidents which seemed to show that both Egypt's internal constitution and her international sovereignty were a sham. The British were still the real masters. Even Egypt's economic gains were partly an illusion. Her industries had developed, but the cost of living had risen sharply. The £300 million sterling balances earned by Egypt during the war were blocked by Britain who doled them out to suit her economic convenience or her political purpose. The end of the war-time boom meant more unemployment.

The old parties and the political system were discredited: in the eyes of the younger generation they had achieved neither of the aims of the 1919 revolution – neither complete national independence nor a genuine constitutional system. To these aims there had been added in recent years the need for solutions to

Egypt's growing social and economic problems: the growth of her cities and her population, the effects of her increasing industrialization. Then there were new problems posed abroad by the semi-responsibility assumed by Egypt and other Arab states for their foreign policies, the most urgent of these problems being Palestine.

The new wave of the revolution was aimed at making Egypt's sham independence real, at finding a political system that was both effective, representative and capable of dealing with the crushing problems of health, education, housing, employment; and at developing Egypt's leading role in the newly emerging Arab world. In the process educated Egyptians sought above all a self-esteem which they had lost from half a century of frustrated struggle and disillusion.

The new political movements in Egypt drew their inspiration from a variety of sources. The most important were the Islamic revivalism of the Muslim Brothers and the growing left-wing groups which stretched across a wide spectrum from the small clandestine Communist party, through fellow-travellers, 'peace partisans' and struggling labour unions to the social democratic left of the Wafdist youth. The left had been stimulated both by the wartime respectability and performance of Russia as an ally and also by the growth of socialist ideas in Britain and Western Europe. The originally Fascist-inspired 'Young Egypt' movement of Ahmed Hussein had also switched to a more left-wing nationalist line and changed its name to the Islamic Socialist Party. On the extreme secular right were the survivors of the old National Party of Mustafa Kamil. All these groups had something in common. They all hated Western imperialism and wanted to get rid of the British military presence once and for all. Their deep suspicion of British motives and influence everywhere led them to advocate a mistaken policy of asserting Egyptian sovereignty over the Sudan, an error compounded by King Farouk's own royal vanity. They were contemptuous of the Egyptian parliamentary system as a sham structure based on collaboration with the British (though the Muslim Brothers were willing at times to cooperate with the king and even some of the revolutionary officers still nursed hopes of a rejuvenated Wafd).

Most of them, especially on the Islamic nationalist right had in common a taste for violence and conspiracy and a new awareness of social as well as political problems. Another feature of these movements was their new type of leadership. The old parties, including the Wafd, had drawn their leadership chiefly from the *élite* of land-owners and the upper strata of the official and professional classes which had emerged under the Khedives and Cromer. Now there were leaders from humbler social layers, more middle-class professional men, merchants and some workers.

What was the role of the army and of Nasser's group in this ferment?

Most of the accounts of the development of Nasser's secret army movement written by its members after the revolution, such as that in Anwar es-Sadat's *Revolt on the Nile*, give a picture of a clear, consistent, planned development under Nasser's far-sighted leadership, which it probably did not have. Nasser's own account gives perhaps more convincingly the flavour of confusion, improvisation and groping for ideas and means of action which were typical of the atmosphere of Egypt at that time. Sadat, for example, with some vagueness about dates and sequences of events, describes how the year 1945 'saw the opening of a new phase in the history of our secret preparations. ... From now on, our actions were controlled by a carefully-thought-out plan, aiming at a specific target. ... Gamal Abdul Nasser was taking careful stock of the situation, choosing the moment when he would give the signal and the fight for freedom would begin.' Nasser, says Sadat, was working on a theory of gradual infiltration and refused to rush things. He quickly vetoed a proposal by Sadat to blow up the British embassy and everyone in it after rumours that the ambassador, Sir Miles Lampson, had snubbed the prime minister, Mohammed Nokrashy Pasha, when he called to remind him of Egypt's national claims. Nasser recalled the British reprisals after the murder of Sir Lee Stack, Sirdar of the Egyptian army, in 1924.[1]

Nasser's group had at first been divided into two sections, a military section under Nasser himself and a civilian section headed by Sadat. Nasser also devised an administrative system for the movement, dividing it into five sections dealing with economic affairs, combat personnel, security, terrorism and propaganda. It is difficult to know just how seriously to take all this. The 'economic section', for example, was not to deal with future economic policy but with the finances of the movement itself and to help the families of any member sent to prison. The most violent action of the terrorist section, according to Sadat, was when a coastguard officer threw a shoe at Nahas Pasha, the Wafdist leader! Later, not long before the 1952 revolution, Nasser and others did make an unsuccessful attempt to kill General Hussein Sirry Amer, the most hated and corrupt man in the army. There is a long emotional passage in Nasser's book *The Philosophy of the Revolution* describing the ambush and his remorse afterwards as he heard the screams of the women and children in the intended victim's house. He tells of his relief at hearing that the victim had survived and his reinforced conviction that assassination was not the answer to the country's problem. Previously, he recalls, he and his colleagues had seriously considered a plan to assassinate the king and some thirty of the leading politicians associated with him, but had rejected it.

The propaganda section was hampered by the need for secrecy and relied on personal contacts and discussions. It was not until in 1949, after the Palestine war, when the movement had grown bigger, that it came out in the open sufficiently to distribute mimeographed tracts signed 'Free Officers'. The most important sections appear to have been 'Security', which vetted new recruits, and 'Combat Personnel', which was responsible for arms and training. The cell organization, which began after the war, developed seriously only after 1949. There were cells of five members in which each member knew only his own cell-members and those others whom he had personally recruited to form another cell. Liaison was established with each branch of the army. Only Nasser and Abdul Hakim Amer knew the exact number and the names of all the members.[2] At its peak the movement probably had about 1,000 members of whom several hundred were in the army though of these perhaps not more than one or two hundred were really active. Each member made a monthly contribution to an emergency fund. With these meagre funds, supplemented by windfalls such as the proceeds of the sale of

the mango harvest from the farm owned by the retired General
Aziz al Misry, their 'spiritual mentor', they set up a small secret
workshop in which they made revolvers and manufactured
Molotov cocktails out of tens of thousands of Coca-Cola
bottles.[3]

There is also uncertainty about the combat personnel section
and the movement's relations with the Muslim Brotherhood.
Nasser's group contained several officers who were also members
of the Muslim Brotherhood or sympathizers with it. Nasser had
rejected a merger with the Brotherhood but agreed to cooperate
in military training. This cooperation appears to have been
sketchy because the army officers resented the unquestioning
obedience demanded by the Muslim Brotherhood's Supreme
Guide and the vagueness of his aims. It was closest when volunteers from Egypt were preparing to go to fight in Palestine in
support of the Arab irregulars at the end of 1947. It was broken
off when the Muslim Brothers took increasingly to terrorism and
were suppressed by the government.

Thus, at least during the first post-war years, Nasser's group
was probably one of several within the army and was not very
extensive, coherent or influential. The main opposition force in
Egypt at that time within the parliamentary system was still the
Wafd, though it had begun to be a party dominated by rich men
and to lose some of its popular roots. The main revolutionary
force outside parliament was the 'anti-imperialist front' stretching from Muslim Brothers to Communists which evolved rapidly
and violently as Britain and official Egypt once more failed to find
a military and diplomatic *modus vivendi* to match the passionate
hopes and fears of the times.

On 20 December 1945 Mohammed Nokrashy Pasha, who had
succeeded his murdered friend and colleague, Aly Maher, as
premier, approached the British officially to negotiate a revision
of the 1936 Treaty. Egypt's claims had already hardened. Under
nationalist pressure Nokrashy was demanding the complete and
immediate withdrawal of British troops from Egypt and the Sudan
and the unity of the two countries under the Egyptian Crown.
The demands were popularly expressed in the slogans of 'Evacuation' and 'Unity of the Nile Valley'. The emphasis on the Sudan

had been increased. King Farouk was anxious to assert his title to the Sudan. Egyptians were also suspicious that the moves already made towards self-government in the Sudan were part of a British plan to circumvent Egyptian rights in the condominium there and set up a separate Sudanese state linked exclusively with Britain. Out of office, the Wafd, supported by the left-wing and the Muslim Brothers, moved further towards a policy of neutrality. It rejected any new alliance or joint defence arrangement with Britain or even any negotiations on these topics.

Nokrashy's proposal to the British was coldly received. The British agreed to talks but declared their belief that the events of the war had shown the soundness of the principles on which the 1936 Treaty was based. The reply was doubly disappointing because it came from the newly elected Labour government in London of which the Egyptians had high hopes. It led to serious student riots in Cairo in which there were 170 casualties from police fire at the 'Abbas Bridge Massacre', and riots by workers in Alexandria and elsewhere. There had already been large-scale industrial strikes as well as bomb outrages and other attacks on British troops. Some British forces were still in Cairo and Alexandria.

Nokrashy was forced to resign and was replaced by Ismail Sidky Pasha, the strong man of the 1930s, still intelligent and ruthless, but now aged seventy-one and in poor health. Sidky, while suppressing agitation with his usual iron hand and trying to deal with some of the country's economic problems, opened negotiations with the British.

The talks took place against the background of a rapidly changing situation in the Middle East and throughout the world. In 1919 the Egyptians were dealing only with Britain. France was absorbed with her share of the Ottoman spoils in the Levant. America and Russia were hardly in the Middle East picture. Egypt then had little political connexion with the rest of the Arab world. Now France had gone from the Middle East altogether and America and Russia had begun to take a serious interest in the area. A new system of Arab states of varying degrees of independence was emerging. Although Egypt, with British encouragement, had assumed the leadership of the new

Arab League, she was herself not yet as independent as Syria and
the Lebanon from which French troops had reluctantly departed
under British pressure. Iraq and Jordan were, like Egypt,
nominally independent but tied by treaties to Britain. Libya had
been promised freedom. In Palestine, 650,000 Jews had established themselves and, driven into fierce desperation by Hitler's
massacres, were in revolt against Britain, demanding statehood,
while the Palestine Arab majority claimed at least the same degree of independence that had been accorded to other Arab
states.

The anti-imperialist revolt in the Middle East was part of a
vast uprising throughout Asia against European rule – especially
in India, Indonesia and Indochina. At the other end of the Arab
world the French were struggling to reimpose their rule in North
Africa.

Yet for a short time – perhaps a year or two – after the Second
World War, Britain's power over most of the Middle East and
the Arab world was complete and real. If used swiftly and with
imagination it might then have produced a general political
settlement comparable with that achieved in India and Pakistan –
or at least everywhere in the Middle East outside Palestine,
thereby also perhaps limiting the effects of the Palestine conflict.
But the basis of this power was fragile and evanescent. The British
economy, impoverished by the war, could not support the British
military machine in the Middle East for long, especially after the
withdrawal from India and the loss of the Indian army. Britain
was forced to call on the United States for help in dealing with
the civil war in Greece, and in backing Turkey and Persia against
post-war Russian pressure. This help and the economic aid she
needed herself also meant that Britain must pay greater attention
to American views on Palestine and face the fact of American
public and political support for Zionism.

Henceforward, the Palestine problem and its later manifestation as a conflict between Israel and the Arab states were to
become inextricably interwoven with the relations of Egypt
and the Arabs with Britain and the Western Powers and also with
the relations between the Arab states themselves. The Palestine
dispute was one of the chief obstacles to the general Middle

East policy initiated by Ernest Bevin, the British Labour Foreign Secretary and carried on in broad outline by his successors. This aimed at putting Britain's relations with the Arab states on a more equal and cooperative footing by a new system of treaties which would have involved the withdrawal in peace-time of all or most of the British forces from those states. But the biggest obstacle of all in Britain's dealings with Egypt was not Palestine but the fact that she still over-estimated her own strength. She had still only partially realized the underlying change in her power position in the Middle East. She still counted on being able to fall back on her existing military positions, her bases and old treaties, if her terms for revised alliances were not accepted. She had not realized that once she was no longer able or willing to rule by force she could only usefully keep her troops in Arab states by consent based on the persuasion of common interests. Lord Stansgate, who led the first British treaty delegation to Egypt in 1948, later said that 'If we had accepted the principle that our troops would only be in Egypt by consent of the Egyptian Government, there would have been agreement in a month'. Whatever the legal niceties on either side about the continuation of the 1936 Treaty in Egypt, for example, the political and military realities were – or should have been – quite clear. An army which stays on the territory of another sovereign state without that state's consent and in defiance of its request to leave becomes, in practice if not in law, an occupying and not an allied force. Such a force and the state to which it belongs has to be strong enough to take over the occupied country entirely in the last resort or else find itself a beleaguered garrison, a strategic liability rather than an asset. The first people to demonstrate this fact in the post-war Middle East were not the Egyptians or the Arabs but the Palestine Jews. In Egypt the British were not strong enough to take over Egypt and govern it themselves. But they were strong enough to resist physical eviction, to inflict damage on those who tried to drive them out, and to make Egypt ungovernable by anyone else. No post-war Egyptian government could survive for long which did not at least attempt to obtain the withdrawal of British troops. Since none of them was strong enough to drive the British out they had only two other courses open to them. They could either pay a political and military price in negotiation for the British withdrawal or they could try so to limit the usefulness and increase the expense of maintaining the British base in the Suez Canal Zone that the British would decide to withdraw voluntarily. From 1946 to 1951 negotiation was tried but the British price in terms of military alliance and the status of the Sudan was more than Egyptian governments could accept and survive. In 1951 the Wafd tried the second course: they attempted to make the British base in the Canal Zone uselessly expensive by non-cooperation and guerrilla harassment. But this policy got out of hand, brought down the Wafd and hastened the revolution in Egypt without getting rid of the British. It proved a point, however, which was not lost on the British government. When, finally, agreement was reached between the British and Nasser in 1954 it was partly because Nasser had combined both the previous tactics of negotiation and the threat of guerrilla warfare.

The draft treaty between Sidky and Bevin in September 1946 was the nearest Britain and Egypt came to an agreement before the 1952 revolution, but it broke down over the Sudan clauses. When Sidky resigned, Mohammed Nokrashy came back as prime minister. In January 1947 Nokrashy announced that the dispute would be taken to the United Nations Security Council, while Bevin told the House of Commons that Britain would continue to stand by the 1936 treaty and wait for a 'more representative government' in Egypt to resume negotiations. Britain could not simply withdraw 'leaving a vacuum'. A fortnight later, on 18 February 1947, Bevin announced that Britain was taking the Palestine dispute to the United Nations, with the clear implication that she intended to hand over responsibility and herself withdraw from Palestine. In the same year Britain began her withdrawal from India, Pakistan, Ceylon and Burma, setting in motion the great but gradual imperial retreat caused by a growth of principle and a decline in power. In Egypt and other Arab states of the Middle East the principle was for another decade only half applied and the loss of power only half realized. One reason was perhaps that these countries were only half imperial in status. Another was that an even stronger principle for the Labour government than the liquidation of imperialism was the welfare of the British worker: Middle East oil was a more important factor in the British economy than any profit from India. The Middle East also seemed more vulnerable to Russia.

The United Nations was not of much help to Egypt over her problems or to Britain over Palestine. Egypt's complaint to the Security Council was eventually heard in September 1947 and reached no conclusion. The legal arguments were nicely balanced. On moral and political grounds Egypt had a strong case for the withdrawal of British troops from the Canal Zone. But she had a weak moral case on the Sudan where her policy was confused and she seemed to be opposing Sudanese self-determination which was advocated by the British. In any case the political complexion of the United Nations at that time, dominated by the Western Powers, would probably have ensured the defeat of any important resolution on Egypt not desired by Britain, unless the United States were supporting it. The United States at that time had little interest in Egypt. In the Middle East she was concerned for strategic reasons with Turkey and Iran; for domestic political reasons with the Jews of Palestine; and for oil reasons – mildly – with Saudi Arabia. Otherwise she left the Arab states to the care of the British. But in the case of Palestine, the support of both the United States and Russia ensured the passage of a resolution which the British did not like.

The disillusion of Egyptian nationalists with the rebuff in the Security Council was soon overlaid by Arab anger over the decision of the United Nations General Assembly in November 1947 to approve the partitioning of Palestine into separate Jewish and Arab states. The anger was not merely over the fact of partition and the creation of a Jewish state but also over what was regarded as the wildly unfair nature of the division. The Jewish state was to include almost as many Arabs as Jews and much of the more fertile land of Palestine.* The Arab state would contain only about half of the Palestine Arabs, with mostly poor hill land. Moreover, the Jewish state had been awarded the southern desert triangle of the Negev, thus breaking land contact between Egypt and the other Arab states of the north and east.

*The Jews, who owned six per cent of the land in Palestine, were to be given fifty-six per cent of the area of the country for their state.

The Arab League decided to oppose the partition plan, by force if necessary. At a fatally leisurely pace, arrangements were made to recruit volunteers for an unofficial 'Liberation Army' to go to the support of the Palestine Arabs. By the end of 1947, five months before the British mandate ended and the regular armies of the Arab states entered Palestine, the Palestine war had already begun. The Palestine Arabs were already fighting with the Jewish armed organizations, Haganah and the unofficial terrorist groups, the Irgun Zvai Leumi and the Stern Group, for control of territory vacated by the British as they concentrated their forces to prepare for eventual departure.

In Egypt there was no lack of volunteers for the war. The Muslim Brothers were in the forefront but there were recruits from the army, too, with official encouragement. General Neguib has described how a whole battalion under his command unhesitatingly stepped forward to volunteer.[4]

During the previous year or so Nasser's group had been lying low. The political police were keeping a watch on the army and seemed to be on their track. There had been few meetings and Nasser himself was absorbed in studying for his final Staff College examination. He debated with himself whether he should give up his examinations to join the officers who had volunteered for Palestine or wait another month. He had already met the Mufti, Haj Amin el Husseini, the Palestine Arab leader, at Zeitoun, near Cairo, the day after the partition resolution and offered his services and those of his colleagues as volunteers or instructors. The Mufti had told him he must get the permission of the Egyptian government. In Nasser's case, this had been refused. Should he now leave his army uniform to join the fight, after the Arab League had officially endorsed the creation of a volunteer 'Arab Liberation Army' for Palestine? At a meeting of the 'Free Officers' at Nasser's house in April 1948, it was decided that some members should join the guerrillas at once and others wait their turn.[5]

Kamal ed-din Hussein left at once to join the volunteers fighting under the command of the Egyptian colonel, Abdul Aziz, round Hebron. Two other officers from Nasser's group, the air force men, Abdul Latif Baghdadi and Hassan Ibrahim, had already gone to Damascus to try to arrange for air support for the 'Arab Liberation Army' of irregulars under Fawzi el Kawukji which was being assembled and trained in Syria. But within a few weeks Nasser, as well as Zacharia Mohieddin, Abdul Hakim Amer and others of his friends, was on his way to Palestine as part of the Egyptian regular army. For the Egyptian government, after some hesitation, had decided to intervene openly and officially in support of the Palestine Arabs.

Only a few days before this decision, the prime minister, Nokrashy Pasha, had told a secret session of the Senate that Egypt would not intervene openly, since she was not militarily prepared.[6] Nokrashy was speaking with the advice of the Egyptian army leaders. Neguib, who was to be appointed second-in-command of the Egyptian expeditionary force, was against open intervention. He thought that Egyptian action should have been limited to unofficial support for the Palestine guerrillas.[7] Egypt might then not have won the war, he later commented, but she would not have lost it so disastrously. But Nokrashy quickly reversed his position, apparently under pressure from King Farouk, and the Egyptian army was ordered to prepare to enter Palestine on 16 May, the day after the British mandate ended.

Nokrashy appears to have reassured the dubious army leaders, aware of their lack of preparedness for a major campaign, that they need expect little serious fighting since the main aim was to occupy territory in order to establish political claims. The official reason for intervention was to protect the Arabs of Palestine. The king's decision to intervene officially seems to have been inspired by a number of factors. The desire to divert violent revolutionary energies away from home may have been one.[8] But first there was the widespread public belief that the intervention of the Arab armies was needed to support and protect the Palestinian Arabs. In the months of fighting while the British were still there, the Palestinian Arabs had already suffered serious losses. The Jews had been able to seize such important towns as Jaffa and the Arab areas of Haifa and the new quarters of Jerusalem, from all of which the Arabs had been expelled or had fled in fear. There had been the massacre of 250 Arab villagers at Deir Yassin, near Jerusalem, and other atrocities which had stirred Egyptian public opinion. Second, there was the question of maintaining Egyptian prestige as the most important state of the Arab League. Third, there was the problem of the future status of Arab Palestine.

Within the Arab League there had already begun to develop rival blocs. On the one side were the Hashemite rulers of Transjordan and Iraq, in close alliance with the British, who favoured an Arab union based on the Fertile Crescent. On the other were Egypt and Saudi Arabia who opposed these Hashemite plans and wanted a broader and looser Arab League under Egyptian leadership. Lebanon did her best to remain neutral between these blocs, while Syria was divided and changed course according to which Syrian group was in power in Damascus. The signs were that King Abdullah of Transjordan would use his British-officered and British-financed Arab Legion to stake out a claim to part of Palestine, at least the area allocated to the Arabs under the partition plan. He could then develop a variation of his Greater Syria Plan, which he had announced in February 1947, for an Arab Federation of a Greater Syria (composed of Syria, Transjordan and Palestine) and Iraq in which there would be autonomous Jewish and Lebanese Christian states. It was also an idea which the British, after their failure to get a settlement with Egypt, regarded as logical and sensible. Bevin accepted the movement of the Arab Legion into Palestine so long as it kept within the areas allocated to the Arabs under the partition plan. So one motive for the Egyptian intervention was to forestall the seizure by Abdullah of all or most of Arab Palestine. Another was to ensure Arab control of the Negev which was the land link between Egypt and the eastern Arab states.

Whatever the rational calculations of policy or the pressures of royal ambition, it is probable that the strength of public sympathy for the Palestinian Arabs would sooner or later have forced the Egyptian government to intervene.

The Palestine war gave birth to many legends – helped by the absence so far of any comprehensive and serious account of the war by an Arab historian. The most inflammatory legend was also that most common among defeated armies, the theory of the 'stab in the back'. What is certain is that, when the Egyptian army entered Palestine on 16 May, it did so with no clear military or political objective. Moreover, it opened the campaign with a force too weak to achieve a decisive result even against the newly formed Israeli state, itself desperately short of arms and in the throes of military reorganization, and with a population of only about one-thirtieth of that of Egypt. There was no serious co-ordination between the seven different Arab military forces operating in Palestine. In the first phase of the war, the Arab regular armies had more heavy arms, particularly artillery, tanks and aircraft, than the Israelis, but the two sides were more evenly matched in numbers of men mobilized and in the field. The slightly smaller Israeli forces had the advantage of unity of command, clear political and strategic aim, compactness and short-ness of internal lines of communication, and in some cases of better training and greater experience of modern war. They proved themselves superior in command, planning and organiza-tion to all the Arab armies, except the Arab Legion of Trans-jordan. Both sides fought bravely as individuals, the Egyptians better in defence, while the Israelis, with a greater personal and political awareness of the issues involved, showed both fierce determination in holding on to politically valuable ground and greater initiative and daring in attack.

At the beginning of the war the Egyptian army consisted of nine battalions. Four were available for the Palestine campaign, three for the initial advance and one other to follow. In addition, there was the equivalent of a battalion of Egyptian volunteers, mostly Muslim Brothers, already operating in the Hebron area of southern Palestine. Later, at the peak of the war, Egypt was to muster some 40,000 men in Palestine.

Egypt's part in the Palestine war involved four campaigns interspersed with truces of varying degrees of effectiveness. The first campaign was her advance into southern Palestine which brought her to a line running roughly from Isdud (today the Israeli town of Ashdod) on the Mediterranean coast inland through Majdal, Falluja and Beit Jibrin to Bethlehem and the southern outskirts of Jerusalem.

Both Nasser and Neguib in their war memoirs have described the confusion and lack of preparation amid which the Egyptian campaign began. Neguib recalls that when he got beyond the

Egyptian railhead he had to hire local trucks from the Palestinian Arabs to carry his troops forward and was compelled to leave behind some six-pounder guns because there were no tractors to tow them.[9] He was often short of ammuniton for his British-made guns and of spare parts for his British and American tanks. During the first truce when both sides were trying frantically to buy arms on the international black market to get round the United Nations official arms embargo, the Egyptians found themselves supplied with Italian grenades that blew up in the thrower's face, with defective Spanish field-guns and 1912 Mauser rifles. The natural suspicion of soldiers that the civilians were making a fortune behind their backs hardened into a conviction that the king and the government themselves were making money out of buying defective arms.[10]

Nasser described how no provisions were made for any hot meals for the troops and when he arrived with his unit in Gaza he was simply given £1,000 to buy local cheese and olives for the rations. He complained of contradictory orders coming from Cairo, from which the war was being run, and in the early stages of the war of the reckless launching of Egyptian infantry in frontal assaults on strongly fortified positions without armoured cover or even proper prior reconnaissance. He noted the untrue stories of constant victories broadcast from Cairo radio and the ignorance of the ordinary Egyptian soldier about the reason for the war. He asked one of his men what he thought they were doing and the man said that of course they were on 'the Rebiki manoeuvres' – the annual army manoeuvres held in Egypt round Rebiki, east of Suez.[11]

Nasser had graduated early from the Staff College to enable him to take part in the campaign. He said good-bye to his family, now increased by two baby girls, and took the train to Gaza. On the train he met Amer and Zacharia Mohieddin, also on their way to join their units at the front. Together they studied a map and discussed, with some misgivings, the strategy of the campaign.

Nasser was attached as staff major to the sixth battalion which moved up to Isdud. There he observed the slackness of the Egyptians in failing to make use of the first truce in June and July to train and improve their positions, compared with the incessant activity of the Israelis. He attributed this contrast partly to the demoralizing effect on the Egyptian troops of the feeling that this was a 'political war', that its outcome depended less on the efforts of the soldiers in the field than on the pulling of political strings behind the scenes – and not only in Cairo but in other Arab capitals and by the Great Powers at the United Nations. Nasser was gloomy about what he had seen of the war. He criticized the way the small Egyptian forces had been dispersed in small units to occupy as much territory as possible for political purposes, but without any serious mobile striking force in reserve. He talked it over all night with Hakim Amer, as they lay on the camp beds under the stars in an orange grove at Isdud. He found Amer's optimism and serenity comforting.

Largely on the insistence of Egypt and Syria, the Arabs refused to resume the first month's truce. The Egyptian public had been led to expect victories. The Arab leader also believed that the Israelis were gaining more from the truce than they were. The Israelis, with efficient and diligent purchasing missions abroad, had been able to smuggle in large quantities of arms despite the United Nations embargo. Many of the arms came from Czechoslovakia. When the Egyptians resumed the offensive in July, the difference in Israeli strength was at once apparent. The Egyptians made little headway. In the battle for the key point of Negba they lost some ground.

In the unsuccessful Egyptian attacks on Negba, Nasser was slightly wounded by a fragment of a ricochet bullet. At the hospital in Majdal where he was sent he noted the bad medical services and the wounded pouring in from the Negba battle. He reflected, he wrote later on,

war which I detest . . . I said to myself that humanity does not deserve to live if it does not work with all its strength for peace. [When he learned that one of his friends had been killed, he wrote] I swore that if one day, I found myself in a responsible position, I should think a thousand times before sending our soldiers to war. I should only do it if it was absolutely necessary, if the fatherland was threatened, and if nothing could save it but the fire of battle.[12]

During the second truce which lasted from 18 July to 15 October Nasser went to Cairo on four days' leave. After his return to Palestine on 9 September, his unit was moved inland to join the brigade under the Sudanese Brigadier Taha Bey which held the central sector of the front covering the vital Falluja crossroads. In the Falluja area, roads going north and south from Central Palestine to the Negev crossed the main east–west road which went laterally across the Egyptian front from Gaza to Hebron via Majdal and Beit Jibrin. Among the group of small Arab villagers in the Falluja area the key points were the police fort of Irak Suweidan to the west and the village of Irak al Manshiya on the east. Nasser's sixth battalion was posted to Irak al Manshiya to maintain contact via Beit Jibrin with the Egyptian forces in the Hebron hills. It was here that Nasser had his main battle experience of the war and also his first experience of negotiating directly with the Israelis.

During the second truce, international political developments had begun to affect the military situation and plans of both sides. A plan for a political settlement was worked out by the United Nations mediator, the Swedish Count Bernadotte, in July 1948. In a modified form (which proposed internationalizing Jerusalem instead of giving it to Transjordan) the plan was published after Bernadotte was assassinated by Israeli terrorists in Jerusalem in September. It would have given the Negev to the Arabs – to the proposed union of Transjordan and Arab Palestine which became the kingdom of Jordan. Western Galilee awarded to the Arabs in the 1947 partition plans would have gone to the Israelis. The plan convinced the Israelis that they must recover the Negev at all costs. But the Bernadotte plan also widened the already existing political splits among the Arab governments, chiefly between Egypt and Transjordan, since it would have given the lion's share of Arab Palestine to King Abdullah.

The military consequences of these political events were soon to show themselves. On 15 October the Israelis took advantage of Egyptian interference with one of their convoys going south to the Negev settlements under the truce agreement (the Egyptians claimed the convoys often smuggled arms under guise of non-military supplies in defiance of the truce terms) to launch a carefully prepared major offensive. Their aim was to drive the Egyptians out of the Negev.

The Israelis launched heavy attacks on the two hinges of the Egyptian line at Iraq el Manshiya and at Irak Suweidan. The Falluja brigade fought back stubbornly. Irat al Manshiya was held, once after a counter-attack. The Irak Suweidan fort surrendered after withstanding six attacks, the last and seventh launched after the heaviest artillery barrage of the war. The Israelis had cut the communications of the Falluja brigade with Gaza and Majdal. The brigade had orders from the Egyptian High Command on 21 October to prepare to withdraw to avoid complete encirclement. But the order was changed. By the time it was renewed again on 23 October, the Israelis had completed the encirclement of the Falluja pocket.

The Israelis called on the surrounded Falluja troops to surrender. There were parleys under the white flag between local commanders on each side and also between Brigadier Taha and Colonel Yigal Allon, the Israeli commander on that front. But the Egyptians refused to surrender. At these higher-level meetings, Nasser was present as a staff officer. In the final passage of his memoirs of the Palestine war, Nasser described his first meeting of this kind. On 24 October an Israeli armoured car approached the Egyptian lines flying a white flag. A voice blared through a megaphone 'An Israeli officer wants to meet an Egyptian officer'. Nasser jumped into a jeep with two other officers and a sergeant with a tommy-gun. An Israeli officer put his head out of the turret of the armoured car and said 'haughtily' in English 'I am the assistant of the general officer commanding this area and I am instructed to point out to you your situation. You are besieged on all sides and we invite you to surrender.'

Nasser replied, 'We are fully aware of our situation but we shall not capitulate. ... We are defending the honour of our army.' The Israeli officer than spoke in Arabic and again in English, 'less haughtily'. When Nasser maintained his refusal to surrender, the Israeli 'more politely' asked for permission to recover the bodies of the Israeli dead. Nasser agreed.[13]

It was during these truce parleys that Nasser met Captain, later Colonel Mordechai Cohen, an Arabic-speaking Israeli of Yemenite origin on Allon's staff. Cohen later wrote about his talks with Nasser in a series of articles in the *Jewish Observer*.

Nasser himself approvingly quoted the following passage from one of these articles in his own *The Philosophy of the Revolution*:

> The subject Gamal Abdul Nasser invariably discussed with me whenever we met was our struggle against the British, the way we organized our secret resistance movement against them and the way we succeeded in mobilizing world opinion on our side against them.

Yigal Allon himself recalls that Nasser's personality and intelligence made an impression on him at the time.*

The other consequence of the Arab political split was that neither during the October offensive nor during the final Israeli offensive in December was there any serious support for the Egyptian forces from the other Arab armies. The new Israeli offensive on 22 December 1948 was aimed at destroying the Egyptian army, driving it off what Israel now claimed as her territory under the UN Partition Plan and forcing Egypt to agree to peace talks. The main Israeli assault was a drive south inland which was to turn eastwards towards the sea and cut off the entire Egyptian expeditionary force. The Israelis captured the key points of Bir Asluj and El Auja on the Sinai frontier by taking tanks on a round-about way through the desert along an old Roman road. The Egyptians were attacked from the rear and taken by surprise. Swinging round rapidly towards the sea, the Israelis reached the outskirts of Rafah and the main Egyptian base at El Arish. Here they were stopped by a virtual British ultimatum, backed by American diplomatic pressure, ordering them to leave Egyptian territory. At El Auja, for the first time in the war, the Egyptian troops had become so disorganized and demoralized that they had surrendered in large numbers. But in the Gaza–Rafah area they continued to fight hard, and the Falluja pocket withstood more heavy attacks. The pocket had been subjected to heavy air and artillery bombardment and at 2 A.M. on 28 December the Israelis launched a strong attack on Irak al Manshiya, where Nasser was in command. Under cover of darkness, mist and driving rain, the Israelis succeeded in penetrating the Egyptian

---

*Allon in interview with author, November 1967. Allon told me then he was 'disappointed' with Nasser. He thought Nasser had wanted to be 'a second Saladin' and had mismanaged his attempt at 'socialism' in Egypt.

defences at two points. Nasser mounted a counter-attack with all his available forces, about 100 men, including the cooks, and with the help of a barrage from artillery and mortars at Falluja itself a mile and a half away. When the Israelis resumed their attack just before dawn they ran into heavy fire and after a five-hour battle withdrew with heavy losses.[14]

While the Falluja garrison held on, the rest of the Egyptian expeditionary force was threatened with being completely cut off from Egypt and left with no supplies or communications. On 7 January 1949, the Egyptian government asked for armistice talks. The armistice was negotiated at the UN headquarters in Rhodes, with Dr Ralph Bunche, who had replaced Bernadotte as UN Mediator, in the chair, and was signed on 24 February 1949. The armistice left the Gaza strip under Egyptian control and created a demilitarized zone in the strategically vital area of El Auja. Both these places were to become sources of later conflict. The whole of the Negev was left in Israeli hands, except for the south-eastern tip touching the Gulf of Aqaba where the port of Eilat now stands. This was later seized by the Israelis in a quick thrust while the armistice talks with Transjordan were still in progress.

As part of the Egyptian–Israeli armistice agreement, the Falluja garrison was allowed to march out with the honours of war, carrying its arms and with its colours flying, in recognition of its brave resistance.

And so the war was over. Egypt and the Arabs had been badly defeated. For the Palestine Arabs it was a human catastrophe. Three quarters of a million of them, more than half of the Arab population of Palestine, had been driven from their homes. They had lost most of the chief towns, all the main sea ports and railways and a large part of the fertile land and water supply in a country in which they had been a two-thirds majority of the population. Egypt had lost no territory but her geopolitical position had been profoundly changed. The new Israeli state separated her territorially from the Arab states of Asia and controlled the north–south communications between Egypt and the Levant. A new non-Arab state, which the Arabs feared to be of a dynamic and expansionist character and of uncertain external loyalties, had been established on Egypt's border and in a strategically vital part of the Arab world. In its psychological effect on Egypt, the result of the war was comparable with that of Russia's defeat by Japan in 1905.

As one of the defenders of Falluja, Nasser soon returned home to a hero's welcome. Like any returning soldier, Nasser came home with relief. But he was also more determined than ever that things in Egypt must be changed.

Chapter 4

The Road to Revolution, 1949–52

The Palestine defeat has often been cited as a water-shed in the political history of the post-war Arab East. It was not, however, the true cause of the subsequent revolutions and military *coups* in the Arab states. It merely hastened a revolutionary process which had already begun. The old regimes which had dealt with the British and French imperial powers since the First World War, whether as nationalist opponents or collaborators, were being challenged by a new generation of nationalists whose aims included not only complete independence but also social reform and greater unity between the Arab states.

The Palestine war drove home painfully lessons which were already being learned and taught. At the same time it impressed these lessons especially on the army officers and so helped to transform the Arab armies from being the final props of the old regimes into the revolutionary instruments of their destruction.

Retrospectively, in his *The Philosophy of the Revolution* written a year after the 1952 revolution, Nasser outlined the conclusions he had drawn from his Palestine experiences. He recalled his first awareness of the Palestine question and with it his 'first notions of Arab consciousness'. Both had come to him when, as a secondary school student, he went on strike with the rest of the students every year on the anniversary of the Balfour Declaration which favoured the establishment of a Jewish national home in Palestine. His main reaction then was of emotional sympathy with the Palestine Arabs, 'the legitimate owners of the land'. But by the time the Palestine crisis came to a head in 1947–8, his military studies had convinced him that to fight for the defence of Arab Palestine was not merely a matter of ethnic or religious sympathy but of Egyptian national security. When he and his colleagues made secret preparations to help the Palestine Arabs before the official war had begun, their motive was

neither sympathy with our Arab brethren nor love of adventure – it was solely the clear consciousness of our confirmed conviction that . . . our security made it necessary for us to defend the frontiers of our

Arab Brethren with whom we were destined to live in one and the same region.[1]

Sitting in the dug-outs of Irak al Manshiya, and reflecting on the state of Egypt and the Arab world, Nasser saw the whole region with its different Arab capitals as besieged just as he and his men were in the Falluja pocket. The besieging force was 'imperialism'. In this 'political war', the Arab armies were like pawns in a chess game: their governments at home which seemed to move them were in reality themselves being manipulated by the outside forces of 'imperialism' which was at the same time the support and mainstay of Israel.[2]

Nasser's picture, seen with melodramatic clarity, was of a vast conspiracy linking together 'imperialism' (which meant the Western Powers and chiefly Britain, still the dominating force in most of the Arab states), complaisant or self-seeking Arab governments and Zionism. For Nasser decided, from a reading of Chaim Weizmann's *Trial and Error* and his own observations, that Zionism could not have approached its goal in Palestine without the support of a Great Power.[3]

The remedies for the Arabs, Nasser concluded, were greater unity among themselves, a common struggle against imperialism, on whose help Israel depended for survival, and the breaking of the corrupt and selfish Arab regimes through which imperialism operated. Finally, Nasser believed that in this process the army had a role to play as an instrument to express the national concensus – he had not yet evolved the 'Nasserist' doctrine of the army as itself an *élite* instrument of government.[4] Most of these conclusions were to become, indeed to a certain extent had already become, the commonplaces of radical Arab nationalism. It was fairly obvious to all Arabs that the disunity and rivalry of the Arab states had been one of the causes of their defeat in Palestine. Another cause had been the backward state of Arab societies. This had shown itself in the Arabs' poor organization behind the military lines, their lack of political leadership, the sheer poverty and lack of technical experience of most of the Arab peoples, and the absence or scarcity of an educated, politically aware public able to play its full part in a national effort, as the Palestine Jews had done. Then it was also undeniable that the Great Powers had

played an important part in the course of the war and its settlement, throwing their weight sometimes here, sometimes there. It
could hardly have been otherwise. It was also a fact that three of
the Arab states concerned – Egypt, Iraq and Transjordan – were
all subject to powerful military and economic pressures from
Britain. The British had troops or bases in their countries, controlled their arms supplies and also, through the sterling balances
in London, some of their money. The kings of Iraq and Transjordan were British protégés who owed their position to British
power. The king of Egypt was also, however unwillingly, a partner
dependent on the British in the maintenance of the *status quo* in
Egypt.

To many non-Arabs and to most Zionist historians, however, it
would appear that the British government had, in a proper or
mistaken pursuit of its own interests, shown a decided partiality
for the Arab cause and had used its influence to save Egypt and
the Arabs from more serious losses. This was not how British behaviour appeared to most Arabs. The conclusion many Arabs
drew was that Britain had proved herself a weak and ineffective
ally. She had bowed to the Jewish revolt in Palestine and to
American pressure. She had intervened in Sinai at the last moment only to try to force the Egyptians to recognize the validity of
the 1936 Anglo-Egyptian Treaty. What use was she then as an
ally, as far as Arab interests were concerned? The main justification for Anglo-Arab alliances was that Britain should be strong
enough to protect the Arabs and thereby demonstrate a mutual
interest in security. But here was a case where vital Arab interests
were affected and Britain would not or could not act, for fear of
offending Jewish and American opinion. Where British interests
were concerned Britain did not hesitate to use force, if necessary
against Arabs and Egyptians, but if the British were too weak to
deal with the Zionists, how could they stand up to the Russians,
the new bogey which they were using to argue in favour of joint
Middle East defence pacts? The inevitable conclusion drawn by
this Arab reasoning – which ignored the complications of domestic and international politics by which Great Powers often find
themselves trapped in contradictory policies – was a simple one:
the British forces were not in the Middle East to fight the Russians

but to control the Arabs. Moreover, in the broader international context, an alliance with a weak Britain seemed likely to attract Soviet hostility while being unable effectively to deter the possible consequences of such hostility.

The fault of the Egyptian government in the Palestine struggle was not, however, that it fought a 'political war' but that its politics were even worse than its military strategy. It chose the wrong political priorities: it attached more importance to frustrating the territorial ambitions of King Abdullah of Jordan than to the most practical unified action to save as much as possible of Arab Palestine. This policy was prompted partly by the personal rivalries of King Farouk and King Abdullah, and partly by the traditional opposition of Egypt and Saudi Arabia to the Hashemites. Also, an expansion of Transjordan seemed in Cairo to be a strengthening of the British position.

If the weakness and disunity of the Arabs and the dangerous domination of imperialism were indeed the ideas upon which Nasser brooded during the tense nights of the Falluja siege, the state of Egypt on his return home did little to disprove them. The British army sat in force in the Suez Canal Zone and Egypt was in the grip of a ruthless police repression. While the war was in progress in Palestine, there had been a near-revolution at home. A strike of the police in Alexandria in April 1948, leading to riots and widespread looting and army intervention, had shown the savage temper of the growing and neglected slum population of Egypt's great cities. The government had taken some half-hearted measures to try to ease unemployment, but its main answer was to intensify the hunt for 'subversive elements' begun under Sidky. Hundreds of its political opponents were interned in prison camps on charges of 'Communism' or 'Zionism' or both.[5]

Renewed agitation against Britain fed nationalist fervour again into the social discontent. Then came the bitter disappointment of the Egyptian defeats in the Negev. After a stormy summer, there was a more savage explosion of rioting and xenophobic rage in November. Jews and Jewish property and Europeans were the main target. Jewish shops were wrecked and looted in Cairo and 150 Jews were reported to have been killed. The leaders of the campaign were the Muslim Brotherhood. Their strength and influence had been growing rapidly. It looked as if they were preparing for a revolutionary seizure of power. The government had hitherto feared to take action against them because of public sympathy for the courageous performance of their volunteers in Palestine. But the situation in Cairo had begun to frighten the Egyptian ruling class. After the November riots Nokrashy, who never lacked either courage or patriotism, ordered the dissolution of the Brotherhood. Three weeks later, on 28 December 1948, he was assassinated by a Muslim Brother.

Nokrashy's successor, another Saadist leader, Ibrahim Abdul Hadi, struck back ruthlessly at the Brotherhood. Hundreds of its members were arrested, tortured and held without trial in desert camps. On 12 February 1949, the Brotherhood Supreme Guide, Sheikh Hassan el Banna, was assassinated. His murderers were, it is believed, either the government secret police or killers hired by Nokrashy's friends or family. The police claimed to have discovered a widespread revolutionary terrorist organization which included Muslim Brotherhood members.

Investigation of the terrorist wing of the Brotherhood, which had come partly into the open as a result of training volunteers for the Palestine war, had also led the police to look at its army connexions. A warrant was issued for Nasser's arrest. His house was searched by the military police, but they found nothing incriminating. On 25 May Nasser was sent for by the prime minister, Ibrahim Abdul Hadi, and closely questioned about the connexion between the Brotherhood and the army. It was, according to Anwar es-Sadat, 'a stormy interview'. The prime minister more or less accused Nasser of helping to train the Brotherhood terrorists. Nasser, usually calm, lost his temper but apparently convinced Abdul Hadi that he was not involved in any subversive activity.[6]

The officers lay low for a time until the police pressure under Abdul Hadi eased off. Then Nasser, back at the Staff College as an instructor, began to reorganize his secret army network. It was now that the movement set about establishing both a more solid and widespread organization and a more precise programme. It also formally adopted for the first time the name of the 'Society of Free Officers'. The cell system was overhauled and an executive committee of ten officers was set up which was to be the core of the future Revolutionary Command Council. In addition to Major Nasser, who became first president of the committee, this body was composed of five other army officers – Abdul Hakim Amer, Kamal ed-din Hussein, Salah Salem, Khaled Mohieddin and Anwar es-Sadat – and four air force officers, Gamal Salem, Hassan Ibrahim, Abdul Latif Baghdadi and Abdul Moneim Abdul Raouf.[7]

In October 1949, at a secret meeting at Amer's house, the executive committee agreed on a plan of action to prepare a revolution over the next five years. In this programme the struggle against imperialism, meaning in the first instance the withdrawal of British forces from Egypt, was to have top priority. The programme also called for a strong modern army and a democratic parliamentary system.[8]

According to General Neguib, it was at this time that he established his first contacts with the Free Officers. Neguib had won distinction by his personal courage in Palestine where he had been seriously wounded. Amer, who had been on his staff, came to visit him in hospital in Cairo and once brought Nasser with him, obviously to size the general up as a potential senior recruit to the secret movement.[9] From then on Neguib seems to have been in regular contact with the Free Officers but without being let into their inmost secrets.

After months of police terror, King Farouk dismissed Abdul Hadi and replaced him with a caretaker government under Hussein Sirry, charged with the task of preparing elections. The king had an eye on a *rapprochement* with the Wafd. He had grown impatient with the private criticisms from the Saadist ministers of his increasingly scandalous personal life. But he must also have realized that he was becoming too isolated and unpopular and that some concessions would have to be made to public feelings. It was one of the most corrupt of all the king's cronies, his press counsellor, the Lebanese Karim Thabet, who was secretly clearing the path for the return of the Wafd by his personal contacts with Fuad Serag ed-din, the Wafd Secretary-General. Judging from the Wafd's subsequent performance, these two struck a bargain on the basis of 'live and let live' – if the Wafd returned to power, it would not enquire too closely into the corrupt practices of the palace, and vice versa.

In the elections held in January 1950, the Wafd, probably helped by the secret support of the palace and the Muslim Brotherhood, won with a large majority. But even with this help, the Wafd had less than half the total votes. This and the low percentage of the poll indicated the extent to which the great national party of between the wars had begun to lose its mass support. Nevertheless, the return of the Wafd was greeted with high hope and enthusiasm in Egypt and with more cautious optimism in Britain. Egyptians looked forward at least to some relief from the increasingly oppressive and corrupt royal dictatorship of the past five years. They hoped that, under the influence of younger liberal elements, the Wafd leadership had turned over a new leaf and would initiate the social and economic reforms the country needed. It could be relied upon to press the national cause of ridding Egypt of British troops. But in London there was hope that the Wafd, though leading the nationalist clamour, might repeat its statesmanlike performance in making the 1936 Treaty and achieve a compromise settlement of the Anglo-Egyptian dispute over the Suez Canal Zone base and the Sudan.

There was at first some justification for these illusions. The Wafd government included a number of able and honest ministers, such as the Finance Minister, Zaki Motaal; the Minister for Social Affairs, Ahmed Hussein (an internationally recognized expert on Egyptian rural welfare and no relation to the Misr el Fatat leader of the same name); the Minister for Education, the famous scholar and author, Taha Hussein; and the Foreign Minister, Mohammed Salah ed-din. Plans were launched for a limited social security scheme and for universal free education. Police measures and press censorship were relaxed. After a visit by Bevin to Cairo negotiations with Britain were reopened.

Egypt began to breathe more freely again but it soon became clear that the hopes placed in the Wafd were not to be fulfilled. To the public scandal of the king's private life was added that of Nahas Pasha, the Wafdist prime minister himself, governed in his dotage by a younger wife who was herself a member of a grasping political clan. The Wafd collaborated with the palace in stifling enquiry into the purchase of defective arms during the Palestine war, when it looked as if the investigation was nearing the truth. One of the key men reported to be involved in the scandal was a close confidant of the king. He was said to have been responsible for handling a million pounds in arms dealers' bribes, a large part of which went to the king himself.[10] In return, Wafd ministers themselves were left free to indulge in corruption on an even more spectacular scale. The Korean war had driven the price of cotton high and vast fortunes were made by the rigging of the Alexandria cotton market with government connivance.

Efforts to settle the Palestine problem through the United Nations Palestine Conciliation Commission ended in a deadlock that was to continue for years. The armistice was meant to be the first step to a peace settlement, but the result was neither peace nor war, but merely a suspension of hostilities. The Arab states would not consider negotiating a final peace settlement until Israel had complied with the United Nations resolutions on Palestine, including withdrawal to the frontiers laid down by the 1947 Partition Plan. The first step, they insisted, must be the return of the Palestine Arab refugees to their homes. Israel had meanwhile begun to take in hundreds of thousands of new immigrants and refused to consider the return of the Arab refugees or other particular issues separately from a general peace settlement. She argued that the Partition Plan frontiers had been rendered null and void by the Arab rejection of them and the subsequent Palestine war. She made it plain that she would cede none of the territory she had gained, except for minor adjustments, and would take back few if any Arab refugees. The furthest she went, under American pressure, was to offer to take back 100,000 out of some 800,000 refugees. Instead, she offered compensation and said that the refugees should be settled in the Arab countries.

Only King Abdullah of Jordan (who had successfully incorporated the rump of Arab Palestine, except for the Gaza Strip, into his Transjordan kingdom) was prepared to discuss peace terms with the Israelis without prior conditions. He did so in secret, but secrets do not last long in the Arab East, and he paid for his boldness with his life. He was assassinated in Arab Jerusalem on 20 July 1951.

The failure of Israel–Arab peace talks led the Western Powers (the United States, Britain and France) to try at least to prevent the resumption of war. In May 1950, they issued their Tripartite Declaration, guaranteeing the armistice lines against violation and promising to control arms deliveries to the Middle East so as to maintain a balance between Israel and the Arab states. The Tripartite Declaration coincided with a new interest of the Western Powers, especially Britain, in the organization of the regional defence of the Middle East against Russia. It thereby marked the beginning of the dilemma or confusion of policy which was to characterize Western diplomacy in the Middle East for the next decade and to accelerate its decline and the rise of Russian influence in the area. It was a confusion which Nasser himself, when he came to power, was to find constantly baffling, since the resulting western policy appeared to him to reflect no rational consideration of Western, let alone Arab interests.

The dilemma was this: so long as there was no settlement between Israel and the Arab states, there could be no serious Middle East joint defence plan which included Egypt and Israel's other neighbours, Jordan, Syria and Lebanon. This was not only because of problems of geography and communications, but also of arms supply. If the Arab states and especially Egypt were to be treated as equal partners in Middle East defence and adequately armed, what became of the Tripartite Declaration on arms control? The Israel prime minister, Ben Gurion, warned on 12 July 1951 that cooperation between the Arabs and Israel in time of war was 'wishful thinking'. A great part of his subsequent policy of 'activism' (vigorous reprisals against the Arab states and military pressure to maintain and consolidate the political *status quo*) was in fact directed not so much towards the Arab states themselves as to the Western Powers. It was meant to demonstrate that in Western plans for the Middle East Israel must not be left out of the reckoning. Ben Gurion was determined to ensure that Middle East regional defence schemes based on a Western–Arab alliance should work only on the basis of a political–military settlement which guaranteed Israel's survival.

In the resumed Anglo-Egyptian talks there was a new emphasis on the British side on the place of the Suez Canal Zone military base in the regional defence of the Middle East. Previously, especially in the 1936 Treaty, the stress had been on the importance of the Canal as a lifeline of British imperial communications. The new emphasis on regional defence was in line with the development of NATO in Europe and its projected extension to include Greece and Turkey. It also reflected Britain's greater interest in the Arab oil lands farthur east, in Iraq and the Persian Gulf. Stalin's forward policy in Eastern Europe and above all the Korean war had created an exaggerated fear of direct Soviet military attack as the main danger from Moscow in the Middle East, when the real vulnerability of the area to Soviet penetration lay in its internal weaknesses: its social backwardness, its semi-colonial status and its local rivalries and conflicts.

At first it seemed as though there might be room for compromise between Britain and Egypt on the defence issue. While Nahas Pasha stuck to the principle of the complete and immediate evacuation of British troops, he declared himself ready to consider maintaining, with the help of a few hundred British technicians, a base in Egypt to which the British could return in time of war.

But there were several factors which prevented an agreement at this stage. The worsening international situation and the intensification of the cold war led the British to pitch their military demands too high – higher than those proposed by Bevin to Sidky in 1946. The Egyptian government on its side insisted on linking the question of the Sudan with that of the Canal base and itself put its Sudan demands too high. Finally, both governments were operating from a position of domestic weakness. The British Labour government had emerged from the 1950 election with a majority of only six and Bevin, a sick man, had been replaced by Herbert Morrison, perhaps the least skilful Foreign Secretary of this century. The government was being assailed over Egypt not only by the Tory Opposition demanding imperial firmness but also by some of its own pro-Zionist back-benchers. The Wafd on its side was losing popularity at home. It had produced no positive result in talks with the British; it had failed to check the rising cost of living; and there was growing public awareness of its corrupt practices. The lifting of martial law and of press censorship led to a rapid growth of a violently vituperative radical and extreme nationalist press, subsidized, some claimed, from Communist bloc embassies.

The Free Officers, too, were taking advantage of the relaxation of security measures to circulate their mimeographed tracts. At first they had shared the hopes put in the Wafd, but the covering up of the arms scandal soon disillusioned them.[11] Their main targets were still the king and the corrupt higher officers of the army.

Otherwise, their tracts echoed the nationalist demands of the radical wing of the Wafd for complete and immediate British evacuation, no alliances and a policy of neutrality like that of India.[12]

The tragedy of errors played out by two weak governments developed towards a crisis in the summer and autumn of 1951. It was a tragedy because both Britain and Egypt were trying to assert their wills in the two spheres in which they could not succeed, when in fact their final intentions for both defence matters and the Sudan were not vastly different. Egypt insisted on her unity with the Sudan but, in practice was in no position to enforce her claim. Britain insisted on Egyptian military cooperation in defence and the maintenance of a base, but could not force Egypt to co-operate without an unthinkable and impracticable reconquest of the whole country. By encouraging self-government in the Sudan, with or without Egyptian agreement, Britain had been able to demonstrate that Egypt could not effectively prevent the Sudanese march towards self-determination, however legal Egypt's claims as one of the co-domini might be and however legitimate her interests in preventing any hostile control of the waters of the Nile. But the British had not perhaps realized that Egypt could also show that the British base in the Canal Zone in peacetime was ineffective without Egyptian cooperation, however legal the British presence there might be, and however vital Britain's interest in preventing hostile strategic control of the Middle East communications and oil supplies. The vital interests of neither side could any longer be attained by force but only by persuasion; yet each was in a position to obstruct, frustrate and threaten the other. It was a situation ideally designed to produce the maximum of ill-feeling and the minimum of practical results.

In spite of an urgent appeal for delay from Morrison, saying that new defence proposals were on the way, on 9 October 1951 Nahas Pasha announced the abrogation not only of the 1936 Treaty but also of the 1899 convention on the Sudan. Four days later the Western Powers, in the name of the United States, Britain, France and Turkey, presented proposals to Egypt for a Middle East Defence Organization of which Egypt would be a founder-member and which would replace the Anglo-Egyptian Treaty. At the same time, Britain proposed the establishment of an international commission to supervise the preparation of the Sudan for self-government and self-determination. The Sudanese proposals were unexceptionable. Though not immediately accepted by Egypt, they formed part of the eventual Sudan settlement. But the Western defence proposals were incredibly ill-timed and ill-conceived. It did not take much acumen to perceive, as the Egyptian government quickly pointed out, that the terms and the context of the MEDO plan would have meant an occupation of the Canal Zone by four Powers instead of one and a multiple veto on any Egyptian military proposals. It 'invited' Egypt to become a partner in an arrangement already fixed beforehand by four other Powers, one of whom was occupying Egypt against her will, another of whom, France, had just been persuaded to relinquish only with the greatest reluctance her control of the nearby Arab countries of Syria and the Lebanon, while a third, Turkey, was a country from whose suzerainty the Egyptians had struggled for a century and a half to shake themselves free. If there were less long-standing historic objections to the United States, she had recently shown herself the chief friend of Israel and acceptance of her military presence could only mean an inescapable commitment to the East–West cold war in which almost every Egyptian would have wished to remain neutral.

When Morrison told the House of Commons in a belligerent speech on 16 October 1951, on the eve of a British general election, that Egypt's position in MEDO would be no different from that of Britain in NATO, since Britain also had foreign troops on her soil, he was deceiving no one. For the essential point, as every intelligent Egyptian knew, was that if Britain had decided to withdraw from NATO and asked American troops to leave, then the Americans would, though grumblingly and with reason, have gone (as they were to go from France at de Gaulle's request fifteen years later). It would have been inconceivable that they should refuse to leave and should then fire on British patriots who tried to make them move. It was impossible to imagine them occupying British towns and destroying British villages in order to maintain their presence. If they had done so, it would not have been surprising if a British government which failed to dislodge them were itself to be overthrown.

This is what happened in Egypt. The situation which developed between the British and Egyptians after the abrogation of the treaty was extraordinary between two countries arguing about an alliance, since it was one of more or less limited war. But the Wafd was uncertain just how far to go in its militancy. It declared a boycott of labour and supplies to the British forces in the Canal Zone but was ambivalent in its attitude to armed attacks. Officially it was against violence but it condoned and sometimes encouraged the activities of volunteer guerrillas, of students, Muslim Brothers, Communists and sometimes local gangsters, who sniped at and ambushed British troops and raided British stores and camps. Eventually it was forced to take over these 'liberation commandoes', partly in order to keep them under control. At first the police helped to control mob violence, but then stood aside or increasingly, in the case of the auxiliary police, or Boulak el Nizam, gave support to terrorism.

The British commander in Egypt, General Erskine, with a new Conservative government in London behind him, replied to these attacks with ruthless energy. He seized control of the main rail and road communications of the Canal Zone and of Ismailia, the chief town, headquarters of the Suez Canal Company and the home of many British families. Fifty houses of an Egyptian village were demolished by bulldozers and dynamite to protect a water pipe-line near Suez. Scores of Egyptian families were evicted from their homes in Ismailia. Tanks turned their heavy guns on houses sheltering snipers in Suez and elsewhere.

And what were the Egyptian army and Nasser's secret group doing during this extraordinary national crisis? The Egyptian army as a whole remained passive. The British had seized control of the road and railway bridge across the Suez Canal which carried supplies to the Egyptian army division in Sinai. Egyptian forces had also taken up positions on the Cairo–Suez road, covering the approaches to the capital, where a no-man's land of desert separated them from the British outposts of the Canal Zone. All traffic into and out of the Zone was controlled by the British. It was a stalemate. In any case, the Egyptian army was both outnumbered and heavily out-gunned. A straight military encounter between the two armies would have been a massacre.

If the Egyptian army was forced to hold aloof, its feelings were not in doubt. Guerrilla warfare was another matter. The Free Officers were later to join in the condemnation of the Wafd for having recklessly plunged Egypt without proper preparation into a deadly campaign against powerful British forces. But at least one of them (Anwar es-Sadat) recalls that at the time they admired the patriotism of the Wafd in their campaign against the British. They even approached the Wafd, through its Secretary-General and Minister of the Interior, Fuad Serag ed-din, with an offer of support if the Wafd would depose the king. But the approach came to nothing.[13] The Free Officers secretly helped in the training of volunteers for the 'liberation commandoes' and some of them fought themselves in civilian clothes in the Canal Zone. But the Officers already had another preoccupation. They were at grips with the king and his secret police and the struggle was coming out in the open.

The king's unpopularity was increasing rapidly. He had deepened it by appointing, in the middle of the Canal Zone crisis, a new chief of his Royal Cabinet, Hafiz el Afifi, an able and intelligent man but known for his pro-British views. There were violent student-led demonstrations against the king in Cairo and Alexandria. At the same time, the Free Officers decided to challenge the king openly for the first time by putting up their own candidates for the presidency of the executive committee of the Army Officers Club, in competition with the king's nominees. Against the highly unpopular General Hussein Sirry Amer they put forward General Neguib for the presidency and other Free Officers for the Committee. It was a test of strength inside the army, and the Free Officers won hands down. On 6 January 1952, Neguib and all their candidates were elected. The king was furious. He suspected the existence of a subversive army group but did not know who was in it.

The Free Officers and the palace police had been trying to break each other's secrets. While the police tried to ferret out the weak spots in the officers' organization, the Free Officers built up contacts with the palace. The king's doctor and confidant, Dr Youssef Rashad, was cultivated by Anwar es-Sadat, while Major Salah Salem tried to win the confidence of the army chief of staff, General Haidar Pasha.[14]

It was to this cloak-and-dagger period that Nasser was referring when he later wrote,

> I even thought of assassinating the ex-king and some of his confederates – those evil geniuses who played havoc with our rights and liberties and everything we held sacred. ... Many indeed were the plans I drew up in those days. In fact our activities in those days very much resembled those depicted in a detective thriller. ... We had secret symbols and signs. We moved under cover of darkness and stored stacks of pistols and bombs, the anticipated utilisation of which represented our sole aspiration. We actually made many attempts in this direction.

But Nasser had doubts, he said, about such violent courses. 'I was in a state of perplexity mixed with inter-linking factors – patriotism and religion, scepticism and conviction, cruelty and compassion, knowledge and ignorance.'[15] His reflections on the abortive attempt to kill General Hussein Sirry Amer, early in 1952, confirmed his doubts about the use of political assassination as a revolutionary weapon.[16]

Simultaneously with these melodramatic adventures, Nasser was beginning to broaden his political contacts and develop his political ideas more systematically. At the Staff College he read a good deal, mostly works on politics and history and biographies. Among his new friends in the political world was Ahmed Abul Fath, editor of the Wafdist newspaper *Al Misri*,* a radical and neutralist and brother-in-law of one of the Free Officers, Colonel Sarawat Okasha.

---

*Abul Fath later broke with Nasser. He went into exile in 1954 and wrote a book *L'Affaire Nasser*, published in Paris, bitterly attacking Nasser. *Al Misri* was taken over by the government.

By the beginning of 1952 Egypt was on the edge of chaos. The guerrilla warfare and British reprisals in the Canal Zone became increasingly serious. On 25 January General Erskine announced his intention of disarming and expelling at once from Ismailia all the Egyptian auxiliary police suspected of helping the guerrillas. The main police barracks at Ismailia were surrounded by strong forces of British troops and tanks. The British-trained police commander, on instructions from Serag ed-din, in Cairo, to 'fight to the last bullet', rejected a British ultimatum to surrender. After a brief exchange of small-arms fire – the police had no heavy weapons – the British tanks opened up on the barracks at point-blank range. The police resisted bravely for three hours and by the time they were forced to surrender had lost forty-one killed and seventy-two wounded. Three British soldiers were killed.

The assault was a grave political mistake and was considered so by some observers at the time. The power employed was excessive, and insufficient time was given to finding means of enabling the Egyptian authorities and the police themselves to make an honourable retreat. Its consequences were immediate and profound. What all Egyptians regarded as a brutal massacre sent a shock of incredulous revulsion and anger throughout the country.

In Cairo the next day units of the auxiliary police marched out of their barracks and through the streets of the city to the government offices and the Abdin Palace in protest demonstrations. They were joined by students and other demonstrators. At first the demonstrations, though angry, were not violent. But as it became clear that the authorities were taking no precautions to keep order and that the police, sympathetic in any case with the mutinous mood of their comrades, had no orders to interfere, the crowds grew more ugly. New elements took a hand. The riff-raff of the city surged out of the slums in search of loot. Small gangs of political arsonists and saboteurs equipped with inflammable material, demolition equipment and lists of targets, seized the opportunity of the virtual withdrawal of authority from a great city to turn an inevitable explosion of national anger into an orgy of murder and destruction. Most of the destruction was directed at buildings in the central part of the city associated with British or other European interests, or at bars, cinemas and other similar establishments. The chosen targets symbolized the hated alliance of pashas and foreigners. Shepheards Hotel, symbol above all of the Egypt of the 'good old days'; the British Turf Club, where twelve people, including nine British civilians, were murdered with horrible brutality, and Barclays Bank were among the 700 or more buildings burnt down, smashed or looted, as the crowds raged through the streets unchecked. Altogether, seventeen Europeans and fifty Egyptians were reported to have been killed.

At the British embassy, the ambassador, Sir Ralph Stevenson, waited agonizingly poised to 'press the button' which would summon British forces from the Canal Zone to intervene in Cairo to protect British lives and property. He hung on grimly, as the reports of destruction came in, because he knew that a British take-over in Cairo would be a political disaster, putting the clock back seventy years, and he was convinced that eventually the king would be forced to order the Egyptian army to intervene in order to save his own position.[17] When he tried to contact the Minister of the Interior, Serag ed-din, he was told he was out buying a house. The prime minister, Nahas Pasha, was too busy having his corns cut. The king was entertaining many of the army senior officers at lunch at Abdin Palace. But for hours neither the king nor the government moved.[18] Each, it seems, was hoping, by allowing trouble to develop, to frighten the other and force them to take repressive action first. The king may also have hesitated, according to one report, because the army commander, Haidar Pasha, had told him he could not be sure of the loyalty of the army. It was not simply a matter of suspect officers but of whether the rank and file might not join in the savage popular explosion in the capital. According to Sadat, those Free Officers who were in Cairo that day had orders from their organization to do what they could to check the riots.

Finally, in mid-afternoon, when the smoke from burning buildings was already rising in a thick pall over the city and the pavements were covered with broken glass, the blood of victims and the trampled debris of fashionable stores, the king ordered the army to clear the streets. Within three hours the capital was once more under control, but the *ancien régime* of Egypt had been struck a blow from which it never recovered.

Much controversy followed over the responsibility for 'Black Saturday'. No complete or clear picture emerged from the subsequent official enquiries. It seems probable that the gangs of arsonists belonged to Ahmed Hussein's so-called Socialist Party but there has never been convincing evidence of Ahmed Hussein's own complicity or of the story circulating at the time that the arsonists had been paid and organized by a Communist bloc embassy. The hands of the Muslim Brothers and their sympathizers can be seen in the attacks on places of entertainment and in the xenophobic destruction of non-Arabic shop signs. The Wafd and the king may both have connived at some disorder to discredit one another but surely neither foresaw how things would get out of hand. Simply, the day was a combination of the pent-up fury and frustration of the Egyptian masses and the slackening of a police repression which had hitherto kept them cowed. By their killing of the police in Ismailia, the British had helped to destroy one of the main forces that was preserving order and with it British interests in Cairo. The king, the Wafd and the British who between them had ruled Egypt for the previous thirty years had now between them made Egypt ungovernable. It was time for them all to go, and for others to take over.

But before the whole system finally collapsed there was a period of six months of uncertainty and crisis in which four successive prime ministers tried to patch it up again out of its traditional elements. At the same time, Black Saturday had made it plain that the army was now the final arbiter in an already revolutionary situation. While the politicians manoeuvred, the forces in the army which were to deliver the *coup de grâce* were making their final preparations. The first stage, the struggle for control of the army itself, had already secretly begun.

The first to go was the Wafd. Nahas was dismissed by the king the day after Black Saturday and Aly Maher was brought back from a decade in the wilderness to replace him. Aly Maher, a true Trimmer, tried to keep in touch with the Wafd, the king and the British at the same time, while also promising a charter of reform designed to appeal to the militant young. The king's idea of restoring authority and of national reconstruction was, however, simply to take vengeance on the Wafd. Aly Maher was not prepared either to dismiss parliament or to be harsh enough with the Wafdists. So he was replaced by Neguib el Hilaly, an intelligent and honest ex-Wafdist who had been a popular Minister of Education and had resigned from the Wafd in protest against corrupt practices. A gentle intellectual, he hoped to rally the support of the more liberal elements in the Wafd by a drive against official corruption. He agreed to dissolve parliament and to exile Serag ed-din, the Wafd Secretary-General. But the king found Hilaly's corruption enquiries coming too near his own interests.

So on 30 June Hilaly gave way to that old stand-by and mediator, Hussein Sirry. Hussein Sirry was more conciliatory to the Wafd and called for a new general election. He also advised the king to appease the obviously rising wave of discontent in the army by appointing General Neguib as Minister of War. But the king now pushed his folly to the limit. Far from appointing Neguib, he prepared instead to strike vindictively but, in the event, ineffectually at his army critics. On 15 July he ordered the dissolution of the Officers Club Committee and pressed Hussein Sirry to make the detested General Hussein Sirry Amer Minister of War. When Hussein Sirry warned the king of the consequences and gave him the names of officers who were believed to be already hostile to him, the king retorted, 'A bunch of pimps'. Hussein Sirry resigned, and the king called back Hilaly, who accepted the king's brother-in-law, Colonel Ismail Sherin, as Minister of War. The king also began steps to deal with the suspected army rebels. According to one story, he had plans not only for the dispersal and arrest of some of them but also for the eventual assassination by the secret police of those believed to be the leading figures.

News of the king's intentions reached the ears of the Free Officers (one source was Ahmed Abul Fath who tipped off the officers through his brother-in-law, Colonel Okasha) and precipitated the plans for action which Nasser and his group had been discussing for months past.[19]

On 10 February, a fortnight after Black Saturday, the executive committee of the Free Officers had met and decided to carry out a *coup* in the following month. They had been forced to postpone it because they were unable to ensure the support of Colonel Rashid Mehanna, an officer of fickle temperament and high ambition, on whom they had counted to bring in the artillery units under his command. They had meanwhile chosen General Neguib as the senior figurehead they needed, after having unsuccessfully approached General Fuad Sadek. Here the versions of General Neguib himself and of others about his role in the Free Officers movement begin to diverge. According to Neguib, he was elected President of the executive committee in the spring of 1952, but before the *coup* he had in fact met only five of the members of the committee.[20] Sadat says that Nasser remained president of the committee and Neguib knew nothing of its real plans until twenty-four hours before the *coup*. (Other leading Free Officers have told me the same story.) According to Sadat, the decisive pre-*coup* meeting of the executive committee was held under Nasser's chairmanship on 16 July, the day after the dissolution of the Officers Club committee on the orders of the king. The others present were Hassan Ibrahim, Kamal ed-din Hussein, Abdul Hakim Amer, Khaled Mohieddin, Abdul Latif Baghdadi and Sadat himself. Neguib was not there. It was then that the decision to act was taken. The *coup* was planned for midnight on 21 July. There was an alternative plan, opposed by Nasser, for mass assassination of the old regime leaders if the *coup* failed. On the afternoon of 20 July Nasser and Amer went to Neguib's house to tell him of the plans, but because of the presence of other visitors could only talk about the affair of the Club Committee.[21]

Neguib's version is that the decision to strike was made at a meeting at his house on 19 July, the day of Hussein Sirry's resignation, at which Nasser, Amer, Hassan Ibrahim and Kamal ed-din Hussein were present. It was agreed that Neguib should stay at home and take no active part in the first phase of the revolt, since he was being closely watched and his movements would arouse suspicion.[22]

Both versions agree that the *coup* was fixed for 22 July and then postponed twenty-four hours because the preparations could not be completed in time. The delay was nearly fatal to the conspirators. The government had taken alarm. On the evening of 22 July, the army chiefs were meeting with the chief of staff, General Hussein Farid, at general headquarters to plan their action. Tipped off by an army intelligence officer, the Free Officers advanced their own attack on the headquarters. Nasser's comment on hearing of the meeting was, 'It will save us time and trouble. We can take them all together, instead of one by one at their homes.' The attack on general headquarters, led by Amer, was helped by the defection to the rebels of a company of troops that had been sent by the chief of staff to surround the Free Officers' quarters.[23]

The plan of the *coup* had been drawn up in outline by Nasser and worked out in detail by Amer and Kamal ed-din Hussein. Nasser, driving round from unit to unit in his small black Austin car, was the animating and directing commander. At one point he was almost shot by mistake when his car was stopped in the night by rebel troops who did not recognize him.

The operation was planned in three main stages. First, to ensure control of the armed forces; second, to take over civil government and appoint a new prime minister; and finally to get rid of the king. (The original plan was more elaborate: to take over all centres of government at once. Nasser simplified it to concentrate first on gaining control of the army, arguing that if this were achieved, the rest would follow easily.)

While Nasser and Amer, revolver in hand, took over the general staff, other units seized other key points in the city, some government buildings, the radio and telephone exchanges. Gamal and Salah Salem had taken control of the army units in Sinai. A detachment of troops with armour was posted on the road into Cairo from Suez with orders to try to stop any move by the British forces in the Canal Zone to intervene in the capital. At the same time the rebels sent an officer (Squadron Leader Aly Sabry, then chief of air force intelligence and later one of Nasser's chief political advisers) to the American embassy. He informed the Americans of the *coup* and asked them to pass a message on to the British embassy in Cairo urging the British to keep out of what was a purely internal affair, promising protection of foreign lives and property and warning of resistance to any attempted

British intervention. The British took some military precautions but there seems never to have been any serious question of British military action.[24]

Neguib was told of the success of the first phase of the *coup* in the early hours of the morning. He was escorted to the rebel-occupied general headquarters and appointed commander-in-chief of the armed forces. He then emerged as the public leader of the *coup*. It was in Neguib's name that Sadat read a proclamation over the radio at seven in the morning that told the Egyptian people something – not much – of the *coup* and its purposes. The proclamation (said by Sadat to have been written by Amer) spoke of a purge in the army to rid it of 'traitors and incompetents' and to put it in 'the hands of men in whose ability, integrity and patriotism you can have complete confidence'.

The proclamation declared the army's intention of preserving law and order and protecting foreign nationals. It warned that any acts of violence or destruction would be punished as treason.[25]

The news was received in Cairo with popular enthusiasm. And those who were not pleased were cowed by the tanks in the streets and the planes swooping low overhead. No mention had yet been made of the next two political phases of the *coup*. The king and his prime-minister-designate Hilaly still thought it was only a matter of internal army reform which could be settled by a compromise without affecting the civil government. The telephones were kept busy between the king and the ministers in Alexandria and the army headquarters in Cairo. Hilaly offered to support the movement and accept Neguib as commander-in-chief if the rebels proclaimed loyalty to the king. But the rebels had already begun the search for a new prime minister of their own. Their first choice, Aly Maher, agreed to let his name be put forward but cautiously added the condition that he must be called on officially by the king. Hilaly resigned and the king said he was ready to accept Aly Maher as his successor. Aly Maher was primed by the revolutionaries with a long list of demands to present to the king as a condition for accepting office. They included a wide political purge, social and economic reforms and the dismissal of all the king's personal entourage and advisers.

But the revolutionaries were already planning to move on to the final phase of the removal of the king, who was still in Alexandria. They were worried that unless they acted quickly Farouk might, with British help, manage to turn the tables on them. They believed that the British were considering an appeal from Farouk to intervene and that finally it was pressure from the United States which held the British back. The British government, according to Eden, had no intention of intervening to keep Farouk on the throne, but it warned Neguib that it would not hesitate to intervene if necessary to protect British lives.[26]

On the morning of 25 July Nasser told Sadat, 'The king must be expelled today, or tomorrow at the latest.' While troops and tanks under Colonel Zacharia Mohieddin were preparing to encircle the royal palaces in Alexandria to support the revolutionaries' ultimatum to the king, the executive committee had debated the king's fate in the middle of the night. Half of the committee were with Neguib in Alexandria and the rest with Nasser in Cairo. Gamal Salem, who wanted the king tried and sentenced to death, flew from Alexandria to consult those in Cairo, but a majority of the nine who voted, including Nasser and Neguib, decided on the king's exile. Gamal Salem brought back a written note from Nasser which clinched the matter. It said

The Liberation movement should get rid of Farouk as quickly as possible in order to deal with what is more important – namely, the need to purge the country of the corruption that Farouk will leave behind him. We must pave the way towards a new era in which the people will enjoy their sovereign rights and live in dignity. Justice is one of our objectives. We cannot execute Farouk without a trial. Neither can we afford to keep him in jail and preoccupy ourselves with the rights and wrongs of his case at the risk of neglecting the other purposes of the revolution. Let us spare Farouk and send him into exile. History will sentence him to death.[27]

At seven o'clock on the morning of 26 July, Mohieddin's troops began the seizure of the royal palaces of Montazah and Ras el Tin. Six men were wounded in a skirmish with the Royal Guards. Through Aly Maher, an ultimatum was delivered to the king demanding his abdication in favour of his infant son,

Prince Ahmed Fuad, by noon and his departure from Egypt before six o'clock that evening. The American ambassador sent a message to Neguib in Alexandria saying that while the US government was prepared to regard the *coup* as an internal matter for the Egyptians only, it would welcome an assurance that the king and his family would be allowed to leave Egypt unharmed and 'with honour'.[28]

Early that afternoon, the king signed the official document of abdication. He was allowed to leave on board the royal yacht *Mahroussa* to the accompaniment of a twenty-one-gun salute. Shortly before 6 P.M. Farouk took leave of Aly Maher and the American ambassador at the Ras el Tin Palace and, dressed in admiral's uniform, boarded the *Mahroussa* at the palace quay. With him went his queen, Narriman, and the infant prince, as well as his three daughters by his former wife. Over 200 trunks full of the king's personal property had been hurriedly packed and stowed aboard.

Neguib came to say goodbye to Farouk on board the yacht. As Neguib prepared to leave after an embarrassed brief conversation, the king said, 'I hope you'll take good care of the army. My grandfather, you know, created it.' When Neguib replied that the army was in good hands, Farouk added, 'Your task will be difficult. It isn't easy, you know, to govern Egypt. . . .'[29]

While Neguib was attending these historic funeral rites of the 150-year-old Mohammed Ali dynasty and receiving the acclamations of the astonished and excited Alexandrian crowds, Nasser, the chief architect of the *coup* which was not yet a revolution, was hard at work in Cairo in the position of *éminence grise* he was to occupy for nearly two years.

Chapter 5

The Path to Power and the Struggle for National Independence, 1952–4

With the departure of the king, three main problems faced Nasser and his colleagues. The traditional political system of Egypt had collapsed: they had either to try to reform the old structure and put it on its feet again or devise a new one. The British were still in Egypt and the Sudan: they had 75,000 troops and £500 million worth of installations in the Canal Zone; in the Sudan they were working fast to separate the Sudanese from Egypt for ever and to bring them more securely into the British imperial orbit. There could be no political stability in Egypt until the British troops had left, but how in the face of overwhelmingly superior British military power was the evacuation to be achieved?

Then there was the appalling state of Egypt itself. The economy was stagnant: the increase in productivity was beginning to lag behind the rising rate of population growth. The conditions of poverty, disease, illiteracy and exploitation, especially among the peasants who formed two-thirds of the population, were among the worst in the world.

While the countryside seemed sunk in apathy except for an occasional local squatters revolt, 'Black Saturday' had shown something of the fury in the great city slums. Industry, still small with about a million workers, was slack. *Per capita* income in Egypt on the eve of the revolution was £42 ($100) a year, one-tenth of that of Britain. But the income of the poorest was much lower. *Per capita* net income from agriculture was only £22 ($52·8) a year. Landless labourers earned only about ten piastres a day (10 p or 24 cents) and might earn nothing at all for half the year. The average life expectancy of an Egyptian male was thirty-six years compared with sixty-nine for an American.[1] Ninety per cent of the population were estimated to suffer from the debilitating disease of bilharzia and other parasitical maladies.[2]

Egypt had six times fewer doctors per head of population than an average Western European country and eighty times fewer hospital beds per head than in Britain.[3] Seventy-seven per cent of Egyptians over five were illiterate. These were long-term ills requiring long-term remedies. There were also more immediate troubles.

Despite what should have been a substantial gain in the national wealth from the cotton boom during the Korean war, the Wafd administration had left a balance-of-payments deficit of £E38 million, with almost nothing in the sterling working account, a budget deficit of £E81 million and a large unsold surplus of cotton stocks bought by the government at high prices.

Within two years all three problems – the British, the political system and the economy – had been tackled simultaneously and with different degrees of success. An agreement had been reached for the withdrawal of the British troops from Egypt and for the future of the Sudan. Some painful first aid by a conservative finance minister had restored the national finances. The first small but important steps had been taken in the Herculean task of long-term economic and social development by an agrarian reform and the launching of a modest industrialization programme. The attempt to rebuild the political structure on its old basis had been virtually abandoned – if it had ever been seriously intended – and the Free Officers with Nasser now openly at their head had emerged as the nucleus of a new ruling *élite* of army officers, technocrats, administrators, professional men and other members of the middle class who sympathized with or profited from their activities. The search, still in progress eighteen years later for a broader and more popular political framework had begun, but the rule of Nasser and his colleagues was already what it was essentially to remain, a dictatorship but one which included some public consultation and rested on a wide degree of national consent about its aims if not its methods.

These were formative years for Nasser and his regime. By the end of 1954 a pattern had been set in Egypt's internal affairs, if not yet in her foreign policy, which was to dominate the next decade.

Egypt was glad to see the king go but it knew almost nothing of its new rulers. A few Egyptians might have heard of Neguib as a distinguished soldier, and for those politically in the know he was the centre of the recent conflict in the army between the king's men and the would-be reformers. Even to most of the best-informed, whether Egyptian or foreign, the rest of the *coup* leaders were unknown. At first all was done in the name of Neguib, and he seemed to be the leader. Another soldier credited publicly with a key role in the *coup* was Colonel Rashed Mehanna, an idea he himself helped to promote. He was kicked upstairs by the Free Officers Committee to be a member of the Regency Council as the first stage to his eventual disgrace and imprisonment. But gradually the word went around among politicians, journalists and diplomats that behind General Neguib and the civilian government formed by Aly Maher there was a secret military junta which took the important decisions. It met usually at night in what had been King Farouk's yacht house on an island in the Nile, where after hot but casual debate it took its decisions by majority vote. Apart from Neguib, who was a general and aged fifty-four, the rest of the junta were mostly in their thirties and were officers of middle rank. Its most influential member was rumoured to be 'el Bikbashi', the thirty-four-year-old Lieutenant-Colonel Gamal Abdul Nasser. The mysterious junta was in fact the thirteen-man executive committee of the Free Officers which was soon to emerge into the open under the title of the Revolutionary Command Council.

Even those who had read the earlier underground manifestoes of the Free Officers and now listened to their proclamations after the *coup*, would have been hard pressed at first to gain any clear idea of their aims. They wanted to get rid of the British; they wanted reform in the army which could only be achieved by getting rid of the king; they sought clean honest government in the interest of the people and not of the 'feudalists'. Beyond this their political ideas seemed vague and conflicting.

Was this vagueness real or deliberately misleading? Was it Nasser's intention from the first to climb to supreme power on the shoulders of the army? Or was he driven by events and experience to abandon early hopes of a more democratic constitutional system? Support for either thesis can be found in the writings and speeches of Nasser and other Free Officers. Their words mostly stress their early democratic hopes and reluctance to govern, while from the first their actions showed a decided will to power.

Nasser wrote later (in his booklet *The Philosophy of the Revolution* in 1953) that he had at first seen the army's task as that of an advance guard that charges 'the strongholds of oppression' to clear the way for the mass to follow on 'the Holy March to the Great Goal'. He had been dismayed to find that the masses did not follow the army's desperate charge but hung back as onlookers, as their forebears had passively watched the Mameluke cavalry fighting among themselves in the streets of Cairo in the Middle Ages. The politicians and intellectuals had been equally disappointing: they seemed interested only in furthering their personal interests, criticizing each other or patronizingly airing their egos. But even after this disillusion, after the abolition of the 1923 constitution and the dissolution of the political parties, Nasser still declared that the way forward out of the national crisis 'must lead to economic and political freedom. Our role is that of a guardian only, no more and no less, a guardian for a definite period with a time limit.'[4] In the same booklet, Nasser made it plain that he was a man of ambition and wide vision, that he had thought deeply, if not always with precision, about Egypt's political and social condition.

At about the same time as *The Philosophy* was written, in June 1953, Nasser gave another and more pragmatic explanation of the Free Officers' intentions. He said in an interview in the newspaper *Al Ahram* that he and a majority of the Free Officers had deliberately decided against drawing up a precise political programme before the *coup*. They wanted to avoid a split in the army movement, for

the political ideas of the Free Officers differed, according to their temperaments and the family or social milieu from which they came. ... What we all wanted was to purge the army, rid the country of foreign occupation and establish a clean, fair government which would work sincerely for the good of the people. Once in power, we found ourselves faced with the difficult problem of establishing a political, social and economic programme. It was necessary to improvise. We did our best. The divergence of political ideas then obliged us to separate from those who did not agree to apply the majority decisions of the

Council of the Revolution and then those of the Government we set up.

If pragmatism was for long a hall-mark of Nasser's political action, this did not mean lack of a purpose or of a determination to achieve it. Both Nasser and the old politicians approached each other after the *coup* with equal self-deception – a misunderstanding on the one side of the democratic process and on the other of the realities of power. Nasser and his colleagues assumed self-righteously that their early actions or proposals, such as the removal of the king, the purge of the army, the call on the political parties to purge themselves, the introduction of agrarian reform, and the appointment of a Regency Council were self-evidently correct actions which any man of good will must support. They thought that the proper instruments for carrying out these changes were the civilian politicians, the parties and a parliamentary government, provided they had been 'cleaned up' along the lines demanded by the junta. It was a civilian politician, Aly Maher, who had been used to hand the king the abdication ultimatum and to whom the officers had passed their land reform programme for execution.

According to Major Salah Salem, later the junta's public spokesman, the officers had themselves planned to return to barracks in six months. Nasser himself helped to persuade the junta at first to promise parliamentary elections in six months, that is by February 1953, while other officers with Marxist or Muslim Brotherhood leanings wanted more drastic revolutionary action. When the politicians questioned these arbitrarily decided changes, the officers saw such reservations not as a normal hazard of a free political life but as a proof that the politicians were unrepentantly rooted in the rotten society of the past. The officers were led to realize that what they wanted was a revolutionary remoulding of that society and that they alone could ensure the fulfilment of that desire. If the officers did not want power, they at least wanted the fruits of power. If they would have preferred democracy, they also wanted political and social results which could at that time be obtained only by dictatorship.

After years of planning and dreaming, Nasser and his friends must have had strong political intentions. Having risked their necks in a daring and brilliantly successful *coup*, they were obviously not going simply to hand over power to the civilian politicians until they were fairly sure that their most important aims would be carried out. Yet this is apparently what the old political leaders expected.

It is not altogether surprising if at first the professional politicians, including the Wafdist leaders, Nahas Pasha and Fuad Serag ed-din, who had hurried back from Europe, believed the officers were primarily concerned with reforming the army. There was the comforting presence of General Neguib at the head of affairs. He had spoken repeatedly of a quick return to constitutional life. He had called in a well-known civilian politician to be the first prime minister. (The manner in which Aly Maher was summoned suggests he was a last-minute choice: incredibly, after years of secret planning, none of the conspirators had Aly Maher's address and Anwar es-Sadat, who had known him of old, was sent to track him down with the help of a friendly journalist.)[5]

The determination of the junta to remove the king had been a first shock – even to Aly Maher who had 'turned pale as death' when the officers insisted on Farouk's departure despite the king's acceptance of all their demands.[6] But then the officers had put two respected civilian figures together with Colonel Mehanna on the Regency Council. However, more shocks were to come. Aly Maher was dismissed on 7 September and replaced as premier by General Neguib with a government of civilian technicians and a few officers. Aly Maher went because he had objected to the agrarian reform law which had been presented to him by the junta and had shown reluctance to enforce the purging of the Wafd.

The day after Neguib became premier, the agrarian reform law was promulgated. The law provided for a modest but comprehensive agrarian reform, including a redistribution of land. It was the work primarily of Wing Commander Gamal Salem, brother of Salah Salem, with the help of two left-wing 'progressives', the socialist economist Ahmed Fuad and another economist, Dr Rashid al Barawy, translator of *Das Kapital* into Arabic, and later author of a book on the 1952 *coup*.

Egypt's land problem was enormous in both human and

economic terms. There was first the simple shortage of cultivable land relative to the spectacular growth of population. Then within this limited area of cultivation the land was distributed in a manner both startlingly unequal and highly inefficient. The nineteenth-century development of perennial irrigation and of cotton as a cash crop had transformed Egyptian agriculture. It had changed it from a traditional subsistence economy supporting two or three million people into 'a highly commercialized and responsive enterprise' supporting over twenty million. For a poor country, Egypt had a relatively highly developed infrastructure of transport, credit and marketing, but its population density, at 650 people per square kilometre, was among the highest in the world for a predominantly agricultural country. The combination of Mohammed Aly's state monopoly and feudalistic land grants, followed by the *laissez faire* policy under the British and their immediate successors, and the fragmentation of landholdings due to the Muslim laws of inheritance, had also led to a situation where less than six per cent of the land-owners – some 162,000 persons – possessed sixty-five per cent of the cultivated area while over ninety-four per cent of the land-owners, or 2,600,000, owned only thirty-five per cent. Within the former group (defined as owning more than five feddans or acres), twenty per cent was held by large land-owners with more than 200 feddans, who formed 0·1 per cent of the owners.[7]

Many of the landlords, including many small ones with an inherited family share of the land, were absentees who lived in the cities. More than two-thirds did not operate their land themselves but let it out to tenants or sharecroppers on conditions which were usually harsh and not subject to official regulation.[8] Land prices averaged £E400 per feddan, too high for a small farmer to pay. Rents were usually fixed in relation to prices of cotton and other crops and averaged three-quarters of the net income from the land. The landlord usually provided the working capital, but most peasants, being too ignorant to be able to take advantage even of the meagre cooperative and government credit facilities available (the big land-owners knew better how to use them), were in debt to their landlords, to village moneylenders or to brokers. Even worse off were the landless labourers and their families, totalling some eight million souls whose average earnings worked out at £E7 per annum per person.[9]

Some big land-owners were enlightened farmers and might provide clinics for their villagers, but generally speaking 'feudalism' was a polite description for the social condition of the Egyptian countryside. A big land-owner was the boss of his district, able to command the services of the police at his discretion. He often employed his own gang of bravos as well as his agents to extort rents and depress wages. Almost the only restraint on his power – or sometimes its means of transmission – was the existence within the villages of a class of medium land-owners, of leading families who competed for the position of omdah or officially recognized headman. This class, from which Nasser's family came, might espouse rival political parties and, according to circumstance, be either the mainstay of authority or the groundswell of rebellion, as they were from Arabi to Nasser.

Egyptian peasants did not emigrate from the familiar intimacy of the Nile Valley except to Egypt's own cities, and industrial development was not enough to provide jobs for the millions who poured into the slums of Cairo and Alexandria.

The result was an unbelievable misery in the countryside alleviated only by a warm climate, narcotics, ignorance, religion and that humour, intimacy and solidarity that are often characteristic of slum life, whether rural or urban – for most of Egypt was a vast rural slum. These conditions, reminiscent of descriptions of the French peasantry in the eighteenth century before the Revolution or of Macaulay's picture of the savagery of rural life in seventeenth-century Catholic Ireland, were known to Nasser and his friends not only through their family connexions but also because most of their soldiers were drawn from the villages. Against such a background the land reform proposed by the Free Officers was modest indeed. It was all the same a milestone in the social history of the Arab East and was to provide a model for subsequent agrarian reforms in other Arab countries of the Middle East and North Africa. Its most publicized aspect was the decision to limit land holdings to 200 feddans per person, with 100 feddans extra allowed for dependants. Any land held in addition to this was to be requisitioned and redistributed by the state to small farmers, tenants and labourers. The requisitioned land was to be paid for with non-negotiable government bonds repayable over thirty years at three per cent interest. The compensation was fixed at ten times the rental value which in turn was calculated at seven times the basic land tax. This amounted to about half the market value or less, depending on how honest the land-owner had been in paying his taxes. The sale price to the new peasant owners was fixed on the same terms plus fifteen per cent for the administrative costs of the new Government Agrarian Reform Department (later elevated to a Ministry). Repayment was also over thirty years at three per cent interest. The land available for distribution totalled nearly half a million feddans and eventually about a million people – farmers and their families – were claimed to have benefited from rights of full ownership under the land redistribution, as against 10,000 big land-owners who lost.[10]

But the land redistribution – also applied to some lands held by the state and by Waqfs or Muslim religious endowments – was only one of four different aspects of the agrarian reform. A minimum wage was fixed for agricultural labourers at 18 piastres per day (18 p or 43 cents) and agricultural trades unions were legalized. Rents were pegged at seven times the land tax – about half their previous market value – and the conditions for tenancies and sharecropping regulated. Cooperative efforts were encouraged to overcome the fragmentation of land-ownership and farm operation and a new system of agricultural credits was introduced. The state began an increasing control and supervision of land reclamation.[11]

The economic effects of the agrarian reform naturally took some years to make themselves felt. Here we are concerned with the immediate political consequences. The ceiling on land holdings limited, as it was meant to, the local power of the really big land-owners and also their national political influence. This effect was to be produced not only because of the change in land distribution but also because the law demonstrated that the governmental authority was no longer at the disposal of the land-owner but on the side of the peasant.

Yet, even if the promised government compensation for requisitioned land was to prove illusory, the continued ownership of 200 feddans of good land was no mean asset. It represented a capital value of some £80,000 and an annual income from rent of between £6,000 and £8,000. Moreover, landlords had been given a breathing space before requisitioning in which they could sell their surplus land to small farmers instead of waiting for government seizure and compensation. Many did so at cut prices. Some economists and sociologists advising the junta had pressed for a lower ceiling, of fifty feddans for land-ownership. The junta had rejected this advice because they were afraid the administrative problem involved would be too difficult to handle without serious damage to agricultural productivity as a whole.

But 200 feddans was not good enough for the old rulers of Egypt. Aly Maher, supported by Colonel Mehanna, wanted to raise the limit to 500 feddans or to subject the surplus land to progressive taxation rather than confiscation. The Wafd Secretary-General, Fuad Serag ed-din, opposed the law. According to one report, Nasser had been prepared to offer the government to the Wafd and to restore parliamentary government at once if they had accepted the land reform. Nasser was at first outvoted seven to one on this issue in the Officers Committee and had resigned before getting his way.[12] But Nahas and Serag ed-din refused.

The Wafd and the Muslim Brotherhood were the only two groups which had survived from the collapse of the political system with any degree of mass support. Without the backing of the palace and the instruments of state power, the police, the army and the bureaucracy, the minority parties were exposed as only a handful of individuals of varying quality. They were mostly discredited by association with the king. But in spite of the failure of the old Wafdist leaders and the abortive insurrection and then repression of the Muslim Brothers, the Wafd and the Brotherhood both still had mass organizations. They could still count on a following among students and workers and in the villages. They also had sympathizers among the Free Officers, especially the left-wing of the Wafd which shaded off through fellow-travellers into Communists. The Muslim Brothers were particularly strongly represented among the officers, but they mistook the extent to which the junta was committed to their idea of an Islamic state. The junta invited the Muslim Brothers to take part in the government but they rejected the demands of the Brotherhood for a veto power over the Islamic aspects of any legislation and for the right to nominate four ministers. One Muslim Brother, Sheikh Ahmed Hassan el Bakhoury, was appointed Minister of Waqfs (Religious Endowments) but then split from the Brotherhood.

The combination of Wafdists, Muslim Brothers and Communists, operating sometimes separately and sometimes in a united front, sometimes directly and sometimes indirectly through the Free Officers themselves, was to provide the main opposition to Nasser and the junta during the years to come. The first blow in the struggle with this opposition was struck by the Free Officers. When the political parties showed little sign of voluntarily purging themselves in accordance with the officers' wishes, the junta issued a law requiring the reorganization of the parties and their registration after certain conditions had been complied with.

The political leaders now began at last to realize that effective power lay with the army. But the Wafd was still defiant. The Free Officers replied by arresting Fuad Serag ed-din and sixty other leading politicians, including two former prime ministers. The Wafd bowed its head, suspended Serag ed-din from the Secretary-Generalship and nominally replaced the aging Nahas Pasha as leader by the less tainted Saleh Fahmy Gomaa. But the prestige and the influence of the party had been broken.

Most of those arrested had been released by the beginning of December but on 14 October Colonel Rashad Mehanna was dismissed from the Regency Council and placed under house arrest. He was suspected of being the focal point of a counter-revolutionary movement developing on a broad front, including old-regime politicians, land-owners and the Muslim Brothers and their sympathizers in the army.

By the beginning of December the junta had made up its mind to abandon its earlier ideas of working with the purged parties and of holding elections by February 1953. Elections, it considered, would simply mean going back to the abuses of the old system, with the removal of Farouk the only change. They must also have been faced with the old revolutionary dilemma of how to get off the back of the tiger: a parliament dominated by Wafdists and Muslim Brothers might very well now try to make sure that the revolutionary officers were themselves eliminated from positions of power in the army. On 9 December, therefore, General Neguib announced the abolition of the 1923 Constitution and the postponement of the promised elections for another three years. Within the next six weeks the junta took a series of steps finally to liquidate the old party system and to ensure that at least for the next three years of the 'transition period' its own political power should reign supreme. After serious student riots in the early days of 1953, it was announced that a plot against the government had been discovered. Many people were arrested and accused, including Colonel Mehanna and twenty-four other leading politicians, a number of Muslim Brothers and forty-eight persons said to be members of the Communist party. One of the army officers, Colonel Damanhoury, was sentenced to death for incitement to mutiny but was reprieved. Colonel Mehanna, tried later, was sentenced on 30 March to life imprisonment. But Serag ed-din and other arrested politicians were not tried until September 1953. They then appeared before a special revolutionary tribunal composed of three leading members of the junta, under the chairmanship of Wing Commander Abdul Latif Baghdadi, on charges of corruption and plotting with a foreign power for the overthrow of the government. These were political and not judicial trials. Designed for their propaganda effect, they were the junta's first large-scale public venture into political cynicism and the distortion of justice. Serag ed-din was sentenced to life imprisonment and so was Karim Thabet, the former favourite and press counsellor of Farouk. The former Saadist premier, Ibrahim Abdul Hadi, the bitter foe of the Muslim Brothers, was sentenced to death but reprieved. The wife of Nahas Pasha was heavily fined. At the same time groups of Communists were tried on charges of subversion.

The junta had already shown its anti-Communist bias by its harsh reaction to the riots at the textile works of Kafr el Dawar near Alexandria in August 1952. The managers had called in the police to break a strike believed to have been organized by the illegal Communist party which had through strike action successfully forced union recognition and a wage rise in a neighbouring plant. A riot developed in which cars were set on fire and the company offices attacked. Nine people, including a policeman and two soldiers, were killed and twenty-three seriously wounded.

A military tribunal set up on the factory grounds sentenced two men, considered the ringleaders, to death. One of them, a young man of twenty-four named Mustafa Khamis, was offered by Neguib personally a commutation to life imprisonment if he would disclose the names of those who had inspired his action. He refused and was hanged together with the other man.[13] The final decision on execution was said to have been taken by a majority of the junta, with Nasser among three voting for clemency.

The arrests of political leaders were followed on 16 January by the dissolution of all the political parties – except for the Muslim Brotherhood, which was still given favoured treatment as a social and religious organization – and the confiscation of their property. In a speech on 23 January, the anniversary of the first six months of the revolution, Neguib announced the outlines of the proposed transitional political regime, and a provisional constitution was promulgated three weeks later. Full sovereign powers were vested in Neguib as 'Leader of the Revolution' on behalf of the Council of the Revolution, which was in fact composed of the Free Officers executive committee. Legislative and executive powers were vested in the cabinet, a mixture of civilians and officers. The 'general policy of the state' was to be directed by joint meetings of the Council of the Revolution and the Cabinet. A new political organization, the Liberation Rally, would replace the political parties during the three years' transition. On 6 February it was announced that the Secretary-General of the Rally, which, in its claim to be a national but not a party body, was reminiscent of General de Gaulle's Rally of the French People, would be Nasser. Members of the junta, Nasser and Neguib among them, had already begun to tour the country making speeches to try to rally popular support behind the regime, to counteract discontent caused by the economic austerity measures, the revival of press censorship and the crushing of party political life.

The true power structure of the regime was beginning to emerge. Its core was the Council of the Revolution. Neguib's genial and modest manners, his pipe and his kindly words, had won him enormous personal popularity. Neguib also re-assured foreign opinion, as well as the apprehensive Christian and Jewish minorities in Egypt. But to those who had serious business to transact with the Egyptian government it was becoming increasingly clear that the man who counted was Nasser.

When Neguib spoke on the six months' anniversary, Nasser stood at his right hand, a tall, dark, awkward figure. His appearance symbolized the reputation Nasser was beginning to earn as the vaguely sinister man behind the scenes, the austere 'fanatic' who was blamed, rather than the 'moderate' Neguib, for harsh or unpopular actions. The emphasis of the regime, tempered verbally by Neguib, was on order and authority, on responsibility and a Cromwellian puritanism, rather than on the traditional flowery rhetoric and promises of Egyptian and Arab political leaders. The slogan announced by Neguib for the Liberation Rally was 'Unity, Discipline and Work'. With his assumption of the Secretary-Generalship of the Rally, Nasser moved officially for the first time out of the shadows and nearer to the limelight. At first his only official position had been that of head of Neguib's personal staff as commander-in-chief. In that capacity, his first concern had been characteristically to ensure the solidity of the regime's power base by purging and reorganizing the army. In the junta he had one vote in the taking of majority decisions, like the other members. He appears to have dominated their councils by sheer personality and capacity for work – and by the fact that he had from the first been the main organizer of the Free Officers and shared only with Abdul Hakim Amer the special power given by complete knowledge of the secret army network. Now, as the chief organizer of the Liberation Rally, he would also have in his hands the main civilian organization supporting the regime. On 19 May he became official Vice-President of the Revolutionary Command.

After the abolition of the monarchy and proclamation of the

republic in June 1953 Nasser entered the cabinet for the first time as Deputy Premier and Minister of the Interior. Neguib was both provisional President and Prime Minister. In the re-organized Cabinet there were five officers and ten civilians. Wing Commander Baghdadi became Minister of War and Hakim Amer, promoted major-general, succeeded Neguib as commander-in-chief of the armed forces. Later in the year Nasser handed over the Ministry of the Interior to another of his closest associates, Lieutenant-Colonel Zacharia Mohieddin. He and his most trusted and able friends thus between them controlled the main security forces of the country and also the only permitted mass political organization. Nasser was in an increasingly strong position to establish his own authority and defeat the challenge of any rival.

The challenge – and a contest which, in spite of all precautions, Nasser was within an ace of losing – was not long in coming. Within weeks of the proclamation of the Republic, there were rumours of disagreement within the regime between Neguib and the Revolutionary Council. At the same time the Muslim Brothers showed signs of stirring; there was dissension within the Brotherhood ranks between those who pressed for more violent action and the more passive conservative leadership of the Supreme Guide, Hassan el Hodeiby. One reason for this unrest was the displeasure of the extremists that the regime had reached an agreement with Britain over the Sudan, had begun negotiations with Britain over the Canal Zone and was keeping more violent measures of boycott or guerrilla attacks against the British under tight control.

At first there was no apparent connexion between the split within the regime and the pressure of the Muslim Brotherhood. The split had arisen largely because Neguib, having become both President and Prime Minister and increasingly aware of his personal popularity, began to feel that he should have more real authority. He was no longer satisfied with the role of figurehead. He complained that the young officers of the junta often met secretly behind his back to arrange decisions before he took part in meetings of the RCC or the Cabinet.

The junta on their side objected that Neguib often made

public statements of policy without getting their prior approval
and sometimes without full knowledge of the facts. The dispute
was one of personality and authority rather than over clear policy
issues, though the political trials in September 1953 may have
been one cause of dissension. Neguib himself later claimed that
it was primarily a difference of 'psychology' and tactics rather
than strategy.

> Abdul Nasser believed [he wrote], with all the bravado of a man of
> thirty-six, that we could afford to alienate every segment of Egyptian
> public opinion, if necessary, in order to achieve our goals. I believed,
> with all the prudence of a man of fifty-three, that we would need as
> much popular support as we could possibly retain. I further believed
> that it would be better to sacrifice, or at least delay, the attainment of
> some of our objectives in order to ensure the attainment of others.[14]

Specifically Neguib wanted more personal authority to dismiss
and appoint ministers and army officers. He demanded a form of
veto over decisions of the cabinet, of the Council of the Revolution and of the commander-in-chief. The junta wanted to maintain its control of policy and its own system of majority vote.

The two disputes, with Neguib and with the Muslim Brothers,
came to a head within a fortnight of each other. On 12 February
1954 there was a clash at Cairo University between armed
Muslim Brothers and student supporters of the Liberation Rally.
A score of students were wounded before the police restored
order. The government reacted immediately by abolishing the
Brotherhood and arresting several hundred of its leading members, including the Supreme Guide. The ban on the Brotherhood
was later lifted (until its final dissolution on 26 October 1954) and
most of its leaders released on a promise to confine the Brotherhood's activities to religion and social welfare.

On 23 February 1954 Neguib submitted his resignation in a
letter to the Council of the Revolution, declaring, 'I can no
longer carry out my duties in the manner that I consider best
calculated to serve the national interests'.[15] Neguib's resignation
was a clear challenge to the authority of the Council of the
Revolution and of Nasser in particular. In attempting to force
the junta's hand, Neguib was obviously counting on both his

popularity in Egypt and his key position in dealing with the Sudan – he was about to fly to Khartoum for the inauguration of the Sudanese parliament five days later.

Nasser's first reaction – it was to become a characteristic tactic for him – was to play for time. He sent two of the junta, Gamal Salem and Hussein esh-Shafei, to try to persuade Neguib to withdraw his resignation and, if this failed, to ask him to keep it secret for two weeks until the Sudan visit was over and the Council of the Revolution had had time to consider the question. To this latter suggestion Neguib agreed. But the next day the Council met without him and, according to some reports, under pressure from Salah Salem, who as Minister for Sudan Affairs resented Neguib's initiatives on the Sudan, and other officers, voted to remove him.[16] That night while Neguib was at home his house was surrounded by troops and his telephone cut. He was put under house arrest.[17]

The news of Neguib's removal brought big popular demonstrations in Cairo in his favour. They were organized by the remaining cadres of Wafdists and the left-wing groups who, with the Muslim Brothers, could still bring masses of students and workers on to the streets. This united front of the Brotherhood, the left and the Wafd aimed to use Neguib's popularity in the hope of forcing the junta to restore the political parties, parliament and a freer press. But more worrying to Nasser than this massive support for Neguib in the streets was the split created in the army and inside the Council of the Revolution itself. On 26 February, there was a stormy meeting of Neguib partisans in the barracks of the cavalry corps to which Khaled Mohieddin, the youngest and most left-wing member of the Council, belonged. Khaled Mohieddin had previously opposed the abolition of political parties and urged a quicker return to a form of democratic life through the election of a constituent assembly. Nasser himself went to the meeting for talks which lasted through the afternoon and part of the night. There were rumours that at this time Nasser was himself isolated and in danger of arrest at the cavalry barracks. Khaled Mohieddin has maintained that the cavalry corps were not preparing a *coup* and Nasser was never in danger of arrest, though some of the officers present may have tried to make Nasser think their tanks had the barracks surrounded.[18]

To avoid the split spreading through the army and destroying the power basis of the revolution – and perhaps to escape from an awkward personal situation at the cavalry barracks – Nasser persuaded the Council of the Revolution to adopt a compromise. Khaled Mohieddin was to become premier and Neguib was to be asked to come back as President.

Early next morning Khaled Mohieddin and seven other young cavalry officers went out to Neguib's suburban home, got through the cordon of troops and barbed wire and told the general the news. Neguib was ready to accept the compromise, but the game was by no means over. An hour later, intelligence officers under instructions from Nasser took Neguib away from his home, first to the artillery headquarters near Al Maza airport on the outskirts of Cairo and then, when this was surrounded by demonstrating soldiers, out to a hiding place in the desert. At the same time sections of the Free Officers who had rejected the compromise and supported Nasser had begun to organize counter-action against the cavalry corps. The cavalry barracks were surrounded and were over-flown by aircraft. While demonstrations continued in the streets and an official Sudanese delegation flew to Cairo to urge Neguib's release and safety, a new compromise was proposed. Neguib should return as President but with Nasser as premier instead of Mohieddin. Neguib again accepted.

There was an emotional public reconciliation between Neguib and Nasser, but it was not to last for long. Nasser was obviously relieved to have escaped a crisis which had looked as if it might sweep away the whole of the revolution. But the events had also shown the depth of the rift with Neguib and the dangers involved. Disagreement in the Council continued over the question of the return to parliamentary life. Neguib had publicly announced that he had returned to the Presidency on the understanding that parliamentary life would be restored. A few days later, after his return from the Sudan, Neguib announced plans to create a constituent Assembly and provisional parliament before 23 July, the second anniversary of the revolution. He also announced the abolition of press censorship.

On 9 March Nasser handed over the premiership to Neguib until free elections should be held. Nasser was said to be suffering from great strain and to have been advised by his doctor to rest. It looked as if Neguib had won all along the line. But Nasser had already begun to organize what was virtually a second *coup*, reminiscent in its timing and subtlety of Mark Antony's speech on the death of Caesar. It was a masterly combination of force and political finesse. The preparations had begun while Neguib was in Khartoum. Nasser ordered the arrest of several hundred people accused of trying to exploit the Neguib–Nasser crisis to bring about a counter-revolution. He had already made use of his ten days as prime minister to carry out a quick purge of pro-Neguib elements in the army, especially the cavalry corps. Khaled Mohieddin was sent on a 'special mission' to Europe which was a prelude to his dismissal from the Council of the Revolution and exile for two years. Sixteen other cavalry officers were arrested and three months later tried and sentenced to prison terms. At the same time prison sentences were imposed on twenty-two civilians alleged to be Communists. Nasser also tightened his hold on the trades unions and other workers' organizations by appointing one of his loyal Free Officers, Major Kamal ed-din Hussein, to be Minister of Social Affairs. While preparing his forces, and eliminating potential opposition organizers, Nasser had been letting Neguib have his head. His aim was not only to gain time but also to let Neguib work himself eventually into an untenable political position. Nasser saw clearly that, whether Neguib intended it or not, a return to parliamentary life on Neguib's terms would mean the end of the army movement and probably of most of what it had set out to achieve. The public, like Neguib, might mistakenly think that it could have both the fruits of revolution and a return to the old party system. Nasser's plan was to make it plain that they had to choose one or the other.

On 25 March, the Council of the Revolution majority voted to issue a communiqué announcing the restoration of political parties and stating, 'The Council of the Revolution will surrender its powers to a constituent assembly on 24 July 1954 at which time it will proclaim the end of the Egyptian Revolution'. As Nasser had planned, the announcement of the impending self-dissolution of the Council of the Revolution came as a shock to all those in the army and in the public who had opposed the old regime and feared its return to uninhibited power. Acting through the Liberation Rally and the trades unions, Nasser was able to canalize this feeling into large demonstrations demanding the maintenance of the Council and calling for Nasser instead of Neguib. The demonstrations were backed up by a general transport strike. More important, Nasser was given a free hand to settle the crisis by an assembly of the Free Officers.

Nasser thus demonstrated conclusively that, whoever might hold the titles, he held the keys to power – in the army, among the workers and in the streets. It was only a matter of time before he took the titles, too. On 17 April, Neguib, suffering from a nervous breakdown, still popular but shorn of organized support from any source, was forced to resign again as prime minister. He was also dropped from the Council of the Revolution. Nasser took over the premiership once more, keeping Neguib as President. But increasingly Neguib became only a figurehead until his final removal from office in October.

With Nasser's return, the army dictatorship was re-established. The elections were again postponed until the end of the three years' transition. Once more political parties were banned and the press censored. Thirty-eight former ministers and twenty-three journalists were deprived of political rights for ten years. The only concession to democratic sentiment was the creation of a National Advisory Council of 240 members appointed by the Cabinet.

So the parliamentary constitutional system which Egyptian liberals had struggled so long to establish and which had suffered so many abuses was finally destroyed. Did Egypt's parliament deserve to die? What would have happened if Neguib had won? It might be argued that with all its faults the parliamentary system in Egypt at least held out some prospects of a political evolution which might gradually reduce its corrupt basis and enable an increasing educated public to learn from political discussion. British parliamentary life until the last century was also corrupt and dominated by land-owners. Against this has to be weighed three probabilities. First, a parliament dominated once again by the Wafd would probably have undone the land reform and held up other economic and social reforms. There would have probably also been no High Dam and a slower industrialization. Second, there would have been no negotiated agreement with the British over the Canal Zone base, because no political group, even if it wanted to, would have been strong enough to make such an agreement. Third, even if Neguib had won and the parliament had been recreated, it is probable that it would before long have broken down again in the throes of a revolution more violent and bloody than the 1952 *coup*. For the combination of social and economic pressures and of a possible resumption of the struggle against the British in the Canal Zone would almost certainly have been more than the old parties could cope with. Disillusion would have been widespread and the way would have been open for action by the Muslim Brothers and the Communists waiting in the wings.

Before there could be any political stability and real progress in Egypt there had above all to be a settlement with Britain. The consolidation of Nasser's power enabled him to complete a settlement which had been hanging fire for eighteen months.

As we have already seen, the secret tracts of the Free Officers before the *coup* had echoed the radical nationalist slogans of the time, demanding unity of the Nile Valley and immediate and unconditional British withdrawal from both Egypt and the Sudan. They had rejected any negotiation with Britain, denounced schemes for joint defence and called for a policy of neutrality.[19] But when the Free Officers came to power they had to face the realities of the dilemma of dealing with the British. Should they continue and perhaps intensify the physical pressure of boycott and guerrilla warfare against the British base in the Suez Canal Zone, which had hastened the ruin of the Wafd? Or should they adopt the course of negotiation which had hitherto produced no results, which was condemned by most of the more extreme nationalists and which would certainly be used against them by their opponents? In the event, they employed a mixture of pressure and talks; the emphasis was on negotiation but the boycott was kept up and the threat of guerrilla warfare maintained, though in practice it was kept at a low level. At the same time, the junta was preparing for two important policy decisions which helped to clear the way for a negotiated settlement. The first was to recognize the Sudan's right to self-determination, the right to choose independence rather than union with Egypt if it wished. The second was to negotiate with Britain on the Sudan and on the Canal Zone base as separate issues.

A series of meetings at the end of 1952 between General Neguib and leaders of the four main Sudanese parties led to an agreement between them on 10 January 1953. Egypt and Britain reached agreement on the Sudan a month later. They recognized the right of the Sudanese to self-determination, to an eventual choice between independence and union with Egypt. There were to be early free elections for a Sudanese parliament to be followed by a three-year transitional period of self-government. During this period sovereignty would be held in reserve and the Governor-General would be advised in its exercise by a five-man commission composed of an Egyptian and British representative, two Sudanese and a Pakistani chairman.

In Egypt, the agreement was regarded by the Muslim Brothers and others as breaking the cherished unity of the Nile Valley. In Britain there were misgivings from the right-wing imperialist group in the Conservative party at the apparent abandonment under Egyptian pressure of the possibility of bringing the Sudan into the British Commonwealth. On the British side the clinching argument for the Sudan agreement came not from the British embassy in Cairo but unexpectedly and irrefutably from the British authorities in Khartoum. The Civil Secretary of the Sudan government, Sir James Robertson, told the British government bluntly that if Britain did not give the Sudanese their freedom she would have to fight them, and this was inconceivable. Britain had only a brigade of troops and a few hundred officials in the Sudan. The whole vast country, as big as Western Europe, was really ruled on the basis of confidence.[20]

The agreement did not end the contest between Britain and Egypt in the Sudan but brought it within the more manageable limits of competition for local political influence. When the National Union party won the first parliamentary elections and formed the first Sudanese national government under Ismail el Azhari at the beginning of 1954, there was jubilation in Cairo and shock in London. But two years later it was Ismail el Azhari who led the Sudan into complete independence, after forcing both Britain and Egypt to accept a simple declaration of independence by the Sudan parliament in place of the more elaborate process of self-determination originally envisaged.

The Sudan continued to be a source of friction in Anglo-Egyptian relations. In particular it nourished the animosity and suspicions of the British conservative press and the imperialist back-benchers in the House of Commons and so inhibited the British government's diplomatic dealings with Egypt. But it ceased otherwise to be a major obstacle to an agreement on the British military base in Egypt. More serious was the problem of reconciling views on the base itself. The Egyptians demanded the complete withdrawal of British forces and rejected any joint Middle East defence commitment. The British insisted that a military base must be kept available in the Canal Zone for the regional defence of the Middle East. There were problems of a military strategic character as well as those created by an emotionally aroused and ill-informed public opinion on both sides. But other factors made for agreement. On the British side, defence strategy was being reviewed in the light of the hydrogen bomb and the possibility of a 'thaw' in the cold war after the death of Stalin. Both of these developments would reduce the likelihood of a direct Soviet military attack as the main threat against which Western policy in the Middle East must guard. The H-bomb also made it likely that a huge base such as that in the Canal Zone was now obsolete because it was too vulnerable: more dispersed and smaller bases would be better. There was a growing realization – already shared by the British commanders in Egypt – that to try to maintain the base in the Canal Zone in the face of Egyptian hostility was counter-productive from a military point of view. There was continued pressure for an Anglo-Egyptian settlement from Washington where the new Republican administration under President Eisenhower and his Secretary of State, John Foster Dulles, was beginning to take a wider interest in the Middle East.

Churchill and Eden sought the support of Eisenhower for a new joint approach to Egypt. In talks in Washington at the beginning of 1953, Eden presented Eisenhower with alternative British plans for the maintenance of a base in Egypt. 'Plan A', which the British hoped to get Cairo to accept, would have left 7,000 British soldiers in uniform in Egypt to maintain the base so that it could be 'reactivated' in the event of an attack or threatened attack on the Arab states, Turkey or Iran. The plan also provided for joint air defence and continued British military command over the Canal base. Eisenhower, while agreeing to the principle that the Canal base was needed for Middle East defence and promising diplomatic support for Britain and the carrot of economic and military aid for Cairo, declined to join in a united front against Egypt. He later expressed doubts whether the British 'Plan A' could be made acceptable in Cairo in view of the state of Egyptian national sentiment. He thought the British 'Plan B' – which would put the Canal base under Egyptian control with a smaller number of British or Allied supervisory staff and technicians – was more realistic.

The first move towards a settlement came from Nasser. In April 1953 he gave an interview to the Cairo correspondent of the *Observer* in which he said that Egypt would be willing to allow a limited number of British technicians to stay in the Canal Zone to maintain the base for reactivation in war-time, provided Britain did not try to make this presence into a disguised occupation of Egypt.[21] This was correctly interpreted by the British as opening the way to talks. The negotiations began in Cairo on 28 April 1953. Nasser led the Egyptian side, together with Salah Salem, Amer, Baghdadi and the Foreign Minister, Mahmoud Fawzi. Fawzi and Salah Salem did the day-to-day talking but the key man was Nasser. At first the British team was led by Sir Ralph Stevenson, together with General Sir Brian Robertson (now Lord Robertson), the commander-in-chief, British Land Forces, Middle East, a calm and sensible soldier who had already skilfully played a politico-military role as the chief British representative in Germany during the Berlin blockade.

Stevenson had later to go on seven months' sick leave and was replaced by Robin Hankey of the Foreign Office. But this first round of talks lasted only a week. The British, working on their 'Plan A', tried to engage Nasser in a detailed discussion of the technical problems of maintaining the base and of its war-time reactivation. Nasser refused to be drawn and insisted that he could not discuss details until the British had accepted the principle of complete evacuation of their troops. The base must be under Egyptian military command. The continued presence of British technicians in uniform would in the Egyptian public's eyes have amounted to less than complete withdrawal. When the British declined to give this assurance of their departure until they knew what they could leave behind, Nasser broke off the talks on 6 May. He declared, 'we preferred not to waste our time'.

Churchill, taking advantage of the absence through illness of Anthony Eden, his more flexible Foreign Secretary, was inclined to be tough. He hated the idea of leaving Egypt. In a letter to Eisenhower he complained that

the Egyptian dictatorship had washed its hands of discussions with the British, timing this move with Foster Dulles's visit. . . . If as a result of American encouragement Neguib decided to turn his threats into action, bloodshed might well result, bloodshed for which the British would disclaim all responsibility.[22]

The American Secretary of State had seen Neguib and Nasser in Cairo on 11 May as part of a tour of Middle East countries and Pakistan.

Despite the formal breaking off of talks and threatening activities by the Egyptians in the Canal Zone, including the formation of a National Liberation Militia, informal contacts between the British and Egyptians continued during the rest of the year. General Robertson privately regarded the Canal Zone base, he said later, as 'a military nonsense': 'The Egyptians were sitting in the Delta and could swoop down at night and shoot up members of the forces and their families. Protecting the Canal Zone base already took the best part of three divisions – more than the British army could afford to keep in Egypt.'[23]

During the talks, which were held secretly at General Robertson's villa at Nasser's request, Robertson found Nasser 'intelligent and straight, but inexperienced in the government of a country'. In negotiation, 'he was fluent and had done his homework. He was polite and clear. . . . Nasser emphasized during the talks his ambition for a united Arab state of which he saw himself the leader. This was a fixed thing at the back of his mind.'*

In January 1954, the continued quiet discussions in Cairo between Nasser and Stevenson produced an important concession from Nasser: he agreed that the Canal base could be reactivated in the event of an attack on Turkey, a condition Egypt had hitherto rejected. The question was now whether Britain would on her side concede complete evacuation – which meant Egyptian control of the base and technicians in limited numbers without uniform. When the British showed no signs of giving way on these points Nasser allowed or encouraged an increase in armed attacks on British troops in the Canal Zone. For the first few months of 1954, the political situation in both Egypt and Britain held up further progress towards an agreement. By mid-summer political conditions on both sides were quiet enough for the final move to a settlement. The British agreed to withdraw all their forces from Egypt and to maintain the base with civilian technicians under contract to British firms. The British Minister for War, Anthony Head, was sent out to Cairo, to negotiate the principles of an agreement. He and Nasser initialled the agreement on 27 July. It was then negotiated in detail by the British Minister of State for Foreign Affairs, Anthony Nutting, and finally signed by him and by Nasser on 19 October 1954.

The agreement ended the 1936 Treaty and provided for the complete withdrawal of British forces from Egypt in stages over the next twenty months. The remaining installations of the Canal Zone base would then be under Egyptian command but would be maintained by a maximum of 1,200 British civilian technicians for seven years. During this time British forces could reoccupy and make use of it if there were an armed attack on Egypt or on any

---

* Sir Ralph Stevenson gained a slightly different impression. He told the author in September 1968. 'Nasser had few illusions about the Arabs; his views on them were vitriolic. "No Arabs have ever been able to work together," Nasser said, "The only agreement I can hope to get is to use our nuisance value in more or less the same direction." '

other Arab country which had signed the Arab Collective Security
Pact, or on Turkey.

After the signing ceremony, Nasser declared, 'The ugly page of
Anglo-Egyptian relations has been turned and another page is
being written. . . . There is now no reason why Britain and Egypt
should not work constructively together.'²⁴ A fortnight later the
United States agreed to grant Egypt $40 million in aid. Britain
announced the resumption of arms deliveries. Nasser had achieved
the great national aim. British troops would soon leave Egypt
after an occupation lasting seventy-two years. But for some of the
more extreme nationalists among his compatriots, the price Nasser
had paid for securing British withdrawal was too high. He had already let the Sudan go and now, instead of insisting on complete
neutrality, he had linked Egypt with the West in a Middle East
defence system. Among the fiercest of these critics were the Muslim Brothers. Though the Free Officers had had a complex and
changing relationship with the Brothers, Nasser had never had
much sympathy with their mixture of religion and politics. He was
himself a practising Muslim of a sincere but conventional kind
and Islamic traditions coloured his view of the world, but he was
no fanatic and his nationalist politics were firmly secular.

Since Nasser's victory over Neguib, the Muslim Brothers had
been quiet in Egypt but some Brotherhood militants had gone to
Syria to conduct a campaign against Nasser from there, denouncing him as a tyrant and a collaborator with the West. After the
overthrow of the military dictatorship of Adib Shishakli in February 1954, the pan-Arab neutralism of the Baath (Arab Renaissance) Socialist party had begun to set the dominant tone of
Syrian politics and Syrian attitudes towards the West. During the
summer of 1954, Nasser had also deliberately lifted the press censorship sufficiently to allow the Brotherhood to raise their heads
again and to attack him in the Egyptian press.

On 26 October 1954, while Nasser was speaking to a huge
public meeting in Alexandria, a member of the Muslim Brotherhood, a carpenter named Mahmud Abdul Latif, fired six shots at
him from a range of a few feet. Every bullet missed its mark, but
two men beside Nasser were hit. While the crowd began to panic
and those with Nasser on the platform ducked for safety, Nasser

stood his ground and called on the crowd to keep their places. In a voice with a shrill edge of nervous tension but still under control, he shouted, 'Remember that, if anything should happen to me, the Revolution will go on, for each of you is a Gamal Abdul Nasser'. He continued with his speech while the police carried off the would-be assassin.

This attack gave Nasser an opportunity to strike a crippling blow at the Muslim Brothers, who had emerged as his most determined and dangerous opponents. In the process he was also able finally to eliminate General Neguib from power.The Brotherhood was once more, and this time finally, banned and its leaders and many thousands of its followers arrested.* The police claimed to have discovered large arms dumps belonging to the Brotherhood's terrorist section which was alleged to have been planning a large-scale insurrection. The Supreme Guide, Hassan el Hodeiby, who disclaimed responsibility for the Brotherhood's terrorist organization, and other leaders were tried before a special military tribunal presided over by Gamal Salem. Witnesses who told of plans to kill Nasser and overthrow the military regime also alleged that Neguib was involved: he would have been asked to take over the government and calm the nation after the Brotherhood's seizure of power. Within a few days, on 14 November 1954, Neguib was deposed from the Presidency of the Republic and placed under house arrest in a villa in a Cairo suburb. It was alleged that he had allowed himself to be used as a tool by the Muslim Brothers and Communists. It was all done quietly and there was no visible public reaction. Neguib was still popular with the Egyptian man-in-the-street but he had receded into the background since his defeat in March. All the activists who had then inspired the demonstrations in his favour, the Muslim Brothers, the Wafdists and Communists, whether among the students or in the army, had now been brought under control by Nasser.

Nasser's agreement with the British and his ruthless action against the Muslim Brothers had already brought him under severe attack by diverse elements in many Arab countries. His critics ranged from radical nationalists, neutralists and religious

*In a speech to the Arab Socialist Union in December 1968 Nasser gave the figure as 18,000.

leaders to those, like the Syrian left and centre, who had only just got rid of their own military dictator and regarded Nasser's regime as equally oppressive. His unpopularity was deepened by the dismissal of Neguib, who had been seen as a moderating and restraining influence. When Hassan el Hodeiby and six other Brotherhood leaders were sentenced to death and all but Hodeiby were hanged, despite pleas for clemency from many Arab governments, the Arab world was swept by a storm of protest. In several Arab capitals mobs attacked and burned Egyptian embassies.

By the end of 1954, Nasser was established as the new head of state and president of the Council of the Revolution. He was now master of Egypt, if somewhat precariously still, and he had, at least on paper, achieved the national aim of British withdrawal from both Egypt and the Sudan, which was to be completed within a matter of months. But as a personality he was still relatively unknown to the general public, both in his own country and abroad. And what was known about him – or thought to be known – was not usually liked. To the public he still appeared a taciturn, ascetic and ruthless figure who lacked the personal appeal of the easy-going Neguib. Few in the west realized that he had been more ready to compromise, for example over the Canal base, than Neguib, a weak leader, would ever have been able to. In Egypt, the effects of the land reform – which had so far resulted in the distribution of only 75,000 feddans – had not yet been enough to offset for the masses the austerity measures taken to stabilize the economy.

Moreover, the enforcement of the new reduced land rents and higher minimum farm wages was proving difficult because of the severe land shortage and huge unemployment. But the austerity measures had succeeded in liquidating the deficits in both the budget and the balance of payments. The regime had not yet worked out any clear economic ideology of its own, except a vague attachment to industrial development and social welfare. It had promoted the land reform and encouraged trades unions – though under its own control and without the right to strike. Its general economic practice, however, had not differed greatly from that of its predecessors in relying mainly on private enterprise.[25] Various junta spokesmen had spoken against socialism, though sometimes also against the 'domination of monopoly capital'. In January 1954, the government announced a Charter of Cooperation 'between capital, labour, science and technology, free from the exploiting aspects of capitalism and the stifling effect of socialism'. The regime appeared eager to encourage Western investment and economic aid, and its general economic doctrine was in tune with its apparently pro-Western and especially pro-American political orientation.

The tight control of the press, especially the suppression of the famous Wafdist newspaper *Al Misri* and other journals, had aroused the resentment of the Egyptian intellectuals. But other sections of the middle classes were inclined to welcome Nasser's strong hand as a deliverance from the old violence of the streets and from the twin threats of the Muslim Brothers and the Communists. Businessmen, both Egyptian and foreign, welcomed not only the chance of stability but also the prospects of better trading relations with the West.

To militant Arab nationalists outside Egypt, Nasser was suspect. He was the man who had compromised with the British, who was thought to be considering a peace settlement with Israel and who might take Egypt along an isolationist or pro-Western path. Nasser had not at that time set foot outside Egypt except for his military service in the Sudan and a combined official visit and pilgrimage to the Hejaz in 1953. His main international dealings had been with the British, though he had had visits from Nehru, Tito and some Arab leaders.

He had already, however, shown his ability to charm and impress in private. Sir Ralph Stevenson, who got to know Nasser well during the Canal base negotiations, recalls his impression at that period:

During our negotiation, I always found that if Nasser agreed to something, he stuck by it. I went to visit him at his home and met his wife and children. I liked the way he lived in his colonel's quarters out near the barracks. His style of life was simple and he seemed disinterested in money, interested rather in his own, not very profound, ideas. He was vastly inexperienced politically.

Nasser was then aged thirty-six, an age when many Western statesmen are only just finishing the first stage of a long apprenticeship in politics and preparing for a slow climb up the ladder of office. He was largely self-educated apart from the sketchy instruction given in a sporadically attended secondary school and the narrow curriculum of the Military Academy and Staff College. If his intelligence was formidable and his industry tireless, his general culture was limited. As a soldier he had only a limited experience of modern war from the unsuccessful Palestine campaign in which he had fought bravely. Before becoming the titular as well as the actual ruler of Egypt, Nasser had had only two and a half years of active public political experience, after a decade of secret brooding, study and conspiracy.

In the crisis with Neguib, in the attempt on his life and the abuse from other Arab countries, he had already tasted some of the bitterness as well as the sweets of power. More troubles were to come only too soon. But few would have then guessed that within little more than eighteen months, this young man would be the central figure of the biggest international crisis since the Second World War, the hero of the Arab world and the villain of the West.

Chapter 6
The Arabs, Russia and the West, 1954–6

During the first two and a half years of their revolution Nasser and his colleagues had been concerned chiefly with the consolidation of their regime and the settlement of Egypt's dispute with Britain. The next two years, culminating in the Suez crisis, were to see the fulfilment of Nasser's aims of national liberation and the establishment of what were to prove the key-points in his foreign policy: non-alignment, involving a shift towards closer relations with the Soviet Union; Arab unity; the struggle with Israel; and the search for economic aid without 'political strings'. All these aims were inter-related: their pursuit by Nasser sprang as much from his analysis of Egypt's national interests as from sentiment, ideology or a desire for a personal 'empire'. They, perhaps inevitably, brought Nasser into conflict with the Western Powers, especially Britain, whose policy was broadly speaking to uphold the *status quo*.

Nasser was criticized in the West for not having concentrated on home affairs and eschewed foreign 'adventures', for having spent Egypt's scarce resources on arms instead of economic development. (Ironically, this view was often held most strongly by those who ignored the important social and economic changes that were being attempted inside Egypt and paid attention only to the more flamboyant aspects of Nasser's foreign policy.) Such an admirable course might have been more feasible for Egypt if the Western Powers themselves, or indeed Israel, had been able to practise what some of them preached. But at that time Britain and France were straining their own economies and weakening their international position in trying to hold on to the remains of their empires in the Middle East, North Africa and South-East Asia, while at the same time maintaining powerful armed forces in Europe against a feared Russian attack. Israel was spending a very high proportion of her budget on arms not only to survive but also to hold on to the considerable areas she had gained in the 1948 war over and above the territory allocated to her in the United Nations partition plan.

There is some evidence (e.g. budgetary allocations) that at first Nasser's intention was to avoid heavy arms expenditure so as to concentrate on domestic development. But to some extent a more active foreign policy was forced on him, whatever his own inclinations might have been, by the political circumstances of Egypt and the Arab world, and by the actions of the Western Powers and Israel. It was difficult for any Egyptian leader simply to opt out of the two main political conflicts convulsing the Arab world: the nationalist revolt against British and French imperial control and the unsettled struggle with Israel.

Nasser had, it is true, shown in *The Philosophy of the Revolution* his awareness of the importance to Egyptian security of the support of the other Arab states. This conclusion was one which had already been reached by previous Egyptian governments from that of Aly Maher in 1939 onwards. It had become as much part of Egyptian foreign policy, especially as regards Palestine and Syria, as the defence of the Low Countries had become part of British foreign policy. What was new in Nasser's policy was his broader vision of Arab geopolitics. He grasped as no other Arab leader had before the bargaining power the Arabs could exert through their geographical position and oil resources, provided they were united, at least in their policies if not in their political institutions. He had noted the special position of Egypt as the largest Arab state, as a centre of Islam and as a part of Africa.[1] Nasser's analysis was derived, intellectually, from his strategic studies at the Staff College, as recently as 1951; practically, from his experiences in the Palestine war; and, emotionally, from a long nationalist commitment to Arab causes. This part of *The Philosophy of the Revolution* was to be belatedly discovered by Anthony Eden, Guy Mollet and other Western leaders and publicists and denounced as a blue-print for empire-building and a plan for conquest, like Hitler's *Mein Kampf*. (Nasser was later to comment ironically, 'Why Hitler alone? Eisenhower has suggested that I am not only Hitler but Stalin as well! What they are frightened of really is the impact of the Afro-Asian revolution on their economic interests and they inject into this basic difference all types of racial and religious propaganda. They must know that they have got to appreciate nationalism and learn to live with it or their economic interests will be affected adversely.')²

In fact, the part of *The Philosophy of the Revolution* which dealt with Egypt's role in the three Arab, Muslim and African 'circles', was but little different in character and motive from Winston Churchill's description of Britain's position at the intersection of the three spheres of Europe, the Commonwealth and the Anglo-American alliance. But Nasser's booklet is also impregnated throughout with an emotional sense of Egyptian–Arab history, seen as a long story of foreign oppression, and with a passionate hatred and suspicion of imperialism. Nasser's basic sympathy with Arab nationalist causes everywhere would no doubt sooner or later have led him into further conflict with Israel and with the Western Powers – certainly with France in North Africa and possibly with Britain elsewhere in the Middle East, especially in the Arabian Peninsula, if the process of decolonization there were too long delayed. Egypt was already committed to at least unofficial support of Arab liberation movements: the North African nationalists, for example, had been operating from headquarters in Cairo since 1945, with the backing of the Arab League.

At the end of 1954, however, Nasser appeared to be inclined to adopt a more passive policy of partial military cooperation with the West, of comparatively modest armed forces, a quiet border with Israel and a limited interest in the revolutionary movements of the Arab world. His prime concern was the economic and social development of an independent Egypt for which the West then seemed the only source of indispensable economic aid. But pressure from the Western Powers to bring the Arab states into a new regional military alliance and the parallel adoption of a more aggressive 'activist' policy by Israel under the leadership of Ben Gurion, who feared the rise of a strong Arab leader, stimulated restive forces inside Egypt. The army on which Nasser depended for support demanded more weapons and a more militant attitude to Israel. The radical nationalists of the extreme left and right, who were then Nasser's chief opponents in Egypt and other Arab countries, pressed for a more active neutralist and anti-imperialist (which in this context inevitably meant anti-Western) policy.

Nasser might have continued to resist the pressure of his radical neutralist opponents had he been able to prove to the Egyptian army that cooperation with the West would produce the results they desired, namely more arms and a policy towards Israel which at best forced her to make concessions and at least restrained her militancy. But while Britain and the United States made a concerted effort during 1955 to produce a compromise settlement of the Arab–Israeli dispute, they appeared to be either unwilling or unable to exert serious pressure on Israel to this end. And their price for anything more than token arm supplies to Egypt was, in the case of the United States, a peace settlement with Israel, and, in the case of Britain, Egyptian membership of or cooperation with a Western-controlled Middle East defence pact. At that time Britain and the United States were so obsessed with the formation of military pacts against possible Soviet invasion or Communist subversion, that they failed to understand that Arab nationalist sentiment regarded both Israel and Western military bases as greater threats than Russia or Communism. So soon after the 1954 agreement with Britain, which had nearly cost him his life, it is highly doubtful whether Nasser could have paid the Western price and survived. It was also impossible for him to take the lead in the politically dangerous enterprise of seeking a settlement with Israel if in other ways the leadership of Egypt among the Arab states was not recognized by the West. If the West would not supply the weapons demanded by the Egyptian army in the face of Israeli pressure, then they had to come from somewhere else: the only serious alternative source of supply was the Soviet bloc.

These conflicting pressures were already approaching an explosive point when Sir Anthony Eden passed through Cairo on 21 February 1955 and met Nasser for the first and only time at dinner at the British embassy. Eden was still Foreign Minister but soon to be premier. He was on his way to a SEATO meeting in Bangkok, accompanied by the British Chief of Imperial General Staff, Field Marshal Sir John Harding. Describing the meeting in his memoirs, published in 1960, after Suez, Eden wrote,

Sir John gave an excellent strategic appraisal with which Nasser entirely agreed. Nasser declared that his interest and sympathy were with the West, but he argued that the Turco-Iraqi pact [about to be signed a few days later], by its bad timing and unfortunate content had seriously set back the development of effective collaboration with the West by the Arab states.

I was familiar with this plea [comments Eden], it is never the right time for some. We used every argument we could to persuade Nasser at least to restrain his criticisms and, if the agreement were reasonable in terms, to cease his opposition. I do not think, however, that we made much impression. Colonel Nasser, whom I thought a fine man physically, was friendly throughout our talks. He referred repeatedly to the great improvement in Anglo-Egyptian relations, to the importance which his Government attached to this improvement and to his hopes for its continuance in the future. Nasser was not, however, open to conviction on the Turco-Iraqi enterprise. I commented on this in my report to London at the time, adding: 'No doubt jealousy plays a part in this and a frustrated desire to lead the Arab world.'[3]

In an account by Nasser of the same meeting, Eden 'didn't say anything. He just listened while I told him and Harding about my ideas on defence, and why I thought the Baghdad Pact was a mistaken way of defending the Middle East. Harding spoke, but Eden's face said nothing.'[4] On his way back from the Far East, Eden stopped in Baghdad. In the more congenial company of his old friend, Nuri es-Said, the Iraqi prime minister, and King Feisal, an Old Harrovian, he put the finishing touches to a new military agreement with Iraq. This, together with Britain's adherence to the 'Baghdad Pact', as the Turco-Iraqi agreement was then called, was officially announced on 4 April 1955.

This action, which provoked an angry response from Nasser, and Eden's subsequent comments on his meeting with the Egyptian leader showed an astonishing insensitivity to the real state of political opinion in Egypt and the Arab countries. They displayed also an almost frivolous indifference to the relative political importance of Egypt in the Arab world, not to speak of the position of Nasser himself on whose cooperation Britain now depended for the maintenance of her huge Canal Zone base. Neither Eden nor Nasser, each absorbed in his own problems, was able to appreciate the extent to which in making the 1954 agreement the other had gone out on a limb. Each felt he had taken great risks to make the concessions which brought the agreement about and so afterwards expected more in return than the other could give.

Nasser expected recognition from Britain of Egypt's leading position in the Arab East, more sympathy for the Arab position *vis-à-vis* Israel and increased supplies of arms and economic aid from the West. He hoped for a respite of a year or two before having to review Egypt's foreign policy in the light of her newly-gained independence and before considering any formal ties with the West. Eden had made the 1954 agreement with Nasser in the teeth of opposition from within his own party. He also had to reckon with a Conservative press and public opinion which regarded Nasser as an implacable enemy and saw the withdrawal from Egypt as the most humiliating example to date of British imperial weakness and decline. Eden therefore expected Nasser to help him by avoiding any further trouble[5] and refraining from attacks on British interests or activities elsewhere in the Middle East or Africa. But there was a sharp contrast between the nature of their respective internal difficulties: Eden faced a few 'rebels' on the Tory back-benches and at worst the danger of losing the next election; Nasser lived on top of a simmering volcano of revolution where the risks were of personal death and public anarchy.

When in 1953 Britain and America had again taken up plans for Middle East defence pacts, Nasser had tried to persuade Dulles not to press the Arabs into any new alliances. During Dulles's visit to Cairo in May 1953, Nasser told him that, because alliances with outside powers were suspect and unpopular with the Arab peoples, to try to create them was self-defeating. It would only weaken the Arab governments and help the Communists. The strength of the region had to be built on Arab nationalism and on policies of social reform and progress, since the greatest Communist danger was not the external military threat but from within.[6]

Not long after this meeting, the Egyptian military regime set up the 'Voice of the Arabs' transmission of Cairo radio, the only transmission from an Arab country addressed to the Arab world as a whole and destined to become one of Nasser's most powerful political weapons.[7]

Dulles had at first begun to develop the idea of the 'Northern Tier', an alliance between Turkey, Iran and Pakistan, to complete the chain of pacts and bases surrounding the Soviet Union and China. The first move in this direction was the overthrow, engineered with American help, of the nationalist government of Dr Moussadeq in Iran in 1953.[8] The second step was the treaty of friendly cooperation between Turkey and Pakistan signed on 2 April 1954. Concentration on these countries reflected not only the chief American aim of containment of the Communist Powers but also the desire of Dulles not to become too deeply involved in the political quagmires of the Arab world. Dulles hoped to be able to safeguard America's strategic interests without being forced to take sides in Arab rivalries, in the Arab–Israel dispute or in Britain's troubles with Arab nationalism. The Arab–Israel conflict was always a dangerous and unrewarding issue in American domestic politics because of the powerful Zionist lobby. But Dulles was prepared to promise a limited amount of arms and economic aid to Egypt in order to persuade Nasser to settle with the British. And in April 1954 he agreed to military aid to Iraq, whose government was openly friendly to the West and which had no frontier with Israel.

The British interest in Middle East defence differed from the American in one important respect. While the British shared with the Americans the desire to keep the Russians out of the Middle East, they were far more concerned with the maintenance of their own political influence in the area so as to protect their oil interests and their communications against a threat from the Arabs themselves. This meant being in a position to give support, military if necessary, to those regimes, chiefly at that time in Iraq, which were friendly to Britain and who could be trusted not to interfere with the oil business. The close partnership thus developed between these rulers and the British was more than a military alliance for external defence: it became also a tacit commitment to uphold a particular local political and economic system, regardless of how unpopular it might become with its subjects. Britain successfully urged the rulers of Iraq to set aside seventy per cent of the oil revenues for economic development. She also turned a blind eye on the political jobbery, corruption and straight police repression by which Nuri es-Said and others bought the support of a parliament of big land-owners and crushed the radical nationalist opposition.

This motive of British political control over the oil countries increased proportionately in importance as the military justification for Middle East bases diminished after the advent of the hydrogen bomb. It was doubtful whether Nuri es-Said, back in power in Baghdad, would long be able to resist nationalist pressure for a revision of the Anglo-Iraqi treaty and for a withdrawal of the British forces from Iraq, after the conclusion of the 1954 evacuation agreement with Egypt. In any case, the Anglo-Iraqi Treaty was due to expire in 1956. But some way had to be found to buttress the ruling group in Iraq and maintain their partnership with Britain.

Nuri es-Said, who was genuinely concerned about possible Russian attack, saw the answer both to this problem and to that of the Anglo-Iraqi treaty in the creation of a new western-backed Middle East defence system linking the Arab states with the 'Northern Tier' alliance sought by the United States. The link between the two would be Turkey. Nuri approached Nasser about this proposition. There followed talks between Nuri and Major Salah Salem, the Egyptian Minister for National Guidance, at Sarsank in northern Iraq in August 1954, and a meeting between Nuri and Nasser in Cairo on 15 September 1954. The talks showed a wide gap between the ideas of Nuri and Nasser and they ended in misunderstanding.

In his negotiations with Britain, Nasser had for long tried to confine the reactivation of the Canal Zone base to the event of an attack on the Arab states, rejecting the inclusion of Turkey. When he had finally accepted Turkey, 'he knew that he had virtually attached Egypt to NATO by the back-door'.[9] He was preparing for a *rapprochement* with Turkey after the 1954 agreement but he did not want to go as fast or as far in this direction as Nuri es-Said. In any case, the agreement with Britain was only for seven years. Above all, Nasser wanted to wait until British troops had left the Canal Zone and Egypt could enjoy the feeling of complete independence before taking any further decision about the future alignment of Egyptian policy. Nasser envisaged a defence system built on the Arab collective security pact under Egyptian leadership and in a relation of benevolent neutrality to the West which would supply and train the Arab armies for regional defence. The position of the Arab states jointly would be like that of India, close to the West in ideology, economic interest and military organization, but diplomatically and militarily independent and non-aligned.

This policy depended on the other Arab states following Egypt's lead. If they chose to ally themselves with an outside power, Egypt would have to break her alliance with them in the Arab pact or see her own neutrality endangered. So, already in 1954, before the Baghdad Pact or the Bandung Conference, Egypt was campaigning in Arab Asia against outside treaties and Nasser had attacked the Turco-Pakistan pact as harmful to Arab interests. But there was still considerable confusion in Nasser's mind about the nature of his neutralism. Even up to the time of the Baghdad Pact in 1955, he was still thinking in terms of a unified Arab military system which would have been linked with the West through Britain's bilateral agreement with Egypt, Jordan, Iraq and Libya. Nasser would not then have opposed an agreement between Iraq and Britain similar to the Anglo-Egyptian agreement. Iran could have been brought into a reactivation clause of such an agreement in the same way that Turkey was brought into the Anglo-Egyptian agreement on the Suez base.[10] In practical terms it is difficult to see how the effect of such an arrangement would have differed from that of the Baghdad Pact. The ultimate commitments, involving Britain and Turkey and through them a link with NATO and other Western alliances, would have been the same. Apart from the motive of jealousy cited by Eden, why then should Nasser have been so upset by the Baghdad Pact? The main reason seems to have been his conviction that a system which appeared to give primacy to an Arab grouping would arouse less hostile reaction from Arab opinion than one which seemed to originate from the strategic interests of the Western Powers. The difference was one of public presentation, but in the political context of the Arab countries it was a vital difference.

The weakness of Nasser's policy was the weakness of the Arabs, while Egypt was a far more fragile power base than India from which to conduct an ambitious regional diplomacy. On the other hand, Nasser's vision probably corresponded closely to the political mood of the Arabs and to what it was realistic to expect from them in the way of foreign commitments.

The weakness of the Arabs was never absent from the mind of Nuri es-Said, a man of few illusions, except, in the end, about his ability to manipulate his own countrymen. Iraq was geographically the nearest Arab country to Russia. Nuri had no faith in neutralism and no confidence that the Arab collective security pact would ever prove more than a piece of paper. He believed Iraq's defence could be assured only by an effective alliance with the Western Powers. To this argument, Nasser is said to have replied that Egypt would continue her policy and 'the future will judge between us'.[11]

The basis of Nuri's disagreement with Nasser and his own policy of commitment to the West were perhaps never better expressed than in a passage from an article by him which was not published until a month after his death.* Nasser, wrote Nuri, had undoubtedly won wide Arab support,

> But he failed to understand that the West would not tolerate Russian influence in the Middle East. He failed to understand that the West would not grant the Arabs the luxury of neutralism, that this area is too decisively vital to the West for that sort of foolishness. He failed to understand that the Middle East is inextricably tied to the West economically – there is no other big market for Arab oil, for example. Despite a soldier's background, Nasser overlooked the military reality of Russia's incapacity to defend the Arabs if they made an enemy of the West. . . .[12]

But in September 1955 Nuri had not yet given up hopes of agreement with Nasser. He came away from their meeting in Cairo apparently believing that, though Egypt could not join in his plan now, she might do so later; meanwhile she would not object if Iraq went ahead without her. Nasser's impression, however, was that Nuri had promised not to rush into any new schemes. This misunderstanding was deepened rather than resolved when the Arab Foreign Ministers met in Cairo in December 1954.

* 'The Last Testament of the Iraqi Premier', *Life*, 18 August 1958.

But Nuri was already preparing a decisive step. By the end of the year, he had worked out with the British and the Turks a new plan for Turkey to join the Arab collective security pact with the backing of Britain and the United States.[13] The British were hesitant at first but their hand was forced. During a visit by Menderes to Baghdad, he and Nuri issued a joint communiqué announcing the early conclusion of a defence pact.

In the words of Sir Ralph Stevenson, then British ambassador in Cairo, when Nasser heard the news, 'he flew straight off the handle. He took up a hard and fast position from which it was difficult for him to retreat.' Stevenson went to see Nasser and pointed out that he was working himself into a corner. Nasser told him, 'It's your fault. You didn't tell me.' Stevenson assured him that the British had not known in advance that Nuri and Menderes would agree so quickly. Nasser admitted he had lost his temper, but said in so many words, 'Don't let it happen again. Unless you warn me of such things I am liable to take hasty action.'[14]

Nasser called a meeting of Arab prime ministers in Cairo on 22 January, the first Arab conference he himself attended. His aim was to condemn Iraq and secure a declaration rejecting outside pacts. Nuri refused to attend but sent a delegation. A delegation from the conference, including Salah Salem, went to see Nuri in Baghdad on 30 January. Nuri's parting words to Salem after this meeting were, 'I am not a soldier in Abdul Nasser's army. Please tell him that I will never obey his orders.'[15] The prime ministers' conference ended on 6 February without a decision.

The conference was one of the most fateful in the post-war evolution of the Arab world. The clash between Nasser and the Iraqi delegation led by Fadil el Jamali was no shallow conflict of personal or national pride (though these played their part) but a serious confrontation of two carefully thought-out and sincerely held rival policies. These policies above all reflected two opposing views about the relations of the Arabs with the Western Powers. Nasser believed that if the Arabs exploited their bargaining position in a united front, the West would in its own interest give the Arabs the arms they needed without further Arab commitments. The Iraqis argued that this was unrealistic and that the West would not supply arms without some defence commitments from the Arabs. Nasser overestimated the rationality of Western policies and underestimated the political pressures at work in Western countries.

Tactically, the struggle at the conference centred round Syria, foreshadowing the key role this country was to play in Nasser's Arab policies, for if the Syrians had voted with Iraq they would have been supported by Lebanon and Jordan. But Syria refused to join either in a condemnation of Iraq or a rejection of pacts, though she agreed not to commit herself to any outside alliance. As the conference ended, Cairo radio began a violent campaign against Nuri es-Said as a traitor to the Arabs. In Damascus the Syrian government fell and gave way on 13 February to a pro-Egyptian and anti-Iraqi coalition. It included leaders of the neutralist, left-wing Baath and the independent Khaled el Azm who favoured seeking support from Russia against Israel.

On 25 February 1955, Nuri es-Said and Menderes signed their new alliance in Baghdad. Its birth led eventually to a fierce struggle between Nasser on the one side and Nuri, backed by Britain and, more tepidly, by the United States on the other, for the allegiance of the other Arab states. But at first there was a temporary lull after Sir Ralph Stevenson, on instructions from London, had assured Nasser in the spring of 1955 that no attempt would be made to extend the Baghdad Pact to other Arab states than Iraq. In reply to this assurance, Nasser told Stevenson that he would not regard it as an action hostile to Egypt if non-Arab states, such as Britain, joined Iraq and Turkey as members of the Pact.[16]

But the tranquillizing effect of this understanding about the Baghdad Pact was reduced by the coincidental increase of pressure on Nasser from another direction (though Nasser was inclined by nature to see a conspiracy in every coincidence). On 28 February 1955, breaking six years of comparative quiet on the Egyptian–Israeli border since the armistice, the Israel army made a heavy attack on an Egyptian military camp in the Gaza Strip. On the Egyptian side, thirty-six soldiers and two civilians were killed and twenty-nine soldiers and two civilians wounded, most of them Palestinians. The Israelis lost eight killed and nine wounded. It was the worst clash on the Egyptian–Israeli border since the 1949 armistice.

Like the Baghdad Pact, the Gaza raid had a long history. After the armistices between Israel and the Arab states were signed, hopes that they would lead to a speedy peace settlement were disappointed. As the peace efforts collapsed, friction grew on the borders. The armistice lines had not been intended as viable frontiers. They were both militarily insecure and in many places humanly intolerable, often shutting off Arab villages from their lands and livelihood. Border incidents gradually multiplied in a bloody cycle of infiltration and shooting, retaliation and reprisals. Most of these incidents were on the long and heavily populated Jordan frontier; the Egyptian border – mostly desert except for the Gaza strip – was relatively quiet. The chief manifestation of tension between Israel and Egypt was the latter's refusal to allow Israeli ships to pass through the Suez Canal. Egypt claimed the right of blockade since she regarded herself as legally still in a state of war with Israel, the armistice being only a suspension of hostilities. The 1888 Convention on freedom of passage through the Canal permitted her to take such measures for her own defence in time of war. The Security Council in September 1951 rejected this interpretation of the armistice and called on Egypt to let Israeli ships through the Canal. Egypt ignored the resolution – no Egyptian government could have implemented it and survived, so long as Israel on her side refused to implement other United Nations resolutions, such as that calling for the right to return home of the Palestinian Arab refugees – but in practice the Egyptian authorities turned a blind eye on the passage through the Canal of non-warlike cargoes to and from Israel in non-Israeli ships.

A new situation began to develop when the Egyptian revolution was followed in 1953 by signs that London and Washington were revising their policies towards the Middle East. Under the pressures of the Cold War, the new Eisenhower administration was turning away from the pro-Israeli commitments of President Truman and looking for friends, if not for open allies, in the Arab world. The British were beginning to consider a withdrawal of their troops from Egypt.

Israel's leaders saw several causes for alarm in these developments. Egypt, the biggest and most developed Arab country, had found a more militant and dynamic leadership. Though the revolutionary regime in Cairo did not in its early stages pay much attention to Israel, a British withdrawal from the Canal Zone would remove a possible buffer between Israel and Egypt and leave control of the Canal irrevocably in Egyptian hands. The pursuit by both Britain and America of Arab cooperation in a Middle East defence system would, the Israelis believed, both weaken the guarantee to Israel under the 1950 Declaration and at the same time mean more Western arms for the Arab states. Although Israel was still militarily stronger than any of her Arab neighbours or any combination of them, the future trend seemed to be towards a gradual tipping of the balance of power against Israel.

The reaction of the Israeli government was three-fold. It sought more arms from the Western Powers, especially from France, which appeared a more likely source than Britain or the United States. It tried to obtain the enforcement of free passage for Israeli ships through the Canal before the British agreed to withdraw from Egypt. It asked for an assurance from Washington that if the United States formed any new defence alliance with the Arab states, she would give a parallel guarantee of Israel's security.

In February 1954 Israel brought the Suez Canal question once more before the Security Council, but to little effect. On 28 September 1954, when the negotiation of the Anglo-Egyptian agreement on the Canal Zone was in its final stage, she sent a test ship, the Israeli vessel *Bat Galim*, with an Israeli crew on board, to approach the southern end of the Suez Canal. The Egyptians arrested the ship and jailed the crew on the grounds that they had attacked Egyptian police. The case of the *Bat Galim* went before the Security Council in mid-October, but the debate was adjourned until January 1955. By that time the Egyptians had released the crew and offered to hand over the vessel and cargo to any consignee named by Israel, provided they did not pass through the Canal. The Egyptians also disclosed that they had not been preventing the passage through the Canal of non-Israeli ships bound for Israel with cargoes which were not considered contraband of war. The *Bat Galim* incident did not affect the conclusion of the Anglo-Egyptian agreement. Nor was this aim achieved by another Israeli operation which later became a *cause célèbre* in Israel under the name of the 'Lavon affair'. While the 'Lavon affair' failed to achieve its intended result of preventing a British agreement with Egypt, it helped to worsen relations between Egypt and Israel.

When Ben Gurion had resigned from the premiership in Israel at the end of 1953 and retired to meditate and work in the pioneer kibbutz of Sde Boker in the Negev desert, he had handed over the Ministry of Defence to Pinhas Lavon, a leader of the Israeli Labour party (Mapai). Noted among his colleagues for both energy and arrogance, Lavon was believed to be Ben Gurion's candidate for his succession. He had once been against the 'activist' policy of Ben Gurion but changed to become an over-zealous advocate of massive reprisals.[17] In mid-July 1954, Lavon is said to have approved a proposal by the Israeli military intelligence to stage a series of bomb attacks on British and American official establishments in Egypt: the explosions were to be made to appear the work of Egyptians. By so envenoming the atmosphere between London, Washington and Cairo, it was hoped to wreck the Anglo-Egyptian negotiations and ensure that British troops would remain in Egypt.[18] What Lavon apparently did not know was that by the time he gave his approval the operation was already over and had been a failure. Some explosions had taken place but the small and rather amateur spy ring of Zionist-minded young Jews in Egypt who had been recruited to do the job had mostly been caught by the Egyptian secret police. It was revealed years later that one of the Israeli intelligence agents sent to organize the spy ring was himself a double agent working also for the Egyptians. The arrested men (and one woman) were held incommunicado for some months and their arrests were kept secret until the beginning of October. It was only then that the Israeli prime minister, Moshe Sharett, began to hear the truth about the case, for the controversy behind it was leading to a split inside the Israeli Defence Ministry between Lavon and his army chiefs and officials. The trial of the spies came hard on the heels of the attempt on Nasser's life and the trial and execution of the Muslim Brotherhood leaders. Two of the Jewish accused, a Dr Marzouk of Tunisian origin and French nationality, and Samuel Azzar, a teacher, were sentenced to death: six, including the woman defendant, Marcelle Nino, were given long prison terms; and two were aquitted. Another of the accused, Max Bennet, committed suicide in his prison cell. The trial was itself fairly conducted and in public, but Marcelle Nino declared in court that she had been ill-treated during interrogation.

'There followed,' according to a well-known Zionist writer, 'an ill-advised Israeli public and private campaign to exert pressure on Nasser to save the two sentenced to die.'[19] But, four days after sentence, Marzouk and Azzar were hanged. Nasser is said to have given a promise to an American intermediary, Roger Baldwin, chairman of the American League for the Rights of Man, that the two men would be reprieved, but to have been over-ruled by his colleagues. The affair had a double impact in Israel. It roused public feeling against Nasser and it brought about – or at least hastened – a momentous change in Israel's government and in her policy.

Lavon resigned a few days after the executions and Ben Gurion came back from retirement to take his place. At the Defence Ministry, Ben Gurion's first preoccupation was to restore the morale of the Israel army, which had suffered in the quarrel with Lavon, and the confidence of the public, shaken by the fiascos of the *Bat Galim* and the spy affair. Exactly a week after his return to the Defence Ministry, Ben Gurion authorized the attack on Gaza, claiming that it was a reprisal for raids into Israel by Egyptian intelligence agents and saboteurs. Though there had been incidents of this kind, General Burns, the United Nations truce supervisor, said in his report to the Security Council on 17 March 1955 that, 'the number of casualties prior to the Gaza incident reflects the comparative tranquillity along the armistice demarcation line during the greater part of the period November 1954–February 1955'. The Egyptian government claimed to Burns that such raids as there were into Israel were being organized by their political opponents in Egypt (thought to be Muslim Brothers) with the purpose of aggravating tension on the border.

At their first meeting in November 1954, Nasser told General Burns, the UN truce supervisor, that he wanted no trouble on the border with Israel and no military adventures. Burns comments,

> It is difficult to determine exactly what weight to give to Nasser's words. He speaks with an air of sincerity and simplicity; there is no bluster, no menace, instead an appearance of reasonableness. Nevertheless, one remembers that he is a politician who has reached power by way of conspiracy and revolution.[20]

But Burns concluded from an analysis of Nasser's policy that Egypt was unlikely to be planning to wage all-out war against Israel, since this could not be combined – except as a remote objective – with Nasser's main aim of uniting the Arab states of the Middle East under Egypt's hegemony.

Sharett, who had authorized the raid on Gaza in principle, was appalled at the scale of the casualties,[21] especially as he had just begun to discuss with the United States a possible new approach to a peace settlement with Egypt. The US State Department at that time saw Egypt under Nasser as the Arab country most likely to lead the way to a realistic settlement with Israel. It was the biggest Arab state and Egyptian public opinion was thought to be less emotionally involved in the dispute with Israel than public opinion in other Arab countries.[22] But, for Ben Gurion, the Gaza raid was the first step in a stronger security policy of 'active defence' destined to develop eventually into 'preventive war' against Egypt. Whether intentionally or not, the timing of the Gaza attack only three days after the signature of the Baghdad Pact was reminiscent of the attacks made by Haganah, the Jewish underground army, on strategic points in Palestine when Britain was reviewing her policy there at the end of the Second World War. It was a demonstration to the Western Powers of Israeli strength and a warning that Israel could not be overlooked in any military arrangements for the Middle East then being considered by the West. Its main effect, however, was sharply to accelerate the arms race between Israel and Egypt, and to inaugurate a new and far more bloody cycle of terrorism, guerrilla raids and reprisals.

The Gaza raid intensified the pressure already being exerted on Nasser from the Egyptian army to acquire more arms. For although Egypt had begun to receive a trickle of modern arms from Britain after the Canal Zone agreement (chiefly Centurion tanks ordered long before and whose delivery had been held up), Nasser knew that Israel was also beginning to get substantial quantities of new weapons from a new source – France. The outbreak of the Algerian rebellion in November 1954 had strengthened Israeli arguments in Paris, used especially to the French military leaders, that Israel and France should cooperate against the Arabs as a common enemy. At the end of 1954, the Israeli and French Ministries of Defence signed an agreement for the delivery of tanks, planes, guns and radar to Israel.[23]

There were also other less official transactions. In January 1955, Nasser sent for the British ambassador in Cairo, Sir Ralph Stevenson, and banged his hand angrily on a pile of papers on his desk. He said they were copies of bills of lading for 100 Sherman tanks and 100 seventy-five-millimetre guns with turrets (the guns and tanks put together formed 'Super-Shermans') which had apparently been shipped direct from England to Haifa in Israel. 'You are supposed to keep a balance of arms between us and the Israelis,' said Nasser. 'What are you going to do for me now?' Stevenson replied that he would have to check the information but added that in any case Britain had given Egypt Centurion tanks which could out-gun the Shermans. Nasser retorted that 100 Shermans in the hands of the Israelis gave them a very strong striking force and unless he obtained arms he could not count on the continued support of the army for his regime.

Stevenson's enquiries confirmed that the French had been secretly breaking the 1950 tripartite arms control agreement. French interests had bought the Shermans from Britain for scrap: after they had been shipped from Britain to Cherbourg they had been rerouted direct to Israel.* Nasser then asked Stevenson to send a personal message from himself to Eden saying that unless

* A statement by the British Foreign Office on 8 October gave the number of Shermans supplied to Israel as seventy-five, of which twenty were sold direct from Britain and fifty-five through France (Documents on International Affairs 1955, RIIA).

he could get arms from Britain or the United States he would have to get them where he could. Stevenson was certain that Nasser would do as he said.[24]

The British made it plain that any substantial arms supplies to Egypt would depend on a more cooperative attitude by Nasser towards the Baghdad Pact. In February the Americans turned down a request from Nasser for $27 million worth of arms, ostensibly on the grounds that Egypt could not afford to pay cash for them. Nasser had already rejected an earlier offer of American arms because of the accompanying proviso that he should receive an American military mission.

While he continued this unrewarding search for arms in the West, Nasser answered the pressure of the Israeli army by the same tactics that he had used against the superior British military strength in the Canal Zone. He began to organize terrorist and sabotage raids inside Israel on a large scale by guerrilla commandoes or 'fedayin' (which means 'self-sacrificers').

In April of 1955 Nasser made his first important appearance on the international stage at the Afro-Asian conference at Bandung in Indonesia. He showed an impressive capacity for the quiet and effective conduct of business in committee work behind the scenes. His experience in Bandung gave his political picture of the world new dimensions. He heard an echo from the leaders of more than a billion people of Egypt's – and his own – deep hatred of colonialism and European imperialism. This revelation of the vast political hinterland of rebellious Afro-Asia and his visit to India on the way home strengthened Nasser's inclination towards neutralism which had already been encouraged by his earlier contacts with Nehru and Tito and by his opposition to the Baghdad Pact. He also made his first contact with a Communist leader in the persuasive form of Chou En-lai, the brilliant Chinese prime minister, for whom the Bandung conference was a personal diplomatic triumph. Nasser asked Chou En-lai if China could supply Egypt with arms. Chou temporized, promised to buy some Egyptian cotton, and told the Russians of Nasser's enquiry.

Nasser himself has stated that his first contact with the Russians about arms was in June 1955 through the Soviet ambassador in

Cairo.[25] In the same month Nasser told the American ambassador in Cairo, Henry Byroade, that he had had an offer from the Russians and that he would accept if he could not get arms from the United States. Byroade told his British colleague, Stevenson, who reported the news to London and was instructed to warn Nasser that if he took Russian arms he would get no more from Britain. Nasser reacted angrily. He later told Sir Humphrey Trevelyan (who succeeded Stevenson in Cairo in August 1955) that he considered the British message as a threat which he could not accept and that from that time on he decided to have no more talks with the British about arms.[26]

Israel had put some of her new French planes and tanks on show in her Independence Day parade in May and the election campaign for the Knesset that summer was full of debate about the pros and cons of 'activism'. The right-wing Herut (Freedom) party led by Menahem Beigin, former leader of the Irgun Zvai Leumi terrorist group openly advocated an expansion of Israel's frontiers – some slogans said 'from the Nile to the Euphrates' – and a preventive war against the Arab states. In the new Israeli parliament Herut became the second strongest party and the activists of right and left were a majority of the members. The alarm caused in Cairo by these developments was increased by more heavy fighting along the Gaza Strip borders during August and early September. On 22 August Israeli forces attacked and occupied an Egyptian army post near the armistice line five miles east of Gaza, killing three Egyptians and wounding three others. The Egyptians retaliated by once more sending fedayeen into Israel in a series of raids which killed eleven Israeli soldiers and civilians and injured nine. For the previous three months these attacks, begun after the first Gaza raid in February, had virtually ceased.[27] On 31 August, the Israeli army attacked the police fort at Khan Yunis in the Gaza Strip and other Egyptian positions, killing (according to Egyptian figures) thirty-six soldiers, policemen and civilians and wounding thirteen. The Egyptian commander-in-chief, General Amer, wanted to mount a counter-offensive but was restrained by Nasser.[28]

This episode and the continued failure to obtain promises of arms in substantial quantities from the Western Powers must have decided Nasser on his bold new course. When Trevelyan called on Nasser on 27 September, to enquire about rumours of an impending arms deal, Nasser confirmed that he had made an agreement for Russian arms, though he said it had been made through Prague. The Foreign Office, without further consultation with Trevelyan or Nasser, revealed this news at a press briefing the following day. Nasser was again angered by what he considered as a breach of confidence and an attempt to 'put him in a corner',[29] and the same evening made a defiant speech announcing the arms deal. The reports of the deal had also brought a special envoy from the US State Department, George V. Allen, flying to Cairo, to try to persuade Nasser to change his mind. His mission, like the further protests from London, was unsuccessful.

In a speech at an Armed Forces exhibition in Cairo, Nasser announced that during the previous week Egypt had signed a 'commercial agreement' with Czechoslovakia for a supply of weapons in exchange for cotton and rice. Describing his unsuccessful quest for weapons in the West, Nasser claimed that 'France always haggled with us, telling us that they would give us weapons on the condition that we did not criticize their policy in North Africa: that is, they asked us to abandon our Arab nature, to abandon our humanitarianism, to ignore the butchery that was going on in North Africa'. America had attached the unacceptable conditions of a mutual security pact. Britain, after having promised arms, had delivered them in insufficient quantities. At the same time, Israel had been receiving arms from several Western countries; the Western newspapers, alleged Nasser, had said that the Israeli army was stronger than the Egyptian army in arms and equipment and could defeat all the Arab armies combined.

A week later the Israeli government declared publicly that Cairo reports of Israel's alleged superiority in arms were 'absolutely unfounded' and announced its intention of acquiring more arms. The same day, however, the Director-General of the Israeli Defence Ministry, Shimon Peres, gave a different picture. Reviewing the two-year-old rearmament plan in a speech to employees of his Ministry, Peres said, 'With regard to the acquisition of arms, we have provided Israel with superiority over the Arab states'.

Israel had greatly expanded her armoured units and acquired modern aircraft 'which gave us a new air superiority'.[30]

The precise terms of Nasser's first arms deal with the Soviet bloc (he later admitted that the deal was in fact with Russia not Czechoslovakia) have never been officially revealed. According to an American official estimate, Egypt purchased between eighty and 100 Mig jet fighters, thirty to forty-five Ilyushin-28 light jet bombers, 100 Stalin and T34 tanks, several hundred armoured troop carriers, as well as artillery, trucks, bazookas, small arms and ammunition, all to be paid for with cotton and rice deliveries over a long period of years. The value of the deal was variously estimated in Washington at between $90 and $200 million.[31] A British estimate put the cost at about £150 million and included in the material 300 medium and heavy tanks, more than a hundred self-propelled guns, two destroyers, four minesweepers and twenty motor torpedo-boats.[32]

The crisis between Egypt and Israel had begun with the agreement to withdraw British troops from the Canal Zone: the Czech arms deal brought it into a new and acute phase. Overnight Nasser's prestige and popularity soared among the Arab publics to a height no modern Arab leader had reached before. He was admired for his boldness and for his refusal to submit to an arms control system imposed by the Western Powers which seemed to leave the Arabs at the mercy of the Israeli army. Where other Arab leaders had only talked, he had dared to act. Few Arabs paused to think of the wider international implication of the deal. The Arabs knew that neither they nor Nasser were Communists or desirous of becoming Soviet satellites. So, they thought, why should Egypt not get the arms she desperately needed from Russia, if the Russians, unlike the West, would supply them without political strings? To all those Arabs living round Israel's borders, except perhaps for the Maronite Christians of the Lebanon, Israel appeared a more immediate and real danger than Russia.

The Soviet arms deal did not bring the Cold War into the Middle East: it was already there and had been intensified by the moves to set up Western-backed regional defence systems, culminating in the Baghdad Pact. But the arms deal ensured that henceforward the Middle East could no longer be regarded as a purely Western sphere of influence. The West could no longer hope simply to seal off the Arab world from Soviet penetration. Russia had re-established herself as a Middle East power after an absence of nearly forty years. She had secured at a cheap price a valuable political foothold in the most important Arab country whose influence also extended into Africa. The West could no longer count on treating the Arab countries as if they were rebellious satellites. The struggle for influence there had taken on a new style. It was part of the competition between the West and the Communist bloc for the sympathies of the non-aligned Third World, a conflict ushered in by Khrushchev and Marshal Bulganin with their doctrine of 'peaceful coexistence', and their highly publicized journey to India. But the Western Powers were slow to grasp the changed setting in the Middle East. For Dulles, in particular, neutralism was 'immoral', while the British found it hard to adjust to a struggle of political and economic manoeuvre, rather than the direct exercise of military and administrative power, in dealing with the Arab countries.

At first, however, before the clumsy panic which led up to Suez, Dulles and Eden made some attempt to recover lost political ground. The months between the first Gaza raid and the Soviet arms deal saw not only a sharp increase in tension between Egypt and Israel but also an effort by Dulles, supported by Eden, to bring about a negotiated peace settlement between the two countries, an effort which was also continued during the months following the arms deal. This peace attempt arose partly in response to Israeli approaches to Washington for an alliance or military guarantee parallel with the Baghdad Pact.

The Anglo-American approach to a settlement, which appears to have aroused Nasser's interest, was based on the assumption that the key points in a peace were frontiers, the refugees and the status of Jerusalem. For Nasser the first two were the more important. He considered that Israel must be ready to take back a substantial number of the Palestinian Arab refugees and pay compensation to the rest. If the Arabs were to accept less than their claim for the return of all the refugees to their homes in Israel, they would have to be given at least some token *quid pro quo* in the form of a territorial concession. At the same time, the biggest grievance of Egypt arising out of the armistice lines was that she had lost her land communication with the eastern Arab states because of Israeli control of the Negev. The biggest difficulty for Jordan was her lack of access to the Mediterranean. Nasser's first claim – perhaps his first bargaining position – was for the re-establishment of a land link with Jordan by the cession to Egypt of most of the Negev south of Beersheba.[33]

Among various complicated schemes discussed in London and Washington for crossroads and corridors which might link Egypt, Jordan and the Gaza Strip without impeding Israeli access to Eilat, there was one which seemed to be most favoured by the Americans. It envisaged the cession by Israel of a narrow strip of land parallel with the Sinai border running from the Gaza Strip down to the Jordan frontier at the head of the Gulf of Aqaba.[34] This corridor would not cut across the centre of Israel or any seriously populated area and it would link Jordan not only with the Mediterranean and with the Palestinians in the Gaza Strip but also with Egypt. It would run through barren desert incapable of agricultural development. If demilitarized, it would also be a buffer between Israel and Egypt. Some way might be found to give Israel access across it to Eilat.

The snags were obvious. Apart from the Egyptian claim to more of the Negev including Eilat, there was the general Israeli objection to giving up an inch of the territory gained in the 1948 war. Even more important was that the Israelis, and Ben Gurion in particular, attached great material and sentimental, almost mystic importance, to the Negev and to their foothold on the Gulf of Aqaba. They saw their access to both the Mediterranean and the Red Sea as a valuable geopolitical advantage enjoyed by only one other country, Egypt. Eilat was intended to be the gateway to an expanding trade and political influence for Israel in Africa and Asia. It would be a port for oil coming in to Israel from Iran, which could not go through the Canal because of the Arab blockade. Perhaps it might even one day be the terminal of not only a pipe-line but also another canal, rivalling Suez, across the Negev from Eilat to the Mediterranean. There were long-cherished hopes of rich mineral deposits in the rocky wastes of the southern Negev and Ben Gurion dreamt of the northern Negev, half-desert, half-steppe, as an open pioneering frontier, providing the place for Israel's future expansion of population, especially if the three million Jews of Russia were ever allowed to emigrate.

Nevertheless, the possible advantages of the American proposal to Israel were not negligible, provided it led to a real peace settlement. For such a result, the price might reasonably be considered not excessive. For the Americans and some Israeli economists believed that some of the dreams of settlement and expansion in the disputed area were likely to remain dreams, because agricultural development of the Negev, particularly of the completely barren south, was not economic. It was doubtful whether the expected mineral deposits existed in worthwhile quantities and the transport problems were formidable. Once the Suez Canal was open to Israeli shipping and the Arab oil blockade was lifted, as would happen if a peace were signed, the usefulness of Eilat would be greatly diminished.

An oblique public reference to these American ideas for a settlement was made by Dulles in a speech on 26 August 1955. He offered American help for the resettlement or compensation of the Arab refugees and an American guarantee, by formal treaty, of agreed frontiers between Israel and the Arab states. Expressing the hope that other countries would join in the guarantee and that it would be sponsored by the United Nations, Dulles said that the difficulty of agreeing on permanent frontiers was 'increased by the fact that even territory which is barren has acquired a sentimental significance'. The Dulles proposals were endorsed the following day by the British government. They were coldly received by the Arab states because they implied recognition of the Israeli state. The Arab states came nearer to accepting the proposals for a settlement of the Jordan waters put forward by the American special envoy, Eric Johnston, but, on Syria's insistence, rejected them on 12 October.* Israel's reaction to the Dulles proposals was even more negative and decisive. In a speech to the Knesset on 18 October, Sharett welcomed the suggestion

* For details see Chapter 16.

of a security pact guaranteeing Israel's borders but declared that Israel could not consider any unilateral territorial concessions.[35]

A few days later, Israel's policy took a sharp turn away from thoughts of a negotiated settlement towards plans for a preventive war. On 22 October 1955, Ben Gurion, then still Defence Minister, summoned Major-General Dayan, then army chief of staff, back from holiday in France and instructed him to prepare plans for the capture of the Straits of Tiran in order to ensure freedom for Israeli shipping through the Gulf of Aqaba and the Red Sea.[36] This move was partly a response to action taken the previous month by Egypt to strengthen her blockade of Israeli shipping through the Gulf of Aqaba. No Israeli ships and planes were to be allowed through or over the Tiran Straits; ships and planes of other countries had to obtain permission from Egypt who claimed that the Straits formed part of her territorial waters.

The cycle of border incidents and reprisals, escalating into larger Israeli military action and intensified Arab guerrilla raids and blockade, was already becoming the classic pattern of the Arab–Israeli conflict. Each side could produce strong arguments of emotion, political survival or legal right to justify its actions, but neither Nasser nor Ben Gurion showed much awareness of the dangerous long-term implications of their tactical moves.

Whatever the morality or wisdom of Nasser's action in tightening the blockade of the Straits of Tiran, Egypt's legal case for claiming the right to do so was not negligible. It was, in fact, a particularly complex example of one of the most controversial aspects of the international law of the sea – the case of an almost landlocked gulf, in which sovereignty over a vital part of the shoreline was disputed. The Arabs had from the first rejected Israel's right to be at Eilat: although it was allocated to Israel under the 1947 partition plan, the area had been seized by Israeli forces in debatable circumstances in 1949 after the conclusion of the Egyptian–Israeli armistice and while the Jordan–Israel armistice was in its final stages of negotiation. Moreover, the shores of the Straits of Tiran and the two islands in the middle of them were Egyptian on one side and Saudi Arabian on the other. The coasts of the Gulf of Aqaba also belonged to Egypt and Saudi Arabia, except for a few kilometres at the head of the Gulf round Eilat which were controlled by Israel and another narrow stretch round the port of Aqaba which belonged to Jordan. The passage between the shore and the islands in the Straits of Tiran was only two miles wide, thus falling within the limits of the territorial waters of Egypt and Saudi Arabia. The legal question was whether as Israel claimed, the Gulf nevertheless constituted international waters to which all ships should enjoy free and innocent passage, and also whether Egypt's claim to exercise the belligerent right of blockade, despite the armistice – a claim already rejected by the Security Council in the case of the Suez Canal – had any bearing in the case of the Gulf.

The timing of the Egyptian move against Eilat reinforced the suspicions already aroused in Ben Gurion's mind. He saw it as yet one more sign of a conspiracy to deprive Israel of the Negev as part of a Middle East settlement in which the Western Powers, especially Britain, hoped to appease Egypt at Israel's expense.

The race between peace moves and war plans quickened. During September 1955 the main area of border tension switched from the Gaza strip to the key strategic sector on the Israeli–Egyptian frontier at the El Auja demilitarized zone and the areas on either side of it. This region covered one of the main invasion routes into Egypt from Israel and vice-versa. Israel had established a military foothold in the El Auja demilitarized zone under the guise of a collective farm settlement, in breach of the armistice agreement, while both she and Egypt were maintaining forces in the adjoining areas in dispositions and strength which were also contrary to the armistice. Raid and counter-raid followed each other and the United Nations made vain efforts to get agreement on a withdrawal by both sides.

On 2 November 1955 Ben Gurion replaced the more cautious Sharett as prime minister of Israel. The same day he made a bellicose speech to the Knesset warning Egypt that guerrilla operations and the blockade of the Straits of Tiran could lead to war. He called for full observance of the armistice agreements and offered to meet Nasser and other Arab leaders for peace talks, but declared, 'if acts of violence interfere with our rights on land and on the seas, then we reserve our freedom of action to protect our rights in the most effective manner'. Ben Gurion added, 'We have never initiated and shall never initiate war against anybody; we do not desire a single inch of foreign territory, but we shall not permit even an inch of our territory to be taken from us as long as we have life'.[37]

Despite this latter declaration, Ben Gurion at this time proposed to the Israeli cabinet a military attack by the Israeli army to seize the Straits of Tiran, in other words war against Egypt. The Cabinet 'decided that the moment was not propitious' but added that Israel should act in the place and at the time that she deemed appropriate.[38]

The British and American governments began to show alarm at the growing border tension, but neither they nor the French were prepared to take effective measures to enforce the keeping of the peace, either through the United Nations or under the Tripartite Declaration of 1950. They limited their action to verbal support for the efforts of General Burns and the UN Secretary-General, Hammarskjöld, and intensified their diplomatic pressure to bring about a peace settlement.

On 9 November, President Eisenhower repeated his offer of an American guarantee by treaty of agreed Israeli–Arab frontiers. The same day, in the British prime minister's traditional annual speech at the Guildhall in London, Sir Anthony Eden called for a compromise by Israel and the Arab states on their future frontiers. Eden pointed out that the Arabs had said they were willing to discuss peace terms with Israel on the basis of the 1947 partition plan and other United Nations resolutions, while the Israelis took their stand on the 1949 armistice lines. 'The stark truth' was that if Israel and the Arab states wanted peace, which was in their own interests, 'they must make some compromise between the two positions'.

In making the speech, Eden had in mind his successful initiative to solve the Trieste dispute between Italy and Yugoslavia. The speech was well received by the Arabs but angrily denounced by Israel. Nasser welcomed Eden's initiative as a move in the right direction. He had already let it be known that he thought the Bernadotte plan of 1948 a better basis for negotiation than the 1947 partition plan.[39] The Bernadotte plan drawn up by the then

United Nations mediator would have given the Negev and the Gaza strip to Jordan in exchange for leaving Israel in control of the whole of Galilee, the western half of which had been awarded to the Arabs under the 1947 plan.

Nasser made it plain that any settlement would have to include a choice of return home or compensation for the Arab refugees, though he believed that probably most of them would choose compensation if return meant going back under an Israeli government. Would Nasser, even on this basis, have been prepared for serious negotiations leading to a final peace settlement? As a journalist in personal contact at that time with most of the Arab leaders, including Nasser, I formed the impression that if Israel had been prepared to cede some territory for the sake of the advantages of a permanent settlement, the readiness of the Arab states to accept a final peace, including acceptance of the Israeli state with borders guaranteed by the Great Powers, was greater than at any time since 1949. But the process would have taken time and prolonged bargaining. Nor could it have begun seriously until there was greater quiet on the borders and a truce over the Baghdad Pact. For Nasser, any move towards a peace settlement would have meant a considerable political risk at a time when he was competing with Iraq for the allegiance of the other Arab states, particularly Syria and Jordan, who were more concerned than any other with the problem of Israel. Whether or not Nasser was serious about seeking peace, he was certainly serious about not wanting war. Despite the Soviet arms, Egypt's position vis-à-vis Israel was weak. Eden told the House of Commons on 12 December 1955, that 'Israel is not, in my belief, at a military disadvantage today in relation to any Arab state, or indeed, any combination of Arab states who are on her frontier'. UN military observers, who were in a good position to judge the forces of both sides, believed it would take two years for the Egyptians to absorb and master their new Soviet weapons. The Baghdad Pact and the quarrels it aroused had also weakened the general Arab position by splitting the Arab states and their collective security pact. Under pressure from his army to undertake a counter-offensive operation against Israel, which he knew Egypt was too weak to sustain, Nasser's first concern was to avoid armed clashes on the frontier. He had proposed that Egyptian and Israeli forces on the border should withdraw 500 feet on either side of the demarcation line. This suggestion was incorporated in General Burns's plan which was endorsed by the Security Council. Speculation about Nasser's peace intentions was soon rendered academic. Six days after the Guildhall speech the Anglo-American peace initiative was torpedoed by Israel. In a scathing speech to the Knesset, Ben Gurion denounced Eden's statement as 'a proposal to reduce Israel's territory in favour of her neighbours' and as 'entirely without legal, moral or logical basis and therefore not to be considered'.

Ben Gurion's uncompromising attitude was fortified by the knowledge that, three days earlier, Israel had signed a new arms agreement with the French government of Edgar Faure, under which she would receive another twenty-four Mystère jet fighters as well as more tanks and guns. France had opposed the Anglo-American plans for the Baghdad Pact because of her traditional resentment of possible Anglo-Iraqi designs on Syria, once a French preserve. This attitude led her Foreign Ministry to an ambivalent attitude between Egypt and Israel, who also both opposed the Baghdad Pact. But the Israeli government had succeeded in bypassing the Quai d'Orsay and establishing contact with the French Defence Ministry and with a group of ministers, soldiers and politicians whose foremost concern was the preservation of the French presence in Algeria. These influential and determined men, headed by M. Maurice Bourgès-Manoury, the Defence Minister, had accepted the Israeli thesis that France and Israel had a common enemy in the Arabs, especially in Nasser who was helping the Algerian rebels with arms and radio propaganda. This new Franco-Israeli alliance was to be further strengthened when the government headed by the French Socialist leader, Guy Mollet, took office in January 1956. Mollet's Socialist–Radical coalition had been elected on a promise of seeking peace in Algeria. But after Mollet, on a visit to Algiers in February, had been pelted with tomatoes by angry European workers, he changed his policy to one of more violent suppression of the Algerian Arab rebellion. Simultaneously, the influence of Israel in Paris was strengthened by the personal and ideological ties existing between leading members of the French Socialist party and the Israeli Socialist leaders.

Nasser thus faced a developing Franco-Israeli alliance but, despite the Soviet arms deal, his relations with the United States and Britain had not yet hardened into hostility. Anglo-American policy towards Egypt was to remain fluid for some months, until it finally crystallized into enmity around two questions, the financing of the Aswan High Dam and the future of Jordan. For the Americans, the first was decisive and for the British, the second.

Within a year of coming to power the Egyptian revolutionary regime had begun to study seriously the plan for a giant dam on the Nile south of Aswan. As the project was finally conceived, it would provide long-term storage of the Nile waters, extend perennial irrigation in Upper Egypt and enable another million and a quarter acres of land to be brought under cultivation. It would also generate large quantities of electric power for the industrialization which was needed to provide work for Egypt's rapidly expanding population. The dam was to be $2\frac{1}{2}$ miles long and 365 feet high, holding behind it a lake 344 miles long, the biggest artificial lake in the world. Twelve turbines worked from the dam would generate ten milliard kilowatts of electric power a year.

The plan was to build the dam in two stages over a period of ten years. The cost was estimated at some $1,300 million (£466 million) of which about a third would have to be in foreign currency, the greater part of this in the first stage. To obtain this foreign currency was one of the two main problems involved in building the Dam; the other was to get agreement with the Sudan for a new sharing of the Nile waters and for the flooding of a 124-mile-long stretch of the Nile Valley inside Sudanese territory from which some 50,000 people would have to be moved.

Several European firms, beginning with West Germans, had become interested in carrying out the High Dam project and since 1953 the Egyptian government had been discussing international financial help with the World Bank. The World Bank was reluctant to consider a loan until Egypt was politically more stable. This meant in the first place until she had reached the

Canal Zone agreement with Britain. Then there was the condition of agreement with the Sudan. In 1955 Nasser and his colleagues were still trying to persuade the leaders of the emergent Sudanese state to choose unity with Egypt rather than complete independence. Egypt's interest was obvious – to ensure that the upper waters of the Nile should not be under hostile control, with perhaps the secondary aim of an outlet for her surplus population, though the Egyptian peasant has rarely emigrated. The Sudan's interest in unity was less self-evident: Egyptian support was useful in ending British rule and Egypt was a cultural centre for many northern Sudanese, but Egyptian arguments for future unity included no guarantees of material advantage, such as more money for social and economic development. Egypt's anxiety about the Sudan, sharpened by suspicion of the influence of the remaining British officials there, was reflected in the unscrupulousness of her methods – propaganda was supported by bribery and intrigue among all the rival Sudanese factions in the non-Muslim south as well as the Muslim north. These tactics strengthened the influence of those in the British Foreign Office who believed Nasser was incorrigibly hostile to British interests and could not be trusted to keep an agreement.

British officialdom itself was, however, not averse to a little intrigue. When by the autumn of 1955 it had become clear that the Sudanese were going to choose independence, the British government, under pressure from the governor-general in Khartoum, Sir Knox Helm, proposed that Egypt and Britain should waive the provisions of the Sudan agreement calling for a constituent assembly and jointly declare the Sudan independent. Nasser replied through Trevelyan, the British ambassador in Cairo, that he was now convinced that in a free vote the Sudanese would choose independence, but he could not admit this publicly and had to keep the Sudan agreement in being as long as possible. Trevelyan advised the Foreign Office to stick to the provisions of the agreement but his advice was rejected. Instead the British secretly suggested to the Sudanese prime minister, Ismail el Azhari, that he should himself make a declaration of independence with a promise of British support. Azhari was non-committal but, as Trevelyan had foreseen,

Nasser got wind of the British move. He saw it as a breach of an understanding he had reached with Trevelyan that in dealing with Sudan affairs neither would try to 'put the other in a corner'.[40] When, on 1 January 1956, Azhari, with the agreement of the Sudanese parliament, proclaimed independence, Nasser swallowed his disappointment and, like Britain, at once recognized the new independent state. (One casualty of the failure of Egypt's policy of unity with the Sudan was Major Salah Salem, the Minister for National Guidance and the Egyptian minister chiefly responsible for Sudanese affairs. He was removed from his post in August 1955 and consoled with a job as a newspaper columnist.)

Although agreement on the Nile waters still hung fire, the World Bank was stimulated to a more urgent approach to the High Dam finance by a new interest of the United States and Britain provoked in turn by Russia. In October 1955 Russia had followed up the news of the Soviet arms deal by expressing her readiness to offer a loan of £100 million towards industrialization in Egypt, including the supply of material and technicians for the High Dam. Alarmed at the prospect of increasing Soviet economic and political penetration into the Middle East and thence into Africa, the British and American governments decided to join in a preemptive bid to ensure Western rather than Soviet financing of the High Dam. On 17 December they announced that they would contribute part of the foreign exchange costs of the first stage of the Dam project and would also 'consider sympathetically in the light of the then existing circumstances' further support for the later stages, together with the World Bank.

For the first stage the United States offered a grant of $56 million (£20 million) and Britain $14 million (£5 million) as a joint collateral for a World Bank loan of $200 million. The rest of the cost, in Egyptian currency, would be borne by Egypt herself.

When Eden and Eisenhower met to discuss Middle East policy in Washington in February 1956 they agreed that Nasser's attitude towards this High Dam offer would be an important indicator of the prospects for his cooperation with the West.[41]

The contacts between Nasser and Eugene Black, President of the World Bank, had already begun to show Nasser's extreme suspicion and caution about the terms for the Anglo-American aid and the World Bank loan. The Anglo-American conditions were that Egypt should promise to refuse aid from Communist sources, should give the Dam priority over other projects and award contracts for the work on a competitive basis. The World Bank also put some conditions of its own about the conduct of Egyptian government finances, as regards both the budget and the balance of payments. Nasser baulked at what seemed to him a demand for a close outside supervision of the Egyptian economy. It was explained to him that the World Bank was an international institution, an agency of the United Nations whose officials were international civil servants and whose rules were the same for every country. He pointed out with some truth but little tact that the United States and Britain supplied so large a proportion of the Bank funds that presumably they had considerable influence over its lending policy.

The British and American governments attributed Nasser's wariness to the fact that he had – or thought he had – an offer from Russia up his sleeve and was trying to get the best possible terms by playing one side against the other. But they underestimated the degree to which Nasser was influenced by Egypt's history. He was obsessed with the fear that the country's newly won independence might be lost again through the domination of foreign creditors, just as the debts of the Khedive Ismail had led first to European financial control and then to the British occupation.

Such misunderstanding over the High Dam might have been overcome but for other developments which weakened confidence between Nasser and the Western Powers. Early in November King Hussein of Jordan told the British that his country was now ready to join the Baghdad Pact. Once again the Turks were the prime movers in the affair; Hussein had made up his mind during the visit to Jordan of the Turkish President. The British were delighted at the chance of getting another Arab state to join the Pact, for Iraq felt isolated as the only Arab member. Such a move would be a clear breach of the assurance given to Nasser only a few months before that the Pact would not be extended to other Arab countries. But the British might argue that

Nasser's Soviet arms deal had created an entirely new situation. To counter the anticipated propaganda opposition from Egypt, Eden decided to make what he thought would be an impressive demonstration of the value of the alliance to Jordan. He sent the Chief of the Imperial General Staff, General Sir Gerald Templer, to Amman bringing a gift of ten Vampire jet fighters, the promise of substantial quantities of other military equipment, and the draft of a new agreement to replace the Anglo-Jordan Treaty, once Jordan signed the Baghdad Pact. General Templer, who was in Amman from 6–14 December 1955, told the Jordan government that Britain would provide the Arab Legion with the equipment and finance for two more infantry battalions, a medium artillery regiment and a regiment of tanks.[42]

In an attempt to cover up the breach of the earlier assurance to Egypt, Trevelyan was told by the Foreign Office to inform Nasser that the Templer mission was not intended to press Jordan to join the Baghdad Pact but to discuss the supply of arms, during which the Pact question had arisen. But Nasser knew this to be 'a misleading statement' and consequently intensified Egyptian propaganda against Britain and the Pact, to the further detriment of Anglo-Egyptian relations and the situation in Jordan.[43]

The Jordan government split and fell when four Palestinian ministers resigned rather than accept the Templer proposals. The ministers, claiming to reflect the majority of public opinion – which was now formed numerically at least by the Palestinians in Jordan, including the refugees – opposed Jordan's membership of the Baghdad Pact because it would mean isolation from Egypt. The Palestinians believed that they could not risk losing Egypt's support on the front against Israel. The cabinet crisis was accompanied by widespread strikes and demonstrations. General Templer was obliged to return to London empty-handed, except for an agreement that he should come back to continue the negotiations when the Jordan government felt strong enough to do so. Fears, encouraged by Cairo radio, that the attempt might be renewed by a new government of king's men and anger at the failure to hold new elections led to more rioting in Jordan, especially in the west bank towns, early in

January 1956. At least seven people were killed and hundreds wounded and many buildings set on fire.[44] The British prepared to fly in troops to Amman and King Hussein asked for troops from Iraq. But in the end neither British nor Iraqi forces moved. Selwyn Lloyd, who had replaced Harold Macmillan as Foreign Secretary, sent a message to Nasser containing a mixture of protest, threat and conciliation. The message warned Nasser that Britain's future relations with Egypt depended on the ending of Egyptian hostility in Jordan and especially of the anti-British campaign of Cairo radio. Lloyd assured Nasser that Britain was not trying to isolate Egypt and wanted good relations between Cairo and Baghdad.[45]

From the time of the Templer mission onwards, Nasser began to believe that the British government, with the help of Nuri es-Said, were pursuing a hostile policy towards him by trying to isolate Egypt and make her once again dependent on Britain. Both Nasser and the British claimed that each was only reacting to the hostile moves of the other. In spite of Nasser's suspicions, he seemed prepared to consider a new proposal for a diplomatic truce sketched to him by Trevelyan in a meeting on 1 January 1956.[46] This proposal would have revived the previous understanding by which Nasser agreed to drop his attacks on the Baghdad Pact provided it was not extended to any other Arab states. But, at the time, the British government was still anxious to extend the Pact, apparently believing that its prestige and that of Nuri es-Said was now committed to a struggle with Nasser for influence in the Arab states, which, if lost, would mean a precarious isolation for Nuri and the Baghdad regime.

There was a strange blindness or lack of coordination in the British diplomatic timing. Eden's initiative for a Palestine peace settlement depended for its success on the Arab side chiefly on the reactions of Egypt. Opposition from Nasser could kill it immediately, while only Egypt and Nasser could provide the influence and leadership that might bring a settlement about. Yet at the very same time Eden was preparing to bring Jordan into the Baghdad Pact, a move certain to arouse Egyptian hostility and suspicion. Moreover, it was a move peculiarly calculated to destroy the prospects of obtaining Arab support for a compromise settlement with Israel. Jordan, with its long frontier with Israel and two-thirds of its population Palestinians, was at the heart of both a peaceful settlement of the Palestine problem and of the Arab military front 'containing' Israel. In Nasser's eyes, the inclusion of Jordan in the Baghdad Pact would mean that eventually Egypt and Syria would be left to face Israel alone. Syria herself might be the next target for inclusion in the Pact after Jordan. As if to warn Syria not to rely on her Egyptian alliance, Israeli forces, on the personal order of Ben Gurion, made a heavy attack on Syrian army positions and villages near Lake Tiberias on 11 December 1955, while General Templer was in Amman. Fifty-six Syrians were killed. The attack was ostensibly a reprisal for alleged Syrian shooting at Israeli fishermen, but was in reality a clumsy diplomatic demonstration.[47] The *Jerusalem Post* newspaper, which usually reflected the views of the Israeli government wrote, 'We hope that the Israeli raid has convinced many Syrians that the military pact with Egypt has increased the danger to Syria instead of guaranteeing Syria's defences.' The result of the raid was, however, not to break the Egyptian–Syrian alliance, but to strengthen it. It helped to destroy the prospects of either Syria or Jordan joining the Baghdad Pact, overcame the last resistance inside the Syrian cabinet to a Syrian purchase of Soviet arms and ensured the supremacy in Damascus of the advocates of closer ties with Egypt. (There was a joke in Israel at the time that the attack on Syria had been ordered by a special committee of three, made up of the prime minister, the defence minister and the foreign minister – Ben Gurion was then occupying all these posts, as the Foreign Minister, Sharett, was in the United States trying to buy arms – a mission which was not helped by Ben Gurion's action.)

Nasser's reaction was not to recoil from the challenge but to stress the seriousness of his new commitment to Syria. He informed the United Nations Secretary-General that any further aggression against Syria would be met with the whole of the Egyptian armed forces. The repercussions of the attack on Syria also ensured that no serious attention would be given in the Arab capitals to Israel's counter-proposals for a peace settlement which were made known a week later. Rejecting any major territorial changes, Israel proposed mutual adjustments of the 1949 armistice lines, compensation but no return for the refugees and a loan for their re-settlement in the Arab states. To Egypt she offered land and air transit rights for trade with the Lebanon and across the Negev to Jordan. To the Jordanians, she offered a right to free port facilities in Haifa and transit rights to them from Jordan.

The Syrian raid and the upheaval in Jordan over the Baghdad Pact led to new attempts by the Arab states to find a common policy towards Israel and the Western Powers. There also followed a more intensive search through the United Nations for a peaceful *modus vivendi* between Israel and the Arab states. In this operation Hammarskjöld appeared for a time to have the unusually unanimous backing of the Great Powers, including Russia. But the Secretary-General's peace-making efforts eventually broke down, largely because the Western Powers attached more importance to their own hostility to Egypt than to the maintenance of Arab-Israeli peace; Britain and France believed that Nasser threatened their interests in the Arab oil countries and in North Africa, and the United States chose to strike at Russia's wooing of the neutralists by making an example of Egypt.

The Baghdad Pact and the Soviet arms deal had internationalized the local struggle for power in the Middle East. They brought America and Russia more actively into an area where hitherto the dominant Great Powers had been Britain and France. But the struggle was fought out still in local terms and Britain was still the main foreign power involved. Nasser's policy of Arab unity and independence under Egyptian leadership was a challenge to the hegemony of the two powers which had dominated the Middle East militarily since the Palestine war – Israel, and Britain acting through the Hashemite regimes of Jordan and Iraq. Eventually this struggle came to a head in open war, in which Israel and Britain found themselves in reluctant alliance against Egypt. Until then it was fought out politically and centred on Syria and Jordan. Israel used her military strength to try to keep Egypt, Syria and Jordan apart. Egypt competed with Britain and Iraq for influence in Amman and Damascus.

The British government saw Nasser's opposition to Anglo-Iraq influence and to the Baghdad Pact as a breach of the promise of better relations after the 1954 Canal Zone agreement. But the Pact – as Nasser had warned Dulles – had brought the opposite results from those intended: it had increased the instability of Arab Asia and helped the growth of Russian and Communist influence there. Russia appeared more able than the West to accommodate itself to the underlying neutralism of Arab nationalist opinion. The Baghdad Pact had drawn new lines in the Arab world. Nasser, the more orthodox neutralists, the Baathists and Communists were thrown together in a common 'anti-imperialist' front. They were against the vestiges of Western military and political control in the Arab countries and the suspected attempts, such as the Baghdad Pact, to maintain Western hegemony by new means. A strange but temporary ally in this anti-imperialist camp was Saudi Arabia which, under King Saud, had quarrelled with Britain over the Buraimi oasis, and which sided with Egypt in opposition to Hashemite ambitions. Syria was torn between pro-Iraqi and pro-Egyptian factions and between those desiring an alliance with the West and those favouring neutralism. The Syrian neutralists leaned towards Russia as an insurance against the converging pressures of Israel, Turkey and the Anglo-Iraqi partnership. Jordan was also divided internally between King Hussein and his east bank supporters, who looked to Iraq and the West, and the Palestinians, mostly on the west bank, who clung to Egypt as their chief ally against Israel.

During the first six months of 1956, Nasser tried to reduce this turmoil rather than increase it; his policy was one of containment rather than militancy. In the absence of any serious prospect of a peace settlement with Israel, he was ready to cooperate with the United Nations Secretary-General in stabilizing the armistice and pacifying the borders. In April, after talks with Hammarskjöld in Cairo, Nasser agreed to a cease-fire agreement with Israel which included a promise to cease all hostile acts by both regular and irregular forces. Jordan agreed to a similar cease-fire. But the lack of real peace and the continuation of the arms race meant that Israel and Egypt went on looking for arms and allies to improve their position in case the armistice broke down.

While Ben Gurion turned increasingly to France, Nasser tried
to establish a common front round Israel's borders with Jordan
as well as Syria. He also tried to reach an understanding with the
Western Powers about 'freezing' the Baghdad Pact. He needed
a period of quiet and of better relations with the West for internal reasons. He had begun negotiations in January with
Eugene Black of the World Bank about the High Dam loan.
At the same time he had taken the first step towards the construction of a new political system in Egypt with the publication
in January 1956 of a draft constitution. The last British troops
were leaving Egypt. In June, after they had all gone, the post-
revolutionary transition period would officially be over and the
new constitution, after approval in a plebiscite, would come into
force.

But the momentum of Arab nationalism in Jordan and in
Algeria, the intractability of the Arab–Israeli conflict, the
pressures of Western domestic politics and Western–Soviet
rivalries, combined to wreck all attempts to stabilize the Middle
East. The intensified war in Algeria and the failure of French
efforts to secure an end of Egyptian support for the nationalist
rebellion led to a strengthening of French ties with Israel. In
Jordan, the dismissal of the British commander of the Arab
Legion, General Glubb, by King Hussein on 1 March, was
wrongly attributed by Eden to Nasser. It led the British prime
minister, under attack at home for lack of decisiveness, to
the abrupt and angry decision that Nasser was a dangerous
and irreconcilable enemy of all British interests in the Middle
East, an enemy to be brought down before he did more serious
damage.

The dismissal of Glubb was not Nasser's work: it was rather
the hasty personal decision of King Hussein. It was a result of
personal antagonisms and jealousies between a monarch of
twenty-one, anxious to show his sympathy with the young
nationalist generation, and a man more than twice his age who,
however devoted to his adopted country, was a foreign soldier
and a surviving symbol of an older paternalist imperial relationship. Egyptian propaganda attacks on Glubb no doubt influenced
Hussein indirectly, because of the climate of opinion they helped

to create in Jordan. It was nevertheless Hussein who took the decision, without consulting Nasser or any other Arab leader.[48]

The timing of Glubb's dismissal was unfortunate from Nasser's point of view. The news broke just as Selwyn Lloyd was in Cairo during a tour of the Middle East. Lloyd had come to Cairo, despite considerable criticism of the visit in Britain, partly with the aim of exploring a possible *modus vivendi* with Egypt. Lloyd was given a message about Glubb as he was returning from dinner with Nasser. He apparently believed that Nasser was responsible and consequently that Nasser had deceived and mocked him in their talks. Nasser's account was that he heard the news after he had left Lloyd that evening and thought at first that Glubb had been withdrawn by the British government. This, he considered, was a sensible British move and he told Lloyd so when he saw him the next morning before Lloyd flew off. Lloyd thought Nasser was making fun of him and was angry. Nasser could not understand the reason for Lloyd's bad temper until he heard the full story of Glubb's dismissal after Lloyd had left.[49] This misunderstanding helped to confirm the violent reaction of Eden over the Glubb episode. It ensured that his fury was directed against Nasser rather than Hussein. Nasser was made to appear not only relentlessly hostile but also totally untrustworthy. Anthony Nutting, then Minister of State at the Foreign Office, later recalled, 'On that fatal day he [Eden] decided that the world was not big enough to hold both him and Nasser. The "Egyptian dictator" had to be eliminated somehow or other, else he would destroy Britain's position in the Middle East and Eden's position as Prime Minister of Britain.'[50]

In the House of Commons, Eden stated his position more diplomatically. On 7 March, he said,

> To disrupt a treaty between Jordan and ourselves is utterly inconsistent with assurances of friendly relations. If the Egyptians genuinely want friendly relations with the Western Powers, they can be obtained, but not at any price. One way of ensuring that Egypt does not get them is to pursue a policy which, on the one hand, professes friendship and on the other incites hostility.

Selwyn Lloyd had taken away with him from Cairo a proposal from Nasser, based on his earlier talk with Trevelyan, for a new truce over the Baghdad Pact provided it were not extended to any other Arab states. Nasser would have agreed to a link between the Pact and the Arab League Collective Security Pact, of which Egypt was a member, through Iraq's membership in both alliances. When after three weeks Lloyd had sent no reply to this proposal, Nasser made his ideas public in interviews with two British Sunday newspapers. The move was intended to be conciliatory but brought a sharp response from London. The same day that the interviews were published a Foreign Office spokesman commented that, while Nasser professed to offer cooperation, he was really bent on destroying British interests, and that any agreement to exclude new Arab members from the Baghdad Pact was impossible. According to the British ambassador in Cairo, 'Nasser took this statement as a declaration of war'.[51] He saw it as a public rejection of his private truce proposal to Lloyd and launched into a fierce press and radio campaign against Britain.

British relations with Hussein were patched up and the subsidy to the Arab Legion maintained. But although there was ample proof that Nasser had not engineered Glubb's dismissal, from that time on British policy towards Nasser began to change. It moved away from attempts to gain Egyptian cooperation and towards the isolation of Egypt and if possible the destruction of Nasser's regime. As an illustration of this change and of Eden's mood, Nutting records an extraordinary conversation with the British prime minister shortly after the Glubb episode. Nutting had sent Eden a memo suggesting means of neutralizing Nasser's attack on British interests in the Arab world without launching into a damaging head-on clash with Egypt. Eden rang Nutting in the middle of dinner with the American disarmament delegation and, according to Nutting, shouted down the telephone, 'But what's all this nonsense about isolating Nasser or "neutralizing" him, as you call it? I want him destroyed, can't you understand? I want him removed, and if you and the Foreign Office don't agree, then you'd better come to the Cabinet and explain why.'[52]

Eden found a ready ally for this new policy in France. The French prime minister, Guy Mollet, plunging ever deeper into a ruthless war of repression against the Algerian nationalist rebellion, already saw Nasser as the arch-enemy of France. For him Nasser was not only the inspirer and supplier of the Algerian rebels but an aggressive dictator like Hitler whose ambitious designs had been plainly laid out in *The Philosophy of the Revolution*, as Hitler's had been revealed in *Mein Kampf*. The comparison, later to be adopted and repeated by Eden and his colleagues in Britain, was inspired by the hysteria of political warfare rather than by a sense of history. In addition to the totally different power and political situations of pre-war Germany and Egypt, there is scarcely anything in common between the two books or, indeed, the personalities or the historical contexts of their authors. Mollet's view was not shared by his Foreign Minister, Christian Pineau, who, at the suggestion of Pandit Nehru, visited Nasser in Cairo a few days after the visit of Selwyn Lloyd. On his return to Paris, Pineau told Mollet he did not think Nasser was a second Hitler, but a man without much political experience who would never be the dictator of the Middle East.[53] But this meeting, like Selwyn Lloyd's, produced a misunderstanding which left the same feeling in Paris as in London of Nasser's untrustworthiness. Pineau appears to have believed – appears, because over the years he has made different statements about this episode – that Nasser had given him an assurance that Egypt was not giving military help to Algerian rebels, and that Nasser subsequently went back on this pledge. Nasser has denied giving any promise to Pineau not to help the Algerians. He said that he had told Pineau that the Algerian revolution came from inside the country not from outside, and a settlement was the responsibility of the Algerians themselves. There were no Egyptians fighting with the Algerians but Egypt had trained Algerians because 'It is our responsibility to help our Arab brothers everywhere'. When Pineau asked Nasser, 'Are you training them now', Nasser appears to have said, 'No', since 'there were no Algerians at that time in the country for training as soldiers'. Perhaps Pineau inferred from this that Nasser was assuring him that this training had ended finally and not temporarily.[54]

Eden's increased anxieties about Nasser's policy in the Middle East showed themselves during the visit to Britain in April of the Soviet leaders, Khrushchev and Bulganin. Khrushchev, having just denounced Stalin in his famous Twentieth Congress speech and dissolved the Cominform, was in a conciliatory mood. On the eve of the British visit, the Soviet government announced its support for the Middle East peace mission that the Security Council had asked Hammarskjöld to undertake. In London, Eden told Khrushchev and Bulganin bluntly that Britain considered her Middle East oil supplies so vital that she would fight to ensure their continuance. The Russian leaders assured Eden that they recognized the importance of British economic interests in the Middle East. When Eden raised the question of controlling arms supplies to the Middle East, the Russians did not reject the suggestion but indicated that the scope of such a control would have to be broadened beyond the Arab states and Israel to other 'Middle East' states such as Turkey.

Just before these talks took place, the Baghdad Pact Council had been meeting in Teheran and the United States had announced closer military and economic cooperation with the Pact. Another sign that the United States was also beginning to reconsider its Egyptian policy and to move closer to the new Anglo-French front against Nasser came during the May meeting of the NATO Ministers when agreement was reached between the Western Powers on the sale of more planes, tanks and warships and other arms to Israel. Dulles agreed to the sale by Canada and France of thirty-two Sabre and Mystère jet fighters while Britain was to deliver two destroyers to the Israeli navy. In addition to this agreed sale, the French also delivered at least another twelve Mystères and large quantities of other arms to the Israelis in secret.

American suspicions that Nasser was becoming too friendly with the Communist bloc were strengthened when on 16 May he decided to recognize Communist China and to break off relations with Formosa. To Western diplomats Nasser explained that he had taken this step because of reports (they were inaccurate) that Russia might agree to Western proposals for an arms embargo for the Middle East. If the embargo cut off Russian arms supplies to Egypt, he might be able to find another source in Peking. But if this was a reason for recognizing Peking, it was probably not the only one: Egypt had already sold £10 million worth of cotton to China and a Communist Chinese mission was already establishing itself in a large villa in Cairo.

Nasser's decision angered the American administration just at a time when it was being urged by the British and French, and also by its friends in the Baghdad Pact, to take a tougher line with Egypt. Nasser was not, however, looking for trouble abroad at this time, for he was nearing the end of a historic chapter in the consolidation of Egypt's independence and his own political position at home. On 13 June the last British troops left Egyptian soil. In punctual fulfilment of the 1954 agreement, they slipped away quietly by sea from Port Said to avoid any embarrassing publicity, a few days before the ceremonial Egyptian take-over had been planned. On 18 June, Nasser, with tears in his eyes, hoisted the Egyptian flag to the masthead over the Port Said Navy House, the former British naval headquarters. As jet fighters flew overhead and an Egyptian frigate fired a twenty-one-gun salute, Nasser told the vast, cheering crowds

This is the most memorable moment of a life-time. ... We have dreamed of this moment which had been denied to our fathers, grandfathers and our brothers who have fought for years to achieve this moment and to see the Egyptian flag alone in our skies. Citizens, we pray God no other flag will ever fly over our land.[55]

Egyptians at last felt they were really independent. In Cairo the occasion was celebrated by an elaborate military parade at which Nasser took the salute at a march-past of detachments from all the Arab countries. One of the foreign guests was the newly appointed Soviet Foreign Minister, Dmitri Shepilov. A week later Egyptians voted in a plebiscite to approve the new constitution and to elect Nasser as the first President of the Republic.

The transitional period of the Egyptian revolution, begun with the military *coup* deposing Farouk four years before, was officially over. The Council of the Revolution, composed of the army officers who had organized and directed the revolution, was dissolved. Henceforward, Egypt was supposedly to be governed on the basis of the new constitution. The plebiscite was not democratic by Western standards, although voting at the booths appeared to be secret. Nasser was sole candidate for the Presidency, and the plebiscite was not preceded by any serious public discussion of the merits of either the constitution or the presidential candidate. The majorities were embarrassing: over ninety-nine per cent in each case. The constitution itself was vague on important points. Although martial law was abolished, press censorship lifted (it was reimposed later during the Suez crisis) and political detainees released, there remained an ever-present consciousness of military and police power in the background. Nasser still kept all the main sources of real power in his hands but the new constitution meant that in future he would have to use this power within certain limits unless he wished to abandon the attempt to create a more representative legitimacy in place of the purely revolutionary regime.

The constitution, drafted by a small committee appointed by Nasser, listed in its preamble the six main aims of the Revolution: the elimination of imperialism; the abolition of feudalism; an end of monopolies and of the domination of capital over government; the creation of a strong army; the achievement of social justice; and the establishment of a 'healthy democratic life'. The first article of the Constitution declared for the first time that Egypt was an Arab state and the Egyptian people 'part of the Arab Nation'. Only in Article Three was Islam declared the state religion.

Under the constitution the President became both chief of state and chief executive, on the American model. His office was for six years and he appointed his cabinet ministers. Future presidents were to be elected by majority vote of an elected legislature, the National Assembly, and the choice submitted for ratification by a popular referendum.

The chief promise of greater political freedom or at least wider popular consultation lay in the National Assembly. All laws were to be approved by the Assembly which would have the right to over-ride the presidential veto, question ministers and remove them by a no-confidence vote. It could also impeach the President and ministers for high treason – if it dared. But the likelihood of these powers being boldly exercised was limited by other factors. There were to be no political parties of a normal parliamentary type. Candidates for election to the Assembly would be chosen by a nebulous 'National Union' representing all citizens and organized in a form which the President was to prescribe. The 'National Union' was destined to replace the 'Liberation Rally', the regime's first unsuccessful attempt at a mass political organization. The main purpose was said to be to exclude the former members of the old pre-revolutionary regime, variously described as 'reactionaries', feudalists and tools of imperialism. But it would also give Nasser an opportunity to exclude any other potential opponents, too.

It was clear that the first assembly would be hand-picked. It was due to meet in November 1956, but its election was postponed until the summer of 1957 because of the Suez crisis. There was some hope that an assembly of 350 members, however carefully selected, meeting in public session would in time have a certain effect on the political life of the country and that it might eventually show the courage to exert the powers given to it under the constitution. But, at least for the time being, until he could form an effective political organization of his own, Nasser continued to rely on the Free Officers movement in the army as his ultimate source of power. In the new cabinet which he formed after the dissolution of the Revolutionary Council, he dropped two of his leading revolutionary associates, Gamal Salem and Anwar es-Sadat, but kept Amer and Zacharia Mohieddin in charge of the army and the police respectively. He also appointed civilianized army officers to a number of key administrative and diplomatic posts.

But even if the plebiscite which elected him had been completely free and contested, there is little doubt that Nasser would have won an overwhelming majority as the man who had achieved the long dream of Egyptian nationalists and secured the withdrawal of all foreign troops. It was perhaps Nasser's mistake not to have seized this opportunity to create a more solid constitutional base for his power by permitting a more truly democratic system and giving real life to the paper promises of the constitution. He revealed later that he had at that time been considering introducing a two-party system.[56]

Nasser's relationship with the Egyptian public as he became President was a peculiar one. He did not touch spontaneous popular affection as General Neguib had done. In public he did not relax easily; his speeches were heavy, earnest and repetitive, awkward in style and laboured in delivery. He found it hard to communicate in public the passion which drove him or the sardonic humour that enlivened his personal relations. But he enjoyed great prestige in an aloof way. The average Egyptian seemed to accord him the reluctant admiration and slightly awed respect that schoolboys give to a vigorous and high-minded headmaster who is determined to ginger up the standards of the school. Among educated Egyptians the attitude towards Nasser varied from enthusiastic support to cynical acquiescence. Some, especially journalists and intellectuals, resented the heavy hand of military bureaucracy. Others suspected the sincerity of Nasser's professions of a return to constitutional life or feared that his widening ambitions might lead Egypt into unwanted adventures and a dissipation of her resources. But even many of his critics gave Nasser credit for having ended the humilitating scandals of the old regime, launched desirable social reforms, stimulated new vigour and hope in the country, and devoted an immense and unflagging energy to the promotion of what he believed to be the public good rather than his private gain. In addition to the land reform, the anti-corruption drive and the departure of the British troops, the regime had some other positive achievements to show. It had begun to expand education and the welfare services, it had given greater encouragement to the spread of trades unions and cooperatives, though both remained under close government control. Its dissolution of the special religious courts which administered the Sharia or Islamic law, dealing with personal status, and the absorption of the Sharia and its administration into the normal civil legal system was a landmark in Egypt's social life, after many years of hesitant change in that direction. Within the limited funds available for development, the regime had begun a government-backed industrialization programme. The pride of this programme were the £10 million iron and steel plant at Helwan, being built by a West German firm, and the hydro-electric power station on the Aswan Dam. But the greatest hope lay in the Aswan High Dam. Negotiations about the financing of the Dam were still under way with the World Bank, Britain and the United States, while Russia hovered in the background invitingly but not fully committed to help.

Internationally, Nasser appeared to be in a strong position – at least on the surface. The Western Powers and Russia were competing to give him economic aid. Now that the Western attempt to extend the Baghdad Pact to other Arab countries had been abandoned for the time being, relations with Britain and France, though cool, were not openly hostile, except in press and propaganda. In Syria and Jordan, the political trend was in Egypt's favour, though the general mood of the Arab world was quieter and less inclined to follow Egypt in adventure or upheaval. Moderate Arab opinion hoped for an end to the quarrel between Nasser and the West. The main obstacle seemed to be the violence of anti-British propaganda from Cairo radio, including its encouragement of African nationalist rebellions, such as the Mau Mau in Kenya, and the suspicious hostility of the British press, which fed on each other. In May 1956, Nasser had received the British ambassador in the last attempt at reconciliation on either side before the Suez crisis. Trevelyan then argued that there was no longer any specific Anglo-Egyptian dispute. The last British troops were leaving Egypt and the Sudan was settled. So why not a period of quiet on both sides? Why shouldn't Nasser follow Ataturk's example and devote himself to reform at home?[57] Nasser answered such exhortations with the claim that Egypt could not be indifferent to the area surrounding it and that his activity outside Egypt was mostly in reaction to the hostile moves of others. Trevelyan concluded that Nasser regarded himself as 'the destined champion of Arab nationalism' and was 'at heart still a revolutionary conspirator'. It was at this meeting that Nasser told the ambassador, 'You cannot carry out a gunboat policy against me as you could against Farouk. I have no throne, no hereditary position, no fortune.'[58]

In his speech at the independence celebrations, Nasser was moderate in his usual references to imperialism and expressed the wish for better relations with Britain. The shadow of the conflict with Israel still loomed over all and the border remained tense, but there was some hope that, with the backing of the Great Powers, the new cease-fire agreement negotiated by Hammarskjöld might lead to a stabilization of the armistice. The Soviet Foreign Minister, Dmitri Shepilov, during his visit to Cairo for the independence celebrations and subsequently to Damascus, had made the most of the popularity won by the Soviet arms deal and had hinted at a new Russian offer to finance the High Dam. At the same time he had emphasized that Russia wanted to reduce international tensions in the Middle East and had refused to be drawn into any Russian commitment against Israel. Khrushchev himself, in an interview with the Egyptian newspaper *Al Ahram*, made it plain that the intensified Soviet wooing of the Arab states would be kept within Moscow's new broad policy of 'competitive but peaceful coexistence' with the Western Powers. The competition would be primarily of an economic and propaganda kind, and Russia would avoid provocative new diplomatic or military commitments. Over Israel, Khrushchev counselled patience to the Arabs and warned that Arab–Israeli hostilities held the danger of a third world war.

Nasser listened to what Shepilov had to offer in the way of economic aid and also on 20 June received a flying visit from Eugene Black. He wanted the High Dam aid to come from the West so as to avoid a further heavy dependence on Russia which might endanger his policy of non-alignment. But he was still worried about the financial controls asked for by the West. He had reached an agreement with Black about these controls but its signature depended on Egypt's also reaching agreement on the terms set out in British and American *aides-mémoires*. Nasser had offered a revised version of the *aides-mémoires* which seemed to the British ambassador to be unobjectionable. After some delay the British government approved most of the Egyptian revised version, but the State Department delayed its reply further because the Americans were reviewing their policy towards Egypt. Both the British and American ambassadors in Cairo urged their governments to keep the Dam offer open and to clinch it before Nasser went to Moscow.[59]

But there were already some ominous signs from Washington and London that the Americans and British might be less keen on the project than before. Powerful groups in the Congress and the House of Commons were opposed to any aid for Egypt. Indeed, the British government was already considering withdrawing its loan offer for the Dam. This change flowed naturally from Eden's new but not yet public policy, crystallized by the Glubb episode, of treating Egypt under Nasser as an enemy rather than as a potential partner or even a neutral.

Eden also invoked economic reasons – Britain's own financial stringency and Egypt's allegedly deteriorating financial position because of payments for the Soviet arms deliveries – but the main motive for refusing aid was political. Britain's financial share in the Dam loan was, in any case, only £5 million. Eden was more concerned with the hostile activity of Egyptian agents and radio propaganda in Arab countries whose governments were friendly to Britain. In Iraq, Nuri es-Said was complaining that Nasser got more aid by bullying than he (Nuri) did by co-operating.[60] Similar complaints came from the Conservative back-benchers in the House of Commons.

Selwyn Lloyd sounded out the State Department about the Dam and found they shared the British doubts. So in mid-July the British government decided to withdraw from the Dam project, though Eden 'would have preferred to play this long and not to have forced the issue'.[61] The US Administration was itself already considering withdrawing its own Dam offer, for domestic as well as foreign policy reasons. The Congress was being difficult about the whole foreign aid programme and several strong lobbies had formed against aid to Egypt in particular. The pro-Zionist lobby was trying to persuade the Administration to press Egypt into lifting the ban on Israeli shipping through the Suez Canal.[62] The cotton lobby of the Southern States saw no good in lending money to Egypt to help it expand its cotton acreage while there was a huge cotton surplus in the United States. Then Nasser's abrupt recognition of Peking had not only angered Dulles but also roused the pro-Chiang Kai-shek lobby. There was also a strong anti-neutralist trend in the Congress which was shared by Dulles himself. The Administration was under pressure to switch aid from neutralist or sometimes hostile states such as Egypt to their allies and friends.

Two other factors helped to tip the balance. The first and
decisive factor in Dulles's mind was the belief that the Russians
had made a better offer to build the Dam and that Nasser was
playing Moscow and Washington off against each other to
squeeze out the best terms. Dulles thought the Russian offer
was a bluff. By withdrawing the American offer he would be
able to force the Russians to choose between backing down or
investing in a project they could not afford. At the start of Soviet–
American competition in aid throughout the Afro-Asian
countries, this would be a resounding blow to Russian prospects.
Nasser's let-down would be a sharp lesson to other neutralists
who thought that by playing both sides they could do better out
of Washington than America's 'stalwart allies'.[63] The second
factor was the feeling that Egypt's economic plight and her
political attitudes were such that she might prove both a bottom-
less and politically unrewarding pit for aid. The Western Powers
might find themselves involved in a costly enterprise which could
not fundamentally improve the Egyptian economy but which
might earn them abuse rather than kudos because of the burden
of cost it put on the Egyptians themselves.[64] This kind of cruel
assessment was also to be heard among British Middle East
experts, comparing the prospects for developments in Iraq and
the lack of them in Egypt. It was equivalent to saying that
twenty-three million Egyptians should be left to sink steadily
deeper into destitution and despair instead of being helped to
pull themselves out of it.

The Egyptian ambassador in Washington, Dr Ahmed Hussein,
himself an agrarian expert, had warned Nasser of the changing
climate of American opinion. In mid-July Hussein returned to
Cairo and persuaded Nasser to drop his counter-proposals,
overcome his suspicions and take up the High Dam offer on the
Western terms without delay. Nasser told Hussein that he
believed the American and British governments had already
decided not to go ahead with the project. However, he authorized
Hussein to tell the Americans that he accepted their offer unconditionally. At the same time he casually mentioned to the
startled Hussein the possibility that if, as he expected, the
Americans backed out, he might get the foreign exchange he

needed to build the Dam by nationalizing the Suez Canal Company.[65]

The nationalization of the Canal Company had often been discussed in Egypt in past years, both publicly and inside the government. In 1954 the project had been re-examined by Nasser. He had rejected it in favour of negotiations to increase Egypt's share of the foreign exchange earnings of the Canal during the period until the Company's concession ended in 1968. It was almost inevitable that the concession would not then be renewed. The Canal was a deeply emotional national symbol, because of the sacrifices Egypt had made for its construction, the little profit it had brought her and the belief that it had paved the way for the British occupation. Nasser had therefore appointed a special group to study the operation of the Canal and prepare plans for taking over when the concession ran out. Meanwhile negotiations took place with the Canal Company in 1955 and 1956 on plans for the development and widening of the Canal, on greater 'Egyptianization' of the company staff, and on the investment in Egypt of a greater proportion of the Canal Company's earnings.

The Egyptian government had no shares in the Company – the 177,000 shares, forty-four per cent of the capital, originally subscribed by the Khedive Ismail had been sold in 1875 to the British government for £4 million. Half of the privately owned shares were in French hands. In 1955, Disraeli's famous bargain of eighty years before earned Britain £3,300,000. The Egyptian government in the same year received £2,300,000 in taxes and other payments. But Nasser was more concerned about the fact that although the Canal Company was at least nominally an Egyptian company, most of its foreign exchange earnings were invested in Britain, France or America and did not contribute to Egypt's balance of payments. On 10 June 1956, agreement was announced between the Egyptian government and the Canal Company to transfer over £20 million to investment in Egypt over the next seven years. A week earlier, the Egyptian government's chief representative on the Suez Canal Board (the Company had thirty-two directors of whom five were Egyptian, ten French, nine British, one Dutch and one American) had stated that Egypt would not extend the Company's ninety-nine-year concession when it expired in 1968.

On 17 July Ahmed Hussein returned to the United States and announced to the press that Egypt intended to take up the West's High Dam offer. He sought an early interview with Dulles to give him Nasser's decision. Dulles kept him waiting until 19 July. Then in a short meeting at the State Department Dulles handed Hussein a statement announcing withdrawal of the American offer. Hussein's eloquent plea for reconsideration for the sake of better future relations between Egypt and the West was of no avail: the ambassador's final desperate stratagem of invoking the prospect of an alternative offer from Russia only confirmed Dulles's determination.[66]

Almost as soon as Hussein had taken leave of Dulles the American statement was in the hands of the press. Whether intentionally or not, its terms were harsh. (Dulles later claimed, in a letter to Eisenhower, that the statement had not been intended to be offensive.)[67] The reason it gave for the withdrawal decision were that the two necessary conditions – an agreement on the Nile Waters and the ability of Egypt to make enough resources available for the Dam project – had not been fulfilled. But the impression conveyed was of the general weakness of Egypt's economy and her lack of credit-worthiness. There was an obvious underlying assumption that the other countries concerned with the Nile would probably never agree to the scheme, and that the whole High Dam project would never get off the drawing board. The only conciliatory note was an assurance that the United States hoped to maintain friendly relations with Egypt and remained ready to consider other economic development schemes, including other schemes for the Nile.

It was the manner of the announcement and its wording rather than the fact of the American withdrawal itself which infuriated Nasser when he learned the news. He received the text when he arrived in the middle of the night at Cairo airport on his way back from a meeting in Brioni in Yugoslavia with Nehru and Marshal Tito; Nehru had accompanied him back to Egypt. The timing of the American decision, when the three neutralist leaders were in conclave, also seemed significant and insulting. It is uncertain whether Nasser discussed his riposte with Nehru the next day before the Indian prime minister flew on to Delhi. On 21 July he began to study seriously the possible nationalization of the Canal and to evaluate the international reaction it would cause. He concluded that it could be done without serious danger of military intervention from Britain, the country most likely to react violently because most affected. Before taking a final decision he discussed the plan with his cabinet.

So on 23 July the decision was taken. The next day at a ceremony at Mostarod, five miles outside Cairo, inaugurating a new oil refinery and the Suez–Cairo pipeline, Nasser made a coldly furious speech attacking the United States in which he said that he would give his answer to the High Dam action in two days time. He declared,

> When Washington shamelessly and without regard for the principles on which international relations should be based, and without any basis in truth, aims to cast doubt on the Egyptian economy, then I turn to them and say, 'You may die of your fury, for you will not be able to dominate us or to control our existence, for we know our way – the road of honour, freedom and pride'.[68]

Just before he spoke, Nasser told the director of the Egyptian Petroleum Authority, Mahmoud Yunis, to prepare a plan to take over the operation of the Canal. Yunis was a former army engineer officer with a high reputation for efficiency. He organized several small teams of soldiers, technicians and administrators ready to take over the company's headquarters in Ismailia and the other two chief control points of the Canal in Port Said at the northern end and Port Tewfik at the south. Troops were held in reserve in case of emergency or resistance. The teams were to seize physical control of the Company and ensure the continued operation of the Canal, as soon as the signal came from Nasser. The signal was to be the words 'Ferdinand de Lesseps' (the name of the builder of the Canal) in a broadcast speech by Nasser in Alexandria on the evening of 26 July. The greatest secrecy was observed. Only Yunis knew the full significance of the operation. The others in his teams received their orders in a sealed envelope to be opened only when they heard the codeword. Yunis authorized any member of the group to shoot any other who refused to carry out the orders or tried to give away the secret.[69]

At 7.40 P.M. on 26 July, Nasser began his speech from a balcony overlooking the main Liberation Square in Alexandria to a crowd estimated at a quarter of a million. He spoke for two hours and forty minutes. It was one of the great speeches of his career, not only for its historic announcement but as a dramatic performance. It began slowly with a repetitive attack on Western imperialism for trying to maintain a sphere of influence in the Arab Middle East: Israel, military pacts and the control of arms supplies were means used by the West to dominate the policies of Egypt and other Arab countries. But Egypt, Nasser claimed, had established a free and independent policy which made her and the Arab nation a power to be reckoned with in the world. The days were gone when Egyptians waited round to take their orders from high commissioners and ambassadors. But still

the imperialists want us to be their dependents and when they issued an order to respond to it. . . . They want us to hear their orders about Israel which they say exists as a matter of fact, and they say that they will pay money to the Arabs of Palestine. We have pride in Arabism and our land cannot be sold for money. They want us to give in to Israel on all points and forsake Palestine and our brothers in North Africa and to agree as the Security Council agreed, to the slaughter in Algeria. They want us to execute the policy dictated to us. Egypt has refused to do this and wants to have an independent personality.

The nature of the speech, its angry defiance of the Western Powers and its uncharacteristic tone of colloquial and often humorous intimacy, the voice of a self-assured popular leader close to his audience, began to emerge more clearly when Nasser described how he had dealt with the special American envoy, George Allen, who had come to see him with a letter from the US government at the time of the Russian arms deal. Because he believed the letter to contain threats to Egypt, Nasser had said he would not accept it and if Allen came and tried to present the letter he would have him put out of his office. 'I said I am not a professional prime minister but have become a prime minister as a result of a revolution. . . . They thought we were professional politicians, but Egypt was able to protect her dignity and her prestige.'

The real leitmotiv of the speech soon appeared when Nasser stressed that economic independence was as important as political independence. He gave his version of the High Dam loan negotiations in the same intimate and picturesque detail and described how he had reached the conclusion that the conditions imposed by the World Bank and by British and the United States amounted to 'a conspiracy to dominate our economic independence'. The withdrawal of the loan offer was intended 'to punish Egypt because she refused to stand on the side of military blocs'.

They punish us by delaying the raising of our standard of living. . . . They claimed that we threatened their oil supplies but I said that we will not be the sphere of influence of any one. We have no objection to your legitimate economic interests.

While he was talking to Eugene Black, the President of the World Bank, said Nasser, he had been reminded of 'Ferdinand de Lesseps coming to Egypt in 1854 to persuade the Khedive Ismail to build and help finance the Suez Canal'. The mention of de Lesseps gave the signal to Mahmoud Yunis and his men waiting in the Canal Zone to begin the take-over of the Canal Company's installations. At the same time it served to introduce the main subject of the speech.

As a result of de Lesseps' persuasion of Ismail, said Nasser, the Suez Canal had been built by Egyptian labour – 120,000 Egyptian workers had died while digging it – and largely financed by Egypt. The Khedive Ismail had subscribed forty-four per cent of the shares and then had been virtually cheated out of them by the British government. As a result, out of the Canal's annual revenue of $100 million (£E35 million) Egypt now received only $3 million (or £1 million). History would not be allowed to repeat itself 'by treachery and deceit'. Egypt would build the High Dam herself and would pay for it out of the revenues of the Canal. She would collect the $100 million a year Canal revenue for her own benefit and would have no need to wait for the American aid which amounted to only $70 million. 'Whenever a statement emanates from Washington, I will tell them "die of your fury".'

After reading the law nationalizing the Suez Canal Company, Nasser concluded, 'At the moment, some of your brethren, the sons of Egypt, are now taking over the Egyptian Suez Canal Company, and directing it. We have taken this decision to restore part of the glories of the past and to safeguard our national dignity and pride.'

Chapter 7

Suez and Sinai, July 1956–May 1957

On 21 July after Nasser's return to Cairo from Brioni, he had
drawn up an 'appreciation', in staff officer style, of the likely
international consequences of nationalizing the Suez Canal
Company. Later Nasser gave slightly varying versions on different
occasions of the contents of this document.[1] But the main gist of
it was that he concluded that the strongest reaction would come
from Britain. France, he thought, was too preoccupied with
Algeria and she also disagreed with Britain over the Baghdad Pact
and other matters in the Middle East. Britain was, however, unlikely to use force because of her relations with the other Arab
states, the risk to her oil interests in the Middle East, and the effect
on the already shaky position of sterling if the Canal were
blocked. For the same reasons, Nasser thought, she would
certainly not ally herself with Israel. And even if the British were
to contemplate using force, their military dispositions were such
that they could not act for two or three months. By that time
Nasser had a good chance of securing diplomatic settlement of
the dispute or of benefiting from the creation of an international
climate against a settlement by force. Nasser's impression was
that the United States would reject any use of force. He appears
not to have considered seriously an attack on Egypt by Israel
alone.

Nasser said nothing concerning his predictions at the time
about Russian reaction. There is no evidence to suggest that he
asked for Soviet support before nationalizing the Canal Company,
but he no doubt counted on – and received – Soviet diplomatic
backing, particularly at the United Nations.

Nasser was wrong in almost all his calculations, except his
estimate of the American position. The world crisis over 'Suez'
culminated in a jointly planned attack on Egypt by Britain,
France and Israel. As he admitted years later, Nasser had under-
estimated the extent of French bitterness over Algeria.[2] Nor did
he realize the extent to which Eden had already come to regard
him as a personal enemy and as a threat not only to Britain's

interests and prestige in the Middle East but to her very national existence. In spite of his previous concern over Franco-Israeli military collaboration, Nasser did not foresee the opportunity the crisis would provide for the preventive war that had long been in Ben Gurion's mind. This neglect of the Franco–Israeli combination may have been partly the result of mental habit: for a decade, after the departure of the French from the Levant, Britain had been the main outside Power with which the Egyptians had had to deal in the Middle East, and Algeria, though a matter of keen sympathy, was still a far-off side show for the Middle East Arabs.

Nasser's analysis was another example of his failure to take into account Western emotions as well as interests in his political calculations. There was a paradox in his picture of the Western governments. He saw them as blinded by an outdated imperial outlook which led them to try to act beyond their strength. At the same time, he saw them still as Great Powers who could be expected to act upon rational calculations of their interests, rather than in the emotional manner that was excusable in small nations struggling to assert their independence and dignity. A recurrent theme in Nasser's interview and speeches is his puzzlement at Western, especially British, policy which seemed to him constantly to run counter to British interests and to surprise him by its irrationality. Perhaps because he had no first-hand experience of any Western European country or of public opinion and politics in Europe, he found it difficult to sense the emotional problems created by a decline of power and a changed position in the world.

In any case, his own national problems, both material and moral, were so great as to be excusably obsessive. For Nasser, the nationalization of the Canal Company had two main purposes: to provide more foreign exchange for Egypt's economic development; and to show that a poor, weak country would not accept continued degradation.

Legally Nasser had a strong case. He could produce substantial evidence to support his contention that the Canal Company was an Egyptian company subject to Egyptian law. The Canal itself was, as he claimed, indisputably an inseparable part of Egyptian territory. It was an established precedent in international law that a state could nationalize a private enterprise under its jurisdiction, provided it paid adequate compensation. Nasser had broken no agreement except the Company's concession, which was not an international treaty but a contract between a private company and the Egyptian government.

The legality of the nationalization of the Company as such was, in fact, scarcely questioned by the British and French governments. The main legal argument employed by the Western Powers, on the initiative of Dulles, was a more sophisticated echo of a widespread public confusion between the Canal Company and the Canal itself. This argument was that the Canal Company was 'an international agency' with rights beyond its concession, the rights being rooted in the Constantinople Convention of 1888 which guaranteed freedom of navigation through the Canal at all times. The convention, it was argued, set up a system of operating the Canal so as to ensure freedom of navigation, and the Canal Company was intended as its prime instrument.[3] The British had thought this argument flimsy. It was easily demolished by Nasser who pointed out that there was no connexion between the operation of the Canal and the obligations of the 1888 Convention: while the Company's concession would in any case have ended and reverted to the Egyptian government in 1968, the Constantinople Convention, with no time limit, would have continued. The Suez Canal Company had never been at any time responsible for freedom of navigation through the Canal. This had been (at least since the British recognized Egypt's sovereignty in 1922) legally the responsibility of the Egyptian government.[4] In practice, also, since the departure of British troops from her soil, Egypt had been in sole physical control of the Canal; even while the British troops were there she had exercised this control. Egypt's much criticized refusal of passage of Israeli shipping had taken place while British troops were in the Canal Zone. The only international treaty governing the Canal was the 1888 Convention and Egypt had reaffirmed her intention of observing it. This situation had in no way been changed, in the Egyptian view, by the nationalization of the Canal Company. The Egyptians argued that the stopping of Israeli ships was permitted to them under the Convention since the Palestine armistice had not ended the state of war between Egypt and Israel. This argument had been rejected in the Security Council Resolution of 1951 which had called on Egypt to allow Israeli ships through the Canal. Nasser offered to take this question to the International Court. Knowing themselves to be weak on the legal side, the British and French, especially the former, had some hopes of supporting their arguments for an international authority to control the Canal on technical and financial grounds. Only thus, they argued, could they be sure that the Canal would be operated efficiently and would neither break down under Egypt's inexperienced management nor have its tolls raised excessively and its revenue exorbitantly milked for the development of the Egyptian economy. But Nasser was able to prove, when the British and French pilots of the Canal Company were withdrawn on 15 September, that Egypt could run the Canal efficiently without them. On the financial side, he offered to negotiate an agreement with the Canal-users on the fixing of tolls and on guarantees for the use of a fair share of the revenue for development.[5] But for the British and French governments the main issue was political: would control of the operation of the Canal enable Egypt to discriminate against countries with whom she had political disputes by preventing or delaying the passage of their ships? Would she eventually, if Nasser succeeded in dominating the Arab oil countries, use her control of the Canal to 'hold Western Europe to ransom' – for either economic or political gain – by cutting off the supply of Middle East oil (half of Britain's oil imports passed through the Canal)? If Nasser were to succeed in his *coup*, would not this so increase his prestige that his will would eventually prevail in those Arab countries still friendly to Britain and where British oil interests were concentrated, such as Iraq, and also in Algeria where the French were struggling to maintain their authority against an Arab rebellion they believed to be supported and encouraged by Nasser?

The British and French governments totally lacked confidence in Nasser's word and feared that he was implacably hostile to their interests. They were interested in the legal, technical and financial arguments about the Canal only in so far as these provided a public justification for their political aim of destroying Nasser's influence in the Arab world or removing him from power altogether. In Eden's view, the assertion of international control over the Canal was the test: this would both provide the necessary guarantees in place of Nasser's suspect word and at the same time constitute probably a fatal personal defeat for Nasser. If this result could be achieved by negotiation, well and good; if not, then force must be used.

It seemed obvious, however, that an international authority could not be maintained in the Canal area against the will of the Egyptians or without their active cooperation, unless the whole country were conquered. Yet this would simply revert to the days of the British occupation, a quagmire from which Britain had only just extricated herself through the 1954 Canal Zone agreement. The dangers and difficulties of this course were pointed out to Eden by Eisenhower in a letter on 31 July 1956.[6] Such a policy could be justified only on the assumption that Anglo-French military intervention would swiftly bring about the collapse of Nasser's regime and that an agreement could be then made with a successor government. Such a misreading of the political possibilities in Egypt was surprising in view of the difficulty Britain had found over nearly forty years in finding an amenable Egyptian negotiating partner. It may be explained partly by the undue reliance of Eden on dubious sources of information in Egypt and partly by sheer wishful thinking. For on both sides in the dispute the driving force was emotion rather than logic.

The withdrawal of the High Dam offer by Dulles had been widely interpreted, in the Arab world as elsewhere, as not merely an economic decision but as a deliberate blow at Nasser's neutralism and his claims to political leadership in the Arab countries. Similarly, the nationalization of the Canal Company was at once understood as being not merely a means of gaining Egypt more foreign exchange but also as a deliberate challenge to Western claims to dominant political influence in the Middle East. It was the equivalent in the economic sphere of the Soviet arms deal in the military – a defiant move to break away from dependence on the West. Its manner was clearly intended to be as insulting to Western prestige as Nasser had conceived Dulles's

High Dam communiqué to be to the reputation of Egypt. In fact, the manner only concealed the underlying realities. Suez was only the *coup de grâce* to a system of military–political–economic control of the Arab world by European Powers and Western capitalism which was already hollow and crumbling away.

Among the Egyptian and Arab publics, the news of Nasser's move was received with a mixture of enthusiasm and apprehension, for it was obvious that it would mean a showdown of some kind between Egypt and the Western Powers. Some anti-Nasser and pro-Western Arab leaders, chief among them Nuri es-Said of Iraq, while publicly approving, let the British government know secretly that they would be glad to see Nasser taught a lesson. Their inability to face their own public with such thoughts revealed the weakness of their own positions and their limited value as allies or advisers. Nuri and King Feisal of Iraq were dining in state at 10 Downing Street with Eden when the news of Nasser's *coup* was received. Nuri, it is said, advised Eden to 'hit him [Nasser] hard and hit him now'.[7] This advice was later repeated, but with the rider that Britain should not act with either France or Israel.[8] Eden needed little encouragement. His immediate reaction was that on the outcome of Nasser's action would depend 'whose authority would prevail' in the Middle East 'from Agadir to Karachi. ... In our judgment the economic life of Western Europe was threatened with disruption by the Egyptian seizure of the Canal.'[9] Britain could not tolerate having Nasser's 'thumb on her windpipe'. Eden saw the Canal Company nationalization as one step in a vast programme of conquest by an ambitious dictator. This vision assumed nightmare proportions as the crisis wore on, until Eden saw Nasser not only dominating the Middle East but also setting out in league with Russia to control the destiny of all industrial Western Europe by cutting off the oil supplies. (The purpose of such a programme was not evident and could not be explained, except possibly as a belated revenge for the Crusades.)[10] In Eden's mind, Nasser was like Hitler and the Canal was the Rhineland. He had to be stopped now, by force if necessary. The French prime minister, Guy Mollet, shared this view while Pineau used the Rhineland analogy early on in talking to the Americans.[11] But the main French concern was with Algeria; and to a lesser extent with Israel. The French mistakenly saw Nasser as the mainspring of the Algerian rebellion. They believed that if he succeeded in the Canal *coup* an Algerian settlement on the lines then envisaged by France would become impossible.

Israel's first reaction to the Suez *coup* was to keep quiet and let it be known that she did not consider the dispute between Egypt and the Western Powers over the Canal Company to be her affair. Ben Gurion later wrote that Israel was not opposed in principle to the nationalization. But he saw it as an 'ominous' occasion because it 'represented a new and alarming stage in the development of Nasser's arrogant self-confidence which had been fortified in proportion to his build-up of Communist arms'.[12]

In the United States, Eisenhower from the outset considered the future of the Canal and the problem of Nasser's influence in the Arab world as two separate issues, neither of which could be solved by rushing to war. Dulles's action over the High Dam had been the first move towards 'cutting Nasser down to size' (a favourite phrase of American diplomats in private and of American journalists in public at that time) by economic pressure and diplomatic isolation. Now Dulles, who was away in Peru when the Canal news broke, wanted to 'play it long', as Eden had originally wanted him to do over the High Dam. For the United States the Canal was far less important economically than for Britain and Europe. Eisenhower was not convinced by Eden's panic picture of Nasser bringing European industry grinding to a halt. A study by American experts soon revealed that, by a combination of rerouting round the Cape and increasing supplies from the Western hemisphere, Western European oil supplies could be maintained. The cost, it was true, would be about $600 million (£215 million) a year, two-thirds of which would be for British oil imports.[13] This was burdensome but not catastrophic.

The most important points about the Suez Canal for the United States were that it should be operated efficiently and that navigation through it should be free to all nations in accordance with the 1888 Convention.[14] The only possible justification for military intervention would be if traffic through the Canal were stopped, either because the Egyptians could not make it work or because they were breaking the 1888 Convention. Even so, every means of peaceful settlement would have to be exhausted before resort to force. From his experience of the Panama Canal Eisenhower believed that it would not be as difficult to operate the Suez Canal as the British and French, on the advice of the Canal Company, believed. He was supported in this view by Admiral Arleigh Burke, US Chief of Naval Operations.[15]

Dealing with Nasser's influence was seen in Washington as a long-term process. The Canal was a bad issue on which to try to bring Nasser down because of its 'colonialist' associations: Egypt could count on widespread Arab and Afro-Asian sympathy as she faced the two old imperial Powers, Britain and France. But the American opposition to the use of force did not become publicly clear until some weeks after the crisis began. During the first period, the United States neither advocated force nor ruled it out. Dulles wanted to avoid encouraging the British and French to think they could go ahead with a policy of force with American support. On the other hand, he wished to keep the possibility of force open as a form of pressure on Nasser in the negotiations. The most important thing for him was to get negotiations going and to play for time: he knew that there were six weeks before the British and French would be ready to strike.[16]

At a meeting on the day after nationalization, the British Cabinet had approved Eden's policy of taking the Canal out of Nasser's control, by force if necessary. Instructions were given to the chiefs of staff to prepare a military plan for the seizure of the Canal as soon as possible. Some 20,000 reservists were recalled, and troops, ships and aircraft despatched to the eastern Mediterranean 'as a precautionary measure'. The Canal Company assets and the Egyptian sterling balances in London were frozen, and an arms embargo imposed. On 27 July Eden sent Eisenhower a long cable which the President found 'disturbing', informing him of the Cabinet decision. The immediate threat, Eden declared, was to the oil supplies of Western Europe, a great part of which flowed through the Canal. Unless 'we take a firm stand . . . our influence and yours throughout the Middle East will, we are convinced, be finally destroyed'. 'My colleagues and I,' Eden wrote, 'are convinced that we must be ready in the last resort to use force to bring Nasser to his senses. ... For our part we are prepared to do so.'[17]

Eisenhower sent Robert Murphy of the State Department to London to try to delay any rash action until Dulles could be summoned back from Peru. Murphy found the British ministers in a bellicose mood, determined to fight rather than 'sink to the status of the Netherlands'.[18] Dulles joined him on 1 August and at a meeting with Selwyn Lloyd, the British Foreign Secretary, and Pineau, the French Foreign Minister, agreement was reached on the principle of international control of the Canal. The ministers also agreed on an American proposal to call a conference in London on 16 August of the chief maritime Powers, the eight signatories of the 1888 Convention and the sixteen main users of the Canal (Israel was not invited and protested at her exclusion – the three Powers were in agreement at that stage to keep the Arab–Israeli dispute separate from the Canal question). Meanwhile, Eden in a statement to the House of Commons on 30 July, had set out publicly his main requirement for a settlement: 'No arrangements for the future of this great international waterway could be acceptable to Her Majesty's Government which would leave it in the unfettered control of a single power which could, as recent events have shown, exploit it purely for purposes of national policy.'

There had in any case to be some weeks for talking, because the Anglo-French military planners found that, short of a risky operation by airborne troops alone, they could not mount an invasion of Egypt before 15 September. The date was later postponed, first to 26 September and then to 5 November, a limit set by the American presidential election and by the Mediterranean weather. Because of lack of good harbours in Cyprus, the seaborne invasion fleet would have to muster at Malta, six days from Egypt. At British suggestion, the landing would be preceded by a week or more of aerial bombardment and psychological warfare, in the hope apparently that the Egyptians might collapse or overthrow Nasser even before the invaders arrived.[19]

While the military preparations went ahead, invitations for the London Conference were sent out, together with a statement by

Britain, France and America, issued on 5 August, outlining their joint proposal for an international Canal authority. This proposal was later introduced by Dulles at the London conference and formed the basis of what became known as the Eighteen-Power proposals. Egypt and Greece (hostile to Britain over Cyprus and with many Greeks in Egypt) rejected the invitation. In a statement on 12 August Nasser gave his reasons. He rejected the thesis of the three Western Foreign Ministers on the 'international character' of the Canal Company and the argument that it formed part of one system with the 1888 Convention. He declared that any attempt to confuse the Company and freedom of navigation was only intended to find an excuse for interfering in Egypt's internal affairs. The proposal to set up an international authority for the Canal was 'nothing but a polite form of international colonialism'. The invitation to the conference was issued under the threat of a 'large scale international conspiracy to starve and terrorize the Egyptian people' by freezing their funds and mobilizing troops and warships against them. Finally Nasser stressed Egypt's intention to guarantee freedom of navigation and proposed a conference of the signatories of the 1888 Convention and of Canal-users to reconsider the Convention.

Nasser later revealed that he had at first been determined to accept the invitation to the London conference and attend in person, against the advice of his ministers and advisers who thought he would be insulted to no useful purpose. But Eden's television interview in which the British prime minister had attacked Nasser's 'black record' had convinced him there was no point in trying to negotiate with Eden round a table.[20] Instead of going himself, Nasser sent his chief political aide, Aly Sabry, to the London conference as an observer. Egypt's point of view was in any case well defended in the conference by Russia and India.

While the London conference was in progress, Nasser himself left Cairo for a few days' rest and reflection to prepare himself for the critical days to come. From the moment of his fiery outburst at Alexandria, Nasser had behaved with circumspection in order to avoid any further provocation. His aim was to impress on the world that it was 'business as usual' at the Suez Canal despite the change of management. As in the negotiations over the Canal

Zone base, the crucial question was that of recognition, in fact as well as on paper, of Egyptian sovereignty. Nasser was from the beginning determined not to give up sovereignty and full control over the canal to anyone. This was his sticking point. Almost as important was the opportunity to increase Egypt's foreign exchange resources from the Canal revenue. He was prepared to make an increasing range of concessions on other matters, technical and financial, provided they were on a basis of cooperation and not of outside control. Meanwhile his policy was to keep the Canal working and to avoid giving any excuse for military intervention. He reaffirmed on 31 July Egypt's intention of maintaining freedom of navigation in accordance with the Constantinople Convention. He began advertising for pilots to be trained to replace the British and French pilots in case they were withdrawn, and, possibly on the advice of India, he did not enforce his original threat to imprison those who stopped work.[21] He allowed those pilots who wished to leave to go, but they were asked by the old Company to stay on until further instructions were given to them. (There were 187 pilots from thirteen nations of whom fifty-six were French, fifty-two British and thirty-two Egyptian. Apart from a dozen Greeks, the rest were from other Western countries.)[22]

Nasser did not insist that all ships pay their Canal dues to the new Egyptian authority. When the British and French ordered their ship-owners not to pay dues to Egypt but into the accounts of the old Company in London or Paris, he continued to allow British and French ships to pass through the Canal. In spite of the threatening British and French troop movements and the freezing of Egyptian assets (perhaps also because of these actions), there was no molestation of British or French nationals in Egypt or interference with their property. The freezing of Egyptian assets in London, Paris and to a limited extent in the United States, deprived Egypt of the use of £110 million and $50 million and meant that Egypt had reserves of only some £4 million in free foreign exchange to finance her imports.[23] She was able to survive by restricting imports to the barest minimum, by obtaining credits from friendly countries, especially later from the Soviet Union for vital wheat imports, and by her increased foreign exchange earnings from the Canal. Despite the British and French boycott, some fifty-five per cent of the Canal dues were paid to Egypt, including those of American ships and of the large number of American-owned ships flying the Panamanian and Liberian flags of convenience.

Militarily, Nasser had taken such precautions as he could. Egyptian army reserves had been called up, plans were made to develop the National Guard militia into an 'Army of National Liberation', and troops were moved from Sinai (possibly half of the force usually there) into the Canal Zone. He tried to keep the border with Israel quiet. The fedayin were called off for the time being. In August there were only a few minor incidents along the Gaza Strip. Yet the border remained tense and dangerous.[24]

Nevertheless most of the game was still yet to play. The angry speeches made at the London Conference were further evidence, after the parliamentary debates and newspaper editorials in Britain and France, of the belligerent and emotional state of Western European opinion.

The London Conference ended with eighteen of the Powers present adopting the Tripartite proposals drafted and introduced by Dulles. The Eighteen-Power Declaration* published on 23 August embodied the principles of international control and management of the Canal to ensure its fair and efficient operation and, in the cant of the time, 'to insulate it from the influence of the politics of any nation'. Operation of the Canal would be entrusted to an international board, on which Egypt would be represented, the other members being chosen with regard to use of the Canal, pattern of trade and geographical distribution. The declaration said that it recognized Egypt's sovereign rights and proposed to guarantee her 'a fair return' for the use of the Canal.[25] A mission representing the eighteen Powers was appointed to explain the proposals to Nasser, but was not em-

---

*The eighteen Powers were Australia, Denmark, Ethiopia, France, West Germany, Iran, Italy, Japan, the Netherlands, New Zealand, Norway, Pakistan, Portugal, Spain, Sweden, Turkey, the United Kingdom and the United States.

The other four Powers at the Conference – Russia, India, Indonesia and Ceylon – supported an Indian proposal for an international board with only advisory powers.

powered to negotiate or discuss alternative proposals. It was headed by the Australian prime minister, Robert Menzies.

It was already clear that Nasser would not accept proposals intended to remove the Canal from Egyptian control, whatever lip-service they might pay to Egyptian sovereignty. Moreover, the take-it-or-leave-it manner in which the proposals were to be presented against a background of gathering military forces – on 28 August it was announced that French forces had joined British troops in Cyprus – gave the mission the air of an ultimatum. It was, however, in Nasser's interest to keep talking as long as possible and the mission had its first business meeting with Nasser in Cairo on 4 September. The Menzies talks were the only direct encounter between Nasser and a 'Western' statesman throughout the Suez crisis. Nasser and Menzies strikingly contrasted the old imperial order and the new world of decolonized Afro-Asia. Though from a 'new' country, Menzies was a man of the old Empire, the British-centred white Commonwealth. He was red-faced, stout and sentimental, a lover of port, cricket and English ceremonial tradition. He was also a shrewd, fluent lawyer and politician.

In a private letter to Eden, Menzies gave his personal impressions of Nasser.

I was told that Nasser was a man of great personal charm who might beguile me into believing something foreign to my own thought. This is not so. He is in some ways quite a likeable fellow but so far from being charming he is rather gauche, with some irritating mannerisms, such as rolling his eyes up to the ceiling when he is talking to you and producing a quick, quite evanescent grin when he can think of nothing else to do. I would say that he was a man of considerable but immature intelligence. He lacks training or experience in many of the things he is dealing with and is, therefore, awkward with them. He will occasionally use rather blustering expressions, but drops them very quickly if he finds them challenged in a good-humoured way. His logic does not travel very far. . . .[26]

Ten years later, in his memoirs, Sir Robert Menzies produced a slightly mellower version of this encounter.

In spite of some irritating mannerisms – and I suppose we all have some – I got the impression that we were dealing with a patriotic

Egyptian who had a strong sense of responsibility and of the gravity of the issue. Nasser was a man of imposing physical presence, obviously the master of his government, of much intelligence, but with some marks of immaturity and inevitable lack of experience. But he was impressive and clearly courageous.[27]

After five days of intermittent discussion and exchanges of letters, Nasser, as expected, rejected the Eighteen-Power proposals. Menzies reported that he had tried and failed to persuade Nasser that the position of Egypt *vis-à-vis* the proposed international board to run the Canal would no more contravene Egyptian sovereignty than the position of a landlord receiving rent from a tenant would affect the landlord's ownership.

The exchanges between Menzies and Nasser illustrate two cardinal points in the conflict between Western ideas of the Middle East and those of Nasser and the Arab nationalists, a misunderstanding of which Suez was the prime example. The first was the failure of most Western statesmen to understand the *nature* of the relationship they were trying to maintain or re-establish with Nasser and the Arabs; it was essentially a relationship of force rather than consent, and recognized as such by the weaker party, whatever the smooth verbal covering. While trying within the narrow limits of his brief to be as accommodating as he could to Egyptian national pride, Menzies seemed to be genuinely surprised that Nasser did not accept his analogy of the landlord and the tenant. Yet it was plain to any Egyptian that this was not a case of a landlord free to let his property and to choose his tenant and get the best rent he could, but rather an attempt at forceable requisitioning. Nor would it be a rent at the market rate: for Menzies regarded it as an unacceptable prospect that, if the Canal dues were left within Egypt's sole control, there was 'the strong possibility that they would be raised to the maximum that the traffic would bear'. This fear of 'blackmail', which underlay Eden's nightmares not only about the Canal but about a Nasserite empire controlling Middle East oil, was really a fear that Nasser, like a trade-union leader or a skilful company financier, might be able to organize the Arabs to squeeze the maximum profit out of their unique combination of oil resources and geographic position on the world's communications which were in fact the main assets available to these backward countries to finance their own development. Yet this was all according to the rules of Western capitalism. The British and French reaction, apart from the overtones of sentiment and pride, was that of nineteenth-century strike-breakers, upholding their 'company union' leaders in Iraq and Algeria, and using armed force to deal with the militant radicals. At one point in his exchange with Dulles, the French Foreign Minister, Pineau, exclaimed despairingly that if Nasser succeeded in the Suez *coup*, the West would henceforward be dependent on 'the goodwill of the Arabs'. Yet the plain fact was that, short of the power to dominate the Arab world over a long period by force, which Britain and France no longer possessed, the relationship of the two former imperial powers with Egypt and the Arabs was bound to be one based primarily on goodwill and common interest. The semi-monopolistic position of the Arabs in oil and communications and their valuable strategic geography made it essential to cultivate their friendship if they could no longer be physically controlled. And, if the Arabs sought to exploit their position too ruthlessly, then prudence suggested that Western Europe's best answer was not a military threat but the economic counter-measure of reducing its dependence on the Middle East oil and communications system by developing alternative sources and routes of supply. If the Arabs really wanted more money, self-interest would show them the limit to which they could apply a squeeze. To wealthy Western Europe this might be 'blackmail', to the poor of the Arab world it was a fair application of the West's own market doctrines.

But the second point the Menzies talks revealed was the inability of Nasser himself, like other Arab radicals, to find the language which would persuade the West of these underlying realities while at the same time promoting the confidence which would enable the British and French to put away their nightmare fears. For Nasser found it difficult to realize that the West was as full of historical 'complexes' as Egypt and the Arabs. Though the old relationship had broken down, neither side had been able to work out a mutually convincing new system for the partnership both needed.

In his letter finally rejecting the Eighteen-Power proposals, Nasser said that the system proposed was 'bound to be considered and treated by the people of Egypt as hostile, as infringing upon their rights and their sovereignty; all of which precludes real cooperation'. To keep the negotiations going, Nasser also offered his first concessions. Reaffirming Egypt's intention to earmark an adequate percentage of the Canal revenues for development of the Canal, he declared that the Egyptian government was also ready 'to enter into a binding arrangement concerning the establishment of just and equitable tolls and charges'.[28] He also proposed in a memorandum issued on 10 September a new Suez conference not only to review the 1888 Convention on freedom of navigation but also to discuss the development of the Canal to meet future shipping needs and the establishment of fair tolls and charges. As an immediate step, Nasser proposed the formation of a negotiating body representing the Canal-users. These proposals were curtly dismissed by a British government spokesman.

Eden had foreseen the failure of the Menzies mission and he and the French had already begun to prepare the next move. Nasser having, in Eden's eyes, spurned a peaceful settlement, the next step would be to go to the Security Council to get the record straight before going to war. Dulles opposed recourse to the Security Council at this time. He feared that the British and French meant only to make a cover for war. Instead, he proposed a new plan of his own for an association of Canal-users, a kind of cooperative which would deal collectively with the Egyptian government. If necessary it would arrange to pilot its own ships through the Canal and collect dues from its members. Dulles conceived SCUA (Suez Canal-Users Association) as a means of negotiating with Egypt and of delaying the British and French resort to force. But Eden appears to have believed that Dulles meant SCUA to be an instrument of coercion against Egypt, which would in the last resort be backed by armed force. Even before the SCUA proposal was taken up and adopted at the second London Conference on Suez on 19 September, it had become clear that Eden was mistaken or had been deceived.

On 12 September, Eden had alarmed the Labour Opposition in

the House of Commons by a speech announcing the SCUA plan. He had implied that, if Egypt refused to cooperate with SCUA, then force would be used to take ships through the Canal. The previous day, as a result of a meeting between Eden and Mollet on 10 September, the Suez Canal Company had instructed British and French pilots still in Egypt to leave by 15 September. Talk of war became more widespread in Western capitals. Bulganin, the Soviet premier, wrote a remonstrating letter to Eden. Nasser for the first time began to show real concern about the possibility of war.[29]

On 13 September the Egyptian ambassador in Washington informed Dulles that Egypt would regard any move by the proposed SCUA to force a way through the Canal as an act of aggression and she would resist it 'even if it means national martyrdom'.[30] The same day Dulles told a press conference in answer to questions about SCUA that the United States had no intention of shooting a way through the Canal. If her ships were stopped she would send them round the Cape instead. Two days before, Eisenhower had declared at a press conference that the United States was not 'going into any kind of military action under present conditions' and 'will not go to war while I am occupying my present post until the Congress is called into session and Congress declares such a war'.[31]

These American statements caused relief in Cairo and anger in London and Paris. It seemed as if the war threat might begin to recede. Tension remained high but gradually easing during the next ten days after the Canal Company pilots had been withdrawn, while the second London Suez conference on SCUA was held and until the British and French decided to take their case to the United Nations Security Council.

On 15 September, the day the British and French pilots left, Nasser in a speech to Egyptian air force cadets at Bilbeis denounced SCUA as intended to rob Egypt of the Canal and deprive her of her rightful Canal dues. He affirmed Egypt's intention to resist threats or the use of force, in defence of her sovereignty and independence. 'Those who attack Egypt will never leave Egypt alive. We shall fight a regular war, a total war, a guerrilla war. Those who attack Egypt will soon realize they brought disaster upon themselves. He who attacks Egypt attacks the whole Arab world.' This was Nasser's most violent and defiant outburst since his nationalization speech at Alexandria. It may have been a reflection of his increased confidence that Egypt would not in fact have to fight. Or perhaps its tone was intended to raise the morale of his military audience and of the country at a time when outwardly Egypt appeared to be facing its worst crisis so far in grappling with the operation of the Canal without the British and French pilots.

During the following week Egypt passed this crucial test. She demonstrated that she could run the Canal efficiently without the withdrawn pilots. The remaining Egyptian and Greek pilots, together with new, hastily trained pilots recruited from Russia, Yugoslavia, Germany, the United States and the Scandinavian countries, under the supervision of the dynamic Mahmoud Yunis, worked extra shifts to keep the Canal open and took through more than the previous daily average of ships.

Faced with the impending fiasco of SCUA and the failure of the withdrawal of the pilots to provide either a means of coercion or an excuse for intervention, Eden and Mollet seemed to have come to a point of decision: either they had to accept the possibility that Nasser might get away with most of his gains or they would have to go to war without a convincing pretext and without the support of the United States. From Cairo it looked as if the worst was over. But unknown to Nasser – and at that time to Eden, too – a new element was entering the picture. The Arab–Israeli dispute, which all concerned had hitherto striven, at least in appearance, to keep separate from the Canal conflict, was becoming involved in the crisis in two ways: through Israel's relations with France and through the situation in Jordan and Jordanian relations with Britain.

From the beginning of the Suez crisis, the Director-General of the Israeli Defence Ministry, Shimon Peres, had been in close contact with French military and defence officials. (On 27 July France asked for and got agreement from America and Britain for the sale of twenty-four of her latest Mystère fighters to Israel – in fact she sent sixty.) Early in August they had begun to discuss informally the possibility of a concerted attack on Egypt. On

7 August France agreed to supply a large amount of military equipment to Israel to mount an attack.[32] By the beginning of September the military talks had become more formal and Israel knew the details of the Anglo-French military plans against Egypt. By the last week in September, Ben Gurion had given his agreement in principle to Israel's participation in a joint operation. General Dayan, together with the new Foreign Minister, Mrs Golda Meir, who had replaced the too pacific Moshe Sharett, then flew to Paris with an arms shopping list. They came back with a promise of 100 Super-Sherman tanks, 200 large half-tracks, 300 four-wheel-drive trucks, twenty tank transporters, 1,000 bazookas and a squadron of transport planes.[33]

The original Israeli plan had been for a limited operation to destroy the fedayin bases in the Gaza Strip and the Egyptian army in Sinai and to seize and open the Straits of Tiran. It was to be a large-scale lightning raid or *coup de main* to be completed in four days after which most of the Israeli forces would withdraw. The Israeli army would concentrate the equivalent of three divisions first against the one Egyptian regular division and National Guard forces scattered through Sinai and then against the weak Palestinian division in the Gaza Strip. The Israelis convinced some of the French officers sent to Israel for talks that, in combination with this operation, France could herself, using only limited forces, easily seize Port Said or some other piece of Egyptian territory as a pledge or guarantee.[34]

To meet French wishes, Ben Gurion agreed to extend his original plan to include an Israeli expedition to the vicinity of the Suez Canal and hence the conquest of most of the Sinai Peninsula. By 2 October, Dayan was in a position to tell his General Staff to make preparations for a campaign along these lines. The campaign was to be launched within three weeks – although the Israeli government's final decision had not yet been taken. For the French government, too, the plan was still officially only 'the Israel hypothesis', but on 10 October, Franco–Israeli staff agreements were signed in Paris and at a secret conference the details of French support for the Israeli operation were agreed upon.[35]

There is some doubt as to when precisely the British were told of the Franco–Israeli negotiations. Eden may have had wind of the general idea by the end of August.[36] But it seems clear from the evidence of Anthony Nutting that the first serious discussion between Eden and the French of possible British participation in the Franco–Israeli plan occurred on 14 October, when two French emissaries, Albert Gazier, Minister of Labour and acting Foreign Minister in Pineau's absence at the United Nations, and General Maurice Challe, deputy chief of staff, came secretly to see Eden at Chequers.[37]

In the meantime other important events had taken place which had a bearing on Eden's reaction to the French plan. The Second London Conference on Suez opened on 19 September and ended on 21 September with an agreement to set up SCUA. But it became more than ever clear that Dulles now conceived of SCUA as means of collective bargaining and cooperation with Egypt rather than as an instrument of coercion. Therefore, after the London conference, on 23 September, Britain and France referred the dispute to the Security Council, asking for a debate on 3 October, two days after the establishment of SCUA. The Security Council was also seized of the other aspect of the Middle East crisis through the report on Arab–Israeli frontier tensions submitted to it by Secretary-General Hammarskjöld, on 27 September.

The promises of peace given to Hammarskjöld by Egypt, Israel and Jordan during his last Middle East visit on 19–23 July had, after a short lull, begun to break down. While the Egyptian–Israeli border remained fairly quiet there were more incidents on the Jordan frontier. Jordan was internally in political effervescence. King Hussein had dissolved the parliament on 26 June after it had voted to replace the Anglo-Jordan treaty by an agreement with Egypt and Syria. Elections were being prepared and the rival Arab camps – the Hashemites of Jordan and Iraq on the one side and the Egyptian–Syrian–Saudi Arabian alliance on the other – were competing to influence the outcome. Israel was also watching closely to ensure that there was no change in the military and political *status quo* in Jordan which might seriously affect her security. In the event of such an upset, which might come from, for example, the arrival in Jordan of troops from Iraq or from other Arab countries, she had declared that she reserved the right to intervene. Her intervention would probably have taken the form of an occupation of Jordan's West Bank.[38]

On 10 September, the Israel army launched the first of four large-scale 'reprisal' raids of increasing strength against Jordanian army and police posts on the border. The later reprisals were also intended to divert attention from Israel's plans to attack Egypt. They may also have been meant to put pressure on the British to agree to the attack on Egypt rather than face possible complications arising from the Anglo-Jordanian treaty.

Eden was concerned about the possibility of British involvement in support of Jordan. He encouraged King Hussein to seek the support of Iraq and on 14 September Hussein went to Baghdad to confer with his cousin King Feisal. A week later Nasser flew to Saudi Arabia to confer with King Saud and President Shukri Kuwatly of Syria. Nasser and his allies repeated their long-standing offer of aid to Jordan to replace the British subsidy and proposed linking the Jordan army with the Egyptian–Syrian joint command. The offer was not then accepted because Hussein was negotiating for closer military coordination with Iraq. But Hussein's efforts failed. The despatch of Iraqi forces, after initial British encouragement, was held up by British hesitation and by Israeli threats.

The day after Nasser had flown back to Cairo from Saudi Arabia (on 25 September), Israel launched her third assault on Jordan, killing thirty-nine Jordanians at the police fort of Husan. By now the attention of Ben Gurion and the Israel military leaders was already centred on Egypt, not Jordan, as their real target. But during the first half of October it still looked to the United Nations truce observers as if an Israeli attack was most likely to fall on Jordan.[39] This impression was increased when the Israelis made their fourth and heaviest raid on the Jordan frontier town of Qalqilya, killing some fifty Jordanians and losing eighteen dead themselves.

While the Qalqilya raid may have served as a useful cover for the well-advanced Israeli preparations for an attack on Egypt, it was not divorced from the situation developing in Jordan. Its repercussions suggest that Eden, who had gone to Paris with Lloyd for secret talks with Mollet and Pineau on 26 September, had not yet been told of the Franco-Israeli plans. For the reaction of Eden, perturbed by King Hussein's call (unanswered) for British air support during the Qalqilya attack, was to cable Nuri es-Said to expedite the despatch of an Iraqi brigade to Jordan, in order to dissuade Hussein from turning to Nasser for support.[40] At the same time, Selwyn Lloyd condemned the Israeli action at the Security Council and reminded Israel of British obligations under the Anglo-Jordanian treaty. Nuri and Hussein agreed to the Iraq army move but the Israelis, through the French, protested that it would be a threat to them. Ben Gurion suspected that Eden's move might be part of a British–Iraqi plan not merely to keep Jordan out of the Egyptian orbit but to bring about a general Arab–Israel settlement at Israel's expense.

According to Nutting, Eden was reluctant to call off the Iraqi moves completely, in spite of the French insistence on Israel's behalf. It was for this reason that Mollet was forced at that stage, on 14 October, to take Eden into his confidence about the Franco-Israeli plans for attacking Egypt. Clearly it would not do for Britain to find herself defending Jordan against Israel when at the same time her ally France was supporting Israel against Egypt. There were other reasons why Mollet should broach the matter now. First, the Franco-Israeli plans were so well advanced that the time for putting them into operation was running out, if the Anglo-French target date of 6 November was to be kept. Secondly, the British were needed if the French promise to Israel of neutralizing the Egyptian air force were to be fulfilled: only the British could provide bombers able to strike at Egypt's airfields. Third, and perhaps most important, was Ben Gurion's desire to make certain that the British would not back out at the last moment and double-cross him. Might they not use the occasion of an Israeli attack on Egypt to support Jordan and Iraq in a campaign to seize some Israeli territory? The best way of ensuring that he would not suddenly find the British as his opponents was to make certain they were involved on Israel's side.[41] Finally, there was the fact that Eden was approaching the end of both his pretexts for taking military action and his reasons for postponing it. Dulles had finally dashed his hopes of American support for a policy of force and the dispute had already gone through the Security Council. The day after the formation of SCUA, the American Secretary of State, by now increasingly suspicious of British and French intentions to resort to war, had declared at a press conference that he was not aware of any 'teeth' in the SCUA plan. For the Americans, especially for Eisenhower, it was clear that Egypt's demonstrated ability to keep the Canal open, despite the withdrawal of the British and French pilots, had been a turning point; it removed the last valid reason for using force. In Eisenhower's view, the West's quarrel with Nasser over his relations with Russia and his influence in other Arab countries were political problems requiring different treatment: they were part of the 'long haul' of the cold war.[42]

Eden dismissed Dulles's plea for the efficacy of economic and moral pressure: 'Nasser was unnegotiable', he declared, and further delay would simply enable him to consolidate his prize.[43]

In fact, in the Security Council proceedings which opened on 5 October and in the private talks held between Selwyn Lloyd, Pineau and Mahmoud Fawzi in Hammarskjöld's office between 10–12 October, the Egyptians showed themselves willing to negotiate. They were ready to compromise on virtually all aspects of the Canal except on the principle of their ultimate national as opposed to international control. Nasser appeared, however, to accept for the first time such a degree of organized participation by the users, in the settling of such matters as the level of tolls and the allocation of funds for maintenance and development, as could be considered a form of partnership between the Egyptian government and the users.

In the private talks agreement was reached on what became known as the 'Six Principles'. These were:

1. Free and open passage through the Canal without any discrimination.
2. Egyptian sovereignty to be respected.
3. The operation of the Canal to be insulated from the politics of any country.
4. Tolls to be fixed by agreement between Egypt and the users.

5. A fair proportion of the revenues to be allocated to development.

6. Egypt and the old Suez Canal Company to accept arbitration on unresolved questions between them.

The two sides still disagreed about the methods of implementing these principles. Fawzi rejected the Anglo-French demand for an international board on the lines of the Eighteen-Power proposals, but he was ready to consider suggestions for 'organized cooperation between an Egyptian authority and the users'. He was also prepared to accept a broadening of the 1888 Convention to include commitments about the question of maximum tolls, maintenance and development and reporting to the United Nations.[44]

Selwyn Lloyd thought that some progress had been made in the talks with Fawzi. But Eden was impatient. He instructed Lloyd to press for a Security Council vote on an Anglo-French resolution setting out the Six Principles but calling for implementation through the Eighteen-Power proposals. Egypt accepted the first part of the resolution but not the second. In the vote on 13 October the whole resolution won nine votes out of eleven in the Council but its second section on implementation was vetoed by Russia. Despite the vote, Selwyn Lloyd and Fawzi remained in contact with Hammarskjöld with a view to resuming negotiations in Geneva on 29 October.[45]

The Egyptian attitude at New York may have been only a 'conciliatory tactic', as Nasser is reported to have told the Indian ambassador in Cairo at the time.[46] But Nasser was also under strong political pressure, from his friends and supporters, as well as some economic pressure from his opponents, to make a compromise settlement. The Indians were urging him to be conciliatory. The other Arab states were also anxious for a settlement. Nevertheless, after the Security Council vote, Eden could claim, publicly at least, that hope of peaceful redress through the United Nations had been blocked and so resort to force was justified. This situation and the tangle over Jordan formed the setting when the French envoys, Gazier and Challe, arrived on their secret visit to Chequers on 14 October. The two Frenchmen did not beat about the bush. After appealing once more for the British to stop any Iraqi troop movements into Jordan, Gazier asked what the British reaction would be if Israel were to attack Egypt. According to Nutting, who was present, Eden 'replied with a half laugh that he could hardly see himself fighting for Colonel Nasser'.[47] Challe then outlined a plan by which Britain and France could seize control of the Suez Canal in concert with an Israeli attack across the Sinai Peninsula. Israel would be given time to capture most of Sinai; the British and French would then order both Israel and Egypt to withdraw their forces from the Canal so as to enable an Anglo-French force to occupy the Canal and separate the combatants.[48] Eden agreed to let the French government know his views on the plan as soon as possible.

Nutting says that from Eden's remarks after the meeting he knew that the British prime minister had already made up his mind to cooperate in the French plan. At a meeting of British ministers on the morning of 16 October Nutting urged in vain the obvious objections to the French plan – the damage it would cause to British oil and other interests in the Arab countries, the fact that it would be a breach of the UN Charter, the inevitable American opposition it would arouse and the division it would create in the Commonwealth. Lloyd, urgently recalled by Eden from New York, told Nutting on arrival that he disapproved of the plan, but he was won over by Eden. That same afternoon, Eden and Lloyd flew to Paris for secret talks with Mollet and Pineau. On their return Lloyd told Nutting that Eden had fully endorsed the French plan and that there would be further talks in Paris between the French and Israelis.[49] According to one well-informed French source, Eden later showed signs of changing his mind under American pressure, but eventually confirmed his decision to go ahead when the French and the Israelis threatened to carry out the plan without the British.[50]

Ben Gurion himself, accompanied by Dayan and other Israeli leaders, arrived in France secretly by air at dawn on 22 October to conduct the final negotiations with Mollet and Pineau. These are believed to have taken place either at a private villa at Sèvres, a Paris suburb near the military airfield at Villacoublay, or initially in an unused airfield building. Selwyn Lloyd came from London to take part in the first day of the talks, together with a senior Foreign Office official, said to have been Mr (now Sir) Patrick Dean, who stayed on to draft and sign on 25 October the still officially non-existent 'Treaty of Sèvres' between Britain, France and Israel. The agreement provided that Israel would attack through Sinai on the evening of 29 October. The attack would begin with a paratroop drop near the east bank of the Suez Canal. An announcement broadcast by Israel that her units were at the approaches to the Canal would be the signal for Britain and France to deliver an ultimatum to Israel and Egypt calling on each side to withdraw its forces ten miles from either side of the Canal and to allow an Anglo-French force to move in. The presumed Egyptian rejection of the ultimatum would lead to an immediate British bombardment of the Egyptian airfields. The bombing would continue daily until British and French troops had landed at Port Said six days later, first by air and then from the sea, and occupied the Canal Zone.[51] The British and French would simply put into effect the military plans they had already worked out for the occupation of the Canal Zone.

Immediately the agreement was concluded, Israel began mobilizing. On 28 October Ben Gurion won the support of the majority of his cabinet and also of the Israeli opposition leaders for the plan. More French arms and equipment continued to pour into Israel. The French planes, pilots and warships that were to provide Israel's air umbrella and naval protection took up their stations. The impression given to the Israeli public, to deceive the rest of the world, was that the military preparations were connected with the situation in Jordan.[52] The Jordanian developments indeed provided an excellent cover. On 21 October the pro-Egyptian nationalist groups in Jordan had won the parliamentary elections. Nuri es-Said, warned off by Eden after the Chequers meeting, had not sent any Iraqi troops into Jordan. Instead, on 25 October, the Jordan government decided to join the Egyptian–Syrian joint military command and so to put Jordanian forces under an Egyptian commander-in-chief in time of war.

After the decisive Paris meeting between Eden and Mollet on

16 October, the Americans had ceased to receive information through the usual military channels from their allies. Eisenhower thought that Israel might be planning to seize the west bank of the Jordan since the Jordan state seemed to be in danger of disintegration. He sent several personal messages to Ben Gurion asking him to show restraint and warning him not to count on the paralysis of the US government by the impending presidential elections.[53] In his second message Eisenhower spoke of consulting Britain and France, co-signatories of the Tripartite Declaration. This evoked from Dayan the dry comment in his diary:

> From both his signals it is apparent that he [Eisenhower] thinks the imminent conflict is likely to erupt between Israel and Jordan and that Britain and France will cooperate with him in preventing this. How uninformed he is of the situation! In all its aspects the reality is the reverse of his assumptions.[54]

Lulled by the apparent intention of Britain, France and Egypt to continue the negotiations on the Canal begun in New York, increasingly preoccupied by the final phase of the presidential election campaign and by the developing Polish and Hungarian revolutions against the Russians, Eisenhower, with all the vast intelligence resources at his disposal, appears not to have suspected a joint Israeli–French–British attack on Egypt. Neither did Nasser. He had confidently ruled out such a combination of forces because it appeared to be so obviously contrary to British interests in the Middle East. He may have feared that the British, alone or with the French, might still attack – he told a British journalist, Tom Little, in mid-October that he thought no compromise with Britain was now possible because 'Sir Eden intends to attack me and there is nothing I can do about it'. When Little suggested that Egypt could not hold out against Anglo-French forces, Nasser is reported to have said, 'But I do not intend to fight them. I intend to stand back and wait for world opinion to save me.'[55]

Even after Ben Gurion's speech to the Knesset on 17 October, which named Egypt as Israel's main enemy, and after the Israeli mobilization, Nasser still did not strengthen his forces facing Israel. He did not reverse the decision he had made at the beginning of the crisis to withdraw a good part of his army from Sinai to guard the Canal Zone and the Delta against what he saw as the main threat from Britain and France. Of her total army strength of 90,000, Egypt was estimated to have usually some 60,000 troops in Sinai and the Gaza Strip, composed of four divisions and an armoured brigade. During August and September, Nasser had withdrawn two divisions and the armoured brigade to the west of the Canal.

Most of the remaining Egyptian forces were concentrated in the northern part of Sinai in defensive positions based on the triangle formed by Rafah (on the southern edge of the Gaza Strip), El Arish, farther west along the Sinai coast, and Qusseima in the south. The other main road farther south across Sinai to Ismailia was defended by the strong point of Abu Agheila. The Gaza Strip – which was virtually indefensible once the loss of Rafah cut its communications with Egypt – was garrisoned by about 5,000 troops, most of whom were Palestinian or National Guard units.

South of Qusseima in the vast desert expanses of Sinai, the frontier and the desert tracks were held by posts and patrols of about 1,500 men of the lightly armed motorized Frontier Force. At Sharm esh-Sheikh on the southernmost tip of the peninsula, covering the entrance to the Gulf of Aqaba through the Tiran Straits, there was an Egyptian garrison of about 1,200 men, mostly reserve units and National Guard, and batteries of coastal guns.

Egypt's armoured forces in the Sinai and the Gaza Strip consisted of some 100 Sherman and Soviet T34 tanks and fifty Archer self-propelled anti-tank guns.

According to Israeli estimates Egypt's operational air force then consisted of fifty-seven jet fighters (thirty Migs, fifteen Vampires and twelve Meteors), twelve Ilyushin bombers and sixty transport planes.[56] Only part of this force was used in the Sinai battles. Nasser kept the rest back in the early stages and then had them flown out of the country.

Against these Egyptian forces, Israel used six infantry brigades, a paratroop brigade and three armoured brigades (about 45,000 men) including some 300 Sherman, Super-Sherman and French AMX tanks. The Israeli air force had an operational strength of fifty-three jet fighters (composed of sixteen Mystères, twenty-two

Ouragans and fifteen Meteors) plus sixty-four piston-engined planes and nineteen transports.[57]

Thus the Israelis at first had the edge in numbers and armour while French air support (from sixty jet fighters) gave them an advantage there too.

The Sinai campaign included some remarkable feats of arms by the Israel army and revealed some lamentable weaknesses in the Egyptian forces, especially the officer corps. But it was not quite the swift and humiliating rout of superior but unresisting Egyptian forces that some contemporary accounts made it out to be. It is clear from later, franker and better informed versions including that of General Dayan himself, that there were several hard-fought engagements. The Egyptians showed themselves strong in static defence and weak in mobility and counter-attack. These accounts also showed that the intervention of the British and French air forces and the threat of Anglo-French landings played an important part in the speed and manner of the Egyptian defeat and so probably helped at least to minimize Israeli casualties.

The Israeli attack on Egypt began at five o'clock on the afternoon of Monday, 29 October 1956, when 398 paratroopers of the airborne brigade were dropped at the eastern end of the Mitla Pass, about forty miles east of the southern end of the Suez Canal. This was the force whose descent, publicly announced over the radio, was to provide the 'military threat to the Canal' and so the pretext for Anglo-French intervention. At the same time, Israeli army forces crossed the frontier into southern Sinai at three points and quickly over-ran a series of small Egyptian border posts. One brigade moved from Eilat at the head of the Gulf of Aqaba and seized the small post of Ras en-Nakeb, eight miles inside the Egyptian border. From here it was later to advance down the rough desert tracks along the coast of the Gulf to assault Sharm esh-Sheikh, as soon as the Egyptian air force was no longer a threat. The rest of the airborne brigade crossed the frontier at Kuntilla to advance across southern Sinai and link up with the paratroops at the Mitla Pass. It captured two Egyptian posts at Thamad and Nakhl and its advance units linked up with the paratroopers at Mitla by six o'clock on the evening of 30

October. The third thrust by an infantry brigade supported by an armoured brigade was across the frontier at Sabha to attack Qusseima, the southern outpost of the main Egyptian defensive positions in northern Sinai. Thamad and Nakhl were quickly seized, though not without resistance which cost the Egyptians nearly 100 dead; for part of the Qusseima position there was a stiffer engagement lasting for three hours before it was occupied. Dayan's plan to conceal his main attack until the following day, was almost wrecked by the premature advance of the armoured brigade in this thrust through Qusseima to the outskirts of the Abu Agheila strong-points. By this time, in any case, not only Nasser and the Egyptian command, but indeed the whole world had become fully alerted.

At first, however, the Egyptians had been taken by surprise. Their commander-in-chief, General Amer, was away on a visit to Syria and Jordan to discuss the decision of these countries to form a joint command with Egypt. As soon as Nasser received news that evening of the Kuntilla attack and the air drop at Mitla, he alerted all the armed forces. He at once sent reinforcements to Mitla and instructed two infantry brigades and an armoured brigade to be ready to move into Sinai along the central and coastal roads, where the Egyptians expected the main Israeli thrust to come. The Egyptian air force was slow to react but the next day it flew fifty sorties and a hundred the day after, mostly in ground attacks on Israeli troops. By midnight it was clear that the Israeli operation was more than a raid. Nasser ordered the alerted reinforcements to move across the Canal, thus increasing his forces in Sinai by some 10,000 men and by a mixed force of tanks and other armoured vehicles.

The Syrian army asked to join in the war but Nasser advised them to stay out for the time being. He did not want, he later claimed, to give Israel an opportunity to open another front or to enable the British and French to invade Syria and other Arab countries. According to Nasser, no other Arab state except Syria offered more than moral support. Throughout the next week's fighting, first against the Israelis and then against the British and French, the Egyptian forces stood alone.[58] Nasser also said that the Arab states did not join the battle because he warned them

not to. Nevertheless Cairo radio broadcast appeals for support
from the Arab peoples. If the struggle had remained one with
Israel alone, perhaps the Arab states might later have been called
by Nasser to join in. But by the evening of 30 October a new situation had developed: the conflict had broadened into an international crisis. That afternoon, Eden and Mollet, after a final
consultation in London, had issued their prepared ultimatum to
Israel and Egypt to withdraw their forces ten miles back from the
Suez Canal and permit the occupation of key points in the Canal
Zone by British and French troops. They claimed to be acting to
'separate the combatants' and ensure the security of the Canal.
Egypt and Israel were given twelve hours in which to reply. Israel
accepted and Egypt, as expected, refused. Nasser immediately
saw that compliance would have penalized Egypt, which was
being attacked, and favoured Israel which was the attacker.
Egypt would have had to withdraw her forces over 100 miles,
leaving the Israelis to advance and occupy most of Sinai without
resistance and permitting the British and French to occupy the
Canal Zone, both areas part of Egyptian territory.

Nasser received the British ambassador, Sir Humphrey Trevelyan, at nine o'clock that evening to give him Egypt's reply. Nasser
told Trevelyan that Egypt would fight but gave him a promise to
protect the lives and property of British subjects in Egypt. The
promise was honoured even after British bombs began to fall on
Egypt and British troops invaded the country. A number of
British people were interned, for their own safety and for security
reasons. They included British journalists and the 400 British
civilians working at the Canal Zone military base which the
Egyptian army took over completely. They were well looked
after. It was not until weeks later, when Nasser was trying to
hasten the departure of British and French troops in accordance
with United Nations resolutions, that he began to expel British
and French subjects from Egypt and to sequestrate their property.

The news of the ultimatum, which had been carefully concealed
earlier that day from the United States government by its British
and French allies, was announced just as the United Nations
Security Council was preparing to meet, at the urgent summons of
the American delegate, to discuss the Israeli attack. An American

resolution was tabled calling for an immediate Israeli withdrawal behind the armistice lines. It urged all member states to refrain from the use of force or threat of force in the area and to deny any help to Israel. It was vetoed by Britain and France. A similar Soviet resolution was also vetoed. A resolution was then put forward by Yugoslavia calling for a special emergency session of the General Assembly, under the 'Uniting for Peace' procedure designed to circumvent the veto. It was approved by the Security Council on 31 October by seven votes to four.

Nasser appears to have thought at first that the Anglo-French ultimatum was a bluff intended to help Israel by pinning down substantial Egyptian forces in the Canal Zone to meet the possible threat of intervention.[59] For the time being he did not change his military dispositions. He neither sent more reinforcements to Sinai nor recalled those already on their way. But he kept part of his air force out of the Sinai battle to meet the new threat. It was not until the British air attacks began the next evening, at 6 P.M. on 31 October, twelve hours after the ultimatum had expired, that he was sure that the Anglo-French threat was serious.

Nasser was now faced with a situation of the utmost danger and complexity. In addition to what was obviously a formidable Israeli offensive, which even all Egypt's available resources might not be sufficient to check, he was facing attack by two major European powers with vastly superior forces. In conventional military terms there was little he could do for long against such a combination. But he did not lose his nerve. As the crisis unfolded, he displayed both the strength of his own character and of his position in Egypt. Totally dominating his colleagues, he coolly manipulated the many strands of an intricate international situation and at the same time took bold military decisions. He showed the qualities which distinguished him as a leader from the lesser men around him: his intelligence and moral courage; a broad and quick grasp of essentials and concentration on them; a fine sense of political timing; a capacity to command and be obeyed.

His first thought was whether the morale of the Egyptian public might not crack under the British bombing. When from his house Nasser heard the Canberra jets and the bombs exploding on the outskirts of Cairo, at the Al Maza airfield, he drove out through the streets of the blacked-out capital to the Presidency to get the feel of the city. He was reassured by the crowds who shouted to him, 'We shall fight, we shall fight'. He felt he could count on popular support in organizing Egyptian resistance.[60]

After British bombs put the Cairo radio transmitter out of action, he went to the Al Azhar mosque, a traditional rallying centre for patriotic sentiment, to make a fighting speech. When he heard that a group of former politicians and leading business-men were considering coming as a deputation to urge him to compromise with the Anglo-French demands, he threatened that anyone who came to talk of surrender would be shot on the spot in the presidency garden.[61]

After reassuring himself about national morale, the next essential was to save what he could of the Egyptian forces in Sinai. If the British and French landed in the Canal Zone, any Egyptian troops still in Sinai or Gaza would be completely cut off.[62] More-over, if any territory had to be sacrificed temporarily it was better it should be the empty Sinai desert than any of the rest of Egypt, especially the Delta and the Canal Zone, the populated heart of the country. The British and French could in the long run be checked only by a combination of diplomacy and guerrilla action. But every weapon and soldier that could be brought back across the Canal would help in this political–military conflict.

The international reaction to the Anglo-French intervention showed Nasser that Egypt had powerful political support, from both the United States and the Soviet Union as well as from the Arab world and the Afro-Asian countries. Nasser was neverthe-less cautious in his dealings with the Russians at this time. He wished to avoid offending the United States, especially as from 1 November onwards Russia was herself engaged in crushing the Hungarian Revolution. Even in Britain Eden's action aroused bitter opposition in parliament and in the press; public opinion was deeply divided and already there were open accusations of 'collusion' with Israel. Abroad, Eden was facing increasing pres-sure from the United States and the Commonwealth as well as the United Nations.

But Nasser realized that all these assets might still crumble away to nothing but words in the face of a military *fait accompli*, unless Egypt herself resisted as best she could. If her regular armed forces were overwhelmed, as they were likely to be, she had to be prepared for a guerrilla war and to be ready to play her only other trump card of blocking the Canal. Nasser ordered blockships, which had been held ready, to be sunk in the Canal. Forty-seven were sunk in the next forty-eight hours. By 1 November, the Canal was closed. The other main channel for Middle Eastern oil supplies to Britain and France was blocked two days later when Syrian army engineers blew up three pumping-stations on the IPC pipeline that crosses Syria from Iraq to the Mediterranean. In support of Egypt, Saudi Arabia banned oil shipments to Britain and France. Eden's action had thus brought on the very nightmare of disrupted oil supplies that he had dreaded.

Nasser also authorized the issue of 400,000 rifles to civilians for the formation of popular resistance groups. That evening (31 October) Nasser ordered a general withdrawal of all Egyptian forces from Sinai. The forces in the Gaza Strip were told to surrender at a suitable moment to avoid casualties to the large civilian population there. In the event, part of the Gaza Strip garrison, the Palestinian brigade at Khan Yunis, refused to surrender and was overwhelmed by an Israeli attack with tanks and aircraft. Such was also the fate of the garrison of Sharm esh-Sheikh whose commander decided to fight on when it became obvious that his force could not be evacuated.

Nasser is said to have had to threaten to resign in order to get the army chiefs to agree to his orders to withdraw. By that time the Sinai battles had entered a new and critical stage. The Israelis had begun their assault on the main Egyptian positions at Abu Agheila and at Rafah: they had also become unintentionally involved in a fierce battle at the Mitla Pass. At Abu Agheila, the Israeli armoured brigade coming from Qusseima broke through the outer defences from the south and west. Together with a new thrust by an infantry brigade from El Auja, it had almost encircled the two main Egyptian redoubts, Um Katef and Um Shihan, but the Egyptians in these two positions held firm and drove back repeated Israeli attacks on them. An attempt by an Egyptian tank force from El Arish to relieve Abu Agheila by a counter-attack was driven off. The Egyptian infantry and

armoured units which were sent along the coastal road to reinforce El Arish and along the central road to join the battles at
either Abu Agheila or Mitla had been held up by Israeli air
attacks in which French planes were now joining. A French
cruiser also joined that night in the bombardment of the Egyptian
positions at Rafah as preparation for the Israeli attack there.
Another French warship, the frigate *Kersaint*, had taken part in
the crippling and capture of the Egyptian destroyer *Ibrahim el
Auwal* off Haifa early on 31 October even before the Anglo-
French ultimatum expired.[63]

At the Mitla Pass, the Israeli paratroop commander, contrary
to orders from Dayan not to seek battle, had on 31 October
decided to try to occupy the pass, a narrow mountain defile with
steep sides. The paratroop column found itself trapped by heavy
fire from Egyptians in caves along the sides of the defile and on
the surrounding heights. The battle lasted for seven hours before
the Egyptian positions were stormed. The admitted Israeli losses
were thirty-eight killed and 120 wounded, as well as a number of
vehicles. The Israelis claimed 150 Egyptian dead. The rest of the
Egyptian force, of battalion strength, withdrew under cover of
darkness.[64]

In New York, an emergency General Assembly of the United
Nations met on 1 November and at 3 A.M. on 2 November passed
an American resolution calling for an immediate cease-fire, for
withdrawal behind the armistice lines and for a halt to the movement of military forces into the area. It also called for steps to
open the Canal. At the end of the debate the Canadian foreign
minister, Lester Pearson, with the support of the United States,
proposed the establishment of a United Nations force to keep
the peace in the Middle East. Egypt announced that she would
accept the cease-fire if the attacking armies stopped their aggression.

By this time the main battles in Sinai and Gaza were almost
over. Rafah had fallen and the Israelis had entered El Arish to
find it deserted by Egyptian troops. By the end of the day (2
November) the Gaza Strip had been occupied and the Egyptians
had withdrawn from their remaining strongholds at Abu Agheila.
Israeli tanks advancing along the central road westward from

Abu Agheila had clashed twice with the rearguards of the Egyptian armoured brigade withdrawing from Bir Rod Salim and Bir Gifgafa. These were the only straight tank battles of the campaign and there were some losses on both sides. The retreating Egyptian columns deprived of air cover had begun to suffer heavily from Israeli and French air attacks. After the Anglo-French bombing of the Egyptian airfields, Nasser had restricted the activity of the Egyptian air force so as to save the pilots and had sent the surviving Migs and Ilyushins off to Luxor, Syria and Saudi Arabia. The roads in Sinai were choked with damaged and burning Egyptian vehicles and abandoned equipment. Thousands of Egyptian soldiers took to the desert, throwing off their uniforms, equipment and boots to try to struggle home on foot across the sand dunes. It was at this stage that an at least partially organized withdrawal became a disordered flight.

There now began a race between the diplomats and the soldiers. Peace-making efforts, designed to produce a cease-fire and prevent an Anglo-French invasion, centred on the Canadian proposal of a United Nations force. The promoters of the proposal saw it as a means of forestalling Anglo-French intervention. The British and French saw it as a possible means of legitimizing the planned operation of their expeditionary force which was already at sea on its way to Egypt. The French were determined to carry through the attack on Egypt come what may, but Eden's political difficulties were accumulating. The British prime minister clutched at the hope that it might still be possible to make the Anglo-French operation internationally respectable by getting agreement that it should occupy the Canal Zone until the UN force arrived, or that British and French troops should themselves be considered the advance guard of the United Nations. Both the United States and the Afro-Asian countries at the United Nations, led by India, made it plain they could never accept such a suggestion.[65]

Israel was not primarily concerned with whether the Canal Zone was occupied by the Anglo-French forces or by the United Nations. Her main interest lay in completing her own war aims, the most important of which was the capture of Sharm esh-Sheikh and the Straits of Tiran, before international pressures forced her to accept a cease-fire. Nevertheless, Ben Gurion hoped that the British and French would intervene. He was moved chiefly by the 'cold calculation' that it was better for Israel 'not to appear alone as an aggressor who disturbs the peace and ignores UN resolutions' but rather to have Britain and France in the dock with her.[66] But the speed with which the Israeli campaign in Sinai was being completed, as the Egyptians tried to withdraw, looked like ending the fighting before the planned Anglo-French landings on 5 November. This threatened to rob Eden of his required pretext. He would no longer be able to claim that he was acting to separate the combatants and to stop the war from spreading.

In the evening of 3 November, the General Assembly began to debate an Afro-Asian resolution, which reiterated in stronger terms the demand for a cease-fire forthwith, and a Canadian resolution calling for the Secretary-General to report in forty-eight hours on a plan to establish a United Nations force for the Middle East. Both resolutions were passed in the early hours of Sunday, 4 November, while in Hungary the Russian army was going into action in Budapest to crush the Nagy government. Egypt abstained in the vote but later said she would accept the resolution and was ready for a cease-fire by eight o'clock that evening. With the Israeli forces already having completed the occupation of almost all Sinai and the Gaza Strip and mustering for the final assault on Sharm esh-Sheikh, the Israel delegate also felt safe in announcing to the Assembly that day his government's acceptance of the cease-fire provided Egypt did likewise. But under British pressure, the Israelis later retracted this acceptance until the Anglo-French landings in Egypt had begun. For, despite the news from the United Nations, the British cabinet had decided to go through with the military intervention.

The following morning, 5 November, at dawn, 600 British paratroops landed at Port Said and 487 French paratroops at Port Fuad, on the opposite side of the Suez Canal, followed by further detachments in the early afternoon. They were supported by aircraft from naval carriers lying offshore. Port Fuad fell to the French and in Port Said, after some heavy fighting, the Egyptian commander agreed at 3.30 P.M. to a truce to discuss surrender terms. But Nasser ordered the Governor of Port Said to reject any surrender and two hours later the fighting was resumed. Local resistance groups sprang up, organized by the Muslim Brothers and Communists, as well as by the government and the Nasserite Liberation Rally. The people of Port Said were encouraged to resist by broadcasts over loudspeaker vans saying that London and Paris had been attacked by missiles in a new world war. Russia had, in fact, that evening virtually threatened Britain, France and Israel with nuclear rocket attack, in letters from Bulganin to Eden, Mollet and Ben Gurion. (According to Nasser, these letters were sent at the suggestion of President Shukri Kuwatly of Syria who was then visiting Moscow.)[67] The Soviet premier also wrote to Eisenhower suggesting a joint Soviet–American military intervention to stop the fighting in the Middle East. The Soviet press began the next day to talk of 'volunteers' to help Egypt. It is doubtful whether this Soviet intention was serious.[68] In any case, at this time Nasser was pinning his hopes on the United Nations and on American pressure against Britain and France. He did not then want Soviet volunteers, whose arrival would inevitably lose him American support and who might prove as hard to get rid of later on as the British had been – or as the Russians were proving themselves to be in Hungary. Nasser told the American ambassador in Cairo, Raymond Hare, on 8 November, 'Don't worry about these Soviet moves, I don't trust any big Power'.[69] Nasser later said that he had had no contact with Russia about possible support until the Soviet letter of 6 November.[70] Nevertheless, the possibility of Soviet bloc 'volunteers' was taken seriously by many at the time. It was one reason for the urgency with which the United Nations Emergency Force was established and for the strength of American pressure to make the British, French and Israelis withdraw their forces.[71]

The temporary coincidence of Soviet and American support for Egypt did not mean any diminution of the cold war between the Super-Powers. This fact was underlined when Eisenhower replied to Bulganin rejecting any Soviet intervention, with or without the United States, and warning that any attack on Britain and France would bring American retaliation against Russia.

During the first day's battle in Port Said, the Israelis had completed the capture of Sharm esh-Sheikh. Battered by the unopposed Israeli air force, the Egyptian garrison surrendered after a nine-hour battle in which they lost 100 killed and thirty-one wounded. Her conquest of Sinai having been completed and the Anglo-French landing begun, Israel accepted the United Nations cease-fire. At the United Nations, Hammarskjöld had been working round the clock with the Canadians and others to complete plans for a United Nations force. That day a Canadian resolution setting up such a force, known later as the United Nations Emergency Force (UNEF), under the command of Major-General E. L. M. Burns, the Canadian chief of the UN Palestine Truce Supervisory Organization, was approved by the General Assembly.

At dawn the next day, 6 November, British and French commandoes and support troops landed from the sea at Port Said and Port Fuad. In a battle lasting until the late afternoon, the British and French troops, led by tanks and supported by naval planes, gradually gained control of the town from the Egyptian army which was helped by a considerable number of armed civilians. Egyptian casualties were heavy.*

After the surrender of Port Said, a British armoured column began advancing down the Canal towards Ismailia and Suez. But it had penetrated only as far as El Cap, a village twenty-five miles south of Port Said, when the British government announced its acceptance of the UN cease-fire to take effect from midnight.

There were many political and diplomatic reasons for the British government's decision, but an economic factor may have been decisive. Whether the British and French fought on or stopped, for many weeks to come there would be no oil coming through the Canal or the Syrian pipelines. The United States government let it be known that its financial help needed to meet the extra dollar cost of alternative oil supplies and to support the pound would depend on the British accepting an early cease-fire and this economic pressure was maintained to secure an Anglo-

---

*A British mission of enquiry (carried out by Sir Edward Herbert, President of the Law Society) later put the Egyptian casualties at 650 dead. The Egyptians said there were over 1,000 killed.

French withdrawal.[72] The severity of the American pressure on London and Paris was not only a measure of Eisenhower's anger at being deceived by Eden and Mollet. Nor was it aroused only by concern for the American position in the Middle East. The American administration seems to have seen the Middle East and Hungary together as part of a broadening world crisis which could, if unchecked, drag the United States and Russia with their huge nuclear arsenals into a dangerous confrontation. In this situation the British and French, by insisting on landing in Egypt, were like children playing with matches near a leaking tank full of petrol.

So the fighting stopped, except for occasional clandestine Egyptian guerrilla harassment in Port Said. Nasser now faced months of clearing up and of close diplomatic struggle to secure the withdrawal of the British, French and Israeli troops, the re-opening of the Canal and some kind of political settlement. Egypt had been saved from the terrible human and material consequences of prolonged guerrilla warfare and from the ever-present danger that the conflict might spread into a more destructive world war by proxy. But the diplomatic struggle in which Nasser was now to engage was in some ways more difficult than the week of war just ended. It demanded skill, tenacity and a shrewd assessment of international politics to be able to reverse the military *fait accompli* and produce a peaceful retreat of the occupying forces. For though in the heat of war Egypt had wide international sympathy and support, it was bound to be more difficult to maintain support at this intensity if the Anglo-French-Israeli occupation dragged on for too long and negotiation took the place of shooting.

Apart from a world opinion that might prove fickle, the three main weapons in Nasser's hands were all dangerously double-edged. There was the fear of a clash between the Western Powers and the Soviet bloc if the latter introduced 'volunteers', and the anxiety of the United States and Russia to prevent each other from gaining influence in the Middle East in the wake of the British and French collapse. Nasser had to keep this danger alive but not so acutely that it would force the United States into supporting the British and French rather than urging them to withdraw. There was the delay in unblocking the Canal and pipelines which, together with American pressure and the threat of guerrilla warfare against a prolonged Anglo-French occupation, was Nasser's chief weapon against Britain and France. But this, too, was risky. It was damaging economically to Egypt herself and, if too prolonged, would have lost her friendly support. Finally, in securing the withdrawal of Israeli forces the only effective means was once again American economic pressure. But Nasser had to try to secure this American action at a time when he was resisting American pressure on the Arab countries to accept the new 'Eisenhower Doctrine' which aimed to establish an American anti-Soviet sphere of influence in the Middle East. He could not pay the price of accepting the 'Eisenhower Doctrine', not merely because he was opposed to becoming part of the sphere of influence of any Great Power, but also because to do so would have alienated the Russians when he still needed their support as well as that of the Americans.

Similarly, in his dealings with the United Nations, through Hammarskjöld, over the conditions for the operation in Egypt of the United Nations Emergency Force, especially in the Gaza Strip, Nasser felt the need to tread warily. He tried to ensure that Egypt gave away as little as possible of her political sovereign rights, but he was always in danger of losing international sympathy by a too protracted and stubborn bargaining.

In accepting the cease-fire, Britain, France and Israel had not at the same time promised the rapid and unconditional withdrawal of their forces demanded by the United Nations. For the next three weeks the British and French sought to make their withdrawal conditional on the establishment of UNEF in the Canal Zone with a mandate to carry out what would have been the Anglo-French task – to clear the Canal and ensure its security until an agreement was reached on its international control. But Eisenhower rejected anything but unconditional withdrawal. General Burns told Nasser, when the latter expressed fears about such a UNEF role at a meeting on 9 November in Cairo, that it was inconceivable that the General Assembly, with its then majority views, would ever allow UNEF to be used to compel Egypt to internationalize the Canal.[73]

Burns met Nasser in the President's temporary offices in the old
Revolutionary Command Council headquarters on the Nile. The
building was blacked out and heavily guarded (Burns had
noticed on his way into Cairo the tanks at street corners and a
lively movement of troops, presumably, he thought, either to impress the population with the government's remaining power or
to shelter the tanks in built-up areas where they would not be
bombed). The atmosphere was 'rather like that of an improvised
field headquarters'. Nasser was wearing 'an ancient grey cardigan
and looked rather tired, but still vigorous and confident'.[74]

The report by Hammarskjöld on the establishment of UNEF,
which had been approved by the General Assembly on 7 November, made it plain that the force, more than an observer force but
not a military occupation force, could be in Egypt only with the
consent of the Egyptian government. As Burns later pointed out,
this legal point was reinforced by practical considerations. A
force of 6,000 men could not impose its will on the Egyptians. It
was dependent on their cooperation and therefore on their consent
for the maintenance of its supply lines and communications. The
terms of this cooperation were worked out in a series of meetings
between Nasser, Fawzi and Hammarskjöld while the build-up of
UNEF was in progress. The advance guard of UNEF arrived
in the Canal Zone by air on 15 November. By the end of the month
the British had told the Americans they would withdraw from
Egypt, though the decision was not formally announced until 3
December by the acting prime minister, R. A. Butler. (Eden had
left for Jamaica for three weeks' rest.) Eisenhower at once
authorized American help in oil supplies for Western Europe and
massive financial support for Britain. His main preoccupation
now was to patch up the Western alliance and to keep the
Russians out of the Middle East.

The Anglo-French withdrawal was completed by 22 December,
after an exchange of 186 Egyptian prisoners for 470 British
technicians from the Canal Zone military base who had been
interned. Nasser had taken over all the base installations and
stores and on 1 January 1957 formally declared the Anglo-
Egyptian agreement of 1954 ended. It was not until 27 December,
after the Egyptian army had reoccupied Port Said in strength and

UNEF had begun to move into Sinai in the wake of the gradual Israeli withdrawal, that Nasser allowed the United Nations to begin clearing the sunken ships from the Canal. The struggle to bring about a complete Israeli withdrawal lasted another two months. Before the Sinai campaign began, Ben Gurion had told his Cabinet that they should not count on keeping control of Sinai, or even annexing the islands in the Straits of Tiran. The United States, he foresaw, would force Israel to give up occupied Egyptian territory.[75] Later he seemed to be tempted to try to hold on to Sinai both for sentimental nationalist reasons, because it was the wilderness where the Israelites had wandered and where God had given Moses the tablets of the law, and for reasons of real-politik, because it was an internationally important strategic area. This victory dream soon passed, but he fought a shrewdly judged diplomatic rearguard action to conserve for Israel the essential gains of the Sinai campaign. These were international guarantees against interference with Israeli shipping in the Gulf of Aqaba and against the resumption of fedayin raids from the Gaza Strip.

The Israeli forces withdrew across Sinai in stages during the months of December and January, destroying roads, railways, buildings and other installations as they went. The UNEF took over in their wake. By the end of January, the Israelis held only the Gaza Strip and the western coast of the Gulf of Aqaba down to Sharm esh-Sheikh. But from there the Israelis refused to move until they received assurances that neither Egyptian military nor civilian control would be restored in the Gaza Strip and that UNEF would take over and stay at Sharm esh-Sheikh.

The United States tried to meet Ben Gurion's demand for assurances. On 11 February, Dulles sent him a secret *aide-mémoire* in which the US government promised to seek to have the UNEF deployed so as to stop raids from either side in the Gaza Strip and to do its part in helping to assure free passage for ships of all nations through the 'international waters' of the Gulf of Aqaba. Israel still refused to move and used all the considerable political and publicity resources of the Zionist movement to try to mobilize American public and Congressional opinion against a threat by Eisenhower to impose economic sanctions.

Faced with resistance from Congressional leaders, Eisenhower took his case for using pressure on Israel direct to the American public over television. Inside the United Nations Assembly, an Arab–Asian campaign for the imposition of sanctions was gathering strength. While Dulles negotiated with Abba Eban, the Israeli delegate at the UN and ambassador in Washington, Hammarskjöld tried to work out a compromise with Nasser in Cairo and with Fawzi in New York, about the UNEF role in Gaza and at Sharm esh-Sheikh.

Hammarskjöld's diplomatic technique in this kind of dispute was to try to separate the legal situation from the practical question of keeping the peace. Thus while publicly recognizing Egypt's rights to reoccupy the Gaza Strip and Sharm esh-Sheikh, he sought to persuade Nasser privately that it would be in Egypt's interest not to seek fully to enforce those rights. He was able to do this more easily in the case of Sharm esh-Sheikh because it was a distant, empty corner of the Sinai desert. But the Gaza Strip was inhabited by 400,000 politically passionate Palestinian Arabs: it was one of the most sensitive symbols of the Arab–Israeli dispute. Nasser could not afford politically to accept an end of effective Egyptian sovereignty or control there and its replacement by internationalization, especially against the wishes of the people of Gaza themselves.

The Secretary-General got from Nasser an understanding not to try to reoccupy Sharm esh-Sheikh and to allow UNEF to stay there once the Israelis had left. He also established a doctrine about the UNEF security of tenure which he believed Nasser had accepted. This doctrine, endorsed in the UN Assembly resolution of 7 November, recognized that UNEF was in Egypt by Egyptian consent. At the same time, it laid down that questions affecting UNEF, such as changes in its disposition or its withdrawal, would be dealt with by an Advisory Committee (of Brazil, Canada, Ceylon, Columbia, India, Norway and Pakistan) under the chairmanship of the Secretary-General. This committee could refer urgent matters to the General Assembly. The Israelis interpreted this procedure as being meant, in Ben Gurion's words, 'to ensure that no lasting step was taken which might provoke hostilities'. (In the negotiations with Hammarskjöld, Fawzi urged that

242   The Egyptian Revolution

UNEF should be placed on both sides of the armistice demarcation lines, but Israel refused to have UNEF troops on her side.) Hammarskjöld confirmed in reply to questions from Eban on 26 February that this procedure of consultation would be followed before any withdrawal of UNEF from Sharm esh-Sheikh.* Four days earlier Hammarskjöld had stated 'with confidence that it is the desire of the government of Egypt that the take-over of Gaza from the military and civilian control of Israel in the first instance would be exclusively by the UNEF'. The statement said Egypt was willing to cooperate in the stationing of UNEF on the Gaza armistice line to separate the Egyptian and Israeli armies and to help put 'a definite end to all incursions and raids across the border from either side'. Hammarskjöld added that there would be further arrangements during 'the period of transition' for good civilian administration, economic development and effective police protection. But in answer to another question from Eban on 26 February, as to whether these arrangements excluded Egypt's return to the Gaza Strip, Hammarskjöld said that nothing in the agreement limited Egypt's right under the armistice agreement (which gave her control of Gaza).

After further negotiations, the Israeli Foreign Minister, Mrs Golda Meir, announced in the UN Assembly on 1 March that Israel would withdraw from the Gaza Strip and Sharm esh-Sheikh in accordance with UN resolutions, but on the basis of certain assumptions. She assumed that the United States, in accordance with its memorandum of 11 February, would support and assert the right of free and innocent passage through the Gulf of Aqaba, and that UNEF would be stationed at Sharm esh-Sheikh and not withdrawn before the Secretary-General had consulted his Advisory Committee. She also assumed that UNEF would take over exclusive military and civil control in the Gaza Strip and maintain it until a definite agreement on the future of the Strip had been worked out. She reserved Israel's freedom to defend her rights if the Gaza Strip reverted to its previous condition. The United States delegate endorsed the Israeli assump-

*The question of UNEF's status in Egypt which became a crucial and controversial issue in the events leading up to the 1957 Arab–Israel war, is dealt with in a note to Chapter 17 on pages 471–2.

tions, but Mahmoud Fawzi for Egypt insisted that the Israeli withdrawal must be considered as unconditional and that the rights of Egypt and the Arab people in the Gaza Strip could not be affected. These differences were to come to the surface when the Israelis moved out of the Gaza Strip on 7 March and UNEF took over. There were demonstrations by the local Arab population and by the refugees demanding the return of the Egyptians. UNEF troops had to use tear-gas and fire over the heads of the crowds. The demonstrations had Egyptian encouragement, though, in the view of General Burns, the UNEF commander, they probably also reflected the wishes of most of the Arabs in the Strip. Hammarskjöld had anticipated that UNEF might remain in full control of the Strip for about a fortnight while more permanent arrangements for some kind of joint control with Egypt were worked out. This seemed to be his interpretation of his 'understanding' with Nasser. He was therefore shocked to hear three days after the UNEF take-over that Nasser had announced the appointment of an Egyptian Administrative Governor for the Gaza Strip who would be taking over his duties immediately. Nasser's insistence on this step, which led to the re-establishment of full Egyptian civil control of the Gaza Strip, while UNEF remained on the borders, aroused Israeli anger and threats to reoccupy the Strip. These eventually subsided, but Nasser's action left behind the belief that he had broken his word to Hammarskjöld and further damaged his reputation in Washington. In his memoirs, Eisenhower, commented wrathfully, 'Colonel Nasser, who had remained in power only through the restraint of the West, failed to seize this opportunity for true statesmanship, thereby depriving his country of the assistance and cooperation of all self-respecting Governments.'[76]

Had Nasser broken his word? The verdict of General Burns, who was in a favourable position to judge, is that if Nasser did go back on his word it was only in the timing and not the substance of his action. Nasser and Hammarskjöld had agreed on exclusive UNEF control only 'in the first instance'. At no time did the Secretary-General or the Egyptian government promise that no Egyptian administrators or military personnel would reenter the Strip. As regards arrangements after 'the first instance', for which Hammarskjöld envisaged shared control, Burns disclosed in his memoirs, 'Later information came to us that President Nasser had disagreed with the wording of the latter half of Secretary General's statement of February 22 ... and had told Fawzi he could not accept it. But this rejection by the President never reached the Secretary General.'[77]

On 8 March, Israeli forces withdrew from Sharm esh-Sheikh and were replaced by UNEF troops. The same day Nasser allowed the UN to start lifting the last two blockships in the Canal, and the Syrian government let the IPC begin repairing its pipeline. The first convoy went through the Canal on 29 March and ten days later the Canal was declared open to the biggest ships. But continued negotiations with Nasser, first through Hammarskjöld and then through the United States, had failed to produce an agreement on the operation of the Canal. The British had tried at first to resume the negotiations where they had been left in mid-October, after the Security Council meeting and the accompanying private talks. But Nasser was now in a stronger position. He was less prepared to make concessions, particularly as after the Anglo-French attack they would not have been understood by the Egyptian public. On 24 March Egypt made a unilateral declaration on the future of the Canal. It reaffirmed that the Canal would be operated by the Egyptian Suez Canal Authority which would have financial autonomy; that tolls must henceforth be paid to this Authority; that the old company would receive compensation and that Egypt guaranteed freedom of passage under the 1888 Convention. All Nasser's former concessions to international participation in such matters as fixing tolls and ensuring maintenance and development had now gone by the board.

At first the British government tried to organize a boycott of the Canal and advised British ship-owners to avoid transit through it. But a month later this advice was withdrawn. On 28 March the Security Council adopted an American resolution saying that the Egyptian declaration on the Canal should be given a trial, although it did not conform with the 'Six Principles' that the Council had laid down the previous October. When the

Council met again to discuss the Canal at French request on 15 May, the debate was adjourned *sine die* five days later. Negotiations on compensation for the Canal Company dragged on much longer. They became linked with Egyptian, British and French financial claims and counter-claims arising out of war damage; the freezing of Egyptian assets and the Egyptian sequestration of British and French property; and compensation for the seizure of the Canal base installations.

One of the most important consequences of the Suez–Sinai war was the destruction, full of personal human tragedy and of great social and economic significance to Egypt, of the foreign and Levantine predominance in Egyptian commercial life. In addition to the expulsion of some 2,700 British and French subjects, some 14,000 Jews – a third of Egypt's Jewish population – mostly of foreign nationality, but also some Egyptian citizens, were driven into exile by police harassment and economic pressure, leaving their property under sequestration or officially 'frozen'. Many of those with foreign passports were from families that had lived in Egypt for generations, having used their foreign nationality to enjoy the privileges of the 'Capitulations', of the consular courts and then the Mixed Courts.[78] Other 'foreigners', apart from Jews or British and French, began to leave during the first half of 1957, after the 'Egyptianization' of all foreign manufacturers and exporters and a decree making Arabic compulsory for all business transactions. In theory, 'Egyptianization' meant that non-Egyptians were replaced by Egyptian citizens in certain jobs and in control of businesses. In practice, whether Nasser intended it or not – and he often made declarations against religious or racial discrimination – 'Egyptianization' often meant a preference in jobs and influence for Egyptian Muslims.

The treatment of the Egyptian Jews was deplorable from every point of view, but it was no worse in total effect than the Israeli treatment of the Palestine Arabs, even in some respects of the Arabs still inside Israel. And it had taken place as a result of war. There was nothing in Egypt comparable with the massacre by the Israeli border police of forty-one Arab villagers – Israeli citizens – in the village of Kfar Kassim in Israel at the start of the Sinai campaign because they were breaking a curfew of which they had not been told. Some 'Egyptianization' of business was probably an inevitable part of the process of social and political change in Egypt. But by rushing the pace in the post-Suez mood of mixed anger, pride and fear, Nasser inflicted unnecessary hardship and Egypt lost, through the combination of 'Egyptianization' and the expulsions, both invaluable economic and technical know-how and some of the most liberal and intelligent members of her society.

In the war, Egypt had lost perhaps 3,000 dead (about 1,000 in Port Said, 1,000 in the Sinai battles and another 1,000 killed in the retreat by air attacks or from exposure and thirst in the desert). She had also lost large quantities of military equipment, but the story that she had lost in Sinai vast numbers of Russian tanks and planes which were being prepared to strike at Israel was largely political warfare fiction. General Dayan's account later showed that one of the main weaknesses of the Egyptian military dispositions in Sinai was their over-defensive character, while he listed the number of their Soviet-made armoured vehicles at twenty-seven T34 tanks (compared with fifty-two American-built Shermans), six SU100 self-propelled guns and sixty armoured troop carriers. Of the planes lost by the Egyptians over Sinai, four were Soviet-built Mig 15s and four British-built Vampires and Meteors.[79] It might well have been that the Egyptian army would one day attempt to fulfil the directive said by Israeli intelligence to have been given to the Egyptian Third Division in Sinai, namely 'the destruction and annihilation of Israel in the shortest possible time and in the most brutal and cruel of battles'.[80] But in October 1956 that day was clearly still far off.

Suez was a political and to a certain extent an economic victory for Nasser. It was the culminating point of modern Egyptian nationalism, making the Egyptians for the first time for seventy-five years fully masters of their own country. It enormously strengthened Nasser's position inside Egypt and encouraged him to engage more deeply in the 'Arab revolution' against the remains of Western imperialism and its allies in the Arab world. It ended the period of British paramountcy in the central area of the Arab Middle East and brought the United States and Russia face to face in that region where the Arabs themselves sought to 'fill the vacuum' between them. It accelerated the British 'retreat from empire' and hastened the process of de-colonization throughout the world and especially in Africa. It was a demonstration of the determination of under-developed countries to be independent and develop their economies, as well as of their unsuspected technical ability to do so, if given financial help.

Nasser himself said he thought that Suez not only gave confidence to the Egyptians and Arabs as a whole but also 'helped many of the African countries to be sure of themselves and insist about their independence'. Historically, he said, 'The meaning of Suez is that there is an end to the methods of the nineteenth century, that it was impossible to use the methods of the nineteenth century in the twentieth century.'[81]

But the result of Nasser's great gamble also had a darker side. While it may have increased the self-confidence of the Arab and Afro-Asian countries, it also introduced a dangerous lack of confidence into the West's future economic relations with them, and into the political relations of the Western Powers and the Arab states. It was only a month or two after the last Israeli, British and French soldiers had left Egyptian territory that these suspicions once more burst out into an international crisis in the Middle East.

Part Two

The Arab Revolution

Chapter 8
Filling the Vacuum:
The Struggle with America, 1957–8

Nasser emerged from the Suez crisis as the dominant leader in the Arab world. As a political nationalist movement, the Egyptian revolution which had begun in 1919 reached its climax with Suez. Henceforward, its emphasis in Egypt was on social and economic change. Its nationalist aspects merged into the broader nationalism of the 'Arab Revolution', the movement for the transformation of all the Arab countries into independent, modernized states and eventually into a unified 'Arab Nation', and into the even wider anti-colonial revolution of the non-aligned and underdeveloped countries.

This closer linking of the Egyptian and Arab revolutions was a result partly of Nasser's deliberate choice and partly of circumstances. Egypt's domestic needs and the demands of the Arab movement were to be often in conflict. Support for Arab policies, such as the confrontation with Israel and the revolution and war in the Yemen which began in 1962, were a diversion of Egyptian energies and resources from construction at home. At the same time Nasser's engagement in Arab affairs was dictated not only by his personal vision of anti-imperialist liberation but also by his view of Egypt's domestic as well as her foreign interests. For if Egypt's economic development were to be able to keep ahead of her rapid population growth she needed substantial foreign economic aid. Nasser concluded that the amount of aid Egypt might get from Russia or the West was likely to be proportionate to her international importance, as a potential ally to be encouraged or a possible enemy to be appeased. As a leading country in the Arab world, in Africa and the non-aligned group of nations, all three spheres in which the two super-Powers were now beginning more seriously to compete, Egypt could turn her foreign policy into an important economic asset (as Mohammed Hassanein Heykal, the editor of *Al Ahram* and often Nasser's spokesman, described it).[1] If Egypt were to be isolated politically from the Arab world, as Nasser had feared was the object of the

Western Powers from the Baghdad Pact onwards, she would simply be left to rot economically and to face the military power of Israel alone and without modern arms.

Suez brought Egypt and the other Arab countries closer together in two ways. It confirmed Nasser's belief that Arab solidarity was an indispensable part of Egyptian security, not only for defence against Israel but also because of the deterrent effect on the West of Arab control of oil-fields and pipelines. (It also perhaps gave him an exaggerated idea of the value of Arab unity as a decisive military asset against Israel). The sympathies aroused by Suez and the admiration for Nasser's success in handling the crisis had created a new emotional bond between Egyptians and other Arabs, especially in Syria.

Nasser himself was also encouraged by his Suez success to seek a more ambitious Arab role. He now saw himself as the leader on the international stage of a group of countries with a great history and strong ties of language, culture and religion who now occupied a strategically important region in which a large part of the world's oil supplies were located. To aspire to lead the mobilization of this potential for the renovation of Arab society was not an ignoble ambition. For a basically weak country like Egypt, however, it entailed many dangers, especially in view of the turbulent political state of most of the Arab countries. Yet it was partly the very weakness and instability of the other Arab states which led Nasser into an increasingly active Arab policy. His motive was not simply to increase Egypt's own influence. It was also to forestall the Americans and the Russians moving into the Arab East as the British moved out, and so prevent the Arab states from falling once more into the spheres of influence of Great Powers whose rivalries might turn the Middle East into a theatre of nuclear war.

The pursuit of the 'Arab Revolution' in the Arab East was to draw Nasser inevitably into conflict with those forces against which the revolution was directed: the remains of Western, especially British, imperialism in the area; Israel; and those Arab governments or groups which were upholders of the *status quo* in terms of political geography, social privilege or international alignment. In the Arab West, the Maghreb, Nasser's commitment to the Algerian nationalists brought continued conflict with France. Eventually, as the Algerian movement developed along Arab revolutionary lines, it also meant hostility with President Bourguiba of Tunisia and the Moroccan monarchy who leaned towards the West.

But Nasser was also to find himself pitted against potential rival leaders of the Arab Revolution, such as the Communists and above all the pan-Arab Socialist Baath (Renaissance) party whose origins were in Syria, the ideological centre of 'Arabism'. For, like the Egyptian revolution, the Arab movement became increasingly an amalgam of nationalist and social, sometimes socialist, ideas. The emphasis was at first on national independence and unity, on the liberation of a single 'Arab nation' that had been artificially divided. But increasingly the stress changed to questions of social change and economic development. While the Communists made little headway in the organization of political power, the social and economic thinking of Arab revolutionaries was increasingly influenced by Marxist ideas, especially of a Yugoslav Titoist kind. At the same time, the struggle with the West in those parts of the Arab world where the Western Powers still sought to hold traditional positions meant that the neutralism of the Arab revolutionaries was tactically modified to make use of Russian support.

Nasser's engagement in the 'Arab Revolution' in the ten years after Suez passed through two distinct phases. What might be called the phase of 'Arab nationalism' lasted from 1957–61. It was followed by the phase of 'Arab Socialism' until in 1967 the third Arab–Israeli war created a new situation for Egypt and the Arabs. In Egypt's international relations this decade included two climactic moments of triumph and disaster: the short-lived but historic merger of Egypt and Syria into the United Arab Republic; and the Arab defeat by Israel in 1967. But for Nasser the dominant theme was still the social revolution in Egypt itself. After the break with Syria he found a theoretical means of reconciling this priority with continued attachment to the Arab revolution – this was the idea of 'Arab Socialism', a new approach to Arab unity: instead of Arab unity being considered the prerequisite for the end of dependence and backwardness, the reverse was proclaimed. There could be real unity only between already liberated Arab states. The promotion of Arab unity entailed therefore both Egypt's own socialist development and the encouragement of 'liberation' movements in other Arab countries. Nasser's 'Arab Socialism' produced at least two results which may be lasting: the accelerated decolonization and radicalization of the Arab world; and increased industrialization and a planned economy in Egypt itself.

*

At first, however, as in 1955, the pace of Nasser's commitment to the Arab revolution was forced by others. As the Suez crisis passed, the temporary international alignments it had fostered began to break up. Old feuds began to reappear. Now that the British had lost their paramountcy in the area, except on the fringes of the Arabian peninsula, the pressures to establish alliances, bases or ideological allegiances came from the United States and Russia. Though Nasser was a hero with the Arab masses, other Arab governments began again to voice their opposition to Egyptian leadership and to Nasser's policy of militant 'positive neutrality', an opposition they had had to stifle while Egypt was being attacked by Britain, France and Israel. They were encouraged to do so by the new policy of the United States who rushed to reassure Britain, France and her Baghdad Pact allies of her continued support and Russia of her vigilant opposition.

The American role in the Suez affair had obscured the fact that it was an American act of cold war policy which had triggered off the crisis. The withdrawal of the High Dam offer had been intended in part at least as the first step towards curbing the influence of Nasser as a neutralist leader who had taken aid from Russia and who appeared to Washington to be helping the spread of Soviet influence in the Middle East at the expense of the West. Eisenhower had disapproved of the use of force against Egypt, especially in the internationally unfavourable context of Suez, but in his correspondence with Anthony Eden he had shared at least partially the British prime minister's fears about Soviet penetration of the Middle East and Nasser's role. He saw this as a continuing problem after a settlement of the Suez Canal dispute and was prepared to put other pressures on Nasser, such as economic measures and the encouragement of Arab rivalries.[2]

On the first day of 1957, Eisenhower told Congressional leaders that 'the existing vacuum in the Middle East must be filled by the United States before it is filled by Russia'. Henceforward the idea of 'filling the vacuum' left by British withdrawal was to dominate Washington's Middle East policies. The 'Eisenhower Doctrine' for the Middle East, set out in an address by the President to Congress on 5 January 1957, covered two main points. It proposed US cooperation with Middle Eastern states to build up their economic strength and thus their political independence. For this purpose it requested aid funds up to $200 million yearly. More significantly, it asked Congress to authorize the President to use American armed forces 'to secure and protect the territorial integrity and political independence of nations desiring and requesting aid, against overt armed aggression from any nation controlled by International Communism'.

Two months later the Doctrine had been approved by Congress and became law on 9 March. Eisenhower later wrote in words which closely echoed Eden's Suez nightmares,

> We had effectively obtained the consent of the Congress in proclaiming the administration's resolve to block the Soviet Union's march to the Mediterranean, to the Suez Canal and the pipelines, and to the underground lakes of oil which fuel the homes and factories of Western Europe.[3]

Eisenhower rejected Soviet proposals repeated by Marshal Bulganin in three letters in 1957 for an understanding on the Middle East based on a declaration against intervention by force, the withdrawal of all foreign troops and bases and control of arms deliveries. In its formulation the Eisenhower Doctrine tried to avoid some of the mistakes made in creating the Baghdad Pact and in the Suez crisis. It did not try to press more Arab countries into new military alliances. It did not propose military intervention in any country unless that country 'desired and deserved' such help. Intervention was supposed to be limited to the case of attack by 'International Communism' or any country controlled by it, thus by implication excluding the case of conflicts arising out of local rivalries.

Though Eisenhower had shown a better understanding than Eden of the repercussions in the Arab world of the Anglo-French military action against Egypt, he shared with other Western leaders a grossly over-simplified view of the relations between Nasser and Russia. He and Dulles failed to recognize the important differences between the Communists and radical nationalists such as the Nasserites or Baathists. They misunderstood the extent to which inter-Arab conflicts were a symptom of local power struggles and internal social change rather than of commitments in the East–West cold war: they did not appreciate the extent to which anti-Communism was a useful invocation for Arab rulers seeking Western support against their local opponents.

While the Eisenhower Doctrine tolerated neutrals in the sense of not requiring an open military commitment to the West, it still demanded from them an un-neutral open commitment against Russia – or against 'International Communism' which everyone took to mean the same thing. But in thus making the Doctrine acceptable to the American public and Congress, Washington also made it unsaleable to most Arab nationalist opinion. As a general warning against open Soviet military aggression in the Arab East, the Doctrine may be claimed as having in the long run had an important effect in stabilizing the world balance of power. As an instrument to limit the growth of indirect Soviet and Communist influence, it was as ill-timed and counter-productive as the Baghdad Pact. As Nehru had warned Eisenhower, it raised tensions in the Middle East instead of lowering them.[4] It sharpened inter-Arab disputes of a largely internal character, such as the communal tensions between Christians and Muslims in the Lebanon, between pro-Egyptian Arab nationalists and the Hashemite kings in Iraq and Jordan, and between radicals and conservatives in Syria. It added a new division in setting Egypt and Saudi Arabia, formerly allies, at loggerheads. Its effect was to divide and weaken the Arab East and provide more openings for Communist penetration, when its ostensible aim was to stabilize and strengthen the Arab states against Russian pressure.

Whatever the view of some Arab governments may have been, Arab public opinion by and large was at that time as a result of Suez emotionally pro-Russian without being pro-Communist, like British opinion in the later years of the Second World War. Moreover, although American help in the Suez crisis had been gratefully recognized, the United States was still freezing Egyptian funds and Egypt was having to rely on Soviet wheat and oil shipments to beat the Western economic blockade.

It was in any case too late to try to exclude Russia entirely from Middle East affairs. She had already become a Middle East power with clients – though not satellites – in Egypt and Syria. At first, Soviet diplomacy, unburdened by considerations of domestic public opinion, showed itself more able than the Americans to adapt itself to the mood of Arab nationalism. But when, after the merger of Syria and Egypt and the revolution in Iraq, the Russians appeared to be interfering in Arab politics to support the local Communist parties, they were met with a rebuke from Nasser as defiant in some respects as any of his attacks on Western interference. The irony of the situation is that if Washington had been able to keep quiet about 'International Communism' when Eisenhower proclaimed his doctrine, it would have found less than two years later that Nasser, whom it saw as Russia's instrument, was denouncing 'International Communism' in the Arab world in terms more virulent than Washington's own. Indeed, an almost absurd state of cross-purposes developed even earlier. Within a year of Nasser's denunciation of the Eisenhower Doctrine, he himself rushed into union with Syria to block Communist influence there, only to see a few months later the landing of American forces in the Lebanon to protect it from an alleged threat from the UAR presumed to be instigated by 'International Communism'. It became clear that the Arabs were best left to deal with their internal Communist problem themselves.

Nasser was opposed from the start to the 'vacuum' theory which lay at the basis of the Eisenhower Doctrine, though his opposition was at first somewhat muted by his need of American pressure to secure Israel's withdrawal from the Gaza Strip and the Straits of Tiran. In Nasser's view there was no 'vacuum' in the Middle East. It was an area filled by Arabs who would defend their independence against East and West, given arms and money, and whose neutrality in the cold war was a necessity both for their own safety and for world peace. Nasser wanted neither an American sphere of influence nor Soviet Communism in the Middle East.

Events were soon to show how far Nasser was able to counter the influence of America and Russia with his own. They proved that while his influence was strong enough to prevent the formation of any large rival or hostile bloc against him in the Middle East, Egypt was also too weak to impose her political will on all the Arab Asian states together or on Israel. This equation, in which the key factors were Syria and Israel, was to hold good throughout the next ten years of the Arab Revolution.

Seen by Nasser from Cairo, the Eisenhower Doctrine was an obvious attempt to isolate Egypt. It was clearly not addressed to Iraq, Iran or Turkey which were already linked with the West through the Baghdad Pact and American military agreements. The Americans must have known that Nasser was in no position at that time to make a public declaration against 'International Communism' which might cost him Soviet support. It could, therefore, only be intended, Nasser reasoned, to wean away from him his then Arab allies, Syria, Jordan and Saudi Arabia, and the uncommitted Lebanon. It was the continuation by more subtle means of the policy of Suez, to destroy Egypt's leadership of Arab nationalism.

This suspicion was strengthened when Eisenhower chose King Saud as the first salesman of his Doctrine to the Arab world. The American administration 'wanted to explore the possibilities of building up King Saud as a counter-weight to Nasser'.[5] The choice was not altogether surprising in view of America's long connexion with Saudi Arabia through the oil business. But it showed little awareness of the new political forces in the Arab countries.

Saud was at first a reluctant emissary. He complained more of Israel and the British than he did of the Russians and told Eisenhower that reports of Nasser's and the Syrian President Kuwatly's leanings towards Russia were exaggerated. They had both told Saud that if the Russians tried to interfere in their internal affairs, they would at once break off all dealings with Moscow.[6]

On Saud's return from Washington, in February, he met Nasser, Kuwatly and King Hussein of Jordan in Cairo. The communiqué after this summit conference showed signs of disunity. It did not mention the Eisenhower Doctrine by name but rejected any idea of a 'vacuum' in the Middle East and approved of 'active neutrality'. On 12 March, Eisenhower sent a special envoy, James P. Richards, a Democratic Congressman, on a tour of Middle East capitals to canvass support for the Doctrine. It was scarcely a profitable journey. The Lebanese government under President Chamoun was the only Arab government in the Middle East to give unqualified public acceptance to the Doctrine, a departure in Lebanese policy the rashness of which was to be a source of much later trouble.

The American diplomatic offensive nevertheless soon put a serious strain on Nasser's four-power alliance. The most sensitive point was Jordan. King Hussein had begun to have second thoughts about the policy of swimming with the radical nationalist tide that he had pursued since his dismissal of General Glubb a year before. The parliamentary elections of October 1956, recognized as genuine by informed foreign observers, had brought into power a coalition of moderate Arab nationalists and left-wingers, headed by the leader of the former, Suleiman Nabulsi.[7] The Nabulsi government rested on a parliamentary coalition which included eleven National Socialists (Nabulsi's party), two Baathists and three Communists or fellow-travellers under the label of 'National Bloc'. Its aims were to abrogate the Anglo-Jordan treaty by negotiation, to follow the Nasser policy of non-alignment and establish closer ties with Egypt and Syria, 'with due regard for Jordan's material interests'.[8] This entailed also adopting a less hostile attitude to the Soviet Union.

In mid-January Nasser agreed with Syria and Saudi Arabia to pay Jordan £12,500,000 a year between them to replace the British subsidy to the Jordan army when the Anglo-Jordan treaty came to an end. Negotiations to end the treaty were completed on 13 March 1957, thus terminating within six months the British military presence, the British subsidy and also the British defence guarantee of Jordan's frontiers.

But King Hussein had already begun to try to reverse the trend of the Nabulsi government's policy. He feared it would not only increase Soviet influence in Jordan but also end in the disappearance of his kingdom, absorbed or partitioned by one or more of his Arab allies. He therefore sought a new life-line with the West through the United States.

It was hard to challenge the elected Jordan government on the grounds of its pan-Arab views for these had wide popular support in the country. Softness to Communism and Russia was a safer charge at home and more attractive in Washington. On 31 January, Hussein wrote – and immediately published – a letter to his prime minister, Nabulsi, warning him against tolerating the growth of Communist influence in the country. He cited such perilous innovations as allowing the Soviet news agency to operate and Soviet films to be shown, as well as the discussion by the government of establishing diplomatic relations with Moscow and possibly Peking. (Arab nationalists were not slow to point out that all these activities had been freely indulged in by Western governments and most of their anti-Communist allies for years past.)

The crisis between Hussein and the government over the control of foreign policy began to come to a head in April. Each side tried to ensure support from the army. But the army was split politically. A nucleus of Arab nationalist officers headed by the chief of staff, Major General Ali Abu Nawar, a Baathist sympathizer, backed the government. The rest of the officers and many of the NCOs and rank-and-file, especially from the mainly Bedouin units, were loyal to the person of Hussein. On 10 April Hussein dismissed Nabulsi. The nationalist officers gave a warning that they could not be responsible for the explosive situation in the army and the country unless the new government was acceptable to all parties. Hussein considered this 'an insolent ultimatum': officers and NCOs loyal to him mutinied at their encampment at Zerka against what they believed to be plans for a *coup* against the king by their nationalist commanders. Their march on Amman to support Hussein was blocked by artillery units under nationalist officers. Hussein himself intervened with courage and decision to stop the fighting and gain complete control of the army. He exiled Abu Nawar and other suspect officers, imposed martial law and imprisoned hundreds of nationalist supporters of the former government. Hussein himself, in his autobiography, has described these events as simply the defeat of a plot by disloyal army officers and radical politicians, encouraged and financed by Egypt, Syria and Russia.[9] The plot, he claims, was to force him to abdicate, to declare a republic and to join a pro-Communist front with Nasser and the Syrians. The losing side and their apologists have seen the affair as a *coup* planned by Hussein himself to smash the radical nationalists, discredit Nasser and gain American support and financial aid. The confused sequence of military movements during the crisis suggests that there were no clear plans on either side for a *coup* or a counter-*coup* with agreed objectives.

The Jordan crisis nevertheless had all the ingredients of the cold war which was beginning to develop in the Arab East between Nasser and the United States and its Middle East allies, with Russia occasionally making warning noises off-stage. Secret services were active; money flowed freely for 'subversion' or 'counter-subversion'; radio stations, secret and public, poured out propaganda and incitement. The American Sixth Fleet periodically moved into diplomatically demonstrative positions. In the West a great deal was heard of Nasser's side of this underground war; the ferocious campaigns of Cairo radio's 'Voice of the Arabs', the suborning of Arab newspapers, the alleged assassination attempts against Arab leaders, the plotting among Arab army officers and the cloak-and-dagger activities of Egyptian military attachés in Arab capitals. The Western public heard little of the battery of radio stations – eventually numbering eleven, according to Nasser, and some of them Western-organized – conducting propaganda against Egypt and its allies; of the money spent by Iraq and later Saudi Arabia in press bribery, of the alleged attempts to buy the assassination of Nasser (the most famous was the bribe of £2 million said to have been offered by King Saud to the head of Syrian military intelligence, Colonel Abdul Hamid Sarraj – and refused, to public wonder – to arrange Nasser's assassination during an aeroplane flight), or of the plotting encouraged from Iraq and, it was alleged, by American agents, for the overthrow of the Syrian regime.

Hussein's crushing of the Arab nationalist leadership in Jordan has been described as 'the first major setback for Nasirism in Arab Asia'.[10] It meant the break-up of Nasser's Arab alliance – at least with two of the governments concerned– and a gain for America's new Middle East policy. King Saud supported Hussein and the United States declared Jordan's independence to be a vital American interest. US Sixth Fleet units were moved to the eastern Mediterranean and Hussein was paid $10 million as an immediate first instalment of American aid. The promptness with which a great democratic republic hurried to reward a king who had overthrown a popularly elected government was mildly shocking even to those used to the more discreet traditions of eastern venality.

But the Jordan affair was something of a pyrrhic victory for the West and its Arab allies, except for Hussein himself. For it set in train a fierce struggle for power in Syria, the Lebanon and Iraq. In little over a year this conflict destroyed the pro-Western elements in Syria and brought that country into complete union with Egypt, overthrew President Chamoun's pro-American government and policy in the Lebanon, swept away the Iraqi monarchy and wrecked the Baghdad Pact. Both Nasser and the Russians strengthened their positions – to such an extent that their rivalry eventually replaced for a time the conflict between Nasser and the United States. The fact that Jordan remained under Hussein and protected by a vague Western defence umbrella may not have been altogether unwelcome to Nasser. Jordan was desperately poor; the defence of its long frontier with Israel was a heavy military responsibility; and any attempt to merge Jordan politically with Syria or Egypt risked bringing about a threatened Israeli seizure of the west bank. From Nasser's point of view there was much to be said for having a useful influence in Jordan through the pro-Egyptian sentiments of the Palestinians there, especially the refugees, while leaving the unpopular responsibility for maintaining the international *status quo* to King Hussein.

During May 1957 the propaganda war between Nasser and his Syrian allies on the one hand and the pro-US Arab governments on the other came out into the open. It found a new focus in the Lebanon. Parliamentary elections there resulted in a massive victory for supporters of President Chamoun and his pro-American policy against the opposition led by the United National Front. The Front had been formed of those who were against Chamoun either because of his foreign policy or because they suspected he was planning to seek election for a second term as president – which would have required a change in the constitution. The opponents of his foreign policy were not confined to supporters of Nasserist Arab nationalism. They included those who believed that in taking sides with America Chamoun was endangering the National Pact, the basis of Lebanese national unity. The essence of the Pact was two-fold: first, the Lebanese Christians recognized that the Lebanon was part of the Arab world on condition that it retained a special independence and neutrality and was not forced into an Arab union or to take sides in Arab disputes. Second, the Lebanese Muslims recognized Lebanon's cultural links with the West and its special position provided this did not involve policies hostile to the rest of the Arab world.

The unprecedented scale of the Chamounists' electoral victory aroused legitimate suspicion that their control of the administrative machine and local security forces had been decisive. President Chamoun's adherence to the Eisenhower Doctrine had already shaken the basis of compromise on which Lebanese politics rested: the elections were a further heavy blow to the whole structure. They forced the opposition more and more into extra-parliamentary methods and increased the reliance of both President Chamoun and his opponents on support from outside the country. The seeds of civil war were thus sown.

The struggle for Syria itself followed swiftly and inevitably after the changes in Jordan and Lebanon. It was a more complex affair and far more important to Nasser. With the defection of Jordan and Saudi Arabia from the Arab alliance and with the pro-Western alignment of Iraq and Turkey and the Chamoun government in the Lebanon, Syria's ruling coalition of neutralists, nationalists and left-wingers felt itself isolated and threatened on all sides. Earlier in the year it had attempted to cow the remaining Syrian advocates of an alliance with Iraq and the West, the leaders of the People's Party, by means of an elaborate conspiracy trial. But the country and the army were still sufficiently divided to make a civil war a possibility if outside pressures increased. For support against Western pressure the regime looked to Egypt and to Russia. The coalition was itself divided about whether Cairo or Moscow should be the main source of help. This division was not primarily one of foreign policy or ideology – except in the case of the Communists – but of internal rivalry. The pro-Moscow group was led by the Syrian Defence Minister, Khaled el Azm. He was a millionaire member of an ancient Syrian family, a man of high intelligence and intense ambition whose lukewarm nationalism under French rule had left him with few ready nationalist allies. The pro-Moscow group included the small but active Syrian Communist party led by an able Kurd, Khaled Bagdash.

Those who looked mainly to Cairo were the pan-Arab Socialist Baath party, then the chief radical driving-force in Syrian politics, and a section of the old nationalist conservatives headed by the President Shukri el-Kuwatly and the prime minister, Sabri el Asaly. But the radicals and conservatives in this pro-Egyptian wing were divided over domestic policy in Syria, and were themselves struggling for control of the army. In the course of this struggle the Syrian commander-in-chief, General Nizam ed-din, a man of the centre, was replaced by a leftist, Colonel Aziz el Bizry. Bizry was appointed not because he was a Communist sympathizer but because he was not committed to any of the main factions in the army leadership, either the Baath or the conservatives.[11] His appointment was, however, one of several other developments which together alarmed the American administration – and later also Nasser – into the belief that Syria was rapidly sliding into the Communist camp. On 6 August, Khaled el Azm signed an extensive economic and technical aid agreement with the Russians in Moscow. A week later the Syrian government expelled three American diplomats whom it accused of plotting to overthrow the regime. American anxiety was fed by alarmist and unfounded stories of secret Soviet air bases and even volunteers in Syria. These mostly emanated from Arab sources in Beirut and Baghdad who wanted American backing in a campaign to bring down the Syrian regime, and to check the influence of Nasserism.

Syrian opinion, stimulated by the Baathists, by Nasser and by America's own pressures, was anti-American and pro-Russian. But it was still largely and essentially Arab nationalist and neutralist. The Syrian Communists were not strong enough to take over and convert Syria into a satellite. Nor would the Russians have been in a position to give them effective military backing if they had tried to do so. It is improbable that the Russians would have risked such an operation. It would have involved not only staving off a possible Western intervention but also alienating Egypt where they had made important diplomatic gains.

During August, September and October 1957 an international crisis rapidly blew up around Syria and almost as quickly subsided, like a summer storm. Washington sent a special envoy, Loy Henderson, a senior diplomat and Middle East specialist, to consult in Ankara with Turkish and Iraqi leaders and with King Hussein of Jordan. He also went to Beirut to see President Chamoun. He did not go to Syria but reported to Washington the 'deep concern' of Syria's neighbours that she might become a base for 'international Communism', the significant phrase that could trigger off American intervention under the Eisenhower Doctrine. Syria and Russia accused the United States of mounting a plot to intervene in Syria. This allegation was given more precision a year later when notes said to have been taken at the meeting with Henderson in Turkey were read at the trial in Baghdad of the former Iraqi Foreign Minister, Ahmed Mukhtar Baban. Henderson was then said to have urged the Arab states to take action against Syria, with an assurance of Turkish support and with the deterrent of the US Sixth Fleet in the background.[12]

President Eisenhower in his memoirs fully confirms that there was a 'plot' between the United States and its Middle East allies to intervene in Syria and overthrow the Damascus regime.[13]

His account also shows that the plot was conceived in melodrama and ignorance, conducted in muddle, and that it expired on a note of farce. Yet on this basis Eisenhower was ready to face what he thought might be the risk of world nuclear war.

For Eisenhower, 'one clear fact was emerging' – 'Syria's neighbours, including her fellow Arab nations, had come to the conclusion that the present regime in Syria had to go: otherwise the take-over by the Communists would soon be complete. A strong Soviet outpost would be in existence amidst this formerly neutral region.'[14]

As in the case of the Baghdad Pact, it was the bellicose Turkish premier Menderes, seconded by Iraq, who took the lead. Supported also by Chamoun in the Lebanon and Hussein of Jordan, he pressed the United States for direct military action before Syria could sign a defence treaty with Russia and become an 'official Communist satellite'. In principle, to assuage any tenderness of conscience in Washington, there was to be no attack until Syria had actually 'committed aggression' against her neighbours and provoked retaliation. But Eisenhower was uneasily aware that pretexts for intervention were only too easy to come by in the Middle East. The plan suggested to the United States was for Turkey, Lebanon and Jordan to mass troops on their borders with Syria so as to disperse the Syrian forces and facilitate Iraqi military intervention from the East. America promised to back the plot by expediting deliveries and stopping any outside interference, for example from Russia or Israel, on condition that the operations were confined to the overthrow of the Syrian regime and there was no permanent occupation of Syrian territory.[15] Harold Macmillan, consulted in London, urged on the affair with a comparison between Syria and Czechoslovakia in 1948. The US Sixth Fleet was sent to the eastern Mediterranean to warn off the Russians. There is something appalling about the almost casual way that Eisenhower was prepared to risk a major war in an ill-judged entry into a Levantine imbroglio.

> If Syrian aggression [he wrote], should provoke a military reaction by Iraq and a difficult campaign should bring the Turks to Iraq's aid, the Soviets might very well take this occasion to move against Turkey.

Should that happen, a much larger war would be almost upon us. The alternative, however – to do nothing and lose the whole Middle East to Communism – would be worse.[16]

From this risk, as reckless and misconceived in its way as Eden's at Suez and Khrushchev's in Cuba, Eisenhower was fortunately saved by the fecklessness or the belated prudence of his Arab allies. The Iraqis began to have second thoughts about their role – not through fear of nuclear war but because they might lose their pipelines and oil revenues. They wanted the Turks to act first. King Hussein went off to Italy on holiday. King Saud bewildered Eisenhower by blaming America for the crisis and talking about Israel and the Gulf of Aqaba instead of the dangers of a Communist Syria. The Turks were still eager for action and President Chamoun was asking for American protection, but without an Arab cover for the intervention the United States was obliged to restrain the Turks.[17] The atmosphere of crisis built up on a slender foundation gave the Russians an excellent opportunity to appear as champions of Syrian independence at little risk to themselves at the moment when in fact the plot had already collapsed. The Soviet premier, Khrushchev, warned Turkey against military intervention in Syria and Moscow once more proposed a Four-Power Declaration against the use of force in the Middle East.

The crisis began to peter out as the recriminations were transferred inconclusively to the United Nations and Saudi Arabia, Iraq and Jordan tried hurriedly to disengage. Eisenhower himself sounded the end of the crisis with an admission that Syria's neighbours now had less cause for alarm. This tactical retreat had become all the more necessary because it was clear that the Syrian regime, while glad of Russian backing, was moving much closer to Nasser. The Western pressures on Syria were producing almost exactly the opposite of what they were meant to achieve. They were further weakening the pro-Western and pro-Iraqi elements in Syria. They were also pressing Syria further into Nasser's arms instead of detaching her from Cairo.

Nasser had watched the progress of Western diplomacy since Suez with mounting anxiety. Hussein's 'coup' in Jordan, the cooling-off of King Saud, the rigging of the Lebanese elections to keep a pro-American government in power, and now the Syrian crisis seemed to confirm his suspicions that although the ultimate aim of the Eisenhower Doctrine might have been the containment of Russia the Americans believed the first step in this direction was to isolate Egypt. The defections of Hussein and Saud were setbacks for Nasser but not decisive. But the loss of Syria to the pro-American camp was a development Nasser would try to prevent even at the risk of plunging deeper into the notorious quicksands of Syrian politics.

The political life of Syria had undergone a progressive fragmentation since the country achieved independence after the Second World War, a process accelerated by the entry of the Syrian army into politics after the Palestine defeat. Syria had neither a closely integrated political structure nor a clear sense of national identity. Its national boundaries had been artificially created as a result of the settlement after the First World War and of subsequent truncations by the French mandatory power. The country was really a cluster of city states, rather like those of Renaissance Italy, Damascus, Aleppo, Homs and Hama and their agricultural dependencies – plus the desert tribes and the minorities of the mountain regions. Above the level of family, city, tribe or religious community, the political and emotional loyalty of Syrians was less to a precarious Syrian national state then to a wider Arab community, of which Damascus, the capital of the first Arab Caliphs, was felt to be the historic heart.

Syrian views of the nature of this wider community varied. The older generation of nationalists who had led the fight for independence from France were drawn largely from the class of conservative notables, land-owners, wealthy merchants from Aleppo or Damascus, and some professional men. They preferred a loose form of Arab union in which the fruits of local power won in their own personal struggle were not entirely lost. Some saw this union in the form of a 'Greater Syria', the combination of those territories, now the states of Syria, Lebanon, Jordan and Israel, which had traditionally formed the geographical entity of Syria under Ottoman rule. Others looked to a closer link either with Iraq in a 'Fertile Crescent' union or with Egypt and Saudi Arabia. The choice of Iraq was influenced by the commercial interests of the merchants of Aleppo, the great northern commercial city, who formed the basis of the People's Party. Their opponents, the National Bloc, based chiefly on Damascus, favoured Egypt and Saudi Arabia partly because of their common opposition to the Hashemite monarchies. Revolutionary groups of middle-class intellectuals had risen to challenge the power of this older nationalist generation. They combined new concepts of Syria's international role with a greater interest in social and economic reform. For five years after the Palestine war and the first military *coup*, two of these groups fought for supremacy through control of the army and the state apparatus rather than through the parliamentary ballot. They were the Baath Socialists and the PPS, the Parti Populaire Syrien. The PPS was a right-wing, pro-American group. It had a pan-Syrian, rather than pan-Arab, vision of a Syrian state extending even farther than 'Greater Syria' to include parts of Iraq, Turkey and even Cyprus. It drew much support from the non-Sunni Muslims and non-Arab minorities. The Baath Socialist party saw Syria as merely one part of 'the Arab nation' which embraced all Arabic-speaking peoples from the Atlantic coast of Morocco to the Persian Gulf and from the Taurus mountains in the north to the borders of Ethiopia in the south. Both these groups had ideas of social reform and governmental economic intervention in place of the *laissez-faire* domestic policies of the traditional nationalists. The Baath had strengthened the socialist content of its programme through a merger with the Socialist party of Akram Haurani. The tough, opportunistic political realism of Haurani and his mass contacts, built on the poor peasants of the huge landed estates of the Hama region of central Syria, contrasted with the milder manners and almost mystical idealism of the founders of the Baath, two French-educated intellectuals, Michel Aflaq and Salah ed-din el Bitar. Aflaq, a gentle Christian Arab historian from Damascus, was the party's chief ideologist, and Bitar, a teacher of philosophy, its main organizer and tactician.

By 1954 the Baath Socialists had defeated the PPS in the struggle to be the chief driving-force behind the scenes in Syria. They had won in an alliance with a section of the old Nationalists and the Communists, all united first against outright military rule and then in opposition to Iraq and to Western military pacts. At this time the Baath was denouncing Nasser publicly as a pro-American military dictator who was suspected of keeping Egypt apart from the Arab struggle and preparing for a separate peace with Israel.

The Syrian Baath party was the only serious ideological rival to Nasser in the struggle to mobilize public opinion in most of the Arab world outside Egypt. Nasser's adoption of 'positive neutralism', his struggle to limit the extension of the Baghdad Pact and his Soviet arms deal transformed his rivalry with the Baath into a tactical alliance. A new element was thus introduced into Syrian politics. Nasser's own brand of Arab nationalism and his personal leadership became both a support for and an alternative to the Baath as a focus of popular feelings in Syria. In addition, the Baath's more conservative Nationalist allies saw Nasserite Egypt as a useful counter-weight to both the Baath and the Communists.

Nasser's ideas on Arab unity were later to appear almost indistinguishable from those of the Baath, particularly when he adopted a more socialist economic policy. They had, however, a different starting point and their different underlying character was constantly to reappear in Nasser's chequered relations with the Baath movement over the next decade. The difference was not unlike that between the ideas of European unity as developed by General de Gaulle and the idea of a supranational state embodying a resurrected historic 'European' community which inspired such original 'Europeans' as de Gasperi, Adenauer and Schuman. Nasser's primary interest in Arab unity was the creation of a common front to preserve the independence of Egypt and the Arab area against outside Powers. His secondary interest was to advance Egypt's economic development. The Arab world offered a wider market for the products of Egypt's industrialization. There were mutual benefits to be gained from a large regional economy, as in the case of the European Common Market, including the hope of obtaining investment funds from the Arab oil states. Unlike most other Arab states, Egypt had a strong sense of her own identity as a nation-state. It was natural for her to think in terms of unified action by a community of states rather than submersion into a supra-national union. Though Nasser had no scruples about appealing to the Arab peoples over the heads of their governments, his purpose at this stage at least was primarily to put pressure on these governments to accept his foreign policy or to replace them if they refused. He foresaw Arab political unity as the natural goal of people sharing the same language and historical consciousness, but he had no particular interest in the short term in pursuing political unification beyond what was needed to ensure a common policy.

Perhaps on this basis new Arab political structures reflecting common interests might emerge, but it would be a long process.

The Baath, however, saw Arab unity as the urgently needed liberation of an already existing 'Arab nation' from political frontiers and pseudo-national divisions imposed on it by foreign interests. The Arab national states and governments were not the bricks with which a new supra-national community would be built. They were merely artificial obstacles to be swept away; their only *raison d'être* was to serve foreign interests or to preserve the social and economic privileges of a local ruling class. This view was also, like the Egyptian idea of the nation state, based on historical experience, for Arab Asia had until recently been a unity without dividing frontiers, although under Ottoman rule.

The anarchic nature of Syrian politics was such that Nasser was driven ever closer to political unity in order to ensure the supremacy of his policy in Damascus. It was no longer possible merely to rely on cooperating with or influencing a Syrian government. It became necessary to create and sustain one.

During 1956 and 1957 the initiatives for union with Egypt still came from Syria, and were inspired by the Baath. While in 1956 Nasser was chiefly concerned with the creation of a joint military command, the Syrian parliament set up a commission to pursue the idea of a federal union. As a result of Suez, the Baath began increasingly to think of Nasser as the instrument who might be used to realize their concept of Arab unity.

Nasser himself was cool to the idea of a constitutional merger on confederal lines when it was put to him by President Kuwatly in February 1957.[18] In March 1957 Nasser said in a newspaper interview,

> I am not thinking in terms of any federation or confederation for the present. . . . I should prefer organizations like the Arab League, for instance, to become strong and formidable links between Arab states.[19]

Nasser was thus still sticking to the main line of post-war Egyptian policy in Arab affairs. His caution was no doubt reinforced by his circumstances: he was only just emerging from the supreme test of Suez; the last Israeli troops had only just left occupied territory.

In August, Kuwatly returned to the charge. He declared that 'Syria's dearest wish was to achieve a union with Egypt which would serve as the nucleus for universal Arab unity'. In early September a commission was created to study an economic merger. But it is doubtful if such initiatives alone would have changed Nasser's attitude. What really modified his detachment was the course of the Syrian crisis in the late summer months. In a press statement on 9 September 1957 Nasser attacked American policy and assured Syria of his unconditional support. Two days later, General Bizry and Colonel Sarraj flew to Cairo for talks with Nasser and Field Marshal Amer. In mid-October a small force of Egyptian troops landed at the northern Syrian port of Latakia to join the Syrian forces defending the frontier with Turkey. The force was symbolic not only of Nasser's commitment to Syria's defence but also of his acceptance of a deeper involvement in Syrian internal politics. He wanted to avoid the danger that Syrian politics would be polarized between a left leaning increasingly on Russia and a right forced to turn to Iraq, Saudi Arabia and the West. If either King Saud, Nuri es-Said or Khaled Bagdash were to be prevented from being the arbiter in Syria's intricate internal struggles, it began to look as if Nasser must act to ensure the invidious role for himself.

The Baath saw this situation as a great opportunity both to safeguard their local position and to push Nasser further on the road to unity. Domestically they were afraid that the Communists might gain ground from them as leaders of the nationalist left. Internationally they were afraid that, though this would not mean a Communist seizure of power, it would provoke a right-wing military counter-action backed by Iraq, Jordan and the West.[20] A closer link with Egypt would reduce both these dangers. Moreover, the Baath leaders believed that Arab union must begin with Egypt, if only because Egypt was strong enough to block any Arab unity move which did not include her and of which she disapproved.[21]

In October the Baathist leader, Akram Haurani, became Speaker of the Syrian parliament and, shortly afterwards, Michel Aflaq went to see Nasser in Cairo. The following month a delegation from the newly elected Egyptian National Assembly visited Damascus where they made a joint declaration calling for a federal union. Nasser still resisted being rushed. He thought any union would need at least five years to prepare.[22] One reason for Nasser's caution was his fear that a merger would unite his enemies and raise an international storm against him with accusations that he was annexing Syria.[23] Yet within three months Nasser had accepted not only a union between Egypt and Syria but a total merger which went far beyond any previous federal or confederal schemes of Arab unity. Why?

The movement towards unity was hastened by dissension within the Syrian army leadership and by fear of Communist influence. In their local struggle for power the Baath had begun to attack the Communists for being opposed to Arab unity, a popular cause in Syria. The Communists were forced to compete with the Baath in their zeal for unity with Cairo, though in Egypt Nasser had ruthlessly crushed the Communist party.[24] The Communists had favoured a loose federation, while the Baath in December proposed a more strongly knit federal state but with effective regional governments and parliaments.

The Communists then raised the stakes. They proposed a total union, expecting Nasser to refuse – and forced the Baath to follow suit.[25] On 12 January 1958, after a violent quarrel between two senior Syrian army officers, a deputation of fourteen army commanders headed by the chief of staff, General Bizry, flew secretly to Cairo to urge Nasser to agree to immediate union. They left behind in Damascus a virtual ultimatum to the Syrian civilian government demanding that it should carry out its pledges about union. Four days later the Foreign Minister, the Baathist Salah ed-din el Bitar, went to Cairo to join the talks between the officers and Nasser.

Fear of anarchy in Syria which might lead to attempted seizures of power by the Communists or the pro-Iraqi right appears finally to have overcome Nasser's caution. In a speech three and a half years later when the Syrians seceded from the union, Nasser said, 'You all know how the union was born. The Syrian army was then divided into clans and parties.'[26] During his campaign against the Communists in 1959, Nasser declared that the Syrian–Egyptian merger had 'disturbed the Syrian Communists who were hoping that the day when they could dominate Syria was near and who believed that Communist infiltration in Syria was so great that it would be possible to set up a Communist government'.[27]

The Syrian Baathists exaggerated the dangers in order to force Nasser's hand and stampede the other Syrian parties. They also appealed skilfully to Nasser's pride and imagination. 'I knew,' Nasser said in his secession speech quoted above, 'that the union in its constitutional form was not going to be an easy but a difficult thing. I told those who asked me for union in 1958, "let us prepare this union slowly; it bristles with difficulties".' The Syrians then replied, 'Are you going back on those aims you have so long proclaimed?' Nasser denied reneging on his principles but said, 'to be sure of the future let us prepare the ground'. The Syrians retorted, 'Is it your intention then to leave Syria a prey to divisions and hatred? Will you leave Syria to perish?' 'I replied,' said Nasser, ' "Never. Syria is a second motherland for me. Syria is a part of the great Arab nation in which I have always believed."'[28]

When it looked as though the prospect of union was serious, both the Baath and the Communists reverted to their former ideas of a federal system, in which they were backed by the majority of the Syrian cabinet. To their surprise and chagrin, Nasser insisted on a complete merger of the two states. He also demanded the dissolution of all political parties in Syria, as in Egypt, and the withdrawal of the Syrian army from politics, as his conditions for union.

Having accepted the risk of union at all with a Syria which seemed so divided as to be incapable of governing itself, it was logical for Nasser to insist on a form of union which would give him complete authority. Events, his view of Egypt's interests, and the pleas of the Syrians themselves pushed him reluctantly to accept responsibility for Syria; to have done so without the power to exercise this responsibility effectively would have been, from his point of view, a double folly.

The Baath accepted Nasser's conditions partly because they hoped, despite their dissolution as a party, to play a leading role within the National Union, the new political body created by Nasser to replace parties. The eleventh-hour attempt of the Syrian cabinet to hold out for a federal scheme was over-ruled by another ultimatum from the Syrian army leaders who had decided to accept Nasser's terms. The officers, headed by Bizry, packed off the cabinet to Cairo with a warning that their destination was either Egypt or a notorious Syrian jail.[29] At a joint session with the Egyptian cabinet the next day on 1 February 1958, union between Syria and Egypt was proclaimed, subject to confirmation by a plebiscite. The new state was to be known as the United Arab Republic and Nasser was to be its first president.

Three weeks later the union under Nasser's presidency was approved in a plebiscite by a vote of 99·99 per cent in Egypt and 99·9 per cent in Syria. However ornamental the figures, there was no doubt about public enthusiasm, especially in Syria where huge crowds celebrated. Later the Syrians thronged the streets and house-tops to welcome Nasser on his first visit to a land with which he had joined his fate but which he had never until then seen.

In a speech in Cairo after the plebiscite results were announced, Nasser said that the UAR was the first state created by the Arabs themselves and not imposed on them by foreign powers; it was formed from two states which were completely freed from foreign control. Its creation was the first step to Arab liberation. To reassure those who feared how this 'liberation' might be achieved, Nasser declared that the UAR was a state that 'shuns extremism and takes no sides' and pledged that 'no Arab arms shall ever be raised against Arab people whatever the circumstances may be'.[30]

Earlier, in addressing the Egyptian National Assembly, Nasser had warned of troubles ahead. There were those, he said, who would try to destroy the new union and he appealed for caution in dealing with the 'dreams and hopes let loose in flood by the removal of imperialism'. In a very Egyptian metaphor, he spoke of the need 'to dam our aspirations and to regulate the flow, otherwise it may overwhelm us as a strong high flood'.[31]

But less than three weeks later, faced by the delirious seething crowds of Damascus and Aleppo, he felt himself swept along by this same emotional torrent, so much more powerful in Syria than in Egypt. In Syria, 'the throbbing heart of Arabism', he felt 'the happiest moments of my life'. He spoke of 'this sweeping avalanche, this overpowering flow of sentiment' and of the 'hope for an all-embracing Arab unity that would include all Arab peoples in every country'. It was, he said, 'our responsibility to back the Arab nation in the four corners of the Arab world' and 'to work untiringly to free the Arab nation from imperialism and its agents'. He faced 'a great task, a responsibility so big that it fills the heart with awe'.[32] After a week of celebrations he called on the new nation to return to work. There was much to be done.

Chapter 9

The Syrian Challenge:
The Formation of the UAR, 1958

Although the union of Egypt and Syria lasted for only three and a half years, it was an experiment that continues to haunt the Arab consciousness. Apart from the liberation and development of Egypt herself, it was Nasser's most ambitious political venture and brought out both his gifts and his weaknesses as a statesman. It showed perhaps his most valuable contribution to Egypt and the Arabs: his seriousness of purpose, his resistance to inertia and despair, the determination with which he was prepared to try to translate words into acts and dreams into decisions. In accepting the union against his early misgivings he doubtless felt not only the dangers of inaction but also the challenge of a great adventure and the appeal of a historic vision.

Egypt and Syria, like other Arab countries, spoke the same language, mostly shared the same religion, culture and historical experience. They were not much more different than, say, Piedmont and Sicily, or Prussia and Bavaria. But the difficulties of the enterprise were formidable. Nasser's weaknesses as a ruler, especially his reluctance to share power, his suspicious fear of conspiracy and his excessive readiness to fall back on secret police methods rather than to master the open play of competing political forces, were more clearly exposed in the unfamiliar individualistic turbulence of Syrian public life than in the more docile atmosphere of Egypt, accustomed to millennia of authoritarian administration.

Speaking of his compatriots, the Syrian President Kuwatly is said to have told Nasser when the UAR was proclaimed, 'You have acquired a nation of politicians; fifty per cent believe themselves to be national leaders, twenty-five per cent to be prophets, and at least ten per cent to be gods'.[1]

Egypt and Syria had been united before in such high moments of history as when together they stemmed the Mongol invasions of the Near East and when the great Saladin combined their forces to drive the Crusaders finally out of Palestine, precedents

Nasser became fond of quoting with a picture in his mind of himself as potentially a second Saladin. But the two countries were different in the temperaments of their people and to a certain extent in their economic and social structures: they were widely disparate in size of population (some twenty-five million Egyptians to five million Syrians) and were geographically separated. Not only had they no common frontier but what should have been their natural overland communications passed through 200 miles of hostile territory in the state of Israel. Apart from its border with Israel, Syria was surrounded on all sides by states – Jordan, Iraq, the Lebanon, Turkey – who opposed the policies of Nasser and his Syrian allies, feared the extension of their influence, and were ready to work for their downfall.

As Nasser had predicted, the creation of the UAR aroused international storms. It had an electrifying effect on Arab mass opinion and wide repercussions on the other Arab governments of the Middle East and on the attitudes of the Great Powers.

Russia publicly welcomed the union but regarded it with mixed feelings. For while it appeared to strengthen the neutralist Nasser relative to the pro-Western Arab governments and to ensure that Syria would not topple into the Western camp, it also meant the eclipse of Communist influence in Syria. The Syrian Communist party, like the Egyptian party, welcomed the merger as an extension of the anti-imperialist front but opposed Nasser's condition that political parties must be dissolved. The Syrian Communist party split. Its leader, Khaled Baghdash, refused to dissolve the party or to sign the union proclamation and left the country for the Soviet bloc.[2]

The Egyptian Communist party also bowed to pressure from its rank and file and condemned the suppression of 'democratic liberties' in Syria as well as Egypt.[3]

This did not prevent the Russians from welcoming Nasser on 28 April on a three-week tour of the Soviet Union, a visit fixed two years before. It was Nasser's first visit to one of the Great Powers and his first to a Communist country, except Yugoslavia. He met Khrushchev and other Soviet leaders for the first time in Moscow and also visited Leningrad, the Ukraine and the republics of Azerbaijan and Uzbekistan with their largely Muslim populations. In a speech at a lunch given by Khrushchev in the Kremlin on 30 April, Nasser paid tribute to Soviet aid which he said was without strings and entailed no interference in the UAR's independent policy.

Experience has shown that our cooperation with the Soviet Union is founded on a sincere desire to help us get rid of spheres of influence, develop our economy and industrialize our country. If someone wants to subjugate a country he cannot possibly help it to achieve strength whether in the military field or in the field of industrial development.[4]

He was impressed both by Russia's own industrial development and by the degree of religious freedom allowed to Muslims in the USSR. He found the mosques he visited well filled though mostly with older people.[5] But, above all, he was moved by the fact that the Russians treated him, the Egyptian people and the Arabs with seriousness, dignity and respect. On his return home from Russia he told the Cairo crowds in front of the Presidency that the Russians held the Arabs in 'great esteem'. The Soviet Union was 'a friendly country with no ulterior motive'. Khrushchev had signed a joint communiqué supporting the rights of the Palestinians and Algerians to self-determination and had denounced British aggression against the Yemen.[6]

It was not until later that Nasser revealed a less harmonious side of his Moscow talks. Khrushchev had asked him to allow the Syrian Communist party to operate more freely. Nasser objected that this request amounted to internal interference in the UAR. Khrushchev did not press the point then but later returned to it publicly at the Twenty-first Communist Party Congress.

In the same speech on his return, Nasser disclosed that before starting on his Russian visit, he had been informed by the United States 'that it was adopting a new policy towards the UAR, that it respects our neutrality and our independence'. Nasser's answer was that the UAR desired friendship if those intentions were sincere. The policy of non-alignment had at last triumphed, Nasser claimed. It was acknowledged by the two greatest Powers in the world, the Soviet Union and the USA. But the struggle was not ended until all Arab countries were as free as the UAR. There seemed some justification for Nasser's exultant claim in a speech two months before on his return from his triumphant Syrian tour, that, after struggling for many years, 'We have reached a stage in our struggle that places us on a sunlit summit'. But the road ahead was still full of hazards. Neither the setback to the Communists in Syria nor Nasser's offer of neutrality towards the West and of peaceful coexistence with other Arab states were enough to overcome the suspicions of the United States, Britain and their Arab allies.

The Iraqi government denounced the Syrian–Egyptian merger as having been carried through by force, a charge that Nasser had little difficulty in ridiculing before the huge crowds that flocked to hear him in Syria. When, within a fortnight of the proclamation of the UAR, the Iraq and Jordan governments announced the federation of their two countries, Nasser skilfully heaped coals of fire on their heads by welcoming any step towards greater Arab unity, even if, as *Al Ahram* wrote, it was carried out by a Nuri es-Said 'who must one day disappear'. Nasser did not maintain this benevolent indifference for long: Cairo and Damascus radios were soon going full blast once more against the 'imperialist stooges' of Baghdad and Amman. The Iraq–Jordan federation was – geographically and economically – a more logical union than that of Syria and Egypt. But it aroused little popular enthusiasm. During its brief five-month existence it never developed much beyond a paper arrangement, the chief effect of which was to emphasize and legitimize the senior role of Iraq in a Hashemite alliance.

An even greater artificiality marked the arrangement by which the Yemen, under its fierce old medieval despot, Imam Ahmed, joined the UAR in March in a paper confederation called 'The United Arab States' (see Chapter 14). Another sign of Nasser's growing impact in the Arabian peninsula was the announcement, a fortnight after the Yemen's adherence to the 'United Arab States', that in Saudi Arabia King Saud had handed over full powers as prime minister and foreign minister to his brother Feisal, the Crown Prince. Feisal was reputed to be more competent, more progressive and more flexible in his attitude to Nasser than Saud: within five years he had become one of Nasser's bitterest enemies.

Among the crowds that greeted Nasser in Damascus and the Arab delegations that came to pay him their respects there were many thousands of Lebanese, mostly Muslims or Arab nationalists, who had streamed across the frontier to the Syrian capital only fifty miles from Beirut. It was a portent of the next crisis in which Nasser was to be involved and which centred on the Lebanon.

The Lebanon holds a special position among the Arab states: it is educationally the most advanced and has the freest Arabic press; its population of some two million is evenly divided between Christians and Muslims; and it has a unique political system designed to hold the balance between eleven different groups into which the two main religious communities are subdivided. The main justification for Lebanon's existence as a separate state is to satisfy the desire of the Christians, especially the main Christian sect, the Maronite Catholics, for an autonomous existence within the predominantly Muslim Arab world. With the departure of the French, their traditional protectors, the Maronites had to rely on the bargain of the 'National Pact'* struck with the Lebanese Muslims and by implication with the Arab nationalist movement in Syria and elsewhere in the Arab world (a movement in which Lebanese Christians, especially intellectuals, had played a prominent part). The Christians' political position was buttressed by their greater wealth compared with the Muslims and by their alliance with some of the more wealthy Muslims on a basis of class interest. But this also created a situation in which communal and class tensions dangerously reinforced each other in times of crisis, as in the previous year. Lebanon's internal conflict was intensified by the creation of the UAR, a new and powerful magnet just across the border for Muslim feelings and for supporters of Arab nationalism and of social change among both communities. Nasser's declaration that the UAR would be a centre of support for Arab nationalism everywhere encouraged the resistance of the Lebanese opposition to the Chamoun regime. It also sharpened the anxieties of those Christians who feared that their autonomy

*See Chapter 8.

might be submerged in a predominantly Muslim Arab nationalist flood. Nasser was aware of these fears and had no wish for a break-up of the Lebanon which might bring Western forces back into the Levant. So, while he continued his attacks on Chamoun's pro-Western policy, he tried to give reassurances to all the Lebanese, Christian and Muslim alike, that he had no designs on Lebanese independence. He told the delegations of Lebanese admirers who came to see him in Damascus that, although naturally he would welcome unity with the Lebanon, this could only be as a result of a unanimous decision of the Lebanese people. On 9 March 1958 the Maronite Patriarch, Paul Ma'ushi, who had criticized Chamoun for dividing the country, announced that he had had a letter from Nasser and from the former Syrian president, Shukri el Kuwatly (now known officially in the UAR as the 'First Arab Citizen'), saying that 'the Lebanon in its present status is a structure with complete sovereignty and independence which will not be touched'. 'These brothers,' said the Patriarch, 'want only one thing from the Lebanon, and that is that it is not a centre for plots and intrigues against them.'[7]

It proved difficult for Nasser to hold the balance between pressure and reassurance. The more the opposition pressed for a change in foreign policy to align Lebanon closer to Nasser, the more Chamoun blamed this pressure on interference from the UAR and himself leaned on America for support. Each side began secretly to arm itself with foreign help.

On 8 May 1958, a left-wing Christian newspaper editor, a critic of the regime, Nassib Matni, was shot as he left his office in Beirut. The opposition blamed the killing on government supporters and called for a nation-wide general strike until Chamoun resigned. The strike developed into riots, armed clashes between rival political groups and finally into an armed rebellion. The small Lebanese army, some 9,000 men, contained the revolt without reducing it. Its commander, General Fuad Chehab, was afraid that the army, the sole remaining guarantee of national unity, would itself split along communal lines if he tried to use it more actively to crush the rebellion as President Chamoun wished.

Claiming that the rebellion was fomented and inspired by the UAR, with Russia in the background, Chamoun appealed to the United States for help. He claimed that Nasser was making a massive attempt to overthrow his regime and that, unless the United States supported him, every other pro-Western regime in the Middle East, including those of Jordan and Iraq, would fall to Nasser.[8]

On 13 May President Eisenhower and Dulles discussed an enquiry from Chamoun as to what action the Americans would take if he called for help. Their reaction was typical of the confused state of Washington's Middle East policy at that time. Dulles knew that Chamoun's 'political error' in seeking a second term had sharpened Christian–Muslim rivalries and that his pro-Western policy deepened the cleavage in the country.[9] Eisenhower's own special envoy, Robert Murphy, confirmed a few weeks later that the situation had scarcely anything to do with Communism. He found that

... much of the conflict concerned personalities and rivalries of a domestic nature, with no relation to international issues. Communism was playing no direct or substantial part in the insurrection. ... The outside influences came mostly from Egypt and Syria.[10]

Yet Eisenhower could still write, 'behind everything was our deep-seated conviction that the Communists were principally responsible for the trouble', and that President Chamoun was a staunch pro-Western ally motivated only by a strong feeling of patriotism.[11] Eisenhower and Dulles were, however, less concerned with the niceties of Lebanese politics than with what seemed a good opportunity to demonstrate to the Russians and Moscow's friends, among whom they included Nasser, that the United States, despite its caution over Suez, was not afraid to intervene militarily to support *its* friends. They saw the Lebanon impatiently as 'one more Communist provocation' in a Soviet political offensive in the 'Third World' of Afro-Asia and Latin America which the United States had found hard to handle.[12]

Eisenhower decided to assure Chamoun of US support on certain conditions: he should drop his plan for a second presidential term; any request from him for US help should be backed by another Arab country; and the mission of a US force of intervention would be to protect American lives and property and help the legal Lebanese government. This intervention would be only a last resort.[13] Meanwhile Sixth Fleet amphibious units were moved to the Eastern Mediterranean and American airborne battle groups in Europe were alerted.

For a time it looked as though they would not be needed. In the Lebanon a stalemate developed in the civil war while attempts were made to reach a diplomatic settlement of the Lebanese government's complaints against the UAR. After rejecting a compromise settlement through the Arab League, the Lebanese government took its complaint to the United Nations Security Council. There its Foreign Minister, Charles Malik, accused the UAR of 'massive, illegal and unprovoked intervention' in the Lebanon, through large-scale supply of arms to the rebels, the training and direct employment of terrorists, and a hostile radio and press campaign. The UAR delegate, Omar Lutfi, denied these allegations and pointed out that the 'rebels' included a former Lebanese president, four ex-premiers, two former Speakers of Parliament, three other ex-ministers and a former Secretary-General of the Ministry of Foreign Affairs.[14]

On 11 June the Security Council decided, with Russia abstaining and no dissent from the UAR, to send a United Nations observer group to the Lebanon to ensure that there was no infiltration of arms or men across the borders. The observers' task was not easy. The terrain was mountainous; only eighteen out of 324 kilometres of the border with Syria was under Lebanese government control; there was kinship and traditionally easy movement between people on either side of the border. The UN observers found in their first report little evidence of 'massive interference' from outside.

There is little doubt that Nasser was willing, through the Syrian army '*deuxième bureau*', to supply enough arms and money to the Lebanese rebels to ensure that they could not easily be crushed and that Chamoun's policy would have to be modified. At the same time he was trying behind the scenes to bring the conflict to a negotiated compromise. He raised no objections to the despatch of UN observers and approached the US government with an offer to use his influence to end the conflict. Nasser's conditions, comments Eisenhower,

were not wholly unreasonable. They were that President Chamoun should finish out his term; that General Chehab, who many of our specialists felt was the strongest Lebanese politician outside of Chamoun, should succeed him; and that the rebels within Lebanon should be accorded amnesty. This message we passed on to President Chamoun through diplomatic channels, making certain he understood that our Government was only a messenger in this regard and that we were not joining hands with the United Arab Republic against him. Apparently mistrusting President Nasser's motives, President Chamoun did nothing to follow up this lead.[15]

This studied American detachment no doubt contributed to Chamoun's negative decision, for a similar settlement was accepted by the Chamounists two months later when the United States, through Robert Murphy, threw her weight behind it.

In mid-June heavy fighting broke out again and Chamoun renewed his appeals for American help. But when on 8 July Chamoun announced publicly for the first time that he would definitely give up the presidency on the expiration of his term on 23 September, it looked as if the crisis would subside without American intervention. Chamoun had, however, been canvassing help from the Muslim members of the Baghdad Pact, especially Iraq, who were due to discuss the Lebanon at a meeting in Istanbul on 14 July. During a visit to London before the meeting, Nuri es-Said, prime minister of the Iraq–Jordan federation, made it plain at a press conference that he believed the Western powers should intervene to support the Lebanese government against what he claimed was Russian interference through the medium of Nasser. He hinted that Iraq or the Iraq–Jordan federation might itself send troops to the Lebanon if President Chamoun asked for them.[16]

The British, after Suez, were cautious, for Nuri's main target was not the Lebanon but the UAR itself: he thought that Syria could be detached from Egypt, given help from outside.[17] As Nuri flew back to Baghdad to prepare for the crucial Istanbul meeting, two brigades of Iraqi troops were ordered to move into northern Jordan. To their officers it looked like the first step towards a military intervention in the Lebanon – which could only take place by invading Syria, since Jordan and the Lebanon had no common frontier. As they moved apparently to carry out their orders, the two brigades swept instead into Baghdad in the early hours of 14 July and seized control of the key points in the capital. Their two commanders, Brigadier Abdul Karim Kassim and Colonel Abdul Salam Aref proclaimed a revolution and the end of the Hashemite regime. They announced a new policy based on neutrality in the cold war, Arab unity, political freedom and social reform. The royal palace was surrounded and King Feisal, the Crown Prince and former Regent Abdul Ilah, and other members of the Royal Family were shot down (possibly by mistake – according to one version Abdul Ilah opened fire as the king and the rest of the family were going down the palace steps to surrender; the waiting troops then fired back, killing or wounding them all). Nuri es-Said at first escaped from his house. He was recognized in the street the next day as he moved, disguised under a woman's cloak and veil, from one hiding place to another. He was killed and his body dragged through the streets and torn to pieces by the mob.

Although the suspected army move against Syria provided the opportunity for the overthrow of the regime, the *coup* had been secretly planned by Kassim for three years past.[18] A popular revolutionary upsurge was released by the *coup*. It reflected the widespread discontent which had been gathering among all classes beneath the surface of the old regime. Among the middle classes, the mainspring of the revolution, this discontent sprang chiefly from what was regarded as Nuri's cynical indifference to public opinion, whether in the repression of civil liberties, the tolerance of corruption or in his isolation of Iraq from the mainstream of Arab nationalist feelings. Despite the much-publicized devotion of seventy per cent of Iraq's oil revenues to economic development, Nuri was bored with economic and social affairs. He loved politics and the international power game. Partly because he counted on the big landlords and tribal sheikhs for political support, he failed to pay proper attention to the social aspects of the development programme.

Many Iraqis under-estimated the skill required and for long supplied by Nuri in merely holding together a new, deeply divided and somewhat artificial state. They felt with a deep sense of shame that they were saddled with a reactionary and incompetent government which served the interests of the Western Powers rather than their own. This position was symbolized by Iraq's membership of the Baghdad Pact.

The pact seemed to be less a military alliance against Russia than a kind of police club, like the Holy Alliance of nineteenth-century Europe, for the suppression of internal radical or revolutionary movements which were indiscriminately branded with the name of 'Communism'.

It is difficult to over-estimate the psychological shock caused in London and Washington and among their remaining Arab allies by the Iraqi revolution. It destroyed in a few hours the main pillar of Anglo-American policy in the Arab world. Suez had ended the already fading British hopes of a Western-controlled Arab regional defence bloc including Egypt and the Canal base. The revolution in Baghdad wrecked the American as well as British hopes of using Iraq and Saudi Arabia to bring the whole of the Fertile Crescent, including essential Syria, firmly into the Western system, while isolating Egypt unless and until Nasser chose also to join in. The formation of the UAR had dealt a blow to these plans but so long as Iraq remained intact there seemed always the hope, nursed by Nuri, of winning back the fickle and unstable Syrians. Now Nuri and his regime had been destroyed by a *coup* which seemed inspired by Nasser's ideas if not engineered by his actions.

President Chamoun in the Lebanon and King Hussein in Jordan felt their backs to the wall and appealed urgently for Western support. The British and Americans were themselves shocked and uncertain, confused by their own tendency to identify all manifestations of Arab radicalism and neutralism with Nasser's alleged empire-building and to link both with Communism and Soviet expansion. In Washington, Allen Dulles, the CIA chief, had reported that the Iraqi *coup* had been made by pro-Nasser elements of the Iraqi army but that 'We have no information that Nasser himself is behind the *coup*'.[19] Nevertheless Eisenhower decided that, 'This sombre turn of events could, without vigorous response on our part, result in the complete elimination of Western influence in the Middle East'.[20] After consulting sceptical Congress leaders, Eisenhower called for a United Nations Security Council meeting, while within twenty-four hours of Chamoun's call for help, American marines from the Sixth Fleet began landing in the Lebanon. Two days later the first of 2,000 British paratroops began flying into Jordan, through Israel's air space, to protect Hussein.

At the heart of this potentially disastrous international crisis there was an element of farce. In spite of Eisenhower's insistence that the American intervention was the result of a request from the legal Lebanese government, the American forces went ashore on the beach near Beirut airport in deployed formations ready for action – not because of anticipated opposition from the rebels but because of the 'unknown' attitude of the Lebanese army. General Chehab had, in fact, asked for the landings to be put off for twenty-four hours while negotiations took place to ensure that his troops would not open fire, but at this crucial moment the American ambassador was out of radio contact with the Sixth Fleet.[21] Some of the Lebanese army blocked the road into Beirut with tanks and forced a parley, involving Chehab and the American commander, as a result of which the US troops were confined by agreement to the airport area and the harbour.

Eisenhower was prepared if necessary for a wider action in the Middle East. He ordered military precautions to reinforce the area of the Persian Gulf and Saudi Arabia and readiness to use nuclear weapons, if necessary, to defend Kuwait.[22] He warned Nasser, through the US ambassador in Cairo, against involving the UAR directly or indirectly in hostile acts against the US forces in Lebanon. Russia and the UAR denounced the American intervention as an act of aggression. The UAR pledged its support for Iraq against any attack.

Nasser heard the news of the Iraqi revolution and the Western moves while he was on holiday in Yugoslavia, visiting Tito. He had no doubt had some inkling of the secret disaffection within the Iraqi army, but was as surprised as the Western Powers by the *coup*. He was also as uncertain as the Western Powers at that moment about the potential scale of the crisis. The formidable

size of the American military movements, partly intended to safeguard against a possible Russian riposte, left open the possibility
that they were meant eventually to go beyond the Lebanon and
Jordan and perhaps to include the seizure of Syria and the reconquest of Iraq. Nasser at once flew to Moscow to confer with
Khrushchev. He wanted an assurance of Russian support against
any extension of the Western moves to Damascus and Baghdad.
But he also wanted to ensure that the Russians themselves would
not intervene unilaterally or do anything likely to provoke a
Western invasion or turn the Middle East into a nuclear battlefield. On his return to Cairo he reported in a speech on 22 July
that he had discussed in Moscow 'means of preventing aggression
against Arab countries, preserving their independence and also
preserving world peace'. Nasser later revealed during his public
quarrel with Moscow in 1959 that the Russians had given him no
assurance whatever of military support. When, on his return to
the UAR he met the Iraqi revolutionary leader and deputy
premier, Colonel Aref, in Damascus on 18 July and repeated his
public pledge of support for Iraq against any aggression, Nasser
was 'definitely certain at that time that we were the only country
that stood by Iraq and the only state that would fight side by side
with Iraq in the event of any aggression or imperialist attack
launched against it'.[23]

Instead of a military pledge to defend the UAR and Iraq –
which the Russians would have found logistically difficult to
fulfil without risk of a nuclear war because of the interposing
barriers of Turkey and Iran – Khrushchev confined himself to
threats and a call for a five-power summit meeting. By including
India and not China as the fifth power, Khrushchev angered
Peking. Nasser supported the summit proposal, saying, 'We are
tired of the cold war, we are tired of military groupings, we are
tired of the division of the world into two camps and of the world
being dragged to the brink'.[24]

Before he went to Damascus, Nasser had already taken the
bold decision to link his fate with that of the Iraqi revolutionaries
and give them as much military aid as possible. The UAR supplied the Iraqis with small arms for 'popular resistance squads',
ammunition for heavier weapons and planes and radar equip-

ment. She also concluded a military pact with the new Baghdad regime. 'We were at that time,' admitted Nasser, 'gambling with our destiny and our independence ... for we believed that the independence of Iraq would consolidate our independence.'[25]

For Nasser this was a moment of high triumph and of deep danger. His most formidable Arab rival had been eliminated, as he had predicted. Iraq, once the keystone of Western influence, had joined the UAR camp of the 'liberated' neutralist Arab states. The Arab nationalist movement aimed at freeing all the Arab countries from 'imperialism' and ending foreign spheres of influence in the Arab world was rapidly gathering momentum. Speaking in Damascus in the presence of the Iraqi delegation, Nasser declared, 'Arab nationalism has at last been unchained. The Arab peoples are confident in themselves and in their fatherland. . . . The banner of freedom will also fly high over Amman and Beirut. . . .' Nasser was also conscious that all could be disastrously lost if the crisis led to war. He tried to assuage Western anxieties and appealed to the Western world to realize that 'the occupation days are over', to try to understand the real meaning of Arab nationalism and the Iraqi revolution.

Asking why America should be against 'the free men of Iraq', especially now that the Iraqi leaders had assured the West that Iraqi oil would continue to flow to its factories, Nasser said in one of his most eloquent and dramatic speeches,

We want independence for our country. We want to preserve our nationalism and our dignity. We are working for peace, for peace is our aim and war means total destruction. . . . When the people of Iraq and the army of Iraq rose, they rose only against tyranny, against oppression. They rose only against destitution and assassination. They rose only against despotism and corruption. . . . In speaking of peace [said Nasser], I am talking to the rulers of the Great Powers who, carried away by fury, are today leading the world to the brink of the precipice, in other words to war.[26]

Within a few days the panic began to subside all round. It became clearer to the Western governments that the revolution in Baghdad was primarily an Iraqi affair. After the initial atrocities of the Baghdad mob, Kassim showed that he was in control of the situation in Iraq and there was no serious organized opposition. He made conciliatory pronouncements to the Western Powers, declaring his intention to continue Iraq's international obligations, including the oil concessions. He did not immediately withdraw from the Baghdad Pact, but Iraq became a sleeping partner and then withdrew after giving legal notice. His regime was soon recognized by Britain and America. Although Nasser and Aref had an emotional public meeting in Damascus as fellow-Arab nationalist revolutionaries, neither Kassim nor Nasser was in any hurry to rush into a union between Iraq and the UAR.

Khrushchev's call for a summit meeting was quietly dropped. At the same time, with the help of the American envoy, Robert Murphy, a political compromise was reached in the Lebanon. General Chehab was elected next President on 31 July, as Nasser had earlier suggested. Four days later, Chehab announced that he intended to ask the American troops to leave. A new compromise cabinet was formed on the basis that there should be 'no victor, no vanquished' as a result of the civil war.

At the United Nations, where a special session of the Assembly had been called, there was also a compromise based on a resolution drawn up by the Arab states themselves. They pledged themselves to refrain from interference in each other's internal affairs and agreed to measures through the United Nations to help prevent 'indirect aggression', such as arms smuggling and radio incitement. On this basis American troops were to be withdrawn from Lebanon and the British forces from Jordan. A United Nations official, representing the Secretary-General, would act as a 'watchdog' to see that the agreement was fulfilled.

On 8 October the United States announced that its troops, already reduced from their peak of 14,000, would be withdrawn. The United Nations observer group were also to go. The British withdrew from Jordan by the end of the year.

Although the Iraq revolution had been politically the more spectacular event, the Lebanese civil war was a far more bloody affair, costing perhaps as many as 3,000 lives.

During his Middle East mission, Robert Murphy visited Cairo for talks with Nasser. Nasser gave 'a long dissertation about the

United Arab Republic, explaining the necessity of Arab unity for the security of a small weak country like Egypt'. When Murphy introduced the subject of Israel, 'Nasser shrugged his shoulders with the intimation that nothing could be done about that situation'. Nasser's view that 'no matter what the issue, the United States would be found on the side of Israel' had been shaken but not destroyed, Murphy found, by American policy over Suez.

There could be no doubt [concluded Murphy], about the intensity of Nasser's patriotism and devotion to the Arab cause, and I respected him for his struggle with the crushing burden of trying to do something for Egypt's impoverished millions. But I left with a feeling of uneasiness about the pressures on Nasser which could lead to methods not conducive to peace.[27]

By the end of the year, when American and British troops had gone, the international crisis was over. It marked, to Nasser's satisfaction, the end of an era in the Middle East. He had won the second stage of his struggle with the Western Powers, the attempt by the United States, after the Suez débâcle, to bring the whole area within its sphere of influence. The period of direct military intervention by the Western Powers in the central area of the Arab world was finished – for some years at any rate. The 'neutrality' of the area was tacitly recognized by the Great Powers, who during the next decade confined their competitive activities there to gaining influence through economic aid, arms deliveries and propaganda. The former imperial powers, Britain and France, withdrew their military and administrative presence to the periphery of the Arab world. Britain clung to her footholds in the Arabian peninsula and the rich oil sheikhdoms of the Persian Gulf. France, now under the new leadership of de Gaulle, fought on with an increasingly destructive and costly war in Algeria, but also with decreasing conviction about the formula of 'French Algeria'.

The 'vacuum' allegedly left in the Middle East by the Anglo-French defeat and withdrawal after Suez was not filled militarily or diplomatically entirely by either Russia or the United States. Neither was it to be filled, as Nasser had hoped, by a united bloc of the Arab states themselves. So long as the UAR stayed united, it remained a focus of potential stability for this area, but continued quarrels between Nasser and other Arab governments and the break-up of the UAR itself were to leave a fluid situation in which eventually, and perhaps temporarily, Israel was to emerge as the dominant military power.

Even before the American and British forces had withdrawn, it had become evident that the 'year of victory' for Arab nationalism, as Nasser called 1958, had also brought new problems. The new-found revolutionary solidarity between Iraq and the UAR soon began to show signs of strain. Within seven months it had cracked into open hostility with a propaganda feud between Nasser and Kassim as fierce as that with Nuri es-Said. At the same time, and contributing to this split, Nasser's conflict with the Arab Communists was intensified and burst into an open ideological quarrel with the Soviet Union.

The Iraqi officers who had carried out the 14 July revolution were of similar background and outlook to the Egyptian Free Officers: mostly middle or lower middle class, nationalist, radical and Puritan, in an ideological spectrum stretching from mild Marxism to Islamic egalitarianism. But their relationship with the civilian political forces was different from and weaker than that in Egypt.

As the threat of Western intervention receded, the revolutionary forces in Iraq began to divide over two main issues: how far Iraq should go towards political unity with the UAR, and how far and how quickly party political life should be restored. Because of their suppression under Nuri and their record of underground struggle, the former opposition parties in Iraq were less discredited than the parties had been in Egypt before the 1952 revolution. As a result of their underground experience, the Communists were also stronger and better organized than in either Egypt or Syria, while the Iraqi Baathists were weaker, younger and less experienced than their Syrian counterparts. Two other factors entered into Iraqi calculations about Arab unity: the large Kurdish minority in the north, and some of the Shia Muslims who formed perhaps half of the Iraqi Arab Muslims, opposed any tight Arab and predominantly Sunni Muslim union in which their influence would be reduced.

While all the parties, especially the Communists, pressed the military leaders for a return to legalized party activity and constitutional life, they were split over Arab unity, a split which soon extended to the military leadership itself. The Baathists, the Istiqlal, some of the National Democrats, and non-party 'Nasserites' among the army officers wanted a quick move towards unity with the UAR, if necessary under Nasser's leadership. Except for the Baathists and Nasserites they wanted a merger less complete than that between Syria and Egypt, a kind of federation which would leave Iraq greater autonomy and the continuation of its own party political life. The Communists, the Kurds, some of the small but influential left-centre National Democrat party and sections of the army, while paying lip-service to Arab unity through a loose federation, were secretly opposed to any merger. The Communists clearly hoped that they would be able to establish a firm political base in Iraq from which they might eventually regain the influence they had lost in Syria since the formation of the UAR.

Colonel Aref, the deputy premier, an impulsive, energetic and rather simple extrovert, was the leading 'Nasserite' in the Iraqi revolutionary regime. He put Arab unity before the problem of the Iraqi parties and wanted to suppress the Communists, but at the same time urged a radical land reform. General Kassim, premier and defence minister, was cautious, intense, secretive and devious. He feared that any premature move towards unity would increase the danger to both Iraq's international position and to her internal unity. Having neither the strength nor perhaps the temperament entirely to impose his own will, Kassim tried to steer a middle course – nationalist, neutralist and moderately left – between the rival factions, leaning now on one side and then on the other.

Nasser later claimed that he had shared Kassim's caution and thought Iraqi unity more urgent than closer ties with the UAR. Several Iraqi leaders, such as Kamal el Chaderchi, veteran leader of the National Democrats, came to Cairo to discuss the pattern of unity with the UAR.

I told them [said Nasser], not to be in a hurry but to go back and consolidate the revolution. . . . Our objective never was any form of constitutional unity between the UAR and Iraq, but the greater emotion of Arab national solidarity. ... In pursuit of this policy, I sought to meet Kassim several times. He avoided me with feeble excuses.[28]

Why, if both Nasser and Kassim appeared to want the same thing, did they clash so fiercely? The answer is to be found partly in the egos and suspicious characters of both men. More important was that neither was fully in control of their supporters or allies in Iraq. Above all, there was Nasser's concern about the effect on Syria of increased Communist influence in Baghdad. Nasser's personal popularity in Iraq was great and the Nasserites of Iraq were apt to be tactlessly more Catholic than their Pope. The brash and outspoken Aref was quickly in conflict with Kassim. He was dismissed and sent as ambassador to Bonn. After he had suddenly returned to Baghdad unauthorized, he was arrested, charged with plotting against the regime, and condemned to death but not executed. Kassim used to visit him regularly in prison. Kassim, believing Nasser was intriguing against him, leaned more on the Communists to counter the Arab nationalist pressure.

The Communists had no ministers in the government and were still legally banned as a party, but they or their sympathizers had secured several important official posts in the administration. The more influential the Communists seemed to grow in Iraq, the more anxious Nasser became. He began to see the struggle in Iraq as repeating that between Arab nationalism and Soviet-backed Communism that he had finally intervened in Syria to prevent. Nasser had earlier in 1958 complained privately to Khrushchev that Soviet diplomats appeared to be encouraging Communist intrigues against the union in Syria. He also expressed his concern at Khrushchev's critical remarks at the Twenty-first Party Congress about Arab 'annexation' and suppression of 'democratic liberties'. He believed the Communists were developing a campaign against him, similar to that of some Western newspapers, accusing him of wanting to annex Iraq for the sake of its oil. During the autumn of 1958, Nasser's counter-attack was muted. He was waiting until the international crisis was over, and he was also engaged in crucial economic negotiations which resulted in

October 1958 in a Russian agreement to help to finance and build the Aswan High Dam. The Russians agreed to grant credit of up to 400 million roubles (£33 million) for the first stage of the Dam and to supply experts and technicians.

In a speech on 23 December 1958 at Port Said, Nasser allowed himself the first light blow back in public. He attacked the Syrian Communists as opportunists and separatists, 'new enemies who saw the triumph of Arab nationalism as the end of their interests'. He made no direct reference in this context to Iraq or Russia, but did so obliquely through an obvious historical analogy. Often before, in urging the value of Arab unity, Nasser had spoken of how Egypt and Syria together under Saladin had defeated the Crusaders, the imperialists of that time coming from the West. Now he recalled that under Saladin the united Arabs had also defeated the Tartars (coming from the East) who had invaded Baghdad and reached Syria.[29]

The climax of the new quarrel came in March 1959 after an abortive rising in the northern Iraq city of Mosul by pro-Nasser army elements led by a Colonel Shawwaf. The rebellion was directed against the growth of Communist influence and the terrorizing excesses of the 'Popular Resistance Forces', an armed militia in which the Communists were influential. Nasser denied Kassim's charges that the revolt had been engineered from Syria.

Speaking in Damascus, shortly before the Mosul revolt, Nasser reaffirmed that his policy was one of non-alignment and independence of either the Western or Eastern blocs. He accused 'imperialists' of trying to stir up trouble between the UAR and Russia and revealed that he had written to Khrushchev to ask whether there was any change in the Soviet policy of support for the Arab liberation movement on a basis of equality. He had just received, he said, a ten-page reply from Khrushchev assuring him of Russia's continued support, despite ideological differences, and asserting that as far as the attitude of the UAR towards Communism was concerned, the Soviet Union did not wish to interfere in the UAR's home affairs.[30]

But with the suppression of the Mosul revolt, Nasser launched into a bitter, hard-hitting campaign against Kassim, the Communists and eventually against Khrushchev himself. Punning on the Arabic meaning of Kassim's name, he called him 'Kassim el Iraq', the 'Divider of Iraq'. He accused him of imitating Nuri both in his regime of terror and in trying to split Iraq from Arab nationalism. He attacked the Communists in both Egypt and Syria as being agents of outsiders who were trying to bring the Arabs into a sphere of influence. Having been foiled in their plans to dominate Syria, 'the Communists had emigrated to Baghdad in order to turn Iraq into a Communist state from which Communism will spread to the rest of the Arab countries, thereby creating a Communist Fertile Crescent'.[31]

On 17 March Nasser issued a statement replying to a speech made by Khrushchev at the signing of a technical and financial aid agreement between the Soviet Union and Iraq. Khrushchev had said that 'when the UAR President talks about Communism and Communists, he arms himself with the language of the imperialists' but that relations between the UAR and the USSR would continue as before. Khrushchev alleged that Nasser was insisting on the unification of the UAR and Iraq, but such unification must be decided by the peoples concerned. While the Arabs had a common interest in resisting imperialism, after liberation each country might have different interests which could not be disregarded. The Soviet Union had not interfered and was not interfering in such affairs, said Khrushchev, but 'is not indifferent to the situation which is developing in a region not far from our frontiers'. This ominous hint of a Soviet right to intervene to support and protect the Arab Communist parties was immediately and vigorously rejected by Nasser as 'unacceptable' and 'a challenge to the will of the Arab people'. He denied that he had insisted on unification with Iraq; he had urged Arab solidarity and declared that for any merger it was absolutely essential to have the unanimous approval of the people concerned. Nasser said he appreciated Soviet friendship on the basis of non-interference and co-existence, but 'the Arab people who fought for liberation from imperialism will never agree to become satellites'.[32]

Instead of dropping his anti-Communist campaign after Khrushchev's strictures, Nasser intensified it. In a speech in Damascus, on 22 March, he replied with proud and angry irony to the Soviet premier's comment that 'Abdul Nasser is a young man, passionate and hot-headed'. He said,

> Abdul Nasser is not the only one who is passionate and hot-headed, but the whole Arab people. ... Without this hot-headedness the Arabs would not have achieved their successes in the struggle against imperialism, against the Baghdad Pact, against the British and French at Port Said and then the Iraqi revolution. Between 29 October and 6 November 1956, Egypt had fought against Britain, France and Israel single-handed with passion and hot-headedness. ... No country stood by us and we had no agreement with the Soviet Union. ... Had it not been for this passion and hot-headedness, our country would have been turned into rocket bases against the Soviet Union and into Western bases against the Socialist and Communist world.

Nasser dismissed the Communists' championing of 'democratic life' as a 'false slogan'. He said he did not want political parties, neither a reactionary party financed and supported by Western imperialism nor a Communist party inspired by foreign Communism and trying 'to tie us to the wheel of dependence'.

Ridiculing the idea that the UAR wanted to grab Iraq's oil, Nasser pointed out that Iraq's oil revenue of £E75 million a year was only as much as Egypt earned from Suez Canal dues and her own oil production. Egypt's national income was £E1,000 million and her budget £E360 million, and she earned £E120 million from cotton sales, while Syria's budget amounted to another £E75 million. Apart from oil, Iraq's budget was only £E45 million. So, asked Nasser, who wants money from whom?

The Syrian Communists had resumed their activities after the Iraqi revolution. Attacks on the UAR by Arab Communists were published in the Soviet bloc press, said Nasser. 'We were suddenly faced by a flagrant interference in our internal affairs by the Soviet Union,' because of the link between the Arab Communists and the Soviet leaders.

As part of the anti-Communist campaign, Nasser carried through a purge of suspected Communists and fellow-travellers in both Egypt and Syria. A week after the Port Said speech, in the early hours of 1 January 1959, 280 leading members and officials of the Egyptian Communist party were arrested. Many were sent to the notoriously brutal desert concentration camp of Abu

Zabaal and to military prisons, where several were reported to have died as a result of torture.[33] In March 1961, Nasser told the American journalist C. L. Sulzberger that there were then still 280 Communists in jail but 340 others had been released. Public ideological discussion that had been tolerated, indeed encouraged, by Nasser through the left-wing Cairo newspaper, *Al Massa*, edited by Khaled Mohieddin, was curtailed. On 12 March, after the Mosul rising, Khaled Mohieddin was dismissed together with most of his staff and a week later there were many hundreds more arrests of suspected Communists or fellow-travellers in Egypt and Syria.

The Egyptian Marxist left faced a painful dilemma in trying to reconcile support for Nasser's anti-imperialist neutralism and the growing trend towards socialist planning, with the regime's anti-Communism and suppression of democratic liberties.

The breach between Nasser and Moscow was gradually papered over. The reconciliation was helped by the fact that the Communists in Iraq overplayed their hand and became intensely unpopular. Kassim began slowly to turn against them. By the middle of 1960, though Kassim had accepted large-scale economic and military aid from Russia, it was plain that the Communists in Iraq were in decline and had lost their chance of taking over the country. With no serious prospect of a Communist political base in Iraq or Syria, there was no longer any incentive for the Russians to endanger their relationship with Nasser by giving preference to Kassim or the Arab Communists. Instead, they decided to invest heavily in the UAR. In August 1960 they agreed to be responsible for the whole of the foreign exchange costs of the construction of the High Dam instead of only the first stage, granting an extra credit of 900 million roubles (£81 million). They had already pledged £33 million for the first stage of the Dam and another £60 million for the UAR industrialization programme. The Soviet industrial credits were on highly favourable terms – 2·5 per cent interest, repayable over twelve years with repayment beginning one year after the factory concerned had been built and begun producing.[34]

At the ceremony laying the foundation stone of the High Dam on 1 January 1960, Nasser paid a fulsome tribute to Russia's 'wholly unconditional aid'. He declared that though the material purposes of the Dam were of 'tremendous importance', the greatest value of the Dam was as a symbol of 'the determination and independent will of the Arab people'. It showed that 'nations, no matter how small, are capable of doing great works, if determined enough'.[35]

Fifteen months earlier, as the 1958 international crisis was subsiding, Nasser had declared in a press interview that while the UAR could not abstain from supporting liberation movements, at the same time she wanted 'matters to return to normal' so as to be able to deal with 'urgent problems of political consolidation, economic stability and domestic productivity'. By early 1960 it looked as if a more 'normal' situation were being established in the Middle East. There was less interference by either the Western or Soviet blocs: America and Russia were themselves seeking better relations with each other through personal contact between Khrushchev and Eisenhower. The inter-Arab struggle was also more subdued: there was less talk of union and more of solidarity among independent states.

In a speech on 9 July 1960, to the inaugural session of the General Congress of the National Union of the UAR, Nasser reaffirmed that a common history and common language made the Arabs one nation, but went on to redefine the principles of 'our work towards unity'.

First, unity should be through free and independent choice and will. Second, an Arab people seeking unity must first have completed 'the potentialities of its national unity within the limits of its existing borders before entering into commitments outside those borders' (which could be taken to refer to countries such as Iraq, the Sudan and the Lebanon which have serious problems of maintaining national unity between different communal or ethnic groups). Third, the Arab people concerned must be determined and sure of their wish for unity.

'On these bases,' added Nasser, 'we believe that unity should be continuously evolving and should not take place by a *coup*.'[36]

Nevertheless Nasser's polemics with Kassim continued with fluctuating degrees of violence for the next two years until in February 1963 Kassim was overthrown and executed in a *coup* led by Colonel Aref and supported by the Iraqi Baathists. In 1961, Nasser found himself in the unusual position of being virtually a temporary ally of the British – and at the same time in conflict with the Russians – in the defence of the oil Sheikhdom of Kuwait against what seemed to be a threat of invasion by Kassim. A small unit of UAR technical troops was briefly among the mixed force from the Arab League states sent to Kuwait to take over there from the British brigade which had been rushed to the newly independent sheikhdom in the summer of 1961.

Nasser's quarrel with King Hussein of Jordan also simmered on and boiled over from time to time. In November 1958 a private plane carrying Hussein had been dangerously buzzed by UAR Migs while flying over Syrian territory. Hussein believed it was a deliberate attempt by the UAR authorities to kill him.[37] Nasser scornfully denied this accusation. He claimed that it was one of many similar incidents and was due to the fact that Hussein's plane had not identified itself properly. In the following year, after Nasser's campaign against the Communists and Kassim, relations between Amman and Cairo were resumed. But the truce was brief. The radio war was re-opened and in August 1960 the Jordan prime minister, Hassan al Majali, and ten other people were killed by a bomb placed in his office. The suspected killers escaped to Syria. Hussein again put the blame on the UAR and attacked Nasser himself in violent terms. In February 1961, there was another attempted *rapprochement* between Nasser and Hussein, as the Arab League tried to close its ranks against Israel, because of the threatened diversion of the Jordan waters. But the feud burst out violently again six months later when Hussein rushed jubilantly to recognize the secessionist regime in Syria within twenty-four hours of the Damascus *coup* which split the UAR.

The UAR continued its support for the Algerian nationalists, who by 1961 were in sight of victory with the opening of talks with France at Evian. But Nasser was at loggerheads with President Bourguiba of Tunisia who accused him of sending Egyptian secret service officers to plan his assassination. There was a reconciliation in 1961 after the UAR supported Tunisia in the 'battle of Bizerta', in which 1,000 Tunisians were killed by French army fire, and Nasser and Bourguiba met for the first time in three years at the Belgrade non-aligned conference. Nasser also launched a virulent attack on the Shah of Iran and broke off relations with Teheran because of Iran's closer relations with Israel (Iran was secretly supplying the oil to go through the new sixteen-inch pipeline laid by the Israelis from Eilat on the Gulf of Aqaba to the refinery at Haifa).

Nasser was thus never short of friends or foes, especially the latter. But in comparison with earlier years, Nasser's attention outside the UAR between 1959 and 1961 was less absorbed by the Middle East and Arab problems of unity or disunity than by the affairs of the non-aligned world in general and of Africa in particular.

Chapter 10
The 'Sunlit Summit':
Nasser on the World Scene, 1958–61

The early 1960s marked the peak of Nasser's influence on the world scene. His control of the united Egyptian–Syrian state, the most powerful in the Arab world, was then briefly combined with a leading role among the rapidly growing number of independent African countries. This period was also the apogee of the influence of the wider group of non-aligned countries, built round a majority of the Afro-Asian states and Yugoslavia. It was partly Nasser's ability to operate through both the Arab and African blocs that enabled him to establish himself as one of the 'Big Five' of the leaders of 'neutralism', with Nehru of India, Tito of Yugoslavia, Nkrumah of Ghana and Sukarno of Indonesia, both at the 'summit' meeting of the United Nations General Assembly in September 1960 and at the Belgrade conference of non-aligned states in September 1961.

As their efforts to hasten the end of colonialism successfully produced more and more independent countries, the attention of the non-aligned countries began to turn more insistently to other world problems. The Belgrade Conference was as much concerned with limiting the East–West cold war and checking the nuclear arms race as it was with anti-colonialism. Bridging the gap in economic development between rich and poor countries was a dominant theme at the Cairo conference of non-aligned countries in 1964. But as the non-aligned and Afro-Asian groups grew in number, so also their cohesion began to weaken under the pressure of different national interests and priorities. The process began with the splits among the Afro-Asian states over the Congo crisis in 1960.

More serious blows to the influence of the non-aligned countries as a 'third force' (they claimed they never desired to be a third 'bloc') in world affairs came at the end of 1962 with the Chinese border attack on India, the Cuban missile crisis between America and Russia and the growing Soviet–Chinese split. The world picture of two monolithic cold war blocs in East and West with the non-aligned group able to manoeuvre in between began to change. America and Russia dealt more directly with each other; their own blocs were loosening up; and for the Afro-Asian countries the struggle between China and Russia added a new dimension to the older competition between the Western Powers and Soviet Communism. India, shaken first by the Chinese attack and then by the death of Nehru, ceased to be a serious driving force in the non-aligned group. In this situation Nasser became increasingly a key figure among the non-aligned leaders. He held the middle balance between those tending to lean more towards the West, Russia or China (himself leaning more to the Russians), especially as the three-way contest spread into Africa.

In 1960 and 1961 Nasser, in common with other neutralist leaders, was most concerned with three problems: keeping the East–West cold war from becoming mixed up with the anti-imperialist struggle in Africa, especially in the Congo and Algeria; the growing tension and arms race between America and Russia after the collapse of the Paris summit; and the effect of these crises on the future of the United Nations.

Nasser's campaign against the Communists in Syria and Iraq as well as in Egypt and his defiance of Khrushchev in 1959 had helped to ease his relations with some of the Western Powers, particularly the United States. By 1960 Nasser had settled with Britain, France and the Suez Canal Company the financial consequences of the Suez affair: compensation for the Canal Company nationalization, the war damage, the freezing of Egyptian assets and the sequestration of British and French property in Egypt. Diplomatic relations were resumed with Britain in 1959 but ambassadors not exchanged until the spring of 1961, while diplomatic relations with France were not fully resumed until 1963. In Washington for a time Nasser came to be regarded in some quarters as a stabilizing anti-Communist factor in the Middle East, especially after Kennedy succeeded Eisenhower. American aid to the UAR was resumed on a substantial scale. In 1959–60 American aid for Egypt totalled £54 million and in August 1960 the United States sold 900,000 tons of wheat to Egypt for £20·8 million in local currency (sixty-five per cent of which was to be spent on financing economic development in Egypt). Altogether, until US aid to Egypt, much of it in surplus food, was suspended in 1965, it totalled about a billion dollars (£350 million).

The basic mistrust between Nasser and the Western Powers continued, however. It fluctuated in intensity between attempts at coexistence and active hostility, according to the development of the anti-imperialist liberation struggle in the Arab countries and Africa, the degree of Western support for Israel, and the temperature of the East–West cold war. Nasser's commitment to support liberation movements in the Arab world prevented a real *rapprochement* with France until the Algerian war ended with de Gaulle's recognition of Algerian independence in 1962. Even then it was still inhibited by the fact that France was the main supplier of arms to Israel. The chief obstacles to better relations with Britain were the continued British military and administrative control of Aden and the Persian Gulf sheikhdoms. Not only was Nasser committed to active support of local Arab liberation movements against the remnants of imperial rule in the Arab world. He also believed that, in order to maintain her position in Arabia and the Gulf against the Cairo-supported local Arab revolutionaries, Britain was encouraging and organizing the enemies of the UAR, whether at one stage Kassim in Iraq, or later Jordan and Saudi Arabia in an 'Islamic alliance' with the Shah of Iran and other members of CENTO (Central Treaty Organization), the successor to the Baghdad Pact after Iraq's defection.

Nasser's identification of the UAR with the African liberation movements and the most radical and militant group among the African states was another cause of tension with Britain and also with the United States. After the Kennedy administration took over in Washington in January 1961, the United States adopted a more flexible and understanding policy towards Afro-Asian anti-colonialism and neutralism. Kennedy began a friendly private correspondence with Nasser and other Arab leaders on Middle East problems. But Nasser's clash with Saudi Arabia, an American protégé, over the Yemen after September 1962 combined with American support for Israel to limit the extent and warmth of American–Egyptian cooperation.

Western opinion found it difficult to reconcile the idea of positive neutralism or non-alignment with the fact that Nasser and the UAR press and radio usually adopted a much more critical and hostile attitude towards Western policies and actions than towards those of the Communist bloc. The discordance was attributed at best to a hypocritical 'double standard' on the part of Nasser and other non-aligned leaders or, at worst, to a secret alliance between Nasser and the Russians to destroy Western influence in the Middle East and Africa.

Nasser made many attempts in speeches and interviews to explain his conception of non-alignment. It was, he said, different from 'neutrality' on the Swiss model. It did not mean that a country never took sides, but that its policy was independently formed: it judged each case on its merits rather than adopting automatically the attitude of an alliance or bloc. For the UAR, 'our friends are our friends and our enemies are our enemies'. If the UAR criticized the United States and the West, it was not out of anti-Americanism or anti-Westernism, but because of what it considered unjust American or Western policies. To be aligned meant you supported someone else's policies, right or wrong; non-alignment meant: 'We say what we believe, whether this pleases or displeases'.[1]

However commendable such an attitude may be, it is one which neither nations nor individuals are usually able to maintain unless they are either very powerful or prepared to pay a price in suffering and hardship.

While the non-aligned countries were concerned about the arms race and cold-war tension, they could not avoid being committed in the struggle against imperialism and colonialism or against what they called 'neo-colonialism', an alleged attempt to replace the old imperialist rule by economic domination or military pacts. In this struggle they could not be neutral, even though they did not want to belong to either of the two world blocs, and wanted friendship with both East and West. But neither did it mean they were ideologically or morally neutral: Nasser remained anti-Communist while accepting Soviet aid.

Addressing the inaugural session of the National Union General Congress in Cairo on 9 July 1960, Nasser said that in pursuit of positive neutrality and non-alignment 'we extended our hand to the United States and the Soviet Union as the greatest powers today and expressed to them our desire for cooperation'. The Soviet Union gave 'a warm response enabling us to establish firm friendly relations based on equality between the Arabs and Russian peoples. This friendship was characterized by close economic cooperation that reached its climax in the Soviet Union's participation in the High Dam and the Soviet Union's firm stand on our side in our great battle against imperialism.' But, said Nasser, it was 'a matter of great regret for us' that the United States, despite its attitude during the Suez crisis, had not given the desired response. For this he blamed American policy's relationship 'with the imperialist powers and world Zionism' and its failure to appreciate that 'the Arab people are their own masters and free to decide their own destiny'. (Yet Nasser's relationship with Moscow was also to continue to have its periods of coolness.)

In a world threatened by the nuclear arms race and the mounting cold war between the Great Powers, only the developing non-aligned countries, Nasser concluded, could provide the world's 'conscience and voice of right and truth'.[2]

In the summer of 1960 the world was alarmed at the collapse of the Paris East–West summit meeting which seemed to have wrecked the growing hopes of better relations between Russia and America. The non-aligned leaders, Nasser among them, were deeply worried by this turn for the worse in the cold war. Their main effort at the famous United Nations summit meeting, the Fifteenth General Assembly, that autumn, was to help Moscow and Washington to reopen summit talks. Their anxiety was sharpened – and their role as would-be mediators made more difficult – by the Congo crisis which that summer brought the cold war into the heart of Africa and threatened the existence of the United Nations itself.

From the earliest days of the Egyptian revolution, Nasser had emphasized the importance of Africa to Egypt. In *The Philosophy of the Revolution*, he defined the African continent as the second of the three circles with which the revolution is linked, the first being the Arab circle, and the third the Islamic world. Of the African circle, he said

We cannot under any condition, even if we wanted to, stand aloof from the terrible and terrifying battle now raging in the heart of that continent between five million whites and two hundred million Africans. We cannot stand aloof for one important and obvious reason – we are ourselves in Africa. Surely the people of Africa will continue to look to us – we who are the guardians of the Continent's northern gate – we who constitute the connecting link between the Continent and the outer world.[3]

Africa was in any case closely linked with the Arab and Islamic circles. Apart from Egypt herself, five other Arab and predominantly Muslim states – Sudan, Libya, Tunisia, Morocco and Algeria – were in Africa while several other non-Arab African states were either entirely Muslim, like Somalia, Mauretania, Mali and Senegal, or had large Muslim populations, like Nigeria. But, as in the case of his dealings with Asia and the Arab east, for Nasser the question of Islam or even of Arabism was less important than that of a common foreign policy and of solidarity in the anti-colonial and anti-imperialist struggle. Just as Nasser was closer to neutralist India than to Muslim Pakistan, and was hostile to Nuri's Iraq although it was Arab, so in Africa he worked closely with radical, non-aligned Ghana under Nkrumah and often clashed with Arab Tunisia and with partly Muslim Nigeria.

Nasser's words quoted above, with their rather grandiose conception of Egyptian leadership, now sound exaggerated and out of date. But in 1953, when they were written, Egypt was the only African state formerly under imperial or colonial rule to have attained independence, except for Libya which achieved independence in 1951. The only other independent states on the continent were Liberia, Ethiopia and South Africa. Egypt and South Africa were also the most developed states of Africa. The rest of the continent, whether 'Black Africa' south of the Sahara, or the Arab countries of north Africa, or the Sudan, which was an Arab–African hybrid, was in greater or lesser degree still controlled by the European colonial powers. Britain and France ruled most of the continent, with Belgium, Portugal and Spain still controlling important territories.

Egypt's first African preoccupation then was with the Sudan, though she had already begun to play a part through the United Nations in bringing Libya and Somalia to independence and, through the Arab League, had given her support to the nationalist independence movements in Arab north Africa, the Maghreb. Her hopes that, once freed from British rule, the Sudanese would choose union with Egypt and so ensure the unity of the Nile Valley were dashed when the Sudan achieved independence in 1956. Hard bargaining by the Sudanese over the Nile waters was one of the obstacles to an agreement on the building of the High Dam and relations with Egypt were strained over Egyptian military pressure during a border dispute at the beginning of 1958. After a *coup* in Khartoum established a military regime in the Sudan under General Ibrahim Abboud in 1958, relations with Egypt improved. Nasser paid a successful visit to Khartoum. Eventually a Nile Waters agreement was signed and the way opened for the beginning of work on the High Dam in 1960.

There were several strands in Nasser's African policies. Apart from Egypt's geographical position, her interest in the Nile waters and in Arab and Muslim Africa, Nasser saw Africa as one of the great theatres of the struggle for national liberation against imperialism and for peace through positive neutrality. This struggle, that had been given its first international ideological formulation at the Bandung conference in 1955, formed perhaps the most potent emotional and intellectual element in Nasser's world picture. As in the case of Arab unity, so African unity seemed to Nasser to have a positive and a negative side. Greater unity or closer cooperation between the African states would be positively beneficial in strengthening their diplomatic influence and their economic power as developing countries. In a more negative sense, African solidarity, like that of the Arabs, could be a defensive weapon in protecting the African states and Egypt herself from foreign and especially Western imperialist pressures. The liberation of African states would mean usually the departure of Western, and particularly British troops; the adoption of non-aligned policies by the liberated states would lead to the removal of Western military bases. This would reduce the dangers of the East–West cold war in Africa. It would also remove bases from which Egypt herself might be threatened with reconquest or politico-military pressures, an anxiety never far from Nasser's mind and which was reinforced by the Suez war.

By supporting the African liberation movements, Nasser hoped not only to keep British and French imperialism at bay but also to build up useful friends and allies for the future. With their independence, the African states would gain votes at the United Nations and a certain influence in world affairs. Nasser wanted to be able to mobilize this support behind Arab causes such as that of the Palestinian Arabs and the Algerian nationalists, as well as disputes in which Egypt herself might be more directly involved. In later years, as Israel began to woo the Black African countries, the limitation of such Israeli influence became another of the important – and eventually least successful – aims of Nasser's policy in Africa.[4]

Nasser saw the potential of a united Afro-Asian bloc as a bargaining factor in world politics. He hoped for advantages for Egypt in prestige, influence and possible material aid in playing a leading part in such a bloc.

As in his response to and mobilization of Arab nationalism, Nasser approached African nationalism on two levels – through governments and through peoples or non-governmental organizations. At first the emphasis was on popular movements because there were few African governments to deal with. Egypt gave encouragement and refuge to African nationalist movements, some of whom set up their headquarters in exile in Cairo and were given special programmes for their propaganda on Cairo radio. At the beginning of 1958, the Afro-Asian Solidarity Movement, a mixture of governmental and non-governmental organizations, held its first conference in Cairo where it also set up its permanent secretariat with an Egyptian Secretary-General. This organization, unlike the Bandung conference, included Russian as well as Chinese representatives. The main Egyptian official argument for their inclusion was that the chief concern of the Afro-Asian peoples had become the struggle against imperialism in which there was no question of neutrality between East and West. The real reason may have been the Egyptian sense of obligation to the Russians for their economic support since Suez and the prospects that they might agree to build the High Dam.[5] Nevertheless, by

Egyptian contrivance, the Afro-Asian Solidarity Movement gradually became a gilded cage for the Russians and Chinese rather than a power-house of their influence in Africa. As more and more African countries gained independence, Nasser's interest shifted to the African governments and their developing organizations. At the first conference of independent African states held in Accra in April 1958, five of the eight states represented were Arab and Muslim – the UAR, Sudan, Libya, Tunisia and Morocco. The others were Liberia, Ethiopia and newly independent Ghana. At the second conference of African states at Addis Ababa in June 1960 the number of countries invited had risen to fifteen (two did not come). The Arab countries were now in a minority, despite the addition of the Algerian provisional government-in-exile.

The resolutions of the Accra conference had laid down the lines of a common policy of support for the liberation of all Africa from colonialism, for the Algerian nationalists and of opposition to racialism in South Africa. They supported non-alignment between the hostile world blocs and called for the creation of an 'African personality' to be expressed through a unified foreign policy based on the principles of Bandung and the United Nations Charter.

Nasser was closely involved in the first major test of the African states' ability to play an effective international role when the Congo crisis developed in the summer of 1960. He promised the then Congo prime minister, Patrice Lumumba, full support, including arms, when Lumumba canvassed African help in case neither the United States nor the United Nations would help him to end the secession of Katanga and get rid of the Belgian troops and mercenaries. The UAR was one of the thirteen African states which took part in the African 'Little Summit' convened by Lumumba in Leopoldville in August 1960. UAR troops, 500 paratroopers, were among the contingents from the African and Asian states which formed part of the United Nations force sent to the Congo, though they were withdrawn within a few months after the controversial split in the Congo central government between Lumumba and President Kasavubu.

At first the African states were able to maintain a common

policy in dealing with the Congo. At Leopoldville they agreed to support the United Nations action in the Congo and condemned the 'secessionist and colonialist manoeuvres of Katanga'. But by the time that Nasser went to attend the UN 'summit assembly' between 23 September and 4 October 1960, this African unity had begun to crack. The split began over the breakdown of the Congo Central government, when President Kasavubu dismissed Lumumba from the premiership with the help of General Mobutu, an action that Lumumba rejected as unconstitutional. Even more controversial than the *coup* itself was the action of the United Nations officials in the Congo which accompanied it. At Kasavubu's request, the United Nations closed the Congo airfields and radio stations to all except United Nations aircraft and personnel. This meant that Lumumba was unable to rally his followers by broadcasts or to mobilize his military support in the provinces through the use of the Russian aircraft then at his disposal. The United Nations representative, Andrew Cordier, who took the decision, justified it on the grounds that it was necessary to prevent a breakdown of the Congo into civil war. But its effect was to handicap the Lumumbists and infuriate the Russians, who, together with the ambassadors of the UAR and Ghana, were expelled from the Congo by Kasavubu. Nasser blamed Belgian influence in Leopoldville and retaliated by seizing and nationalizing all Belgian property in the UAR, valued at about £15 million. Khrushchev, in a series of angry speeches at the United Nations, demanded the resignation of Hammarskjöld, with whom he refused any further cooperation. He called for a reorganization of the United Nations secretariat on the lines of a 'troika'–replacing the Secretary-General by a committee of three representing the West, the Communist world and the neutrals, whose decisions would have to be unanimous. This would have meant extending the veto from the Security Council into the executive operations of the Secretariat, including the carrying out of Assembly decisions.

All the Afro-Asian states, including the UAR, rejected the Soviet 'troika' plan which would have crippled their own influence in the Assembly. Almost all, again including the UAR, supported Hammarskjöld, though many were critical of the

United Nations officials' handling of Congo affairs. But they were divided over the question of who was the legitimate Congo government and on the degree to which they regarded the exclusion of Russian influence from the Congo with pro-Western or neutralist eyes. This division, basically over how neutral neutralists should be, was accentuated by several other new factors of African disunion. First there was the new independence of the thirteen French-speaking African states, many still under strong French economic and military influence.

Then the division between radicals and moderates, between the more and the less neutral, was complicated by the dispute over Morocco's claim to Mauretania. This led to a quarrel between Morocco and Tunisia which supported most of the other French-speaking African states in recognizing Mauretania's independence.

Over these questions the African states split into three main groups: the first evolved into what became known as the Casablanca Powers. Nkrumah, Nasser and Sekou Touré of Guinea were its leading spirits. It included the most radical states, the strongest supporters of the Lumumbists and those most critical of Western policy and of the conduct of the United Nations officials.

At the other extreme were eleven of the French-speaking African states, in which the leaders were the Ivory Coast, Congo (Brazzaville) and Madagascar. They later formed the nucleus of the Brazzaville and Monrovia groups of African powers. Under strong French influence, they were unequivocally for Kasavubu against Lumumba and indulgent towards Katanga separatism. They supported Western policy largely on anti-Communist and anti-neutralist grounds and were critical of the other more radical African states. In between these two groups was a third group of influential 'moderates' which included Nigeria, Tunisia, Ethiopia, Liberia and the Sudan. They were less committed as between Lumumba and his opponents and less critical of both the United States and the United Nations Secretariat.[6]

On 23 September Nasser flew to New York (stopping on the way in Madrid to see General Franco), to attend the United Nations General Assembly. At the initiative of Khrushchev, most of the world's leading statesmen, except General de Gaulle (and, of course, Mao Tse-tung), were present at this Assembly, leading their national delegations. It was Nasser's first visit to a Western country, except for European visits to Greece and Yugoslavia. He did not, regrettably, visit any of America outside New York City. It was also his first public appearance before a fully international conference not confined to Afro-Asian countries. He behaved with dignity in his public appearances and his meetings with Eisenhower, Khrushchev, Macmillan and other world leaders. When he addressed the UN Assembly on 27 September he spoke quietly and with comparative restraint. He was critical about 'imperialist designs' in the Congo, attacked French policy in Algeria, where he called for self-determination through a UN-supervised plebiscite, and restated the Arab case on Palestine. But the main emphasis of his speech, as in his private talks, was on problems of world peace and the need to reduce cold war tensions between the two blocs. The United Nations, he said, must be supported as the best organization for keeping the peace, and the non-aligned states had a great role to play in keeping down the temperature of the cold war.

On his return home Nasser reported on his visit in two public speeches, one to the National Assembly. He said that he had gone to New York because, after consulting other Afro-Asian and positive neutralist leaders, he had felt that as a result of the collapse of the Paris summit conference the world was going through a crisis that could destroy it: its fate should not be left in the hands of the conflicting camps. 'When the war comes we cannot be sure where the first atomic bomb will drop.' The newly independent countries might be able to help bridge the East-West gap. It was a 'misunderstanding' to think that the non-aligned countries wanted world tension so as to get aid from both blocs, for the expansion of military blocs could only lead to war. That was why neutralist leaders (himself, Nehru, Nkrumah, Tito and Sukarno) had drafted a resolution for the Assembly calling on Eisenhower and Khrushchev to meet.[7]

The proposal of the five neutralist leaders had failed to secure a two-thirds majority in the Assembly but the vote showed, Nasser claimed, that a majority of the states in the world supported it. This proposal and his speech to the Assembly were two of the most important aspects of Nasser's visit; the third was his meetings with world leaders. Eisenhower told him the United States wanted friendship with the UAR. Nasser replied that the UAR wanted this, too, but Israel and the supply of Western arms to her were an obstacle to closer relations. The UAR would also resist any 'imperialist influence' in Africa. Nasser felt the meeting was 'a constructive step towards Arab-American friendship'.[8] (Eisenhower, recording his impression of Nasser at this first meeting, wrote: 'In presence he was impressive, tall, straight, strong, positive. His features, dark eyes and dark hair with greying temples, gave him a vivid appearance. . . . He quickly got to specifics.')[9]

Nasser said he had had a friendly welcome in the United States and had tried to explain Arab views to the American people.

World Zionism tried to picture us [the Arabs] as savages and trouble-makers. . . . the citizens of New York were expecting to see Abdul Nasser shout and rant the way the Zionists say I do in their efforts to deceive the American people. The American people saw a different picture. The picture they saw was a reflection of this free and independent people.[10]

Nasser mentioned briefly his two meetings with Harold Macmillan, who had succeeded Anthony Eden as British premier. These led to an agreement to restore diplomatic relations with Britain at ambassadorial level. He had a 'most absorbing' talk with Castro with whom he felt a bond as a fellow-revolutionary.

But his warmest references were to his two meetings with Khrushchev. They had renewed 'an old friendship based on mutual respect for the viewpoints and ideologies of the other'. He had had a 'frank talk' with Khrushchev about the crisis in their relations in 1959 in order to consolidate the foundation of their friendship.[11]

By the end of the year the split in the Congo and between the African groups had deepened. Under heavy American pressure, the United Nations Assembly had recognized President Kasavubu's appointees as the legitimate Congo government. This was followed by the arrest of Lumumba and the establishment in

Stanleyville in Orientale province of a Lumumbist government under Gizenga, claiming national legitimacy.

At the invitation of the king of Morocco, a 'summit' conference was held in Casablanca in January 1961 between Morocco, the UAR, Ghana, Guinea, Mali, Libya, Ceylon and the Algerian nationalist provisional government. It was Nasser's first visit to the Maghreb, the Arab west.

The Casablanca meeting was essentially one of pro-Lumumbist countries and its discussions centred on three main topics: the Congo, Israel and the concept of African political union. At the conference Nasser urged that the Casablanca Powers should carry out the threats some of them had made to withdraw their troops from the UN force in the Congo, unless Hammarskjöld and the Assembly accepted the need for a new mandate, and that they should give direct military aid to the Gizenga government. The UAR then had a thousand of its troops among the 17,500-strong United Nations Congo Force. It had shown itself the only country prepared to give substantial aid to the Gizenga government, but the Sudan had refused to allow through to Stanleyville any supplies not sanctioned by the United Nations.[12]

Stanleyville's chief contact with the outside world was through Cairo, but direct UAR aid was limited to the supply of a radio station and some technicians.

Nasser yielded to the arguments of Nkrumah for a more cautious policy. Nkrumah opposed unilateral military support of Gizenga, and urged continued action through the United Nations. Geography and the lack of equipment of the African states would have made direct military help to Gizenga a risky enterprise. Such action, especially if suspected of having Communist backing, would also produce counter-balancing help for the Kasavubu regime, thus embroiling the Congo more deeply in civil war and outside interference. Partly as a *quid pro quo*, Nasser secured the agreement of Nkrumah to a resolution condemning Israel as an 'imperialist base' – the last time he was able to get agreement from an African states conference on a resolution condemning Israel. His insistence this time may have been spurred on by rumours that had begun circulating in the Western press that Israel was making an atomic bomb from her secret nuclear reactor set up with French help at Dimona in the Negev. Shortly before coming to Casablanca, Nasser had declared that if this were confirmed, the UAR would have to wage a preventive war 'even if we have to mobilize four million people'; if Israel were given nuclear weapons by imperialist states, 'we will secure atomic weapons at any cost' as the matter then would be one not of neutrality but of future survival.

The resolutions of the Casablanca conference called for African solidarity in the political, economic and military fields and for an African Charter based on the ending of colonialism and foreign military bases on the African continent.

Assessing the results of the conference in a speech to the UAR National Assembly, Nasser described it as 'a historic event incarnating African unity and the common anti-imperialist struggle and making nonsense of the imperialist attempt to divide the continent at the Sahara between Arab and Black Africa'. Nasser was already conscious of a trend among some of the 'Black African' states to prefer an organization of their own which would exclude Arab states, some of whose interests – for example, their dispute with Israel – lay outside the African continent.

This is not the place in which to follow in detail the subsequent evolution of the Congo: the murder of Lumumba in Katanga which deeply shocked most Africans, for whom he had become a nationalist symbol; the various attempts at a negotiated settlement; the fiasco of the first Katanga clash with United Nations forces in September 1961; the death of Hammarskjöld in a plane crash in November 1961; and the second and more successful United Nations action in Katanga a year later under the new Secretary-General, U Thant. Nor is it possible to give a full account of the various manoeuvres and conferences by which the rival African groups were eventually brought together into one body, the Organization for African Unity, formed at the Addis Ababa conference of heads of African states in May 1963. Suffice it to say that for the next two years at least African unity and unity in the Congo proved almost as elusive as Arab unity. In the struggle surrounding both objectives Nasser played an important part, though his influence in African affairs diminished as more African states and their leaders came to the fore. Even

among the Arab states of Africa the revolutionary pace was set
by the militant Algerian leader, Ben Bella, soon after Algeria
gained her independence in 1962. Nasser was, however, able to
prevent the split between Arab and 'Black African' states that he
had feared. The fact that he threw in his lot with the more militant
and radical African states, such as Ghana and Guinea, helped to
strengthen the influence of their ideas in the eventual agreed commitments of the OAU to the cause of the African liberation
movements and to positions of international non-alignment or
non-commitment. It also helped to maintain African pressure
behind the Algerians' demand for self-determination and independence. This was a factor which must have weighed in de Gaulle's
decision to end a war which cost hundreds of thousands of
Algerian dead and twice brought France herself to the brink of
civil war.

   For the UAR itself, however, the gains from Nasser's militant
African policy, other than moral satisfaction and prestige, were
less obvious. Nasser was unable to block the growing influence of
Israel, achieved through skilled diplomacy and technical aid, in
the Black African states – an aid he suspected of being secretly
financed and encouraged by the United States as a means of
combating the influence of the UAR and its associates. The
Americans on their side were apt to see Nasser's policy in Africa
as simply an extension of that of the Russians, with Nasser acting
as Moscow's instrument in repayment for Soviet support in the
Arab world. The main gain from Nasser's policy may have been
the extent to which his ability to play an active role in Africa as
well as the Middle East secured him a desperately needed economic development aid from both Russia and the United States.
Would he have received as much if he had played a more modest
and moderate role in African affairs like, say, the Sudan or even
Nigeria? Probably not, but he would also have avoided some of
the constant and economically damaging friction with the Western
Powers created by his African militancy.

   All these calculations of interest no doubt entered into Nasser's
mind. A different calculation might have sometimes changed the
style and scope of Nasser's policy in Africa, but it is unlikely that
it would have changed its substance. For as well as being a

calculating statesman, Nasser was a man of emotion and intense convictions, indeed one might fairly say a deeply moral man, however immoral some of his methods may have appeared. It would be unjust not to recognize that among his most sincere feelings was a passionate hatred of any form of 'colonialism' or 'imperialism' (words which Westerners like to write sceptically in quotation marks but which few people in Asia or Africa have any difficulty in recognizing as symbols of hateful real experiences that they have lived through). He had an equally passionate sympathy with the efforts made by those who have suffered from imperialism, whether in Africa, Asia or the Arab world, to stand in dignity on their own feet and to catch up socially and economically with the richer and more advanced parts of the world. It was in the impatience of his desire to see imperialism end and these efforts succeed that he was a revolutionary.

But in the summer of 1961 the turmoil in Africa was once more overshadowed by what seemed the even greater dangers of a war between the two great nuclear Powers. The summit meeting in Vienna in May between Kennedy and Khrushchev, far from reducing tension as the non-aligned leaders had hoped, appeared to have increased it. Khrushchev decided to put on the pressure over Berlin. Kennedy, determined to prove to Khrushchev that he was no weakling, reacted by despatching more American troops to Europe and increasing the American military commitment in South Vietnam. Khrushchev countered with the building of the Berlin wall dividing the city in two. He also resumed nuclear testing in the atmosphere, which had been suspended for two years past while a test-ban treaty was being discussed in Geneva.

It was against this sombre background that Nasser joined with leaders from twenty-three other non-aligned nations in the Belgrade conference on 1 September 1961. The preparatory committee of the conference, meeting in Cairo, decided that to qualify as non-aligned a country must pursue an independent foreign policy based on peaceful coexistence: it should take part neither in multilateral alliances such as NATO or the Warsaw Pact, SEATO and CENTO, nor in bilateral military alliances with Great Powers. It should not willingly have foreign military bases on its territory. Finally, it should be committed to support movements for national liberation and independence.[13] Only ten of the twenty-eight African independent states attended the conference in Belgrade. Tunisia and Nigeria were invited at the last minute: the offended Nigerians declined.

The composition of the Belgrade conference and its definition of non-alignment suggested that the conference would show a bias in its neutralism against the Western Powers because of their colonial activities and their recent policy in the Congo, and a more benevolent attitude towards the Soviet Union. Led by Nehru and Tito, who were supported by Nasser, the conference gave more attention, however, to the danger of a Soviet–American clash than to anti-colonialism. In his speech to the conference, Nasser stressed the need for peaceful coexistence and disarmament and later proposed that the conference should appeal to Khrushchev and Kennedy to reopen negotiations.

Nasser attacked Western military bases and neo-colonialism and condemned the use of NATO weapons by France and Portugal against the Algerians and Angolans. He also criticized the Soviet decision to resume nuclear tests which, he said, 'shocked me just as it shocked world opinion'. The failure to record a similar censure of the Soviet tests in the Belgrade conference final communiqué caused anger in Washington. The conference decided to send special missions to Washington and Moscow to urge the two blocs to start talks to reduce tension and avert the war threat. While Nehru and Nkrumah set off for Moscow to plead with Khrushchev and Sukarno and President Modeiba Keita of Mali flew to Washington to try to persuade Kennedy, Nasser returned to Cairo to face a crisis of his own. The UAR was on the verge of breakdown.

Chapter 11

The Rise and Fall of the UAR, 1958-61

As the immediate international pressures on the UAR relaxed after 1958, Nasser turned more of his attention to the internal affairs of the new state. He found himself grappling with increasing difficulties as he tried to graft on to Syria a political system and an economic planning structure which were still experimental in Egypt itself and which sprang more naturally from Egypt's circumstances than from those of Syria. When the merger of the two countries took place, Nasser's ideas about the organization of society were still largely fluid and unformed. But the way his mind was moving was indicated in his choice of a non-party national political organization outlined in the 1956 Egyptian constitution and in his call in the following year for the creation of a 'democratic, socialist and cooperative society'. In the trend of his thought there was a discordance which the union with Syria was to accentuate. Politically, the trend was towards the 'right', not only in the suppression of Communists but also in the emphasis on central authority plus some consultation and discussion rather than on any real popular share in policy or decision-making. Economically, the trend was towards the 'left', towards public ownership and state planning, culminating in the launching in the summer of 1961 of what was virtually a 'second revolution' with the extension of nationalization and land reform.

In Egypt this discordance could be overcome because of the strength of Nasser's own personal position and the powerful military and bureaucratic apparatus he controlled. The Egyptian left was weak; on the other side, a large part of the industrial and commercial capitalism that was initially brought under public control was not Egyptian but foreign. In Syria the situation was different. Despite much socialist talk, Syria had scarcely begun the social revolution which in Egypt had already started to affect both agriculture and industry. To carry through an increasingly socialist programme in Syria, where the ground had not been prepared politically or economically, and where he lacked the kind of reliable power apparatus that he had in Egypt, Nasser needed the active cooperation of the Syrian left, especially (in the absence of the Communists) the support of the Baath Socialists, the pioneers of the union. But for political reasons, Nasser not only got rid of the Communists but also snubbed the Baath. He did not trust the Baathists. His aversion to them was increased by the intrigue and quarrelling he found among the Baath leadership.[1] He sought more reliable allies in Syria among army officers who were less doctrinally committed and among political independents of a more conservative kind. He also made a genuine effort to avoid economic dislocation as a result of the union, and so at first tried to appease the Syrian business class. The consequence was that when his movement towards socialist planning was suddenly accelerated with the major series of nationalizations in 1961 (largely for reasons connected with the economic and social structure of Egypt), he found that the Syrian bourgeoisie, relatively strengthened by the subduing of the Syrian left and freed of their fears of Iraq, where Kassim had also begun to curb the Communists, were able successfully to revolt against him. In his dealings with Syria, Nasser was torn between controlling it too tightly and not controlling it enough. The political needs of Syria required compromise with the right while the social needs of Egypt drove Nasser towards the left. To meet Syrian grievances and avoid charges of Egyptian domination, he sometimes tried to limit the dictatorial tendencies of his Syrian instruments, such as Colonel Sarraj, in favour of persuasion and more liberal policies. But he was not prepared to accept in Syria such a degree of democratic discussion as might give a foothold for outside influences from the West or from Russia or that might by contagion spread eventually through the UAR and thus undermine his political will in Egypt. The result was that Nasser interfered in Syria arbitrarily enough to arouse Syrian hostility but not powerfully enough to make his policies finally effective.

In Egypt the implementation of the 1956 constitution had been delayed by the Suez crisis. The constitution provided for an elected National Assembly and for a single political organization, the National Union. In May 1957 the executive committee of the

National Union, newly appointed by Nasser and consisting of three of his closest associates, Abdul Latif Baghdadi, Zacharia Mohieddin and Abdul Hakim Amer, began screening the 2,500 candidates for the Assembly elections, rejecting nearly half of them. The voting in July for the Assembly's 350 seats had two interesting new features: it was compulsory and it was open to women for the first time. Most of the candidates and those elected, apart from government ministers, were middle-class, professional men, lawyers, journalists, doctors, senior civil servants, ex-army officers, some businessmen, land-owners and farmers, village headmen and local mayors. There were few candidates from the poorer classes largely because of the £E50 deposit required. Among those elected were four workers, seven company employees, two women – but no poor peasants.[2]

The Assembly opened its first meeting on 22 July 1957, the fifth anniversary of the revolution, with an inaugural speech by Nasser. The candidates had been hand-picked, but the Assembly members were not all mere official echoes. They included some who had been associated with older political groups, both on the right, including the Muslim Brothers, and the left. Before the Assembly was dissolved in March 1958, with the creation of the UAR, it was the forum for some criticism of the government's treatment of political detainees and also of its tightening of political control over the universities. The pressure for the removal of political discrimination against students entering universities was strong enough to force the Minister of Education, Kamal ed-din Hussein, to resign. Nasser reinstated him.[3]

In November 1957 the main body of the National Union was formed in Egypt with Anwar es-Sadat as its Secretary-General. Its constitution was laid down by presidential decree. Its first article defined the aim of the National Union as 'the creation of a socialist, democratic, cooperative society free of all political, social and economic exploitation'.

The slogan of a 'socialist, democratic and cooperative society' was to remain the vague guiding principle of Nasser's groping search for an effective political and economic doctrine until the regime crystallized in 1961-2 into a more definitely socialist pattern.

During those years, broadly speaking 'democracy' meant for Nasser the National Union, with its controlled mass organization, and the National Assembly, with its limited scope for discussion; 'socialism' meant state control of planning and investment and limited redistribution of wealth. The most important word was 'cooperative'. This meant not only the practice of extending cooperatives in the traditional sense in agriculture, but also the principle of 'cooperation' between government and private enterprise in both farming and industry.

The idea of 'cooperation' gave a certain homogeneity to Nasser's political thinking at that time. He saw the National Union as a political framework in which inevitably conflicting class interests could be resolved by discussion and cooperation in the interests of national unity, rather than by a Marxist class struggle.[4]

One of the six original principles of the Free Officers in 1952 had been to eradicate not only 'feudalism' but also 'the domination of capital and monopoly over government'. They appear to have had in mind the political influence exercised over the national economy, like that of the great land-owners, by a few of the biggest industrialists, such as Abboud Pasha who controlled a sugar, textile and shipping empire with the help of government funds and privileges obtained through the Wafd. But just as land reform left agriculture still in private hands, subject to some state control, so the Free Officers saw the development of industry, which Egypt desperately needed, as being carried out by a mixture of public and private effort. In the first years after the revolution, before Suez, the regime made little change in the structure of Egypt's economic system, apart from the limited land reform and some social welfare measures. This was partly because it was absorbed with completing the 'political revolution' of securing complete national independence. The aim of a balance between public and private enterprise was embodied in the 1956 Constitution.

The movement from a basically free enterprise economy, through a phase of 'Guided Capitalism'[5] to an at least partially socialist society, did not take place in accordance with a clear and pre-determined ideological doctrine, but pragmatically in response to economic and political pressures. Nasser later said, 'we reached our ideologies through our experience. We extracted our ideologies from the details of events we passed through and did not permit any ideology to force itself on us.'[6]

One of the first and most important experiences pushing Nasser along the road towards greater government intervention in the economy was the affair of the High Dam and Suez. The withdrawal of the Western offer to help finance the High Dam and the Western 'economic blockade' during and after the Suez crisis confirmed Nasser's fears of Egyptian dependence on foreign capital. They also indicated that his former hopes of relying heavily for Egyptian development on Western aid without political strings might have to be abandoned for some time to come. (These fears proved exaggerated, though Western aid never reached the level once hoped for.) At the same time, the Western 'blockade', through the freezing of Egypt's foreign assets, meant that the government, while keeping a tight control over imports, also encouraged local manufacturing to replace imported goods. Egypt needed industrialization more rapidly than ever and she would have to rely more than before on her own capital resources for investment. The nationalization of the Canal Company had itself seemed to point to one of the methods to be employed, both to make more capital and foreign exchange available and to reduce dependence on foreign investment. The 'Egyptianization' of all foreign banks, insurance companies and commercial import–export agencies in January 1957 (they had to become Egyptian-owned companies within five years) was accompanied by the creation of a National Planning Committee and of the 'Economic Organization'. A semi-autonomous government body, the Economic Organization was to control all industrial and commercial concerns which the government fully or partly owned – including steel, minerals, chemicals and textiles – and also to take over the sequestered British and French property. The latter included most of the commercial banking and insurance business of Egypt. Nasser's decision to hand over most of the sequestered and Egyptianized firms to the Economic Organization rather than sell them to Egyptian private enterprise was one of the first big steps on the road to public ownership and a planned economy.

While the National Planning Committee, staffed by a technical secretariat of 200 and some foreign experts, was charged with drawing up a long-term plan for social and economic development, a new Ministry of Industry prepared a five-year industrial development plan which went into effect in 1958. The aim of the industrial plan was to increase the annual growth rate of industrial output from about six per cent to sixteen per cent over five years. The government was to provide sixty-one per cent of the investment required, mostly in heavy industry or industries new to Egypt, but it still hoped to attract more private capital into industry (this had also been one of the aims of the land reform).

The failure to achieve this private investment on the hoped-for scale (at a time when foreign aid was comparatively scarce) and the difficulty of exercising effective planning control over private enterprise led Nasser into conflict with the Egyptian business class and on towards increased public control of investment and eventually extensive nationalization. Once the process had begun it was further stimulated by political factors. Nasser saw the resistance or reluctance of the leading Egyptian capitalists from 1960 onwards as a challenge to his power. He also feared that the mixture of public control and private ownership was opening the door to a new form of corruption. Officials were more liable to be bribed to grant contracts for development schemes and to help friends and relatives in the import–export business (there was one notorious case of a senior official and his engineering adviser who received a one per cent commission on construction work for the Liberation Province, the big expensive agricultural development scheme). There was the greater danger that the capitalists might buy their way back into the very centres of government power by building financial and social connexions with the new ruling group of ex-officers and technocrats.[7]

These anxieties were reinforced by the feeling that in other ways, too, the revolution was beginning to run down and lose sight of its social aims. The land reform was in difficulties. Economically it was a success. Production on redistributed land had risen, with the incentive of ownership and the help in credit and technical advice given by the government through the system of 'supervised cooperatives'. As a measure of social justice, the reform had been less successful. The redistribution of land had benefited perhaps a million people, farmers and their families, but this was only about five per cent of the peasantry. Many millions still had no land at all and the rest owned or rented only tiny holdings. The laws controlling rent and fixing minimum agricultural wages were being widely evaded, often with the connivance of the tenants and farm workers themselves, owing to the acute shortage of land and jobs. There was criticism in the press of the amount that farmers had to pay the government in interest and annual repayments for the land they acquired under the agrarian reform. All these grievances were more deeply felt in 1960–61 because it was a bad year for cotton, with the crops ravaged by cotton worm. There was also evasion of the law limiting the amount of land that could be owned by one person or his family. By exploiting the allowance made for relatives and the use of 'straw men', it was possible for a former big landowner whose personal holding should not have exceeded 200 feddans to control effectively as much as two or three thousand feddans. Thus he was able to maintain in his district the kind of power and influence over the peasantry that the revolution had branded as 'feudalism' and had tried to eradicate.[8]

Internationally, Egypt had run into quieter waters after the 'year of victory' in 1958. The quarrel with Kassim in Iraq continued and Nasser still had problems in Syria. But in neither of these troubles did the Egyptian public feel deeply involved. 'Arab nationalism' was not exciting enough to stir the Egyptians as a whole except at a time of international crisis. Nasser must have felt the need of a new political dynamic to keep the revolution going and to generate the energy required for a more rapid social and economic development. For Egypt had to move faster if she were not to be left even further behind by her increase in population and by the progress of the more advanced countries. Socialism, in the sense of state-planned development and more equal distribution of wealth, was one answer. Its adoption also involved making a new choice in the dilemma that had faced the revolution from its beginning, whether to give priority to efficient production and economic motives or to social justice. The regime had at first given priority to production and efficiency rather than to redistribution of wealth. The economic gains from this policy seemed not enough to compensate for the political disadvantages. So more weight had to be given to equalizing wealth, while the state took over the task of mobilizing investment.

To gain control of investment sources, the government in 1960 nationalized the Bank Misr, Egypt's most powerful and oldest established financial, commercial and industrial complex, comprising not only the country's largest commercial bank but also factories contributing some twenty per cent of Egyptian industrial production. This was the first of a series of nationalization measures in 1960. Newspapers and magazines were 'socialized' by being given a form of self-administration responsible to the National Union, but the effect was to end the independence of the Egyptian press in the eyes of its readers, for whom this was an unpopular move.

At the same time the government adopted the first comprehensive five-year plan – the first stage of an ambitious plan to double the national income over a decade. The five-year plan called for a total investment in Egypt of £E1,577 million to increase the national income by forty per cent. Investment in Syria was to total 2,720 million Syrian pounds (about £270 million).[9] By 1960 the government had assumed control over at least three-quarters of Egypt's capital investment but had still little control over actual production. Some two-thirds of all national production in Egypt, including almost all of agriculture, was still outside government control.[10]

In his speeches to the first session of the General Congress of the National Union of the UAR in July 1960 and to the opening session of the new National Assembly (400 nominated members from Egypt and 200 from Syria), Nasser stressed the theme of social justice as well as increasing production, but still talked in terms of a mixed economy. But within less than a year Nasser had reached the conclusion that cooperation between government and private capital in carrying out the five-year plans would not work. This may have been due to the recalcitrance of the capitalists or the inefficiency of the planning methods, or both. Nasser's solution was not to modify the plan but to take over direct control of production. He then launched the UAR into what was described as the 'Social Revolution', or 'The Second Revolution' (the first being the 'Political Revolution' which had established independence and broken the power of 'feudalism'). In June 1961 there began a new series of nationalizations and other sweeping government economic measures. The whole of the cotton trade was taken over by the government and all import–export firms brought under government control. On 23 July 1961, on the ninth anniversary of the revolution, Nasser announced the nationalization of a large part of Egyptian industry and commerce, including all banks and insurance companies, all heavy or basic industries, among them electricity and motorized transport. In eighty-six medium-sized companies, the state expropriated half of the share capital and in 117 others limited the private individual share holding to £10,000, the rest of the shares going to the state. Small-scale light industry and 'non-exploiting' professions and services were left free.

At the same time there were new measures aimed at redistribution of wealth and increasing workers' control in industry. The limit of land-ownership was cut from 200 to 100 feddans and a maximum of fifty feddans for rented land. Farmers would no longer have to pay interest on loans from the Mortgage Agricultural and Cooperative Credit Bank. (The government had already reduced the interest and lengthened the repayment period for farmers who had bought land redistributed under the agrarian reform.) No incomes in any organizations were to exceed £5,000 a year, and there was to be a new progressive income tax of up to ninety per cent on all incomes over £10,000.

Workers and employees were to have the right to a twenty-five per cent share in the profits of their firms. They would also have elected representatives on the management boards of their firms in the proportion of one to seven. Working hours were to be cut from eight to seven hours a day without a reduction in wages.

Speaking on 23 July in Alexandria, Nasser said the new measures ushered in a 'new era of equality without hate or violence or spirit of revenge. ... We meet today in the framework of a new society. ...' He stressed the need for a more equal sharing of wealth but claimed that there had been no confiscation without compensation: the land-owners had been generously treated, being left with 100 feddans while the landless peasant received only five.

If we want to have an idea of the way of life of our people [said Nasser], we should not look at the lights of Alexandria, Cairo or Damascus ... we must look at our problems far from the sparkling lights of great cities. We must look at the rural sector to know how the fellah lives. He lives on wages in the service of a land-owner; as an agricultural labourer working four or five months a year and unemployed the rest of the year. He can scarcely find enough to eat, to subsist, for himself and his children. How does an itinerant agricultural worker live? He lives with the lowest wage a worker can get. Five years ago I visited Kom Ombo [in Upper Egypt near Aswan] and the factories there. For lunch each worker was eating dry bread and an onion – all of them the same. None of us can accept such living conditions.

Without economic justice and social equality, Nasser claimed, using a familiar argument, there could be no real democracy. Nevertheless, there were soon to be signs that one of the main weaknesses of the new 'social revolution' was the lack of an effective democratic political organization for carrying it out.

Although the July decrees did not turn Egypt or the UAR into a fully socialist country – agriculture, in which two-thirds of the population were engaged, was still in private hands and so were many small urban enterprises – they involved a major change in the structure and direction of Egyptian society. Yet they were decreed by Nasser with scarcely any preliminary public discussion either in the National Union, the National Assembly or the press and radio. They were administrative decisions to be carried out by administrative means, through the government apparatus. There might be free criticism in detail of the way the measures were applied but no serious discussion of basic policy.

In Egypt, at least, there had been some preparation over the years for this radical change, as a result of the gradual increase in public control and ownership. But in Syria, there had been little alteration in the free enterprise system, except for the recent land reform and the imposition of exchange control. So to the Syrians the nationalization came like a bombshell. In neither half of the UAR did there yet exist a political organization capable of handling such important economic and social changes effectively in a democratic manner.

Despite the elaborate network of the National Union, and the creation of the National Assembly, Egypt continued in practice to be ruled administratively by Nasser himself through a powerful bureaucracy. Since the revolution, ex-army officers and technocrats had become a dominating element in the ministries as well as in publicly owned or controlled economic and cultural bodies. All major decisions flowed from Nasser himself, in sporadic consultation with his ministers and with the inner core of his old revolutionary associates of the Free Officers group. In any time of crisis, Nasser's power base, apart from his mass popularity, was still the network of loyal Free Officers which now extended not only through the army but through all the key posts of the administration, especially in the intelligence and security services. Nasser was always aware of the need to broaden his political base. But in the absence of political parties, which Nasser would not accept, he and the Free Officers seemed never to be clear in their minds about the rule of organizations such as the National Union. They were said to be intended for the mobilization of national political energies behind the objectives of the revolution. They were to be linked with government at different levels and to discuss and advise on government policy. In that case, what was their real relation to the National Assembly which the top layer of the National Union seemed to duplicate? One explanation is that Nasser was trying to overcome public passivity of the kind that he despairingly recorded when he wrote that during the 1952 revolution the army vanguard charged the barricades of the old regime and looked round to find no one following it. At the same time, he was still afraid of public extremism in a crisis, such as occurred in the years leading up to the revolution. He distrusted the capacity of politically conscious Egyptians to avoid destructive factionalism or to refrain from seeking foreign support, whether from West or East. So there was an ambiguity about the regime's attitude towards the National Union, as towards its predecessor, the Liberation Rally, and its successor, the Arab Socialist Union. Were these organizations to be instruments for the regime's control of the masses to guide them more effectively along the road of social and economic planning? Or were they meant to give the public more control over the regime, that is, greater responsibility and participation by the public in political life? Probably Nasser had both aims in mind – he wanted both to mobilize and educate the masses politically but also to keep ultimate power in his own hands. Where the two aims clashed, as they were bound eventually to do, it was the second which prevailed.

The National Union was organized on a pyramidal structure and its greatest value, both to the regime and to the population, was probably at the lower levels of village, town and district. Its local committees were intended to help both to decentralize and democratize Egyptian local government, and to provide centres of initiative in social and cultural affairs among a conservative peasantry. The top of the pyramid, the Higher Executive Committee, was chosen by Nasser from among his chief ministers and Free Officer supporters.

In Syria, on the other hand, until the merger with Egypt there was an active party life and a parliament which was able not only to talk but to take decisions, though in practice its powers had become limited by the attempted terrorization of the opposition and by the influence exerted by army factions behind the scenes. After the merger, the Syrian parties were dissolved. The intention was to replace them by a National Union for the whole of the UAR. Under the provisional constitution for the UAR promulgated on 5 March 1958, there was to be a single National Assembly for the UAR – 400 members from Egypt and 200 from Syria – appointed by President Nasser. Half of the Assembly was to be appointed from the Egyptian Assembly and the Syrian parliament. The other half was to be selected from the General Congress of the National Union.

There was to be a central cabinet for the UAR and separate executive councils for the two 'regions' – Egypt was the 'Southern Region' and Syria was the 'Northern'. The first UAR cabinet announced on 6 March 1958 included fourteen Syrians among its thirty-four members. Two Syrians, Akram el Haurani of the Baath and Sabry al Asaly, the National bloc leader and former premier, were among two of the four Vice-Presidents. The former President of Syria, Shukri el Kuwatly, retired into the background with the honorific title of 'First Arab Citizen'. In Syria itself, the formidable and heroically incorruptible Colonel Sarraj became Minister of the Interior.

Though the Baath had theoretically dissolved itself in accordance with the official abolition of parties, it continued for a time to be the main political influence, together with the Baathist and Nasserite army officers, in the day-to-day government of Syria. In Egypt Nasser ruled as before. In the joint affairs of the UAR, Nasser and his own personal apparatus in the army and bureaucracy were responsible for decision-making. The Syrian ministers in the central government, like the Syrian officers brought down to serve in Egypt, found they were decreasingly consulted. With handsome offices and titles in Cairo, they were cut off from their home political base in Syria, but without compensating influence in the UAR as a whole.[11]

From the start there was a basic misunderstanding between Nasser and the Baath, who considered themselves the chief architects of the union. The Baath saw the purpose of the merger as, in the words of Salah ed-din el Bitar, 'the Arabization of both Egypt and Syria' as the first step towards an even wider union of Arab states. They had accepted the abolition of parties and their replacement by the National Union in the belief that the Baath would have a leading role in the National Union and the government. They hoped that the form of the National Union for the UAR would not be simply an extension of its pattern in Egypt, but would reflect in its ideology and structure an agreed ideological blend of Baathism and Nasserism, a blend which would apply not only to Syria but throughout the UAR and any future expanded Arab union. They saw Nasser as a splendid capture or recruit whose personal prestige would add power to the Baath's ideas.[12]

But to Nasser, the Baath were only one factor in the Syrian political scene. He relied in the first place on his links with the

Syrian army and security officers, headed by Sarraj. He did not at first wish to alienate other important and more conservative groups in Syria by making the Baath his exclusive ally. His first concern was to check Syria's political disintegration, especially while there was any danger first of Western intervention and then of Communist pressure from Kassim's Iraq. He wanted to consolidate the UAR itself and did not want to bring other Arab states into the union at that stage. He only wanted their cooperation and support for his foreign policy of neutralism.

In these circumstances he could count on widespread support in Syria, without the Baath, from all sections of the population, including the business community, who wanted stability and feared Communism. For many Syrians, too, disillusioned with their own political leaders, Nasser was welcome not as an intruding Egyptian, but as a strong Arab leader. To them the Baath began to seem simply 'Nasserism without Nasser'.[13] Moreover, Nasser had no desire to give the Baath a share in the ideological formation of the UAR as a whole, since this would have given them a political influence in Egypt of which he was suspicious. The Baathists believed that all the influence of Egypt's new ruling *élite* of ex-army officers and bureaucrats was also thrown against a more democratically based political system which might have curtailed their influence and privileges.

For the Baathists, 'Arabism' and Arab unity were a missionary cause: their zeal found an echo in Syrian popular emotion, though they remained a small minority party in parliamentary terms. Nasser himself may have been enthused by the same kind of vision, but the general Egyptian approach was based on interest rather than emotion. Part of Nasser's task was to persuade the sceptical Egyptian public of the value of the union, in both sentimental and practical terms. To support his persuasion, the official propaganda machine concentrated on the Arab centuries of Egypt's history and the Arab aspects of her civilization. But the average Egyptian bureaucrat or technocrat was inclined to look on Syria, with its five million people, compared with Egypt's more than twenty-five million, as a country Egypt had taken over to help to administer in her own interest. To the touchy and sophisticated Syrian middle class this often looked like a patronizing attitude verging on colonialism. This did not necessarily mean that Egypt was trying to exploit Syria economically in any damaging sense. On the contrary, Syria benefited from additional public investment and from the help of Egyptian technicians and professional men in certain fields. Syrian businessmen profited more than Egyptians from freedom of trade between the two countries.

In his speech on the first anniversary of the UAR, Nasser was able to claim a number of important internal achievements in the first year of the merger, a year which had been, he said, chiefly devoted to planning and the study of economic development. Perhaps the most important changes affecting Syria were the introduction of land reform, the abolition of tribal law in the desert areas, and the launching of a five-year industrialization plan to cost some 560 million Syrian pounds (about £56 million). Schools and university places, agricultural projects and road-building had substantially expanded. In Egypt there was progress towards the building of the High Dam and the development of the New Valley. The latter was an ambitious scheme for agricultural development in a large area linking a string of oases in the desert parallel with the Nile valley. The iron and steel plant, built at Helwan outside Cairo, with the help of West German capital and technicians, had begun production. This plant was to prove of more value as a morale-raising symbol of Egypt's determination to industrialize and as a training ground for technicians and management than as a profitable economic investment. For years it ran at a loss and under capacity, absorbing large quantities of precious public investment capital.

The merger of the Syrian and Egyptian economies ran into four main difficulties. The first was intractable natural disaster. A three-year-long drought severely cut Syrian agricultural production and reduced the Syrian national income in 1960 by a third. It wiped out Syria's profitable grain exports and forced her to import wheat instead.

The second difficulty, temporarily aggravating the first, was the manner in which the land reform, a landmark in Syria's social history, was implemented. The land reform in Syria was both more extensive and more drastic than in Egypt. It affected sixty per cent of the cultivated land as compared with ten per cent in Egypt. But it was criticized for making insufficient allowance for the variety of land and the different types of cultivation and farm organization in the various regions of Syria.

The third cause of trouble was the attempt to bring Syria into line with Egypt's strict system of foreign exchange control. Syrian merchants had a well-developed import–export trade on a free exchange basis. If exchange control were to be extended to Syria at all – and this was probably inevitable if the economic merger of the two countries was to make sense – it needed to be done both more rapidly and with more careful preparation to avoid the massive flight of Syrian capital abroad which took place. Finally, the most serious difficulty arose from the introduction of a new progressive income tax and the large-scale nationalization of banks, insurance companies and industrial enterprises decreed in July 1961, following the public control of their operations under the state planning system.

Much has been written about the virtues of Syrian free enterprise and its incompatibility with the *étatism* imposed from Egypt. In fact, there is little doubt that Syria needed more planning of its economy and more public investment. Even the operation of private enterprise suffered from the weakness of the public sector which had failed in many cases to provide the investment in infrastructure, such as roads, railways, irrigation and state social and technical services, required for a developing country. Nor, despite Syria's advantage of plentiful land, underpopulation and greater literacy, was the distribution of wealth in Syria more socially just than in Egypt, whether before or after the revolution. Land reform was as great a social need in Syria, especially in certain areas, as it had been in Egypt.

The conditions in each country were, however, clearly sufficiently different to require different methods of economic and social planning. Perhaps nationalization of Syria's small but efficient industrial sector was less urgent or important economically than in Egypt and created a disproportionate political opposition. The process could have been more gradual. But the biggest weakness in Nasser's attempts to introduce economic and social change in Syria lay in his failure to find a suitable political framework. It was this failure that led to the breach between Nasser and the Baath, who should have been his natural partners in Syria if his aim was socialism. The breach was to have fateful consequences for years after the break-up of the UAR in Nasser's dealings with Syria and Iraq and eventually in contributing to the outbreak of the 1967 war with Israel.

In October 1958, a new central cabinet for the UAR was formed, bringing Haurani, Bitar and other Baathists to Cairo and leaving Sarraj virtually in control of Syria. The Baathists were not even dominant in the Syrian regional cabinet which was headed by a non-Baathist former civil servant, Dr Nur ed-din Kahhale. In October 1959 Nasser appointed Abdul Hakim Amer as his viceroy in Syria with full powers to deal with the economic and political situation there. Amer agreed to some liberalization of economic controls to appease the Syrian businessmen. Politically, his first task was to supervise the last stages of the National Union elections. In fact, it was Sarraj who 'fixed' them. The results were the last straw for the Baath leaders, who had already clashed with Nasser over the land reform and his policy towards Iraq. The Baath won less than five per cent of the 9,500 seats on the higher committees of the National Union in Syria. The majority elected were 'independents' from the traditional and conservative elements in Syrian society.[14] The Baathist leaders, Haurani and Bitar, resigned from the UAR Central Cabinet and two other Baathist officers left the Syrian regional cabinet. The thirty-four-year-old Sarraj, whose star was steadily rising, became controller of the National Union in Syria (his counterpart in Egypt was Kamal ed-din Hussein, the Minister of Education). He was the most important of six Syrians in the eighteen-man Higher Executive Committee of the National Union for the whole UAR appointed by Nasser in June 1960. Five months later Sarraj was appointed chairman of the Syrian executive council, the equivalent of prime minister of the regional government, and Nasser brought Amer back to Cairo. By this time the Baath and its army sympathizers, except for Sarraj, had been completely ousted from the government of both Syria and the UAR as a whole.

In June 1960 Nasser appointed the 600-man National Assembly of the UAR and seven months later asked the Assembly to work out a new permanent constitution. In Syria, however, the withdrawal of Amer and the promotion of Sarraj marked a tightening of the police state controls which paralleled Nasser's plans for radical changes in the UAR economic structure. In a speech at Latakia during a visit to Syria in February 1961, Nasser showed his awareness of the various sources of discontent in the country. But he scoffed at the Beirut newspapers 'in the pay of the imperialists' who said the union could not last. 'Crocodile tears' were shed about economic freedom in Syria but where, he asked, was Syrian industry? The only factory he could see in Latakia was a lumber mill. As for complaints about political freedom, 'By God, anyone who wants to have a conversation in his house can do so without fear. We shan't do anything to him. But let them come and say to the people what they say among themselves "We want civil liberties, we want democracy, we want political parties."' When there were parties, Nasser added, the Syrian parliament had never been able to discuss land reform or social questions.[15]

Nasser was not deterred by these symptoms of unrest from pressing on with the radical economic changes in the UAR which had already been taking shape in Egypt during the previous years. The nationalization decrees of July 1961, a leap forward in the centralized control and planning of the economy, were issued without consulting the Syrian Minister for National Economy.[16] They were followed three weeks later by the centralization of the UAR government under a single cabinet. On 28 August Nasser told the cabinet that the aims of the new central government in 'the new phase of the revolution' were unity and socialism. 'Henceforward the struggle is engaged to eliminate regionalism.' Ministerial portfolios would no longer be allocated on the basis of national origin. The central government would meet in Damascus from February to May and for the rest of the year in Cairo or Alexandria. There would be strict centralization for all economic planning but a wide autonomy and decentralization in carrying out decisions.

As part of this process Sarraj was made Vice-President for internal affairs and brought to Cairo. The removal of Sarraj from Damascus was intended by Nasser partly as a measure of reassurance to the Syrians who had been becoming increasingly restive under Sarraj's heavy policeman's hand. But while Sarraj was an unpopular goad to Syrian public feelings, his security apparatus was also the most effective safeguard Nasser had left for the control of Syria, at least during this critical time when he was estranged from the left and when his economic policy was bound to antagonize the right. Above all, Sarraj's 'promotion' removed Nasser's most efficient watchdog over the Syrian army officers, among whom there had been growing jealousy and frustration at their subordinate place in the UAR military hierarchy.

Like other Syrian ministers before him, Sarraj found that his post in Cairo was without serious power or responsibility. After two months, on 15 September, he went back to Syria, apparently without even asking Nasser's permission, and resigned eleven days later. Several officers of his security organization were then dismissed by Nasser. On 28 September 1961 a group of army officers, profiting from the virtual paralysis of the regime's intelligence apparatus in Damascus, staged a swift *coup* which led within a week to the secession of Syria from the UAR. An armoured column moved into Damascus from a nearby military camp, seized the radio and army headquarters. The UAR vice-president, Field Marshal Amer, and General Jamal Feisal, commander of the UAR First Army, were held virtually under arrest.

The leaders of the *coup* were professionally disgruntled or right-wing army officers in alliance with civilian politicians connected with the Syrian business class. Prominent among the latter were men associated with the 'Khamissiya' or 'Group of Five', who controlled a powerful concentration of banking, insurance and industrial interests. The legal adviser to the 'Khamissiya', Dr Mamoun el Kuzbari, who had been a minister under the former military dictator, Shishakli, became prime minister of the first secessionist government, formed mostly of technical experts and businessmen, especially bankers. In one of their first radio communiqués, the rebels accused the UAR of having tried to impoverish and degrade the Syrian people. 'We revolted,' it said, 'against those who betrayed their national responsibilities, misspent public and state funds, enforced a police-state type of government and ousted the best military personnel from the army.'[17]

The *coup* leaders at first hinted that they did not want to break up the union but only to change its form. They offered talks on this basis with Amer, but Nasser refused to discuss a compromise, considering probably correctly that the offer was made largely to gain time. Amer and General Feisal were then released and allowed to fly back to Cairo.

Nasser heard the news of the *coup* almost at once when he tuned into Damascus radio at two or three in the morning. It was, he said later, 'one of the bitterest moments of my life'.[18] At nine o'clock the same morning he broadcast to the nation. Speaking quietly, but with his voice shaken by emotion, he said that what was happening in Syria was more serious than the Suez invasion because it was not an external aggression but 'an attack on the long struggle for the creation of the Arab nation and Arab nationalism'. He declared that he would never proclaim the dissolution of the UAR. It would be maintained as the bastion and vanguard of the Arab struggle. 'We want to avoid bloodshed,' he said, but announced that 'the First Army is now converging on Damascus from all sides to repress the mutiny'.[19]

At midday, believing that the northern Syrian cities of Aleppo and Latakia were still holding out against the rebels, Nasser ordered 2,000 paratroopers to be flown from Egypt to support them, followed by the entire UAR navy and more troop reinforcements in ships. But the next day, after learning that the Aleppo and Latakia garrisons had gone over to the rebels, Nasser countermanded these orders. The aircraft and ships were turned back. The 120 paratroopers who had already landed at Latakia were instructed to surrender without firing a shot. Nasser declared, 'Shall an Arab fight an Arab?' and added, 'I could in no circumstances transform this union into a military operation'.[20] Militarily and logistically he knew a reconquest was impossible unless a substantial part of the Syrian army remained loyal to the union.

Instead, he wisely made a virtue of necessity. The same day

(29 September 1961) he made the first of several speeches to the Egyptian people over the next few weeks in which he explained the difficulties encountered by the union, analysed the causes of its breakdown and prepared Egyptian and Arab opinion for the inevitable acceptance of Syria's secession in a mood of sorrow rather than anger. Above all, he made it plain there was no question of abandoning Egypt's attachment to Arab nationalism. His chief concern was to avoid a reaction in Egypt against commitment to the Arab world. He also wanted to clear himself before Arab opinion as a whole of responsibility for the break-up of the first serious experiment in Arab unity.

With Amer at his side, he addressed a large crowd outside the National Union headquarters in Cairo. He said that the Egyptians must not let bitterness overcome reason and wisdom, the UAR 'must remain the fortress and focus of Arabism'. Blaming the *coup* on 'reactionary, separatist and imperialist' elements, Nasser predicted – accurately as events proved – that the Syrian people would not give up the social gains they had made under the UAR – the end of agricultural feudalism brought about by the land reform, and the end of the domination of capitalism.[21]

Three days later, speaking at Cairo University, Nasser continued the post mortem but also began to formulate what was to be one of the driving forces behind his new policy of Arab socialism – the belief that the 'setback' ('one of the gravest moments for Arab nationalism') was due to a mistaken softness and compromise with 'reaction'. The 'setback' could be converted into an irresistible drive to eliminate reaction in all parts of the Arab world.[22]

Nasser denied allegations of Egyptian imperialism and of a police state in Syria. There had been, he claimed, only ninety-five political detainees in Syria, seventy of them Communists and twenty Shaabists (People's party). How could people say it was a despotism when he had travelled all through Syria in an open car without fear? There had been no exploitation of Syria by Egypt. Egyptians who had been working in Syria and were now being expelled were army officers, doctors and engineers defending and serving the Syrian people. The nationalization decrees affected only fifteen Syrian companies compared with 300 in

Egypt.[23] Again, on 5 October, Nasser refuted charges that Egypt had exploited Syria economically. He quoted figures of expenditure in Syria under the union on industrial and agricultural development and other projects. These totalled 2,862 million Syrian pounds (about £280 million) in three-and-a-half years. The Syrian gold reserves had been untouched. Syria had shared in the revenue from the Suez Canal and her military expenditure had been cut by 40 million Syrian pounds.

It was not until this speech, a week after the *coup*, that Nasser first publicly admitted the end of the union. In a broadcast from Cairo he announced that he would not oppose Syria's applications for renewed membership of the United Nations and the Arab League. He said he spoke with 'a broken heart' but called for national unity as the first priority in Syria. Egypt would keep the name, flag and anthem of the UAR. The great experiment was, at least temporarily, over.[24]

In Syria, in spite of Nasser's continued personal popularity among the Syrian public, there was no great upsurge of public demonstrations against the secession. But neither were the Syrians fully united in support of the change. The right-wing rebel alliance of officers and politicians proved as fragile as the usual coalitions in Damascus. The Baath leaders themselves were divided in their reaction to the secession. Akram Haurani and Salah Bitar both signed the declaration of secession by the Syrian parliament. But whereas Haurani continued to support the secession, cooperated with the conservatives and carried on a bitter personal campaign against Nasser, Bitar came to regard his signature of the declaration as a regrettable error. Bitar and Aflaq still hoped to find a new basis for cooperation with Nasser, and for the restoration of unity.

Years later, Bitar described the causes of Nasser's political failure in Syria as he had observed them as a Baath leader and a member of the UAR government during its first year and a half.

President Nasser was very able, but the others, both Egyptian and Syrian, were very far below his level and their own responsibilities. There was no really free discussion or any debate of broad ideas among the ministers. Nasser was the first in everything – in foreign and home policy and in economic and social policies. I did not at all contest his capacities or his leading place – he deserved that place, but I contested the idea that others had no place. From this sprang the absence of the institutions needed for the regime of the union. There was also a difference between Nasser and the other Egyptian leaders about Arab national consciousness. Nasser detached himself from the Egyptian view in favour of the Arab national view . . . a certain personal view of greatness pushed him to take the leadership of Arabism. . . . But the rupture between Nasser and the Baath ministers in 1959 was caused by a certain Egyptian hegemonic view of the union.

Bitar added – the words were spoken in 1968 after the Arab defeat by Israel in the previous year –

Nasser was the first and only Arab leader capable of taking the leadership of an Arab renaissance. But he failed to accept a necessary association of other Arab progressive leaders in the management of the Arab cause and its policies.[25]

Chapter 12

Arab Socialism and the National Charter, 1961–2

The break-up of the UAR was a great blow to Nasser's prestige. The blow fell when he was at the peak of his international influence as an Arab, African and neutralist leader. It coincided with a critical period inside Egypt when the sweeping new changes made by Nasser in the economic and social system had aroused deeper discontent among the former wealthy class. The double shock of the secession and the socialist measures also shook the confidence of the middle classes and the army officers.

Nasser believed the regime was facing a real crisis, perhaps its most serious internal challenge since the Neguib affair in 1954. The successful Syrian *coup* was an encouragement to those who sought Egypt's isolation from the Arab world and to those who would like to reverse the socialist changes in Egypt by similar means. It was a threat to what had become Nasser's key concepts of Arab nationalism and socialism.

After a brief hesitation and reappraisal, Nasser reacted with characteristic vigour and defiance. He re-organized his government with five of his old revolutionary associates grouped round him as vice-presidents, and passed from the defensive to the attack. Far from heeding those who urged him to change both his domestic and Arab policies, he launched a more intense revolutionary drive at home and abroad. He reaffirmed Egypt's Arab nationalist role and Arab socialism as the bases of his policy but presented the relation between them in a new formulation of the 'Arab Revolution'. This formulation enabled him effectively to shift the stress on to Egypt's own development without abandoning her claim to Arab leadership. Henceforward, Egypt's main Arab role was to be to provide the example and inspiration of a liberated, socialist Arab state. She would be ready to help other Arab states to 'liberate' themselves, whether from foreign rule or from their own 'feudalists and reactionaries'. But she would not accept political union with another Arab country unless it were already 'liberated'. For there could be no real constitutional unity between states with different social and political systems: the most that could be expected would be unity of policy. In this way, Nasser combined the preaching of a new revolutionary doctrine with a partial return in practice to the old Arab policy of Egypt, as it was before the union with Syria, the aim of which was a common Arab attitude towards the rest of the world under Egyptian leadership.

The first trumpet blasts of the 'Arab Revolution' were sounded by Nasser in a televised speech to the nation on 16 October 1961. He proclaimed, 'Socialism is our only road to justice'. Socialism, as Nasser understood it, meant that the national income must be shared among citizens, to each according to the efforts he makes to produce it. But there had also to be equal opportunities.

From the Syrian upset, Nasser drew three broad lessons for the future. First, he had gone too far in appeasing the 'reactionaries', because of a misplaced trust in their patriotism. They had shown that they were one of the main supports of imperialism against Arab unity and nationalism. Nasser presumably had in mind his attempts to compromise with the Syrian conservatives, but his warning of tougher measures was intended for the restive propertied class in Egypt. The second lesson was that the regime had failed to evolve a system of government to fit its revolutionary tasks. The bureaucracy was a cause of paralysis rather than an instrument of revolutionary change. The structure of the state must be overhauled. The third and most important conclusion concerned the need for greater popular drive behind the socialist revolution. It had been a mistake to open the National Union to 'reactionary forces' who had turned it into a façade. The National Union had to be reorganized to make it 'a revolutionary instrument of the national masses'.

Nasser ended with a reassurance to those who feared the end of all private property under socialism. He was not against individual ownership but against 'exploiting ownership'. Under the new conditions, land-ownership and real estate were no longer 'exploitation'. Investment was still open to individual activity in all fields and taxed profits from it were legitimate, so were the earnings of the liberal professions. 'Our socialist society is a promising field for all who want to work but there is no place in it for millionaires.'

Immediately after the speech Nasser struck an intimidating blow at 'reactionaries and feudalists' in Egypt whom he suspected might try to exploit the crisis against him. At the same time he carried further his socialization programme at the expense of 'the capitalists'. Some forty once-prominent people, including politicians of the old regime such as Fuad Serag ed-din, the former Wafd Secretary-General, and members of former big land-owning families, were arrested; hundreds more had their property confiscated. Those arrested were released a few months later, but thousands – eventually totalling 12,000 – were 'isolated', that is stripped of political and civic rights, and barred from political or public activity, including membership of trades unions and cooperatives. The sequestrations continued over the next few months. Many of those who lost their property were of Lebanese, Syrian, Greek or Jewish origin, though of Egyptian nationality. The exodus of people of foreign or minority origin, especially of Greeks, which had begun as a result of the nationalization laws, reached a new peak in the spring of 1962. They took with them, like those who left after Suez, valuable skills and knowledge.

Some of the fortunes confiscated were enormous: that of Abboud Pasha, the sugar magnate and industrialist, was said to be £E33 million and that of François Tagir £E12 million, while the biggest fortune of all belonged to the Badrawis, a large clan of land-owners. Concessions were also made to the poorer classes; rents, fares and the prices of consumer goods were reduced and school and university fees lowered.

On 5 November, after a long cabinet meeting, Nasser announced details of the reorganization of the political system he had called for in his broadcast. This was to take place in three stages. First, a preparatory committee of 150 people appointed from all walks of life – except 'reactionaries' – would prepare the election of a 'Congress of the Popular Forces of the Nation' to meet in January 1962. Nasser would submit to the Congress a 'Popular Charter of National Action' which would be discussed in public. On the basis of this charter there would be general elections for

National Union committees who would form a Grand Congress of the National Union. The Grand Congress would be the highest legislative authority of the country and would be responsible for drafting the UAR permanent constitution.

The new Preparatory Committee of the Congress met in Cairo on 25 November against a background of tension, police repression and alarmist reports in the controlled press of imperialist-inspired plots from all directions. Nasser's changed ideas on the future of the National Union were set out in uncompromising fashion when he gave a long address to the opening session. He had, he said, intended the National Union to be a forum in which there would be a reconciliation of conflicting interests and a 'bloodless settlement of the class struggle'. But the reactionaries had exploited this desire for peace and had made the class struggle inevitable. Now the National Union and political life would be open only to those who genuinely supported the socialist revolution.

In certain discussions, said Nasser, 'some have proposed we form two parties and a parliamentary system like the West with a governing party and an opposition. I perhaps thought of this myself in 1956 – but I saw that there existed a political and social revolution and that the parties and the democracy they spoke of were only the expression of the dictatorship of capital.' There had, he claimed, been only pashas and beys and no workers in the pre-1952 parliaments.

This question of political liberties was, however, raised again in the televised debates of the Committee in which Nasser continued to take part. One of Egypt's best-known writers, a liberal and Islamic reformist, Khaled Mohammed Khaled, called for an immediate restoration of civil liberties, an end to the political persecution of the left and the restoration of parliamentary life. Addressing Nasser, he said, 'Your adversaries, Mr President, and we ourselves have only one single argument: Where is Parliament? Where is the Constitution? Where is the Opposition? I think we should answer these points before we do anything else so that we may go forward under your banner to political maturity . . .'[1]

In his reply Nasser claimed that the Muslim Brothers had been arrested and tried because they had 'a secret army ready to descend on the people', while the Communists had been imprisoned not because they were Marxists but because they took their instructions from a foreign power.[2] Nasser's definition of those he thought fit or unfit to play a part, even if only a consultative one, in the future political system of the country was illustrated in the Committee's decisions on the composition of the elected Congress and on those who were to be 'isolated'. The seats in the Congress were to be shared out between certain political and social categories by a complicated method which ensured that the representation of the professional, industrial, commercial and bureaucratic middle class and the intelligentsia would be substantially weighted as against workers and peasants, though the latter would be more strongly represented than in any previous Egyptian parliament.

Out of a total of 1,750 seats peasants were to have 375 seats and workers 300. The rest were allocated as follows: National Capitalism (representatives of industry and commerce), 150; members of professional associations, 225; non-unionized civil servants, 135; university teaching staff, 105; students, 105; women, 105.[3]

The main categories of persons defined by the Committee as subject to the penalty of isolation included: land-owners affected by the nationalizations of 1960 and 1961; those hostile to the Revolution and who had been subjected to arrest or sequestration at the end of 1961; and persons guilty of trying to influence public opinion in favour of political corruption.[4]

Of the thousands of isolation orders made, some 1,600, chiefly those applied to liberals and left-wing sympathizers, were rescinded within a matter of months before the National Congress of Popular Forces met.

Nasser next turned his fire on the 'reactionaries and feudalists' elsewhere in the Arab world. In a speech at Port Said on 23 December he officially launched the 'Arab Revolution' outside Egypt with a fierce attack on the Arab kings, especially Hussein of Jordan and Saud of Saudi Arabia. The kings, he alleged, were not only keeping their own countries backward but also were in league with imperialism to destroy Arab socialism and to attack the UAR's attempt to create a socially just state. He announced the end of the federal links between the UAR and the Yemen in the 'United Arab States'. The links had never been more than paper ones and the Imam Ahmed had already begun to attack the Egyptian regime and to denounce its socialist ideas.

The assault on the Arab kings and other 'reactionaries' was carried further in a speech by Nasser on 22 February 1962, the anniversary of the union of Egypt and Syria. He tried first to answer the question he said he had heard some asking, 'Why don't we leave the Arabs alone and concentrate on our own affairs?' In spite of the unscrupulous behaviour of some Arab rulers, he said, 'We are Arabs and we have no choice to be otherwise'. Arab unity was an 'inevitable process of nature' and disunity was something imposed through the division of the Arab world by imperialism in alliance with certain Arab rulers. These 'puppets' should not be confused with the Arab peoples, but so long as they were in power there could be no real unity. Just as the Arab world had to go through a political revolution to get rid of imperialist powers and their agents and spheres of influence, so it had also to undergo a social revolution to overthrow the 'exploiters, monopolists and rich parasites' and overcome its backwardness. Some people were calling for the closing of the Arab ranks, but unity of aims was more important than unity of the ranks.

The promised National Charter was presented to the National Congress of Popular Forces by Nasser in a five-and-a-half hour speech on 21 May 1962. The Charter is a key document for an understanding of Nasser's political thought and of his aims in Egypt and the Arab world. In the very first paragraph, the Charter reaffirmed the Arab character of Egypt, already proclaimed in the 1956 Constitution. It claimed that the Egyptian revolutionary experiment had had far-reaching repercussions not only on the life of 'the whole Arab nation', but also on the liberation movement in Africa, Asia and Latin America. But the greater part of the Charter was devoted to Egypt's domestic problems.

The Egyptian revolution was set apart from both capitalism and the Marxist class struggle. The Egyptian people, said the

Charter, resisted capitalism because it attempted to exploit national independence and national economic development needs for its own interests. At the same time, they 'rejected the dictatorship of any class and decided the dissolution of class differences should be the means of real democracy for the entire people's working forces'. One of the 'guarantees' of the revolution was the decidedly un-Marxist one of 'unshakeable faith in God, His Prophets and His Sacred Messages'.

The Arab Revolution, said Nasser in the Charter, had three aims of freedom, socialism and unity and needed a 'consciousness based on scientific conviction arising from enlightened, thorough and free discussion, unaffected by the forces of fanaticism and terrorism'. Its course was affected by radical changes which had taken place in the world since the Second World War. These changes included the emergence of the anti-imperialist nationalist movements in Asia, Africa and Latin America and the development of the Communist camp as 'an enormous force'. There was also the increasing weight of 'moral forces in the world, as in the United Nations, the non-aligned states and world opinion'.

In this situation, Nasser argued, imperialism had begun to employ new indirect methods to dominate through economic blocs, monopolies and cold wars. Therefore freedom could not be obtained 'by placating the imperialists or bargaining with them' – as had been shown in the Suez crisis and in Algeria. In a characteristic Nasser formulation, imperialism was condemned as 'not merely a looting of the people's resources but an aggression on its dignity and pride'. Hostility to imperialism in any form and stress on the struggle for economic development were two of the most constant themes in the Charter.

The Charter included a long review of Egyptian history, in which Nasser answered those Egyptian nationalists of the 'Pharaonic' school whose arguments that Egypt should not become embroiled in Arab affairs had been revived by the failure of the merger with Syria. He argued that Egypt had never lived in isolation from the surrounding area, even in Pharaonic times. The 1919 revolution in Egypt had failed not only because its leaders, being from the land-owning class, as was in the nature of the time, 'overlooked the need for social change', but also because 'they failed to extend their mission beyond Sinai' and failed to deduce from history 'that there is no conflict whatsoever between Egyptian patriotism and Arab nationalism'. The Arab nationalist struggle had thus been deprived of Egyptian revolutionary energy at a grave moment of crisis, because the Egyptian national movement thought that the division and domination of the Arab lands did not concern it.

In achieving Arab unity, as well as freedom and socialism, historical and natural factors imposed on the UAR and its revolutionary leadership the responsibility of being 'the nucleus state'. But the methods of seeking unity need not, in Nasser's view, repeat those of the nineteenth-century experiments in national unity, such as those in Germany and Italy. Unity could not be imposed. It had to have a popular basis, to be peaceful in character and to be crowned by unanimous popular acceptance. Differences between the Arab governments stemmed from the social struggle in the Arab world through which the same revolutionary currents were flowing.

Nasser then laid down some definitions of the stages towards real unity under his new concept. 'In the Arab world any nationalist government representing the will and struggle of the people within a framework of national independence is a step towards unity. Any partial unity in the Arab world expressing a popular will of two or more of the Arab peoples is an advanced step towards unity.' The UAR must propagate its call for unity and its principles 'without hesitating for one moment before the outworn argument that this would be considered interference in the affairs of others'. The UAR 'feels it her bounden duty to support every popular national movement'. But it should not become involved in local party disputes in any Arab state. In other words, Nasser was more interested in the broad policies of other Arab governments than in their detailed composition or in the day-to-day handling of their internal affairs. Formerly he had been chiefly concerned that they should be in step with Egypt's foreign policy of independence and non-alignment. Now he proposed to judge them also by their social policies. The aim of the UAR, according to the Charter, was to establish a union of cooperation between the 'nationalist popular progressive movements in the Arab world'. 'World imperialist forces and monopolies' aimed 'to put the Arab territory from the [Atlantic] Ocean to the [Persian] Gulf under its military control, in order to continue its exploitation and loot its wealth.' To defend the Arab area was 'primarily the responsibility of the armed forces of the UAR'. Nevertheless, the best defence was self-development and the effectiveness of armies lay in the national, economic and social power behind them.

In the Charter Nasser laid down some of the principles of Arab socialism on which this power was to be built. He began with the premise that a 'socialist solution' for under-development was inevitable because local capitalism's links with imperialism made it impossible for it to lead a national drive for economic development. A socialist solution did not, however, require the nationalization of all means of production or the abolition of rights of private ownership and inheritance. It was enough to have a 'capable public sector' with chief responsibility for the development plan and a private sector operating inside the plan framework and under public control. All the basic infrastructure of the economy – roads, railways, ports, airports, dams, sea, land and air transport and other public services, as well as financial institutions, banks and insurance companies – should be within the framework of public ownership. Heavy, medium and mining industries should be either publicly owned or controlled and in light industry there must be a 'guiding role' for the public sector. Foreign trade and at least half internal trade must be under public control.

Land was not to be nationalized, but individual land-ownership should be kept within limits that ruled out the possibility of 'feudalism', that is the exercise of political and social domination by big local land-owners. 'Arab socialism' as applied to agriculture meant not only limited land-ownership but also a co-operative system for technology and credit, together with public services in irrigation and drainage. There had to be industrialization in the countryside to reduce rural unemployment and an effort to 'raise the level of civilization in the villages'.

Though priority had to go to the development of heavy industry it would not be so ruthlessly applied as in Soviet Communist doctrine: the Egyptian masses had been so long deprived that consumer industry must be developed to meet their needs and hopes. There would be a seven-hour day in industry (a measure intended primarily to increase the number of jobs) and, as already announced by Nasser, workers would share in profits and in management. In the private sector of industry, free competition and private investment would continue. The 'battle of production' was the chief challenge to the survival of Arab society, the Charter declared. Family planning was also needed if the increasing rise in the population was not to prove 'the most dangerous obstacle' to the Egyptian drive to raise the standard of living.

The proposals of the Charter for a political system of 'true democracy' drew lessons from both the basic Marxist thesis of economic power and also Egypt's own recent past. The political system, it was argued, reflected the controlling economic interests in the state. Thus the parliamentary system in Egypt had reflected the ruling alliance of 'feudalism and exploiting capital'. Peasants had had to vote according to the wishes of their feudal lords. While 'reaction' had to be fought, there was a natural and inevitable class struggle which could be resolved peacefully in the framework of national unity. This framework would be provided by cooperation within the new Arab Socialist Union, as the reorganized National Union would be called. The new UAR Constitution should guarantee that in the ASU and in political and popular organizations at all levels, including the National Assembly, half the seats should go in free and direct elections to farmers and workers. There should be other measures to strengthen democratic control. The authority of the elected popular councils should be above that of the executive machinery of the state and local government should gradually be transferred from the hands of the state to that of the people. Cooperatives and trades unions should have a 'leading democratic role' and to further this purpose agricultural labour unions should be set up.

At the highest level of the state 'collective leadership' was imperative (Nasser later rejected a proposal by the Congress to make him President for life) and there was a 'dire need' for a new political organization, an active cadre within the ASU.

The Charter called for freedom of speech and guarantees for freedom of the press (a call never to be clearly answered). It claimed that the law of press organization had led to 'the ownership of the press by the people', through the Arab Socialist Union. Freedom of worship was 'sacred' but the nation was warned against attempts 'by reactionary elements to exploit religion' (an obvious reference to the Muslim Brotherhood).

In the social field, the Charter proclaimed the aim of 'equality of opportunity'. It spoke of the right to medical care, education and work and the need for old-age and sickness insurance on a wider scale.

Nasser further elaborated on his ideas in public discussions with the National Congress of Popular Forces following his presentation of the Charter. He was frank about what could realistically be expected, for example, in social welfare. It was impossible, he said, to hold out hopes of unemployment insurance, or insurance for sickness and old-age pensions for those working in agriculture. Nor was an enforceable minimum wage for agricultural labourers something that could be achieved tomorrow.

Nasser pointed out some differences between his version of socialism and that of Marxist-Leninism. Apart from the fact that it did not approve of the dictatorship of one class over another, 'Arab Socialism' did not advocate nationalization of land and also left a place for private capital in industry. Finally, Arab Socialism, unlike Marxist-Leninism, acknowledged religion.

Nasser later claimed that in working out his socialist ideas, he had studied many models. He rejected the suggestion that he had closely followed Tito's pattern and said he had looked at doctrines and practice in Russia, China, India, Cuba, Sweden and other countries, as well as Yugoslavia, to see what might be usefully adapted to Egypt's needs.[5]

For six weeks the debate on the Charter continued in public not only in the Congress itself but in the press, on radio and television and in professional groups. To Nasser's disappointment the Congress members were more concerned with their particular professional interests than with general questions of principle, perhaps because the intellectuals among them, especially those of liberal or left-wing tendencies, were still too wary of the police-state aspects of the regime to be really frank. One subject of general principle, however, provoked heated debate: this was an unsuccessful move by Muslim religious leaders to ensure that the Charter and any further constitution should reaffirm Islam as the state religion and the primacy of Islamic law in Egyptian society. On 30 June the Congress unanimously approved the original draft of the Charter. Two days later Nasser explained to the Congress his ideas on the creation of the new political organization, the Arab Socialist Union. Its structure would closely resemble that of the National Union which it would replace. It would be a pyramidal mass organization based on popular committees at each level of the state structure from the village upwards, and including also publicly owned or controlled firms and factories, and government departments. It would differ from the National Union in excluding 'feudalists' and 'reactionaries' and deliberately ensuring a fifty per cent representation of workers and peasants. It was to be the forum for political action to ensure that the provisions of the Charter both as regards socialist economic measures and political democracy were carried out. But Nasser made it plain that the ASU would not have any executive power. He seems to have intended it chiefly as a means of mobilizing popular support behind the new socialist policies and also as a forum for the political education of the humbler classes. The latter needed encouragement if they were to overcome long traditions of passivity and subservience and bridge the deep cultural gap between themselves and their better-off or better-educated compatriots.

Meanwhile Nasser announced that the ASU would have a Provisional Executive Committee and that the first task of an ASU Congress would be to prepare elections for a National Assembly which would work out a new Constitution.

Such were the broad outlines of 'Arab Socialism', its doctrines and proposed institutions. How was Nasser to apply them in practice?

Chapter 13

Developing Egypt:
The Five-Year Plans and the Political System, 1962-7

In the five years between the National Charter and Egypt's defeat in the third Arab–Israel war, Nasser faced four main problems as he embarked on his Arab Socialist Revolution. Foremost was the political, economic and social development of Egypt. This entailed carrying through the first five-year plan which included extensive industrial and agricultural investment and continued work on the High Dam and other major projects. The effort to expand production had to face several hazards: the demand for present rather than future consumption so as to raise the country's miserable living standards had to be reconciled with the need for investment; the inexorable pressure of population increase rising to a million people a year threatened to swallow up any gains in production; the lethargic traditions of Egyptian society and especially of the government machine were a constant brake on progress, there was the risk of a too-heavy foreign indebtedness if funds for investment could not be raised from Egypt's own resources. Linked with the drive for economic and social betterment was Nasser's attempt to create a more dynamic but still obedient political system. Central to this attempt was the expansion of education and the restless role of the intelligentsia, some of whom were estranged from the regime because of the lack of liberty.

Nasser's second problem was the impact of the Arab Revolution on the rest of the Arab world (the main subject of Chapters 14 and 15). The revolutionary upheavals of those years in the Yemen, South Arabia, Iraq, Syria and North Africa would probably have occurred whether or not Nasser had proclaimed the Arab Revolution. Only in the Yemen, and there to a limited degree, was Nasser in control of the revolutionary situation which he had encouraged but not created. In some cases, as with the Baathist revolutions in Syria and Iraq from 1963 onwards, with the overthrow of Ben Bella in Algeria by Colonel Boumédienne in 1965, and the final victory of the National Liberation Front in South

Arabia in 1967, the upheavals brought to power leaders with whom Nasser or his protégés had quarrelled. But for good or ill, Nasser and Egypt were identified with these revolutionary movements and inspired and helped some of them. This identification was a complicating factor in Nasser's third problem, his relations with the Great Powers. His support for 'liberation movements' in the Arabian Peninsula and in Africa, though pleasing to the Soviet Union, brought him into sharp collision not only with Britain but also eventually with the United States. The impact was softened only by the Western desire to ensure that Nasser should not be absorbed completely into the Soviet camp.

Nasser's concept of non-alignment also underwent a change. From 1962 onwards, when an international economic conference of non-aligned countries was held in Cairo, Nasser placed more stress on the economic problems of the Third World than on the political aims that had chiefly preoccupied the Belgrade Conference. He saw the developing countries as forming a large group of the world's under-privileged who should coordinate their efforts to get more trade with and aid from the richer countries. This switch to the economic rather than the political was partly a response to Egypt's own material needs, but it was also a reflection of the changed political situation of the non-aligned countries. Instead of being arbiters or mediators between the Great Power blocs, the non-aligned states were threatened increasingly with becoming victims. The Third World became the battlefield of the new three-way struggle for influence between America, Russia and China, in which the United States showed an increasing readiness to use military or paramilitary means to overthrow or prevent the installation of regimes it suspected of favouring the Communist states but of not having Moscow's direct military protection.

In these years Nasser walked a tight rope between East and West, between non-alignment and militant anti-imperialism, between the demands of domestic development and those of the Arab revolutionary movements. What finally caused him to lose his balance was ironically the fourth problem, that he had put at the bottom of his list of priorities, the Arab conflict with Israel.

*

While Nasser was formulating his new ideology of Arab Socialism he was also grappling with serious practical difficulties at home. In the early months of 1962 the crisis of confidence created by the Syrian secession was aggravated by economic difficulties and by a crisis in Nasser's relations with the army and the Free Officers. The loss of foreign exchange from reduced cotton sales – half of the 1961 cotton crop was ruined by cotton worm – coincided with the need to import more food because of a fall in domestic food production. Egypt's foreign exchange reserves fell to £10 million and she sought a $150 million loan from the International Monetary Fund as well as increased surplus food deliveries from the United States. An agreement was reached with Washington for the supply of 200,000 tons of American wheat and for other food aid.

At the beginning of his correspondence with President Kennedy, Nasser is said to have addressed a letter to Kennedy as from the ruler of the oldest but poorest country of the world to the President of the youngest but richest country in the world. He thought that it must be difficult for Kennedy to have much idea of the kind of problems an Egyptian leader faced: as the next best thing to Kennedy's coming to see for himself he suggested that Kennedy should send a trusted adviser to watch the Egyptian government at work at close quarters and report back to him.[1] In the spring of 1962 Kennedy sent Dr Edward Mason, his economic adviser and a former Harvard economic professor, to Cairo where he had several long talks with Nasser and with other ministers. Mason took away a fairly optimistic picture of the general state of the Egyptian economy in which the increase in the national income was keeping two to three per cent ahead of the increase in population.

The crisis with the army in which the central figure was Nasser's closest friend, Abdul Hakim Amer, was not revealed until more than five years later, after the 1967 war with Israel and Amer's subsequent disgrace and suicide. It was then described at the trial of Amer's associates and by Heykal in *Al Ahram* as a kind of 'silent *coup*'. Both Heykal and Nasser then still referred to the nature of the crisis in vague terms though they described it as the origin of the 'centres of power' (in the army and intelligence) and the 'special political control' over the army which were blamed for the military disaster of the 1967 war. The fact that Amer and the army became the scapegoats for the disaster naturally leads to caution in assessing criticism of their earlier roles. There is, however, some independent non-Egyptian evidence which tends to confirm that there was a crisis of this kind and that it led during the subsequent years to a certain duality of power between Nasser on the one hand and Amer and his army entourage on the other. At least Amer and his men were one important group which Nasser had to balance against others round him.

In the early days of the Revolution Amer had been appointed commander-in-chief of the armed forces. Nasser wanted to have a Free Officer in charge of the army as a military force and also to act as his chief political link with the cadre of Free Officers who had remained in the army. During the years after Suez Nasser paid less personal attention to military affairs and gave Amer a more or less free hand with the army. Then, after the creation of the UAR, came Amer's appointment as Nasser's viceroy in Syria, his first big political job. After the Syrian secession Amer returned to Cairo demoralized by the failure of his mission which had ended humiliatingly with his arrest in Damascus in the middle of the night in his pyjamas. Amer himself had been well liked in Syria, but many of the complaints against the Egyptians there were directed against his entourage, most of whom were army intelligence officers. This and the need to tighten up security in Egypt led Nasser to have a new close look at the army. At the same time, he reorganized the government to create round him a new policy-making group of five vice-presidents. Amer was one of the five. Two of the others, Abdul Latif Baghdadi and Kamal ed-din Hussein, wanted to prevent Amer from retaining the position of *de facto* number two to the President which his control of the army and close personal friendship with Nasser had given him.

For both military and political reasons, Nasser decided there must be changes in the high command and the officer corps and that the political and military control of the army should be separated. After the introduction of the National Charter he divided the officers into two distinct groups: those who would remain professional soldiers and those who would be employed in civilian jobs in the government and the public sector of the economy. The latter had to resign from the army. Nasser told Amer that while remaining politically in charge of the armed forces he should give up the post of commander-in-chief. In future the commander-in-chief should be an officer chosen for purely military purposes. His professional qualifications would have to be more up-to-date and he would be replaced regularly every three or four years. Nasser also proposed the formation of a Presidential Council. This would have exercised collectively the political authority of the President, while individual vice-presidents would be responsible for different subjects. Amer would be responsible for army affairs. Amer agreed to these propositions, but his rivals among the vice-presidents insisted further that army appointments from battalion commander upwards should be approved by the Presidential Council as a whole. Amer was upset and accepted this agreement only under protest.

Amer was by all accounts a brave, generous-natured, impulsive but weak man, impetuously loyal to his friends, with all the attractive, softer side of the Saidis or Upper Egyptians. His army entourage encouraged his resentment and his doubts about handing over the army to a new commander-in-chief. One day in March 1962, when the appointments question was being discussed in the embryo Presidential Council, Amer insisted on maintaining his right of veto, resigned and walked out. He disappeared and turned up later in Alexandria amid rumours of army officers rallying to his side and troops on the move.

Nasser was angry and would not see him. But when Nasser heard that at a meeting with the other vice-presidents Amer had agreed to resign altogether and leave the country for Europe for a time, he quickly intervened. He feared the result would be a split inside the army and possible civil war. Moreover, quite apart from his friendship for Amer, the latter was still his key contact with the Free Officers network inside the army, the instrument on which in the last resort his power depended. Perhaps he may also have thought that if Amer's rivals were able to get rid of him completely it would also strengthen their position vis-à-vis Nasser himself. (Both Baghdadi and Hussein were, in fact, to lose their posts within the next two or three years, for different reasons.)

To prevent an army split Nasser was prepared to compromise. He persuaded his colleagues to withdraw the agreement about control of appointments and made a deal direct with Amer. The latter was to remain deputy supreme commander with the same authority as before but agreed to the later appointment of a professional commander-in-chief.

The outcome of the clash with Amer was to prove doubly dangerous. Amer's position and the influence of the ambitious young staff officers round him became, if anything, greater than before. In March 1964 when the Presidential Council was dissolved, he became officially Nasser's deputy with the title of First Vice-President. Political control over the army became divided, in practice, between the 'general political control' exercised by the President and the government as a whole, and the 'special political control' exercised by Amer and his staff. The military efficiency of the army inevitably suffered, for the reason that Nasser had foreseen: Amer was no longer professionally equipped to plan or command a battle or campaign, and the professional leadership of the army was not kept up-to-date or given enough authority. Herein lay at least some of the seeds of the 1967 disaster.*

What is difficult to judge is how far, before the 1967 war, Amer and his supporters in the army and intelligence services, headed by General Salah Nasser, chief of intelligence, and Shams ed-din Badran, later Minister of War, were able or willing to act independently of Nasser or to put pressure on him, or how far they were Nasser's chosen instruments of power, whose mistakes or shortcomings in military matters or whose increasing economic and social privileges he condoned in order to ensure their loyalty.

Certainly, despite his popular support and his efforts to build up a civilian political organization through the Arab Socialist Union, Nasser continued to rely in the last resort on the state security services – the army, police and intelligence. The military

*The foregoing account was pieced together from different and sometimes conflicting Egyptian and other Arab sources, including Nasser himself.

intelligence services were also active outside Egypt in supporting and promoting pro-Egyptian Arab revolutionary movements. Nasser's relationship with Amer continued to be intimate, both personally and professionally. He sent Amer as his representative on several crucial political missions, to Saudi Arabia, to Moscow and to Paris to see de Gaulle. Nor can Nasser escape responsibility for the state of the armed forces or the operations of the intelligence services; either he knew what was going on and willed it or turned a blind eye to it, or was not effective enough to prevent it; or he did not know what he should have known.

There were episodes from 1962 onwards during the Yemen civil war and the nationalist rebellion in Aden and South Arabia in which it seemed sometimes as if the Egyptian intelligence services were taking initiatives of their own and sometimes as if Nasser was being compelled to adapt his policy to the pressures of Amer and the army.*

Inside Egypt itself the failure of Nasser to put through his plan for a clearer separation of the political and military control of the army probably contributed to his decision from 1964 onwards to devote more of his personal attention to the development of the Arab Socialist Union.[2]

The ASU was slow in developing and never really came politically alive. Six weeks after announcing the National Charter, Nasser presented a draft proposal for the Arab Socialist Union to the 'Congress of Popular Forces' and in October 1962, the statutes of the ASU were promulgated (along the lines already sketched in Chapter 12.) It was to have 7,000 'basic committees', with a membership of over four million.

After its formation the ASU was supposed to approve a new electoral law for the National Assembly and the new Assembly was to meet on 23 July 1963. But events outside Egypt, including talks on a possible constitutional union between Egypt, Syria and Iraq, held up the announcement of the electoral law until 17 November 1963. Candidates for the 350 elected Assembly seats (ten more were filled by appointment) had to be over thirty years of age, able to read and write and to be members of the ASU. Half of them had to be workers or peasants.

* See Chapter 14.

The Assembly was elected and held its first meeting in March 1964. The day before it met, Nasser had proclaimed a provisional new constitution and lifted martial law, but as he issued new emergency laws the following day there was little change in the internal security powers exercised by the government.

At the same time Nasser reorganized his government in line with the provisions of the new constitution. The Presidential Council was abolished and Abdul Hakim Amer became the first among seven vice-presidents. The Executive Council was transformed into a Council of Ministers and its chairman, Aly Sabry, became prime minister. The Assembly nominated Nasser for re-election as President. In March 1965 his term was renewed for six years by a plebiscite, with a meaningless majority of 99·999 per cent of the votes.

Nasser was then forty-seven and more than twelve years of power had left their mark. When I met him in Cairo for a newspaper interview a few months earlier in July 1964, the physically powerful, ebullient young man seen nine years before had been transformed into a calmer, slower figure, with a hint almost of physical frailty. It was the figure of a man approaching middle-age who had borne an enormous continuous burden of work and responsibility. All political passion was not yet spent and could suddenly animate his heavy face. But he gave the impression of a man seeking tranquillity and a way out of endless problems rather than of a revolutionary eager to blaze new trails.[3]

He was still living in the same unpretentious style with a sharp division between his public and private life. He was happily married. His wife was rarely in the public eye though not secluded in the old-fashioned Muslim way. She preferred to give most of her time to their five children. Nasser himself had no taste for social life or high living. He had made it a rule for himself never to go to restaurants or night-clubs that he had not been to before he came to power. He preferred plain Egyptian food and his friends with more sophisticated palates regarded it as a culinary penance to have to dine at the President's house: the menu seemed never to vary, nearly always the same dish of chicken, rice and vegetables – the Cairo middle-class equivalent of meat and two veg.

Nor had Nasser any special interest in the arts or in intellectual society, though he read widely in politics and history. He liked seeing films and playing tennis. Apart from Amer and his other political associates, his closest friend was Heykal. With Heykal he discussed broad political and social ideas. Heykal was also his Boswell, keeping a full diary of his daily activities and thoughts. It was Heykal who helped him produce the final draft of *The Philosophy of the Revolution*. But neither Heykal, nor any other associate, then or later was in any sense a power behind the throne as Nasser was behind Neguib. In the varying influences round Nasser, Heykal represented certain trends of political thought. He was an advocate, for example, of Egypt's role in the Arab world, of the need to keep open Egyptian contacts with the Western Powers and to liberalize the political system at home, just as Zacharia Mohieddin or Aly Sabry or the Amer group represented other trends. But Heykal never had a power base of his own and in power terms was completely dependent on Nasser.

When Nasser began his new term as president in March 1965, one of his first pressing concerns was the state of the Egyptian economy. The first five-year plan was nearing its end. It had some notable achievements to its credit, but the attempt to combine a high level of investment with increased consumption, more employment and a militant foreign policy was producing signs of strain. There were the familiar symptoms of a too rapid expansion: inflation, balance-of-payments deficits and increasing foreign debt. The direct and indirect costs of Egypt's share in the Yemen war* (including the loss of US wheat aid) added to the balance-of-payments burden. But the main problem for the new socialist economy was how to shift the financing of investment from foreign to domestic sources and at the same time keep a balance between the popular demand for a quick rise in living standards and a high rate of long-term economic growth.[4]

The broad structure of the socialist economy inaugurated in the 1961 nationalization decrees and described in the National Charter had already been laid down, although in agriculture an important new reorganization was just beginning. By the end of

*See Chapters 14 and 15.

1964 almost all big companies of any kind had been nationalized, making a total of some 800 industrial and commercial concerns in the public sector.[5]

The government had also extended its control over the businesses still in private hands, especially in the retail and wholesale trades.[6] But the fact that land and houses were also not nationalized meant that two-thirds of the national wealth was still privately owned. Thus socialist Egypt was in reality a mixed economy. Its chief economic characteristic was central planning and control. The central planning involved little more, however, than the control of investment and the allocation of foreign exchange, with the national plan providing targets and guidelines for various government agencies.

Nasser did not envisage public ownership of land, but rather an increase in the number of farmers owning their own land and an extension of the cooperative system. By 1965, successive agrarian reform laws and other government measures had made some 1,250,000 acres (about twenty per cent of the cultivable area in 1952) available for redistribution.[7] About 840,000 acres had already been redistributed to over 300,000 formerly landless farmers, representing families totalling 1,500,000 people.[8] But these were still only about ten per cent of the rural population, the vast majority of which were either tenant farmers, landless labourers and their families or smallholders with one acre or less. Some of these might hope to get land made available through future reductions in the land-ownership limit (in July 1969, Nasser announced the lowering of the limit to fifty acres) and through government reclamation schemes. But meanwhile their livelihood was most affected by the availability of work, the rate of wages and rents and the nature of tenancy and share-cropping agreements. Efforts to enforce the official minimum agriculture wage of eighteen piastres (about 18p or 43 cents) a day proved difficult owing to the seasonal demand for labour and the huge numbers of surplus workers. New laws in 1962 and 1963 had tried to enforce stricter compliance with the regulations controlling rents, tenancy and share-cropping. They provided for longer leases, greater security of tenure and heavier penalties for evasion.[9] Farmers who acquired land under the agrarian reform also benefited from cuts in their repayment and interest terms in 1961 and 1964.

All sections of the rural population, including the landless, profited to some extent from the expansion of social services in the countryside. The introduction into the villages of combined rural welfare centres and clean drinking water, together with an intensive campaign against bilharzia, trachoma and malaria, dramatically improved health standards and worked slowly towards raising standards of hygiene, in spite of the conservatism and poverty of the peasants. The combined rural centres included health and maternity clinics, agricultural and craft schools. By 1966 there were nearly 700 such centres, or one to roughly each 20,000 of the rural population. Little was done, however, to improve village housing compared with the substantial slum clearance and cheap house-building in the main cities and towns, nor were farm workers able to secure the advantages of the trade-union organization and the limited social security insurance enjoyed by an increasing number of urban and industrial workers. Both rural and city workers profited from the rapid expansion of free education and from the increasing number of jobs made available in the urban areas.

When the first five-year plan was introduced in July 1960 *per capita* income in Egypt was about £E50, but in agriculture it was less than £E30 and for landless labourers usually smaller still. Egypt's population in 1960 was twenty-six million: it was expected to rise at the rate of 2·8 per cent a year to reach thirty-two million in 1976 and fifty-three million by 1990.

The plan, which called for a total investment in Egypt of £E1,577 million, aimed at increasing the national income by forty per cent or of achieving a growth rate in terms of GDP (Gross Domestic Product) of seven per cent a year. The official figures claimed that growth achieved under the plan was 7·5 per cent a year or thirty-seven per cent altogether, of which 17·8 per cent increase was in agriculture, 50·2 per cent in industry, 128·6 per cent in electricity and 96·6 per cent in construction. A critical estimate by a non-official foreign expert put the growth rate at between five and six per cent. Taking account of the population increase, this represents a net growth in GDP of just under three per cent a year, a substantial achievement for a developing country.[10]

Apart from electricity, construction and transport, which achieved a bigger expansion than planned, the growth of industrial production, to which more than a quarter of investment was directed, was not much more than half what was hoped for. The main reason appears to have been a tailing off of investment and of production owing to the shortage of foreign exchange. Another reason was the priority given to expensive and relatively unproductive heavy industrial projects, especially iron and steel and such enterprises as the Nasr Motor Car works built with the help of Fiat at a cost of £30 million.[11] The Nasr works was one of several factories that were forced to close down for a time (it has since reopened) or to work at only part capacity owing to the lack of foreign exchange to buy imported raw materials or parts for processing and assembly. The slow expansion of industrial output may have been partly due to the lack of trained management and skilled labour, and the priority given by the government to creating more jobs. Nationalization had led in many cases to a proliferation of an already overgrown bureaucracy in which too few officials were adequately trained or willing to take responsibility. The government sought to remedy this situation by a training scheme for managers and by expanding the number of technical secondary schools.

Throughout the economy the numbers of workers employed rose by 1,300,000 over the five years, an increase of twenty-two per cent compared with a fifteen per cent population increase. 225,000 of the new jobs were in industry. The share of wages in the national income also increased, the biggest beneficiaries being those formerly unemployed. While average industrial wages rose by 22·8 per cent over the five years, the cost-of-living index rose slightly more, by 23·2 per cent, but industrial workers made gains through the expansion of free or subsidized social services, especially in education and health and to a lesser extent in cheap housing.[12]

The plan had provided for an investment of £E392 million in agricultural development including irrigation, drainage and the first stage of the Aswan High Dam. Agricultural output was to be raised by five per cent a year but the actual increase achieved was 3·3 per cent.

The land reform had increased production – partly because of the greater government help given in the land reform areas – but its main purpose was social and political. A bigger increase in production was needed to reduce reliance on imports of foreign food for the country's rapidly growing population. There was some controversy among the experts about whether this was compatible with the growth of small private holdings. The fragmentation of land-holdings was one of the obstacles to efficient farming. Was collective or state farming needed to replace the big land-owners if the advantages of consolidation and planning were not to be sacrificed, especially in the new land to be made available under the High Dam scheme? The first answer found was an ingenious attempt to combine the virtues of private land-ownership with larger-scale production planning and technical control through the system of 'supervised cooperatives'.

The system was based on a combination of the agricultural cooperatives and the government technical supervision which had been set up in land reform areas, together with a new method of crop consolidation. The system was tried out first in land reform areas over which the Agrarian Reform administration and the Ministry of Agriculture still retained a greater degree of control. It was then decided in 1960 to extend it to all areas where there were agricultural cooperatives (there were about 3,500 of them, mainly concerned only with supplying credit and buying farm equipment).[13] In 1965 the aim was proclaimed of eventually introducing the system throughout the country.

Under the system small land-holdings were consolidated and reorganized for production purposes (without changing their ownership) into units of 1,500 feddans. These units were managed by new cooperative societies set up under the supervision of a graduate from a college of agriculture and two graduates from agricultural and secondary schools. The aim was to improve the management of the land, including the introduction of an agreed crop rotation over a large area, without losing the initiative and social benefit of farmers working their own land. This cooperative management was backed up by an intensified government effort to improve drainage, irrigation and seeds, and to increase the use of farm machinery, fertilizers and insecticides. Between 1952 and 1964 the use of chemical fertilizer – sixty per cent of it produced in Egypt – doubled and there was a sixty per cent increase in machinery horsepower. During the same period the number of trained agriculturalists and veterinarians also doubled.[14]

From 1961 onwards farmers obtained loans free of interest through the village cooperatives from the state-owned Agricultural Credit and Cooperative Organization. By 1965 farmers were also selling all their main products at fixed prices through government-controlled agencies. These credit and marketing facilities also provided the government with some leverage for the introduction of the 'supervised cooperatives' system outside the land reform areas where official authority was weaker.

The other factor in agricultural production was an increase in the area of cultivated land. Half a million acres of land had been reclaimed by 1960 and it was hoped to raise the rate of reclamation to 150,000 acres a year during the following seven years as the High Dam came into operation.

When its electric power installations were completed in July 1970 and new canals built, the Dam would not only provide the electricity for the country's industrial and urban expansion but also enough water to irrigate 1·3 million new acres and convert another 700,000 acres to perennial irrigation. By 1970 the Dam power station was already providing half Egypt's power needs and an increasing number of the country's villages had electricity. 500,000 more acres were being cultivated.

Two other experiments in large-scale land reclamation were less successful. The Liberation Province and the New Valley scheme, though technically productive, proved extravagantly uneconomic and investment in them was curtailed. Nasser had held high hopes about the New Valley scheme in particular. Surveys had suggested that within about ten years a million and a half acres might be brought under cultivation along the line of south-western oases between Dakhla and Siwa. If the optimistic estimates of sub-soil water in the area proved correct, there could be developed a 'New Valley' parallel with the Nile Valley. In 1959

Nasser set up an Organization for Desert Reclamation, mostly staffed by army engineers and other military personnel, which organized experimental development in the 'New Valley' as well as running reclamation schemes in the Sinai desert and elsewhere. During the first five-year plan, 22,000 acres were brought under cultivation in the Kharga and Dakhla oases. Wells were sunk, land levelled and roads, model villages, school and clinics and a new township of modern flats built at Kharga. Special incentives in high pay, free housing and cheap air fares to Cairo were offered to professional people to go and work in the new community. But so far the hopes of an abundant water supply waiting to be tapped have not been fulfilled on a scale to justify a large-scale expansion.

To finance investment under the five-year plan without cutting home consumption, Nasser had to rely heavily on foreign credit. The plan had aimed at ending foreign borrowing and achieving a balance-of-payments surplus of £E40 million by the end of the five-year period. In fact, it ended with a payment deficit of £76 million in 1964–5. The total deficit over the five years of the plan was £413 million. The situation was made just manageable by the increase in foreign exchange earnings from the Suez Canal. After the nationalization of the Canal Company, the Egyptian government had widened and deepened the canal to take bigger ships. Between 1961, when this programme was completed, and 1965 the Canal transit receipts rose from £E51–86 million.

In 1965 and 1966, when Egypt was having drastically to cut imports and faced the extra burden of finding £50 million a year more to pay for the wheat hitherto supplied by the US surplus food programme, new discoveries of oil in the Gulf of Suez and the Western Desert held the promise of a valuable new source of foreign exchange earnings (see Chapter 19).

The expansion of employment and earnings, combined with the priority given to capital goods over consumer goods in both imports and home investment, led to inflation, shortages and rising prices. Home agricultural production was not rising fast enough to meet the increased demand for food, and other consumer goods such as clothing were in short supply. The government attempts to control supply and prices through cooperatives led to a parallel black market and shortages of goods at official prices. By the summer of 1965 it was clear that a change of course in economic policy was inevitable. Nasser gave way to those economic advisers who argued that after the attempt at rapid expansion there had to be a cooling-off period to reduce foreign indebtedness, check inflation at home and increase the amount of domestic saving. This meant reducing imports and trying to reschedule the repayment of short-term foreign credits; seeking continued or increased aid from the two main aid sources, the United States and Russia; and taking unpopular measures at home to restrain consumption by higher taxes and by reduced consumer subsidies.

After his return from a visit to Moscow in August 1965, Nasser appointed Zacharia Mohieddin prime minister in place of Aly Sabry to carry out this austerity policy, while he himself began his attempt to reduce the burden of the Yemen war by seeking a settlement with Saudi Arabia. During the following year some greater balance was achieved in the economy at the cost of slowing down development, restraining wages and consumption and sharply increasing the cost of living. The growth rate for 1965-6 dropped to about 4·5 per cent and during the following year preceding the war with Israel it was even lower.

At the end of 1966 a three-year interim plan consisting of a list of investment projects was drafted. But the second five-year plan was skipped and after the 1967 war work was concentrated on a third five-year plan due to start in 1970.

The new deflationist policy did not last long. In September 1966 Nasser dismissed Mohieddin and replaced him by Sidky Suleiman at the head of a government, several of whose leading members were former army officers with technical training and more radical ideas. Nasser seemed to be preparing for another change of course, back to economic expansion at home and to a more militant pursuit of the 'Arab revolution' abroad. A more expansionist budget was being prepared for 1967 when the war with Israel broke out and defeat brought an entirely new situation (for the post-war economic development, see Chapter 19).

The strains resulting from the first five-year plan, the Yemen war and the socialist measures of nationalization were reflected in symptoms of political unrest. Discontent was felt among the working class at the rising cost of living and among some of the professional class and businessmen who had been affected by the nationalizations. The emergence of a new privileged group of army officers holding influential jobs in the expanding bureaucracy and the strengthening of the army's position through the Yemen war also aroused resentment among the middle class and the intelligentsia. Then there were, of course, the former rich who had lost at least part of their wealth and all their political influence.

The Arab Socialist Union and the National Assembly provided neither an adequate safety valve for opposition nor a serious instrument for checking and influencing government policy. The real political struggle, limited as it was, remained clandestine: it was conducted either through what was left of Nasser's two most active challengers, the Muslim Brothers and the Communists, or by local notables who still maintained a hold on the countryside against the influence of the government machine; or within the regime itself between rival power groups, including the army.

The Muslim Brothers, it appeared, were still the most formidable threat to the regime. The Brotherhood had been ferociously suppressed ever since the attack on Nasser's life in 1954, so there was general surprise when in August 1965 Nasser announced that as many as 400 people had been arrested as a result of the discovery of another alleged plot by the Muslim Brothers to kill him and other leading ministers. The surprise was caused not only by the numbers but also by the character of those arrested: they included many educated professional people, engineers, doctors, lawyers and army officers not usually associated with the Brotherhood's archaic, theocratic vision of society.

As usual on these occasions, some Communist plotters were discovered and charged at the same time to keep the political balance of repression. They were from the pro-Chinese faction because the rest of the Egyptian Communist party was now officially cooperating with the regime. A number of imprisoned Communists had been released in 1964 on the eve of Khrushchev's visit to Egypt. In line with the Soviet policy of supporting friendly nationalist governments rather than local Communist parties in the Third World, the Egyptian Communist party voted in April 1965 to dissolve itself and support Nasser. Many more of its followers were then released from jail. Communist policy then was to create a revolutionary political cadre within the Arab Socialist Union. On the understanding that the Communists and their sympathizers would not try to operate an organized party opposition, Nasser allowed a few Marxists to fill influential posts in government ministries and in the press.

In April 1966, the regime launched a wide-spread drive to eliminate the remaining influence of 'feudalists' in the country-side, alleged to have survived their political 'isolation'. The immediate cause of the drive, which led to the seizure of the proper-ties of scores of suspect land-owners, was the murder of an ASU village official. The murder was said to have been an act of revenge because the victim had begun to upset the local 'feudalist' ruling group composed of old land-owners and new officials whom they had corrupted. Field-Marshal Amer headed an anti-feudalist commission which set up committees of investigation throughout the country.

Whatever the truth of the murder, the affair seemed to throw light on some real problems facing Nasser in his attempt to build a new political system round the ASU to carry through socialist changes. In the countryside the land reform and the suppression of the former political parties, especially of the Wafd, had broken the political power of the top layer of big land-owners and their hangers-on. But power and influence had not been transferred to the poorer peasants. It had gone in the first instance either to government officials or to the medium farmers and lesser not-ables. Some of the latter still retained considerable wealth and were also often minor members of big land-owning families. The creation of the ASU and the provision that it and the National Assembly should have half its elected members and officials from among workers and farmers were meant in part to challenge and change this situation. But the definition of a 'worker' and a 'peasant' was at first so elastic that anyone drawing a salary or wage without responsibility for hiring or firing, including high-grade professional men, specialists and technicians, or anyone working on their own land up to a substantial acreage, could claim to stand for election in these categories. For the same reason, the statutory two 'workers' seats on the management boards of firms were at first often filled by high-grade staff members rather than lower-paid workers. The ASU was intended to be a kind of people's watchdog over the conduct of local government and administration at every level through its local elected committees. In trying to fulfil this task, the ASU was bound to run up against vested interests of all kinds which had grown up under the revolution within the government machine and among those connected with it, including some who enjoyed opportunities for corruption, privilege and abuse of power. In a countryside still largely peopled by illiterate and almost destitute peasants, it was not difficult for a new network of those enjoying such vested interests to take control.

At a higher level, the ASU was nevertheless a potential threat to the influence of the army and the 'army class', an alternative source of political power of a more radical kind. The opposition of Amer and the army to a more radical development of the ASU was hinted at by Nasser in a speech to the National Assembly in 1966 when he referred for the first time to the existence of 'power centres'. This occasion was recalled by Heykal in April 1968, shortly after Nasser had announced measures to strengthen the ASU. 'Certain elements,' wrote Heykal, 'which took part in seizing power in 1952 from the old alliance between the British occupation, the Royal Court and the Egyptian upper classes did not see the need to transfer authority to the new alliance of the people's working forces. . . .'[15] To reinforce the ASU and his own grip on it, Nasser created his own 'power centre' inside it. This was what later became known as the 'secret organisation', a personally controlled network of loyal supporters in key positions, a kind of civilian equivalent of the old Free Officers' group within the army.

But Nasser himself was obviously in two minds about the ASU. He wanted it as a new popular basis for his power, as a guide to public feeling and as an instrument of education in political responsibility which might in time overcome the ingrained inertia and subservience of the Egyptian masses. But because he would not risk a real threat to his authority, he was unwilling to agree to the conditions required to bring the ASU to life. Without a cadre of genuine political activists within it, the ASU remained in its lower echelons almost as tame and inert an organization as the National Union before it, although on the village level it developed a degree of local democracy and collective discussion in place of the simple ukase of a policeman, headman or official. To a large extent the ASU was run administratively rather than politically by officials and ministers. Only at the top, in its Supreme Executive Council, did it have an influence on policy-making as one of the power groups surrounding Nasser.

For while Nasser aimed at the development of a new political consciousness and of a future leadership at the lower level through local self-government and through cooperatives and trades unions, the political drive to make the ASU really effective in the short run could come only from the educated class, supported by a free press and radio capable of supplying informed criticism. But, as one Egyptian left-wing critic remarked, Nasser 'wanted to build socialism without socialists'.[16] Moreover, the Egyptian urban middle class was traditionally very status-conscious and separated from the poor, whether peasants or workers, not only by economic interests but by a wide cultural gap.

This cultural gap between a largely westernized and urban *élite* and the traditional Islamic and rural society of the masses has been perhaps the most fundamental obstacle to political development in modern Egypt. It is gradually being narrowed by the spread of education, by the growth of industry and an organized urban working class, and by closer contact between town and country.

Nasser and his associates gave energetic attention to education. By building new schools at the rate of one a day, they increased the number of children receiving primary education from 1,300,000 in 1952 to 3,400,000 (1,300,000 of them girls) in 1966. Primary schooling is free and compulsory from six to twelve and in 1969 about three-quarters of this age group, varying from town to country, were attending school. In the next three-year preparatory stage about forty-five per cent of the eligible age group were attending government schools and some were in private schools. At the secondary stage, which also lasts three years, education is divided into vocational (industrial, agricultural and commercial) and general arts and sciences. In 1969 there were 80,000 graduates from the secondary schools of whom 24,000 were admitted to universities and another 10,000 into other institutes of higher education. University tuition is free but students have to support themselves; especially gifted poor students are eligible for small grants and there is a student bank which lends money, up to £60 a year, for repayment after graduation. Egypt's four universities, two in Cairo, one in Alexandria and the fourth in Assiut, opened in 1957, had in 1969 a student population of 120,000. Another 30,000 students were in other higher institutes and 15,000 at the ancient Islamic university of Al Azhar, modernized in 1961. 35,000 of the students were women, to be found in all faculties, including engineering, a figure which indicates the progress made in recent years towards the emancipation of women among the educated classes in Egypt.

Medicine, engineering (21,000 students) and other sciences are now the most flourishing faculties as a result of the new emphasis placed by the government on technical and scientific education rather than the arts subjects which dominated before the revolution. In vocational schools at primary and secondary levels, the numbers of students increased from 15,000 in 1953 to 100,000 in 1969.[17]

The rapid expansion of schools and universities was perhaps inevitably accompanied, especially in arts subjects, by a decline in quality. The primary schools particularly suffered from a shortage of qualified teachers, overcrowded classes, and too much nationalistic political indoctrination during lessons. Standards of secondary education were also affected by the forcible incorporation in to the state system – as part of 'Egyptianization' – of the three hundred or more foreign schools which once educated most of Egypt's former cosmopolitanly cultured ruling élite.

The fact that 'Egypt's new élite is composed of scientists, doctors, engineers, architects, factory managers and army officers'[18] is part of a cultural change that has contributed both to the strength of Nasser's regime and to one of its notable weaknesses, namely the friction and ambiguities in its relations with the 'non-technical' intellectuals who are an indispensable creative element in the national life.

Nevertheless, the expansion of education must be accounted as one of Nasser's most positive achievements.

Chapter 14

The Yemen War:
Arabia and Arab Unity Moves, 1962–3

In the year following the Syrian secession and Nasser's proclamation of the 'Arab socialist revolution', Egypt's position in the Arab world was one of increasing isolation, at least as far as the Arab governments were concerned. Nasser was not only in open conflict with the Arab kings, especially the rulers of Saudi Arabia, Yemen and Jordan, but also with his fellow-revolutionary, General Kassim in Iraq, as well as with the republican but 'reactionary' secessionist regime in Syria. The Libyan and Moroccan kings, though less directly under fire, could not be expected to welcome Nasser's revolutionary onslaught on the monarchies. The Republican President Bourguiba disliked Nasser for other reasons. He suspected him of interfering through subversive agents in Tunisia's internal affairs and he feared the alliance between Nasser and the more radical elements of the Algerian nationalist leadership. Only in Algeria could Nasser find clear cause for encouragement. In March 1962 the Évian agreements brought the Algerian war to an end. On 3 July, after a referendum, Algeria was formally declared independent by France. A few weeks later Ben Bella emerged on top in the struggle for power inside the Algerian leadership and became prime minister of the first fully independent Algerian government.

Nasser could legitimately claim some share of the credit for Algeria's achievement of independence. The Algerian revolution was primarily a home-made affair. The main outside support for the revolution had come from Tunisia which had supplied a military base, sanctuary and training area, as well as diplomatic help. But Nasser had also given unswerving if limited support from the beginning in arms, money, propaganda and diplomatic backing. He had also helped behind the scenes, at French request, to bring about the final peace negotiations which led to Algerian independence. Ben Bella, the new prime minister, was an anti-imperialist revolutionary, non-aligned and socialist in the Nasser style.

In Syria, although Nasser had wisely cut his losses after the secession, he had not given up hope of recovering his position. He counted on continued popular sympathy and retained secret contacts with the remaining Nasserite officers in the Syrian army. The Syrian government for its part alternated between seeking reconciliation and conducting a vigorous propaganda campaign against Egypt and Nasser.

In June 1962 the Baath party split on the question of how far it was possible to work with Egypt and Nasser for Arab unity. The party's Syrian regional command, influenced by Akram Haurani, believed Nasser was a dictator with whom no compromise was possible. The new national command set up in the Lebanon called for a return to a union between Syria and Egypt in a federal rather than unitary state and on a democratic basis which would allow political parties.

Nasser continued to appeal to the Syrian people over the heads of their government. Through the editorials of Heykal, he denounced the Baathists as the wreckers of the union, and laid down new conditions for the re-establishment of unity. In an article in *Al Ahram* on 11 June, Heykal wrote that the Syrian secession had shown that in future a different form of Arab unity would be needed. Within the unity framework, national entities must remain clearly identified, with their own local governments responsible to elected popular authority. Unity must be complete in defence, foreign policy and in 'a programme of social work based on socialism and democracy'. A united Arab state should have a central parliament in which national entities were fairly represented and to which the central government should be responsible. The UAR, said Heykal, was ready to discuss steps towards unity with any Syrian government provided it spoke on behalf of the free Syrian popular will and that it proved its own sincerity and goodwill by an enquiry into the 'unjust accusations' made against Egypt after the secessionist *coup*.

Instead, the Syrian government's complaint against UAR interference was intensified and was carried officially to the Arab League. A special meeting of the League to consider it was called at Shtoura in the Lebanon in August. It precipitated the worst crisis inside the League since its creation seventeen years before. Saudi Arabia and Jordan supported the Syrian complaint. But the other members of the League were reluctant to become too closely involved in the quarrel between Egypt and her opponents for fear that an Egyptian withdrawal might wreck the League completely. After an uproar in which the police had to be called in, the Egyptian delegation walked out of the meeting in protest against the hearing of the Syrian government complaint. The UAR government then announced its intention of leaving the League unless Syria was condemned by the League for her attacks on Nasser as an alleged American stooge. But if Nasser had ever intended a final break with the League he may have been prevented from taking this step by the re-election as Secretary-General of the Egyptian Abdul Khalek Hassouna on 15 September as a gesture of appeasement to Egypt.

It was in this atmosphere of embattled isolation that eleven days later Nasser received news of a new Arab revolutionary outbreak from an unexpected direction, not from Syria, the most sophisticated of the Arab states, but from the most backward of them, the Yemen. On 26 September 1962, a group of army officers seized power in a *coup* in Sanaa, the capital of the Yemen, and proclaimed a republic in place of the ancient theocratic monarchy of the Imam.

The *coup* was only partially successful. The Imam, believed at first to have died in the ruins of his palace when it was shelled by the rebels, escaped to the mountains, raised support among loyal tribes and help in money and arms from Saudi Arabia. The rebels appealed to Nasser for help and he responded immediately. The first Egyptian planes, arms and army staff officers and specialists were flown into the Yemen on 6 October, followed soon afterwards by the first shipload of Egyptian troops and heavier arms.

Within a matter of weeks, as both the Republican revolutionaries and the royalists gathered strength, the Yemen was plunged into a ruthless civil war. Sustained by outside intervention, the war was to become a running sore in the Arab world, especially for Egypt, for the next five years. There is little doubt that Nasser did not foresee the burden he was assuming when he sent his forces to the Yemen, any more than President Kennedy or President Johnson foresaw how heavily they would eventually commit the United States in Vietnam.

Although the Yemen revolt was unexpected at the time it was not surprising. The country had been in a state of incipient revolution for many years. There had already been several unsuccessful attempted *coups*. Yemen's natural condition over the centuries had been an anarchic balance of power between rival religious sects and tribes: foreigners came or were called in to tip the balance one way or another, but, if the foreigners became too dominant, the country united temporarily to get rid of them and establish a precarious unity and independence until anarchy crept back again.

In the 1962 revolt and the abortive *coups* which had preceded it since 1948, there was a new element. These upheavals were concerned not merely with a change of dynasty or the rivalry of religious sects but with the transformation of Yemen society, with an attempt to bring a country which in most respects was still in the Middle Ages into the modern world. They were the first waves of the Arab nationalist revolution washing into the most remote corner of the Arab world. The desire for modernization and a better government cut across old sectarian differences.

The Yemen's medieval condition was due not to lack of natural resources or any mental limitations of its people, but largely to its isolation. Situated in the south-western corner of Arabia, the Yemen is not a desert country like most of the peninsula but a land of fertile coastal plain and magnificent jagged mountains, some rising to 8,000 feet and cultivated on their lower slopes in careful and intricate terraces. The Yemenis are mostly not desert Bedouin but almost equally hardy farmers organized in tribes but living in villages, often remote and inaccessible as fortresses on mountain ridges; or they are merchants and skilled artisans, living in small towns remarkable for their strange and beautiful architecture of tall multi-storeyed houses of stone and mud. The Yemenis have most of the traditional Arab characteristics of individualism and personal courage, a fierce pride and a love of poetry and of learning. They are often people of sharp intelligence and natural eloquence.

The decisive religious and social pattern of the Yemen, still persistent today, had already emerged by the end of the ninth century with the establishment among the mountain tribes of a heretical Shi'ite sect of Islam, the Zeidis, under their own Imam or priest-king. The plainsmen and townspeople mostly remained orthodox Sunni Muslims of the Shafei sect, who did not recognize the Imam as a spiritual leader and only accepted his temporal rule under force of arms. For several centuries thereafter the Yemen had close links with Egypt. The Zeidis looked for support to the Shi'ite Caliphs of the Fatimid dynasty in Cairo. Then after Saladin had become Sultan in Egypt one of his lieutenants conquered the Yemen. The connexion with Egypt continued to be close until the Egyptian Mamelukes in Cairo were overthrown in 1517 by the Turks who also occupied the Yemen. It was resumed briefly in the early nineteenth century when the Egyptians, the Wahabi rulers of Arabia and the British were already engaged in the rivalry for influence in southern Arabia that they were to repeat during the past decade. After the defeat of the Wahabis by an Egyptian army under Ibrahim Pasha, son of Mohammed Ali, the Egyptians were already in the Yemen when in 1839 the British occupied Aden. Encouraged by the British, the Turks returned to the Yemen in 1849 and stayed until 1918. When the Turks withdrew under the terms of the armistice which ended their participation in the First World War, they handed over the government in the capital, Sanaa, to the Imam Yahya, a devout Zeidi leader and a powerful personality who had led several risings against Turkish rule.

Yahya maintained peace and unity in the Yemen for thirty years but at the cost of stagnation and isolation from the outside world. Scores of thousands of Yemenis left the country to seek education and employment and to escape from the Imam's repressive and barbaric rule. Two main opposition groups developed among the *émigrés*. One was the Free Yemeni movement, founded in 1943 in Aden and supported by Yemeni businessmen there, which demanded constitutional government with an assembly and a limitation on the royal family's powers. Another group established itself in Cairo and aired its ideas through the Egyptian press.

In 1948, at the age of eighty, the Imam Yahya was assassinated. Another Zeidi chieftain, Abdullah Ahmed al Wazir, proclaimed himself Imam with the support of the 'Free Yemenis'. But he was quickly overthrown by the Crown Prince Ahmed, a strong and ruthless personality, who gathered a force of tribesmen in the mountains. Al Wazir and thirty-two members of his government were beheaded and their heads displayed on the gates of Sanaa. Others, including future revolutionary leaders such as Abdullah Sallal and Abdullah Mohammed Nomaan, a moderate constitutional reformer, were sent to the dungeons in chains. Sallal remained there for seven years.

The new Imam Ahmed tried at first to continue the policy of his father, relying on tyrannical rule by fear and keeping out foreign and modernizing influences. The internal opposition was essentially formed of the more educated townspeople, mostly Shafeis. It included liberals of the Free Yemeni type, a few army officers and notables and tribal leaders who resented the dominance of the Imam's family.

In March 1955, Ahmed crushed another attempted *coup*, this time by one of his brothers. It was followed by new repression against the reformers, some of whom, including Nomaan, took refuge in Cairo. But they found no support from Egypt. Nasser's policy at that time was to back the Crown Prince Mohammed al Badr and to bring the Imam into the Egyptian alliance with Saudi Arabia against the British and their Hashemite allies. The Imam gained the backing of Egypt and the Arab League against the British plan for a South Arabian federation which Arab nationalists saw as a British device for retaining control of Aden as a military base.

In April 1956, the Imam Ahmed ventured out of his country as far as Jeddah in Saudi Arabia where he signed an agreement for mutual aid with King Saud and Nasser. He established diplomatic relations with Russia and China and Crown Prince al Badr went to Moscow where he made an arms agreement with the Russians.

The Suez war had a double effect in Southern Arabia. It stimulated the growth of Arab nationalism and anti-imperialist feeling. At the same time the loss of the Suez Canal base increased the importance to the British of Aden as a base from which to protect the Gulf oil sheikhdoms where their main Middle East interest had now shifted.

In early 1957 there was a revival of border warfare between the Yemen and the Aden Protectorates. At the end of the year Badr was invited to London for peace talks but they ended in deadlock. More Egyptian, Chinese and Russian technical aid advisers came to the Yemen and in March 1958 the Yemen joined the newly formed United Arab Republic in the 'United Arab States'. The Imam's aim was to get more Egyptian support for his campaign to force the British to abandon their plan for a South Arabian federation, which was discussed at a conference on London in February 1959. He considered the plan to be a violation of the 1934 Anglo-Yemen treaty since it changed the '*status quo*' (the Imam interpreted the *status quo* agreement to refer to the general political status of the Protectorates and Aden which he claimed as part of Yemen, while the British considered that it referred only to the line of the frontiers). The Protectorate rulers and tribesmen were themselves divided about the federation proposal, many being hostile to it. The main support for the plan came from local rulers who wanted British support against possible domination by the Zeidi dynasty in the Yemen, and from some of the Adeni business class. The latter feared the growing power of the pro-Nasser left-wing Arab nationalist movement which was then centred in the Aden Trades Union Congress and People's Socialist Party.

By throwing in his lot with Nasser and the United Arab Republic in 1958, Ahmed had risked the hostility of Saudi Arabia, for King Saud had now become Nasser's leading Arab opponent instead of his chief ally. As part of this strange new equation of power, Nasser also began to switch his support for the opposition groups in Aden and the Protectorates away from the South Arabian League, a more conservative party which was strongest in some of the Protectorate sheikhdoms and which had close Saudi Arabian links, to Abdullah al Asnag's TUC and Socialist party in Aden. Asnag's group also preached unity of Aden and the Protectorates with the Yemen, although in practice they wanted union only after the Yemen had liberalized its regime.

By 1960 the Imam Ahmed's relations with Egypt had deteriorated. He disapproved of Nasser's trend towards socialism and feared his influence in the Yemen. In June 1960 the Yemen representatives on the Council of the United Arab States were recalled from Cairo. Ahmed welcomed the Syrian secession as a setback for Nasser. He saw himself as one of the targets for Nasser's subsequently proclaimed Arab Socialist revolution and onslaught on the Arab kings. In December 1961 he wrote and had broadcast a sixty-four-line poem attacking Arab socialism as ungodly and deriding Nasser's claim to speak for the Arabs (though without actually mentioning Nasser by name). Nasser replied by denouncing Yemen's membership of the United Arab States and launching a campaign for revolution in the Yemen over Cairo radio.

Nasser would no doubt, as a matter of principle, have preferred a more progressive regime to replace that of the Imam in the Yemen: but there were other reasons why he began to lend his support to the revolutionary movement in the country. Apart from personal pique at the Imam's attack on him and a desire to maintain prestige in the Arab world after the failure in Syria, there was the developing struggle for power within the regime in Egypt. This struggle was partly connected with a dispute over Egypt's foreign policy. Amer and his army supporters backed Nasser's policy of pan-Arab leadership; indeed, they sometimes pressed it further even than Nasser wanted to go. Others among the leading Free Officers, notably Baghdadi and Zacharia Mohieddin, wanted a more cautious policy of 'Egypt first'.

Nasser was probably more concerned with his campaign against Saudi Arabia and against the British in Aden than he was with internal changes in the Yemen. But the contradictions between his alliance with the Imam, the most backward of all the Arab kings, his hostility towards the Saudi monarchy allegedly on account of its reactionary character, and his support for left-wing socialists in Aden who wanted union with the Yemen but not under the Imam, were becoming too blatant. The Imam's defection must have come as something of a relief. It was followed by an attempt by Nasser to work out a policy of 'national liberation' for southern Arabia which would resolve some of these contradictions. As a result, the conduct of propaganda from Cairo for the 'Yemeni liberation movement' was entrusted to a group of three men. The leader was one of the older generation of reformists, Mohammed Mahmoud az-Zubeiri. The other two were younger and more radical revolutionary intellectuals from the Yemen and from Aden. Muhsin al Aini was the Cairo representative of the Aden TUC with the International Confederation of Trades Unions. He was born in the Yemen but educated in Cairo and at the Sorbonne before working in Aden as a schoolteacher. Abdur-rahman al Beidhani, an economist, was born in Cairo, the son of a Yemeni *émigré*. He had been educated in Egypt and married the sister of Anwar es-Sadat, one of Nasser's close associates. After serving for some time as an economic adviser to the Crown Prince al Badr in the Yemen he withdrew to Cairo again in 1959 when the Imam was on the rampage against the reformers. Beidhani favoured the creation of a Yemeni republic on modified Nasserite socialist lines rather than a constitutional reform of the Imamate.

All through the first nine months of 1962 the ailing Imam had been losing his grip on the country. As his well-meaning but weak son, al Badr, waited to take over, plots multiplied round him. The discontent and the terror under the Imamate, as well as the lack of public confidence in al Badr, would probably have made a *coup* against him by one faction or another inevitable sooner or later. Sallal used to say to journalists who came to interview him after the revolution, 'How can you expect the people not to rise against such a state of affairs? Even if this country were inhabited by monkeys they would have revolted against the Imam and his inhuman regime.'[1] There appears to have existed a secret revolutionary committee in the Yemen loosely linking together different opposition elements – army officers, intellectuals and middle-class reformers, the latter mostly from among the merchants. They were a small but determined group. Out of the Yemen army's 400 officers, eighty-six were in or linked with the committee.[2] Many of them had become revolutionaries while training abroad in Egypt or Iraq. The Yemen also had about eighty graduates from foreign universities who, together with some of the merchants, provided the intellectual section of the new movement. Both army officers and intellectuals covered a wide spectrum of political views: reformers, Nasserites, Baathists, Muslim Brothers and Marxist sympathizers.[3] But they all wanted to overthrow the Imamate and modernize the country. They were more interested in radical social change than most of the merchant class whose main aim, like that of the older generation of liberal nationalists, was a constitutional reform which would give them a greater share of power, break the royal family's monopoly of trade and create a modern administration. These reformers were prepared to accept the continuation of the Imamate if it were democratized.

Two other groups were also plotting the downfall of the Imam and of al Badr should he succeed his father. There were the leaders of the powerful Hashid tribal confederation whose paramount sheikh and his son had been executed by the Imam. They were in touch with Abdullah Sallal who, after seven years in the Imam's dungeons, had regained favour through the Crown Prince and had been promoted brigadier and later army chief of staff. Finally there were the rivals for the royal succession, including some of the young princes who wanted to preserve the Imamate while carrying through reforms. They considered al Badr too erratic in his habits and for other reasons too lacking in capacity to carry out this task. They gave their backing to the Imam's brother, Prince Hassan, a long-time aspirant to the throne.[4]

The Egyptians had made contact with all these groups, none of whom, however, can fairly be described as Egyptian 'instruments'. The main Egyptian link was with the army officers and particularly with Abdullah Sallal, who stood somewhere between the more conservative and more revolutionary factions of the opposition. According to one well-informed Yemeni, Sallal was approached by the Egyptians with proposals for a revolutionary *coup* but rejected them as showing ignorance of the tribal situation in the Yemen and of foreign reaction.[5] When the *coup* came it was begun by another group of younger and more revolutionary officers, and took Sallal by surprise.

The crisis came to a head when the Imam Ahmed died on 19 September 1962 and was succeeded by the Crown Prince Mohammed al Badr. The opposition was caught divided and unprepared. The secret committee split. Some were for immediate revolution; others, encouraged by promises of reform from the new Imam, wanted to wait and see whether al Badr would develop into a constitutional monarch. Sallal was for caution: he wanted to make sure of tribal as well as army backing.[6] The younger army officers led by a twenty-five-year-old lieutenant, Ali Abdul Murny, were for action.[7] The young officers decided to force the hand of the reformists in the secret committee by attempting to assassinate the new Imam. On the evening of 26 September, as al Badr was leaving a cabinet meeting in his palace in Sanaa, an officer of his guards tried to shoot him but failed and was arrested. When this attempt went wrong, the new revolutionary officers launched an attack on the Imam's palace half an hour later with tanks and artillery. It was not until the shooting had begun that Sallal was approached and agreed to join the revolutionaries as the future President. The officers (after locking some of their troops in the barracks – the reverse of the usual revolutionary situation) seized the radio station and occupied the palace after shelling it all night.

The rebels believed at first that the Imam had died under the rubble of the palace, and this news was broadcast to the world from Sanaa and Cairo. But he escaped, slipped out of the city and made his way to the mountains. He gathered the support on the way of several thousand loyal Zeidi tribesmen and set up a headquarters in caves in the mountains of northern Yemen near the Saudi Arabian border which he reached eight days later.[8] He then sent messages to the Arab governments denouncing the rebellion as having been engineered by Nasser.

In Sanaa the rebels had set up a Revolutionary Council under Sallal. They proclaimed the end of the Imamate and the establishment of the Yemeni Arab Republic. The new revolutionary government announced in Sanaa on 28 September was joined by the three exiled leaders from Cairo. Beidhani became deputy prime minister under Sallal, with Muhsin al Aini as Foreign Minister and Mohammed az-Zubeiri as Minister of Education.

The revolution was at first generally welcomed in the towns and among part of the countryside, but the revolutionaries were apprehensively aware that previous *coups* had been crushed by surviving members of the royal family with the help of loyal tribes and support from Saudi Arabia. In a panic measure, the revolutionary officers massacred during the first few days a score or more of the former leading supporters of the Imam, members of the royal family, tribal notables and officials. The traditional public execution of beheading by the sword was abolished but replaced by the firing squad.

The revolutionaries turned to Nasser for support against possible foreign intervention, either from Saudi Arabia or from the British in Aden. They also wanted Egyptian technical and administrative help in a country where the machinery of modern government scarcely existed. Nasser's first response was to strengthen the Egyptian military mission in the Yemen with more technicians and advisers and to send some units of the Egyptian air force. The Yemen army had only twenty old York transport planes, few of them operational, and only one pilot.[9] At first it looked as though the revolution had been almost completely successful and that this limited Egyptian intervention would be sufficient to enable the new regime to consolidate its position. The new regime seemed to be sufficiently in control of the country for the British and American diplomatic missions in Taiz to recommend that it be recognized by their governments.

The revolution had, however, an immediate impact outside the Yemen which forced not only Nasser but other governments to treat its outcome as something more than an internal Yemeni affair. It was hailed enthusiastically by public opinion in most Arab countries as a progressive move to emancipate a notoriously backward country. It was the first modern revolutionary movement in the Arabian peninsula. As such it was bound to arouse the apprehension of the traditional monarchic, theocratic and sheikhly regimes which still ruled all the rest of Arabia except for the British colony of Aden. In Saudi Arabia, particularly, it could be expected to strengthen the pressures already being felt for the reform or overthrow of the Saudi monarchy, pressures which Egypt's propaganda and intelligence services were encouraging as part of Nasser's campaign against the Arab kings. In Aden the Yemen revolution was joyfully welcomed by the nationalist opposition of Asnag's party and the TUC, many of whose members were Yemeni workers. It strengthened their hopes of eventual Yemen unity. It also stiffened their opposition to the British plans for a South Arabian federation which would merge the comparatively advanced town of Aden with the more backward Protectorate sultanates. At the same time it cemented the alliance between the Protectorate rulers and the British. The sultans were afraid of being crushed between the pincers of radical unionist movements in Aden and Sanaa.

The main purpose of the British was to hold on to their military base in Aden and to prevent Nasser's influence from spreading to the oil sheikhdoms of the Persian Gulf. The idea of the South Arabian federation had originated in a benevolent colonial service desire for administrative efficiency and progress. It had subsequently acquired an additional and perhaps eventually more powerful attraction. A South Arabian state dominated by sultans beholden to Britain for their survival could, it was hoped, provide a political framework within which Britain might be able to hold on indefinitely to the Aden base from which she could continue to support a military presence in the Persian Gulf.

The Yemen was the first Arab country in which Nasser had intervened openly with Egyptian forces to support a local revolution. He had sent troops to Syria only at the request of a Syrian government whose legitimacy was not in dispute. There was another dangerous new aspect of his intervention. It was to become – though this was probably not Nasser's original intention – an attempt to extend Egyptian military power into the Arabian peninsula for the first time since the expedition of Ibrahim Pasha over a century before. Just as Mohammed Ali's challenge to the Turkish sultan's suzerainty in Arabia and Syria roused the hostility of Palmerston's England, pledged to back the enfeebled Ottoman empire against the Russians, so Nasser's challenge to the traditionalist regimes of Arabia brought him up against the opposition not only of the British, already suspicious of him, but also of the United States. For apart from their oil interests and long-standing political ties with Saudi Arabia, the Americans were also assuming an almost-Palmerstonian stance in supporting anti-Communist regimes in the Middle East.

For Russia, on the other hand, these British and American interests were reasons for backing the Yemen revolution and giving Nasser such help in economic aid, arms and technical advice as he might need if he intervened to protect it. The Russians could hope to secure the accelerated departure of the British military presence from Aden and the undermining and perhaps eventual collapse of the Anglo-American system of protection and influence in Arabia and the Persian Gulf. The Russians were, however, cautious about committing themselves directly in the Yemen, beyond supplying arms, aid and technicians. They were at that very time learning in the Cuban missile crisis the dangers of military commitment in an area where they were logistically at a disadvantage compared with the United States and where their local protégé was not fully under control. They were sceptical, too, about the Yemen revolution itself. On 23 November 1962 *Izvestia* wrote, 'To believe that there exists in the Yemen a coherent front of partisans of renovation is to take desires for reality.'[10]

Nasser later admitted that his military intervention in the Yemen was a 'miscalculation. We never thought it would lead to what it did.'[11] At the time the risks were not so obvious as they later appeared; the risks of doing nothing and letting the Yemen revolution collapse may have appeared greater. For at first the outside reactions were confused. The Imamate regime in the Yemen had been so notoriously brutal and backward that no government liked to come out openly in its defence. Moreover so long as the revolutionary regime seemed to be establishing itself successfully there was a reluctance to antagonize it or to support a lost cause. In addition, the revolution and Egyptian support for it presented both the British and Americans with a dilemma. The Zeidi Imamate had been the main external challenge to the British position in Aden through its claim over the whole of historical Yemen including the Protectorates. If the new regime were to show more interest in reform at home, instead of pressing this claim, there might be some advantage in the change, in spite of increased Egyptian influence in Sanaa. For the Americans, there was a conflict of interest between their protection of Saudi Arabia and their desire to be on good terms with Nasser as a useful anti-Communist influence elsewhere in the Arab world. Finally, there was the recognition that to stifle the revolution in the Yemen would not really protect the Saudi Arabian regime: that could be done only by internal reforms in Saudi Arabia which would make a Yemen-type revolution there unnecessary.

In Saudi Arabia, in the absence at the United Nations of the Crown Prince Feisal, the reaction of King Saud and his advisers was hesitant and divided. Part of the Saudi cabinet favoured recognition of the revolutionary regime: all commoners, they reflected the view of the new middle class that the Yemen revolution would affect the whole of Arabia and lead to an inevitable similar upheaval against the Saudi monarchy.[12] This view was shared by some of the younger royal princes, four of whom, led by Prince Talal, a former Minister of Finance and half-brother of King Saud, fled the country and declared their sympathy with Nasser. But while King Saud himself wavered other members of his family and their supporters had already begun to organize help for the Yemeni royalists. They were encouraged in this by King Hussein of Jordan who was the first to leap into the struggle as a means of hitting back at Nasser.

By the middle of October money, arms and other supplies were going across the border from Saudi Arabia to the tribal armies that were being formed in the Yemen mountains under the command of the surviving Zeidi royal princes. Jordan sent planes down to the Saudi Arabian border and some arms and technicians to train the Yemenis in their use. Larger numbers of Egyptian troops began to arrive in the Yemen by sea. In the last week of October and the first week of November Egyptian planes attacked supply bases and training camps in and around the Saudi Arabian border town of Najran and shelled a Saudi Arabian village on the Red Sea coast from the sea.

Crown Prince Feisal returned from New York on 24 October to become prime minister in place of his brother King Saud. He broke off relations with Egypt and decisively increased Saudi support for the Yemen royalists. He obtained arms for the

Yemenis from Pakistan and Belgium, while Iran sent money. Nasser suspected a combined operation against him by the CENTO powers* backed by Britain and America.[13] Feisal sought help from the United States in deterring Egyptian attack and if possible persuading Nasser to withdraw his forces. At the same time he tried to strengthen the position of the Saudi monarchy by some long-overdue reforms at home. He relaxed the strict Wahabi laws on public morality and ordered the final abolition of slavery – the latter already decreed in the Yemen a month before by the republican government.

A month after the Sanaa *coup* the Republicans still controlled the main towns and the greater part of the country. But the royalists, with the help of Saudi money and arms, were gathering strength among the tribes in the northern and eastern mountains and deserts. It looked as if the Republicans would need greater Egyptian military support if they were to extend their control to the whole country and perhaps even to ensure their survival. Nasser sent Amer and Anwar es-Sadat, his chief adviser on Yemen political affairs, to the Yemen at the end of October to report on the situation. Amer called for troop reinforcements. The Egyptian army was confident that with more men it could bring the country under control. Nasser now faced a crucial decision. He had not expected to have to supply more than some arms, money, a few advisers and technicians and aircraft. Now he was being asked to commit substantial ground forces in a war in a far-off country which many Egyptians had scarcely heard of, or which they thought of as a savage backwater of no interest to Egypt. Moreover, conflict with Saudi Arabia would bring him trouble with the United States with whom he had recently been trying to improve his relations and whose economic aid was valuable to Egypt's development programme.

On the other hand, the political risks of not intervening were considerable. If the Yemen revolution were crushed with Saudi Arabian help after appealing to Nasser for support, his leadership of the 'Arab revolution' would be dealt a heavy, possibly fatal blow. It was little more than a year since the failure of the UAR

*Central Treaty Organization consisting of the former Baghdad Pact Powers minus Iraq.

through the Syrian secession. Egypt was isolated among the Arab governments, with Algeria almost her only friend. At home Nasser had been struggling to preserve his Arab policy against 'Egypt first' critics and the compromise by which he had ended the crisis with Amer in the spring of 1962 had left him in a weak position *vis-à-vis* the Egyptian army. He needed a boost to his prestige in the Arab world and in Egypt and he could not afford to offend the army. The army, through Amer, assured him that with moderate reinforcements they could quickly crush the royalist resistance and teach Saudi Arabia a lesson. While Amer and the army were eager for military victory, Nasser was chiefly interested in the survival of the Yemen Republic: if this could be achieved by political means at smaller cost in blood and money, so much the better. So while he agreed to send more troops to the Yemen he also entered into negotiations through the United States for a political settlement which would enable him to disengage his forces once the Republican position was assured.

The first American reaction to the Yemen revolution was to accept it as a genuine manifestation of Arab radical nationalism, while at the same time reassuring Saudi Arabia against any threat from the Egyptian forces moving into the Yemen. On 25 October President Kennedy wrote to Feisal to assure him of full American support for the maintenance of Saudi Arabian integrity. A month later Kennedy wrote to Feisal, King Hussein and Nasser proposing the outlines of a Yemen settlement. He suggested as the first step the withdrawal of Egyptian forces and the end of Saudi and Jordanian aid to the royalists. United States recognition of the Yemen Republican regime was understood to be part of the deal, though it is unclear to what extent this recognition was to be conditional on an Egyptian commitment to withdraw. At the same time, a squadron of US air force planes was sent to make a show of force over Ryadh and Jedda in order to warn Nasser against extending his air attacks on Saudi territory.

When the United States recognized the Yemen Republic on 19 December 1962, the Republican government promised to honour its international obligations and treaties and to live at peace with all its neighbours – a statement understood as a pledge to respect, among other agreements, the Anglo-Yemen treaty of 1934. The Egyptian statement supported the Yemen declaration and announced the willingness of the UAR to 'undertake a reciprocal expeditious disengagement and phased removal of its troops from the Yemen' as Saudi and Jordanian support for the dethroned Imam was terminated and 'whenever the government of the Yemen Arab Republic should make such a request'.

A number of other Western countries – West Germany, Italy, Canada and Australia – also recognized the Yemen Republican regime. The British government declared its non-involvement in the Yemen and withheld recognition on the grounds that the Sanaa government was not in full control of the country. But there were other reasons for the British attitude, connected with the position in Aden.

Nasser had tried to limit the repercussions of his intervention in the Yemen by assuring the British that he had no designs on Aden. He persuaded Sallal to soft-pedal the Yemeni claim on the Protectorates and offered the British a deal by which the Republican regime would quietly drop the claim in return for British recognition. The Foreign Office, recognizing the reality of the Arab revolutionary ferment which underlay the Yemen revolt, was inclined to accept the proposition and to delay the development of the South Arabian federation until the situation had clarified. It believed that Nasser did not want to weaken the British position in Aden at that time because he did not want Iraq to seize Kuwait – Aden was the base for British forces operating in the Persian Gulf.[14] But other British ministries, particularly the Commonwealth Relations and Colonial Office then under Duncan Sandys, and senior British officials in Aden, successfully insisted that there should be no deal with Nasser and that the merger of Aden and the former Western Protectorate states into one South Arabian federal state should be pushed through as fast as possible. To this end there should be no early recognition of the Sanaa regime which would upset those sultans, especially the ruler of Beihan, whose support was crucial to create the new federation. Instead a blind eye was to be turned to aid for the royalists going through British-controlled federal territory.

This policy was backed by an analysis of the Yemen conflict which attached prime importance to the tribal and religious differences. If the Egyptians withdrew, the Zeidi tribal warriors in the mountains who were supporting the royalists were bound, it was thought, to crush the less warlike Shafei plainsmen who provided the main backing for the Republic. If the Egyptians stayed, they would be bogged down in a long and costly war against the mountain tribes. Either way Nasser would suffer. If he cut his losses and left the Yemeni Republicans to their fate, his prestige as an Arab revolutionary leader would be shattered and the rest of Arabia would have a respite from his influence. If he stayed and fought, his resources would be absorbed in a remote and fruitless war, weakening his position at home and restricting his activity elsewhere in the Arab world.[15]

Both this analysis and that which stressed the strength and irreversibility of the Yemen revolution were proved partly right and partly wrong. The Egyptians were pinned down in a long war but the royalist strength based on the Zeidi tribes was shown to be exaggerated. While the Egyptians and the Republicans at first neglected the tribal and religious aspects, those who backed the royalists to win underestimated new social and economic factors. The Zeidis and the tribes were divided. Some supported the Republic because they had hated the temporal rule of the Imam. Some of the tribes supported the royalists because they were paid to fight and changed sides when it suited them. These divisions encouraged the emergence of a 'third force' of moderate republicans who were prepared to compromise in order to end both Egyptian and Saudi intervention in the country.

In some ways the new regime in Sanaa had begun well. Its first measures included the abolition of slavery, the end of the tribal hostage system used by the Imam, plans for reform of taxation, education and municipal administration. Beidhani, the deputy prime minister, drew up a two-year economic plan based on a mixture of public and private enterprise. Private trade was encouraged in place of the old monopolies run by the royal family. A semi-public national bank for reconstruction and development was set up and a new silver currency established. There was thought to be no need for land reform on the Egyptian pattern because the agricultural problem was not one of land shortage, but the royal estates, comprising a quarter of the country's best farm land, were confiscated.[16]

Egyptian advisers, doctors, teachers, engineers and army officers came in to help the few trained Yemenis to modernize the administration and to set up schools, hospitals and farm services, as well as to train the army. The number of children in school in the Republican territory doubled in the first year from one in twenty to one in ten.[17]

The new regime promised the replacement of arbitrary rule by democratic principles, human rights and modern civil and penal codes.[18] These promises were embodied in the new provisional constitution of April 1963 which was modelled on that of the UAR. Sallal became President, commander-in-chief and chairman of the Presidential Council.

The first weakness of the Republic was in the composition of its government. It included at first too many unknown faces, too many Shafeis instead of Zeidis, too many returned *émigrés* from Cairo suspected of being Egyptian nominees, and not enough notables and tribal leaders to impress what was still essentially a deeply conservative and traditional society. Sallal himself, though he had risen to high military office and was a Zeidi, was handicapped by his humble origins: he was the son of a blacksmith. Sent to Baghdad for military training in 1936, when Iraq was under a military dictatorship, he returned to the army in the Yemen with political ideas of Arab nationalism and reform. His political beliefs earned him two spells in prison under the Imam Yahya. When Yahya was assassinated he was sentenced to death but reprieved. During the seven years he then spent in the Hajjah fortress he is said to have studied Nasser's *The Philosophy of the Revolution* and books on the French Revolution. He owed his release and subsequent advancement to be army chief of staff to the influence of the Crown Prince. Though he eventually became heavily dependent on Egyptian support, Sallal was not simply an Egyptian stooge. He was a Yemeni patriot who had, like other Yemenis, risked his life for his beliefs.

In its summary abolition of the Imamate, the revolutionary regime had unwisely neglected the importance to the Zeidis of the Imamate's spiritual role, even among those Zeidis who had opposed the Imam's temporal rule. Some of the young officers were hasty and brutal in dealing with the religious susceptibilities of the Zeidi tribes. The resentment thus caused was compounded by the arrival of the Egyptians. The latter were not only foreigners, regarded by the fiercely independent northern tribes as would-be conquerors, but also Shafeis by religion. They were resented for their condescension even where their help was accepted. Nor was the Republic in a strong position to buy the loyalty of those tribesmen who were wavering. It took over an empty treasury and its foreign assets were blocked by Saudi Arabia.

By the beginning of 1963 the broad pattern of the Yemen war had already begun to emerge. The republicans and Egyptians, the latter by then with some 15,000 troops in the country, held the coastal plains, including the port of Hodeida and Taiz, the diplomatic capital; these were all areas predominantly Shafei in allegiance and republican in sympathy. But the main axis of the republican military position was the long mountain massif stretching from Sanaa, the administrative capital, northwards to Sadah. The mountains outside the main towns were mostly inhabited by Zeidi tribesmen living in inaccessible villages. By no means all the Zeidi tribes backed the royalists. Part of the two big confederations, the Hashid and the Bagil, at first supported the Republic and others were divided or wavering in their loyalties. The republicans and Egyptians, pushing along the valleys in armoured columns or dropping paratroops, had established outposts to the north-east and south of the Sanaa–Sadah mountain line, but they had failed to cut the royalist lines of supply and communication with Saudi Arabia and the South Arabian federation. The royalists on their side held the northern mountains and the eastern desert areas and part of the mountains round Sanaa. They were able to harass the republican lines of communication, forcing some of the outposts to be supplied by air, and preventing the Egyptians from advancing further. But they were unable to cut the republican supply lines to the port of Hodeida or to capture Sanaa. By a combination of armoured thrusts and air attack, the Egyptians were able to prevent the royalists from mounting a decisive offensive. The war was conducted with brutality on both sides. The royalists often killed or mutilated their prisoners, cutting off their ears and noses, and took savage reprisals on villages suspected of changing sides. The Egyptians were ruthless in their use of air attack on royalist villages, including on several occasions the dropping of gas bombs, and in other reprisals against hostile or suspect tribesmen. The Egyptian air attacks helped to check the royalist military operations, but they created bitter anti-Egyptian feeling among Yemenis on both sides and increased the tribal support for the royalists.

Neither side showed any signs of carrying out President Kennedy's disengagement plan. After another visit to the Yemen by Amer and Sadat, more Egyptian reinforcements were despatched. At the end of February 1963 the Egyptians launched their first serious offensive. They aimed at finishing off the war with a decisive blow at the royalists' headquarters in the north-east and at their communications with Saudi Arabia and the South Arabian federation. After capturing the towns of Marib and Harib in the south-east and penetrating into royalist territory in the north-east, the offensive petered out. The offensive thus failed in its main objective but it broke the royalist threat to Sanaa and forced the royalists on to the defensive.

Unable to secure a quick military decision, Nasser turned once more to diplomacy. He felt in a stronger bargaining position not only because of the improved military situation in the Yemen but because the tide had begun to turn again in his favour in the Arab world. In Iraq, his rival, General Abdul Karim Kassim, was killed in a military *coup* on 8 February and was succeeded by Colonel Aref, who had been imprisoned by Kassim for his Nasserite sympathies. The *coup* was carried out by Aref and other army officers but the new Iraqi government contained a strong Baathist element. A month later a similar combination of pan-Arab army officers and Baathists, but with the latter in a more dominant position, seized power by a *coup* in Syria. Two days after the Syrian *coup*, the new Iraqi regime proposed the creation of 'military unity' between the five 'liberated Arab countries – Iraq, Syria, Algeria, the UAR and the Yemen'. In April, at the urging of the Syrian and Iraqi governments, talks on constitutional unity began in Cairo between Iraq, Syria and Egypt.

Nasser's 'Arab Revolution', which had looked in the doldrums, now seemed to be in full sail again. Egypt was no longer isolated. There was once more a feeling throughout the Arab world that Nasser and the Baath between them were the tide of the future that would sweep the Arab countries towards unity and social justice. The Yemen was just one battlefield in the wider conflict between the Arab Revolution on the one hand and the Arab kings and reactionaries, supported by the imperialist powers, on the other. This broad alignment had crystallized not only on the side of the revolutionaries but also on that of their opponents. American planes and warships were providing an umbrella for Saudi Arabia. In January Britain resumed diplomatic relations with Saudi Arabia after a break of nearly eight years caused by the dispute over the Buraimi oasis. At the same time, on 18 January, she rushed through the merger of Aden with the South Arabian federation on a minority vote in the Aden Legislative Council and in the teeth of local nationalist opposition. There was renewed friction on the border between the Federation and Republican Yemen. But with Syria and Iraq apparently now joining in the 'Arab Revolution', the Yemen became less vital as a test of Nasser's policy and prestige. He had greater freedom to choose whether to compromise or fight there.

The international aspects of the Yemen situation, threatening to involve not only the local contestants but also the Great Powers, led to a new initiative by the United States and the United Nations to reach a settlement based on disengagement. In March 1963 Ralph Bunche, the United Nations Under-Secretary, went to the Yemen and to Cairo. In Cairo Nasser assured Bunche that the UAR was ready to withdraw its troops if the Saudis stopped helping the royalists. Nasser gave the same assurance to the American envoy, Ambassador Ellsworth Bunker, who visited him at the beginning of April. Bunker had previously had talks in Ryadh with Feisal who was sceptical of the disengagement plan, even when accompanied by promises of US protection.

These two missions led to a disengagement agreement and Security Council approval for the despatch of a 200-man United

Nations observer mission to the Yemen in June 1963, to supervise its execution. UN observers were to watch, report and prevent any Saudi moves to supply the royalist forces, and to supervise the eventual Egyptian withdrawal from the Yemen. There would be a cease-fire as soon as the agreement came into force.

The disengagement agreement was to fail in its main objective. The Egyptians did not withdraw and it is probable that the Saudis continued at least some of their aid; because of the wild mountainous terrain, the language problems and the limitations of observation by night, it was extremely difficult for the UN observers to know whether supplies were getting through to the royalists or not. The observer mission was eventually withdrawn over a year later (in September 1964) when it had become obvious that its efforts had failed to stop the resumption of the war.

The disengagement agreement and the mission nevertheless produced two useful results. They prevented the threatened escalation of the war to a point where it might have involved the Great Powers. They also led to a lull in the fighting, accompanied by a series of local tacit and open truces, from April to September 1963. In the last three months of the year fighting was resumed in a number of limited and inconclusive engagements.

By this time the tide of Arab affairs had once more begun to turn, less favourably for Nasser. The spring flood of the 'Arab Revolution' ushered in by the army–Baathist coups in Baghdad and Damascus was ebbing in a winter of disillusion. From the (almost) verbatim account of the Cairo unity talks published by the Egyptians, it is clear that from the beginning Nasser himself had few illusions about the prospects for Arab unity opened up by the Iraqi and Syrian revolutions.[19] He was too deeply suspicious of the Baathists whom he blamed for their share in the Syrian secession in 1961. Moreover, the Baath party was itself still deeply split.

The Baghdad coup had been welcomed in Cairo for its overthrow of General Kassim who had become an open enemy of Nasser. The new Iraqi president, Colonel Abd as-Salam Aref, was known as a friend of Egypt. The army officers who carried out the coup in Syria a month later also included several sympa-

402   The Arab Revolution

thetic to Egypt and to Nasser. When the new Iraqi and Syrian regimes took the initiative in approaching Nasser to discuss unity between the three countries Nasser could hardly refuse, for Arab public opinion had been fired with enthusiastic expectations. Nasser recognized that if it could be achieved 'the unity state would extend from the oil wells through the pipelines to the Suez Canal – from Asia to Africa. This would bring the Iraq army to the Israeli borders. Its potential might perhaps be more than France. Its population would be forty million.' The creation of such a state would prompt the Arabs to seek further unity.[20]

But he was not only sceptical of its being achieved; he also was aware of the new dangers and burdens in which Egypt would be involved if it were. Iraq, in particular, had serious problems. If Egypt's socialization programme were to be applied in Iraq to the foreign oil companies it could bring Nasser into serious conflict with the Western Powers, as over the Suez Canal. Unless union meant central control of the economy, Egypt might find herself having to accept responsibility for the possibly grave consequences of a purely Iraqi decision to nationalize the oil companies. Then in Iraq there were the Kurdish rebellion, another expensive guerrilla war like that in the Yemen, and the suppression of the Iraqi Communists, both of which had brought growls of disapproval from Moscow. Union with Iraq also meant being prepared to face hostility from neighbouring Turkey and Iran and from the British who would see another threat to their interests in the Persian Gulf. The movement of Iraqi forces to the Syrian–Israeli border might provoke an Israeli attack, especially if the tripartite union were to lead to the fall of King Hussein and the adherence to it of Jordan.

The talks which began in Cairo between Egypt and the Syrian and Iraqi delegations, after preliminary discussions in the latter half of March, soon showed that Nasser and the Baath leaders were approaching the subject of unity on two different levels. On one level there was a sincere belief in the value of Arab unity and the desire to attain it. This was expressed mostly in discussions of legalistic forms and abstract ideals and concepts. On the other level, the talks were concerned more with the appearance of unity than its reality. They were tactical; each group was trying to use the unity movement for its own domestic political purposes.

Nasser was alarmed at the prospect that the Baathists might emerge as the dominant force in both Syria and Iraq and then unite these two countries under their control. After his experience with Syria in the UAR he would have preferred to move slowly towards unity, so long as there were friendly, nationalist governments in Iraq and Syria which shared his policy objectives. But he said he was prepared to try again because unity was 'the hope of all Arabs and it is in my heart'.

The Baathists, both Syrian and Iraqi, though committed to Arab unity as their main ideological principle, were wary of a form of unity like that of the UAR which had threatened their political identity and might once again subject them completely to Nasser's control. They sought unity talks with Nasser primarily to stave off pressure from public opinion and from the pro-Nasser unionist army officers who had played a prominent part in the *coups* which brought them to power. The Baathists knew that these elements were still too strong for them to risk a unity move which excluded Egypt. What the Baathists really wanted was a declaration of principle about the formation of a future federal state which would effectively disarm any threat to their position from Nasser or his supporters while being sufficiently vague and distant to leave the Baath freedom of action in Syria and Iraq at least for the next two or three years.

The Egyptian verbatim report of the Cairo talks is a fascinating document. It is the most intimate account of a secret Arab political negotiation and of Nasser in political action in private that has yet been published. It throws a revealing light on the nature and quality of Arab revolutionary thinking: its strange combination of directness and deviousness, of earnestness and superficiality, of reckless idealism and petty shrewdness; its confusion between principles and personalities; the wide range of its intellectual sources and the parochialism of their application, the naïveté of its strategy and the subtlety of its tactics. The report also illuminates the strengths and weaknesses of Nasser's political character. He dominated the talks by intellectual capacity, tactical skill and sheer force of personality. He artfully switched his moods. Sometimes he listened and argued patiently and showed an apparent readiness to compromise. Then suddenly he moved into a ruthless, sometimes vindictive attack or a penetrating and often humorous analysis of opposing themes or personalities. There was a relentless, tigerish mocking quality in his dealings with the Syrian Baath leaders, the two mild intellectuals, Bitar and Aflaq, and a stubborn concentration on the realities of power behind the slogans and the constitutional formulae discussed. He could be savagely frank but was hypersensitive to criticism. He understood the dialectic of power but not the power of the dialectic. He impressed rather than persuaded. He towered over his associates and most other Arab leaders in his ability realistically to analyse and grasp political problems and strip them to their essentials. But he was too suspicious seriously to share power, so he failed to find the way to mobilize the goodwill of those who shared his aims but disputed his methods.

When it was agreed that the form of any future union should be a federal rather than a unitary state, the Baathists, especially the Syrians, wanted to concentrate on defining the constitutional structure and the precise division of powers between the central and regional governments. But Nasser insisted that the first essential was to agree on the nature of the collective political leadership and on a unified army, without which the federal constitution would be no more than a disguise for the continued existence of separate sovereign states. Nasser was determined that in the central political leadership he should not find himself faced with Syrian and Iraq delegations consisting entirely of Baathists working together. For the Baathists might thereby control two-thirds of the federation and also possibly outvote Egypt in matters affecting the whole state.

No agreement was reached on the composition or powers of the central command of a unified political organization and the talks then concentrated on two other matters: the terms of an agreed National Charter for Political Action, based on Nasser's National Charter for Egypt, and the drafting of a federal constitution. As the talks were nearing their conclusion, the Baathists suddenly reversed their positions. They had hitherto urged speedy agreement on the principle of a constitution and stressed the need for it to have a parliamentary democratic form (though a democracy limited by the banning of parties or individuals deemed to be feudalists, capitalists or enemies of Arab nationalism). Now they asked for the constitution to be shelved and for the transition period until elections and a federal union to be extended from months to years. During the transition they wanted only a loose kind of unity between the three states under a joint but not unified revolutionary council.

Sensing that the Baathists were now in retreat from the whole unity concept, Nasser taunted them with going back on the ideals of democracy which they had preached while accusing him of personal dictatorship.

To avoid the talks ending in open disagreement, which would have angered Arab public opinion, a compromise agreement was reached and published in a joint declaration on 17 April. It proclaimed the agreed aim of unifying Egypt, Syria and Iraq in a federal state under a single President, a post for which Nasser was the inevitable choice. There was to be an agreed political 'Charter of Unity' as well as a constitution, and a central political leadership based on national fronts in the three regions. Within five months a referendum would be held to elect the President and his deputies and to approve the constitution and political charter. Within a further twenty months the federal constitution, providing for a house of representatives and a senate on American lines, would come into force and elections would be held. During this transition period there would be a loose unity maintained through the President ruling through a Presidential Council and Cabinet.

At first sight it appeared a more prudent and sensible approach to unity than the hasty merger of Syria and Egypt into a single state in 1958. But the hollowness of the agreement was soon exposed and Nasser's sense of the realities of power, whatever its motives, shown to be accurate. In Nasser's view everything depended on the growth of confidence between Egypt and the Baathists. The test of this from his side would be the extent to which the Baath cooperated with the other pro-Nasser unionist elements in Syria and Iraq.

During most of May Nasser was away from Egypt. He paid

a triumphal twelve-day visit to Ben Bella in Algeria and then went on to see Tito in Yugoslavia. Nasser and Tito noted an easing of tension between the world blocs following the solution of the Cuban missile crisis and the impending agreement between Russia, America and Britain on a partial nuclear test ban. But the clash between India and China and the growing rivalry between Moscow and Peking presented the non-aligned countries with new problems. On 22 May Nasser flew to Addis Ababa for the meeting of African heads of states which founded the Organization of African Unity. His international prestige seemed to have swung back to its highest peak since just before the Syrian secession in 1961. He was President-designate – in principle, at least – of a new federal union bigger than the original UAR. As a result, King Hussein of Jordan was showing signs of seeking a *modus vivendi* with him. In the Yemen the fighting had virtually stopped and there seemed a good chance of a political settlement that would leave the new Republic intact. Nasser was improving Egypt's international relations in other directions, too, except with Morocco, where Egypt and Algeria were supporting the left-wing radicals led by Ben Barka against the king and his conservative allies. Egypt had resumed diplomatic relations with France and Turkey and had received the first visit of a British minister since Suez in the person of Frederick Errol, the President of the Board of Trade. The West German Minister of Economics, Dr Scheel, had also visited Cairo, and Bonn had granted Egypt an 800 million D-Mark long-term loan on favourable terms for development projects. Nasser was playing a leading role among the African states now formally united in one organization, and Nehru's preoccupation with the Chinese pressure on India's border had given greater prominence to Nasser and Tito as the activists of the non-aligned group. Part of Nasser's neutralist activity was to try to mediate with other non-aligned countries in the dispute between India and China. When his prime minister, Aly Sabry, went to Peking in April 1963 to try to persuade the Chinese to accept the non-aligned mediation proposals, he also stopped in Moscow on the way. Sabry was believed to have reassured the Russians that the current moves towards Arab unity were not an attempt to form an anti-Communist front and that Cairo would try to persuade the Iraqis to ease up on their persecution of local Communists.[21] Nasser also tried to avoid involvement in the growing Soviet–Chinese competition for influence in the Afro-Asian countries. When the Chinese premier, Chou En-lai, came to Cairo at the end of the year during his missionary tour of Africa, Nasser made it plain that his friendship with China could not be at Russia's expense and that the Afro-Asian countries did not want to import revolution from anyone but to settle their own problems in their own way.

Soon after Nasser's return to Cairo he received a visit – long postponed at Egyptian request – from President Sallal of the Yemen. Sallal had earlier in the year quarrelled with the leading pro-Egyptian in his cabinet, Beidhani. He had dismissed Beidhani who had gone off to Aden and then back to Cairo. Now Sallal was anxious to strengthen his own prestige by jumping on the new Arab unity bandwagon as one of the 'liberated states'. He was rebuffed by Nasser who clearly had no intention of bringing the Yemen into a projected Arab federal structure which was already shaky and problematic enough.

By this time, in any case, the shadow of new Arab dissension had again begun to fall across Nasser's bright new prospects. Within a month of the conclusion of the Cairo agreement, a three-sided struggle for power had begun in Syria and Iraq between two rival factions in the Baath party and their non-Baathist and pro-Nasser unionist allies. In Syria pro-Nasser unionists were purged from the army and the administration. The more radical Baathists began to gain in influence: they favoured 'going it alone' if necessary, without local allies and without Nasser, to establish a union between Syria and Iraq under a Baathist left-wing socialist regime.

On 17 May, through Heykal in *Al Ahram*, Nasser let it be known that he could no longer cooperate or coexist with the Syrian Baath leadership. But worse was to come. In July some of the moderate Baathists in Syria who opposed an open break with Nasser were expelled from the government, which was taken over by a Baathist officer, General Amin el-Hafiz, of more radical views. On 18 July some of the unionists who had been excluded from power attempted a *coup* against the new government of General Hafiz. It failed and twenty-seven of the alleged plotters, thirteen officers and fourteen civilians, were executed. It was the bloodiest repression of a *coup* in modern Syrian history. Arab opinion, accustomed to a milder Syrian tradition which usually decreed imprisonment or exile for unsuccessful *coup*-makers, was deeply shocked.

The executions were nevertheless a tremendous rebuff for Nasser and for Egypt. In two speeches on 22 July in Cairo and four days later in Alexandria, Nasser launched a violent attack on the Baath and declared that Egypt considered herself no longer bound by the 17 April federal agreement. The Baathists who had taken over in Damascus were 'fascists, opportunists and secessionists' to whom unity meant 'domination, terrorism, murder, blood and the gallows'. The Syrian Baathists replied by accusing Nasser of being a 'dictator' and 'secessionist'.

The Iraqi President, Colonel Aref, tried to mediate in the new conflict between Nasser and the Baath with the hope of rescuing the April agreement. He went to see Nasser in August and in September went to Damascus where he made an agreement for Syrian–Iraqi military and economic cooperation to be followed eventually by a federation, as provided for in the Cairo agreement. On 7 October Syria and Iraq announced the unification of their armed forces. But a crisis was growing within the Baath leadership in Baghdad and between the Baathists and the nationalist army officers. The crisis had its origins in the national convention of the Baath party in Damascus. This meeting, held from 5–23 October, was a turning-point in Arab politics and in the relations of the Syrians with Nasser. The composition of the party's national command and the policy adopted there revealed a sharp move towards the left and towards the younger generation of pro-Marxists. The convention decided in favour of a federal union between Syria and Iraq, while leaving the door open for Egypt to join the union at a later date. The union was to have a socialist economy and collective farming. While maintaining the foreign policy of positive neutrality, the convention called for stronger ties with the socialist (Communist) camp.[22]

The more radical Iraqi Baathists, led by Ali Salih as-Saadi, the former Minister of the Interior, pressed for the implementation of the new party programme, even at the cost of a conflict with Nasser and his supporters in Iraq. This led to a split within the Iraqi party. The crisis which now developed in Baghdad was, however, not only over the policy to adopt towards Egypt and Syria. It was also over the growing power of the 'National Guard', the Baathist militia controlled by as-Saadi. The 'National Guard', formed to offset the Baathists' lack of influence in the army, had begun by a bloody persecution of suspected Communists and had then established a general reign of terror in the streets.

On 18 November, the army, under President Aref's brother, Brigadier Abdul Rahman Aref, seized the opportunity of continued wrangling among the Baathists to intervene in Baghdad, break up the National Guard and overthrow the government. President Aref took over full powers as head of an all-military revolutionary council and formed a new government of army officers, moderate Baathists and non-party administrators and technical experts. He was at once acclaimed by Cairo radio for having saved Iraq from the 'criminal, agnostic, anti-Arab and anti-Islam Baath gang'.[23]

At the end of 1963, with Syria and Egypt again at loggerheads, Iraq in crisis, the fighting flaring up again in Yemen, a state of emergency declared in Aden after a bomb explosion at Aden airport, Morocco and Algeria fighting over a border dispute, and a civil war breaking out between Greeks and Turks in Cyprus, the Middle East was in a not unfamiliar state of ferment. But yet another element of conflict, not new but comparatively quiescent for the previous seven years, reappeared and began paradoxically to ease some of the other troubles. Israel's plans for the diversion of the Jordan headwaters into her national irrigation system were about to mature. The Arab states who had shelved any counter-action over the past two years were now faced with a challenge containing the danger of war, just when their hopes of unity had been dashed again.

For Nasser the Jordan waters presented a particularly delicate problem. If he were called upon to risk war with Israel to stop the diversion, it would be on behalf of Syria and Jordan that he would have to act. Both countries were ruled by regimes which were, for different reasons, his bitter enemies, and with whom all collaboration, including military, was now practically non-existent. Moreover, he knew quite well that in other respects, including his own military commitment in the Yemen, which had now crept up to 40,000 men, the Arabs were in no position to fight a successful war against Israel. Yet if they attempted to interfere militarily with the Israeli water diversion they must be prepared for the fighting to escalate. If the Israeli challenge was to be taken seriously, the Arabs needed to put their quarrels on one side and strengthen their armed forces. Meanwhile they would have to find some non-military riposte to the Israeli diversion. Otherwise Egypt would find herself having to bear the brunt of a war triggered off by others and which she could not win. Yet, having assumed the role of Arab leader and being in competition now not only with the kings and 'reactionaries' but also with rival revolutionaries in Syria and Iraq, Nasser could not simply opt out of the Israeli problem, a matter which particularly stirred Arab opinion in Syria and Jordan. His only alternative, then, was to modify his 'Arab Revolution' policy and accept co-operation or at least coexistence with opposing Arab regimes. He might hope thereby both to produce a more united front and to induce caution among the Arab leaders by spreading the responsibility for choosing between peace or war more widely.

Perhaps in the light of the mounting cost of the Yemen war and the failure of the second attempt at closer Arab unity, Nasser was in any case glad of an opportunity to revise his Arab policy and disentangle himself for a time from fruitless quarrels and expensive commitments. On 23 December he issued a conciliatory call for a meeting of the heads of the Arab League states to discuss the Jordan waters. At the same time he suspended his propaganda campaign against his Arab opponents – King Saud, King Hussein, General Hafiz and the Baathists in Syria, and King Hassan of Morocco (attacked by Cairo over the Algerian border dispute).

On 13–17 January 1964 the first of a series of Arab 'summits' met in Cairo.

Chapter 15

Arab Conflict and Arab Coexistence: Yemen, Saudi Arabia, the Baathists and the Maghreb, 1964-9

The Cairo summit ushered in a period of about two years in which Nasser tried to pursue a policy of 'coexistence' in the Arab world and of political and economic consolidation in Egypt. In Arab affairs his main effort was directed towards a peace settlement in the Yemen and the adoption of a cautious unified Arab policy towards Israel. In place of his previous insistence that cooperation was possible only with states which shared his socialist and anti-imperialist policy, he went back to an older Egyptian policy of seeking cooperation with other Arab states within the Arab League framework, irrespective of ideology, provided they were not actively hostile to Egypt. Nasser's relations with King Hussein of Jordan and with Iraq improved. This change was symbolized in Jordan's recognition of the Yemen Republic in June 1964 and in the agreements between Nasser and Aref in May and December 1964 for an Egyptian–Iraqi 'unified political leadership' (which meant in practice regular consultation between Aref and Nasser and their respective governments). But the Arab Revolution was not forgotten and all was not sweetness and light between the Arab governments.

Tension continued between Nasser and the Baathist regime in Syria and intermittently with Saudi Arabia. The Syrian regime became increasingly isolated – and for a time almost blockaded economically – by hostility from Egypt, Iraq and Jordan, while the internal struggles of the Baath party took it zig-zagging further towards the left. In the Yemen, in between the peace moves, the war flared up in brief, hard-fought battles, continuous guerrilla operations and air bombing. In North Africa, Nasser suffered a setback with the overthrow of his Algerian ally, Ben Bella, by the army leader, Colonel Boumédienne, in June 1965, and the assumption of full powers in Morocco by King Hassan at about the same time. A few weeks earlier Nasser had once again quarrelled with President Bourguiba of Tunisia.

Nor had Nasser abandoned the Arab liberation struggle: he encouraged the nationalist rebellion against the British and the sultans in Aden and South Arabia, and one of his themes from the Cairo summit onwards was the demand for an end to all foreign bases in the Arab world. The latter demand was directed against British bases in Aden and the Persian Gulf and the British and American bases in Libya.

Nasser's attitude towards the Western Powers alternated between defiance and conciliation. In July 1964 he publicly offered the British government a deal over South Arabia. If taken up, it might have secured what then appeared to be Britain's long-term strategic interest in Aden; it might also have assured South Arabia's orderly transition to independence. In a newspaper interview, Nasser declared that he was ready to recognize a truly independent South Arabian state. He drew a distinction between the maintenance of a British military staging-post in Aden, to which he had no objection, and a full-scale military base which might be used to intervene in Arab countries. He saw an independent South Arabian state as being achieved through negotiations between the British and the South Arabian nationalist opposition, but did not insist on its unity with the Yemen.[1]

With the Soviet Union Nasser's ties of interest grew closer while he continued to assert his ideological as well as national independence. The two strands of this curious relationship were exemplified in Khrushchev's visit to Egypt for the inauguration of the Aswan High Dam in May 1964 during which he and Nasser exchanged good-humoured but tenacious debate on the rival merits of Communism and Arab nationalism.

Khrushchev spent sixteen days in Egypt together with his wife and his son-in-law, Alexei Adzhubei, the editor of *Izvestia*. He addressed the Egyptian National Assembly, supporting the Arabs' 'just demands' over the Jordan waters and Nasser's call for an end to foreign bases in Aden, Libya and Cyprus.

On 13 May Khrushchev, in Nasser's presence, inaugurated the diversion of the Nile round the High Dam site: he set off the charge which blew away the sand dam holding back the waters in the Aswan gorge. With Nasser, he sailed over the Aswan Dam site. Suffering from the extreme heat, he cut short his tour of the Luxor antiquities, but he found time to lecture Nasser and the other assembled Arab leaders, including Sallal, Ben Bella and President Aref of Iraq, on the internationalist principles of Marxism. In a public speech he said the Arabs should think of Lenin's 'Workers of the World Unite', rather than of a superficial, purely Arab unity of all classes. 'The Arab farmer and Arab worker,' he said, 'is much closer to my heart than the Arab feudalist and capitalist.'²

In Cairo a few days later, apparently provoked by some remarks of Aref about Arab nationalism, Khrushchev declared that Arab unity should be based on the forces of the working people, not on nationalities. Unity should be not just between Arabs but between all peoples, between all socialist states and all liberated peoples. In reply, Nasser defended the Arab nationalist idea and said that Egypt's goal of unity was not racial.³ The day before Khrushchev left for home, Nasser announced that the Soviet Union had given Egypt a new long-term loan of £100 million for industrial projects.⁴

The moves towards an agreement on the Yemen between Nasser and the Saudi rulers, which were begun at the Cairo summit, were slow to develop. They were held up partly by the launching of a military offensive by the Yemeni royalists which for a few weeks cut the road communications between Sanaa and Hodeida. At the Cairo summit the meeting between Nasser and King Saud, a sick man, was little more than symbolic of conciliatory intentions. But in March Nasser sent Field Marshal Amer to Ryadh. Amer and Crown Prince Feisal agreed on a communiqué announcing the resumption of diplomatic relations between Egypt and Saudi Arabia and declaring that neither state had ambitions in the Yemen. At the end of March there was a palace revolution in Ryadh. A majority of the royal princes, backed by the religious leaders, obliged King Saud to surrender all his powers to Feisal. For another seven months Feisal ruled as king in all but name until on 2 November Saud was formally deposed and Feisal succeeded to the royal title as well.

Meanwhile in Sanaa a split was appearing in the Republican

ranks. Those who counted on Egyptian help to secure a republican victory were challenged by the so-called 'third force' who considered that the continuation of the war and of the Egyptian military presence were now greater evils for the country than a compromise with the royalists. There was also conflict between Sallal's military regime and those who wanted a more liberal constitution. The Egyptians tried to persuade the republicans to form a coalition which would be ready to negotiate but only on terms which would not entail a breach with Cairo or an undignified and precipitate Egyptian withdrawal. Nasser himself joined in these conciliation efforts when he paid his first visit to the Yemen in April 1964.

It was not until the second Arab summit meeting in Alexandria in September 1964, during which Nasser conferred with Feisal, that real progress towards a Yemen settlement began to appear. To strengthen their bargaining position at the conference, the Egyptians had launched their biggest military operation to date. They attacked royalist positions in the north-west Yemen, using tanks, armoured cars and paratroops, as well as infantry supported by tribal irregulars. By July Nasser believed the offensive was a complete success and that victory over the royalists was in sight.[5] But his optimism proved ill-founded. The main Egyptian aim of cutting royalist communications with Saudi Arabia was not realized. The Egyptian forces eventually withdrew after suffering substantial losses.

At their meeting in September both Nasser and Feisal appeared to be ready to press their respective protégés in the Yemen to compromise. At a subsequent secret meeting on 2 November at Erekwit in the Sudan between royalist and republican representatives, in the presence of Egyptian and Saudi observers, agreement was reached on a cease-fire to be followed on 23 November by a political conference between all the Yemeni factions. The aim of the conference would be to set up a coalition national government until a plebiscite could be held to decide the country's future regime. But the conference was never held: no agreement could be reached on its composition and agenda. The republicans wanted to exclude any members of the ex-Imam's family from the conference. The royalists wanted to limit the agenda to the creation of an interim government, leaving any discussion of the future constitution until the Egyptian forces had gone. The republicans insisted that before the Egyptians withdrew there must be agreement that the future Yemen state would be a republic and not a monarchy.

The failure of the conference led to a breakdown of the cease-fire and to more argument among the republicans. Hundreds of dissident republicans, tribal sheikhs, religious leaders and officials, were arrested by Sallal and the Egyptians. In December 1964, three leading liberals, Abdul Rahman Iryani and Mohammed Mahmoud az-Zubeiri, both deputy premiers, and Ahmed Mohammed Nomaan, then president of the consultative council, resigned their posts. They denounced the 'corruption, impotence and bankruptcy' of Sallal's regime and called for a more liberal constitution.[6]

These defections brought the uncompromising General Hassan al-Amri to the premiership while the Egyptians carried out a new military offensive, in which they again suffered considerable losses for little gain of territory. Some of the influential republican tribes, who had been showing signs of increasing restiveness at the Egyptian military presence, threatened to occupy Sanaa unless General Amri was replaced by Nomaan as prime minister.[7]

Faced with an unpromising military and political situation, Nasser decided in the spring of 1965 on an important change of policy. He ordered the withdrawal of the more remote Egyptian military outposts and concentrated Egyptian forces on the central southern massif where the main republican strongholds could be protected more easily and cheaply. At the same time, he agreed to the formation of a new republican government with Nomaan as prime minister, as the prelude to a new attempt to bring about a peace settlement.

Nomaan was an intellectual with western liberal ideas about constitutional and social reform. He had once been the tutor of the ex-Imam al Badr. Like Sallal and other revolutionaries he had spent several years in the Imam Ahmed's fortress prison. Between 1955 and 1962 he had been in exile in Cairo. He formed a capable and independent-minded government, but it lasted only ten weeks.

When Sallal, without consulting his ministers, set up a supreme armed forces council to deal with all war matters, Nomaan resigned and flew to Cairo to appeal to Nasser.

Nomaan believed that most of the difficulties between the Yemeni republicans and Egypt over peace negotiations resulted from a conflict within the Egyptian leadership. Nasser, he thought, favoured peace and disengagement through political conciliation, while the Egyptian military, headed by Amer, constantly sought an escalation of the fighting in pursuit of a prestige military victory. Nasser had personally advised Nomaan not to insist on calling the Yemen a republic if this stood in the way of an agreement with the royalists.[8] Nomaan has described how when he tried to reach an agreement with Saudi Arabia before submitting it to Egypt for approval, the Egyptian authorities in the Yemen stopped financial aid to his government to bring it down. When he flew to Cairo to see Nasser, he found the Egyptian President in full agreement with his peace plan. But the next day at a second meeting with Nasser – at which Anwar es-Sadat was present – the tone was changed. Nasser said they must take the matter to Amer. So they all went to Amer's house. When Amer declared that Egypt could not accept a solution negotiated independently by the Yemenis, Nasser reversed his earlier attitude and opposed Nomaan's plan.[9]

Nomaan and several of his supporters who had flown to Cairo to join him were detained in the Egyptian capital and not allowed to return to the Yemen. Several dozen more of Nomaan's followers were arrested in Sanaa, where Sallal formed a new predominantly military government and once more appointed Amri prime minister.

Peace looked further off than ever. The Egyptians were reported to be reinforcing their army in the Yemen, bringing it up to over 50,000 men. In a speech on 22 July 1965, Nasser threatened to resume the bombing of bases in Saudi Arabia if Feisal did not stop supplies to the royalists. But only a month later the picture had changed again and Nasser was flying to Jedda to negotiate a new peace agreement with Feisal.

One of the reasons impelling Nasser to seek peace was the growing cost to Egypt of the Yemen war in economic as well as political terms. The Egyptian army casualties were running into several thousands. Tens of millions of pounds had been spent on the war as well as on economic and technical aid to the Yemenis.* The war was not unpopular with all of the Egyptian army, because of the bonuses for service in the Yemen and the chance it gave to buy and bring home foreign goods unobtainable in Egypt. But it was felt as an onerous burden by the Egyptian public. Lives and money, it was believed, were being squandered in a remote and ungrateful country in which Egypt had no real interest, at a time when Egypt herself was running into ever heavier debt to try and finance her own five-year development plans. The economic strain of rapid industrialization was causing discontent among the middle class and signs of political unrest. The burden was aggravated by the international impact of the Yemen war.

In the autumn of 1964 the Johnson administration in Washington had made it clear to Nasser that he could not count on economic support from the United States unless he made a greater effort to settle the Yemen war and withdrew his forces. The US administration was itself already under pressure from anti-Nasser lobbies in the Congress to suspend aid to Egypt. Unluckily Nasser's agreement to the Erekwit cease-fire in the Yemen was quickly followed by a clash with the United States over the Congo. By one of the strange twists of Congo politics, Tshombe,

---

*There is little reliable information on either the human or material costs to Egypt of the Yemen war. Dana Adams Schmidt, for example (*Yemen, The Unknown War*, pp. 234–5) quotes a figure – which he claims was obtained by a foreign intelligence source from official Egyptian army records – of 15,194 Egyptians killed and four times that number wounded or captured between October 1962 and June 1964. This is obviously far too high – it would amount to some 75,000 casualties, or more than the total number of the Egyptian army likely to have been in the Yemen during that period and out of whom it was unusual for more than one or two thousand to be engaged in active operations at one time. Western estimates of the financial cost to Egypt varied from £10 million to £20 million a year, though some put it as high as £50 million or even twice that amount during the first year of the war. A senior Egyptian economic official told me in July 1969 that he estimated the foreign exchange costs of the Yemen war at £10 million a year at first but that this figure was reduced when the army cut down its special allowances and economized on operations.

the former Katanga secessionist leader, had emerged at the head of the Congo Central government. He was still anathema to the more radical African nationalists as the man considered responsible for the murder of Lumumba and for his reliance on the Belgians and on white mercenaries. At the first meeting of the heads of state of the Organization for African Unity in Cairo in July 1964, a majority of the delegates voted to exclude Tshombe from the conference, although he was the Congo prime minister. When Tshombe arrived in Cairo to the embarrassment of the Egyptian government, he was held for a time under what amounted to a polite form of house arrest. Tshombe's rise to power in Leopold-ville led to a revolt against his government by the remnants of the more radical Lumumbists and Gizenga supporters in Stanley-ville. When attempts by the OAU to settle the Congo civil war proved unsuccessful, Nasser gave moral support to the Stanley-ville rebels – material support was limited by the refusal of the Sudan to let arms and supplies go to the rebels across its territory. He thus found himself on the opposite side from the United States which was supporting the Congo central government.

American planes carried Belgian paratroopers who joined with Congo government troops and white mercenaries in the capture of Stanleyville and the rescue of European hostages held there. The Stanleyville operations roused protests among African nationalists. In Cairo riots took place in which the United States embassy library was burned down. President Johnson's angry reaction was strengthened by an unrelated incident: an American private plane belonging to one of his personal friends was shot down by Egyptian anti-aircraft fire when it strayed off course over Egypt and failed to respond to a challenge. Johnson let Nasser know that US aid to Egypt would be suspended unless Cairo took a line more friendly to the US. Nasser replied with a petulant, defiant speech in December 1964. Egypt could do without aid, he said, if it meant accepting political strings, and he rudely told the Americans they could take their aid and 'drink up the Red Sea' (or in American terms 'go jump in the lake'). The United States suspended further supplies of surplus wheat, but a complete break in relations was avoided. Egyptian apologies and payment of damages prepared the way for a patching up of the quarrel. But from then on confidence between Cairo and Washington was shaky to say the least, and American aid uncertain. Such was the background of Nasser's meeting with King Feisal in Jedda. After two days of secret talks, they signed an agreement which reaffirmed the principles of a cease-fire in the Yemen and a national political conference, which had already been agreed on at Erekwit but not implemented. Egyptian troops were to be withdrawn within ten months, beginning from 23 November 1965. Saudi Arabia was to stop aid of all kinds to the royalists or the use of its territory for military operations in the Yemen. A plebiscite would be held on the Yemen's future form of government not later than 23 November 1966, that is, two months after the last Egyptian soldier had left. To decide on a transitional regime and provisional government until the plebiscite was held, a conference of fifty members, half nominated by the republicans and half by the royalists, was to meet at Haradh in the Yemen on 23 November 1965.

There may also have been a secret agreement between Nasser and Feisal to exclude both President Sallal and the ex-Imam al Badr from the national conference and from the Yemen while a settlement was negotiated.[10] In any event Sallal left the Yemen for Cairo and stayed in Egypt until September 1966 when he returned to Sanaa to take over power again. Al Badr moved to Taif in Saudi Arabia and became even more of a cypher among the royalist leadership than before.

The absence from the Yemen of Sallal and al Badr, the chief symbols of a rigid revolutionary republicanism and of the old theocratic monarchy, may have been calculated to help the Yemenis find a compromise answer to the still disputed question of what the transitional status of the Yemen should be called. Should it be named a republic or simply the 'state of the Yemen', which would leave the door open to the restoration of the Imamate? Partly because of its failure to settle this question the Haradh conference ended in deadlock after nearly a month's talks. The intransigence of the Yemenis themselves was largely responsible. But, while the deadlock continued, confidence between Egypt and Saudi Arabia began to break down again. Feisal's suspicions were aroused because a month after the Haradh conference began the Egyptians still showed no signs of withdrawing any troops. The Saudis believed the Egyptian promise to withdraw was unconditional; the Egyptians claimed it was conditional on the conclusion of an interim political settlement. The Saudis on their side had aroused Nasser's disquiet by a big arms deal with the British. In collaboration with the Americans, the British had contracted to supply Saudi Arabia with over £100 million-worth of jet fighters, ground-to-air missiles and radar equipment, with technicians to train the Saudis to use the new weapons. Reports of the deal had followed a visit to Ryadh by the British Minister of State at the Foreign Office, George Thomson, in September 1965. Thomson also went to Cairo to see Nasser. His arrival there coincided to the day with the British decision to suspend the constitution in Aden in the face of growing nationalist disturbances. Nasser refused to see him.

Nasser believed that the British were now building up Saudi Arabia as a partner and eventual successor in protecting the South Arabian federation and the Gulf oil sheikhdoms against local Nasser-inspired revolutionary forces. (In fact the new Labour government of Harold Wilson was never more than half-hearted in this policy; it found difficulty in making up its mind whether to try to hold on to its remaining military toeholds in the Middle East or to attempt a new political deal with Nasser and local Arab nationalists. It wobbled confusingly between the two and achieved neither. The Saudi arms deal was not made primarily for reasons of Arabian policy. It was partly a commercial export *coup* and partly an arrangement to help pay the Americans for the F111 aircraft which had been ordered to support the 'East of Suez' policy, the British plan for a continued Anglo-American naval and air presence and communications system in the Indian Ocean area.)

Nasser's belief was strengthened by the tough measures taken by the British in Aden to put down the growing rebellion against the hastily constructed South Arabian federation. It looked to him as if, in the event of their having to give up their Aden base, the British were determined to leave behind a client state in South Arabia run by the sultans and allied with Saudi Arabia, with both states armed by the British and supported by a British air and naval presence in the background. Nasser saw this prospect as a device for frustrating the Arab liberation movement in the Arabian peninsula and ensuring that if British imperialism went out by the door it would climb back by the window. In his eyes it was a direct contradiction of the spirit of the Jedda agreement. The Jedda settlement had been made between Arabs themselves without the interference of foreign powers: it was basically an agreement by Egypt and Saudi Arabia not to interfere militarily in the working out of a revolution and its consequences in an Arabian state.

The Saudis could fairly argue that their purchase of British planes and American missiles was a natural defensive response to Egypt's bombing of their territory – with planes bought from Russia. Why they asked, should they not be as free to buy arms from the West as Nasser was to buy them from the Russians? But Nasser's suspicions were further sharpened when Feisal, on a state visit to Teheran, joined with the Shah of Iran in a call for a conference of Islamic states. The move was obviously intended as a counter to the Arab League summits and to Nasser's appeal to Arab nationalism. Nasser considered the Shah an enemy of the Arabs because Iran half-recognized Israel and supplied her with oil. Iran was also a member of CENTO, the successor to the Baghdad Pact. She had sent money and arms to the Yemen royalists, was believed to be secretly helping the Kurdish rebels in Iraq, and laid claim to the Arab sheikhdom of Bahrein and to the future leading role in the Persian Gulf.

The Islamic conference idea – never put forward as a proposal for an alliance as Nasser usually described it – was muddled and ill-timed. It was a result of the same misconception of the role of Islam in Arab politics that had led the United States to encourage King Saud to match himself against Nasser as a leader of the Arab world at the time of the Eisenhower Doctrine. If its motive was transparent, its conception was vague. In itself it never constituted a serious threat to Egyptian influence, and did Feisal little good. But Nasser saw it as a symbol of Anglo-American intentions to play a more active part in backing 'reactionary' or counter-revolutionary forces in the Arab world, as the United States appeared to him already to be doing in other parts of

Africa and Asia. This could mean that Saudi Arabia and the South Arabian sultans might combine to crush the Yemen revolution as soon as the Egyptian army had left.

In a speech at Port Said on 23 December 1965, Nasser denounced the new move by Feisal and the Shah. He warned the royalists in the Yemen that if they renewed the war, as they had threatened, the republicans would fight back. Two months later the British government announced in its Defence White Paper that it intended to withdraw its forces from South Arabia and give up the Aden base by 1968 after South Arabia became independent.

The British announcement appears to have been decisive in confirming Nasser's change of mind about an early withdrawal of Egyptian forces from the Yemen. His Yemen policy now entered a new phase. Henceforward it was geared not to the needs of a long-term political settlement within the Yemen, but to the short-term aim of keeping Egyptian troops there until the British had withdrawn from South Arabia.

In the Yemen the attempt to defeat the royalists and gain control of the whole country was to be abandoned. The main republican territory in the central massif, the coastal plain and the south was to be securely but defensively held. Nasser's main offensive operation would be an indirect one aimed at hitting the presumed alliance between the Saudis, the British, the Yemen royalists and the South Arabian sultans at its weakest spot – in South Arabia and Aden. Here, by supplying arms, training, money and political support to the nationalist rebels, Nasser could intervene as cheaply as the Saudis had in the Yemen, and with more hope of decisive effect. He believed – rightly as it turned out – that the South Arabian sultans and the Aden conservatives who supported the Federation were even more dependent on British backing for their position than the Yemen Republic was on the Egyptian army. Nasser may have had in his mind, as some believed, a far-reaching plan for the spread of the Arab Revolution throughout the Arabian Peninsula and the Persian Gulf, by which the rump of a Yemen Republic would be joined with South Arabia – itself overrun by a combination of nationalist guerrillas and the Egyptian army after the departure of the British – to form a revolutionary base. According to these theories, the revolution would spread through guerrilla networks of 'Arab liberation movements' along the Arabian coasts from South Arabia up to the oil sheikhdoms of the Gulf, and eventually into the heartland of Saudi Arabia itself. Through a system of Arabian satellites Nasser would then be master of the main Middle East oil supplies. He could flourish them as a political weapon against the West and he could milk the oil revenues to finance economic development for Egypt's teeming millions.

These theories seemed to ignore both some hard facts of geography about the Arabian peninsula, its huge distances and lack of land communications, and also much of the previous evidence about Nasser's political thinking and the conduct of his policies. Nasser certainly believed in 'Arab liberation' as part of the world-wide anti-colonialist and anti-imperialist struggle. He considered that in the Arabian peninsula the rule of the kings, sheikhs and sultans was archaic, helped to keep most of the peninsula in the Middle Ages, and should be changed. He thought that the Arab states could strike a better bargain with the rest of the world over their military, political and economic (including oil) interests if they acted together rather than separately. And if they were to have a unified foreign policy it could only be one of non-alignment, because it was impossible to have unity between countries allied differently with the Western or Eastern blocs. But Nasser had few illusions left about achieving a close political unity between the Arab states, either by the kind of constitutional merger twice tried unsuccessfully with Syria or through the empire-building by conquest attributed to him by some Western political leaders. However blinded by ambition, Nasser could scarcely fail to see from his own experience that as soon as an Arab state became truly independent it would want in the first instance to be independent of Cairo as well.

The nationalists of South Arabia proved to be no exception to this experience. Nasser at first supported the more moderate of the South Arabian nationalist rebel groups, FLOSY (Front for the Liberation of South Yemen) formed in exile in Taiz and Cairo. FLOSY's creation followed the proclamation of the state of emergency in Aden, the suspension of the constitution, the outbreak of terrorism and the arrest or exile of leaders of the Aden Trades Union Congress and the Peoples Socialist Party. It was formed by Abdullah al Asnag and other Aden TUC and PSP leaders, together with the former Aden chief minister, Abdul Qawi Hassan Mackawee. These leaders were at first opposed to terrorism and Asnag was prepared for a negotiated settlement with the British through the mediation of the United Nations. But FLOSY was gradually forced to adopt more extremist positions under pressure of the terrorist exploits of its chief rival, the National Liberation Front, and because of the delay by the British in offering political terms which Asnag and his colleagues could accept with a hope of survival. The NLF demanded simply the unconditional departure of the British and the end of the Sultan's rule. The NLF had begun as only a handful of determined young revolutionaries, but it swiftly gathered support, especially as the British army began to lay a heavier hand on the Aden population in counter-terrorist operations.

At one period it seemed as if the rivalry between FLOSY and the NLF reflected a conflict within Egypt's policy like that over the Yemen. There is some evidence that while Nasser was still supporting Asnag and Mackawee in a policy of negotiation, Egyptian military intelligence in the Yemen was building up the NLF in the conviction that only terrorism and not talking would persuade the British to leave Aden. It may be that Nasser was keeping two strings to his bow, but as the rebellion grew and the NLF gathered more strength, the Egyptians officially switched their support to the NLF, though without entirely dropping FLOSY. In the British press, the NLF was constantly referred to as a simple terrorist tool of Egypt, until the last stages of the rebellion when the NLF began to show the deep native roots it had grown and asserted its independence of Cairo. Then it was the FLOSY leaders, beaten on their home ground in Aden by the NLF, and operating from exile in the Yemen and Cairo, who were labelled as Egyptian stooges.

Perhaps one of the most striking things about Nasser's Yemen adventure was his lack of a plan. He had intervened with the general idea of supporting the Yemen revolution and beating off a Saudi attempt to crush it. The move fitted his general aims and his political purposes of the moment, but the subsequent vacillations of his policy between peace and war, between disengagement and reinforcement, between conciliation and conflict with Saudi Arabia, suggested not only political differences at home but also how little his Yemen policy was related to a coherent broader strategy for Arabia and the Gulf. Characteristically, it was not until he saw what he thought to be the crystallization of a clear and hostile strategic concept by his opponents that he began to clarify his own purposes.

If he could hang on in the Yemen until the British had left South Arabia and, with luck, the sultans there had been overthrown or forced to compromise with the nationalists, then what he took to be a British-backed pincer movement directed against the Yemen republic would have been frustrated. Even if he did not count on an Egyptian-backed union between the Yemen Republic and a nationalist South Arabia, he could hope to be in a stronger position to resume negotiations with Feisal. At worst the departure of British forces from South Arabia would enable him to claim a share of credit for yet another act of Arab liberation and so make it easier for him to withdraw his own forces from the Yemen without loss of face.

The holding operation Nasser consequently initiated in the Yemen had four elements. The territory held by the republicans and Egyptians was further contracted to enable the central bastion of the Republic, which contained a majority of the country's population and main towns within the Sanaa–Taiz–Hodeida triangle, to be held more easily. A republican government was required reliable enough to accept the continued Egyptian presence and tough enough to suppress those Yemenis who might want to end it too soon. A greater effort was made to consolidate the revolutionary regime and strengthen Egyptian influence by economic and social development aid. Royalist attacks and royalist attempts at political consolidation were to be kept in check, especially at a later stage, by the ruthless use of air attack against the mountain and desert villages from which the royalist tribes operated. This air attack included gas bombing.[11]

Nasser was probably encouraged to adopt this policy by promises of Soviet military and economic aid, not only for Egypt but also for the Yemen Republic. It was in Russia's interest to expedite the departure of the British from Aden. The Russians also professed to believe they were facing a world-wide American counter-revolutionary offensive against national liberation movements, of which Vietnam was only the most violent example. They saw the British 'East of Suez' policy as meant to help the United States in its allegedly self-appointed role of 'world gendarme' against revolutionaries of the Third World. In this new phase of the cold war, in which the revolutionary competition of China had also become a serious factor for Moscow, Soviet policy sought to bring about a closer association between the 'progressive' Arab states – Egypt, Syria, Iraq, Yemen and Algeria. The Russians wanted especially a *rapprochement* between Nasser and Syria where on 23 February 1966, a militantly left-wing group of the Baath party seized power and established closer ties with Moscow. This *rapprochement* was one of the purposes of the visit to Cairo in May 1966 of the Soviet premier, Kosygin.

The period of Arab 'coexistence' symbolized by the Arab summits was over, though its demise was not officially declared until July 1966 when Nasser refused to attend the next Arab summit, planned to be held in Algiers in September. Several events in the autumn of 1966 indicated that Nasser was battening down the hatches for a new period of revolutionary storm. In Cairo, Zacharia Mohieddin, an apostle of economic retrenchment and abstention from Arab adventures, who had been appointed prime minister after the Jedda agreement, was replaced by Sidky Suleiman. The new premier was an engineer-officer who favoured a policy of more rapid economic expansion but had no independent political stature or views. A new defence agreement was signed with Syria and a violent propaganda campaign launched against the Saudi Arabian monarchy. President Sallal was sent back to the Yemen to take over the government there and to suppress the growing agitation among the republicans for more independence from Egyptian control. After the breakdown of the Haradh conference and the resumption of the fighting, the Egyptians had kept Sallal in Cairo and relied on his deputy, General Hassan al Amri, to run the government. But Amri had proved less reliable than expected. He had found the Egyptian control in

Sanaa increasingly irksome, especially when the Egyptian army prevented him from receiving Soviet bloc military aid direct and distributing the weapons to suit his own purposes. He had begun to move closer to Nomaan and Iryani and other liberal republican leaders. Nasser decided to send Sallal back to take over as prime minister as well as President. Despite Amri's protests, Sallal arrived by air in Sanaa on 12 August. Amri tried to prevent Sallal's landing by force but was frustrated by Egyptian tanks. Unable to leave the country any other way, Amri flew to Cairo with some of his liberal allies to appeal to Nasser. Instead of being received by Nasser they were placed under house arrest.

Six weeks after his return, Sallal began a purge of his republican opponents. Hundreds were arrested or fled into exile, some executed. Eight senior army officers and officials accused of high treason were publicly executed by machine-gun fire in Sanaa's main square.

Feisal, as well as Nasser, was having trouble keeping his Yemeni protégés in line. In August 1966 he briefly cut off supplies to the royalists to discourage them from mounting an offensive for which their leaders were pressing. For Feisal, as for Nasser, winning the war in the Yemen had become secondary to other concerns at least for the time being. So long as the Egyptians were withdrawing from territory instead of advancing, he was content for the royalists to mark time and not waste his money. He also needed to gain time to complete the new air defence system being installed by the British at emergency speed on the Yemen border.

By the spring of 1967, on the eve of the Arab–Israel war, the Yemen Republic, despite resentment at Sallal's police repression and the continued presence of some 40,000 Egyptian troops, appeared to be developing a political solidity of its own, unmatched by anything comparable on the royalist side. The old ruling class of the royal family and the sayyeds or nobles had been replaced by a new class of officials, army officers and businessmen, strengthened by an inflow of young educated men from a rapidly expanding education programme. There were modern schools for boys and girls in every town and primary schools in many villages, as well as hospitals, clinics, water systems and new roads which were helping to end the isolation in which most Yemeni villagers had lived for centuries. There were three Russian-built vocational training schools in Sanaa, Taiz and Hodeida and 2,000 Yemeni students had been sent abroad, 1,000 to Egypt and 900 to the Soviet Union. Egypt had supplied hundreds of teachers, doctors, engineers and other experts and advisers. Substantial aid was also coming from other sources. Kuwait helped with primary education. The Americans had built one of the country's main roads at a cost of $22 million and the Chinese the other. Communist bloc aid in the form of cheap loans totalled $118 million of which $28 million came from China and $72 million from Russia for industrial and agricultural projects. There were believed to be several hundred Russian technicians in the country, about half of them military.

There was little fighting. In the mountains and deserts, outside the Sanaa–Hodeida–Taiz triangle held by the Egyptian army, the royalists could move about and even infiltrate as far as the outskirts of Sanaa, though liable to air attack if they were in more than small groups. But with limited aid from Saudi Arabia, little help from anywhere else and few local economic resources, they could not hope to lay the basis of a state administration or develop an economy. In the no-man's-land from which the Egyptians had withdrawn, their air bombardment had left a trail of ruined villages.[12]

Although the Yemen continued to place a heavy extra burden on Egypt's over-strained economy, it is probable that but for the war with Israel, Nasser could have continued to hold his position there for some time, at least until the British left South Arabia. But after the defeat by Israel in June 1967, he needed every man and every piastre to defend Egypt herself and maintain her economy.

At the Khartoum conference of Arab heads of state at the end of August 1967, Nasser and King Feisal reached agreement on the withdrawal of Egyptian troops from the Yemen by the end of the year – the date by which Britain was also due to withdraw her forces from a newly independent South Arabian Federation. The Saudis would stop their subsidies to the royalists when the Egyptians had gone. A tripartite Arab commission headed by the

Sudan prime minister, with the acting Foreign Minister of Iraq nominated by Egypt and the Moroccan foreign minister nominated by Saudi Arabia, were to try to arrange a peace conference and settlement between the Yemeni republicans and royalists.* Sallal angrily denounced the Khartoum agreement as a betrayal by Egypt. When the tripartite peace mission arrived in Sanaa it was met by demonstrations in which Yemenis and Egyptians were killed. It stayed less then twenty-four hours. But a month later on 3 November Sallal, fearing an imminent military *coup* against him, left the Yemen, ostensibly for Moscow but in fact for Baghdad, leaving a letter of resignation behind him.

On 5 November after anti-Sallal army units had taken control, a new government was formed in Sanaa. Sallal was replaced as head of state by a presidential council of the three liberal leaders, Iryani, Nomaan and Mohammed Ali Uthman. The new prime minister was Muhsin el Aini. Nomaan soon resigned because his colleagues still refused to negotiate with the royalists unless the Imam's family were excluded from the talks. He was replaced by General Amri who returned from Cairo. On 18 December Amri also became premier.

As the last Egyptian troops withdrew between 1–15 December 1967, the royalists closed in to lay siege to Sanaa. But the general prediction that the Republic could not survive without the Egyptian army was dramatically proved wrong. The siege of the capital lasted seventy days. It was broken by the determined resistance led by General Amri and the *élite* units of the new Yemen republican army, the paratroops and commandos. Young civilian townsmen, intellectuals and workers, shopkeepers and artisans organized popular resistance forces and stopped panic in the city.[13] The mainly Shafei citizens of Sanaa were prepared to fight rather than risk the looting and killing that would have followed surrender to the royalist Zeidi tribesmen; a similar bloody experience in the early years of the century at the hands of the Iman Yahya and his men was still remembered.

The republican resistance was stiffened by more Soviet arms supplies, including, it was said, some planes urgently flown in. It seemed that over the years the Republic with Egyptian help had

*For further details of the Khartoum conference see Chapter 19.

built better than itself and most of the world knew. The new ruling *élite* thrown up by the revolution and trained under the Egyptians could stand on its own feet and was prepared to fight to preserve its gains. It might be long before they could bring the royalist guerrillas in the mountains under control, especially if the Saudis continued to pay the tribes. But the royalists were themselves shown to be a hollow threat with no chance of taking over the state. The situation was a stalemate, but the odds for the future favoured the Republic, especially now that in neighbouring South Arabia, even before the British withdrawal was completed, the federal government of the sultans had totally collapsed and the National Liberation Front had seized power with the acquiescence of the federal army and set up the South Yemen Republic.

The chief obstacle to peace in the Yemen became the vested interest of the tribes in keeping the war going for the money and arms they got in bribes from each side. After Saudi Arabia began to cut off its subsidies, fighting died away. Royalists and republicans once more began to seek a political settlement, but this time on the basis of the royalist acceptance of the Republic. By the summer of 1969, though peace had not yet been formally agreed upon, the war seemed virtually over. Fighting broke out again at the end of the year, but a few months later Saudi Arabia formally recognized the Yemen Republic.

The war had cost Egypt dear in men, money and international goodwill. It played its part indirectly in the events leading to the disaster of the 1967 war with Israel. Nasser was then obliged to make what seemed at the time a humiliating settlement with Feisal at the Khartoum conference. If he had hoped to retain a permanent military foothold for Egypt in Southern Arabia he had lost it. But it is unlikely that such was his aim. In the event, he could claim that if Arab liberation and social revolution were necessary and desirable, then Egypt's sacrifices in the Yemen had not been in vain. The Yemen Republic and revolution had undoubtedly been saved by the Egyptian army, and consolidated with Egyptian civil aid.

The liberation of South Arabia from British imperial rule as well as from the local sultans by the nationalist rebels owed something to Egyptian help and to the Yemen revolution. The pressures generated by the revolution in the Yemen had hastened the introduction of governmental and social reforms in Saudi Arabia itself. They had even helped Feisal to take over the throne from his brother.

Nasser was not alone to blame for the prolongation of the Yemen war, nor for the Aden rebellion and the repeated failure of peace negotiations, though his responsibility for discouraging conciliation, especially in South Arabia, at certain critical times was heavy indeed. Feisal's support for the royalists was also measured in accordance with his own interests rather than those of the Yemeni people. In trying unsuccessfully to force through the South Arabian federation and in leaving serious negotiations with the nationalist opposition until it was too late, the British government also pursued primarily its own strategic and economic interests rather than those of the people of Aden (though until political virtue was restored to it by economic necessity, it had no difficulty in persuading itself that the two sets of interests were identical).

The cost to the Yemen itself in lives and material damage from Egyptian arms was heavy and tragic. To set against it was the beginning of the emancipation of the greater part of the country from a political and social system of cruel backwardness, a system which had been maintained by terrorism in the interests of the privileged leaders of a religious minority.

However crudely and however expensively for Egypt, Nasser in Arabia was on the right side of history.

Part Three

Israel

Chapter 16

The Arabs, Israel and the Great Powers: The Breakdown of the Peace, 1957–67

The picture which most Europeans and Americans have of Nasser was probably formed not by the performance of his regime in Egypt, but by his hostility to the traditional forms of Western influence in the Arab world and above all by his attitude towards Israel. Even those, for example on the European left, who sympathized with Nasser's efforts to reform and develop Egypt, accepted his campaigns against British colonialism and military bases in the Middle East and his support for the Algerian nationalists as a justifiable anti-imperialism, found themselves condemning his policy towards Israel and in some cases approving the Israeli 'preventive' wars against Egypt in 1956 and 1967.

In 1967 many in the West and in Israel once again saw Nasser as a kind of Hitler, this time as the leader or instigator of a genocidal war of annihilation against the Jews of Israel. He seemed to them to be inspired either by a fanatic ambition to establish himself as master of the Arab world or even by a base racial hatred which was simply a Middle East variant of the West's own anti-Semitism. Support for Israel against such alleged Arab intentions and motives became a natural expression of liberal sentiments as well as of sympathy for the Jews. It was reinforced by a subconscious unloading on to the Arabs of the vast Western guilt for Jewish suffering.

But some Western observers believed Nasser was not deeply concerned with Israel. They saw him as the only Arab leader who might have been willing and able to make a compromise settlement with the Israelis, but who had instead been dragged into war because of the inexorable demands of Arab leadership, a miscalculated brinkmanship or the intrigues of Russia. There was one school of thought, including distinguished Zionist historians, which saw the history of Arab–Israeli relations between the Sinai war of 1956 and the war of 1967 as one of a precarious preservation of a *status quo* which was finally upset by the intrusion of a new and decisive element: a Russian attempt to use Nasser for the complete elimination of Western influence in the Arab world through a war by proxy.[1]

These various Western pictures were oversimplified and misleading in different ways. The causes of the 1967 war were complex and deep-rooted. They developed erratically at various stages in the decade after Suez. They involved not only Arab fears and grievances about Israel, but also the course of the Arab anti-imperialist and social revolution, with its conflicts between Arab regimes and leaders, and the fluctuations of the wider international situation. Then there were the actions and policies of Israel herself. It is arguable that two of the most important elements of instability to be introduced into the balance established after the Suez–Sinai war were Israel's decision unilaterally to divert the Jordan waters and her development of a secret nuclear reactor, which would make her capable eventually of manufacturing nuclear weapons. Both contributed to the acceleration of an Arab–Israeli arms race, with weapons supplied by the Great Powers. Russia's aims in the Middle East were a destabilizing factor, but so was the policy of the United States. Perhaps more important was what Nasser and the Russians believed American policy to be. Nasser's actions leading up to the 1967 war became more comprehensible, if not necessarily more excusable, if one realizes the extent to which his interpretation of Israeli moves was influenced by the general world picture that had been growing in his mind. This picture was of an American campaign to subdue the more radical anti-imperialist leaders of the Third World and to break their links with Russia, a campaign in which he felt himself to be marked down as a potential victim, after Egypt had been isolated by the destruction of the revolutionary regime in Syria.

Whatever Nasser's motives for conflict with Israel, anti-Semitism of the European kind was not among them. Nasser was not an anti-Semite. He lived beside Jewish neighbours during his boyhood in Cairo. He claimed that he had no anti-Jewish prejudice and that he maintained contact with some of his Jewish friends from that time. 'I have never been anti-Semitic on a personal level,' he told a British interviewer. 'It is very difficult for a thinking Egyptian to be so. We have so many basic links –

after all, Moses himself was an Egyptian. My feelings and actions against Israel later were inspired solely by the Israelis' actions as a state.'[2]

Nasser was a secular nationalist: his mind, though charged with political suspicion sometimes almost to the point of paranoia, was not of the cast that runs naturally to racial or national prejudices. His attitude towards Jews as a community was probably more liberal than the traditional attitude of Muslim society in which Jews were a tolerated, but not actively persecuted, minority of politically second-class citizens. (It was certainly less racially contemptuous than the attitude of some Israelis today towards the Arabs.) In modern Egypt, as in Iraq, the Jews had established a respected and influential position in commercial and cultural life: it is probably fair to say that but for the development of Zionism and Israel, and especially the effects of the wars of 1948, 1956 and 1967, they would continue to hold this position today, though on a diminished scale. In Egypt, historical circumstances connected partly with the British occupation had created a highly abnormal economic and social structure in which perhaps as much as eighty-five per cent of commercial activity was in the hands of non-Egyptians and non-Muslim Egyptians. It was inevitable that an independent nationalist government in Egypt would take some measures of 'Egyptianization' to change this balance, as African states have tried to reduce the virtual monopoly of commerce in their territories by Asians. It was likely also that in this process favour would be shown to the Muslim majority. The Levantine Jewish community in Egypt would undoubtedly have shared in the economic hardships of 'Egyptianization', but it is improbable that either they or the Jews of Egyptian citizenship would have suffered at Nasser's hands as they did, but for the Arab–Israeli wars.*

As we have already seen (in Chapters 3, 4 and 6), Nasser's hostility to Israel arose primarily from three sources: first, there was the unshakeable conviction he shared with all Arabs that the Palestinian Arabs had suffered a grave injustice in the loss of the greater part of their homeland, an injustice incarnated in the million Palestine Arab refugees who were prevented from

*See Chapter 7.

returning to their homes now in Israel. Second, there was the fact that the creation of Israel introduced a land-barrier between Egypt and the Arab states of Asia. Third, there was Nasser's fear that Israel was a serious danger to the Arab states, not only because it was considered inevitably expansionist by nature but also because he believed it to be the product and instrument of external hostile forces greater than itself, the international Zionist movement and the Western imperialist Powers, principally the United States. Although Nasser was aware that Zionism was a political nationalist movement to which not all Jews were committed, and understood Western sympathy with the Jewish victims of Hitler's persecution, the conflict with Israel had also created in his mind a distorted picture of world Jewry which was no longer untainted by the influence of European anti-Semitic propaganda. For example, complaining of the international influence of Zionist propaganda against the UAR, he once recommended to an Indian journalist that he should read that notorious anti-Semitic forgery, the *Protocols of the Elders of Zion*: 'I will give you a copy. It proves beyond the shadow of a doubt that three hundred Zionists, each of whom knows all the others, govern the fate of the European Continent and that they elect their successors from their entourage.'[3]

Nevertheless, it is not difficult to see how even an intelligent and well-informed Arab, faced with the claim of Zionism to the allegiance of all Jews everywhere and with the success of the dynamic international Zionist organization in mobilizing both wealth and political support for Israel in Western countries, might draw conclusions about the influence of world Jewry which sound sinister or absurd to Western liberal ears.

Similarly, it is not surprising that Nasser or any other Arab should see an intimate connexion between Israel and Western imperialism, despite the fact that the Israeli state was a product of a successful rebellion against the British mandate as well as of war against the Arabs. Among the original British supporters of Zionism, such as Winston Churchill and Leopold Amery, as well as Balfour himself, the idea that a Jewish state could be a bastion of British imperial influence in the Middle East was an important consideration. (A similar idea reappeared in some British Labour as well as Conservative circles after the creation of Israel in 1948 and the gathering drive of Arab nationalism against British military bases.) American official support for Zionism, both diplomatically and in economic concessions over the collection and transfer of Jewish funds from the United States, was obvious. The concept of Israel as the tool as well as the product of imperialism, the instrument by which the West would keep the Arabs in their place, seemed to be shatteringly confirmed by the Franco-British-Israeli alliance during the Suez–Sinai war.

In all this there was, of course, a good deal of gross over-simplification and some sheer fantasy. The Soviet Union had joined with the United States in recognizing the Israeli state in 1948 on the basis of the UN partition plan and arms from Czechoslovakia had then helped equip the Jewish armies. The same two Great Powers found themselves temporarily on the same side again in 1956, but this time opposing Israel and her allies and supporting Egypt. The attitudes of the Western Powers were constantly ambivalent: when they veered further towards Israel it was often not merely because of public sentiment or the influence of Zionist lobbies but because of the hostility aroused by the Arab nationalist drive against Western positions elsewhere.

Western interpretations of Nasser's policy usually exaggerated both his belligerency towards Israel and his ability or willingness to make peace with her. Nasser was neither eager to rush into a war of Arab reconquest nor in any hurry to make a permanent peace settlement, except at the price of radical concessions from Israel. He always regarded the question of Israel as of central importance to the Arab states and to Egypt in particular, but until 1967, because of the extreme difficulty of the problem, he put its solution low down on his list of political priorities (just as there were many in Europe who knew that the German problem was central to a European settlement but put it on one side for the moment as insoluble). He tried to shelve any decisive military action against Israel while giving priority to Egypt's social and economic (and military) development, to the elimination of imperialism from the Arab world, and to the achievement of Arab unity or at least a common Arab foreign policy. He chose these priorities not from idealistic preference but on practical grounds, from respect for the strength of Israel and her friends and believing that only a liberated and developed Arab world with an agreed policy would be able to deal with Israel successfully. At the same time he tried to keep open the options of either a military or political solution of the Israeli problem, though he seems to have thought that any favourable settlement for the Arabs would be more likely to be the fruit of a combination of military power, diplomacy and economic pressures, rather than from a total war with the risk of intervention by the Great Powers.

Nasser did not speak, like other Arab leaders, of 'driving the Jews into the sea' or 'liquidating the state of Israel' in the sense of massacring its inhabitants. He foresaw either the creation of a mixed Jewish–Arab state, just as the Lebanon was a mixed Christian–Muslim state, or a reduction in the size of the Israeli state to a symbolic Jewish sanctuary and the restoration of land contact between Egypt and Arab Asia. The Western Powers might still support such a reduced Jewish state but it would no longer present a serious military or economic danger to the Arabs or a geographical obstacle to their eventual unity.

Officially the basis of Nasser's policy – as of the policy of the Arab League states as a whole – was the implementation of the United Nations resolutions on Palestine: the partition plan of 1947; the return of the Palestine Arab refugees to their homes or their compensation; and the internationalization of Jerusalem. He had also indicated his willingness to explore a territorial settlement on the basis of the compromise suggested in 1955 by Eden in his Guildhall Speech.* The official Arab League policy certainly would have entailed, if not the total destruction of the Israeli state as it was after 1949, at least a drastic change in its character by the reduction of its territory, the internationalization of its capital, the possible return of several hundred thousand Palestinian Arabs, and the probable displacement from areas allocated to the Arabs of many Jews who had come into the country since 1948.

The belated Arab acceptance of the implementation of the principle of partition also meant, however, the recognition of the

*See Chapter 6.

existence of a Jewish state of some kind, however small and changed in character. But when President Bourguiba of Tunisia in 1965 drew this logical conclusion and suggested it should be a basis for negotiation, his suggestion shocked Arab opinion in the Middle East and led to a campaign against him from Cairo.

Nasser's concern with Israel was deepened by his vision of Arab leadership. After the formation of the UAR there was a marked development of his 'Saladin complex' through which he saw himself as eventually leading the united Arabs to the recovery of Palestine as Saladin finally drove out the Crusaders. There was, however, another side to Nasser's analogy of the Crusades: it was a less painful way of telling the Arabs that the struggle with Israel would be a long-drawn-out affair. A matter of decades rather than years, it would depend for its success on avoiding premature military adventures and concentrating on a gradual building up of Arab strength through greater unity and the modernization of Arab society. The chief danger Nasser feared was that Israel might try to strike quickly before the Arab world had time to reorganize itself. While not giving up basic claims or rights, the Arabs should avoid a military confrontation with Israel.[4] Even a less visionary or ambitious Egyptian leader would have been forced by the geopolitics of the Arab world and Egypt's position in it to adopt a policy not much different in its essentials from that of Nasser.

But between coexistence without peace and conflict without war there was a wide variety of possible policies – and Nasser shifted between them at different times over the years between the Suez–Sinai campaign and the war of 1967. With the establishment of the UNEF in Sinai and the Gaza Strip and on the Straits of Tiran, two of the immediate causes of tension between Israel and Egypt were removed. The border was quiet, there were no serious fedayin raids into Israel or major Israeli reprisals, and Israeli shipping went freely up the Gulf of Aqaba to Eilat. The UNEF did not extend round the other Israeli borders with Jordan, Syria and Lebanon. Incidents continued there, especially over the demilitarized zone between Israel and Syria, but for several years they were not on a serious scale. There were other causes of conflict. The continued Arab boycott and blockade of

Israeli ships through the Suez Canal was matched by Israel's continued refusal to take back any Arab refugees. The unsettled dispute over the sharing of the Jordan waters was linked with the continued friction between Israel and Syria over control of the demilitarized border zone near to the Jordan headwaters. The tensions caused by these disputes, especially over the Jordan, were accentuated over the years by the rivalries of the Arab states, the repercussions of the 'Arab Revolution' and the domestic politics of Israel. There was also the competition between the great Powers in providing arms and diplomatic support and between the Israelis and Arabs in seeking this help. Finally a new element helped to spark off the explosive mixture – the emergence of a new Palestinian nationalist and irredentist movement.

When Nasser became the ruler of Syria as well as Egypt he assumed wider responsibilities *vis-à-vis* Israel. His policy was soon put to the test in four ways: over the passage of Israeli ships through the Suez Canal, over Israeli plans to divert the Jordan waters, by the initiative taken by General Kassim to create a 'Palestine entity', and by the disclosure of a secret Israeli nuclear reactor.

Early in 1959, the Israelis tried to send a chartered Danish ship, the *Inge Toft*, through the Canal with a cargo bound for Israel. It was stopped by the Egyptians, the ship arrested and the cargo impounded. Nasser made it plain that he intended to continue to defy the Security Council ruling about the passage of Israeli ships through the Canal, unless Israel herself complied with other United Nations resolutions, particularly on the return of the Palestine Arab refugees.[5] The ship was released in February 1960 without its cargo. Nasser later denied reports that his Foreign Minister, Dr Fawzi, had agreed with Hammarskjöld to let Israeli cargoes go through the Canal provided they were not carried in Israeli-owned or chartered ships. Nasser was determined to retain the Canal blockade, which he called 'one of the remaining trump cards in the hands of the Palestine people'. At the same time he was also resisting pressure from both the Syrian Baathists and Iraq for a more militant policy towards Israel in other respects.

In the autumn of 1959, Israel announced her intention of going ahead with plans for the unilateral diversion of the Jordan waters for her own purposes, in the absence of any agreement with the Arab states. The Jordan is fed by springs and tributaries which rise partly in Israel, Syria, Lebanon and Jordan. The upper reaches of the river, together with Lake Tiberias through which it flows, are in Israel and the lower half of the river is in the state of Jordan. The Israeli plan aroused alarm among the neighbouring Arab states on two counts. First, they feared its possible adverse effect on their own water development schemes, especially in Jordan. Second, the publicity surrounding the project had stressed that the diverted water would be used to irrigate the Negev where millions more Jewish immigrants might then be settled. The Israelis themselves later abandoned the more ambitious ideas of large-scale irrigation of the Negev desert or steppe in favour of the more economical use of water in already cultivated areas farther north and in the development of industry and urban settlement. But in May 1959 the Arab states at the United Nations had already expressed their grave concern to Hammarskjöld over continued Jewish immigration into Israel, which had already raised the Jewish population from 650,000 to some two million. They claimed that it was intended 'to present the world with the *fait accompli*, that there is no longer any room for the Palestine Arabs to return to their homes under the United Nations resolutions; to build up man-power for the ever-expanding Israeli military machine; and eventually to create a crisis of over-population as a pretext for expansion'.

When the Jordan waters problem was discussed in the UAR cabinet in October and November 1959, there was a clash between Nasser and the Syrian Baathist ministers led by Akram Haurani. The Syrians urged military action to stop the Israeli diversion plans. One of the proposals made by Haurani and rejected by Nasser was to reinstate the blockade of Israel shipping through the Straits of Tiran. Nasser's version is that he rejected the Syrian proposals on practical military grounds. According to Heykal, Nasser told the cabinet in November, 'I shall not permit the initiation of war unless I am capable of developing it into an all-out war against the enemy and against all support which may be sent to him, and achieve sure victory'.[6] Since Nasser believed that Israel would probably be able to count on support from the Western Powers, especially the United States, if she were in serious difficulties, it was obvious that the Arabs were in no position to defeat such a powerful combination of forces.

It was largely Syria's objection to any agreement likely to consolidate Israel that had led the Arab League to reject the Johnston plan for the Jordan waters in 1955. A contributing factor to the breakdown of the Johnston negotiations had been Israel's objections to the share of water allocated to her and her dislike of the agreement between Johnston and the Arabs that the whole scheme should be under neutral and international supervision. Under the plan agreed between Johnston and the Arab technical experts, the Arab states would have received a share amounting to sixty per cent of the combined waters of the Jordan and its tributaries, including the Yarmuk (fifteen per cent for Syria and Lebanon and forty-five per cent for Jordan) while Israel would have got the rest after the fixed Arab quota had been fulfilled. This meant that Israel would get under the Johnston scheme an amount variously estimated at between 400 and 490 million cubic metres of water a year; she estimated that by unilaterally exploiting the Jordan waters accessible to her she might get some 550 million cubic metres.[7]

The Israelis justified their unilateral action by giving an assurance that they would not be taking more water from the Jordan (in fact from Lake Tiberias, the main storage area) than they were entitled to under the agreed Johnston plan quotas. The Arabs were afraid, however, that eventually the Israelis would be able to take more than their Johnston quota without anyone being able to stop them except by military action. Instead of trying to make the Israeli diversion a *casus belli*, as the Syrians wanted, Nasser encouraged the Arab League to study the only other alternative to a new international agreement with Israel. This was to take measures to ensure the full use by the Arabs of the waters rising in or running through their territory. In doing so, they might reduce the amount of water available to Israel. At the same time they would try to make sure they obtained at least what they had been allocated under the Johnston plan.

Economically, the dispute was not worth a war for either side. If the Israelis and Arabs had each carried through their unilateral diversion plans the difference between what each side would have got in quantities of water compared with the Johnston plan quotas was almost marginal. The difference between the totals of water to be shared under the two separate schemes or under the Johnston unified scheme was, according to one neutral expert estimate, only about seventy million cubic metres or about one-eighth of the total flow of the upper Jordan.[8] Arab plans for the separate Arab diversion of the Hasbani (in Lebanon), and Banyas (in Syria) and part of the Yarmuk (mostly in Jordan but also partly in Syria and Israel) were no less and no more justified morally, legally and technically than the separate Israel development project.

But the dispute became a test of political will, not economic need. Each side threatened military action to stop the other's schemes if they were put in to effect. While themselves too weak effectively to block the Israeli diversion, the Arab states had to recognize that they could proceed with their own schemes only if they could defend them militarily against Israeli attack. For the time being the contest remained on the diplomatic and political level, except for continued incidents in and around the demilitarized zone on the Israel–Syria border.

The origin of the dispute here was that since the demilitarized zone lay on the Israeli side of the old Palestine–Syria border, Israel claimed it as an area under her sovereignty which she could cultivate and administer. The Syrians considered it an area of unsettled sovereignty, since under the UN-supervised armistice agreement the armistice lines were specifically defined as not being political frontiers. The Syrians supported the rights of the former Palestine Arab inhabitants to continue to farm the zone and resisted their eviction by the Israelis. The UNTSO (United Nations Truce Supervision Organization) was supposed to watch over the demilitarized zone with the help of a Syrian–Israeli mixed armistice commission. But Israel had boycotted the commission since 1951 and had on occasion prevented UN observers from entering and inspecting the zone.

In early 1960 there was a large-scale Israeli raid on the village of Tawafik in the demilitarized zone from which the Israelis claimed their farmers were being fired on. As the raid showed, Ben Gurion, still prime minister in Israel, had not given up his activist policy of reprisals. His main aim, however, was still to convert a precarious coexistence into a more permanent settlement on the basis of the *status quo*, thus consolidating Israel's gains from the 1948 war. Meanwhile he sought to strengthen Israel's arms and alliances. In addition to competing with Nasser for influence among the Afro-Asian states, and cultivating the big Powers, especially the United States, France and West Germany, he also sought and found friends in the Middle East in the anti-Nasser governments of Turkey and Iran. He failed to get a formal guarantee of Israel's frontiers from either the United States or NATO, and de Gaulle stopped the help which the French Defence Ministry had been giving Israel in the development of her secret nuclear reactor at Dimona.[9] But the reactor was by then already established and capable eventually of providing enough material for atomic weapons. It was partly anxiety about this nuclear potential that led President Kennedy a few months after his inauguration to prepare a new attempt at an Arab–Israeli settlement.

On 11 May 1961, just before he was due to receive Ben Gurion in Washington, Kennedy wrote to Nasser and other Arab leaders offering American help in finding a settlement with Israel. He offered American support in solving the Palestine refugee problem on the basis of the United Nations recommendations of repatriation or compensation, also in finding an equitable answer to the Jordan waters question and to other aspects of the dispute.

Kennedy promised continued American aid to 'all Middle Eastern states that are determined to control their own destiny, to enhance the prosperity of their people, and to allow their neighbours to pursue the same fundamental aims'.[10] The latter phrasing reflected Kennedy's aim of persuading Nasser to concentrate on Egypt's domestic development rather than on 'making trouble' in other countries.[11]

Nasser, rather to Kennedy's surprise, wrote back on 22 August a long letter setting out the broad outlines of the Arab view of Palestine and Israel and the damaging effect of the problem on

Arab–American relations. The letter was part of a considerable private correspondence that developed between Nasser and Kennedy on Middle East and world problems. In his letter Nasser was especially concerned to convince Kennedy that the Arab attitude towards Israel was not based simply on emotion but on real experience. It was the result of 'an aggression launched in the past', of present dangers and of fears for the future. Continued Jewish immigration, wrote Nasser, 'creates a pressure within Israel that has to explode and head for expansion'. Israel was constantly liable to be used by 'imperialism' as 'a tool to divide the Arab nation geographically' and also as a base from which to threaten any Arab liberation movement. Nasser said he did not make an identity of views on the Palestine problem a condition of possible understanding with the United States, but appealed to Kennedy to change the situation in which, he said, American interests as well as principles had been neglected in favour of the local political motives of winning Jewish votes in the presidential election. Kennedy's peace-making initiatives petered out, partly because Ben Gurion rejected the President's suggestion that Israel should begin the peace process by taking back some of the Palestine Arab refugees.

In 1961 and 1962, the question of Israel was largely over-shadowed for Nasser by his 'Arab socialist revolution'. There were several meetings of the Arab League to discuss the Jordan waters but the main interest in the Palestine question centred on the political and military organization of the Palestine Arabs.

Hitherto, the Palestinians had been fragmented as a community, both geographically and socially, by the war and exile. Those, numbering about a million, who had stayed on their native soil, were divided between the west bank of Jordan, where both residents and refugees had Jordanian citizenship, and the Gaza Strip where they were subject to Egyptian military and civilian control. Another quarter of a million or so on the east bank of Jordan were also Jordanians by nationality. An additional two or three hundred thousand were scattered in Lebanon and Syria, and a few thousand worked in Iraq and the Arab oil states. While hundreds of thousands still stagnated miserably in UNRWA refugee camps, others had made successful careers in commerce or the professions in other Arab countries. The Palestinians were a majority of the citizens of Jordan; in other Arab countries they had made themselves part of the educated *élite*; but nowhere had they any real organized political voice. In Jordan there were Palestinian cabinet ministers and senior officials but power still rested in reality with the king and his loyal Bedouin troops. In Gaza the real power lay with Egypt. The Gaza Palestine government linked with the Mufti, which had once been the Egyptian-sponsored Palestinian voice in the Arab League, had lost all substance.

Then in 1959 General Kassim in Iraq began to promote the idea of a 'Palestine entity', a Palestinian independent republic with a government-in-exile and a volunteer military force of its own, on the lines of the Algerian nationalist provisional government and its liberation army. The idea was a challenge to Kassim's Arab enemies, Egypt and Jordan, who between them controlled what was left of Arab Palestine. Nasser denounced Kassim's move as 'a base manoeuvre', but it set in motion a competition for the allegiance and control of the Palestinians which was to have a disastrous effect on Arab relations with Israel. Kassim's initiative responded to a growing feeling among the Palestinians, especially of the younger generation, that they should have a greater say in deciding their own future: they felt that the Arab governments were complacently shelving their claims or treating them simply as a refugee problem. King Hussein felt the need to call a Congress in May 1960 at which the Palestinians in Jordan reaffirmed their loyalty to Jordan. Nasser began a special programme from Cairo radio called 'The Voice of Palestine'. In March 1962 the Arab League recommended that 'all Arab states should preserve the Palestine entity and avoid whatever brings its annihilation'. But it was not until September 1963 that an official Palestine delegate was appointed to the Arab League Political Committee. He was Ahmed esh-Shuqeiri, a Palestinian lawyer of demagogic talent, who had previously worked for the Arab League and represented Saudi Arabia at the United Nations. Shuqeiri was an Egyptian nominee but was also supported by the Algerians whom he had helped at the United Nations during their independence struggle.

By this time, the question of Palestine and Israel had again become more acute. Work on Israel's diversion of the Jordan waters from Lake Tiberias was nearing completion and the scheme was due to start operating in 1964. The Baathist regimes which had come to power in Syria and Iraq were more militantly anti-Israeli: they were urging Arab preparations for a military showdown if necessary over the Jordan waters. But, at the same time, the retirement of Ben Gurion and his replacement as premier by the more cautious Levi Eshkol brought a new restraint into Israeli policy towards the Arabs.

Palestine was, however, not only an issue capable of uniting the Arabs but also one which Nasser's Arab enemies on right or left could all use against him. The Syrian Baathists could call for action or for unity on their terms as a necessary prelude to dealing with Israel. Jordan could ask why Nasser claimed to be the leader of the Arabs when he did nothing to stop the Israeli army's assaults on the Jordan and Syrian borders but sat safely behind the United Nations force in Sinai and let Israeli ships into the Gulf of Aqaba. Saudi Arabia could make the obvious point that the Egyptian army would be better employed fighting the Israelis than other Arabs in the Yemen.

On 17 December 1963, Nasser let it be known through the Egyptian press that he believed Jordan, Syria and Saudi Arabia were trying to push Egypt into war with Israel while standing back from the fight themselves. The UAR, he made it plain, was not going to fall into the trap by embarking on any adventures. It would not let itself be pushed into a battle with Israel before the attainment of unity among all the Arab countries. Instead, a week later, speaking at Port Said, Nasser turned the tables on his opponents by calling for a summit conference of Arab heads of state to work out a common policy towards Israel. Whether the decision would be for war or peace or continued uneasy coexistence, the responsibility for it must be shared by all the Arab leaders and not borne by Egypt alone.

At the first 'summit' of kings and presidents, held in Cairo from 13–17 January 1964, the Arab leaders decided against military action to stop Israel's water diversion. Instead they decided in principle to proceed with an Arab Jordan diversion scheme. The Hasbani was to be diverted into the Banyas in Syria and then both were to flow through a canal into the River Yarmuk in Jordanian territory, where a separate irrigation scheme was already under way. The Arab oil states, principally Kuwait, would help to finance this project. The Arab chiefs of staff had recommended that if the Arab diversion works were to be defended effectively, the Arab states must be prepared for escalation into a full-scale war. The Cairo summit, therefore, agreed to set up an Arab Unified Military Command under the Egyptian General Ali Ali Amer. The conference also gave more formal recognition to the 'Palestine entity'. Finally the Arab leaders promised to end their own quarrels and stop hostile propaganda against each other. After two years of the Arab Revolution the era of Arab coexistence had begun.

Though the summit decisions were unanimous there were discordant voices. Major-General Amin el Hafiz, President of the Syrian National Revolutionary Council and the only head of state whom Nasser did not personally receive, clashed with Nasser in the final stages of the conference. He called for action in the Palestine cause instead of speeches, implying that Syria was prepared to fight if Egypt was not.[12]

Israel's reaction was a statement from Eshkol in the Knesset confirming that Israel would in 1964 begin drawing water from Lake Tiberias within the limits of the Johnston plan. Eshkol gave a warning that Israel would act if the Arabs tried to sabotage her water plans.

But the only one of the Cairo decisions to have a rapid follow-up concerned the organization of the Palestine Arabs – and it soon became clear that this was intended, at least by Nasser, as a brake to precipitate action against Israel rather than as an encouragement of it. In June 1964 a Palestine National Congress met in Jerusalem under the chairmanship of Ahmed esh-Shuqeiri. Its 450 members claimed to represent the Palestine people in all Arab countries except Saudi Arabia. It proclaimed a National Charter, and called for the setting up of a Palestine Liberation organization and for military training for all Palestinians. The Charter claimed that 'the Palestine people have a right to self-determination following the liberation of their country'. The

Arab people of Palestine, it said, were the lawful owners of Palestine and were an indivisible part of the Arab nation, but 'Jews of Palestine origin' (presumably those who were already in Palestine before 1948 under the British mandate) 'are to be regarded as Palestinians provided they are willing to abide peacefully and loyally in Palestine'.

At the second Arab summit in Alexandria in September 1964, the Arab leaders, urged on by Ben Bella of Algeria, decided to set up a Palestine Liberation Organization and a Palestine Liberation Army. The new organizations were to have their headquarters in the Gaza Strip. They were to be financed from contributions through the Arab League from several Arab states. The Alexandria conference had already begun to show some of the problems involved in carrying out this agreed Arab programme: they became even more apparent at the next summit meeting at Casablanca in September 1965. The unified Arab command remained little more than a paper operation, because the Arab states neighbouring Israel could not agree on the stationing on their territory of troops from other Arab countries. King Hussein also resisted the demands of the Palestine Liberation Organization to operate freely in Jordan in collecting funds and in mobilizing and training Palestinians for its Liberation Army, for this would have been tantamount to the establishment of a dual authority over his Palestinian subjects, the beginning of a state within a state.

In practice, only Egypt and Syria gave much material or political encouragement to the PLO and PLA, and their aims and motives in doing so were increasingly in conflict. Nasser saw the PLO as a means of canalizing Palestinian national emotions and restraining any rash adventures into guerrilla warfare or more large-scale military operations against Israel. The Baathist regime in Syria, as it moved increasingly towards the left with successive *coups* in 1965 and 1966, continued to preach with greater insistence the doctrine of revolutionary warfare as a means of simultaneously dealing with Israel and spreading social revolution throughout the Arab world. To this end the Syrian regime encouraged the PLO to seek help outside the restraining confines of Egypt, by training on Syrian soil and getting arms from China. It also patronized new unofficial and more militant nationalist organizations which had begun to develop among the Palestinians in exile.

The most important of these was Al Fatah (the word 'fatah' means 'victory' in Arabic but the consonants which compose it also form the initials in reverse of the Arabic words meaning 'Palestine Liberation Front'). Eventually there were a dozen or more Palestinian groups committed to 'direct action', through terrorism or guerrilla operations, to destroy the Israeli state and 'liberate' Palestine. Apart from the PLO and Al Fatah, the two most important, though on a much smaller scale, were the Popular Front for the Liberation of Palestine and 'Al Saiqa' (Thunderbolt). Al Saiqa was the military organization associated with the Baath party, while the PFLP was an offshoot of another pan-Arab group, the Arab National Movement. The ANM was originally a right-wing Nasserist group but moved to the extreme left, to a Marxist anti-imperialist position. Once intermittently patronized and helped by the Egyptian intelligence, it sometimes, as in Aden, ended up in conflict with Egypt. The chief success of the ANM was in Aden and South Arabia, where it inspired the creation of the National Liberation Front which eventually fought its way to power.

Both Al Fatah and the ANM developed among Palestinian exiles chiefly in Kuwait and the Gulf. Al Fatah began in the Gaza Strip. It sprang from the belief that the Sinai war was another defeat for the Palestine Arab cause and that the settlement in 1957 was another demonstration that the Arab governments, especially the Egyptians, were prepared to accept the existence of Israel as a *fait accompli*, whatever defiant words they might still use. The Palestinians, it appeared, could no longer rely on the Arab governments, even Nasser, to regain their lost land: they must act themselves. Their first aim must be to keep the Palestinian cause and the national identity alive. Then they must mobilize a revolutionary guerrilla movement which would prevent Israel from consolidating its position. Finally they must force the Arab governments into more militant action.

Al Fatah began to form cells among the Palestinians in exile at the beginning of 1957 and continued building up a political structure until 1959–60. It began forming its secret military arm 'Al Assifa' (Lightning) from 1959 onwards. '*Élite*' groups were given military and underground training, some of them with the Algerian resistance, and a clandestine infrastructure was built up until the first 'commando' squads were formed in 1964. According to Al Fatah sources, the first operation of these squads was a sabotage attack in 1965 against an Israeli pumping station above Lake Tiberias used in connexion with the Jordan water diversion. From then on the Fatah raids into Israel became more frequent. The Fatah claimed to be completely independent and to be financed by money contributed by Palestinians from all over the Arab world and even beyond, in North and South America. Its leadership was drawn from the younger Palestinian generation of educated professional men or technicians. (The military command of Al Fatah in 1968 was composed of two electrical engineers, two electronics specialists and two mathematicians.) The relations of Al Fatah with the Syrian, Jordanian and Egyptian governments were at first 'cool and reserved', but it had increasing cooperation from the Syrian army as the left-wing Baathist regime in Damascus moved towards the same ideas of revolutionary warfare against Israel as those preached by Al Fatah.[13]

In the first half of 1965 there was growing dissension between Nasser and the Syrians over policy towards Israel. The Israelis had begun to divert the Jordan waters from Lake Tiberias during 1964 without any reaction from the Arabs. The Arab states had not even been able to plan effective joint action to protect their own diversion schemes or to deal with Israeli army raids on the Syrian and Jordan frontiers. The Syrians complained that the UAR was not giving them the needed military backing, especially air support, on their vulnerable border with Israel.

In a speech to the Palestine National Congress in Cairo on 31 May 1965, Nasser spoke with brutal candour of the rifts in the Arab camp. He attacked both Bourguiba for suggesting a compromise settlement with Israel and the Syrians for urging military action. Nasser said that, as a result of the fears of one Arab country of the forces of another passing through its territory, 'the Arab unified command cannot act. . . . If we are unable now to defend, how can we speak of attack?'

Referring to the Syrian Baathists, Nasser said,

They say 'drive out UNEF'. Suppose that we do, is it not essential that we have a plan? If Israeli aggression takes place against Syria, shall I attack Israel? Then Israel is the one which determines the battle for me. It hits a tractor or two to force me to move. Is this a wise way? We have to determine the battle. Israel may wish us to enter a war with it now. . . . Is it conceivable that I should attack Israel while there are 50,000 Egyptian troops in Yemen?[14]

Nasser's policy of caution was endorsed by the next Arab summit conference at Casablanca in September 1965. The conference rejected proposals by the new Algerian leader, Colonel Boumédienne, who had just replaced Ben Bella, for guerrilla operations against Israel. The conference agreed that the Palestine Liberation Organization should discuss with the unified Arab command the formation of Palestinian military units for an eventual Palestine Liberation Army. The main emphasis of the summit was still on inter-Arab coexistence and the avoidance of any military clash with Israel while the Arabs were still weak and divided.

All was not harmony, however. On the eve of the conference Bourguiba circulated a seventeen-page memorandum bitterly attacking Nasser and declaring that Tunisia would boycott the Arab League so long as it was an instrument of 'Egyptian hegemony and tutelage'. 'Never,' wrote Bourguiba, 'in their history have the Arabs been so divided, never have they been killing each other so savagely as since the day when Egypt took upon herself the sacred mission of uniting them.' Bourguiba accused Nasser of trying to overthrow every state in the Arab world: in a 'Pharaonic spirit', Egypt was trying to seek 'living space' for her economic products and giving herself international importance so as to get more aid from East and West.[15]

Bourguiba's quarrel with Nasser had a long history. The ostensible causes this time were differences of opinion over a Palestine settlement and over Arab relations with West Germany. Bourguiba had long argued that the only way to approach a solution of the Palestine problem was by the diplomatic 'gradualism' that had been the Tunisian method of achieving independence – a modest and calculated political step at a time rather than extensive intransigent demands or a revolutionary upheaval. He took his stand on the same principles as those approved by the Arab League and by Nasser – the implementation of the 1947 partition resolutions. But, being further from the conflict and so less vulnerable domestically, he was prepared publicly to accept the logic of this position, which was that at some stage it involved Arab recognition of an Israeli state. By totally rejecting any such recognition – when Israel was already a member of the United Nations – the Arabs weakened the rest of their diplomatic case and produced no practical benefits for themselves. As already noted, in the course of a tour through the Middle East Arab states in April 1965, Bourguiba elaborated on these ideas publicly in Jordan and elsewhere with more truth than tact. He was swiftly and loudly denounced from Cairo and other Arab capitals. He claimed that the real reason for these attacks was not his views on applying the United Nations resolutions on Palestine, but his refusal to follow Nasser's lead in breaking off relations with Western Germany.

The crisis between Nasser and the West Germans arose out of the growing Middle East arms race. Reports of a West German arms agreement with Israel worth more than £20 million and including the promised delivery of 200 American-made Patton tanks had brought sharp protests from the UAR and other Arab states at the beginning of 1965. Under threat of an Arab economic boycott, the West German government decided on 12 February to cancel its arms agreement with Israel, on the general grounds that it was undesirable to supply arms to areas of tension. To placate criticism at home it then considered establishing diplomatic relations with Israel. A fortnight later the East German leader, Walter Ulbricht, was received officially in Cairo. Hints were thrown out of possible UAR recognition of East Germany, if Bonn gave full recognition to Israel. This would have meant forcing Bonn to choose whether or not to break off relations with the Arab states, since its practice under the so-called 'Hallstein Doctrine' was not to maintain relations

with countries which recognized East Germany. A breach between West Germany and the Arab states was a serious matter
for both sides. The Arabs were liable to lose valuable West
German economic aid and a sympathetic ear in the West where
they were short of influential friends. The West Germans were
threatened with the loss of useful Middle East markets which
they had made great efforts to cultivate. More seriously, if all
the Arab states were to recognize East Germany it could start a
landslide of similar recognitions by other still hesitant Afro-Asian
neutralist states. The foundations of the Hallstein Doctrine
would be destroyed.

Neither Nasser in Cairo nor Chancellor Erhard in Bonn
handled this crisis with skill. While Erhard fumbled, Nasser
ranted. On 7 March, Bonn decided to establish relations with
Israel as if in retaliation for Ulbricht's reception in Cairo,
though Nasser had not recognized East Germany. In a speech
next day Nasser fiercely attacked West Germany as 'imperialist,
neo-colonialist, hypocritical', although he had already achieved
the main Arab aim of stopping the German arms agreement
with Israel. In May, the Bonn government established full diplomatic relations with Israel and the majority of the Arab League
states broke off their relations with Bonn. Tunisia was one of
three Arab countries which refused to do so, arguing that it
would harm the Arabs more than the Germans.

Part of the reason for Nasser's fury with Bonn was his belief
that, in agreeing to supply arms to Israel, West Germany had
been secretly acting on behalf of the United States. Nasser's
relations with Washington at that time – as with most of the
Western Powers – were at a low ebb because of his violent reaction to the use of American planes in operations against the
rebels in Stanleyville in the Congo. This was only one of the first
symptoms of a development in Nasser's mind which was to colour
his judgement of both American motives and Israeli intentions
and contribute to the crisis of the 1967 war. In a speech on 23
July 1967, analysing the background of the 1967 war with Israel
and America's role in that crisis, Nasser said, 'I had a presenti-
ment two years ago that something was brewing against us, since
aid was cut off and the United States demanded that we should

not develop our army and march forward with technical and military developments'. The American political and diplomatic role in the 1967 crisis was, he said, to serve 'the end of an American plot against us laid down two years ago for the purpose of liquidating all the revolutionary regimes which refuse to be dragged into spheres of influence'.

The cutting off of aid referred to by Nasser was President Johnson's response to the outburst of anger in Cairo over the American intervention in the Congo (see Chapter 15). The other development which Nasser professed to have found alarming was pressure from America, allegedly using the aid threat, on Egypt to limit her rearmament and to accept American inspection of her weapon development. The Americans had been worried by the possible development of nuclear weapons and rocket missiles in both Israel and Egypt, as well as by the accelerating conventional arms race between the two sides after the Jordan waters dispute came into the open. The Americans were being pressed by the Israelis to supply them with modern weapons, while they in turn were unsuccessfully pressing the Israelis to let them inspect the Dimona nuclear reactor. They did not seriously suspect the Egyptians of being capable of making nuclear weapons, and Nasser was later ready to accept inspection by the International Atomic Energy Authority. But if they were to resist Israeli demands for more conventional weapons, the Americans believed they had to have some effective assurances from Egypt about her weapon procurement – which was chiefly from Russia. In Nasser's eyes this was an unacceptable attempt to re-establish the Western arms monopoly which he had broken with his 1955 Soviet arms deal. He claimed that when the US Under-Secretary of State Talbot came to see him in the spring of 1965, with a message from President Johnson, the US envoy threatened that if Egypt did not accept US inspection of nuclear activities and rocket development and the need to limit the strength of the Egyptian army, Israel would be supplied with all the American arms she required.[16]

During the last few months of 1965, however, Nasser was still pursuing his policy of Arab coexistence and trying to improve his relations with the United States. Nasser's appointment of

Zacharia Mohieddin as premier of the UAR in place of Aly Sabry in September 1965 was widely interpreted as a sign of his intention to follow a more conservative policy of economic retrenchment at home and a more modest Arab role, which would win sympathy and more economic aid from Washington. Zacharia Mohieddin was reputed to be the most 'American' of Nasser's lieutenants: quietly efficient, a cool-headed administrator and an 'Egypt first' man.

In a speech to the UAR National Assembly on 25 November 1965, Nasser said that at the beginning of the year relations with America had reached a crisis but there had since been a great improvement. 'Both sides have made important efforts to stop any deterioration in relations.'[17] A few days after Nasser's speech the US State Department announced the start of negotiations for a new food aid agreement worth about $55 million over a period of six months. The agreement was concluded in early January 1966. The UAR was in desperate need of foreign exchange. In 1965 it had been saved from the serious effects of the cut in American wheat supplies only by Soviet deliveries of 300,000 tons of wheat. Yet, within a month or two, by the spring of 1966, Nasser's policy of Arab coexistence and *rapprochement* with America was in ruins. He was once more turning to the revolutionary struggle in the Arab world, spurning American economic aid and relying on Russia.

Three developments reinforced each other in bringing about this change. The first was the move in December 1965 by King Feisal in collaboration with the Shah of Iran to promote an Islamic 'summit' conference, and the Anglo-American sale of planes and missiles to Saudi Arabia (see Chapter 15).

The second factor was the arms race in the Middle East. This was becoming more than ever a complex three-way affair, as the Western Powers tried to keep a balance not only between Arab and Israeli but also between their Arab friends and their rivals. On 16 February 1966 the US State Department confirmed that it had sold Patton tanks to both Jordan and Israel and was planning to sell Hawk anti-aircraft missiles, already bought by Israel, to Saudi Arabia. In a statement to Iraqi journalists in Cairo on 19 February Nasser said Israel was getting arms secretly and 'We should do the same to prevent Israel's gaining military supremacy'.

The third development which ushered in Nasser's return to the Arab revolution was the *coup* in Syria which in February 1966 brought into power the extreme neo-Marxist left-wing of the Baath party. The very next day President Nkrumah was deposed by a military *coup* in Ghana, while he was away on a visit to Peking, and in Indonesia students, backed by the army, began a campaign which forced Sukarno to hand over ruling powers to General Suharto and led to the banning of the Communist party. The coincidence of these three events was fortuitous but they seemed to have something in common. They were all evidence of the political polarization of the non-aligned world. The cold war was spreading into new fields through a combination of local conflicts and the ideological storm-waves set up by the Vietnam war and the Sino-Soviet split. In Washington and Moscow, the upheavals in Damascus, Accra or Djakarta were chalked up as gains or losses in a global struggle. To Nasser the end of Nkrumah and the eclipse of Sukarno, the last of the old-guard neutralist leaders, except for himself and Tito, looked ominous. The Russians, under fire from Peking for not defending their friends in Indonesia and Vietnam, were anxious to avoid similar setbacks nearer their own borders. As we have already seen in connexion with the Yemen, the Russians, to counter what they saw as an Anglo-American political offensive in the Middle East, tried to encourage the formation of a block of 'progressive', 'revolutionary' or 'liberated' Arab states – the UAR, Syria, Iraq, Algeria and the Yemen – which they would support. In this scheme the Russians still regarded Nasser as the prime mover but they saw new opportunities and new dangers in Damascus. The new Cuban-style Syrian regime included one and possibly two Communists in its cabinet and announced that it would seek closer relations with the 'socialist camp'. However, the new Damascus regime professed views even more extreme than those of its predecessors on the question of military action against Israel. It favoured 'revolutionary warfare' not only as a means of dealing with Israel but also to transform and unify the Arab countries. The Syrian head of state, Dr Nureddin el Atassi, said in Damascus on 8 March that the 'liberation of Palestine' was the keystone of the revolution's plans. Arab unity, he said, 'would be forged in the flames of the liberation war'.[18]

Several of the same elements that had combined to bring about the Suez–Sinai crisis of 1956 had begun to reappear; a real or believed move by the British and Americans to form a new Middle Eastern alliance system, and the reaction to it by Nasser and the Russians; an accelerating arms race between the Arab states and Israel; the key role of Syria in setting the ideological pace for the Arab revolutionary nationalists; the growth of fedayin raids into Israel and Israeli army reprisals. To this was added the belief professed in Damascus and Moscow that – again repeating the patterns of 1956 and 1957 – Syria was the main focus of the inter-Arab cold war and its regime a target for American-backed plots. If such external threats to the Damascus regime existed, they appeared this time, however, to have little to do with the Americans or the British. The latter were now more concerned with checking the spread of Nasser's influence into the oil lands of the Arabian Peninsula and the Persian Gulf than they were with the constantly shifting political kaleidoscope of the Fertile Crescent countries.

Nasser's first reaction was to move nearer to Iraq, for the Syrian Baathists still aroused his suspicions. But the pressure on him to clarify his attitude towards Syria began to increase from both Moscow and Washington. On 7 May 1966, through an article in *Izvestia*, the Russians unveiled their new line of support for the Syrian regime against alleged threats from an Israel armed and encouraged by the United States. Three weeks later a Tass statement accused Israel of 'provocations' against Syria and warned, 'The Soviet Union cannot and will not remain indifferent to the attempts to violate peace in a region located in direct proximity to the borders of the Soviet Union'.[19] During his visit to the UAR from 10–18 May 1966, the Soviet premier, Kosygin, promised continued economic and political support for the UAR. By that time Soviet economic aid to the UAR was estimated to have reached a total of £300 million, including the High Dam and 133 other projects. The new Syrian regime had been promised £50 million-worth of Soviet aid, including a commitment to build the Euphrates Dam, a project as important for Syria as the Aswan High Dam is for Egypt. The total of Soviet aid to Egypt, mostly in the form of long-term low-interest loans, was curiously about the same as that received by Nasser from the United States over the years.

By the middle of June Nasser had made up his mind to a new course. On 15 June he began to hint at the abandonment of his Arab summit policy on the grounds that coexistence was being exploited by Arab 'reaction' in a conspiracy with the Muslim Brothers in Egypt. The reopened Arab rift began rapidly to widen. In the face of hostility from Syria, King Hussein moved closer to Saudi Arabia and declared that all hopes of cooperation with the Palestine Liberation Organization had vanished because it was dominated by 'subversive partisans'. Nasser attacked the British 'pretence' of withdrawal from Aden and the 'false independence' offered to South Arabia. He accused Britain of supplying combat pilots as well as aircraft to Saudi Arabia – which the Foreign Office promptly denied.[20]

In two speeches at the end of July, Nasser finally spelled out the end of Arab 'coexistence'. He confirmed that the UAR would not attend the next Arab 'summit' meeting due to be held in Algiers in September, because it had become impossible to cooperate with the Arab 'reactionary forces'. This did not mean that the UAR would deviate from the 'summit' aim of liberating Palestine, but, said Nasser, 'we shall coordinate our efforts with those of other Arab revolutionaries and shall liberate Palestine in a revolutionary manner and not in a traditional way'.

Nasser also revealed part of the price that this policy would cost Egypt. The US would not renew the wheat agreement which expired in June. The UAR would now have to find $100 million for the wheat which she formerly got from America for local currency: this would adversely affect the second five-year plan.[21]

Another and more onerous part of the price this new policy might entail had already become visible: border incidents between Syria and Israel were developing on an increasingly serious scale. Raids by Al Fatah units based on Syria and sometimes crossing into Israel through northern Jordan, despite the efforts of the Jordan government to prevent them, had been growing more frequent. Israeli reprisals had become heavier. After Israeli planes had attacked the Banyas diversion works on 14 July 1966 with incendiary bombs, Syria complained to the Security Council. Less than a fortnight later there was another border battle round Lake Tiberias involving aircraft and artillery on both sides. In October the Israel government complained to the Security Council of attacks by Al Assifa in Jerusalem, which had been announced officially on Damascus radio and defended publicly by the Syrian authorities.[22] A resolution in the Council requesting Syria to take stronger measures to prevent incidents was vetoed by the Soviet Union.

Thus by the end of October 1966, the Syrian regime was publicly committed to the revolutionary warfare strategy of Al Fatah. It was being backed by the Soviet Union which professed to believe that as the most 'progressive' of the Arab regimes it was the most likely to be a target for American indirect attack. But the Fatah plan would not be complete without the involvement of Egypt; nor could the Syrian regime hope for fulfilment of its wider revolutionary vision unless Nasser were brought into action (perhaps even better from the Baathist's point of view if, in doing so, Nasser himself were to be replaced by a more revolutionary leadership). And the Russians would feel easier if the isolated and exposed Damascus regime had closer support from Egypt, thus reducing Moscow's immediate responsibility for its protection.

For some months Nasser had hung back from complete commitment to the Arab 'progressive front'. While leaning towards the 'progressives' and resuming attacks on the 'reactionaries', he still tried to avoid a break with more middle-of-the road Arab opinion. But on 4 November he took the plunge and signed a new defence alliance with Syria. The chain of commitment to the 'liberation of Palestine', stretching from Al Fatah through Damascus to Nasser, now seemed complete. But Nasser still thought of it as a long and limited struggle. He was aware of his existing commitment in the Yemen. He also knew that although an alliance with Syria alone might enable him to increase the deterrent to any large-scale Israeli attack and so stabilize the situation without war, he could not hope to plan a serious offensive against Israel without the cooperation of Jordan. This may be one reason why on 13 November, to the general surprise, Israel carried out her biggest border reprisal raid for more than ten years, not against Syria but against Jordan. An Israeli army brigade with tanks, artillery and aircraft attacked the Jordanian village of Sammu near Hebron and virtually razed it to the ground. There were eighteen Jordanian military and civilian dead and fifty-four wounded, as well as losses suffered by the Israeli forces. The Israel authorities claimed that this action was a reprisal for thirteen recent acts of sabotage, including the blowing up of a weapons carrier in which three Israeli soldiers were killed and six wounded. The saboteurs were said to have come across the Jordan border and to have sheltered in Sammu. The raid, said the Israelis, was meant to force King Hussein to take more effective steps to prevent the use of his kingdom for such attacks.

The scale and ferocity of the raid and the choice of target shocked Western opinion and roused some controversy inside Israel itself. Since the Israeli official explanations of the choice of Jordan seemed inadequate – for the immediate effect was to weaken King Hussein's authority in Jordan rather than to strengthen it – other interpretations were sought. Eshkol, it was noted, was under pressure from sections of public opinion and from political rivals, especially those associated with Ben Gurion's Rafi group (a break-away from Mapai, the Israel Labour party) which included such 'activists' as Dayan and Peres, to reply more vigorously to the Fatah raids. But a blow of such weight as that dealt at Sammu could not have been struck against the heavily fortified Syrian border without using greater forces and risking heavier casualties. And in any major attack on Syria there was the danger of an escalation which might involve the Soviet Union. The blow against Jordan may also have been intended as a warning to her not to join in the just-concluded Egyptian–Syrian alliance.

The raid led to widespread riots in the Palestinian towns of the west bank of the Jordan and demands for more energetic military measures. Hussein was able, however, to hold his position and avoid any new commitments, beyond those already made on paper, to the unified Arab command. On 7 December the Arab Defence Council held the first of several meetings in Cairo to define the responsibilities of each state in the event of an Israeli attack but failed to produce any practical agreement. At a press conference the Jordan prime minister, Wasfi al Tal, accused the UAR and Syria of failing to support Jordan. Where, he asked, was the promised UAR air cover and why did Nasser not bring back his troops from the Yemen to face the Israelis?

Nasser's answer was to press Jordan to accept the stationing and free movement of Egyptian, Syrian and Iraqi forces on her territory. This was the last thing Hussein wanted. Attacks on Nasser and the Syrians for their inactivity against Israel, in contrast with their hostility to other Arab regimes, became a regular feature of propaganda from Jordan and Saudi Arabia as the struggle between the 'revolutionaries' and 'reactionaries' in the Arab world was resumed. While Cairo and Damascus attacked Hussein and Feisal as 'imperialist stooges', the radios of Amman and Mecca taunted Nasser with sheltering behind the UNEF in Sinai and of letting Israeli ships pass through the Gulf of Aqaba. Jordan was reported to have even suggested officially in the Arab Defence Council meetings in early January that Egypt should ask the UNEF to withdraw.

This suggestion had already been made by King Hussein in an interview in an American magazine at the end of December.[23] He said that the presence of the UNEF prevented Egypt's forces from having any deterrent effect and so allowed the Israelis to increase their pressure on other fronts.

By the end of January 1967 the shock of the Sammu raid seemed to have died down. Although there were continued incidents, neither in Cairo nor in Tel Aviv was there then any serious belief in the danger of a full-scale war. In an interview with me at the end of 1967, Nasser appeared to be only perfunctorily concerned with the problem of Israel. This impression was confirmed in a private talk I had with his Foreign Minister, Mahmoud Riad. The latter considered the situation between the Arabs and Israel as a kind of stalemate. A struggle of political and economic attrition between the Arabs and Israel might go on for years, but Egypt did not wish to be deeply involved from a military point of view unless there were an all-out attack by Israel on Syria.

Nasser was at that time more concerned with the economic situation in Egypt, and with the struggle in South Arabia and the Yemen. But he had already begun to see events in the Middle East in the framework of an Anglo-American 'conspiracy' against the non-aligned radical regimes. At that time he saw this 'conspiracy' at work chiefly in opposition to himself in Arabia, and had not then linked it so closely with Israel as he did later. To at least some Israeli leaders it seemed as if Nasser were still trying to avoid a clash with Israel and that the Arab leaders were more preoccupied with their own conflicts than with planning war against Israel.[24] The Russians, however, continued to paint a more alarmist picture of Israeli intentions towards Syria. Their reasons for doing so are not clear. They could have had no interest in fomenting a war that their Arab clients could not win and in which they risked becoming involved themselves. Perhaps they were trying to build up the world picture of an American counter-revolutionary offensive in which Israel was one instrument, a picture which they may have partly believed and partly developed in order to frighten their own Third World clients into remaining loyal to them. At this time, too, the Soviet government was closely engaged in trying to bring about peace talks between the United States and North Vietnam, during the visit to Britain of the Soviet premier Kosygin. There seems no reason why when the Soviet foreign minister, Gromyko, went to Cairo for three days at the end of March 1967, he should have tried to egg Nasser on to war against Israel, nor is there any evidence that he did so, though he may have urged Nasser to give the Syrians more open support. But within a week of Gromyko's departure from Cairo, there was a new and more serious battle on the Israel–Syria border and the first stage of the crisis leading up to the Arab–Israel war of June 1967 had begun.

Chapter 17

Over the Brink:
Syria, UNEF and Aqaba, May–June 1967

It was not we who started the crisis in the Middle East. We all know that this crisis began with Israel's attempt to invade Syria . . . in that attempt Israel was not working for itself alone but also for the forces that had got impatient with the Arab revolutionary movement.

So Nasser was to claim after the June war.[1] It probably represents what he genuinely believed at the beginning of the crisis: that Israel, encouraged by the United States, was planning a military blow against Syria which would at least bring down the Damascus regime; and that he could not afford to stand by and let this happen. His first moves therefore were to try to deter the feared Israeli assault.

It may be years before some of the questions about the outbreak of the June war can be fully answered but there is little dispute about the beginning of the crisis. On 7 April, there occurred one of those exchanges of fire between Israelis and Syrians over Israeli cultivation of the demilitarized zone which had been a feature of that disputed border for years past. This time it escalated into a battle involving tanks, artillery and aircraft. Israeli aircraft attacked and silenced Syrian artillery posts, and shot down six Syrian jet fighters. Some of the Israeli planes then flew on the fifty-odd miles to Damascus to stage a victory demonstration over the Syrian capital.

Once more there were taunts from the Jordan authorities about the poor performance of the Syrians and Nasser's failure to help them. The Jordan newspaper *Al Quds* asked 'What has Cairo done in the face of this flagrant air aggression on Damascus, the Syrian capital?'[2]

The answer was – nothing, partly because the Syrians had refused to allow the UAR to set up an air base on their territory. Could Nasser go on doing nothing and still hold his own in the revived struggle between the Arab 'revolutionaries' and 're-actionaries'? On 10 April Nasser sent the commander-in-chief of the UAR air force, General Mohammed Sidky Mahmoud, to Damascus where he conferred for twelve days with the Syrian military. The UAR prime minister, Sidky Suleiman, also went to Damascus and there were mutual pledges of joint action against possible Israeli aggression.

The next step-up in the crisis did not occur until the middle of May. During the first week of the month there were two Al Fatah attacks inside Israel which were said to show a higher degree of professional training and equipment than hitherto. This was noted with concern not only by the Israelis but also on 11 May by the UN Secretary-General, U Thant.* During the next few days two developments combined to precipitate the second phase of the crisis. The Israeli prime minister, Levi Eshkol, and the chief of staff of the Israeli army, General Rabin, made statements on 12 and 13 May which were taken by Nasser to be threats of an Israeli attack to overthrow the Syrian regime. At the same time, reports reached Nasser from the Syrians, from the Russians and from Egyptian intelligence sources that Israel was concentrating large forces on the northern frontier for a possible attack on Syria.

Some mystery still surrounds both these developments which together convinced Nasser that he must act quickly to deter an Israeli assault. There is still some doubt as to precisely what General Rabin or Eshkol said. More mysterious is the question of the Israeli troop concentrations the existence of which the Israelis themselves and the UN observers denied. In a speech on 22 May 1967 to the UAR Air Force Advanced Command, Nasser alleged that on 12 May 'Israeli commanders announced they would carry out military operations against Syria in order to occupy Damascus and overthrow the Syrian government'. He went on, 'On 13 May we received accurate information that Israel was concentrating on the Syrian border huge armed forces of eleven to thirteen brigades. These forces were divided into two fronts, one south of Lake Tiberias and the other north of the lake. The decision made by Israel at this time was to carry out an

---

*U Thant, at a press luncheon at UN headquarters, said that such activities were 'a menace to the peace of the area' and that it was the duty of all governments to put an end to them.

aggression against Syria as of 17 May. ... The Syrians also had this information.'[3]

Nasser later (after the war) said: 'Our parliamentary delegation headed by Anwar es-Sadat was on a visit to Moscow and our Soviet friends informed Anwar es-Sadat that the invasion of Syria was imminent. ... There was a joint defence agreement between us and Syria, not merely ink on paper. It was imperative that we take concrete steps to face the danger threatening Syria'.[4]

On 12 May, in a speech to Israeli Labour party leaders, Eshkol had warned Syria that there would be no immunity for any state which aided and abetted sabotage acts on Israeli territory. In a radio interview the same day, he said that nowadays it seemed as if Syria had taken upon herself the leadership in the battle against Israel. However, Syria's forces were not great and 'not without reason is she looking for protection among larger countries'.[5]

The next day, Eshkol said that the Arab states ought to know that 'any border which is tranquil from their side will also be quiet from our side', but added that Israel 'may have to teach Syria a sharper lesson than that of 7 April'.

General Rabin's remarks at this time have been variously reported. According to one version, he said that so long as the Syrian regime continued in power, the Fatah raids would continue. According to another, he declared that only the overthrow of the Damascus regime could end the raids.[6]

But more alarming were the obviously officially inspired press reports coming out of Israel that week-end, which appeared to be based on these statements. The gist of these reports was that Israel was preparing a large-scale military action against Syria which would go further than any previous reprisal raid. A United Press despatch from Jerusalem quoted 'a highly placed Israeli source' as saying that 'if Syria continued the campaign of sabotage in Israel it would immediately provoke military action aimed at overthrowing the Syrian regime', even at the risk of Egyptian intervention.[7]

In his report to the Security Council on 19 May on the aggravating factors of the crisis, U Thant noted,

Intemperate and bellicose utterances, by officials and non-officials, eagerly reported by press and radio, are unfortunately more or less routine on both sides of the lines in the Near East. In recent weeks however, reports emanating from Israel have attributed to some high officials in that State statements so threatening as to be particularly inflammatory in the sense that they could only heighten emotions and thereby increase tensions on the other side of the lines.

Of the stories of Israel troop concentrations on the Syrian border, however, U Thant reported,

> The Government of Israel very recently has assured me that there are no unusual Israel troop concentrations or movements along the Syrian line, that there will be none and that no military action will be initiated by the armed forces of Israel unless such action is first taken by the other side. Reports from UNTSO observers have confirmed the absence of troop concentrations and significant troop movements on both sides of the line.

The Israeli government later claimed it had made repeated invitations to the Soviet ambassador in Tel Aviv to go to see for himself whether or not there were any Israeli troop concentrations, but he refused.[8] Since Israel could in any case move troops from nearby permanent camps to the Syrian border in a matter of hours, the absence of troop concentrations was not conclusive evidence either way about her intentions towards Syria. For this reason, and because of other signs of Israeli military activity, the conclusions of the commander of UNTSO (United Nations Truce Supervisory Organisation) General Odd Bull, on which U Thant based his report, were not shared by all the UN senior officers in the area.[9]

It has been suggested that the Syrian regime chose to fabricate an external threat to strengthen its position in an internal crisis at home.[10] The Syrian Baathist and army leadership was certainly in some turmoil about this time, partly because of public uproar over an anti-religious article published in an army newspaper. Nevertheless, the concurrence between the Syrian, Egyptian and Russian reports about troop movements is striking. One hypothesis is that during the first two weeks of May, when the Israeli authorities seem to have been trying to scare the Syrians by inspired leaks about massive retaliation, they may also have moved some troops temporarily to make a show of force, only to withdraw them again when Nasser over-reacted, Egyptian

troops began to move into Sinai and the United Nations headquarters asked for an explanation.*

Something of Nasser's general state of mind at this vital
juncture may be gauged from a message he sent to a Palestine
Day rally of Arab students in Britain on 14 May. In it he repeated more clearly than ever before his theme that the 'Arab
revolution' was faced by a coordinated conspiracy in which
'imperialism', meaning the United States and Britain, was acting
together with both Israel and 'Arab reaction'. He alleged that
there was a 'coordination between Israel and the Jordanian
government in their pressure on Syria and in trying to involve
Arab forces in premature battle'. This conspiracy was not confined to the Arab world but was part of a counter-revolution,
led by the United States, 'against aspirations for freedom, progress and prosperity in our nation and in the entire Third World'.
The question, said Nasser, 'is no longer one of Palestine alone
but of the entire Arab destiny. It is a question of confronting
all our enemies at once.'

It was against such a melodramatic, almost paranoid picture
of the world that Nasser judged what seemed to be a new and
serious threat by Israel to Syria. For him what was at stake was
not merely the fate of this particular Baathist regime in Damascus
which he had no special reason to love, nor even only the immediate military security of Egypt. It was rather the morale of
the whole Arab revolutionary nationalist movement that he had
come to symbolize, the readiness of the Arabs to assume mastery

* In June-July 1969, *The Arab*, an official publication of the Arab League
Office in London, published an article by 'A Special Correspondent' who
described himself as having been a United Nations military observer on the
Israel–Syria border at the end of April and the beginning of May 1967
when tension between the two countries was building up. The writer
claimed that he had observed considerable Israeli forces, including dozens
of tanks, moving towards the Syrian border during the first week in May,
movements which the Israelis described as 'manoeuvres'. He said that he
had reported this to the UN headquarters in Jerusalem, whence the reports
were transmitted to New York; by the time the New York headquarters
took the matter up a week later the Israelis had withdrawn again but the
Syrians had already sounded the alarm. The anonymity of the writer and
the place of publication obviously limit the value of the article as evidence,
but its content is circumstantial and has an authentic ring.

of their own fate and to stand up to pressure from the Great Powers. He saw a military humiliation of Syria by Israel as a victory not just for Israel but also for the United States in its supposed design to isolate the UAR, the main powerhouse of Arab nationalism, and to replace Britain as the dominating 'imperialist' influence in the Middle East.

Nasser's reaction to the reports from Israel was prompt and fateful. From 14 May onwards, he began to move Egyptian troops across the Canal into Sinai in increasing numbers. On 16 May he asked the United Nations Emergency Force of 3,400 men from seven nations to withdraw from the posts it had manned along the Sinai frontier with Israel for the previous ten years.

Whatever the practical folly or wisdom of asking the UNEF to leave and the brusque manner in which it was done, there is the still-debated question of whether Nasser was legally within his rights in asking for its departure. U Thant believed he was. As soon as he received a formal request from the UAR government to this effect, which reached him on 18 May, U Thant felt he had no choice but eventually to comply and order the force to withdraw. Could he, as some critics suggested, by more prolonged or adroit delaying tactics, have gained time for diplomacy to slow down the escalation of the crisis, especially as it affected the Gulf of Aqaba? U Thant's strong reasons for thinking otherwise were given in his long report of 26 June 1967. U Thant followed the procedure which had been laid down by his predecessor, Hammarskjöld, and consulted the UN Advisory Committee set up when UNEF was established. The members were divided in their views but agreed in the end that he had no choice but to order withdrawal. The Committee did not, as it could have done, refer the question to the General Assembly. U Thant claims that if this reference had been made it could not have had any early practical result in enabling the UNEF to stay without Egyptian consent – which, in his view, was not possible on either legal or practical grounds.*

* Secretary-General's Report on the withdrawal of UNEF. UN General Assembly document A/6730. Add 3:
The practical reasons were incontrovertible: the UNEF could not have

U Thant had considered making an urgent personal appeal to Nasser to reconsider his request for withdrawal. Nasser sent him a message through his foreign minister advising him that such a move would meet with 'a stern rebuff'. But Nasser agreed that U Thant should come to Cairo as soon as possible. A suggestion by U Thant that UNEF might move on to the Israel side of the border was rejected by Israel as 'entirely unacceptable'. On the evening of 18 May, U Thant ordered the withdrawal of UNEF, though the actual movement of troops right out of Egypt and the Gaza Strip did not begin until 29 May and was not completed until 17 June, after the war was over.

---

continued to operate without Egyptian cooperation and it could not have maintained its position in the face of Egyptian hostility.

Legally and practically the whole basis of its operation was one of Egyptian consent. But the argument about the legality of Nasser's action revolved round the question of whether this basis of consent had been supplemented and qualified by the 'good faith' agreement reached between Hammarskjöld and Nasser when UNEF was introduced into Egypt at the end of 1956. The essence of this agreement was that Nasser accepted the presence of UNEF 'until its tasks were fulfilled'.

But what were the 'tasks' of UNEF in this context? Were they only to supervise the withdrawal of British, French and Israeli forces after the Suez–Sinai war or did they extend in a general way to supervising the observation of the Egyptian–Israeli armistice agreements until a more permanent peace was established? In ten years' practice, they had been accepted as the latter, but while not opposing this interpretation in practice Egypt had never given it her formal endorsement. Those who believed that nevertheless Nasser had broken the 'good faith' agreement quoted in their support an *aide-mémoire* written by Hammarskjöld in 1957 for his private use, setting out his interpretation of his understanding with Nasser. A copy of this *aide-mémoire* was given by Hammarskjöld to Ernest Gross, former member of the American delegation to the UN, who made it public during the controversy over the UNEF withdrawal. U Thant's comment on this paper was, first, that it was a private interpretation and not an official document and had never been shown to the Egyptian government for its comments; second, that it referred to the extended tasks of the UNEF which were assigned to it in February and March 1957 *after* the original 'good faith' agreement had been reached with Nasser in November 1956. U Thant pointed out that he had followed the procedure agreed between Hammarskjöld and Nasser in referring the question of withdrawal to his Advisory Committee. (For a detailed discussion of this and other questions relating to UNEF, see Rosemary Higgins, *United Nations Peace-keeping, 1946–67*, pp. 241–415.)

As U Thant set out for Cairo on 22 May, the Israeli prime minister, Eshkol, was announcing to the Knesset that a partial Israeli mobilization had been carried out to meet the 'grave developments' on Israel's southern border. Eshkol said that in the course of the previous week Egyptian forces in Sinai had been increased from 35,000 to 85,000 men, four divisions of infantry with armour and reinforcements of artillery and aircraft. The Israeli leaders had at first apparently shared the view expressed in other world capitals that the Egyptian move was only a show of force intended to head off a supposed Israeli threat to Syria. As the Egyptian reinforcements continued to pour in, including troops brought in from the Yemen, the Israelis began to take the possibility of Egyptian offensive military action more seriously. But Eshkol assured Egypt and the other Arab states through third parties that Israel had no intention of attacking them and would leave them in peace if they left her in peace.

While U Thant was still on his way to Cairo, Nasser announced the reinstitution of the blockade of Israeli shipping through the Gulf of Aqaba and the crisis entered its second phase. In his speech at Advanced Air Force Headquarters on 22 May, Nasser disclosed that Egyptian forces had occupied Sharm esh-Sheikh and added,

> The Aqaba Gulf constitutes our Egyptian territorial waters. Under no circumstances will we allow the Israeli flag to pass through the Aqaba Gulf. The Jews threatened war. We tell them: You are welcome, we are ready for war. Our armed forces and all our people are ready for war but under no circumstances will we abandon any of our rights. This water is ours.*

*In addition to the legal arguments about the status of the Straits of Tiran already referred to in Chapter 6, the Israeli case had been subsequently reinforced by the 1958 High Seas Convention which defined an international waterway as one connecting High Seas with other High Seas or the territorial waters of a third state. Egypt had not, however, signed this convention. In practice, Israel attached greater significance to the fact that in 1957 the United States and other Western Powers had supported the thesis that the Straits of Tiran were an international waterway and that the US government had pledged its support in ensuring free and innocent passage for Israeli shipping through the Straits. (For a useful summary of the legal arguments on both sides see Rosemary Higgins, *United Nations Peace-keeping* 1946–67, p. 481, fn.)

Had Nasser originally intended to close the Straits of Tiran when he moved into Sinai or was he forced by events to do so? If the latter, when did he make up his mind? Even before the June war broke out, official Egyptian sources were claiming to visiting Western journalists that it had been intended that UNEF should stay at Sharm esh-Sheikh, but that the United Nations Secretary-General had insisted that if UNEF were withdrawn from any part of the area it must be withdrawn everywhere.[11]

Nasser himself made this claim in July 1969 in a talk with me giving his version of the crisis. He repeated it publicly in two newspaper interviews in early 1970. He told me,

> It was not in our plan to close the Gulf of Aqaba at that time. When we moved our troops into Sinai we sent to U Thant asking him to withdraw the UNEF from Rafah to Eilat [the length of the Sinai border] and to keep the UNEF in Gaza and Sharm esh-Sheikh. We decided on this step in order not to face complications about the Gulf of Aqaba. . . . But we received the answer from U Thant in which he said 'either we keep all the UNEF or we withdraw all the UNEF'. I think this was Bunche's idea. . . . There was no choice in front of us except to ask him to withdraw all the UNEF. So we faced suddenly the problem of Sharm esh-Sheikh. It was not in our plan to send troops to Sharm esh-Sheikh and we hastily prepared some troops to go there.

The original story from Cairo was angrily denied in a letter to the *New York Times* on 11 June 1967 by Dr Ralph Bunche, the United Nations Under-Secretary for Political Affairs. There was, he said, 'not a shred of truth to it', and to back up this assertion he quoted from earlier United Nations reports on the Egyptian requests and actual troop movements.

But there remain some curious discrepancies between the version of events given in U Thant's first report of 18 May 1967, and his more comprehensive report of 26 June, after criticism of his handling of the crisis had begun to grow.

In this latter report, U Thant recorded that the Egyptian request for the withdrawal of UNEF was first made in a message from General Fawzi, the UAR chief of staff, to the UNEF commander, Major General Rikhye of India, on the evening of 16 May. The message asked for the withdrawal of 'all UN troops which install OPs [observation posts] along our borders'.

The Egyptian brigadier who delivered the message was said by U Thant to have told Rikhye that he must order the immediate withdrawal of UNEF troops from two localities – Sharm esh-Sheikh and Al Sabha, a key frontier position – so that UAR troops could take over that very night. At noon the next day, after Rikhye had said that he could not withdraw without orders from the UN Secretary-General, General Fawzi asked (according to U Thant's report) for the withdrawal of all the Yugoslav troops who were then manning the posts along the Sinai border, within twenty-four hours, but allowed 'forty-eight hours or so' for withdrawal from Sharm esh-Sheikh. At midday on 18 May, four hours before the Egyptian government's formal request for withdrawal had been received by U Thant, Egyptian officers visited the UNEF camp at Sharm esh-Sheikh (which had a garrison of thirty-two Yugoslavs) and said they had come to take over, demanding a reply within fifteen minutes. (In fact, the UNEF garrison did not leave until several days later.)

In his letter to the *New York Times*, Dr Bunche argued that General Fawzi's demand for the withdrawal of 'all United Nations troops which installed Observation Posts along our borders' unquestionably included Sharm esh-Sheikh 'which was, in fact, a United Nations Observation Post'. The full text of Fawzi's letter suggests, however, that by 'our borders' he meant 'our *eastern* borders', that is those with Israel, to which he refers in the preceding sentence as the area where Egyptian troops were already concentrated: Sharm esh-Sheikh is at the extreme southern tip of Sinai.

U Thant's first report quotes Fawzi's letter in full and also mentions his later statement that the UNEF 'might take forty-eight hours or so' to withdraw from Sharm esh-Sheikh.[12] But it does not mention the verbal demand from the Egyptian brigadier delivering the letter for an immediate withdrawal from Sharm esh-Sheikh, which is quoted in U Thant's second report. Instead, U Thant says,

the exact intent of General Fawzi's letter needed clarification. If it meant the temporary withdrawal of UNEF troops from the line or part of it, it would be unacceptable because the purpose of the United

Nations Force in Gaza and Sinai is to prevent a recurrence of fighting, and it cannot be asked to stand aside in order to enable the two sides to resume fighting. If it was intended to mean a general withdrawal of UNEF from Gaza and Sinai, the communication should have been addressed to the Secretary-General from the Government of the United Arab Republic and not to the Commander of UNEF from the Chief of Staff of the Armed Forces of the United Arab Republic.

U Thant reported that he had informed the UAR government that a request by them

for a temporary withdrawal of UNEF from the Armistice Demarcation Line and the International Frontier, or from any parts of them, would be considered by the Secretary-General as tantamount to a request for the complete withdrawal of UNEF from Gaza and Sinai, since this would reduce the UNEF to ineffectiveness.[13]

In other words, it was at that time by no means as clear to the UN Secretary-General, as Bunche subsequently suggested, whether Nasser was officially asking the UNEF to leave the whole area, including Sharm esh-Sheikh, or only the border with Israel or even only part of the border.

U Thant nevertheless told Nasser that it was all or none: there could be no temporary or partial withdrawal, only a complete one. It was then that Nasser asked for UNEF's complete withdrawal.

These conclusions are further strengthened by a United Nations press release of 3 June explaining the background of U Thant's decision.[14] It refers to the allegation that 'the United Arab Republic first requested only the withdrawal of UNEF from the Line and not from United Arab Republic territory' and says that 'in a practical sense, this is an academic point'. It does not deny the allegation entirely, nor does it refer to the reported verbal request to General Rikhye to evacuate Sharm esh-Sheikh at once. On the contrary, it describes General Fawzi's letter as 'cryptic' and 'unclear in meaning'. It says that the only request considered by U Thant to be official was that which came from the UAR Foreign Minister on 18 May (after U Thant had said 'all or none') and which asked for complete withdrawal.

Apart from the reference to Sharm esh-Sheikh in the verbal

communication said to have been made to the UNEF commander by General Fawzi's emissary, there is sufficient confusion in the sequence of events reported by U Thant to leave open the possibility that Nasser, as he claimed, did not at first intend the UNEF to leave Sharm esh-Sheikh and that he changed his mind after being told that a partial withdrawal was unacceptable. The reports do, however, suggest that if this was Nasser's original intention, he did not make it clear and failed adequately to supervise the execution of his plans by the Egyptian military and diplomatic authorities. General Rikhye's initial impression from his contacts with the Egyptian military was that they were asking for the withdrawal of UNEF from all its posts in Sinai, including Sharm esh-Sheikh, though not from the Gaza Strip.[15]

In his speech of 23 July 1967, Nasser said that before deciding to close the Gulf of Aqaba to Israeli shipping he had discussed the matter with a meeting of the Higher Executive Committee (of the Arab Socialist Union) at his home on 22 May. The closure was 'one of the things our Arab brothers had always insisted on'. But Nasser recognized that it greatly increased the risk of war. He said that when he had concentrated Egyptian forces in Sinai he had estimated the chances of war at twenty per cent. At the meeting which decided to close the Gulf of Aqaba, he had estimated the war chances at fifty per cent, at another meeting at eighty per cent. It was not until the political changes in Israel at the beginning of June that he thought the war risk was 100 per cent. But at the meeting on 22 May only defensive action had been discussed. The aim was to deter an attack on Syria, Nasser claimed; there was no question of attacking Israel if only because Egypt was convinced that the US would intervene to defend Israel.

One report of the testimony given by Vice-President Hussain esh-Shafei at the Cairo treason trials in February 1968 suggests that the possible closure of the Gulf of Aqaba was discussed at the same meeting of Nasser and his colleagues that approved the decision to request the withdrawal of UNEF. It says that Amer gave his full assurance that the armed forces were ready to meet the consequences of both these steps.[16] This suggests that the closure of the Gulf had been considered by Nasser from at least

14 May when he began his military moves in reaction to the supposed Israeli threat to Syria. On the other hand, Egyptian prisoners are said to have told the Israelis that Amer had informed a group of officers on 20 May that it was not intended to close the Gulf of Aqaba.

Nasser told U Thant when the Secretary-General arrived in Cairo on 23 May that he had decided on the Aqaba blockade some time before: he had thought it preferable to announce it before U Thant arrived rather than after he had left. During the talks Nasser assured U Thant that he would not initiate offensive action against Israel. He and his Foreign Minister, Mahmoud Riad, outlined the general Egyptian aim as 'a return to the conditions prevailing prior to 1956' and to full observance by both parties of the Egyptian–Israeli armistice agreement.

U Thant warned Nasser of 'the dangerous consequences which could ensue from restricting innocent passage of ships in the Straits of Tiran' and urged him not to take any precipitate action since Israel had declared that such restrictions would be considered a *casus belli*.[17]

In a rather confused reference to this conversation, Nasser later said that he had agreed to a proposal from U Thant for a 'breathing space' with regard to the Gulf of Aqaba, so there could be time for discussions. The general idea appears to have been that for the time being neither side would take action to force the issue: no Israel ships or strategic cargoes would be sent through the Straits of Tiran and the UAR would not search any ships.[18] The proposition was rejected by Israel and publicly never got beyond a general plea by U Thant for all parties to exercise restraint.

By closing the Gulf of Aqaba and setting himself the aim of re-establishing the situation as it was before 1956, Nasser claimed to be restoring Egypt's sovereign rights that she had been forced to surrender as a result of the Suez–Sinai war. Within a few days he had extended his objectives even further: he was talking of restoring the situation as it was, not before 1956 but before 1948, and of a confrontation with Israel to reopen the whole of the Palestine question.

In a speech to Arab trade unionists on 26 May, Nasser recalled that he had been criticized for waiting to act against Israel, especially over Sharm esh-Sheikh, until the Arabs were strong and prepared, but 'recently we have felt strong enough that if we were to enter a battle with Israel, with God's help we could triumph. On this basis we decided to take actual steps.'

Nasser said that taking over Sharm esh-Sheikh meant confrontation with Israel. Taking such action also meant that we were ready to enter a general war with Israel. It was not a separate operation. ... If Israel embarks on an aggression against Syria or Egypt, the battle against Israel will be a general one ... and our basic objective will be to destroy Israel. I probably could not have said such things five or even three years ago. ... Today, some eleven years after 1956, I say such things because I am confident. I know what we have here in Egypt and what Syria has. I also know that other states – Iraq, for instance – had sent its troops to Syria; Algeria will send troops. Kuwait will also send troops. They will send armoured and infantry units. This is Arab power. This is the true resurrection of the Arab nation, which at one time was probably in despair.[19]

Two days later at a press conference in Cairo, Nasser declared that neither the rights of Egyptian sovereignty over the Tiran Straits nor the issue of the withdrawal of UNEF were any longer open to question. 'Israel's ships shall not pass in Egyptian territorial waters. This is a position from which I shall not budge one inch.' He did not see any hope for negotiating a general settlement of the Palestine problem, but neither did he speak of waging an offensive war to achieve such a settlement.

We have regained the rights which were ours in 1956. ... We have left the next move to Israel. Whether it wants to reply to our exercising our rights with violence or non-violence we are prepared. ... If Israel chooses war, then it is welcome to it.

While taking up an apparently inflexible stand on the Tiran Straits, Nasser had referred only in general terms to the wider issues between the Arabs and Israel. The next day, however, in a speech to members of the UAR National Assembly he spoke of restoring the situation to what it was in 1948.

Now ... we are restoring things to what they were in 1956. This is from the material aspect. In my opinion this material aspect is but a small part, whereas the spiritual aspect is the great side of the issue. The spiritual aspect involves the renaissance of the Arab nation, the revival of the Palestine question, and the restoration of confidence in every Arab and to every Palestinian. This is on the basis that if we were able to restore conditions to what they were before 1956, God will surely help and urge us to restore the situation to what it was in 1948.

We are now ready to confront Israel [Nasser went on]. We are now ready to deal with the entire Palestine question. The issue now at hand is not the Gulf of Aqaba, the Straits of Tiran or the withdrawal of UNEF, but the rights of the Palestinian people. It is the aggression which took place in Palestine in 1948 with the collaboration of Britain and the United States.

Still Nasser did not call for an Arab attack on Israel, though Cairo radio's 'Voice of the Arabs', like other Arab radio stations, was threatening war. On 2 June, he repeated to a British MP, Christopher Mayhew, in a television interview, that he did not intend to attack first. Mayhew asked, 'And if they [Israel] do not attack, will you let them alone?' Nasser answered, 'Yes, we will leave them alone. We have no intention of attacking Israel.'

But other Arab leaders were less restrained; in their talk of war they expressed what Arab public opinion increasingly interpreted Nasser's intentions to be, from the general tenor of his speeches and from the Cairo propaganda broadcasts. The Syrian premier Yusuf Zuayyen in a broadcast speech on 29 May declared, 'We are now on the threshhold of the battle of destiny of all Arab people'. Zuayyen added that the 'economic strangulation' resulting from the Gulf of Aqaba blockade 'will assume its true dimensions when the economic and military installations in the occupied land [Israel] are destroyed preparatory to regaining the usurped Arab right'.[20]

Ahmed esh-Shuqeiri, chairman of the Palestine Liberation Organization, told journalists on 28 May, 'I promise you that zero hour has come. This is the hour our people have been awaiting for the last nineteen years.' In a later press interview in Amman, Shuqeiri was reported to have said that among the Jews who survived the anticipated war those who had lived in Palestine before 1948 would be allowed to stay, but he expected that few would survive.

On 26 May, an article by Heykal in *Al Ahram* declared that 'an armed clash between the UAR and Israel is inevitable'.* Heykal singled out the psychological or morale factor in the balance of power between the Arabs and Israel as decisive. Nasser had set out to challenge and to apply himself Israel's policy of the '*fait accompli*'. The closure of the Gulf of Aqaba meant 'first and last that the Arab nation represented by the UAR has succeeded for the first time, *vis-à-vis* Israel, in changing by force a *fait accompli* imposed on it by force'. 'Therefore it is not a matter of the Gulf of Aqaba but of something bigger. It is the whole philosophy of Israeli security.' Hence, concluded Heykal, 'Israel must resort to arms'. But Egypt must wait for Israel to strike the first blow. 'Let Israel begin. Let our second blow then be ready. Let it be a knock-out.'

Why did Nasser decide to broaden the aim of his operations from the deterrence of attack against Syria to a revision of the political *status quo* or a change in the balance of power even at the risk of almost certain war? Probably the main reason is that, trusting in the assurances from his military commanders, he re-assessed and over-estimated his military bargaining power. According to Heykal, 'some of us [the Egyptian leadership] were dazzled by the spectacle of the force we moved into Sinai between May 15th and May 20th'.[21]

In a later post-mortem on the war, Heykal blamed the military command for having 'overestimated its own strength and under-estimated the enemy's'. It had made another 'fatal mistake' in sending more forces into Sinai as a demonstration of strength without being really ready for action. 'Many in the armed forces GHQ,' added Heykal, 'believed the crisis would not go so far as the use of arms. They believed this in spite of the clear warnings of the highest authorities.'[22]

In other words, Nasser was telling the armed forces to be ready for war. But did he believe that the UAR was now strong enough to launch and win an offensive war against Israel? In view of the lack of coordination which still then existed between the Arab

---

*At that date this was not yet Nasser's opinion – or so Heykal told me in July 1969.

armies, particularly with Jordan and Syria, and the possibility of American intervention on Israel's side if she were the victim of attack, it seems improbable.

However much Nasser may have been misled by his over-confident military advisers or dazzled by the armoured divisions he mustered in Sinai, it is unlikely that he thought in such ambitious terms, or that he was simply concerned to lure Israel into a first strike so that he could then overwhelm her. He claimed later,

> Our estimates of the enemy's strength were precise. They showed us that our armed forces had reached a level of equipment and training at which they were capable of *deterring and repelling the enemy* [author's italic]. We realized that the possibility of an armed attack existed, and we accepted the risk.[23]

Israel's reaction to the closure of the Gulf of Aqaba was immediate and vigorous, and within three days both the United States and Russia were fully alarmed at the possibility of war. On 23 May Eshkol declared that any restrictions on Israeli shipping or cargoes destined for Israel in other ships passing through the Gulf would be 'an act of aggression against Israel'. In a statement to the Knesset he claimed that Israel had the right under article 51 of the United Nations Charter – the right of self-defence – to take any measures needed to ensure free and innocent passage through the Straits of Tiran. The same day the Israeli military leaders, who previously had taken the Egyptian move into Sinai calmly, began to urge the Israeli government to authorize immediate military action.[24]

The Knesset endorsed Eshkol's declaration about the Straits by eighty-nine votes to four, unanimously except for four Communist votes. It thus set on foot the beginning of a movement for a 'wall to wall' national unity government. But the cabinet and the parties were divided about the risks of an immediate resort to arms. Partly influenced perhaps by a message from Washington urging that no attempt should be made to force the Egyptian blockade during the next forty-eight hours, the Israeli government decided to try diplomacy first. It sent the Foreign Minister, Abba Eban, to Washington via Paris and London.

On the same day President Johnson issued a statement saying that

the purported closing of the Gulf of Aqaba to Israeli shipping has brought a new and grave dimension to the crisis. The United States considers the gulf to be an international waterway and feels that a blockade of Israeli shipping is illegal and potentially disastrous to the cause of peace. The right of free innocent passage of the international waterway is a vital interest of the international community.

Johnson also called for a reduction in troop concentrations and said the US was 'firmly committed to the support of the political independence and territorial integrity of all the nations of the area'.

The Soviet government took longer to appreciate the new dangers of the situation. In a statement on 23 May it blamed the crisis on Israeli designs on Syria and supported Nasser's action in moving into Sinai and dislodging UNEF. It added, 'should anyone try to unleash aggression in the Near East, he would be met not only with the united strength of the Arab countries but also with strong opposition to aggression from the Soviet Union and all peace-loving states'.

But the Soviet statement did not mention the Gulf of Aqaba. The Russians later, after the war, let it be known through journalistic channels that they had not been consulted by Nasser about his reinstitution of the blockade. At the time when the Security Council was called to discuss the question on 24 May, the Soviet delegate blocked any serious discussion either in the Council or among the four Great Powers, as suggested by President de Gaulle. On 25 May, the Egyptian Minister for War, Shams ed-din Badran, arrived in Moscow at the head of a delegation, for talks with the Russians. On 28 May Badran brought Nasser a message from the Soviet premier Kosygin saying that 'the USSR supported us in this battle and would not allow any power to intervene until matters were restored to what they were in 1956'.[25] If Nasser's version of the message is correct, the Russians had committed themselves at least to blocking any military intervention by the Western Powers to break the blockade of the Straits of Tiran or restore UNEF to its positions in

Sinai and the Gaza Strip. At the same time, Russia delivered urgent warnings to both Nasser and to Eshkol against launching a military attack. According to French sources, the Russians told the Egyptians and Syrians through their ambassadors in Moscow not only that they would not support them if they attacked Israel and so risked confronting the United States as well, but also that they would not give the two Arab states military support in the event of an attack by Israel alone.[26] There is no evidence that Nasser asked for or wanted Soviet military help in the latter case. Although he constantly claimed that behind Israel stood the real culprit, the United States, he had no wish to see a clash with Israel transformed into a conflict between the super-Powers in which the Middle East countries would surely be destroyed: he saw Soviet support as the means of staving off American intervention – but only if he did not attack first, a vital proviso which was to influence his position in the later stages of the crisis.

The Soviet warnings to Nasser and Eshkol in the early hours of 27 May may have been prompted by reports that both Egypt and Israel believed an attack by the other was imminent. Nasser's speech and Heykal's article of the previous day may also have helped to stimulate greater alarm in Moscow. On that day, too, amid rumours of imminent war, President Johnson received Eban in Washington. Johnson promised Eban that the United States would uphold the pledge given by Eisenhower in 1957 to support Israel's right of 'free and innocent passage' through the Gulf of Aqaba. Johnson believed that Egypt was neither willing nor able to launch a full-scale attack; but he had been advised that Israel might attack, and that if she did so she could quickly defeat not only Egypt but any combination of Arab states. The President is reported to have urged Israel to hold her hand for at least a fortnight to allow time for international action to achieve a peaceful settlement.

Parallel with action through the Security Council and consultation with Russia, the United States had begun to explore the possibility of joint action by maritime nations to secure the recognition of free passage through the Gulf of Aqaba. The first move was to try to obtain signatures from the maritime powers to a declaration upholding freedom of passage, and the second was to canvass support for an international naval force to escort ships through the Straits of Tiran and the Gulf, what became known as 'The Red Sea Regatta'. At the same time the American administration began exploring with Nasser the possibilities of a negotiated settlement. It sent a senior State Department official, Charles Yost, a former ambassador in Damascus, to Cairo where the American ambassador, Richard Nolte, was an inexperienced new arrival. President Johnson also later sent a special envoy, Robert Anderson, a former Secretary of the Treasury, to see Nasser.

The immediate aim of the Great Powers was to prevent either side launching the first attack. President de Gaulle, as well as Johnson and Kosygin, had warned both Israel and Egypt against shooting first. The increasing fears of either side that the other might strike the first blow ushered in the third stage of the crisis. The Israeli military were pressing ever more strongly for quick action, arguing that every day's delay would mean more Israeli casualties in a war that had become inevitable. When the Israeli cabinet met during the night of 27–8 May to hear Eban's report on his Washington visit, it was evenly divided on the question of whether to attack or await the outcome of diplomacy. Eshkol was inclined to go to war but, after receiving an urgent message from Johnson warning against military action, he decided not to force the issue with his colleagues. On 28 May the Israeli cabinet agreed to wait and Eshkol replied to Johnson on that basis. But there was growing pressure from Israeli public opinion for a more militant policy and for a more vigorous leadership, which crystallized round the symbolic martial figure of Major-General Dayan. Just as the military mobilization on each side set up a fatal spiral of suspicion and fear, so the movements of public sentiment and their political consequences in both Israel and the Arab states reinforced each other. Together they generated an accelerating rush towards war. Signs that the Arabs were closing their ranks led to a new political unity in Israel. This in turn increased Arab belief that war was inevitable.

The most spectacular development was the sudden decision of King Hussein on 30 May to fly to Cairo and sign a joint defence agreement with his old enemy, Nasser, under which Jordan's armed forces were to be under the command of an Egyptian general. Two battalions of Egyptian paratroops were flown to Jordan. Perhaps more surprising and more alarming to the Israeli public, Hussein also took back to Jordan with him Ahmed esh-Shuqeiri, the chairman of the Palestine Liberation Organization.

The military link-up between Egypt, Jordan and Syria could not have made any significant difference to the military balance for some time to come. It would have taken time for effective cooperation between the three countries to be established. But the threat of encirclement, however ineffective in the short run, was enough to stir deep public emotions in Israel. It convinced the majority of Israelis that the Arabs were preparing to attack and it undermined the arguments of those among the Israeli leaders who still advocated waiting until diplomacy had been given its chance to deal with the Straits of Tiran. On 1 June, the day after the Jordan agreement, a new Israel government of national unity was formed with Dayan as Minister of Defence and including Menahem Beigin as Minister without Portfolio. Nasser later said that it was the formation of this government that made him believe that war had become 100 per cent certain.

During the next four days diplomacy fought a losing battle with public passions and military fears. As the Arab and Israeli armies faced each other in growing strength the original cause of dispute, the blockade of the Gulf of Aqaba, became overshadowed by the fear of the military on each side that they might lose advantage by delay or that the other might gain advantage by striking first. This was particularly felt on the Israeli side: Israel's strategy was based on a swift offensive; time could only weaken the favourable balance of power she still enjoyed.

On 2 June Yigal Allon, the influential Minister of Labour in the Israeli cabinet, said in a speech in Tel Aviv that war was inevitable unless the Gulf of Aqaba were reopened, and unless there were a mutual reduction of the forces massed on the border and a clear undertaking by the Arab governments to stop guerrilla raids. He added, 'There is not the slightest doubt about the outcome of this war and of each of its stages, and we are not forgetting the Jordanian and the Syrian fronts either.'[27]

The public mood in Israel was to get the ordeal over with rather than wait for what seemed either an inevitable Arab attack or a slow strangulation. In Cairo the mood, as described by an American diplomat who was there, was

an odd mixture of exaltation and fatalism, exaltation over what had been achieved, fatalism before the inescapable realization that Israel might prefer war to a political defeat of this magnitude. There was a clear understanding that Israel might attack at any time, no overweening confidence as to the outcome, but a determination to defend, whatever the costs, the intoxicating gains which had been won.[28]

In Nasser's view of the situation during the first few days of June there were contradictions. Though he thought an Israeli attack inevitable, he still hoped that he could secure at least some political gain through negotiation rather than war. He had promised both Moscow and Washington that he would not strike first. He believed that America had been egging Israel on to attack Syria, with himself as the ultimate target; at the same time he expected that in the final stages American pressure could stop Israel from attacking. He misunderstood the relationship between Israel and Washington, and under-estimated the readiness and ability of the Israelis, especially the Dayan generation, to go it alone. It was his second serious miscalculation in addition to his over-optimistic picture of Egyptian military power.

Because of his belief that Israel was simply an instrument of the United States, he later saw the failure of Washington to restrain Israel, while urging Egypt to negotiate, as a 'diplomatic trick'. But in the same speech in which he blamed the United States for a planned 'deception', he said, 'It was quite clear on any political calculation that Israel was bound to take military action, especially after Iraqi forces had moved and Jordan had joined the joint defence agreement'.[29]

The United States and Britain had meanwhile been drafting the declaration on freedom of passage through the Gulf of Aqaba as an international waterway and of measures needed to ensure it. They hoped to get the declaration signed by as many 'Maritime Powers' as possible. Few of the 'Maritime Powers' friendly to the United States seemed ready to sign the declaration.

Even fewer considered joining in a naval blockade-breaking operation. Nor were the Pentagon or the Congress enthusiastic about an American military commitment in the Middle East while the Vietnam war was still raging.

The American administration was also pursuing the possibility of a settlement negotiated directly with Nasser. On 31 May Nasser had talks in Cairo with President Johnson's special envoy, Robert Anderson. They agreed that Nasser should send his Vice-President, Zacharia Mohieddin, to Washington to see Johnson, while Vice-President Humphrey would come to Cairo for talks with Nasser.

Was Nasser prepared for a compromise? On 4 June, on the eve of war, he said that he would consider any declaration by the Maritime Powers about the Gulf of Aqaba as 'a transgression of our sovereignty' and as 'a preliminary to an act of war'. There were some hints from Arab sources at the time, repeated more strongly after the war, that Nasser might have been prepared to let non-Israeli ships through the Straits of Tiran, though still barring Israeli flag vessels. Apart from the question of whether Israel would ever have accepted such an arrangement, there was also the vital point of whether or not Nasser would allow through oil shipments, which formed the most important inward cargoes to Eilat, even in non-Israeli ships. An indication that the United States and Britain were considering some such compromise at least as an interim solution came during the talks in Washington between Harold Wilson and President Johnson on 2 June. Both American and British official sources let it be known to journalists privately that they estimated that only some two to four Israeli ships of any size had in fact passed through the Straits of Tiran during the previous two years. This information apparently came from the United Nations secretariat among other sources.[30] Wilson also referred to his press conference in Washington to the small number of Israeli ships involved. These reports were quickly denied by Israeli officials who claimed that Israeli ships had been running a regular service from Eilat to Africa and the Far East, passing through the Gulf of Aqaba two or three times a week.

Both the reports and the denials may have been true in the sense that only two or three Israeli ships were involved in the traffic, though they made regular runs, compared with a much larger number of non-Israeli vessels, chiefly oil tankers. How or what Nasser would have negotiated must remain a matter of speculation. According to Heykal, he was prepared to refer the question of whether or not the Straits of Tiran were an 'international waterway' to the World Court.[31] But it seems probable that he would have tried to extend the scope of any talks beyond the immediate question of the Gulf of Aqaba to other aspects of the Arab–Israeli problem. For any points he gave away over the blockade, where he felt in a strong position, he might have tried to get compensation on other matters, such as the Syrian demilitarized zone and the Jordan headwaters, or the Palestine Arab refugees.

While ready to talk, Nasser was also preparing for war. On 2 June, the day he informed President Johnson that he would send Zacharia Mohieddin to Washington, Nasser attended a meeting of all the senior officers of the UAR armed forces at the Supreme Command Headquarters. He told them (he said later) that 'we must expect the enemy to strike a blow within forty-eight to seventy-two hours and no later on the basis of the indications of events and developments'. He added that he 'expected the aggression to take place on Monday 5 June and the first blow to be struck at our Air Force'.[32]

Nasser was under something of the same pressure as Eshkol from his military men to strike the first blow as war began to seem inevitable. According to Shams ed-din Badran at his trial for treason in February 1968, the Egyptian air force commander, General Mohammed Sidky Mahmoud, had wanted to strike first against Israel, since a first blow by Israel would mean the destruction of twenty per cent of the Egyptian air force. He was told by Amer that an Egyptian first strike was impossible because it would lead to United States intervention.[33] Nasser claimed that he had never considered launching an offensive war against Israel because of his conviction that the United States would intervene to implement the guarantee of Israel's borders given by President Kennedy and repeated by President Johnson.[34]

Officially the Israeli government was still committed to its promise to Johnson not to attack for a fortnight as from 26 May

– that is at least until 9 June. The final decision of the Israeli government not to wait any longer but to attack immediately was taken at a cabinet meeting which began on the evening of 3 June and continued the next morning. According to one authority, the Israeli military were urging that no more time be lost and the 'last straw' was the announcement on 4 June that Iraq had joined the Egyptian–Syrian–Jordanian military pact.[35] Though this may have increased the 'backs-to-the-wall' feeling of the Israeli public, there is some doubt as to whether the accession of either Jordan or Iraq to the pact or even the danger of an Egyptian first strike were really decisive arguments for the Israeli leaders against waiting another few days, especially for the military, highly confident of their strength and capacity. Perhaps at least as important were the signs that another few days might bring, not an Arab offensive, but the beginning of a diplomatic negotiation between Nasser and the United States. Israeli envoys returning from Washington through London brought disturbing reports of Western weakness and readiness for 'appeasement'. One such envoy was the head of the Israeli Intelligence Services, Brigadier Amit, who, suspicious of Eban's report of his talks with the Americans, went to Washington 'to find out for himself'. His report to the government is said to have 'played an important part in the later stages of the debate on war or peace'.[36] From his opposite number in Washington Brigadier Amit may perhaps have gained the impression, like the killers of Thomas â Becket from the thinking-out-loud of King Henry, that a swift military victory by Israel would, in the Pentagon's view, save the United States a lot of trouble.

Given the way American and British policy seemed to be drifting, the neutral attitude of France and the hostility of Russia, a negotiation with Nasser would doubtless have seemed to the Israeli leaders bound to end in a political defeat for them. They would then be forced to choose between making concessions or attacking at a time when the enemy was better prepared and when they themselves could expect less sympathy from world opinion. They faced a problem similar to that of Eden when, as time passed after the Suez nationalization and the pressures for a diplomatic compromise increased, he saw his chance of decisively reversing Nasser's *fait accompli* about to slip through his fingers. It is true that an interruption of shipping to Eilat, though damaging, would no more be fatal to the Israel economy than even the closure of the Suez Canal proved to be for Britain. But for the Israelis, as for Eden, it was a wider question of a power relationship. For the Israeli leaders the choice seemed clear. It was between an unexpected opportunity to strike a blow which could cripple Nasser's growing military forces – the only Arab forces they were seriously concerned about – for years to come, or of accepting the beginning of a change in the balance of power in which, at each stage, Israel would be in a weaker position to resist pressure for further concessions. They saw themselves in the position of Czechoslovakia dealing with the Nazis at the time of Munich. Faced with what they believed to be the threat of eventual complete conquest, it was better to fight sooner from strength rather than later from a weaker position. This was an understandable analysis, given the assumptions made by the Israeli government about the rightness and necessity of the position they were defending – the political and territorial *status quo* as it had existed in the ten years after the Sinai campaign. Where the wisdom of Israeli policy may be more justly questioned is in the failure to recognize that the *status quo* itself was inherently dangerous and unstable, not because Arabs were vengeful fanatics but because Israel had long been attempting by a military *tour de force* to maintain a situation which imposed serious human and practical disabilities on her Arab neighbours. The real question was whether or not Israel would have been wiser to use her military power to support a search for a more stable compromise settlement, rather than to rely on maintaining military supremacy alone.

In a curiously similar way, both the Israeli leaders and Nasser felt in this crisis that their future national existence was at stake, not as matter of immediate physical survival (though that was how it appeared to the Israeli public) but as expressed in a political, historical and moral concept. The challenge was not to the lives of all Jews or all Arabs, but to the idea of their self-respect and national identity, of their relations with the rest of the world and with each other, which was embodied in the concepts of Zionism and Arab nationalism. A defeat for Israel might mean an end to the great attempt to break away through Zionist nationalism from the position of defenceless subservience in which Jews had been forced to exist in the Gentile world. Nasser feared a defeat for Arab nationalism which was intended to throw the Arabs back, through the instrument of Israel, into a servile dependence on Western imperialism reincarnated in the United States. Both Nasser and the Israelis saw themselves as taking a desperate stand, like a long-tormented schoolboy finally turning and facing a bully. The fullness of the tragedy of the war that began on 5 June 1967 lies in the fact that two great peoples, who were both trying to escape from the humiliations inflicted by European society, were unable to help each other but instead were thrown by historical fate at each other's throats.

Chapter 18

The Six-Day War: 'The Setback', 5–11 June 1967

The third Arab–Israeli war began at 8.45 A.M. (Cairo time) on Monday 5 June 1967. It was virtually won by Israel within the first three hours, perhaps even in the first few minutes. But before it ended, six days later, there was much hard fighting and thousands of lives were lost.

Israel's victory, or what the Arabs euphemistically called 'The Setback', was a brilliant feat of arms.

Israel opened her offensive with an all-out attack on Egypt's airfields. In three hours of incessant raids, the Egyptian air force was wiped out on the ground and the Egyptian army in Sinai was left without air cover in the ensuing land battles. Out of some 340 serviceable Egyptian combat aircraft, 286 machines, including all the Egyptian medium bombers, were destroyed during the first day's assault. The runways on most of the airfields attacked were made unuseable. The Israeli air force threw almost all its 320 combat planes, half of them bombers or fighter-bombers, into the attack, leaving less than a dozen planes to guard its own bases. It had trained intensively for this preemptive strike, with the help of excellent intelligence. It also used a new weapon a special bomb to destroy airfield runways.[1] But, more important, it achieved complete surprise by a variety of tactics. Some of its planes swept in over the sea from the unexpected direction of the west; others flew low behind the Sinai mountains to beat the Egyptian radar and anti-aircraft missiles; and the first attack was timed when the Egyptian pilots were relaxing on the ground after returning from their dawn patrols (though their planes were dispersed at maximum readiness).

Both the air attack and the land offensive which began half an hour later were also timed – perhaps with foreknowledge, since the Israelis had probably cracked the Egyptian military code – to catch almost the entire Egyptian High Command literally up in the air. At 9 A.M. on 5 June, Field Marshal Amer, the UAR commander-in-chief, and his air force commander, General

Sidky Mahmoud, together with other senior officers were in an aircraft flying from Cairo to an airfield in Sinai. The Egyptian anti-aircraft batteries had been given orders not to fire without special authorization while they were in the air. They could not land in Sinai because all the airfields were under attack and were thus obliged to return to Cairo. For ninety vital minutes they were out of touch with their forces and unable to give orders. To make matters worse, the senior Egyptian field commanders in Sinai had left their command posts to go to the airfield to greet Amer.[2]

After the first Israeli attack on the advanced airfields in Sinai, ten minutes' delay in reporting the attack – due partly perhaps to the traditional Egyptian reluctance to tell bad news to superiors – gave the Israelis time to reach the more distant bases undetected.[3]

The Egyptian High Command was slow to realize the scale of the air disaster and its significance for the land battle. Because it believed its own exaggerated figures for Israeli planes shot down it thought there was still a balance in air power during the second day of the Sinai battles.[4] None of the generals dared at first tell Nasser the full extent of the Israeli blow and he did not learn of it until four o'clock on Monday afternoon.[5] When he welcomed Jordan's entry into the war that morning he thought he still had an air force. When the truth about the destruction of the Egyptian air force could no longer be hidden, at least from Nasser and the government, the air force and the military command tried to explain it away by accusing America and Britain of having shared in the first attack. The original source of this canard seems to have been the Egyptian air force.[6] The accusation was fed by the prevailing bewilderment and confusion. There seemed to be many more planes attacking than the Israelis were thought to possess. Nasser claimed on 9 June that 'the enemy was operating with an air force three times stronger than his normal force'. This impression was probably due to the large number of sorties flown by each Israeli aircraft, as a result of efficient ground organization. Then there was a report that Jordanian radar had detected a large number of planes coming in from the sea to attack Jordan, which could not be Israeli. Just before dawn on Tuesday 6 June, Hussein telephoned Nasser to say 400 aircraft were attacking Jordan. The two leaders then agreed to announce that American and British aircraft were helping the Israelis. The result was a wave of anti-American and anti-British anger throughout the Arab countries, the breaking off of diplomatic relations with Britain and the United States by several Arab countries and the suspension of oil shipments to the two countries by Kuwait, Iraq and Algeria. According to a later Egyptian admission, though 'there were indications that Israel had received extensive aid from the United States' [such as, it was alleged, details of Egyptian airfields, photographed by US spy satellites] 'there was no evidence to show that the US Air Force itself had taken part in the air raids on the Egyptian airfields'.[7] At the time Nasser was ready to believe in Anglo-American intervention because of his conviction that America and Israel were hand-in-glove against Syria and the UAR, and because of the experience of Suez.

By the time Nasser had learned of the loss of his air force, he knew that the Egyptian army was already hard pressed in the land battles in Sinai and would be obliged to withdraw. But he thought that it could still hold a line across Sinai covering the Suez Canal.[8]

The Egyptians had seven divisions, two of them armoured, or about 100,000 men in Sinai and the Gaza Strip. (The total mobilized strength of the Egyptian army was about 180,000 men but some 50,000 were in the Yemen.)[9] They had some seven or eight hundred tanks in Sinai, half of them spread among the five infantry divisions, one of which, in the Gaza Strip, was composed of troops of the Palestine Liberation Army. The main Egyptian forces were in strongly fortified defensive positions covering the two main roads across Sinai to the Canal; in the Rafah–El Arish area in the north, defending the coastal road and railway to Kantara; and in the Abu Agheila area farther south, covering the central Sinai road to Ismailia. An Egyptian armoured division was held in reserve in the Bir Gifgafa area, defending the road from Abu Agheila. A small armoured force farther south covered the Nakhl and Thamad areas on the routes into Sinai from Eilat and the frontier post of Kuntilla.

It was in the latter sector and in the centre that the Israelis had begun their assault in the 1956 campaign. This time they attacked first in the north, directing their main thrust against Rafah, the hinge between the Gaza Strip and Egypt proper, and El Arish. Their plan was to break through the two main Egyptian defence positions there and at Abu Agheila. They would then advance rapidly towards the Sinai mountains east of the Canal in order to cut off the Egyptian escape routes. Finally they would complete the destruction of the Egyptian army in Sinai and occupy Sharm esh-Sheikh.

For this task the Israeli command had allocated three divisional groups, of about 45,000 men, highly mobile, and most of the Israeli armour. The number of Israeli tanks engaged in Sinai was probably about the same as the Egyptian: in some respects they were superior in equipment, the 105-mm gun on the British Centurion tanks, for example, having greater range and penetrating power than the guns of the Egyptians' Soviet-made tanks. The Israeli tank crews and commanders certainly proved better-trained and more enterprising than the Egyptians. The Israeli army had a total mobilized strength of some 260,000. While its main weight was thrown against Egypt, always considered the most serious enemy, the rest of the long frontier with Jordan, Syria and the Lebanon was held with comparatively light forces.

Although they were inferior in overall numbers in the Sinai campaign, the Israelis, more mobile and holding the initiative, were able by better tactics and concentration to secure local superiority in numbers at key points on the battlefield. They had the crucial advantage of air supremacy after the first few hours. It was a devastating air bombardment which paved the way for the most important Israeli breakthrough in the north against the powerful Egyptian defences at Rafah. Here the Egyptians put up a stubborn and courageous resistance and suffered heavy losses. By the end of the first day the Israelis had almost destroyed the Egyptian Seventh Division in the Rafah area. They had cut off the Gaza Strip and captured the key supply base and road and rail junction of El Arish. They had also broken into the first defences of Abu Agheila, and begun to encircle it from the rear. Farther south another Israeli force had begun to advance across the frontier at Kuntilla.

The loss of its air force had a demoralizing effect on the Egyptian High Command. It seemed a repetition of 1956 when the Egyptian air force had been wiped out by British bombers, leaving the army in Sinai to face the Israeli offensive without air cover. There was a breakdown in communications, confusion of authority and conflicting orders. When Nasser went to the High Command headquarters he found Amer personally directing the battle operations, instead of leaving them to the chief of staff, General Mahmoud Fawzi, and the field commander, General Mortagi, as had been planned.[10] He had either to dismiss Amer that day or let him continue. He agreed with Amer that withdrawal was essential but left the details to him.

At six o'clock on Tuesday morning, Amer issued an order for an immediate general withdrawal from the whole of Sinai to the west bank of the Canal. In 1956 it was Nasser who had insisted on withdrawal against the wishes of the over-optimistic military command, on the grounds that the forces must be preserved to defend Egypt proper against the main impending attack from the British and French. This time Nasser argued that a precipitate withdrawal was not necessary. Supported by General Fawzi, he believed the withdrawal must be spread over several nights to avoid a rout and that a stand could be made at the mountain passes in Sinai, at Mitla and Bir Gifgafa. When he heard of Amer's order for a general retreat, he went to the High Command and over-ruled it. The Fourth Armoured Division already under orders to withdraw was told to return to Sinai, but before General Fawzi had completed his new plans for a withdrawal over four nights, Amer had countermanded Nasser's instructions and repeated his own orders for a general withdrawal immediately. During the initial battles it was in any case difficult for the Egyptians to disengage and withdraw in good order. The indecision and confusion of the command increased the difficulties. Operations continued to be directed from Cairo instead of from field headquarters along lines of command 'that existed only on paper'. The atmosphere at the Cairo headquarters was 'like a terrifying nightmare',[11] as the High Command was swept by alternative waves of pessimism and optimism, now ordering a withdrawal across the Canal and then changing its mind. The result was a disorganized race for the Sinai mountain passes in which the Egyptian army suffered its main catastrophe when two divisions collided chaotically with each other and were destroyed by air attack.

There was little cause for any optimism on Nasser's part about the prospects of help for the Egyptians from the other Arab states or from their other friends and allies. It is true that, in contrast with 1956, Egypt was not fighting alone. Jordan and Syria had entered the war, and an Iraqi division was on its way to the Jordan front; Morocco, Algeria, Sudan, Kuwait and Saudi Arabia had promised troops; a few Algerian jet fighters and advance army units had actually arrived in Egypt. But all these forces were weak and incapable of being organized in time to have any serious effect on the course of the Israeli blitzkrieg in Sinai. Jordan's army of some 55,000 men and 250 tanks had to defend a frontier of 385 miles. It was largely dependent on Egypt for air cover, for the Jordan air force had only twenty-four jet fighters. When the war began King Hussein decided to honour the military alliance he had made with Nasser less than a week before. Jordan aircraft made one or two minor raids on Natanya and on an Israeli airfield, and Jordanian artillery began a bombardment of Israeli Jerusalem. The Israel prime minister, Eshkol, sent a message to Hussein through the United Nations truce supervisor, General Odd Bull, warning him against entering the war and promising that if Jordan did not engage in serious hostilities Israel would not attack her. But even if Hussein had wished to hold back, it is doubtful if he could have done so. Such was the pressure of Arab public feeling that if he had tried to keep out of the war, he would have lost control of both his army and his throne. Moreover, if Israel were successful in her assault on Egypt, Jordan would in any case be left more than ever at Israel's mercy.

As the Jordan shelling continued and Jordan troops occupied the neutral territory of Government House on the outskirts of Jerusalem which housed the UNTSO headquarters, the Israelis moved into the attack. Having completed their destruction of the Egyptian air force, their planes turned at midday of 5 June on the Jordanian, Iraqi and Syrian air bases. The entire Jordan air force was quickly wiped out and fifty-two Syrian and nine Iraqi planes destroyed. The Israeli army then began an improvised offensive against Jordanian positions round Jerusalem and farther north round Jenin. The Jordanians fought back stubbornly, and held on to their main positions until dawn on Tuesday 6 June when heavy Israeli air attacks shattered their formations and began to wipe out their armoured columns and supply convoys.

Syria's first contribution to the war was a series of minor air raids on the Haifa oil refinery and other targets and the shelling of Israeli border settlements in Upper Galilee, followed on 6 June by three unsuccessful ground attacks in battalion strength against three of these settlements. Apart from these small-scale forays, the Syrian army, with a force of nine brigades, two of them armoured, in the frontier area, sat tight in its Maginot Line-type defences on the Golan Heights.

As in 1956, Nasser had to deal with a complex diplomatic situation at the same time as a military crisis. This time, though no Great Power was directly engaged in hostilities against him, the United States and Russia were not pushing in altogether the same direction, except in their common desire not to let the war escalate to a point where they might themselves become involved. Moscow's support for Nasser did not go beyond ensuring that there was no American military intervention (whatever Nasser may have thought about American air intervention the Russians did not believe it), together with verbal threats to Israel and diplomatic backing for Egypt at the United Nations.

A statement issued from Moscow demanded that Israel should stop immediately and unconditionally all military operations against the Arab states and warned that the Soviet Union reserved the right 'to take all steps that may be necessitated by the situation'. One step was for the Soviet premier, Kosygin, to contact President Johnson over the 'hot line' about joint action to bring about a cease-fire. General de Gaulle was also in contact with the Russians over his own 'hot line'. He suggested a four-Power meeting on the Middle East and suspended French arms deliveries to both sides in the war, a blow to the Israelis whose aircraft were nearly all French. He had warned the Israelis as well as Egypt not to fire the first shot.

Britain favoured urgent action through the United Nations to secure a cease-fire. But when this action began in the Security

Council on the first morning of the war, the divergences between the two super-Powers began to appear. The Soviet Union, supported by India and a number of other Afro-Asian states, called for a cease-fire linked with a condemnation of Israeli aggression and a demand that Israeli forces be withdrawn to their original positions. The resolution was based on the conviction that the Israelis had begun the fighting and that a cease-fire without withdrawal would leave her in possession of territory gained by aggression. The United States, backed by Britain, urged a cease-fire without conditions. Alternatively, the American delegate, Mr Arthur Goldberg, argued that if there were to be a call for withdrawal to the *status quo ante*, then it should be to the position not simply before 5 June but before 16 May when Nasser asked the United Nations Emergency Force to leave. This would have meant Nasser's accepting the return of UNEF and the lifting of the blockade of the Gulf of Aqaba. The United States made it plain that it considered that, whether or not Israel had fired the first shot, the origins of the crisis lay in Nasser's action in removing the UNEF and above all in closing the Straits of Tiran. It was therefore not prepared to put pressure on Israel to move back behind its borders unless Nasser's actions were also reversed. Nasser at first preferred to fight on rather than accept these conditions or an unconditional cease-fire. It was possibly an unwise decision, in view of the subsequent Israeli gains before the cease-fire was agreed upon. It is unlikely, however, that the Israelis, who had counted on a three-day campaign to reach their main objectives before any effective international intervention, would have been deterred from fully exploiting their victory before accepting the cease-fire. Thus the first day ended with the battle still raging in Sinai and a diplomatic stalemate in New York.

Over the next twenty-four hours the Arab position deteriorated rapidly. During the night of 5/6 June, the Israelis overcame the last Egyptian resistance at Rafah and captured the main defences of Abu Agheila after a seven-hour battle. The fortified positions at Abu Agheila were held by four Egyptian infantry battalions with ninety tanks and six regiments of artillery.[12] Against them the Israelis concentrated some 10,000 men including an armoured brigade, a regiment of tanks, six regiments of artillery and a parachute battalion which was landed by helicopter in the rear of the Egyptian positions.[13] The fighting was fierce and there were heavy casualties on both sides.

By early Tuesday morning, 6 June, the Israelis, with the help of their air power, had begun to break into the Jordan front, capturing Jenin and part of Arab Jerusalem. In the course of the day the Israelis completed their occupation of the Gaza Strip, pushed on past El Arish down the coast road towards the Suez Canal and farther south regrouped their forces for the next phase – an advance to cut off the two main Egyptian escape routes through Bir Gifgafa and the Mitla Pass.

The Egyptians still had two infantry divisions and two armoured divisions intact in Sinai, but the main Egyptian fixed defences had been smashed and the Israelis were complete masters of the air. Contradictory orders from the headquarters in Cairo and the failure of some of the field commanders added to the confusion wrought by the Israeli break-through. The relentless harassment from the Israeli air force continued through this and the next two days. When on Tuesday, 6 June, the Egyptian Fourth Armoured Division was ordered to withdraw from Sinai it had not yet taken any part in the fighting. After it was ordered to go back at once to Sinai, as a result of Nasser's intervention, it went into battle without its commander who had gone to Cairo. This division lost three-quarters of its equipment but less than half a per cent of its men.[14]

At the subsequent trial of the commander of the Third Infantry Division, Major-General Osman Nasser, it was alleged that his division, without its commander, took a wrong line of retreat and became entangled with the columns of a motorized infantry division withdrawing through the Mitla Pass and the two divisions became an easy target for air attack.[15]

By the evening of 6 June it was clear that on both the Egyptian and Jordanian fronts any further fighting could only mean greater losses of men and territory for the Arabs. So at the United Nations the Russians abandoned their attempt to attach conditions to a cease-fire. The Security Council unanimously passed a resolution calling 'as a first step' for an immediate cease-fire and a cessation of all military activity in the area. But the following day saw the climax of the battles in Sinai and Jordan. The

Israelis over-ran the west bank and reached the Jordan river by midday on Wednesday. The same afternoon, after an attack launched in haste that morning, they captured the Old City of Jerusalem before the cease-fire accepted by Jordan came into effect. In Sinai, there were confused tank battles as the Egyptians counter-attacked to try to clear their lines of retreat. In a delaying action on the road to Ismailia they used 100 tanks and lost forty of them. They threw in what was left of the Egyptian air force in an attempt to check the Israeli advance farther north.[16] But by the evening of 7 June an Israeli brigade had seized the Mitla Pass and fought off all Egyptian attempts to break through on the road to Suez. During the day Sharm esh-Sheikh was captured without opposition by Israeli troops landed from patrol boats which had come down from Eilat.

Israel had accepted the Security Council's call for a cease-fire, provided her Arab opponents accepted and cooperated in its implementation. Egypt made no response, while Syria and Iraq rejected the call. Jordan accepted but Israel staved off agreement to implement the cease-fire on the Jordan front until she had completed the capture of the Old City of Jerusalem. By that time, the Security Council, under Russian urging, had passed a new and more strongly worded resolution calling for a cease-fire by eight o'clock that evening. But it was not until the following evening, Thursday 8 June, that Egypt finally accepted. For the first time since the fighting began Nasser broke his silence to announce the cease-fire to the National Assembly. In the early hours of 9 June, the Israeli advance forces reached the eastern bank of the Suez Canal and at 9 A.M. the Egyptian High Command announced that its forces had completed their withdrawal to the west bank of the Canal. In fact, thousands of Egyptian soldiers whose units had broken up or who had been captured and turned loose by the Israelis, were still then and for days after wandering in the Sinai desert. Hundreds, perhaps thousands of them, died of thirst as they tried to walk back to Egypt in the fierce summer heat without supplies of water.

By 9 June, Nasser later admitted, Egypt was no longer capable of defending the line of the Suez Canal. 'The road to Cairo was open and offered no resistance whatsoever due to the paralysis which affected our armed forces.'[17] The only organized force left was the Popular Resistance militia, 5,000 men with rifles, who took over the defence of Port Said and Port Fuad.[18] According to Nasser, the Egyptian forces in Sinai lost 10,000 men and 1,500 officers killed between 5–8 June. 5,000 men and 500 officers were taken prisoner.[19] The Egyptian army lost some 700 tanks, hundreds of guns and thousands of trucks and other vehicles.

But on 9 June the war was still not over. Having finished with Egypt, the Israelis turned on Syria, Nasser's ally for whom he had risked the war in the first place. Throughout 8 and 9 June Israeli aircraft bombarded the Syrian positions. The Syrian government asked for a cease-fire to begin at 3.20 A.M. on 9 June but the Israeli army began its attack at 11.30 that morning. Led by tanks, Israeli troops stormed the slopes of the Golan Heights with immense courage and determination against heavy fire and reached the edge of the plateau on which lay Quneitra, the Syrian army base. The fighting continued until Saturday morning, 10 June, when the Syrians abandoned their positions and withdrew towards Damascus. The Israelis advanced through the remaining fortifications without resistance and occupied Quneitra, a deserted town, without a fight. Shortly afterwards they accepted a cease-fire which came into effect at 4.30 that afternoon. The Six-Day War was over.

It was Nasser's darkest hour. In some ways it was also to prove his finest. From the beginning of the war he had made no public utterance. The only official Egyptian voice was Cairo radio repeating the optimistic communiqués of the High Command and the fatuous rhetoric of commentators such as Ahmed Said still boasting to the Arab world of victory when on the battlefield all had already been lost. The Egyptian public had other means of learning the truth, from foreign radio stations, but, at least until the remnants of the Egyptian army began to find their way home, the public was slow to grasp the full extent of the disaster. So when Nasser announced the cease-fire after his long silence it came as a shock. It aroused anger and criticism of Nasser, bewilderment that the army had given up so soon. This time, despite the accusations of American and British air support for the Israelis, there was not the excuse of 1956 that Egypt faced the attack of two Great Powers as well as of Israel. For Nasser the defeat was far worse than in 1956. Almost the entire air force and eighty per cent of the army had been lost. There was little left of the army except the troops still in the Yemen. The hopes he had placed in the Egyptian army, the creation of the officers who had been the mainstay of his regime, headed by the man who had been his closest friend and associate, Abdul Hakim Amer, were completely dashed. Israeli troops not only occupied the whole of the Sinai peninsula but also held the east bank of the Suez Canal which Egypt had run such risks to regain control of and made such efforts to develop. Egypt's allies had also collapsed. Nasser's work of fifteen years, the liberation of Egypt from foreign troops, the establishment of Egyptian control of the Suez Canal, the rebuilding of national self-confidence among the Egyptians and the Arabs, all seemed to have been brought to ruin in three disastrous days. In the prospects of a humiliating capitulation what he feared most was not the material loss but the breaking of the morale of the Arab national movement, the enforced sub-mission of a people who had dared to raise their heads in pride and independence and to seek a better life. He had risked war above all because he believed that sooner or later the Arabs and particularly Egypt must turn and face the power of Israel or live for ever at the mercy of Israel's political will and her supposed international backers. He had run the risk and failed. Nor was there the hope as in 1956 of snatching diplomatic victory from military defeat. He believed that the United States and Britain were actively helping the enemy while Russia did nothing to stop them or materially to help Egypt. World opinion was no longer overwhelmingly on Egypt's side as it was in 1956.

The pre-war picture of Israel as a beleaguered fortress, threatened by a ring of hostile Arab armies bent not only on her defeat but the actual annihilation of her people, had earned the Israelis wide international sympathy, especially in Europe and the United States. In other countries too, in Asia and Africa and Latin America, there was this time greater sympathy for the Israelis who appeared to have hit back only after having been unreasonably provoked. Even within the Communist countries of Eastern Europe there was public dissent from the pro-Arab policies of the governments. Moreover, by the discrepancies between their threats and their performance, the Arabs had invited the world's derision. This had been skilfully encouraged by Israeli psychological warfare and propaganda which stressed the cowardice rather than the lack of skills of the Arabs and took every opportunity of showing the Arab and especially the Egyptian armies in a humiliating light – for example, by photographing Egyptian prisoners stripped to their underwear or in other unheroic situations. (One of the Israeli aims was to destroy the image of Egypt as a leader and ally among the Arabs.) But these factors alone do not account for the extraordinary flood of public scorn and hatred released in Western countries by Egypt's defeat. On both right and left of the political spectrum in the West there were for a time signs of a kind of racist anti-Arabism akin to anti-Semitism: Arabs were mocked as the Jews once were for their lack of soldierly qualities and pictured physically by the cartoonists of popular newspapers in ways reminiscent of Nazi caricatures of the Jews. On the more extreme right, in Britain and France especially, to see the Arabs being taught a lesson by an embattled 'white' settler state, a bastion of European civilization among the barbarians, seemed to be a sweet revenge for the past humiliations of having to 'scuttle' from the imperial outposts of the Middle East and from Algeria.

Faced with this situation, it is not surprising that, as the bad news came pouring in to Nasser at his home at Manshiet el Bakri, he came near to a nervous and physical collapse. Some of his colleagues, including Vice-President Zacharia Mohieddin, are said to have urged him to seek an understanding with the United States as the only way of salvaging something from the wreckage.[20] He had enough strength and pride left to choose an even more painful course. He decided to accept full public responsibility for the defeat and to announce his resignation, appointing Zacharia Mohieddin as his successor. He was influenced to take this course partly by another tragic event. On 8 June he heard that Amer was intending to commit suicide. He went to see Amer and tried to ease his mind. He told Amer that he intended to resign, and that Amer should also resign his military command. Amer was the only person he told of his decision before he announced it. He did not even tell Mohieddin.[21]

On the evening of 9 June, Nasser spoke to the nation over radio and television. On the screen he appeared a broken man. His features were drawn and haggard, his voice half choking and hesitant as he read the text of his speech. He dealt first with the origins of the war which he blamed on 'the enemy plan to invade Syria'. It had been Egypt's duty not to accept this in silence, for 'Who starts with Syria will finish with Egypt'. Both President Johnson and the Soviet government had strongly requested that Egypt should not open fire first. But the enemy had struck with a stronger blow than had been expected, showing that 'there were other forces behind him which came to settle their account with the Arab Nationalist movement'. Nasser repeated his allegations of British and American air support for Israel.

Nasser declared that he was 'ready to assume the entire responsibility' for the 'setback'. He announced that he had decided to give up all his official posts and every political role and become an ordinary citizen. He had asked Zacharia Mohieddin to take over the post of President of the Republic. 'The forces of imperialism,' he said, 'imagine that Abdul Nasser is their enemy. I want it to be clear to them that it is the entire Arab nation and not Gamal Abdul Nasser.'

Nasser gave a valedictory summing-up of the achievements of the Egyptian revolution which, he said,

I am not thereby liquidating. . . . It has brought about the evacuation of British imperialism and the independence of Egypt. It has defined Egypt's Arab character, fought the policy of spheres of influence in the Arab world, led the socialist revolution and brought about a profound change in the Arab way of life. It has affirmed the people's control of their resources and the product of their national action. It recovered the Suez Canal and laid down the bases of industrial build-up in Egypt, built the High Dam to turn the arid desert green. It has extended generating power networks all over the northern Nile valley and extracted petroleum resources after a long wait.

More important than all this, it has given a place to the workers in the leadership of political action.[22]

Nasser ended with a word of praise for the courage of the Egyptian forces and a rallying call to the nation, 'This is the hour of action and not the hour of sadness'. Even before he had finished speaking, there had begun another of those dramatic reversals of fortune that marked his career. As soon as they heard him announce his resignation, people in Cairo began to pour out into the streets and to appear at the windows of their houses and flats shouting for Nasser to stay. The scene has been vividly described by Eric Rouleau who was then in Cairo as the correspondent of *Le Monde*. In the twilight and the semi-blacked-out streets, hundreds of thousands, some of the men still in pyjamas and the women in nightgowns, came out of their houses weeping and shouting, 'Nasser, Nasser, don't leave us, we need you'. The noise was like a rising storm. A whole people seemed to be in mourning. Tens of thousands gathered round the National Assembly shouting 'Nasser, Nasser' and threatening to kill any deputies who did not vote for Nasser. Half a million people massed along the five miles from Nasser's home at Manshiet el Bakri to the centre of Cairo to watch over Nasser during the night and make sure he would go to the National Assembly the next day to withdraw his resignation. Millions more began to pour into Cairo from all over Egypt to make sure that Nasser stayed.[23]

Many people outside Egypt, especially in the West, found this support for Nasser strange, and explicable only in terms of a stage-managed performance. Nasser had led the Egyptians to a national military disaster, yet they were not demanding his head but clamouring for him to stay. Moreover, if they had wanted to get rid of a dictator here was their chance – he was himself offering to go, but they would not let him. How could this be?

This puzzlement reflected partly the continuing failure of Westerners to understand the nature of Nasser's relationship with the Egyptian people, the decisive element of consent mixed with the authoritarianism of his regime and the significance of what he had achieved inside Egypt itself, compared with his international activities which had chiefly attracted foreign attention. Egyptians did not judge Nasser simply by his success or failure as a military leader, however great his failure then was – and perhaps also the public was even then not yet fully aware of the extent of the defeat. He was rather the man who had overthrown the king, ended the British occupation, given Egypt full control of the Suez Canal, begun to build the High Dam, carried through the land reform and tried to control rents, built more factories and schools, brought clean water and electricity to many more villages, begun social insurance for workers and, within limits, given many more Egyptians a say in the running of their own affairs. This did not mean that he and his regime were immune from criticism or even opposition. Egyptians are in any case traditionally given to scathing satirical humour – in private when not possible in public – about their rulers. But like other peoples, in time of great crisis they tend to close the national ranks.

To the less sophisticated majority, used to centuries of authoritarian or paternalistic rule, Nasser had become established as 'the father of the nation'.[24] Now, at a moment of calamity, the father-figure was about to leave them to their fate. But this emotional reaction was strengthened because people, including the more educated and politically conscious, saw Nasser as the symbol of resistance. The Egyptian army had been defeated but not the nation as a whole. The enemy was occupying a large extent of Egyptian territory, but the main part of the country was still intact and needed somehow to be defended. It was the situation of Russia and Stalin when the Germans reached the gates of Moscow, of Britain and Churchill after Dunkirk, though Egypt's military position was for the moment even more helpless. Egypt and the Arabs had lost a campaign but were not yet ready to surrender.

This was also the reaction all over the Arab world. For Nasser had become the symbol not only of Egyptian resistance but of Arab nationalism. His fall would seem the final proof of Arab defeat and humiliation, the ultimate satisfaction for those who wanted to break the spirit of the Arab national revival. Even those who had opposed Nasser's policies were swept along on a wave of deep, spontaneous emotion in urging him not to resign. Perhaps there was also a conviction in this movement that, despite his mistakes and failings, Nasser was the only Arab leader of sufficient stature to deal with the terrible situation in which Egypt and the Arab states now found themselves.

Did Nasser foresee and calculate this public reaction when he decided to resign? The evidence suggests he did not, that his intention was sincere. If he had hoped for this reaction, he did nothing to prepare or organize it. The demonstrations in his favour were not carefully planned like those in 1954 when he overthrew Neguib. They were spontaneous and uncontrolled, though once they had started the left seems to have tried to canalize them with slogans against the Americans and against Zacharia Mohieddin, popularly identified with a pro-American policy.

During the night, as the world's press prepared his political obituary, Nasser hesitated. By the next day he had made up his mind. He announced to the National Assembly that he had decided to withdraw his resignation, but he would offer it again when the consequences of the war, 'the traces of aggression', had been overcome.

His decision was received with an outburst of public joy.

Chapter 19

The Aftermath:
The Struggle to Recover, 1967–70

For the first few weeks after the defeat Nasser remained in a state of shock and depression. He was, he said later, like 'a man walking in a desert surrounded by moving sands not knowing whether, if he moved, he would be swallowed up by the sands or would find the right path'.[1]

The prospect he faced was daunting. The Six-Day War seemed at the time to have changed profoundly both the political map and the entire power structure of the Middle East. It left Israel more than ever the dominant military power in the area. Her troops were on the Suez Canal, the Red Sea and the River Jordan and held a line on the Syrian plateau only thirty miles from Damascus. Her air force ruled the skies unchallenged. She controlled the whole of former Palestine, including a million Palestinian Arabs on the west bank and the Gaza Strip, and the whole of Jerusalem. She occupied the entire Sinai Peninsula except for a tiny Egyptian bridge-head at the northern end of the Suez Canal, and a thousand square miles of Syrian territory on the Golan Heights.

The war and its aftermath eventually displaced over a million more people from their homes in the Arab lands: 350,000 people fled from the west bank to what remained of Jordan, 150,000 of them refugees for the second time and the rest non-refugee residents of the west bank. Another 116,000 people were refugees in Syria from the villages and farms of the Golan Heights; in Egypt some 700,000 people were to be evacuated from the shell-shattered towns of the Suez Canal zone.

The Suez Canal itself was closed and blocked with sunken ships. The Egyptian oilfields in Sinai were in Israeli hands. The worst hit materially of the Arab countries was Jordan. She had lost her most productive agricultural area, her chief tourist centres and half of her most active working population, acquiring instead a new burden of hundreds of thousands of refugees.

In some ways more important at first than the material losses was the effect of the war on Arab morale. In Egypt the defeat threw into doubt many of the basic assumptions of Nasser's revolution. It shattered public confidence in the Egyptian army as a fighting force and as the political mainstay of the regime. Civilian critics, especially on the left wing, linked the poor performance of the army officers in battle with the emergence of a socially privileged 'army class' which was too closely tied to the bourgeoisie and out of touch with the people. The defeat called into question the personal leadership and judgement of Nasser himself and the regime's method of making important decisions. It raised doubts about 'Arab Socialism' and the extent to which the revolution had been able to bring about social and technological change and to modernize Egyptian society. For the left wing it was evidence that the socialist revolution had politically not gone far or fast enough. It led to renewed criticism of Nasser's Arab policy from the advocates of 'Egypt first' and to scepticism about the value of Russia as a friend and ally. What had become of the 'Arab nation' to have allowed itself to be defeated in less than six days by a nation of two million people? Politically, the Arab world was confused and divided. Nasser's chief Arab allies, Syria and Iraq, had scarcely fought and one of his former enemies, Jordan, had made the best military showing. King Feisal of Saudi Arabia had emerged unscathed, except in reputation. Egypt's relations with the United States were in ruins and her policy of non-alignment in danger.

Nasser was determined to recover Egypt's lost territory by political or military means, but his first concern was to restore the confidence of the Egyptians and Arabs in their ability to learn to hold their own in the modern technological world. He regarded this self-confidence as not only the key to military recovery but also as the main purpose of the Egyptian and Arab revolution which he had inspired. He faced four main tasks: to rebuild Egypt's military strength; to seek a diplomatic settlement of the war; to try to unify the Arab front in support of Egypt; and meanwhile to hold the home front together both politically and economically.

In rebuilding the Egyptian armed forces Nasser's aims were to remedy Egypt's total defencelessness, to give her greater bargaining power and to enable her eventually to force the Israelis to withdraw from the occupied territories, if they could not be dislodged by diplomacy. Nasser divided this military reconstruction into three phases: of defence, deterrence (the ability to hit back on a limited scale) and liberation. His diplomacy had a double purpose of genuinely seeking a peaceful settlement and also of gaining time, since in early negotiations Egypt would have been bargaining from a position of 'unnatural' weakness. But Nasser shared the scepticism of those Arabs who believed Israel really wanted more territory rather than peace. He was convinced that only Egyptian military strength – whether actually applied or simply recognized by the Israeli leaders – would bring Israel to reduce her terms and withdraw completely.

Nasser's first steps on the road to recovery were to consolidate his own authority in Egypt and to begin reorganizing the armed forces. The public demonstrations of support when he announced and then withdrew his resignation gave him the first impetus to shoulder the huge new burden that awaited him. Further encouragement came from the Soviet leaders who wrote him a letter on 10 June urging Egypt to stand fast and promising to help rebuild the armed forces and offering support in all fields.[2] Conscious of Arab criticism that they had not done enough to help the Arabs during the war, the Russians were eager to demonstrate the value of their friendship by anything short of military action or a complete break with the United States. Within a few days of the cease-fire they sent President Podgorny to Cairo to discuss military and economic aid and the diplomatic outlook. Soviet arms supplies were rushed to Egypt and Soviet warships put in an ostentatious appearance at Port Said and Alexandria. When the Middle East situation was debated by a special session of the United Nations General Assembly in the latter half of June the Soviet prime minister, Kosygin, went to New York to head the Soviet delegation and to meet President Johnson at an improvised summit conference at Glassboro.

Nasser began the overhaul of what was left of the army and air force by sacking Marshal Amer and fifty top commanders. He appointed General Fawzi commander-in-chief and himself took personal charge of military affairs.

These first steps forced Nasser within two days of the defeat to face a new threat to his position. On 11 June some of Amer's supporters among the army officers demanded that Nasser should re-instate Amer in his command of the armed forces. They backed up their demands with a show of force. Six armoured cars headed for Nasser's house. The presidential guards had all been sent to the Canal front. Nasser had not yet established his personal control over the army, which was still in the hands of Amer. He slept at night with a pistol under his pillow. In this vulnerable position Nasser played for time but gave nothing away. He promised to set up a committee to deal with the grievances of the malcontents, but he insisted that while he would welcome Amer's continuation as Vice-President he could not accept him as a military commander. On 21 June, he reorganized the government with himself as premier and Zacharia Mohieddin and Hussein esh-Shafei as deputy premiers as well as Vice-Presidents.

The 11 June incident never came to a real test of force but it was the beginning of a conflict between Nasser and the Amer group which was to come to a head two and a half months later with Amer's arrest and suicide. The dispute was partly over responsibility for the defeat and partly over the political role of the army. Amer and his supporters blamed Nasser for having refused to strike first and so allowed the Israelis the advantage of doing so. Nasser put the responsibility for defeat on confusion in the army command and its failure to heed his warnings to prepare for an Israeli attack. He defended himself in his speech on 23 July 1967 at Cairo University, his first public speech since his resignation and resumption of power. He pointed out that if Egypt had attacked first she would have had to face American intervention in support of Israel as well as condemnation from Russia, France and the world community. Nasser then rejected 'an imposed peace [which] means surrender'. He called on the Egyptians not to despair or to abandon their principles. They were not, he said, the first people to lose a battle and he quoted the example of British determination after Dunkirk. He refused to retreat from his commitment to the Palestinian Arabs. 'Despite the setback and despite everything, the only road for us to take is that of safeguarding the rights of the Palestinian people and we will never abandon these rights. This is the essence of the matter.'

Nasser acknowledged criticisms of the weakness of Egypt's political organization. He came down on the side of the civilians against the army and in favour of speeding up the social revolution rather than slowing it down. He admitted indirectly the growth of corruption in the 'army class' and the bureaucracy and promised that 'unjustly acquired' privileges would be ended. It was necessary to consolidate the social revolution in Egypt because the aim of the 'imperialist-Zionist aggression' was not only the occupation of territory but the 'liquidation of the Arab revolution in general'. Egypt and the Arabs, Nasser implied, were facing a challenge which they could refuse only at the cost of slipping back into the despair from which they had tried to escape.[3]

Nasser's tone was sombre, restrained but resolute. Within a few weeks his resolution was to be tested by another deeply wounding personal blow. On 4 September it was announced in Cairo that Marshal Amer had been placed under house arrest, together with the former Minister of War, Shams ed-din Badran, and other army and security leaders. They were accused of plotting a limited *coup* to force Nasser to reinstate Amer in command of the armed forces and to call off the investigations of army officers aimed at establishing the army's responsibility for the defeat.[4]

Altogether 149 people were held for questioning. In addition to Amer and Shams ed-din Badran they included the former Minister of the Interior, Abbas Radwan; the former chief of intelligence, General Salah Nasser; a former army divisional commander, General Osman Nasser; and the former commander of the shock troops school, Lieutenant-Colonel Galal Haridi. These four and Badran, together with lesser figures, were put on trial in January 1968 before a special court under Vice-President Hussein esh-Shafei. The trial lasted three months. The five chief accused were all sentenced to hard labour for life. Two other officers got fifteen years' hard labour. Thirty others received prison sentences and fourteen were acquitted.

Amer did not live to face the humiliation of trial and probable imprisonment. On 15 September it was announced that he had committed suicide by taking poison. According to the official story, he had first taken a large dose of poison on 13 September when he was about to be interrogated at his home in Cairo by officials investigating the alleged plot. He was recovering from this dose in a rest home under medical surveillance when he managed to swallow a second dose of aconite which he had hidden on his body under a piece of sticking plaster. He was rushed to the hospital but died three hours later.[5] Inevitably there were rumours that Amer's death was not suicide but judicial murder. It is conceivable that Amer may have been offered the option of suicide; but there is no evidence to support the suggestion that he was deliberately finished off in the rest house or hospital.[6]

Inevitably, too, after Amer's death there were 'revelations' about his private life and his past professional failings. In his dealings with the army, it was said, he had been easy-going, weak and inefficient. He had allowed corruption to develop in his entourage in the handling of promotions and appointments. His slackness and incompetence had sharply increased during the year or so before the war, then his essentially Bohemian nature had come to the surface. He had fallen in love with a film starlet, taken her as his second wife and begun to live a gayer and more expensive social life. Nasser had been told how things were going but had refused to believe the reports.

Nasser's personal relationship with Amer had been closer than with any of his other lieutenants, despite their differences over policy. Amer's ease and warmth seemed to supply a deep need in Nasser whose intense and serious nature was apt to make him awkward and reticent in personal contacts. Their families were linked by marriage as well as a friendship lasting thirty years. Nasser's younger brother, Hussein, an air force pilot, was married to one of Amer's daughters. However sad for Nasser personally, Amer's death and the arrest of his confederates removed the most serious immediate threat to Nasser's authority. It also left him free to direct the reorganization of the armed forces as he wished. With the help of a large number of Soviet advisers and technicians,* the army and air force were being intensively re-trained and re-equipped. The first step was to strengthen the defensive line along the Suez Canal. The manpower available was increased by bringing back troops from the Yemen, calling up additional men in Egypt and expanding and training the popular militia or Home Guard. While the air force was still being rebuilt, the fire-power of the Suez Canal line was expanded by large reinforcements of artillery. In the summer of 1967 the Israelis still held the whip hand along the Canal. They were able to prevent any movement by Egyptian boats on the Canal or any attempts to clear the waterway. They heavily shelled the Canal towns of Ismailia and Suez, killing and wounding hundreds of civilians and causing considerable damage. They also shelled and set on fire the Suez oil refinery in reprisal for the sinking of the Israeli destroyer, *Eilat*, by Egyptian rocket-fire off Port Said. Nasser ordered the evacuation of civilians from the Canal Zone towns to safe areas. Ismailia and Suez became almost ghost towns. Egypt was then not yet in a position to hit back. By the spring of 1968 Egypt had strengthened her defences along the Canal to the point where Nasser claimed that her armed forces were now 'capable of checking aggression'.[7]

During September and October 1968 Egyptian artillery began to be more active along the Canal and the Egyptian army sent small commando groups across to raid Israeli positions on the east bank. In retaliation, the Israelis carried out an airborne commando raid on 5 November on an electric power station and a Nile bridge and dam in the Nag Hamadi district of Upper Egypt. But the most marked Arab military activity of the year was the expansion of guerrilla operations by the Palestinian resistance organizations, chiefly the Fatah. After a slow start, the Palestinian commandos had made their political mark and caught

*Estimates of the numbers varied at first from 1,000 officers – the figure given by Nasser himself in his interview with *Look* magazine of 4 March 1968 – to 3,000 advisers, the figure given in *Strategic Survey, 1968* of the Institute for Strategic Studies (London, 1969). By March 1970 American official sources believed the number had increased to 6,000, including 2,500 Soviet personnel brought in to operate SAM 3 advanced anti-aircraft missile sites round Cairo, Alexandria and the Aswan High Dam. There was a further increase during the summer of 1970.

the Arab imagination in the battle of Karameh on 21 March 1968. In this encounter a large Israeli armoured force which crossed the river Jordan and attacked the refugee township of Karameh, a commando base in the Jordan valley, suffered substantial losses at the hands of the commandos and the Jordan regular army. (The Israelis claimed to have killed 150 guerrillas and captured others but admitted nearly 100 casualties of their own, including twenty-one killed.) From that time onwards, the Palestinian guerrilla organizations, committed to an all-out revolutionary guerrilla war to regain the whole of Palestine and replace Israel with a mixed Arab–Jewish Palestinian state, became a political factor with which all the Arab governments, including Nasser, had seriously to reckon. In the spring of 1968 both Nasser and King Hussein, without abandoning their commitment to a diplomatic settlement with Israel, announced their support for the military operations of the guerrillas, if not for their political aims.

It was not until the spring of 1969 that Nasser felt the Egyptian forces to be strong enough to pass from the first phase of passive defence to the second phase of active deterrence. The change was signalled by intensive artillery bombardments of Israeli positions along the Canal in an attempt to prevent the Israelis completing the fortifications of the so-called 'Bar-Lev line' (named after the Israeli chief of staff). Nasser's claim, based on a report by General Fawzi, that sixty per cent of the fortifications had been destroyed was derided by Israel.

The Egyptians also increased the scale and frequency of their commando raids and infantry patrols across the Canal. At the same time the Egyptian air force began for the first time to penetrate Israeli air space and attack positions in Sinai. The Israelis replied in the summer of 1969 with heavy air bombardments of the Egyptian positions along the Canal and inflicted substantial losses in air battles with Egyptian planes. The Israeli military leaders later claimed that this air offensive had destroyed Egypt's air defence system, radar and missile sites and forced Nasser to give up hope of an early Egyptian attack across the Canal. In September 1969 the Israelis carried out a spectacular amphibious raid with tanks on an anti-aircraft missile site on the Egyptian side of the Gulf of Suez. Three months later they seized and carried away by helicopter an Egyptian radar installation of a new Soviet type.

Nasser had already declared in a speech on May Day 1969 that, unless the Israelis withdrew, Egypt would not allow them to consolidate their positions on the cease-fire line, even if this exposed Egypt to retaliation.[8] Six weeks later Nasser let it be known that he intended to wage a 'war of attrition'.[9] While avoiding being provoked into large-scale actions before his forces were prepared, he hoped to make it too costly for the Israelis simply to sit tight on the cease-fire line, since if they were allowed to do so the line would become a political border. He told the National Congress of the Arab Socialist Union on 23 July 1969 that Egypt was now beginning the third phase of 'liberation' of which the final stage must be the crossing of the Canal from the west to the east bank. It was impossible for the lightning war of 1967 to be repeated. Egypt must use her man-power superiority in preparing for a long battle to exhaust the enemy.[10]

Nasser's choice of a 'war of attrition' was virtually forced on him by the dilemma in which he found himself. Egypt was too weak to wage all-out war and he could not make peace on the terms Israel wanted, but neither could he remain completely passive in the face of criticism at home and of Israeli consolidation in the occupied territory. The timing of Nasser's declaration of the war of attrition was, however, the result both of the stage reached in Egypt's military recovery and of the lack of progress towards a political settlement of the war during the preceding two years.

Nasser called for a new Arab summit meeting to coordinate Arab action and mobilize Arab resources for the new phase. The appeal was at first unsuccessful and he repeated it in a speech on 6 November 1969 to the Egyptian National Assembly. He then proclaimed more categorically than ever before that, in view of the continued failure to produce a political settlement, Egypt must be prepared for war and for 'seas of blood and horizons of fire'. This time the other Arab states agreed to another summit which met in Rabat (without the presidents of Syria, Iraq or Tunisia) on 21 December but failed to reach agreement on a plan for joint contributions of troops, weapons and money prepared by the Egyptian Minister of War, General Fawzi. On his way back to Cairo, Nasser held a meeting in Tripoli with the chairman of the new Libyan Revolutionary Council, Colonel Muammar al Qadhafy, and the Sudanese prime minister, General Jaafar el Numeiry. They agreed on a closer coordination of the military, political and economic policies of the three countries.

During the first half of 1969 Nasser had made renewed efforts to create a more effective 'eastern front' against Israel by encouraging Iraq, Syria and Jordan to strengthen their forces and cooperate more closely. Political differences between the three countries had hindered this collaboration. The Baathist regimes in Syria and Iraq – representing different party factions – were suspicious of each other and both were enemies of King Hussein. Nevertheless, there were some 15,000 Iraqi troops in Jordan and they were reported to have been joined in northern Jordan in the summer of 1969 by a Syrian armoured brigade. Along the Jordan valley front the Jordan army had dug itself in and withstood constant Israeli air attacks in retaliation for raids and rocket bombardment carried out from Jordan by the Palestinian guerrillas. The latter had been encouraged by Nasser to unite and coordinate their operations. Al Fatah and several other smaller groups combined and took over control of the Palestine Liberation Organization under a committee headed by the Fatah leader, Yasir Arafat. But the guerrilla groups were also loosely coordinated in a Palestine Armed Struggle Command. The Fatah was the dominant group in both the military and political fields, but had only limited control over the other groups, especially the PFLP (Popular Front for the Liberation of Palestine), led by George Habash.

By the spring of 1970, the guerrillas were several thousand strong (estimates varied from 8–15,000; Arafat said in an interview in *Al Ahram* on April 3 that there were 32,000 guerrillas in Jordan but they had only 6,000 guns). They had greatly multiplied the number of their attacks on Israeli targets. They had established operational bases in southern Lebanon as well as in the Jordan Valley and were becoming the strongest political force in Jordan.

But they were also suffering heavy losses and were finding it increasingly difficult to penetrate the Israeli border defences. To avoid Israeli reprisals against the Palestinian Arab population on the west bank, they concentrated on targets in Israel proper, rather than in occupied territory, except in the Gaza Strip where separate guerrilla groups maintained a determined resistance despite draconian Israeli counter-measures against the civil population. Guerrilla operations contributed to the mounting toll of Israeli forces taken by the war of attrition. But the guerrillas and the Syrian, Iraqi and Jordan armies together were still a very long way from providing an effective threat which might draw off some of the weight of Israeli forces from the Egyptian front in the event of full-scale war.

The strategy of the war of attrition was, however, beginning to make itself felt in an increasing casualty rate among the Israeli forces from continuous minor engagements. In the Six-Day War Israel lost 803 dead, of whom 777 were military. According to Israeli official figures, from the end of the Six-Day War up to 31 January 1970, Israel lost 526 dead, of whom 435 were soldiers. Of the 2,026 wounded over the same period, 1,469 were military. About half of the military casualties were from clashes with guerrillas and half from action against Arab regular forces, most of the latter incurred on the Egyptian front. Egyptian losses were also heavy. The Israelis claimed at least a thousand Egyptian dead along the Canal front and the shooting down of fifty-eight Egyptian planes for the loss of eight Israeli aircraft. There were also hundreds of Egyptian civilian casualties from Israeli shelling and bombing of the Canal Zone towns and of targets farther inland. The Israelis also claimed to have killed or captured some 2,000 Al Fatah and other Palestinian guerrillas and terrorists operating in or trying to enter the occupied areas.

At the special session of the United Nations General Assembly in June and July 1967 just after the war, the Arab states were still too shocked, divided and disorganized to develop a coherent, unified diplomatic position. They had already split into two main groups. The first group, led by Egypt and Jordan, believed that every diplomatic effort must be made to achieve a political solution; they were prepared to pay a certain political price to secure an Israeli withdrawal. They believed that, even if diplomacy failed in the end, it would gain them time to recover their strength. In any case, the Arabs must present a more conciliatory face to the world to regain the international sympathy that their talk of 'liquidating Israel' had lost them. The other group, chiefly Syria and Algeria, rejected any political compromise as useless. They called for a continuation of the struggle against Israel by revolutionary guerrilla warfare. In practice, Syria remained militarily the most passive of the Arab states, preventing even any guerrilla operations from her territory. Algeria's contribution was limited to a small military force on the Egyptian front.

Nasser had agreed to the calling of the special UN Assembly largely to satisfy the Russians. The Soviet government wanted to use the Assembly to give a loud public demonstration of diplomatic support for the Arabs so as to offset criticism among some sections of the Arab public of the lack of Soviet military help during the war. They also hoped to reach some understanding with the United States which would limit the liabilities of both super-Powers in any future conflict in the Middle East, and also help to recover as much as possible for the Arab states from the wreckage. Such was the purpose of the Soviet premier, Kosygin, at his meeting with President Johnson at Glassboro on 23 June 1967.

Although the defeat made Egypt more dependent on Russia for protection, and for military and economic aid, and although it had roused Arab opinion against the United States more than against the Soviet Union, the Russians had reasons for wanting a settlement. They did not want a repetition of the kind of runaway crisis beyond their control that had led up to the June war. It was too dangerous. To some extent continued tension between the Arab states and Israel had been to their advantage, but Nasser's Egypt was even more important to them as a political influence in Afro-Asia, as an example of the economic and social benefits of association between developing countries and the Soviet Union. For this Egypt needed to be a flourishing concern. Moreover, the Russians wanted the Suez Canal reopened, for both economic and strategic reasons. They had begun to develop a substantial naval presence in the Mediterranean and looked forward to extending it to the Red Sea, the Persian Gulf and the Indian Ocean.

Nasser had placed a serious handicap on Arab diplomacy by the violence of his rupture with the United States. His hasty accusations of direct American military help to Israel had angered President Johnson who might otherwise have had good reason to feel aggrieved with the Israeli government for having ignored his appeal not to start the fighting. The American administration was now in a mood to write off Egypt, Syria and Iraq as already lost to the Russians and Jordan as being of no great importance. It saw American interest in the Middle East as concentrated in Iran, Turkey and Israel and to a lesser extent in Saudi Arabia, Libya and the Lebanon. The Arab–Israeli conflict was, however, a perennial and dangerous nuisance that must be stopped once and for all. Here there was some common ground with Russia. A final peace, buttressed by an agreement with Russia to limit arms supplies to the area, was the aim of American policy. But the Arabs, especially Nasser, would have to pay something for their defeat and to show them that reliance on Russia was a losing game.

From this first diplomatic battle at the United Nations onwards, Nasser's aim was to secure the withdrawal of Israeli forces from Arab territory for the minimum price in political concessions, avoiding commitments such as full recognition of Israel or an abandonment of the claims of the Palestine Arab refugees. The Egyptian delegates insisted that the withdrawal of the Israelis 'to eradicate the traces of the aggression' should precede any direct political negotiations.

Israel's primary purpose was to obtain a permanent peace settlement, full recognition from the Arabs and more secure borders. Her secondary aim was to retain as much of the occupied territories, particularly of former Palestine, and above all Jerusalem, as she could politically digest without diluting the Jewish character of the state. She insisted on direct negotiations and a formal peace treaty with the Arab states. She declined to reveal her territorial peace terms until direct talks began and refused to withdraw until a peace treaty had been signed.

With the United States and Russia giving qualified support to Israel and the Arab states respectively, the contest in the Assembly ended in a stalemate. The Assembly did, however, pass two resolutions. One of these called on Israel to rescind her virtual annexation of Jordanian Jerusalem. The other appealed for humane treatment and help for the civil population affected by the war and the return to their homes of those who had been forced to flee.

At the beginning of September, Nasser met other Arab heads of state in Khartoum. The main topic on the agenda of this Arab League 'summit' was Arab policy towards Israel but linked with this, as always, was the question of the Arab attitudes towards the Western Powers and disputes between the Arabs themselves, especially the still unsettled Yemen civil war. On the face of it, the declarations of the conference on Israel – 'No peace, no negotiations, no recognition' – showed no sign of compromise in the Arab position, and this was how Israel interpreted them. In fact, the conference was a victory for the 'moderates'. Nasser and Hussein of Jordan, backed by all the other Arab states except Algeria and Syria (who was absent), agreed to try and obtain the withdrawal of Israel's forces by political rather than military means. Arab spokesmen later interpreted the Khartoum declarations to mean no formal peace *treaty*, but not a rejection of a state of peace; no *direct* negotiations, but not a refusal to talk through third parties; and no *de jure* recognition of Israel, but acceptance of her existence as a state. In subsequent statements, both public and private, Nasser and Hussein made it clear that within these limits they were prepared to go much further than ever before towards a settlement with Israel. They were ready to end the state of war with Israel, recognize her existence *de facto* within the pre-war borders and accept international guarantees of her security, rights of access to the Jerusalem Holy Places and free navigation.

In a complex bargain, the Khartoum summit also decided to lift the Arab oil embargo against the United States, Britain and West Germany and re-open the Syrian oil pipelines, while Nasser and King Feisal agreed finally to disengage from the Yemen civil war. As part of these agreements, the oil countries, Saudi Arabia,

Kuwait and Libya, promised to pay £95 million a year to Egypt and £40 million to Jordan to help them overcome their war losses, including the loss of revenue from the continued closure of the Suez Canal. The oil boycott had been intended as a sanction against the Western Powers to get them to compel Israel to withdraw. Although the closure of the Canal was believed to be adding £250 million a year to Britain's bill for imported oil, the boycott was ineffective. It was doing more damage to the Arabs than to the intended victims.

When the attempt at peace-making was resumed at the United Nations in the autumn of 1967, on 22 November the Security Council adopted unanimously a resolution drafted by Britain setting out the outlines of a Middle East peace settlement and the methods to be used to achieve it. The resolution was to become the basis of attempts to reach a diplomatic settlement between the Arab states and Israel over the next three years.

The preamble to the resolution emphasized certain basic principles: the inadmissibility of acquiring territory by war; the need for a just and lasting peace; and the fact that all members of the United Nations were committed to act in accordance with Article 2 of the Charter (which forbids the use or threat of force by one state against another, except in self-defence).

The essence of the resolution was contained in five points. Israel was to withdraw her forces 'from territories occupied in the recent conflict' (the omission of the word 'the' before 'territories' left an obvious ambiguity). All claims or states of belligerency were to be ended and there must be acknowledgement of 'the sovereignty, territorial integrity and political independence of every state in the area and their right to live in peace within secure and recognized boundaries'. Freedom of navigation through international waterways in the area must be guaranteed and a just settlement of the Palestine Arab refugee problem achieved. There should also be guarantees for the 'territorial inviolability and political independence of every state in the area, through measures including the establishment of demilitarized zones'.

The resolution requested the UN Secretary-General to designate a special representative to go to the Middle East 'to promote agreement' and to help bring about a settlement on the lines of the resolution. The next day, U Thant appointed Gunnar Jarring, the Swedish ambassador in Moscow, as his special representative for this purpose.

The Security Council resolution was a compromise and its ambiguous language led to difficulties when Jarring tried to secure its implementation. The Arabs, supported by Russia, insisted that the resolution meant a complete Israeli withdrawal to the 5 June frontiers. In support of this view, they quoted the first principle of the resolution on the inadmissibility of acquiring territory by conquest. The Israelis, partially supported by the United States, claimed that the resolution linked withdrawal with the establishment of 'secure and recognized boundaries', which could not be the same as the 5 June borders. Other differences of interpretation arose. Israel still insisted on direct talks at least in later stages of the negotiations. She considered Jarring's mandate was only to bring the parties together. She regarded the the resolution as merely providing guidelines or a framework for direct negotiations. She still refused to disclose what she considered 'secure and recognized frontiers' until she was able to negotiate with the Arab governments face to face.

Egypt and Jordan, after initial doubts, declared that they accepted the resolution. But they regarded it as a plan to be applied as it stood. Jarring's task was simply to work out as a mediator how it was to be implemented by each side. This could be done by indirect talks but before these began Israel must also declare her readiness to implement the resolution and to withdraw. For nearly a year and a half Jarring travelled to and fro between Israel and the Arab countries from his headquarters in Cyprus and New York trying to work out an agreement or even to get negotiations started, but without success.

As time went on the increase in border warfare and the cycle of Palestinian guerrilla operations and Israeli reprisals and repression in the occupied areas deepened the emotional gulf between the two sides. By the end of 1968 it was obvious that the Jarring mission could make no progress unless the United States and Russia themselves agreed on an interpretation of the Security Council resolution and used their considerable influence to persuade their respective protégés to accept it. The advent of President Nixon's administration in Washington seemed a good moment for a new start.

The Russians took the initiative. On 21 December 1968 the Soviet foreign minister came to see Nasser in Cairo and obtained his approval for a memorandum to be sent to the United States, Britain and France setting out proposals for a settlement.

Talks between the Big Four began in March 1969 but only at the modest level of the permanent delegates at the United Nations in New York. There were also continuous meetings in Washington between the State Department and the Soviet ambassador, Anatol Dobrynin. It soon became plain that it was in the Soviet–American talks that the real business was being done.

Israel bitterly attacked the whole idea of Big Four talks. In his May Day speech in 1969 Nasser said that Egypt supported the Big Four talks on the basis that they were intended to lead to the implementation of the Security Council resolution.[11] But he soon became convinced that a political settlement was improbable because, the United States, he believed, was continuing to give full support to Israel in both diplomacy and arms supplies.[12] He believed that Israel wanted territory more than peace. In support of this view he cited the statements of Israeli ministers who, as the parliamentary elections in Israel approached, were beginning more openly to stake claims to the occupied Arab territories.

In December 1969, Nasser rejected (though not formally) a new American peace plan put forward by the US Secretary of State, William Rogers. The Rogers plan was not unfavourable to Egypt in that it envisaged a return to the former international frontier between Egypt and Israel. But Nasser criticized it on three main grounds: first, it did not expressly call for an Israeli withdrawal from Sharm esh-Sheikh or the Gaza Strip but left the future Israeli role in these two areas open to negotiation; second, it seemed an attempt to divide Egypt from the other Arab states by a separate peace; thirdly, the Rogers proposals made simultaneously to Jordan did not provide for complete Israeli withdrawal or a fair settlement for the Palestine Arab refugees and so were less favourable than the Security Council resolution.

By the beginning of 1970 the respective positions of Nasser and the Israeli government on peace-making appeared to be as follows: Nasser had informed Jarring and the Big Four that Egypt was prepared to implement the Security Council resolution (as she interpreted it). She no longer insisted that Israeli troops should withdraw before anything else was discussed or any other action taken. She would agree to a package deal covering all the points in the resolution, to be signed before withdrawal began and to be implemented in stages according to an agreed time-table. She would not accept direct negotiations, a bilateral peace treaty or formal diplomatic recognition of Israel. But she would enter indirect negotiations through the United Nations mediator. She would sign a multilateral peace document of a contractual character, such as that establishing the neutrality of Laos in 1962, to be deposited with the United Nations Security Council and guaranteed by the Big Four. This document would set out the commitments of both sides and the means by which they were to be fulfilled, including recognition of sovereignty and territorial integrity within secure and recognized borders, guaranteed freedom of navigation through international waterways, and a just settlement of the refugee problem through the offer of a choice of repatriation or compensation. The Israelis would have to withdraw completely, but Egypt would accept the establishment of demilitarized zones and the presence of United Nations forces, provided they were on both sides of the borders. She would also accept United Nations forces at Sharm esh-Sheikh to supervise the agreement on free navigation through the Straits of Tiran for a limited number of years.

Nasser envisaged implementation of these points in two stages: the first would be concerned with 'removing the traces of the aggression' and would include the withdrawal of Israeli forces to the pre-June borders, the temporary establishment of demilitarized zones and a United Nations force, an end of the state of belligerency, acknowledgement of Israel's sovereignty and free passage through the Straits of Tiran pending a decision by the World Court on whether or not they were legally an international waterway. It might also include an agreement on access to and control of the Holy Places in Jerusalem – Nasser was prepared to accept any solution for Jerusalem, including internationalization, that King Hussein would accept. The second stage would be concerned with the substance of the Palestine problem, a definition of 'recognized borders', a settlement of the refugee question and the passage of Israeli ships through the Suez Canal.

Israel accepted the Security Council resolution only as a framework for negotiations. She still regarded direct negotiations as essential. She would not withdraw any of her forces until a definitive and permanent peace was signed. This should be in the form of a contractual agreement directly between Israel and individual Arab states and should lead to normal peaceful relations, including full *de jure* recognition and unrestricted trade and movement. There must be unequivocal freedom of passage for Israeli ships through the Suez Canal as well as the Straits of Tiran. The refugee problem should be solved by resettlement in the Arab countries, not by repatriation to Israel. If demilitarized zones and United Nations forces were established they should be only on the Arab side of the border not on Israeli territory. Israel would not go back to the pre-June borders: new 'secured and recognized borders' must be defined by negotiations before withdrawal. Jerusalem must remain 'united', that is with Arab Jerusalem annexed to Israel, but there might be joint municipalities and Jordan might be given control of the Muslim Holy Places and a share in tourist revenue.

Israel would not officially disclose her other territorial aims before negotiations began. Ministers in the Israel coalition government held different views about how much of the occupied territories should be kept or given back. But there appeared to be a rough consensus on the following lines: Jerusalem, the Golan Heights and parts of the west bank on the approaches to Jerusalem and near to Tel Aviv would in any case be retained. Israeli troops would remain along the Jordan river and probably at Sharm esh-Sheikh, but there were differences about whether Israel should also retain and colonize a strip of territory in the Jordan valley (as proposed by the deputy premier Yigal Allon) and whether she should also annex Sharm esh-Sheikh and a strip of

Sinai leading to it along the west coast of the Gulf of Aqaba (as advocated by the Defence Minister Moshe Dayan). The rest of Sinai would revert to Egypt but would be demilitarized. The Gaza Strip would not in any event go back under Egyptian control, but some Israeli leaders wanted it annexed to Israel and others were ready for it to be linked in some way with the west bank and Jordan.

Right-wing opinion, represented in the Israeli government by Menahem Beigin, Minister without Portfolio, favoured annexation of the whole of former Arab Palestine. Dayan also appeared to support a disguised annexation of the west bank when in July 1969 he spoke of the west bank being open to Jewish settlement and 'Nablus, Hebron and Jericho' (the three main Arab towns, apart from East Jerusalem, of the west bank) forming part of the historic Land of Israel. The annexationist faction in the Israeli cabinet was strengthened when six right-wing ministers entered the coalition after the November 1969 elections.

The Israeli leaders mostly regarded Egypt as the key to either peace or war on the Arab side. With some inconsistency, they saw Nasser as both the main obstacle to peace and as being in a precarious position from which he would collapse if the military, political and economic pressures on him generated by the defeat were maintained for long enough. Every few months there were expectations that Nasser could not last much longer, yet he continued in spite of the heavy pressures, including spells of illness. In the summer of 1968 Nasser suffered a collapse in health from a combination of a diabetic complication in one leg, exhaustion caused by over-work and the strain of such events as Amer's death. He went to Russia for treatment which appeared to be successful.

After his death it was revealed that he had had a heart attack in September 1969 which incapacitated him for six weeks and which at the time was officially passed off as influenza. According to Heykal, Nasser had lived and worked for much of the last two years of his life in agonizing pain, though this was not easily visible.

In the three years after the war until his death Nasser weathered several political storms and the Egyptian economy survived better than most people expected. The economy had gone through a critical period immediately after the June war. With the Suez Canal closed and the Sinai oil-fields lost, there was an acute shortage of foreign exchange. When the war came the government had been preparing for a more expansionist budget after a period of deflation, but the cuts already made in investment and in imports of spare parts and raw materials had to be maintained and extended. Many factories remained closed or worked part time. The development programme was slowed down even further, except for work on the High Dam and related projects. The dam and power station were completed in 1970. The growth rate in GNP terms dropped to only about two per cent, less than the rate of population increase. But by mid-1969 the economy had begun to recover. Aid from the Arab oil states under the Khartoum agreement had more than compensated for the foreign exchange lost from the continued closure of the Canal. Oil production had been more than restored and promised to become a substantial export. Before the June war, oil production in Egypt was 7,500,000 tons a year. With the loss of the Sinai fields it dropped to 2,500,000 tons, but in the next two years rose again to fourteen million tons, mostly from the Morgan fields south of Suez. It was planned to increase production to twenty-five million tons by the end of 1970 and if the promises of large oil-finds in the Western desert were fulfilled the figure might rise to forty million tons in 1972 and eventually even higher. Higher export prices for the cotton and rice crops (which increased by 900,000 tons over 1966 to a record figure), and lower prices for imported wheat in the world markets also helped to improve the balance of payments. In July 1969 Nasser announced that in the previous year Egypt had achieved her first trade surplus since the 1930s, a surplus of £E43 million compared with a deficit in 1967-8 of £E84 million. This was achieved partly by a fall of £E64 million in imports, but also by an increase of £E63 million in exports. The foreign debt problem was eased at least temporarily by negotiated agreements to rephase some repayments and to institute rolling credits (by which a new slice of credit is granted as an old one is paid off). Two-thirds of Egypt's estimated £E1,000 million foreign debt was believed to be with Russia and the Communist bloc, though it was not known how much and by what means Egypt was paying for Soviet arms supplies.* It is possible they may have been paid for over a long term by the Egyptian trade surplus with Russia amounting to about £E16 million a year. But it remained difficult for Egypt to get new credit in Western countries except on the most short-term basis. Major projects went ahead such as the High Dam system and the new iron and steel complex to be completed by the Russians at an eventual cost of £400 million. The electric power from the Dam, the iron and steel complex, and oil output were intended to be the basis of an expanding industrialization programme under a new five-year plan due to start in July 1970. In addition plans were well advanced for a big new oil pipe-line from Suez to Alexandria to provide an alternative international oil route while the Canal remained closed and to supplement the Canal when it reopened.

Industrial production in 1967–8 totalled £1,132 million, and an increasing amount was coming from the private sector. By mid-1969 industrial exports were running at the rate of £E130 million a year and for the first time industry was earning more in foreign exchange than it was spending on imported equipment and raw materials. In the 1969–70 budget with a total expenditure of £E2,413 million, investment was pushed up again to about £E330 million compared with £E290 million actual investment in the previous year. The budget included what was said to be a record allocation for defence. The figure was not given. In his speech to the National Assembly on 6 November 1969, Nasser said that Egypt was planning to mobilize 500,000 men and to spend £E500 million for military purposes. In the budget figures announced in May 1970, £E513 million was allocated to defence.

The overall growth rate of the economy was estimated to have risen to five per cent and the industrial growth rate to eleven per cent. Inflation had mostly been kept in check by austerity measures, by cuts in government spending and in subsidies to food

* In his May Day speech in 1970 Nasser revealed that after the Six-Day War, on 12 June, Russia had promised to replace Egypt's lost weapons free of charge.

and fares. The International Monetary Fund report had given Egypt's internal finances a clean bill of health. But the growth rate was not enough to provide all the jobs needed with half a million extra young people coming on to the labour market every year, as well as with the dislocation caused by the evacuation of civilians from the Canal Zone.

To deal with the population increase at the rate of a million a year, Nasser urged greater efforts to promote family planning, a need which he had at first been slow to recognize and which the regime had only begun seriously to encourage just before the 1967 war when a national programme to distribute contraceptives through government clinics was launched. The government also began for the first time to encourage emigration, but fears of a 'brain-drain' limited its effectiveness.

In a speech to the Arab Socialist Union on 23 July 1969, Nasser announced an important extension of the land reform. He also made some new proposals for the management of the 700,000 acres of new land reclaimed through the use of High Dam water and by other government schemes. The limit for individual land ownership was to be reduced to fifty acres, though it would still be 100 acres for a family. Nasser proposed that the new land should be owned by state companies. These would themselves exploit the land directly and export the produce, or they might lease it to farmers on a long-term basis, or sell the land to new small landholders, with priority to war veterans. Nasser thus left open the debate which had been going on for some years between those who saw an increase in the number of farmers owning land as the first priority and those who believed that large-scale state farming was necessary for economic reasons. In previous speeches Nasser had begun to emphasize the importance of giving proper encouragement to selected private enterprise, especially in industry – perhaps on the advice of the academic economists and technicians who were brought into the government in a big reshuffle in March 1968.

The March changes in the government were part of the next big political crisis faced by Nasser after the Amer affair. In his speech of 23 July 1967 and again on 23 November Nasser had shown awareness of the strong currents of criticism and self-criticism set up in public opinion by the continuing shock of the defeat. In his November speech he noted that the government had been asked for 'serious and decisive action', for an end to privileges, for equality of sacrifices, for 'revolutionary purity' and for more democracy. He announced the release of some of the Muslim Brotherhood political detainees who had been arrested two years before, though members of the Brotherhood secret political and military organizations, numbering 'less than 1,000 persons' were to remain in detention. Some sequestration orders were also ended and more people freed from the ban on political activity.

Nasser claimed that the power of the intelligence service had declined and he considered its fall 'one of the most important negative aspects which we dispensed with in our bid to purge public life in Egypt'. He referred mockingly to reports that there were two rival power groups in Egypt: a 'rightist' trend led by Zacharia Mohieddin and a 'leftist' trend led by Aly Sabry. There were, he said, no longer any such competing power centres and the leadership was united.

Three months later public frustration and discontent burst into the open in riots by workers and students. They were the first such demonstrations since Nasser's conflict with Neguib in March 1954. The immediate cause was angry public reaction to the prison sentences passed on the Egyptian air force commander, General Sidky Mahmoud, and other officers for their failures in the June war. The sentences were considered too lenient, another example of the military protecting their own. The first riots, among workers at Helwan on 21 February 1968, appear, however, to have been the result of an official muddle. The workers were taking part in a demonstration organized officially by the Arab Socialist Union. But the police had not been told and tried to stop them. News of the Helwan demonstration and its suppression brought thousands of students of Cairo university out on the streets. More than twenty students and sixty policemen were injured. One of the students' targets was the offices of the newspaper *Al Ahram* where they chanted demands to the editor, Heykal, for a free and more truthful press.

The driving force of the demonstration was a feeling of frustra-

tion and of dissatisfaction with a regime that seemed to be
fumbling and inefficient and which kept the people in the dark
and under a still suffocating security control. There were protests
against the special police operating in the universities, the
government control of students' unions, and some demands for a
freely elected parliament and for political parties.

The emphasis was on more freedom, but this trend expressed
itself in at least three different groups: liberals associated with
the old middle and upper class who wanted a return of parliamentary life, the Muslim Brothers, and the left wing whose idea
of greater democracy was the creation of a more active and
independent political cadre within the Arab Socialist Union.

Among the expanded *élite* of educated professional men, the
doctors, engineers, economists and the like, there was a widespread feeling that there should be more efficient and qualified
people in responsible positions in government. They wanted an end
of the army officers' 'old boy network' which had grown up during
the later years of the revolution. Since the June war and the
discrediting of the army and intelligence services, Nasser had
been trying to disengage from the 'army class' while reinforcing
his control of the army for military purposes. His rule was based
essentially on his national prestige with the Egyptian masses.
The withering of his former instruments of power through the
security services, the army and the ex-officer administrators,
faced him with the problem of maintaining effective contact and
control not only with the mass of people for whom his name was
still magic but also with the more sceptical educated class.
Nasser's first reaction to the February riots was to reorganize
his government, to promise reforms and to talk himself to student
leaders. His dismissal of Vice-President Zacharia Mohieddin, his
closest political associate after Marshal Amer, marked the
virtual end of the revolutionary old guard except for Nasser
himself. Of thirteen members of the original revolutionary
council, the only one left in government apart from Nasser was
the relatively light-weight Vice-President Hussein esh-Shafei. One
other, Anwar es-Sadat, was speaker of the National Assembly and
a member of the higher executive committee of the Arab Socialist
Union. (In December 1969 he was appointed Vice-President and

Nasser's deputy.) Aly Sabry, not one of the original thirteen, remained as Secretary-General of the ASU until removed after an obscure political episode in September 1969, but was no longer a Vice-President.

To meet the demand for more qualified men, Nasser replaced four of the ex-officers in his cabinet with civilians and included leading university professors in several ministries. But with a largely technical and non-political cabinet, Nasser was more than ever facing the public politically alone. His main intermediaries now were the two still largely hollow institutions of the National Assembly and the Arab Socialists Union. He attempted to throw a bridge across this gulf in a 'programme for political action' which he outlined in a broadcast speech on 30 March, and which subsequently became known as the '30 March programme'. He promised more personal and political freedom but not the free parliamentary elections on a party basis that some had been hoping for: he chose the Arab Socialist Union rather than the National Assembly as the channel for greater democratization, but he did not sanction the kind of political party within the ASU that the left-wing had been urging. He promised a further purge of the bureaucracy and a more modern efficient government of the kind demanded by the middle-class technocrats, but he stressed that socialism had come to stay.

The Arab Socialist Union was to be rebuilt 'by free elections from top to bottom'. The Central Committee would remain in continuous session and would chart national policy in all fields. A committee of the ASU would examine government security measures with the aim of 'guaranteeing protection for the revolution within the framework of the supremacy of law'. The ASU National Congress might also take over from the National Assembly the drafting of a permanent constitution. While the 30 March programme tried to remedy deficiencies in the government machine, it failed to deal with the profound political malaise affecting the educated class of the country. The programme was approved in a referendum on 2 May by a majority of 99·989 per cent – the figure was in itself a sign that not much had changed. Then followed elections to the ASU National Congress which opened its new session on 23 July. Elections were held in the following January for the National Assembly. But both elections passed without a ripple of political excitement. There was scarcely any election campaign. The general mood was one of apathy. This atmosphere was caused partly by scepticism about promises of freedom of expression and of a curb on the operations of the secret police. It was also due to the fact that Nasser himself, still the main dynamo of political action in the country, was virtually incapacitated for weeks during the summer through illness. An Asian diplomat, who saw Nasser frequently, compared his mood of depression that summer to that of Nehru after the Chinese attack on India. Nehru was able eventually to restore both his own spirits and those of the Indian public by going out on long tours round the country into the villages. Nasser found it temperamentally difficult to make that kind of personal contact, though part of his political genius was his instinctive capacity to gauge popular feeling.

Without Nasser's political drive, government relapsed into bureaucratic routine. The lack of real political change or of any spectacular improvement in Egypt's military fortunes led to another unexpected explosion. In November 1968 there were more student demonstrations, this time in Alexandria, Mansoura and Assiut. In Alexandria they degenerated into the most serious riots since Cairo's 'Black Saturday' of pre-revolutionary days. The riots began at Mansoura among Islamic divinity students over changes in the examination system. Four students were killed. In Alexandria the riots began as demonstrations in favour of civil liberties. Of the 491 people arrested, ninety-one were kept in detention and forty-six of these sent for trial.

The Alexandria riots, in which others besides students joined, became an expression of rage against the police and the government in general, with police stations and other government buildings as targets for attack. The main cause of the riots were the political discontents of Egyptian youth. The students and young university lecturers who began the demonstrations in Alexandria were reported to include a group calling themselves 'Free Socialists' but, as in the February riots in Cairo, the participants covered a wide spectrum of political views from Muslim Brothers to Communists with liberals and radicals in between. There were slogans against Soviet imperialism as well as American imperialism and calls for more militant action against Israel as well as demands for more political freedom. The students distributed to journalists a seven-point memorandum drawn up for them by the law students of Alexandria calling for a 'new society' to replace the present one based on 'prefabricated slogans', and demanding freedom of expression and a free press.[13]

Nasser's response to the riots was uninspiring and out of touch. In a speech to an emergency meeting of the ASU National Congress, he blamed the riots on 'counter-revolutionaries' and an 'irresponsible minority' in the universities. He called on the students to accept the over-riding need to preserve national unity in the face of the continued Israeli occupation of Egyptian territory. The riots led to a tightening of internal security and a new round of spy and conspiracy trials. At the end of December seven Egyptians – a government lawyer, the manager of a government-owned construction company, two army officers, a farmer, a clerk and a university medical lecturer – were accused of having planned to assassinate Nasser and other leading figures of the regime in May 1968. They were said to have set up a secret organization called 'The Egyptian National Council' with the aim of overthrowing the regime and concluding a peace treaty with Israel.

During most of 1969 Egypt remained politically quiet though the criticisms and tensions continued under the surface. In Cairo there was a trance-like atmosphere of unreal normality and the mood of the educated public seemed close to despair. The gulf between the government and the critics of the educated class remained largely unbridged. Little more was heard of political liberalization and the press remained as controlled or as careful as before. Public scepticism about the credibility of official statements and of press reporting and comment remained profound.*

*It was partly to try to counter this feeling that Nasser appointed Mohammed Hassanein Heykal to be Minister of Information (National Guidance) in May 1970. Heykal, though himself criticized for the lack of press freedom and credibility, had advocated more frankness in official news of the war.

Nasser's main concern was with the military and diplomatic struggle with Israel and with Egypt's economic development.

Then in September 1969, there were sensational rumours in the Beirut press, promptly repeated in Western newspapers, of a purge by Nasser of the top military and political leadership in Egypt after an alleged attempted pro-Soviet left-wing *coup*, said to have involved Aly Sabry.[14] The rumours were based on a bouillabaisse of disparate facts: in the wake of the Israeli armoured raid on the Gulf of Suez coast, Nasser had sacked the army chief of staff and the commander-in-chief of the navy; he had also dismissed a well-known left-wing newspaper editor and removed the official in charge of the administration of the Arab Socialist Union, who was a protégé of Aly Sabry: Nasser himself was officially stated to be ill with acute influenza. Later it was announced that Aly Sabry had been removed from his post as Secretary-General of the Arab Socialist Union, though he remained a member of the Supreme Executive Committee. This demotion, it was stated, was because on returning from a visit to Russia, Aly Sabry's entourage had tried to bring with them more than the permitted amount of goods in their luggage.

The truth of what happened is still obscure. But the evidence suggests there was no attempted *coup*. Nasser was carrying out another balancing act. Though Aly Sabry was no Marxist, his limited disgrace and that of his protégé and the left-wing editor may have been intended as a warning to the left-wing of the Arab Socialist Union and perhaps also to the Russians about the limits of their influence. Aly Sabry's power had already been considerably reduced. He had had a heart attack in November 1968 and had been working at a slower pace ever since. In March 1969 he was partially restored to favour when Nasser appointed him chief liaison officer between the Egyptian air force and the Russians.

Nasser's own illness, though announced as influenza, was in fact a heart attack. His enforced rest of six weeks enabled him conveniently to avoid attendance at the Islamic summit conference in Rabat on 22 September.

There had been no Arab summit since the Khartoum meeting

two years earlier, despite efforts by Nasser to call one. King Feisal of Saudi Arabia did not want a summit. No Saudi territory was occupied and Feisal seemed to have everything to gain by sitting back and letting Nasser take responsibility for peace or war. Meanwhile, he could limit his contribution to war-like words about the recovery of the Muslim Holy Places in Jerusalem, to the presence of a few Saudi troops in southern Jordan, and to the subsidies he paid to Egypt and Jordan. These payments gave Feisal a means of making his influence felt behind the scenes in Cairo and Amman.

Nasser again pressed for an Arab summit in the summer of 1969 to coordinate Arab military and diplomatic action in view of the continued failure of international diplomacy to bring about a settlement with Israel. Feisal countered by reviving his old proposal for a summit conference of Islamic states. He was given an opportunity of doing so by the burning of part of the Al Aqsa mosque in the Israeli-occupied Old City of Jerusalem in August. The Al Aqsa was one of the most revered shrines of Islam, and its damage roused Muslim opinion everywhere.

Nasser disliked the idea of an Islamic summit for several reasons. He saw it as a continuation of Feisal's old scheme for an Islamic conference, and perhaps a pact aimed at outflanking Nasser's influence on the Arab states by bringing in such Muslim states as Iran, Turkey and Pakistan with more conservative and pro-American regimes. He was also against using Islam as a basis for political action; it was contrary to the secular tradition of modern Arab nationalism and could have serious divisive effects in the Arab world and within Arab countries, such as the half-Christian Lebanon (Egypt herself had some three million Christian Copts); it smacked of the ideas of the Muslim Brotherhood, his inveterate enemies at home; and it was damaging to Egypt's position among the non-aligned countries where her friendship with India was more important to her than her relationship with Muslim Pakistan. Finally, Nasser believed that an Islamic summit meeting could not produce the serious concerted action against Israel that an Arab summit must consider. Among the Islamic states there were some, like Turkey and Iran, which had good relations with Israel and bad or lukewarm ones with Egypt, and others, for example among the African states, which did not feel committed to the Arab side.

Seeing that he could not get a purely Arab summit and might not be able to prevent the Islamic meeting, because of Feisal's financial pressure, Nasser put the best face on it he could. He endorsed the idea of an Islamic meeting and left it to Feisal and King Hassan of Morocco to organize it. At the same time he arranged his own 'mini-summit' in Cairo of the Arab states directly engaged in the Israeli conflict: Egypt, Jordan, Syria and Iraq. The Sudan joined in the later stages of the talks. When the Islamic meeting was called for 22 September in Rabat Nasser stayed away, pleading illness. The Islamic summit did not do Feisal or the Arab cause much good or Nasser much harm. Feisal may have wanted the summit partly to strengthen his position at home which had been threatened by unrest in the army. There were reports during September of the discovery of a plot to overthrow the Saudi monarchy and of hundreds of arrests and some executions not only among the Saudi regular army but also in Feisal's parallel 'white army' of supposedly loyal Bedouin tribesmen.

On the other hand, Nasser's position in the Arab world had recently been strengthened by revolutions carried out by radical nationalist officers of Nasserite sympathies in the Sudan and Libya. In Iraq the overthrow of President Aref by the Baathist faction led by Hassan Baqr in June 1968 had been a setback for Nasser. Although relations between Cairo and Baghdad continued on the surface to be close and friendly at first, the Baathist regime in Iraq became more of a liability than an asset as an ally, and eventually became an open enemy. Its bloodthirsty persecution of its political opponents, its witch-hunt for spies and traitors and its public executions, including the hanging of several Jews, and its resumption of the war against the Kurds (eventually settled by agreement in March 1970) sullied the international reputation of Iraq and damaged that of the Arabs as a whole. At the same time, the Baghdad regime was so preoccupied with these activities at home, with its obscure factional fight with rival Baathists in Damascus and its quarrel with neighbouring Iran (which the Shah was not loath to aggravate), that it was of little use as a military ally against Israel. Yet when in July 1970 Nasser accepted the American initiative for a cease-fire and peace talks with Israel, he was denounced by the Iraqi regime.

Among the Arab masses, Nasser's ascendancy, shaken by the June war, had been largely restored three years later. It was not so much that the Arabs of the Middle East liked or disliked Nasser: he was simply the only Arab leader most of them took seriously. Among his supporters in the Arab intelligentsia outside Egypt his reputation was no longer unflawed. 'He is like a Chinese vase that has been cracked. He will never be the same again', a Palestinian intellectual had declared in Beirut six months after the June war.[15] His performance was measured more critically by the militant young whose heroes were the Palestinian commandos, and by the educated class, who saw the cause of Arab defeat in technological and social backwardness and in their own exclusion from a share of power.

Among these new political cross-currents of growing strength, Nasser seemed to hold a point of balance between forces inside Egypt and the Arab world pulling towards the right or the left or towards the West or Russia, though for most of the time he leaned more heavily to the left and, through force of circumstance, towards Russia. These trends of right and left, West and East, did not necessarily coincide with pressures for peace or war with Israel. Nor was it a matter of a bellicose Nasser whipping up the pacific masses. On the contrary, Nasser and other Arab leaders were more realistically aware of Arab military weakness than were their peoples who were more conscious of humiliation and a feeling of immense injustice. There was, it is true, a strong current among the Egyptian middle class, especially the older generation, in favour of a quick peace with Israel, even at the cost of writing off Egypt's Arab allies; Egypt, they thought, had already sacrificed enough for the Arabs and for the Palestinians in particular: now she should cut her losses. But popular feeling in Egypt and the sentiment among young people and the younger army officers seemed to favour resuming the fight against Israel as soon as possible, if only to restore hurt national pride.

Nasser's position lay somewhere in between. He was not prepared to jettison his whole Arab policy and submit to what he regarded as a new American sphere of influence in order to get the Israelis out of Sinai. It is doubtful whether in any case he could have done so and survived. In any case, he believed that Egypt herself could not survive in isolation from the Arab world. But he was prepared to make a settlement with Israel that would (in the words used to me by one of his entourage) effectively put the whole Palestine question into the 'deep freeze'. Even after the growth of the Palestinian guerrilla movement made this position more difficult to hold, Nasser believed that, provided such a peace included a fair settlement of the Palestinian refugee problem, the guerrillas would not prove a serious obstacle.[16] Meanwhile he was rebuilding the Egyptian forces to fight, if necessary, to regain the occupied territory but he had to counsel patience to those who wanted quick military action.

The post-war developments showed that Nasser had established an extraordinary relationship with the Egyptian public. He seemed to have become an unshakeable part of the modern Egyptian scene, a kind of national monument. Yet he remained a very human figure, if a formidable one. He was by no means spared from criticism or from mockery, yet even his mistakes brought him in a sense closer to the Egyptian people who have a tragic sense of their own history and often pay more respect to what they judge to be rightness of intention than to efficient performance. This intimate family-like acceptance persisted despite, rather than because of, the continued operations of a police state.

Nasser held all the main sources of power in Egypt in his hands. He was not only President, but also prime minister and head of the National Congress and Supreme Executive Committee of the Arab Socialist Union, the only permitted political organization. He was personally supervising the rebuilding of the armed forces. There was no one left around him of significant political stature; all were minor figures, subordinates and instruments of his will, but capable of rivalry and intrigue among themselves to gain influence over him. If there were ambitious young officers in the army secretly plotting to oust him, as he himself had plotted to overthrow Farouk, no one yet knew about them. When asked by a French journalist whether such new would-be Nassers might not

exist, Nasser was reported to have grinned and replied, 'I hope so.'
If Nasser's personal position still seemed strong, his political
machine as a whole was tired and infected with moral decay. He
was perhaps nearing the end of his creative period and Egypt
needed new men to take over.

When I last saw Nasser in July 1969 he seemed to have fully
recovered from his illness and depression of the previous summer.
He looked fit, cheerful and relaxed. He had stopped smoking and
begun taking more exercise. Instead of working until two or three
in the morning and getting up at nine, he went to bed before midnight and rose at 6.30 to play tennis for an hour and a half before
breakfast. His family life remained serene. Of his three sons,
Khaled was studying engineering at university, Abdul Hamid
was at the naval academy and Abdul Hakim still at school. His
daughters were both married and both worked. Mona had a son,
Gamal, and worked in the children's book publishing department
of *Al Ahram*. Hoda had a daughter and a job on the research
staff of the Presidency. Nasser managed to spend some time with
his children and enjoyed visits from his two grandchildren.

Nasser's presidential secretariat was not large but it included
one or two influential aides, such as Sami Sharaf, head of the President's office, who dealt specially with internal and security
matters, and Hassan Kholi, whom he used as his personal
trouble-shooter in foreign affairs.* He preferred to deal direct
with his ministers. The cabinet met weekly every Sunday and
on Saturday mornings there was a meeting of four or five
ministers dealing with economic affairs. Nasser used the telephone a great deal in the conduct of business.He read the Arabic
and foreign press avidly and watched the discussions in the
Arab Socialist Union and the National Assembly for indications
of public opinion.

Nasser held in his hands the three strands of policy-making,
executive government and legislation. The first stretched up
through the Arab Socialist Union, the second through the
cabinet and the third through the National Assembly. The ASU
prepared policy guide-lines through discussion in its central

* In May 1970, several of these aides were moved out of the Presidency
to become junior ministers in the cabinet.

committee and in its branches. A report – on, say, cooperatives
or housing – then went to the ASU Supreme Executive Committee. The Supreme Executive under Nasser's chairmanship
made the final policy decision and gave directives to Ministers to
prepare necessary laws. These laws were then approved by the
cabinet (also chaired by Nasser as prime minister) before being
submitted to the National Assembly for discussion and approval.
Such at least was the theory of the flow of power and for many
things that is how it probably worked, with Nasser trying whenever possible to get the support of a majority in the ASU
Supreme Executive. But in practice there is no doubt that on
important or urgent matters Nasser by-passed much of this
machinery and gave his orders direct.

*

On the third anniversary of the war in June 1970, the Israeli
army was still in Sinai and the Suez Canal closed. Nasser's main
problem was thus still unsolved but, otherwise, he appeared to
have achieved a remarkable recovery. Egypt was financially
solvent (with aid from the Arab oil states) and able to defend
herself, though the military budget imposed a crushing burden.
The industrialization of the country was expanding again.
Egypt's commitment to Arabism and Arab socialism remained,
though the former was more muted than before. Her dependence
on Russia had greatly increased but she was not yet a Soviet
satellite. Both Arab and Soviet commitments were measured by
Nasser in terms of the contribution they could make to his
supreme preoccupation of recovering from the defeat and dealing
with Israel.

Strategically, the military situation between Egypt and Israel
was still one of stalemate. But the 'war of attrition' had begun to
escalate alarmingly and had increased the risks that the United
States and the Soviet Union might be drawn into a dangerous
confrontation.

The Egyptian forces were re-equipped to about the levels of
before the Six-Day War, though probably stronger in tanks and
artillery and weaker in offensive aircraft. They could inflict increasing losses on the Israelis but they were not strong enough to

cross the Canal in force and drive the Israelis out of Sinai. The Israelis could hold the Canal line and inflict punishing air and land raids but were unable to invade and occupy the populated Delta area of Egypt. The Israeli air force was still superior and had begun to receive a formidable offensive reinforcement in the shape of fifty Phantom long-range fighter-bombers supplied by the United States, but the Egyptian air force had shown it was capable of limited attack.

After having crippled the Egyptian radar and anti-aircraft missile system, the Israelis began at the beginning of 1970 to extend their air offensive outside the Canal Zone to targets on the outskirts of Cairo. After one such attack had caused over 100 Egyptian civilian casualties, Nasser secured from the Russians the delivery of a more advanced type of Soviet anti-aircraft missile, the SAM3. The reported despatch of Soviet operational crews with the missiles and, on 29 April 1970, reports that the missiles were being supplemented by Soviet pilots flying 'operational missions' in Egyptian planes, marked a new degree of Soviet commitment to Egypt's defence.

Israel approached the United States for the supply of more Phantom and Skyhawk aircraft, as well as other arms, and, it was reported, a credit of $1,000 million. The US government, which had publicly deplored the 'deep penetration' raids into Egypt, postponed a decision on the Israeli requests pending a new diplomatic attempt to end the war. The Israelis meanwhile stopped bombing targets inside Egypt more than about thirty miles beyond the Canal which might have meant combat clashes with Soviet pilots. They concentrated instead on a massive non-stop air offensive against Egyptian installations in the Canal zone itself. The Egyptian casualties were rumoured to run into thousands but the main Israeli purpose was to prevent the strengthening of the air defences in the zone by the introduction of new Soviet missiles. For if the Israeli air superiority over the Canal could be broken, it would leave the Israeli forces on the east bank more vulnerable to artillery bombardment and eventual land attack.

The Russians as well as the Americans were concerned at the growing international dangers of the situation. There was another cause for anxiety in Jordan where the increasing influence of the Palestine guerrilla movement meant that the longer a peace settlement was delayed the more difficult it would become. In February there was fighting in Amman between the guerrillas and the Jordan army. The Jordan government had attempted to enforce a decree banning the carrying of arms by the guerrillas in the towns. But the guerrilla leaders suspected that King Hussein or some of his entourage were planning to crush them in order to push through a political settlement with Israel in conformity with American plans. In April demonstrations organized by the guerrillas prevented a visit to Jordan by Joseph Sisco, the American State Department official in charge of Middle East affairs, who was on a tour of the area to discuss peace prospects.

In his May Day speech, Nasser appealed to the United States to reconsider its policy of support for Israel. He warned that a turning point was approaching in America's relations with the Arab world. This might be the last chance of avoiding a drift by the Arab peoples into a hostility towards the United States which could last for generations.

As the Israeli bombing offensive continued, the Egyptian army carried out two of its biggest daylight raids across the Canal. The Israeli army made a large-scale attack on Palestine guerrilla bases inside the Lebanon. But the heaviest fighting the guerrillas faced was with the Jordan army. Between 7–11 June, more clashes in Amman and Zerqa were reported to have caused 400 dead and 800 wounded. The Jordan authorities accused the guerrillas of trying to assassinate King Hussein, which the guerrillas denied.

With the help of mediation offered through an emergency meeting of the Arab League in Tripoli, Libya, a cease-fire agreement was reached on 10 July between King Hussein and the guerrilla leaders. Hussein agreed to dismiss his uncle, General Nasser Bin Jamil, from his post of commander-in-chief and another relative, Major-General Zaid Ben Shaker, from command of an armoured division. Both men were suspected by the guerrillas of trying to destroy them. A new government was formed containing Palestinians more sympathetic to the Fatah. The Jordan government granted freedom of movement to the guerrillas who in turn promised to respect internal security needs and to discipline their members. The agreement left the guerrillas in control of many parts of Amman but with the Jordan army ringing the capital.

American plans for a new diplomatic initiative in the Middle East had been delayed partly by President Nixon's decision to intervene militarily in Cambodia. Until this intervention was ended with the withdrawal of American troops by the end of June, the international climate, especially between Washington and Moscow, was not favourable to a new move on the Middle East which would require Soviet cooperation.

But on 25 June the American Secretary of State, Rogers, announced that the United States was taking steps to reactivate the mission of the United Nations mediator, Jarring, and called on Israel and the Arab states to 'stop shooting and start talking'. The new move was, he said, a result of a review of the Middle East situation ordered by Nixon on 29 April. Since this was the date of which Israel had announced the operational activity of Soviet pilots in Egypt, it was clear that the increasing Soviet military presence in the Middle East and Mediterranean was the new factor prompting the American initiative. At a press conference on 1 July, Nixon, while endorsing the peace moves, promised that the United States would uphold the 'balance of power' required by Israel in order to deter a possible Arab attack.

The American peace plan was set out in a letter sent by Rogers to the Egyptian Foreign Minister, Mahmoud Riad, on 19 June. Similar proposals were made to the governments of Israel, Jordan and the Soviet Union. They covered three main points: agreement on a ninety-day cease-fire; a reaffirmation by both sides of their acceptance of the main elements of the Security Council resolution of 1967, namely Egyptian and Jordanian recognition of Israel's sovereignty and Israeli withdrawal from occupied territories; and agreement to peace talks through Jarring. The terms of the cease-fire, separately negotiated, included a standstill on the introduction of any new military material or installations into the cease-fire zone on either side of the Canal.

On 29 June Nasser flew secretly to Moscow for talks with the

Soviet leaders on the American plan. His presence there until 17 July was confirmed in a communiqué on that date issued in Moscow. The communiqué expressed Soviet support for Egypt and the Arabs, condemned American backing for Israel but stressed the continued commitment of both Russia and Egypt to a political settlement in the Middle East in accordance with the Security Council resolution.

The way was thus cleared for Nasser's acceptance of the American plan and this he confirmed in his speech to the Congress of the Arab Socialist Union on 23 July. Nasser claimed that, in accepting the American proposals, he was doing nothing new, because Egypt had consistently declared its acceptance of the Security Council resolution and the Jarring mission. He also warned the Egyptians that if political action failed to liberate their territory they must 'never forget the principal fact . . . what has been taken by force can only be recovered by force'.[17]

The American plan was also accepted by Jordan and Israel and endorsed by the Soviet Union, Britain and France. Both in Israel and in the Arab world its acceptance led to political splits. In Israel, the six ministers of the right-wing Gahal, led by Beigin, resigned from Golda Meir's coalition cabinet. Nasser's decision was denounced by Syria, Iraq and Algeria and by the Palestinian guerrillas. While all the guerrillas attacked the American plan, the Fatah leaders were more cautious than their more extreme colleagues about criticizing Nasser himself. They were anxious to avoid an open break with Egypt, before it was clear whether the peace talks would produce a settlement or not. If the peace talks failed, they would have unnecessarily alienated Egypt, which was their most important military ally, and they risked being left with the support of only Iraq and Syria, neither of whom carried any serious military weight against Israel. Indeed, the fear that the 'eastern front' would be overrun by Israel in the event of renewed war was one of Nasser's reasons for seeking a political solution.

The cease-fire on the Canal went into effect on 7 August and eighteen days later Jarring held preliminary meetings in New York with Egyptian, Jordanian and Israeli representatives. But on 6 September Israel formally withdrew from the talks, claiming that Egypt had violated the cease-fire agreement by introducing new anti-aircraft missiles and missile sites into the Canal zone. The Egyptians on their side complained that Israel had broken the agreement by building new fortifications. Israel, whose claim of violations was supported by the United States, refused to resume talks until the offending missiles had been withdrawn. While the American peace initiative thus ground to a halt, it was suddenly dealt a heavy blow from another direction. In Jordan the acceptance of the US plan had further increased tension between Hussein and the guerrillas. In the first week of September intermittent fighting took place in Amman and on a smaller scale in northern Jordan, mostly as a result of army attacks on the guerrillas. There were hundreds of casualties. Cease-fire agreements were made and soon broke down. Each side was trying to improve its position with an eye on an eventual showdown which appeared inevitable if the American peace move brought a settlement with Israel.

As Jordan drifted to the brink of civil war, the world was startled by the news on 6 September that Palestine guerrillas of the extreme left-wing Popular Front had attempted the simultaneous hijacking of four international airliners. The attempt on one aircraft of the Israeli El Al airline was foiled after a gun-battle in the plane over the North Sea in which one of the hijackers, an American-Nicaraguan, was shot dead and the other, a twenty-four-year-old Palestinian girl, Leila Khaled, was arrested and handed over to the British authorities at London airport. The second plane, a Pan-American jumbo-jet, landed at Cairo airport where it was blown up by the hijackers after the passengers and crew had left it. But the two other aircraft, from Swissair and the American Trans World Airlines, were flown to a desert airstrip in northern Jordan where the passengers and crew were held hostage.

Three days later they were joined by a third aircraft, a British BOAC VC-10 airliner, hijacked on its way from the Persian Gulf to Beirut. Eventually over 300 passengers and crew were being held imprisoned in the three aircraft. The Popular Front threatened to blow up the planes with the hostages in them unless Palestinian guerrillas held prisoner in other countries were released – Leila Khaled in Britain, three men in West Germany and three in Switzerland imprisoned after previous hijackings or airport attacks, and an unspecified number, including two prominent Algerian officials, detained in Israel.

All the five governments concerned agreed that any exchange deal with the guerrillas must include the release of all the hostages. Negotiations on this basis dragged on with the International Committee of the Red Cross and other unofficial agents as the main intermediaries. Egypt, like most of the other Arab governments (with the notable exception at first of Iraq) and the Fatah guerrilla organization, had condemned the hijackings as damaging to the Arab cause in world opinion and called for the unconditional release of the hostages. The British prime minister, Edward Heath, secretly sent a message to Nasser asking him to help secure the safety and release of the hostages. Egyptian diplomacy, backed by Nasser's personal influence, played an important part in bringing about the eventual release of all the hostages, especially in the last and most difficult stages of the negotiation when Jordan was already plunged in a bloody civil war.

The Popular Front at first released some 250 women and children and men of nationalities other than American, British, Swiss, German and Israeli. Then after blowing up the three planes on the airstrip, they brought the remaining fifty-four hostages to secret hiding-places in Amman.

But while the world's attention was concentrated on the extraordinary scene at 'Revolution airport' where the three planeloads of hostages were guarded by affable but armed guerrillas, themselves surrounded in turn by tanks of the Jordan army, the smouldering strife between the royal army and the guerrillas had elsewhere already begun to explode into open war. The way in which the Jordan government was obliged to stand by helplessly while the Popular Front strutted on the world stage and defied all authority, including that of the main guerrilla body, the Palestine Liberation Organization, dominated by Fatah, enraged some of the Jordan army officers. They urged the king – if he needed urging – to seize this opportunity to assert himself and destroy the guerrilla power once and for all before it could take over the whole country. The more extreme left-wing guerrilla groups had also aroused fears of Communism among the propertied class and their less disciplined followers had made themselves unpopular. The Fatah was caught between the two extremes, but, faced with a challenge to the guerrilla movement as a whole, it was bound to close ranks with the Popular Front and other extremists.

On 16 September, the day after yet another cease-fire agreement had been signed, King Hussein dismissed the cabinet and appointed a military government.

Within a few hours the Jordan army had begun an all-out assault on the guerrilla strongholds in Amman and elsewhere in Jordan. The guerrillas resisted fiercely but were outnumbered and had only light arms against the Jordan army's artillery and tanks. The ensuing civil war and the guerrillas' appeals for Arab help faced Nasser with a terrible dilemma. Insofar as the war was about the Palestinian guerrillas' opposition to a political settlement with Israel, as envisaged in the Security Council and the American peace initiative, Nasser was on the side of Hussein and the Jordan government rather than the guerrillas. He had already ordered the closing down of the Fatah radio station in Egypt because of guerrilla attacks on Egyptian policy. On the other hand, on grounds both of international policy and of his reputation as a popular radical Arab leader (and the two were connected, because his effectiveness as a peace-maker with Israel also depended on his prestige with the Arabs), he could not approve of Hussein's attempt to destroy the guerrillas, at least at this stage.

Nasser's attitude to the Palestinian guerrillas had long been ambivalent. While disowning some extremist actions of the Popular Front, such as hijacking, he had given the Fatah arms, money, training and political facilities, such as a radio station in Cairo and a certain diplomatic standing in the Arab world. He sympathized with the guerrillas as a national resistance movement, recognized their popular appeal to the Arab public and considered them a useful instrument in the war of attrition against Israel. In principle he also approved of their aim of creating a unitary secular Palestinian state of Arabs and Jews in place of Israel and western Jordan. In practice, he believed this aim was unrealistic and that the majority of Palestinians, especially those on the West Bank, would, like Nasser himself, accept a compromise settlement if it meant the withdrawal of the Israelis from all the occupied territories. If such a settlement became possible and the guerrillas continued to oppose it, then a tragic conflict might become inevitable, but the conflict might be avoided or limited in scale; in the last resort all but a hard core of the guerrilla leadership would bow to the wishes of the Palestinian majority and those that were still defiant could if necessary be more easily crushed. Meanwhile, so long as Israel's attitude made an acceptable compromise peace still highly problematical, it was madness for the guerrillas and the Arab government to fight each other. Moreover, in the case of Jordan the continued existence of the guerrillas was an assurance for Nasser that King Hussein would not risk making a separate peace with Israel on terms disadvantageous to Egypt.

Faced with the Jordan civil war, Nasser's aims were to stop the fighting as soon as possible, to save the guerrillas from physical destruction and Hussein from political defeat. He was appalled at the bloodshed and the scale of this fratricidal struggle.

Then there was the danger that the civil war might lead to international intervention, either by other Arab governments or by Israel and the United States. Threats of American intervention, if necessary, to save Hussein, especially if there were any serious Arab help to the guerrillas, were assiduously leaked from Washington. Nasser and other Arab leaders took them seriously.*

Nasser believed that without outside help the guerrillas were doomed to be crushed by the greatly superior forces of the Jordan army. So while sending the Fatah arms, ammunition and reinforcements in the shape of men from the three Palestinian regi-

---

*In an article in *Al Ahram* on 16 October 1970, describing the last twenty-four hours of Nasser's life, Heykal retrospectively justified this belief by quoting an article by the *New York Times* correspondent, Benjamin Welles, which described an intervention plan said to have been worked out jointly by American and Israeli officials in Washington on 21 September. The plan was said to have provided for an attack by Israeli planes and armour against Syrian armoured forces entering north Jordan, if these moved south in greater strength, and for an American airborne force to land round Amman, the whole operation being protected by the U S Sixth Fleet and its aircraft against Soviet or Egyptian intervention.

ments of the Palestinian Liberation Army which were on the Egyptian front, he warned Arafat that Egypt could not help him by direct military intervention and used all his influence to try to bring about a quick cease-fire. At the same time he sent a message to the Soviet leader, Brezhnev, asking the Soviet Union to do everything in its power to put pressure on the United States not to intervene. The Soviet reaction was cautious. Whatever private words of warning they may have given in Washington, the Russians appear to have been at least equally emphatic in telling the Syrian and Iraqi governments to keep out of the Jordan fighting and so avoid giving the Americans and Israelis any excuse to intervene.[18] The only direct intervention in the fighting was a brief token sortie from Syria into northern Jordan by troops of the Palestine Liberation Army, the small regular force of the PLO, equipped with Syrian army tanks and possibly with some Syrian technical support. The Iraqi division in Jordan remained passive.

While mutual deterrence prevented a bigger war, the Arab states, meeting in a summit conference in Cairo, were trying to mediate in the conflict. In Jordan itself fierce battles continued for nine days, especially in Amman. The populated areas of Amman, including the Palestinian refugee camps, from which the guerrillas were fighting, were ruthlessly shelled by Jordan army artillery and armour. Arab public opinion was horrified at the picture of an Arab capital besieged and battered by its own army and at reports of streets littered with unburied corpses. Estimates of the casualties, at first exaggerated, varied from 500 to an obviously propagandistic figure of 20,000. A more plausible figure quoted later was 2,000 dead.

On 26 September both sides agreed to a cease-fire negotiated by an Arab mediation mission headed by the Sudanese prime minister, General el Numeiry, and the Tunisian prime minister, Bahi Ladgham. Both Hussein and Arafat flew to Cairo to discuss a settlement with the assembled Arab heads of state and government. Meanwhile the last of the hijacked hostages held by the Popular Front had been released unconditionally in Amman. Leila Khaled and the six men held by Western Germany and Switzerland were freed soon after.

After intense efforts by Nasser and other Arab leaders the new and final cease-fire agreement was signed in Cairo on 27 September. It included provision for a supervisory mission of military and political observers from the Arab states. The guerrillas and the army were both to withdraw from the towns and villages and the guerrillas would concentrate their forces along the Jordan Valley front with Israel.

In the heat of the battle the guerrilla leaders had demanded the departure of Hussein as a condition of peace. Arafat had sworn that cooperation with the king was henceforward impossible because 'a sea of blood divides us'. Nasser had to use all his prestige, charm and powers of persuasion to bring the two men together and produce a new agreement. He was exhausted by the long hours of negotiation and the emotional strain. When friends urged him to rest during the talks, he is said to have replied, 'there are men, women and children dying. We are in a race with death.'[19]

As he was returning home at Manshiet el Bakr the next day, 28 September, after the end of the conference, he suffered a heart attack and died in his home three hours later.

Heykal has given a moving account of the last twenty-four hours of Nasser's life, of his dealings with Arafat in the Cairo conference, and of his collapse and death.[20]

According to Heykal, the final stages of the conference opened on the afternoon of 27 September with a stormy meeting at which Arafat and Hussein were present together for the first time. Heykal describes the tense atmosphere in the conference room at the Hilton hotel before Nasser arrived. Hussein and some of his officers were in one corner of the room and Arafat in another, 'hardly able to control himself'. Both Hussein and Arafat were carrying pistols. Heykal, only half-jokingly, suggested to King Feisal of Saudi Arabia, who was also present, that he should 'carry out a disarmament operation' before the talks began. This was something, said Feisal, that only Nasser could do.

After two and a half hours of talks the meeting adjourned while an attempt was made to draft an agreement. Nasser retired to his suite on the eleventh floor of the hotel and slept for two hours. He then received General el Numeiry and Bahi Ladgham and approved the draft agreement they had prepared. While they were discussing the agreement an urgent message arrived from Arafat saying that the Jordan army was intensifying its attacks on Amman so as to gain control of the city that night. Nasser called in Arafat to discuss this message and to try to persuade him to accept the draft agreement before the plenary session of the talks was resumed. Arafat arrived in a mood of wild Samsonian despair. He angrily asked Nasser, 'How can we trust these people who are trying to liquidate us while we are here holding discussions? It is no use – we have no choice but to pull the world down on their heads and ours, come what may.'

Nasser urged Arafat to control himself and keep in mind the main objective which was to get a cease-fire as soon as possible. He reminded Arafat that he himself needed and had asked for a cease-fire because 'your position in Amman is desperate and your men in Irbid are surrounded'. Nor could Arafat expect direct Egyptian military intervention to help him. All that Nasser could do was to try to gain time to increase the guerrillas' power of resistance so as to achieve 'a reasonable solution' and to prevent 'a deadly blow to the resistance which would hamper the unity of the Arab fighting forces'. With a veiled threat of abandonment of the guerrillas, Nasser warned Arafat that he could end the conference at that moment because from his own point of view it had already achieved much politically. But, Nasser concluded, a cease-fire must remain the objective because it would give Arafat the chance to reappraise his situation and redeploy his forces.

Nasser's mixture of persuasion and pressure, of sympathy and realism, was effective. The agreement was accepted by Arafat and the conference that evening. Meeting Nasser afterwards, Heykal expressed his astonishment. Nasser, laughing, asked him what was the matter. Heykal glumly replied that the agreement had not changed the opinion he had expressed during the fighting. 'I still say that the Arab mentality is reverting to instinct. Our thoughts are ashes and our emotions are fire. . . . we are still tribesmen; we are angry one moment and calm the next. We draw guns on each other and then we shake hands and embrace as if nothing had happened.' Nasser laughed again and said, 'Stop this philosophizing, now ... leave it for tomorrow when you will have time to indulge in it.'[21]

At 1 P.M. the next day, 28 September, Nasser telephoned Heykal at his office at *Al Ahram*. From his voice he sounded extremely tired. He said he would rest after seeing off the ruler of Kuweit at the airport. Heykal suggested he went to Alexandria for a holiday. Nasser replied, 'I cannot go while I am so tired. I will sleep here all day and then I will think about going to Alexandria.'

In perhaps his last political act, Nasser gave Heykal a message for Donald Bergus, the head of the American diplomatic mission in Cairo, to take to President Nixon who was then on a visit to the Mediterranean and the Sixth Fleet. The message was to inform Nixon that Nasser was still striving for a peaceful solution with Israel based on the Security Council resolution, but that 'the up- roar they are creating about the missiles [the anti-aircraft missiles which Israel and the United States had accused Egypt of intro- ducing illegally into the cease-fire standstill zone on the Suez Canal] has gone beyond all limits and is illogical'. Nasser told Heykal 'I do not think they will understand anything. Neverthe- less I want our position to be clear – even if only for ourselves – and let them do as they wish.' Nasser added: 'I might not contact you tonight because I am going to sleep.' Then, writes Heykal, 'I found myself saying impulsively: "Good night." Laughing, Nasser said: "Not yet, it is still day." That was the last time I heard his voice. ....'

As he was saying good-bye to the ruler of Kuweit at the airport Nasser felt dizzy and began to sweat heavily. He was driven home and the doctors were called. When Heykal reached the residence the end was already near. Nasser lay on his bed in pyjamas sur- rounded by doctors. Heykal was joined by Aly Sabry, Hussein esh-Shafei and Anwar es-Sadat who recited some verses from the Koran. General Mahmoud Fawzi 'entered in great dismay just as a doctor said: "Everything is over." General Fawzi said bitterly: "No, impossible. Continue your work. ..." All the doctors cried. Tears fell, a deluge of tears. ....'[22]

The news of Nasser's death was announced officially in a broadcast the same evening by Vice-President Anwar Sadat, who had been appointed Nasser's deputy in November 1969 and under the constitution was his provisional successor.

As the news spread, Egyptians crowded into the streets in wild demonstrations of grief. Men wept, women wailed and scratched their faces. Demonstrators marched through Cairo crying 'Nasser is not dead'. For the funeral three days later, millions of Egyptians poured into Cairo from all over the country and blocked the procession as it passed through the streets. Every vantage point, roof-top, balcony, statue, palm tree, was black with people. The foreign statesmen, including the Soviet prime minister, Kosygin, who had come as official mourners, had to retire from the procession after the first few yards. It was the day of the Egyptian people, the humble millions.[23]

The widespread international anxiety caused by Nasser's death was a recognition – however belated in some quarters – of the importance of his role as an Arab as well as an Egyptian leader. The Arab world seemed to be left without a unifying and responsible leadership at a critical moment both for itself and for world peace. There were fears in both West and East that both inside Egypt and the Arab world Nasser's departure would be followed by a period of confusion and possibly of conflict. In Egypt there might be a struggle between rival army and civilian groups, and between liberals wanting to return to a freer parliamentary system and left-wing radicals demanding a Yugoslav-type political regime. Attention was focused on several possible rivals for the succession – Vice-President Sadat; Vice-President Hussein esh-Shafei: Aly Sabry, a former Vice-President and leading member of the Arab Socialist Union and said to have the blessing of the Russians; former Vice-President Zacharia Mohieddin, in retirement since 1968 and favoured by the Americans; Mohammed Hassanein Heykal, the Minister of National Guidance and editor of *Al Ahram*; and General Mohammed Fawzi, the Minister of War. In the wings stood the lesser known but powerful figure of Sharawy el Gomaa, who as Minister of the Interior had controlled most of the internal security system except for Nasser's own personal ultra-secret service. But at first at least the emphasis was on stability, continuity and constitutional decorum. A collective leadership replaced Nasser's personal rule. All the likely rivals for the succession are said to have met together and agreed on a proper constitutional course to be worked out through consultations between the cabinet, the Higher Executive Committee of the Arab Socialist Union and the National Assembly. Anwar es-Sadat was nominated as the new President by the National Assembly and was confirmed in office by a national plebiscite on 15 October 1970. He pledged himself to continue Nasser's policies in all fields. He appointed as prime minister one of Egypt's elder statesmen, the seventy-year-old Dr Mahmoud Fawzi, a diplomat with an international reputation who was formerly foreign minister and then Nasser's chief adviser on foreign affairs. The appointment and the composition of Dr Fawzi's cabinet were signs that Egypt was looking cautiously for peace abroad and for prudent reassurance and perhaps some greater liberalization at home. One of the first actions of the new government was to renew the cease-fire with Israel for another ninety days and call for the resumption of peace talks through Dr Jarring. Another was to order a cut in price of some consumer goods and services. The position of the Egyptian regime in the Arab world was also strengthened by changes in Iraq and Syria in the aftermath of the Jordan civil war, which brought to the top leaders more favourable to cooperation with Cairo.

It appeared probable that any future struggle for the leadership of Egypt would depend less on particular personalities than on the rival influence of groups and institutions that had developed since Nasser's revolution – the army and the 'army class', the Arab Socialist Union, the bureaucracy and especially the managerial and technocratic class which controlled a large part of the socialized economy. But there was also a reasonable prospect that one of Nasser's main legacies to Egypt would prove to be an enlarged middle class of educated men, capable of ensuring efficient and stable government on a more democratic basis.

When I last saw Nasser, I asked him what he considered his greatest achievement. Nasser thought for a minute or two and then said it was the original *coup* of 1952: although it had been easy, it was long in preparation and without it he could have done nothing that followed. The main achievement of the revolution had been to create greater equality of opportunity and to bring the social classes in Egypt nearer to each other. There was still much poverty in Egypt 'but my driver's son is able to go to university while my daughter could not get in because she had not high enough marks. So I had to send my daughter to the American University here and pay £100 a year for her, while my driver's son got into Cairo university free. Some think the nationalization of the Suez Canal Company or the 1961 nationalization were the main achievements but they were only steps towards the aim of equality of opportunity.'

What of the future of the Arab world, its unity and development? Nasser replied that the present situation, the war and its aftermath, would affect the Arab world in ways that could not yet be foreseen. 'Young people will be the dominant factor in the Arab countries. Education is spreading everywhere and this will change things. . . . There may be a leap – or a dialogue – no one knows.'

Chapter 20
Conclusions

Nasser died when his greatest test of statesmanship in making peace or war was yet to come. But whatever the outcome of the still unsettled conflict with Israel, some of the changes Nasser had already helped to bring about in Egypt, in the Arab world and in the 'Third World' of Afro-Asia and the non-aligned countries are likely to endure and to influence his successors.

The Six-Day War was a colossal blunder with disastrous consequences for the Arabs. Yet if Egypt's defeat by Israel had led to Nasser's fall he would have been remembered by most Arabs, even his enemies, not, as Hitler has been by most Germans, with shame, but as Frenchmen remembered Napoleon in Stendhal's day, with tragic pride. If the rest of the world, especially Westerners, find this difficult to understand, it is only partly because some of them were Nasser's opponents or even his victims. It is also because of several factors which affect Western understanding of the Arabs and their leaders in general and of Nasser in particular. The first is the habit, natural enough but often misleading, of drawing parallels between Middle Eastern leaders and Western political figures. The second is the barrier of the Arabic language, or to be more precise a literary barrier. A third factor was the complexity of Nasser's own character, his lack of understanding of Western society, and the two voices, of reason and of violence, in which he alternately addressed it.

If Western comparisons must be sought for non-European leaders like Nasser, they are probably best found not in the pre-war Europe of Fascist reaction or the aggressive chauvinism of powerful modern industrial states, but rather in the Europe of the mid-nineteenth century, not in terms of Hitler and Mussolini but of Mazzini, Cavour or Bismarck. The Middle East of these past fifty years has resembled that era of ethnic or linguistic nationalisms struggling against multi-racial empires, of the unification of nations on linguistic and cultural bases, of the age of industrialization, the spread of education, the rise of radicalism and the decay of faith under the impact of science.

It is, however, much easier for a European or American to place a Frenchman, an Englishman and a German or even a Russian politically or historically, because of their vast familiar cultural and social hinterland. This already existing backcloth of literature, with the intuitive knowledge fed by novels and a common religious and moral consciousness, enables them to be seen by their fellow-Europeans in three dimensions. With the Arabs this illuminating background is mostly missing. The Arabs themselves have only recently begun to create their culture and literature anew and a vital part of their present revolution is to establish a modern identity for themselves. The growing modern literature of the Arab world is only now slowly becoming available in translation. As a result most Arabs, including political leaders, tend to be seen outside the Arab world as stereotypes or caricatures, flat and faceless figures in a conventional Oriental landscape.

But even without these handicaps, Nasser would still have been a difficult man to assess. His career was full of dramatic changes of fortune and his character was a mass of contradictions. On one side he was a man of determination and broad vision, a patient builder and organizer. He was very Egyptian in his down-to-earth practicality, his humour, his pride and easy magnanimity, his touch of Muslim fatalism and his ability to gain strength from feeling part of an ancient, intimate community. But he strangely combined passion and calculation. There was an emotional, impulsive side to him that, under the sting of pride or the spur of ambition, made him capable of risking much of his patient work on a sudden gambler's throw. The Six-Day War was not his first mistake of this kind. He also initially miscalculated the likely course of events in the Suez crisis but then brilliantly retrieved the situation. He misjudged the degree of commitment he was taking on in the Yemen and its high cost to Egypt, though his basic political assessment of the revolution there proved more accurate than that of his enemies. He rushed ill-prepared and against his own better judgement into the union with Syria, but on the whole this was an honourable failure that did his political reputation less lasting harm than a refusal to accept the challenge might have done.

He was both frank and secretive, a proclaimer of bold truths and capable of unblushing lies. He tried to involve the public in political action to a degree unprecedented in Egyptian and Arab history, but was haunted by conspiratorial obsessions and relied in the end on his personal authority. He had great private charm and a flair for judging popular sentiment but lacked the common touch. He was not a great demagogue except in moments of angry crisis when his passion and sardonic humour flashed to the surface: his oratory tended to be laboured, repetitive and full of clichés, but his earnestness conveyed a certain massive power.

It was perhaps these very contradictions which created his appeal to the Egyptians and the Arab public. He appealed in the first place because of his seriousness. Even his greatest political mistakes did not basically affect his reputation as a man unselfishly dedicated in his public activity and modest and uncorrupted in his private life. But neither such respect nor patient constructive work would alone have served Nasser's need to galvanize the Egyptians and the Arabs out of apathy and into revolutionary energy and greater self-reliance. For this a certain display of daring and audacity was required, to stir the popular imagination and encourage the self-confidence needed to face the modern world. In doing so he risked disaster when the human and material resources at his disposal failed to match his ambitions or the tasks he was attempting. In his zig-zags between plodding reform and bursts of apparently reckless adventure and the lurid language in which his propaganda machine expressed them, he also helped unwittingly to build up around himself and the Arabs an international image of untrustworthiness and violence. But it was primarily on acts not words that Nasser built his Arab reputation: other Arab leaders had radio stations, and some were better speakers. Nasser's main asset was not the 'Voice of the Arabs' but the economic and social reforms in Egypt, the Soviet arms deal, the nationalizing of the Suez Canal Company, the building of the High Dam and the union with Syria.

The failure of the Syrian merger underlined one of Nasser's failings, his inability to share power. He could not find the means of cooperation with groups, such as the Baathists, who had similar aims but different political methods. The fault here was not all on his side. As its subsequent history showed, the Baath was not only extraordinarily resilient and persistent but also confused in its thinking and riven by endless faction fights. But while they were often dangerously wrong-headed, the Baathists also represented probably the most vital creative spark in the political life of Syria and to a lesser extent of Iraq, especially among the younger generation. Nasser failed to find a method of harnessing their energies. Similarly in Egypt he was for long unable to find a common language with part of the intelligentsia whose strongest ties were with European culture, who sympathized with his aims but criticized his methods, and who resented the lack of political freedom.

Nasser's clash with the West was the result partly of his anti-imperialist drive and partly of Western policies. It was also, like his difficulties with Egyptian and Syrian intellectuals, a product of his world view which was influenced by his erratic education and lack of first-hand knowledge of Western countries. He was a man of powerful intelligence and broad practical knowledge, but of limited general culture. In his picture of the Egyptian geopolitical position, with its three circles of the Arab world, Islam and Africa, he exaggerated the strength and possible cohesion of the Arab countries and neglected the link with Europe through the Mediterranean. While stressing Europe's dependence on Arab oil, he failed to grasp the positive ways in which Western Europe and the Near East are strategically, economically and culturally complementary, more so even than North and South America.

Nasser was not inherently or culturally hostile to the West. The norm of a civilized state which he carried in the back of his mind as the aim towards which he hoped to lead Egypt was probably something like the social-democratic welfare states of Western Europe, though he showed only a limited understanding of the way a political democracy works. Nor was there a necessary conflict between his policy and the real, as opposed to the imagined, interests of the Western Powers in the Middle East, except over the status of Israel. But, even apart from the Israel aspect, and even when British and French imperialism had almost vanished from the Arab countries, Nasser was unable to present an attractive and convincing picture of the Arabs as possible constructive partners of the West. He tried occasionally to soothe Western fears – about oil, about the Canal, about Communism and Russia, even at times about strategic needs, as in the 1954 agreement with Britain on the Canal Zone base – but he was never conciliatory in his language for long enough to offset the picture of hatred and trouble-making created by his efforts, as a rebellious and suspicious under-dog, to shake off an old master without taking on a new one. It was true that the West was slow to realize that for Britain in particular, and for Western Europe in general, the only basis for a Middle East policy, once the military power and will to dominate was lost, was Arab goodwill and common interest. But it was equally true that the Arabs needed the goodwill and cooperation of Western Europe if they were not to be dominated by Russia or the United States or both, who *have* the power to impose themselves or at least to divide the Middle East between them.

A similar failure to hold out a constructive or positive alternative to conflict marked Nasser's policy towards Israel. The Arab–Israel conflict is *sui generis* and its nature and history leave the leaders on either side with limited room for manoeuvre. It may very well never be solved until it is overshadowed for both parties by bigger dangers or wider opportunities, or until both Zionism and pan-Arab nationalism give way as political creeds either to more local forms of patriotism or to political doctrines of a more universal kind.

Until 1967, Nasser was more willing and able than most Arab leaders to accept a prolonged coexistence with Israel, but he was unable or unwilling to go further and use such coexistence as a preparation for peace rather than a postponement of war. It is true that Ben Gurion's activist policy of force and no compromise made progress towards peace difficult. But Nasser could not rise above the Arabs' own deep sense of grievance and of danger to address the Israelis themselves in language which showed some understanding of the hopes and fears behind their aggressiveness. In the crisis of 1967 he offered no clear prospect to the Israeli public of a viable settlement but only of a quick or slow surrender. After the 1967 war Nasser was ready to accept an Israeli state in practice while, like most Arabs, rejecting it in principle. But he offered no serious alternative political relationship between the Israelis and the Arabs, except the avoidance of war, on which a future peace could be built. The Palestinian guerrillas appeared to go further in speaking of Jews and Arabs sharing a democratic Palestine state. But this concept needed to be worked out in greater detail and its practical variations, such as federation or confederation, studied for it ever to have any appeal to most Israelis remotely comparable with that of the consolidation of their own separate state.

Similarly, Nasser's refusal or inability to accept direct negotiations with the Israeli leaders or to commit himself to a full and permanent peace, though understandable in the circumstances of Arab politics, weakened Arab influence on world opinion and, perhaps more important, on opinion inside Israel. The most powerful inducement Nasser could have held out to the Israelis to make concessions would have been the prospect of a full and final peace, but this was the one card that Arab public opinion seemed to prevent him from playing, at least so long as Israeli forces were still occupying Arab territory.

Yet Nasser probably went further in the direction of a permanent peace settlement than any other Arab leader could have done without being deserted by the opinion of the Arab majority. And while his long-term view of Arab–Israeli relations may have been less imaginative or ideologically attractive than that of the Palestinian guerrillas, his policy of accepting the state of Israel as part of a compromise settlement was in the short-term far more realistic than the guerrilla programme for a generation of war.

The rigidity was by no means all on one side. If Nasser and the Arab leaders failed to offer a picture of peaceful coexistence which looked convincing to two million or more Israelis, the Israeli leaders' picture of peace did not persuade the Arabs that they had begun to take seriously the needs of the two million or more Palestinian Arabs. Neither Israelis nor Palestinian Arabs had yet really begun to see each other as people with whom they must continue to live side by side; they still mostly thought of each other as merely threats or obstacles to be controlled or eliminated.

Nasser has been compared with Mohammed Ali, for his economic development schemes, his personal rule and his attempts to make Egyptian influence felt in the Arab countries of the East. But Mohammed Ali was a foreigner, not an Egyptian, who saw Egypt as his personal fief to be managed so as to produce the greatest possible revenue for his own purse and his own ambitions. The Egyptian society Nasser was trying to build was more generous and humane than that conceived by Mohammed Ali. His idea of Egyptian action in the Arab world was more coherent and constructive than Mohammed Ali's and less simply imperialistic. Nasser was less ruthless and a less able soldier. He was guilty of some brutalities both inside Egypt and outside. In Egypt there were dark blots like the political concentration camps in the desert where Communists, Muslim Brothers and others were sent. There were torture and spying by the political police, the censorship of the press and radio, and the endless propaganda. Outside Egypt there were the bombing, including gas bombing, of villages in the Yemen and the operation of secret intelligence agents. But among revolutions the Egyptian must be counted as one of the least bloody.

Nasser used arbitrary police action as one instrument of power but it would not be accurate to describe Egypt under his rule as simply a 'police state'. There was a large element of consent, discussion and persuasion involved. Most of the aims of the regime were in line with a broad national consensus. The brutalities and repression of criticism under Nasser were less severe than under many other dictatorships or more truly totalitarian states, including some previous Egyptian governments and other Arab governments to which Britain and other Western Powers had given their blessing and about whose secret police and political prisons the Western press was usually more discreetly silent than in the case of Egypt. Although the secret police kept a close watch to stifle any open organized opposition – in the universities, for example, there were special police to control the students –

there was critical comment both publicly within the Arab Socialist Union and in the National Assembly, and even more in private, even in conversation with foreigners. Censorship, the socialization of the press and government control of radio and television limited the flow of accurate information about public affairs and informed comment on it, though Nasser in many long speeches provided a mass of information. Foreign newspapers were also sometimes cut and foreign broadcasts in Arabic jammed, but the flow of information – especially through foreign broadcasts, books, magazines and newspapers, limited as they also were by foreign exchange shortages, as well as through the many foreign visitors – was still free enough for an educated Egyptian, armed with his strong native scepticism, to obtain in time a reasonably reliable picture of the outside world. In this respect Egypt remained a much more 'open society' than any Communist country; it was more often about their own country's affairs that the regime kept the Egyptians too much in the dark. It is probable that Nasser could have allowed Egyptian society to become a good deal more 'open' – as he had indeed promised in response to the students' protests, but failed to do – without seriously weakening his authority.

Until June 1967, Nasser's reputation as an Egyptian ruler seemed to be securely based on his achievement of complete national independence, the nationalization of the Suez Canal Company, the building of the High Dam and the relative success of a broad programme of modernization, education, social reform and economic development. His success in these respects was qualified by his failure to create a self-sustaining dynamic political system which could dispense with the support of the army, arbitrary police action and censorship, by the ineffective restraints on Egypt's rapid population growth, by the persistence of massive unemployment and rural poverty and by the accumulation of a large foreign debt.

In the Arab world, despite the failure of the Egyptian–Syrian merger, the costly involvement in the Yemen, the lack of progress towards solving the Palestine problem and the suspicion and hostility of other Arab governments, both 'conservative' and 'progressive', Nasser was still the most influential Arab leader. He was the most powerful symbol of radical pan-Arab nationalism with its aspirations of complete independence from foreign powers, Arab unity, modernization and greater social justice. In the 'Third World' he had established himself as one of the leading exponents of non-alignment, but deeply committed to the anti-colonial and anti-imperial struggle in the Arab world and Africa.

How far must this assessment be revised in the light of the 1967 defeat and Nasser's struggle to recover during the last three years of his life?

At first sight, the assumptions most in question concern Egypt's national independence, her Arab leadership and her doctrine of non-alignment – in other words, Nasser's foreign policy. Having at last freed Egyptian territory of foreign military occupation with the departure of the British in 1956, Nasser little more than ten years later saw Israeli forces occupying the Sinai Peninsula and claiming to remain indefinitely in at least one corner of it, at Sharm esh-Sheikh. Having gained full control of the Suez Canal, he then saw it closed and useless and with one bank occupied by the Israelis. Having rejected a Western alliance and protection in the pursuit of complete independence and non-alignment, he found himself relying on Russian diplomatic and military support, with Soviet warships using Egyptian ports, Soviet officers training the Egyptian army in the use of Soviet weapons and taking part in the air defence of Cairo and Alexandria. Having sought financial independence and economic aid without political strings, he was faced with a foreign indebtedness of £1,000 million and dependence on subsidies from other Arab governments, including his chief Arab opponent, King Feisal of Saudi Arabia.

There are, however, grounds for arguing that these developments were of a transitory character and did not fundamentally reverse the changes that established Egyptian independence. The Israelis were unlikely to stay in Sinai for more than a few years longer, whether the issue was settled by peace or war. Even if they kept troops longer at Sharm esh-Sheikh, the political significance of their presence there would be far less than the presence of scores of thousands of British troops in the Canal Zone. The Russians had not yet been able to turn Egypt into a satellite: they had no combat troops in Egypt comparable with the former British forces and capable of enforcing their will as in Czechoslovakia. At the peak of their struggle to hold their military position in Egypt, the British had as many as 80,000 troops in the Suez Canal Zone, an organized fighting army with all supporting arms. The Russians had no such organized combat units in Egypt capable of taking over the country or dominating the government. The bulk of the Russians in Egypt were officers and technicians training the Egyptian forces, with perhaps a few hundred more manning anti-aircraft missiles and flying jet fighters. The rest were working as advisers in industrial installations supplied and built by the Soviet Union. These were gradually withdrawn and replaced by Egyptians as the latter were trained – the number of Russian working on the High Dam had already dropped from 2,000 to a dozen or so supervising the power station. These few thousand scattered Soviet personnel would scarcely have been strong enough in numbers, organization or arms to seize control of Egypt or to resist if at any time Nasser had decided to send them away. Nor would the Russians have been in a position easily to move more substantial forces into Egypt unless they were invited to do so by some new Communist-controlled regime in Cairo.

But what of other forms of Soviet penetration in Egyptian society? The Russians lacked in Egypt the two other main instruments which had enabled them to control their East European satellites – they controlled neither the key positions in the internal security services nor an effective Communist party apparatus. They had no doubt done their best to build up sympathizers within the Egyptian armed services and within the Arab Socialist Union, the main civilian political organization, as well as among the students sent to the Soviet bloc for study, and the technical intelligentsia and industrial workers among whom they worked in Egypt. But although in a general way their influence and prestige had increased, there was no serious evidence that they had succeeded in creating a sub-servient, Communist-dominated political or military network capable of seizing and maintaining power. Nor indeed was it certain that they had tried to do so – they were extremely careful to behave correctly and to give no appearance of interference in Egypt's internal affairs. After all, part of their purpose in Egypt was to prove – as against Peking's thesis of revolutionary solidarity with Communists everywhere – that in certain countries, especially in the Third World, it was better to cooperate with nationalist progressive but bourgeois regimes, even at the expense of local Communists. Indeed, one of the most striking aspects of Egypt when Nasser died, was the extent to which, in its external relations, Egyptian culture and education were still dominated overwhelmingly by Western, especially British, French and American, influences. The majority of students still went to the West; English and French were widely spoken and very little Russian. There were still many important schools and even a university (the American university in Cairo) conducted in the English or French languages – but not in Russian. There were officially supported newspapers published in Cairo and Alexandria in English or French but not in Russian. There were innumerable long-standing ties of a cultural, economic and personal character between Egyptians and Europe and America. Russia was distant and strange, understood as a military or diplomatic power, welcome temporarily as an ally, alien and abstract as an ideological system. As people, Russians were unfamiliar.

This situation was changing slowly, especially as the economic ties between Egypt and the Soviet bloc developed. But Nasser could still at any time have sent away the Soviet officers and technicians with his army, if he had been prepared to pay the price. What stopped him was that the price would have been the weakening of Egypt's defences and the probable loss of Soviet military and economic aid. His relations with Russia were conditioned by the conflict with Israel and by the policies of the Western Powers. A settlement with Israel and better relations with the West would have enabled him to reduce his military and economic dependence on Moscow, without having to engage in the kind of desperate struggle that was required to end the British occupation. Such a change might not have been entirely unwelcome to the Russians themselves. For the Soviet military commitment to Egypt had become both expensive and potentially embarrassing to

Moscow, while both Nasser and the Russians would probably have liked the economic relations built up to continue. Similarly, it was unlikely that the Canal would remain closed for ever. And even if its future importance were reduced by the development of alternative routes and of giant oil tankers, it would continue to earn foreign exchange, supplemented by a parallel oil pipe-line from Suez to Alexandria. There was also a good prospect that within a few years Egypt's own oil exports would enable her to relieve some of her foreign indebtedness, reduce her balance-of-payments deficit and dispense with Arab subsidies.

Nevertheless, the June defeat raised in more acute form the question as to whether a country as materially weak and geographically exposed as Egypt could afford a foreign policy which tried to combine non-alignment and reliance on foreign economic development aid with a militant anti-imperialism. For, in practice, anti-imperialist militancy meant frequent collision with the strongest world power and an important source of economic aid, the United States, as well as friction with Britain and occasionally other Western Powers whose political goodwill and economic help could also have been useful to Egypt. Nasser tried to strengthen Egypt's position and reduce her vulnerability by mobilizing the Arabs behind his policy and relying more heavily on Russian military and economic aid. But the June war showed that the Arabs could not provide an effective military support nor could Russian aid compensate for the hostility of the United States. Yet Nasser's choices were at first limited by the political circumstances of Egypt and the Arab world and by the policies of the Great Powers. Egyptian and Arab opinion was strongly opposed to foreign military alliances. It was both anti-Western, because of the Palestine question and the continued British and French domination of parts of the Arab world, and anti-Communist. Nasser could not have openly aligned himself with either the Western or Soviet blocs. In his early years, he was prepared for a tacit military link with the West, but this was blocked by the unsettled conflict with Israel and the Western attempt to organize a formal Arab alliance through the Baghdad Pact.

To mobilize the Arabs behind non-alignment meant also

espousing Arab causes more actively over Palestine and the remaining Western imperial footholds in the Arab world, as well as resisting attempted Communist penetration. It meant trying to give body to the positive vision of Arab unity which was also in Nasser's mind.

The first element in this vision – an Arab world of independent states free of foreign imperial control or open foreign alliances – had been almost completely fulfilled before Nasser died. The British and French had withdrawn their rule and their forces from all the Arab countries they formerly controlled, except for the last small vestiges of a British military commitment in the Persian Gulf which was due to end in 1971. Since 1952 the number of independent Arab states had doubled from seven to fourteen: in several of them there had been revolutions aimed at making this independence complete and at reforming domestic government. This change was not, of course, all Nasser's doing but he contributed powerfully to the movement of ideas which brought it about.

The second element in this vision, common Arab action in defence and foreign policy, was never fully achieved and occurred only sporadically and ineffectively among small and changing groups of Arab states. The third element, political or constitutional Arab unity, was tried seriously and unsuccessfully by Nasser in the short-lived union with Syria and less seriously in the abortive talks on federation between Egypt, Syria and Iraq in 1963. The experience of the union with Syria led Nasser to the view that constitutional unity was possible only between countries with similar political and social systems and his aim became to set the pattern of common Arab development through the operation of 'Arab socialism' in Egypt itself. Nasser's intervention in the Yemen appeared to contradict this idea of unity and socialism by peaceful example, but it was an opportunist miscalculation rather than a basic change of policy.

The fourth element in Nasser's Arab concept was the coordination of the economic resources of the Arab world to carry out a common regional development programme and in order to strengthen the Arab's international bargaining position. This also made little progress but was an aspect of Arab unity that assumed increasing importance in Nasser's mind in his last years.

Some reflection of how Nasser's ideas of Arab nationalism and unity had evolved in the light of the June defeat may be gained from an article by Heykal in *Al Ahram* at the beginning of 1968, entitled, 'Changes in the Arab land'. Arab nationalism, declared Heykal, had been too concerned with the past and not enough with the future. Although it was true that the Arabs had a common language and a common way of thinking, this did not mean they necessarily had a common future. A common future was governed only by common interests. By virtue of common interests, Western Europe, despite past enmities, was now achieving more united action than the Arabs had achieved through their legacy of unity in the past. Only large continental-size states could now develop alone and the Arabs needed a comprehensive economic development plan. The problem was how to achieve economic unity without creating political disputes between the Arab states which would destroy their consciousness of a common future.[1]

This book has traced Nasser's career through the three phases identified as the 'Egyptian Revolution', 'Arab Nationalism' and 'Arab Socialism'. Some writers* have seen Nasser's career as rising to a peak in 1961 and then, after the break-up of the UAR and the introduction of 'Arab Socialism', going into a decline. It is true that Nasser's international influence and prestige was at its zenith in 1960, as was that of the non-aligned leaders in general. The establishment and breakdown of the UAR also was the high-water mark of Nasser's capacity to create a close Arab political union. His break with the Syrian Baathists also set a limit to his influence over the Arab radical intelligentsia. But, in perspective, it may now be argued that the period of Arab Socialism between 1961 and the 1967 war, far from being one of decline, was precisely when Nasser made his most lasting contribution to Arab development. For his efforts to industrialize Egypt and transform Egyptian society are likely to have a more important effect on the future of the Arab world

*For example, Tom Little in *Modern Egypt*.

than his campaign in the Yemen, his cold war with King Feisal or the Syrian Baathists, or even the defeat by Israel.

The June defeat had at first an adverse psychological effect on the national self-confidence which Nasser had striven to inculcate. The need to rearm and prepare for the recovery of the occupied territories imposed a heavy new defence burden and a diversion of resources from civilian needs. But the defeat nevertheless had surprisingly little impact on the general course of Egypt's economic and social development. What difference did Nasser's domestic policies make to the Egyptian people compared with their situation in 1952? What did 'Arab Socialism' mean to the average Egyptian?

In a country with problems of poverty and over-population on the scale of Egypt's and limited national resources, it was not to be expected that any government, however virtuous or however efficient, could cure them or even substantially reduce them in less than twenty years. But it might be hoped that some of the worst abuses could be ended and a start made along a constructive path. This, at least, Nasser could fairly claim to have done in many respects.

The High Dam and its power station were completed in July 1970; the complementary electrification and land reclamation schemes, though slowed down by the costs of the war with Israel, are moving steadily ahead. They will usher in a new era in both agriculture and industry, though this will not mean a quick alleviation of the crushing poverty that is still the lot of the great majority of Egyptians. The increase in agricultural production had been keeping just ahead of the increase in population, while industry, on which the reduction of unemployment and an increased standard of living must primarily depend, had been expanding more rapidly. By 1970 the population was increasing at the rate of a million a year. Forty-five per cent of the population were under sixteen and health standards were rising. Both a faster economic growth rate and more intensive efforts at birth control were therefore needed if the hoped-for improvements in living standards were to be achieved. Since 1952 there had been a small increase in *per capita* national income and a more equal distribution of national wealth. The benefits had been felt less in increased money incomes than in improved social services – more free schools, hospitals and clinics, cheap housing and limited social insurance – and their effect varied among different classes or groups of the population. Sixty per cent of Egyptians still lived and worked on the land. Among them those who had gained most were the medium farmers and the one-and-a-half million people who had benefited from the land reform. Their incomes had increased from better government-aided production and marketing methods, cheaper credit and to a certain extent from rent control, though this was often ineffective. But for the millions of landless and often unemployed agricultural labourers and their families there was little increase in earnings unless they were able to find work in the towns. The legislation fixing minimum wages for agricultural labourers was almost unenforceable, but they at least shared with the luckier peasants access to the expanded rural welfare schemes and education and health services. A similar division occurred in the towns. The main beneficiaries were the factory workers and the middle class. More jobs were created though there were still huge numbers of urban unemployed. But a man with a job had greater security, usually better working conditions, more active protection of his interests through his trade union and representation on management councils (though both unions and management were too often tamely subservient to the government machine). Rent controls and food subsidies helped to keep down the cost of living. But the unemployed or only partly employed lived in the deepest poverty and often in the most appalling slum conditions. Though they and especially their children also gained something from the expanded social services, cities like Cairo were expanding at such a rapid rate from a combination of high birth rate and influx from the countryside that all the public services were strained far beyond their capacity.

In both town and country, especially in the villages, one intangible but important gain was a certain change in the relationship with authority. Centuries of Ottoman and Mameluke rule ground deep into the Egyptian consciousness the idea that the government and its local representatives were a positive evil, an exploiting bullying force, an idea that may have begun to recede under Cromer's rule but survived under subsequent Egyptian governments in which the big land-owners wielded great influence. Now, cautiously and sceptically, the idea grew to a certain extent that the government might genuinely be on the side of the peasant and the worker and desirous of helping him, however limited and sometimes ineffective that help might still be. Corruption, bullying and abuse of power, especially by petty officials, still existed but they were no longer taken to be the *purpose* of government. The villager or the factory or office worker no longer felt completely at the mercy of a local headman or policeman or land-owner with his thugs, or of the factory boss sure of having the government and police to back him up. But as in India and Pakistan and possibly in China, the great mass of rural poverty in Egypt was still the main incubus on a society in which more buoyant forces were emerging through the spectacular expansion of education and increased industrialization.

Nasser's social and economic policies, especially land reform, the development of cooperatives, industrialization and state planning, stimulated similar developments in other Arab countries. There were two aspects of his 'Arab Socialism' which may be more universally relevant to the problems of developing countries. The first is the manner in which socialist and private enterprise were combined in a planned economy; the second and more original feature is the method by which state planning and technical aid, cooperative management and individual land ownership were linked together in the system of 'supervised cooperatives' in agriculture.

Some have also tried to distinguish a political doctrine or practice of 'Nasserism' with a wider application in developing countries. The essence of 'Nasserism' is said to be the political role of the army as a revolutionary *élite*, with social as well as national aims, in countries where the civilian *élite* is still too weak for this purpose. Nasser certainly saw the army as the vanguard of his revolution and used the army officers for this purpose, but he regarded this as temporary expedient rather than a desirable doctrine. He spent a good deal of time trying to devise a political organization which would enable him to dispense with it.

In this and other respects it is instructive to compare Nasser with Kemal Ataturk whose career he had closely studied. Both tried and failed to transform their dictatorships into something more democratic. Both were defeated in this endeavour by their own reluctance in the last resort to give up real power as well as by the authoritarian traditions of their countries. But Nasser was at once more liberal, more radical and more conservative than Ataturk. He was less brutal in his political methods and more cautious in dealing with popular sentiment, especially as regards the Muslim religion and the customs of the peasantry. In his attitude to the Muslim Brothers he demonstrated an opposition to the intrusion of religion into politics almost as strong as that of Ataturk, but he made no attempt to follow Ataturk's example in the disestablishment of Islam, except in the important reform of the application of Sharia law. Nasser recognized the place of Islam in the state and in society and in Egyptian and Arab culture. He did not bully the Egyptians to change their dress or their way of living in order outwardly to ape that of Europeans. He favoured the emancipation of women and accepted the need for family planning, but because he believed these questions touched strongly entrenched traditional feelings, he was careful not to press such changes too hard or too fast. Ataturk was a militant secularist; Nasser wanted to reform Muslim society not destroy it. But Nasser's socialization of the Egyptian economy and his economic development programmes were more radical and far-reaching than the étatism of Ataturk.

Ataturk began with two advantages compared with Nasser. He came to the task of modernizing Turkey with the prestige of a successful military leader, a popular hero who had led a national resurgence after a crushing defeat and occupation. Moreover the defeat itself had enabled him to shed the burden of Ottoman imperial ambitions and the newer extravagances of pan-Turanism and to concentrate on the consolidation of the Turkish national state. But Nasser could not similarly have cut Egypt off from the rest of the Arab East: the links were far more real and close than those between Turkey and the other Turkish-speaking peoples and were reinforced politically by the continuing common struggle against British imperial occupation and Israel.

What both men have left behind in the form of Kemalism and Nasserism is less a formal doctrine than a state of mind, a determination, pragmatic, rational and self-confident, to look the modern world in the face and to use all the resources of the state machinery positively to promote social progress and national independence.

Both inside Egypt and in the Arab world, Nasser's ideas provided a bridge between the old generation of nationalists who were concerned with political independence and the new generation seeking reform and reconstruction. While many Western observers saw Nasser as an element of mischievous disturbance, he was more often a factor of continuity and stability. At a time when Arab society was in danger of collapse and of leaving the field to the Communists, the reactionary fanaticism of the Muslim Brothers, a narrowly nationalistic military fascism or chaos, Nasser, by providing continuous stable and progressive government in the biggest and most developed Arab state, helped to ensure that in most cases Arab society underwent change in a comparatively bloodless way. (The Yemen was the outstanding exception.) He was accused of stirring up trouble in countries like Iraq under Nuri es-Said and Saudi Arabia under its monarchy, which, it was thought, might otherwise have evolved peacefully into reformed modern states. This was to underestimate the revolutionary pressures already at work under the surface of these apparently stable societies. Nasser did not produce the 1958 revolution in Iraq. There would have been a revolution there in any case, but his influence probably prevented it from being led by the Communists. The same was true of the recent revolutions in the Sudan and Libya and may yet prove true in Saudi Arabia.

Nasser helped to direct the Arabs' attention not only towards the achievement of independence and mastery of their own economic resources, but also to the problems of poverty and social organization. He thereby gave in the Arab world, as in Egypt, 'a national purpose to the professional class and new status to the peasant and worker'.[2] At the same time, his abuse of propaganda and his restriction on free political debate in Egypt lowered the intellectual level of Arab society and deprived it of much needed self-criticism.

At this moment some may have grave doubts about the Arab future. They see the Arab defeat by Israel in 1967 as exposing the hollowness of Arab claims to nationhood. This is short-sighted. In historical terms the Arab revival is only just beginning, but there is no doubt about its reality. Apart from the emergence of many new nations within less than a generation, there are powerful currents of renovation sweeping through Arab society in every direction. Nor can there be any doubt of the importance of this movement, especially to Europe, not only because of the great human potential of a region which is the cradle of Western civilization, but also because of the continuing political and economic importance of its geographical position, its oil supplies and its role as a cultural link with emergent Africa and Asia.

Nasser's career throws light not only on the development of Egyptian and Muslim society and on the evolution of the Arab political mind. It also reflects the experience and outlook of the Third World of under-privileged colonial man. In this experience the central driving force is the struggle for the recovery of human dignity and identity, an attempt to escape the humiliation bred of backwardness and weakness, to catch up against overwhelming odds. The emotions engendered by the colonial experience and its equivalent among oppressed minorities provide a tremendous power for good and ill, for national and personal reconstruction and for tragic conflict.

This most vital force which fired men like Nasser, Ben Gurion, Mao Tse-tung, Nehru and Nkrumah was described by James Baldwin in explaining the desperation of American Negroes. They were, he wrote 'a people from whom everything has been taken away, including, most crucially, the sense of their own worth. People cannot live without this sense; they will do anything to regain it.'[3] Time and again, Nasser's speeches and actions were concerned with 'dignity', with the struggle against national despair and the restoration of the Egyptian people's sense of their own worth after long centuries of humiliation,

oppression and self-doubt. People who have suffered are not
always pleasant, and their struggle to be whole again can be
painful for others. But they deserve understanding and help
rather than further humiliation.

'History will sentence him to death', was Nasser's valedictory
comment on King Farouk. What will be history's verdict on
Nasser? Whether it be kind or harsh, it is unlikely to be one of
quick oblivion.

So far, Nasser remains the most progressive Egyptian ruler
of modern times and the most important statesman thrown up by
the Arab renaissance. His role as a leader of the anti-colonial
revolution, one of the great world political movements of the
twentieth century, is likely to be of enduring interest to historians.

Nasser left his mark on nearly two decades of Egyptian, Arab
and world history. In the tradition of the Pharaohs, the High
Dam will be for centuries his physical memorial. But his influence
will continue to be felt in Egypt and the Arab countries for years
to come in the movement of ideas and the course of political,
social and economic development which he stimulated and helped
to create.

References

Prologue

1. James Henry Breasted, *A History of Egypt from the Earliest Times to the Persian Conquest* (London, 1966), p. 144.
2. Albert Hourani, preface to J. H. Ahmed, *The Intellectual Origins of Egyptian Nationalism* (Oxford, 1960), p. ix.

Chapter 1. A Troubled Youth, 1918–36

1. Jacques Berque, *Histoire Sociale d'un Village Égyptien au XXme Siècle* (Paris, 1957), p. 24.
2. From the short story, 'The Maize Field', by Mukhtar el Attar, translated by Raoul and Laura Makarius in *Anthologie de la Littérature Arabe Contemporaine*, vol. 1 (Paris, 1964), pp. 179 *et seq.*
3. Ikbal Ali Shah, *Fuad, King of Egypt* (London, 1936).
4. Robert St John, *The Boss* (London, 1961), p. 18.
5. Anwar es-Sadat, *Revolt on the Nile* (London, 1957), p. 13.
6. Interview in *Sunday Times*, 17 June 1962.
7. Gamal Abdul Nasser, *The Philosophy of the Revolution* (Cairo, 1954), p. 41.
8. Desmond Stewart, *Young Egypt* (London, 1958), p. 183; also, Nasser to the author, July 1969.
9. Marcel Colombe, *L'Évolution de l'Égypte* (Paris, 1951), pp. 122–8.
10. Nasser, *op. cit.*, p. 43.
11. For a detailed discussion of al Kawakibi's ideas, see Khaldun S. al Husry, *Three Reformers* (Beirut, 1966); also Albert Hourani, *Arabic Thought in the Liberal Age* (Oxford, 1962), pp. 271–3.
12. Georges Vaucher, *Gamal Abdul Nasser et son Équipe*, vol. 1 (Paris, 1959), p. 52. Special number of *Al Mussawar*, Cairo, August 1957. Also Stewart, *op. cit.*, p. 184. I am particularly indebted to Vaucher for information in the preceding section on Nasser's school life and reading.
13. *Akher Saa*, 23 July 1958; see also, Nasser, *op. cit.*, p. 17.
14. Nasser, *op. cit.*, p. 31.

Chapter 2. The Army and Politics: Egypt in the Second World War, 1936–46

1. Nasser, *op. cit.*, p. 20. Sir Anthony Eden, in a letter of reply to Marshal Bulganin on 17 September 1956, distorted this reference

as evidence of Nasser's self-confessed addiction to 'militarism', *Full Circle* (London, 1960), p. 487.

2. Stewart, *op. cit.*, p. 182.
3. Nasser to the author.
4. Information supplied to the author by Nasser's uncle, Taha Hussein.
5. P. J. Vatikiotis, *The Egyptian Army in Politics* (Indiana, 1961), pp. 47–9.
6. Anwar es-Sadat in *Al Mussawar*, quoted in Vaucher, *op. cit.*, p. 109.
7. Vaucher, *op. cit.*, pp. 97–8.
8. See especially Vatikiotis, *op. cit.*, and Anouar Abdul Malek, *Egypt: Military Society* (New York, 1968).
9. Stewart, *op. cit.*, p. 185.
10. Nasser, *op. cit.*, p. 28.
11. Public Record Office, Report dated 29 April 1937 (FO/371/20909/ J2365/244/16).
12. Quoted in Vaucher, *op. cit.*, pp. 105–6.
13. For a brilliant description of *la belle époque* in Egypt at this time, see Jacques Berque, *L'Égypte, Impérialisme et Révolution* (Paris, 1967), pp. 484–502.
14. Sadat, *op. cit.*, pp. 13, 14.
15. *ibid.*
16. Nasser to the author.
17. Sadat, *op. cit.*, p. 17.
18. Vaucher, *op. cit.*, p. 115.
19. Lord Wilson, *Eight Years Overseas* (London, 1950), pp. 39, 53–4. Wilson says the British found Aziz al Misry's copy of their secret plans for defence of Siwa in the Italian headquarters files at Sidi Barrani.
20. Sadat, *op. cit.*, pp. 26–32.
21. *ibid.*, p. 29.
22. Nasser, speech to Arab Socialist Union youth leaders, *Egyptian Mail*, 20 November 1965.
23. Sadat, *op. cit.*, p. 31.
24. George Kirk, *The Middle East in the War 1939–45*, RIIA, fn., p. 200.
25. Barrie St Clair McBride, *Farouk of Egypt* (London, 1967), p. 121.
26. Mohammed Neguib, *Egypt's Destiny* (London, 1955), p. 14.
27. Sadat, *op. cit.*, p. 41.
28. Extracts from letter published in *Al Mussawar*, August 1957, quoted in Vaucher, *op. cit.*, pp. 129, 130, and paraphrased in Nasser, *op. cit.*, p. 15.

29. Sadat, *op. cit.*, p. 44.
30. *ibid.*, p. 49.
31. *Al Mussawar*, August 1957.
32. Nasser to the author, July 1969.

Chapter 3. Disillusion, Defeat and Conspiracy, 1946–9

1. Sadat, *op. cit.*, pp. 56–7.
2. *ibid.*, p. 72.
3. *ibid.*, p. 70.
4. Neguib, *op. cit.*, p. 18.
5. Nasser, *Toute la Vérité sur la Guerre de Palestine* (Cairo, 1955), p. 7.
6. Rashid el Barawy, *The Military Coup in Egypt 1952* (Cairo, 1952), p. 159.
7. Neguib, *op. cit.*, p. 15.
8. *ibid.*
9. *ibid.*, p. 20.
10. *ibid.*, p. 17.
11. Nasser, *Toute la Vérité* . . . , pp. 11–18.
12. *ibid.*; also Vaucher, *op. cit.*, p. 191.
13. Nasser, *Toute la Vérité* . . .
14. *ibid.*

Chapter 4. The Road to Revolution, 1949–52

1. Nasser, *The Philosophy of the Revolution*, pp. 54–7.
2. *ibid.*, pp. 58–9.
3. *ibid.*, pp. 59, 61.
4. *ibid.*, p. 28.
5. Colombe, *op. cit.*, p. 255.
6. Sadat, *op. cit.*, pp. 94–5.
7. *ibid.*, p. 95.
8. *ibid.*, p. 96.
9. Neguib, *op. cit.*, p. 29.
10. *ibid.*, p. 93.
11. Sadat, *op. cit.*, pp. 101–2.
12. Barawy, *op. cit.*, pp. 199ff.
13. Sadat, *op. cit.*, pp. 101–2.
14. *ibid.*, p. 97.
15. Nasser, *The Philosophy of the Revolution*, pp. 32, 33.
16. *ibid.*, pp. 34–6.
17. Sir Ralph Stevenson in interview with the author, September 1968.

18. Neguib, *op. cit.*, pp. 101–2.
19. Ahmed Abul Fath, *L'Affaire Nasser* (Paris, 1962), p. 26.
20. Neguib, *op. cit.*, pp. 32, 110–11.
21. Sadat, *op. cit.*, pp. 111, 112.
22. Neguib, *op. cit.*, pp. 110–13.
23. Sadat, *op. cit.*, p. 116, See also Nasser interview in *Sunday Times*, 24 June 1962.
24. Sir Ralph Stevenson to the author, September 1968.
25. Sadat, *op. cit.*, p. 119; Neguib, *op. cit.*, p. 120; Barawy, *op. cit.*, pp. 205–20.
26. Eden, *op. cit.*, pp. 240–41.
27. Neguib, *op. cit.*, p. 132.
28. *ibid.*, p. 135.
29. *ibid.*, p. 140.

Chapter 5. The Path to Power and the Struggle for National Independence, 1952–4

1. Patrick O'Brien, *The Revolution in Egypt's Economic System* (Oxford, 1966), p. 1.
2. Gabriel Saab, *The Egyptian Agrarian Reform 1952–1962* (Oxford, 1967), pp. 2, 7.
3. Henri Ayrout, *Fellahs d'Égypte* (Cairo, 1952), p. 102.
4. Nasser, *The Philosophy of the Revolution*, pp. 20–6, 44.
5. Sadat, *op. cit.*, p. 120.
6. *ibid.*, p. 125.
7. Saab, *op. cit.*, p. 9.
8. *ibid.*, p. 13.
9. *ibid.*
10. Land Reform Law, Decree Law N 170, 1952 (Cairo, 1954).
11. Saab, *op. cit.*, *passim.*
12. Erskine Childers, *The Road to Suez* (London, 1962), p. 375.
13. Neguib, *op. cit.*, p. 174.
14. *ibid.*, p. 216.
15. *ibid.*, p. 213.
16. Wilton Wynn, *Nasser of Egypt* (Cambridge, Mass., 1959), p. 97.
17. Neguib, *op. cit.*, p. 218.
18. Khaled Mohieddin in conversation with the author, March 1968.
19. Barawy, *op. cit.*, pp. 199ff.
20. Sir Ralph Stevenson in conversation with the author, September 1968.
21. *Observer*, 12 April 1953.

22. Dwight D. Eisenhower, *The White House Years*, vol. 1, *Mandate for Change* (New York, 1963), p. 157.
23. Lord Robertson to the author, July 1968.
24. Interview with Arab News Agency, quoted in Tom Little, *Modern Egypt* (London, 1967), p. 157.
25. O'Brien, *op. cit.*, pp. 68ff.

Chapter 6. The Arabs, Russia and the West, 1954–6

1. Nasser, *The Philosophy of the Revolution*, pp. 60, 64–72.
2. Interview with R. K. Karanjia of *Blitz*, 28 September 1958, Nasser's Speeches, 1958.
3. Eden, *op. cit.*, p. 221.
4. Stewart, *op. cit.*, p. 190.
5. Sir Ralph Stevenson to the author.
6. Childers, *op. cit.*, pp. 120–21; a similar view was repeated by Nasser to the author in an interview in November 1955.
7. Patrick Seale, *The Struggle for Syria* (Oxford, 1965), pp. 196ff.
8. Eisenhower, *op. cit.*, p. 164.
9. Sir Ralph Stevenson to the author.
10. Nasser to the author, November 1955.
11. See account of meeting by Major Salah Salem in Seale, *op. cit.*, pp. 201–4, 206–7; also speech by Nuri es-Said on 16 December 1956, BBC Monitoring, N 126, 18 December 1956, and reply by Colonel Hatem, Egyptian Director of Information, on 20 December, BBC Monitoring, N 130, 27 December 1956.
12. Quoted in Lord Birdwood, *Nuri Es-Said* (London, 1959), p. 251.
13. Eden, *op. cit.*, pp. 219, 220.
14. Sir Ralph Stevenson to the author.
15. Seale, *op. cit.*, p. 217.
16. Humphrey Trevelyan, *The Middle East in Revolution* (London, 1970) p. 56.
17. Michel Bar Zohar, *Ben Gurion* (Paris, 1966), pp. 249–50.
18. *ibid.*, p. 251; *Jewish Observer*, 18 December 1964, p. 12.
19. Jon Kimche, *Jewish Observer*, 18 December 1964, p. 13.
20. Lieutenant-General E. L. M. Burns, *Between Arab and Israeli* (London, 1962), pp. 18–19.
21. Bar Zohar, *op. cit.*, p. 263.
22. Information received by author from American diplomatic sources in 1955.
23. Bar Zohar, *op. cit.*, p. 265.
24. Sir Ralph Stevenson to the author.
25. Nasser in an interview, *Sunday Times*, 6 November 1955.

26. Trevelyan, *op. cit.*, p. 28.
27. Report from General Burns to Security Council, 5 September 1955, UN Doc. S/3430, 6 September 1955.
28. Burns, *op. cit.*, p. 92.
29. Trevelyan, *op. cit.*, p. 30.
30. BBC Monitoring, Part IV, 7 October 1955, pp. 11–12.
31. Eisenhower, *op. cit.*, p. 25.
32. Trevelyan, *op. cit.*, p. 33.
33. *ibid.*, p. 42.
34. American diplomatic sources to the author in 1955.
35. J. C. Hurewitz, *Diplomacy in the Near and Middle East* (Princeton, 1956), pp. 405–12.
36. Major-General Moshe Dayan, *Diary of the Sinai Campaign* (New York, 1967), p. 12.
37. Documents on International Affairs, 1955, p. 381.
38. Dayan, *op. cit.*, p. 13.
39. Interview, *Observer*, 13 November 1955.
40. Trevelyan, *op. cit.*, pp. 18–22.
41. Eden, *op. cit.*, p. 335.
42. *ibid.*, p. 343.
43. Trevelyan, *op. cit.*, pp. 57–8.
44. Ann Dearden, *Jordan* (London, 1958), pp. 114–18.
45. Eden, *op. cit.*, p. 341.
46. Trevelyan, *op. cit.*, p. 59.
47. Burns, *op. cit.*, pp. 170ff.
48. King Hussein, *Uneasy Lies the Head* (London, 1962), pp. 107ff.; Sir John Bagot Glubb, *A Soldier with the Arabs* (London, 1957), p. 427; Eden, *op. cit.*, pp. 347–8.
49. Nasser to Erskine Childers, BBC, *Suez Ten Years After*, p. 34.
50. Anthony Nutting, *No End of a Lesson* (London, 1967), p. 18.
51. Trevelyan, *op. cit.*, p. 69.
52. Nutting, *op. cit.*, 34–5.
53. Pineau to Peter Calvocoressi, BBC, *Suez Ten Years After*, p. 35.
54. Nasser to Childers, *op. cit.*, p. 37.
55. *New York Herald Tribune, New York Times*, 19 June 1956.
56. Nasser's speech to the Preparatory Committee of the Congress of the National Union, 25 November 1961. See Chapter 12.
57. Trevelyan, *op. cit.*, 73–5.
58. *ibid.*, pp. 86, 89.
59. *ibid.*, pp. 53, 54.
60. Eden, *op. cit.*, pp. 420 *et seq.*
61. *ibid.*, pp. 421–2.

62. Nutting, *op. cit.*, p. 44; Eisenhower, *op. cit.*, pp. 31–2; Dulles Press Conference, 2 April 1957; Herman Finer, *Dulles Over Suez* (Chicago, 1964), pp. 42ff.
63. Dulles Press Conference, 2 April 1957.
64. *ibid.*; Eisenhower, *op. cit.*, pp. 30–33.
65. Kennett Love, interview with Nasser, *Nouvel Observateur*, 26 July 1967.
66. Finer, *op. cit.*, p. 48; Robert Murphy, *Diplomat Among Warriors* (London, 1964), p. 376.
67. Eisenhower, *op. cit.*, p. 33.
68. *The Times*, 25 July 1956.
69. Love, *op. cit.*, p. 4.

Chapter 7. Suez and Sinai, July 1956–May 1957

1. Stewart, *op. cit.*, p. 189; Love, *op. cit.*; Nasser in speech in Alexandria on 26 July 1966, tenth anniversary of Canal Company nationalization; Mohammed Hassanein Heykal, *Al Ahram*, 6 October 1966; Nasser to Erskine Childers, *op. cit.*, pp. 43, 44.
2. Love, *op. cit.*
3. Statement of British, French and US Foreign Ministers on 2 August and tripartite communiqué of 5 August, *Suez Canal Problem*, US State Department, pp. 34, 35, 44.
4. Nasser's statement on 12 August rejecting invitation to first London conference on Suez.
5. Egyptian Proposal for a new Suez Conference, 10 September, *Suez Canal Problem*, pp. 327–30.
6. Dwight D. Eisenhower, *The White House Years*, vol. 2, *Waging Peace 1956–61* (New York, 1965), p. 39 and Appendix B, p. 664, for text of letter.
7. Hugh Thomas, *The Suez Affair* (London, 1967), p. 31.
8. Eden, *op. cit.*, pp. 422–4, 446; Nutting, *op. cit.*, pp. 47–8.
9. Eden, *op. cit.*, p. 424.
10. *ibid.*, p. 463.
11. *Suez Ten Years After*, p. 35.
12. Ben Gurion, *Israel: Years of Challenge* (New York, 1963), p. 104.
13. Report from Arthur Flemming, Director of Office of Mobilization, quoted by Eisenhower.
14. Eisenhower, *Waging Peace*, p. 39.
15. *ibid.*, p. 40.
16. *ibid.*
17. Eden, *op. cit.*, pp. 427–8.
18. Murphy, *op. cit.*, p. 463.

19. Eden, *op. cit.*, pp. 430, 533–5; Thomas, *op. cit.*, pp. 65–6, 75–7, 109; Merry and Serge Bromberger, *Les Secrets de l'Expédition de l'Égypte* (Paris, 1957), pp. 77–9, 90–94.
20. Nasser interview, *Sunday Times*, 24 June 1962.
21. Terence Robertson, *Crisis* (London, 1964), p. 96.
22. *Suez Canal Problem*, p. 39.
23. Speech by Nasser to General Cooperative Conference, 27 November 1958, *Nasser's Speeches*, 1958.
24. Burns, *op. cit.*, pp. 170–71.
25. *Suez Canal Problem*, pp. 289–90.
26. Eden, *op. cit.*, p. 471.
27. Sir Robert Menzies, *Afternoon Light* (London 1967), pp. 163, 164.
28. *Suez Canal Problem*, p. 321.
29. Robertson, *op. cit.*, p. 116.
30. *ibid.*, pp. 117–18.
31. *Suez Canal Problem*, p. 332.
32. Michel Bar Zohar, *Suez, Ultra-Secret* (Paris, 1964), pp. 140 *et seq.* and *Ben Gurion, op. cit.*, p. 286
33. Bar Zohar, *Ben Gurion*, pp. 286–90; Dayan, *op. cit.*, pp. 20, 34.
34. General Beaufre, *L'Expédition de Suez* (Paris, 1967), pp. 101–3.
35. *ibid.*, p. 120.
36. *ibid.*, p. 94.
37. Nutting, *op. cit.*, pp. 90 *et seq.*
38. Dayan, *op. cit.*, p. 28.
39. Burns, *op. cit.*, p. 172.
40. Nutting, *op. cit.*, pp. 81ff.
41. Bar Zohar, *Ben Gurion*, pp. 290–91.
42. Eisenhower, *Waging Peace*, pp. 667–70.
43. Nutting, *op. cit.*, p. 71.
44. Exchange of Notes between the Secretary-General of the UN and the Egyptian Minister of Foreign Affairs, 24 October and 2 November 1956.
45. Nutting, *op. cit.*, p. 78; Eisenhower, *Waging Peace*, p. 55.
46. Robertson, *op. cit.*, p. 145.
47. Nutting, *op. cit.*, pp. 91–2.
48. *ibid.*, p. 93.
49. *ibid.*, pp. 97–8.
50. Beaufre, *op. cit.*, p. 121.
51. Nutting, *op. cit.*, p. 105; Robertson, *op. cit.*, p. 162.
52. Dayan, *op. cit.*, pp. 70, 71.
53. Eisenhower, *Waging Peace*, p. 56.
54. Dayan, *op. cit.*, p. 74.

55. *Suez Ten Years After*, p. 45.
56. Dayan, *op. cit.*, Appendix 3, p. 218.
57. *ibid.*
58. Nasser at Huckstep Barracks, 30 March 1959, *Nasser's Speeches,* 1959.
59. Stewart, *op. cit.*, p. 189.
60. Nasser speech on 22 July 1966, BBC Monitoring ME/2221/A/6.
61. *ibid.*
62. Stewart, *op. cit.*, p. 189.
63. Dayan, *op. cit.*, pp. 110–14.
64. *ibid.*, pp. 100–103; Edgar O'Ballance, *The Sinai Campaign 1956* (London, 1959), pp. 131–6.
65. Robertson, *op. cit.*, pp. 197, 214, 226.
66. Dayan, *op. cit.*, pp. 182–3.
67. Nasser interview, *Sunday Times*, 24 June 1962.
68. See John Erickson, *Suez Ten Years After*, p. 21.
69. Eisenhower, *Waging Peace*, p. 97.
70. Nasser speech on 30 March 1959.
71. Burns, *op. cit.*, p. 203; Eisenhower, *Waging Peace*, p. 94.
72. Thomas, *op. cit.*, p. 147; Eisenhower, *Waging Peace*, p. 98.
73. Burns, *op. cit.*, p. 199.
74. *ibid.*
75. Ben Gurion, *op. cit.*, pp. 119–20.
76. Eisenhower, *Waging Peace*, p. 189.
77. Burns, *op. cit.*, pp. 269, 270.
78. World Jewish Congress pamphlet, March 1957.
79. Dayan, *op. cit.*, p. 125 and Appendix 6, pp. 227–9.
80. *ibid.*, p. 150.
81. Nasser to Erskine Childers, *op. cit.*, p. 57.

Chapter 8. Filling the Vacuum: The Struggle with America, 1957–8

1. *Al Ahram*, 21 December 1965.
2. Eisenhower, *Waging Peace*, Appendix D, pp. 669–70, 680–81.
3. *ibid.*, pp. 181–2.
4. *ibid.*
5. *ibid.*, p. 115.
6. *ibid.*, p. 119.
7. Dearden, *op. cit.*, pp. 125–6. Mrs Dearden, who was in Jordan at the time, writes, 'the sampling of public opinion ... was as genuine as could be'.
8. *ibid.*, p. 126.
9. Hussein, *op. cit.*, pp. 134ff.

10. Seale, *op. cit.*, p. 289.
11. *ibid.*, p. 295.
12. BBC SWB N 682, 17 October 1958; see also Seale, *op. cit.*, p. 299.
13. Eisenhower, *Waging Peace*, pp. 196–204.
14. *ibid.*, p. 197.
15. *ibid.*, p. 199.
16. *ibid.*
17. *ibid.*, pp. 200–201.
18. Gordon H. Torrey, *Syrian Politics and the Military 1945–58* (Ohio, 1964), pp. 331–3.
19. Karanjia, *op. cit.*, quoted in Torrey, *op. cit.*, p. 332.
20. Seale, *op. cit.*, p. 317.
21. *ibid.*, p. 311.
22. *Nasser's Speeches*, 1958, p. 139.
23. *ibid.*, 1959, p. 19; also Seale, *op. cit.*, p. 314, quoting UAR Foreign Minister, Mahmoud Riad.
24. Torrey, *op. cit.*, pp. 377–8.
25. Seale, *op. cit.*, p. 318.
26. *Bourse Égyptienne*, 28 September 1961.
27. *Nasser's Speeches*, 1959, p. 200.
28. *Bourse Égyptienne*, 28 September 1961.
29. Seale, *op. cit.*, p. 323.
30. *Nasser's Speeches*, 1958, pp. 28–33.
31. *ibid.*, p. 27.
32. *ibid.*, pp. 28–45.

Chapter 9. The Syrian Challenge: The Formation of the United Arab Republic, 1958

1. Émile Bustani, 'Can Arab Unity Survive?', *New Statesman*, 5 January 1962, quoted in Abu Jaber, *op. cit.*, p. 48.
2. Torrey, *op. cit.*, pp. 379–80.
3. Malek, *op. cit.*, 269–73.
4. *Nasser's Speeches*, 1958, p. 153.
5. C. L. Sulzberger, *New York Times*, 29 March 1961.
6. *Nasser's Speeches*, 1958, pp. 190–92.
7. M. S. Agwani, *The Lebanese Crisis, A Documentary Study* (Bombay, 1965), p. 48.
8. Charles Thayer, *Diplomat* (London, 1960), p. 61.
9. Eisenhower, *Waging Peace*, p. 265.
10. Murphy, *op. cit.*, p. 492; see also Thayer, *op. cit.*, pp. 54–6.
11. Eisenhower, *Waging Peace*, p. 266.
12. *ibid.*

13. *ibid.*, p. 267.
14. Agwani, *op. cit.*, p. 150.
15. Eisenhower, *Waging Peace*, p. 268.
16. Author's own note of the press conference.
17. Birdwood, *op. cit.*, p. 261.
18. Kassim press conference, 24 March 1959.
19. Eisenhower, *Waging Peace*, p. 270.
20. *ibid.*
21. Thayer, *op. cit.*, p. 80.
22. Eisenhower, *Waging Peace*, p. 278.
23. *Nasser's Speeches*, 1959, p. 174.
24. *ibid.*, 1958, p. 240.
25. *ibid.*, 1959, p. 174 *et seq.*
26. *ibid.*, pp. 223–4.
27. Murphy, *op. cit.*, pp. 504–6.
28. Karanjia, *op. cit.*; *Nasser's Speeches*, 1959, p. 534.
29. *Nasser's Speeches*, 1958, pp. 353–6.
30. *ibid.*, pp. 34–6.
31. *ibid.*, 1959, pp. 120–33.
32. *ibid.*, pp. 159–60.
33. Malek, *op. cit.*, pp. 128, 134.
34. Nasser interview to Dana Adams Schmidt and *New York Times* correspondents, 5 November 1959; *Nasser's Speeches,* 1959.
35. *Nasser's Speeches*, 1960, pp. 1ff.
36. *ibid.*, Part 3, pp. 1ff.
37. Hussein, *op. cit.*, pp. 179–85.

Chapter 10. The 'Sunlit Summit': Nasser on the World Scene, 1958–61

1. Nasser interview, *The Times*, 15 May 1961.
2. Nasser's Speeches, 1960, pp. 7ff.
3. Nasser, *Philosophy of the Revolution*, p. 69.
4. Nasser interview, *Al Ahram*, 30 June 1959; *Nasser's Speeches,* 1959, p. 560.
5. Colin Legum, *Pan Africanism* (London, 1962), p. 40.
6. Catherine Hoskyns, *The Congo Since Independence* (Oxford, 1965), pp. 256–8, on which I have drawn heavily for this section.
7. *Nasser's Speeches*, 1960, Part 3 (speech, 5 October 1960).
8. Nasser, speech to UAR National Assembly, 12 October 1960.
9. Eisenhower, *Waging Peace*, p. 584.
10. Nasser, speech of 5 October 1960.
11. Speech to National Assembly, 12 October 1960.
12. Hoskyns, *op. cit.*, p. 292.

13. Legum, *op. cit.*, pp. 60–61; also *Survey of International Affairs, 1961*, RIIA.

Chapter 11. The Rise and Fall of the UAR, 1958–61

1. A detailed picture of Nasser's dealings with the Baath leaders after the union and of their replies to Nasser's criticism is given in the verbatim minutes of the talks on unity between Egypt, Syria and Iraq in the spring of 1963 which were published in *Al Ahram* in June and July of that year. See Chapter 15.
2. Vatikiotis, *op. cit.*, pp. 104ff.; see also Malek, *op. cit.*, pp. 117–18.
3. Malek, *op. cit.*, p. 118.
4. Nasser interview, *Al Ahram*, 2 July 1959, for exposition of his ideas about the National Union: *Nasser's Speeches*, 1959, pp. 567, 578.
5. O'Brien, *op. cit.*, p. 85.
6. Speech to UAR National Assembly, 21 July 1960; *Nasser's Speeches*, 1960, Part 3, p. 52.
7. See Nasser's speeches on 26 July, 16 October and 25 November 1961, *Bourse Égyptienne*.
8. Nasser's speech on 25 November 1961 to Preparatory Committee of Congress of Popular Forces, *Bourse Égyptienne*.
9. *Nasser's Speeches*, 1960, Part 2, pp. 50–51.
10. O'Brien, *op. cit.*, pp. 107–8.
11. Salah ed-din el Bitar to the author, March 1968.
12. *ibid.*
13. Torrey, *op. cit.*, p. 399.
14. Vatikiotis, *op. cit.*, p. 118.
15. Nasser speech at Latakia, 21 February 1961, *Bourse Égyptienne*.
16. Bitar to the author.
17. *Manchester Guardian*, 29 September 1961.
18. Nasser speech at Cairo University, 2 October 1961, *Bourse Égyptienne*.
19. *Bourse Égyptienne*, 30 September 1961.
20. *ibid.*, 30 September and 2 October 1961.
21. *ibid.*, 30 September 1961.
22. *ibid.*, 2 October 1961.
23. *ibid.*
24. *ibid.*, 6 October 1961.
25. Bitar to the author.

Chapter 12. Arab Socialism and the National Charter, 1961–2

1. *Al Ahram*, 30 November 1961, quoted in Malek, *op. cit.*, p. 182.

2. Malek, *op. cit.*, p. 182.
3. *ibid.*, pp. 183–5.
4. *ibid.*, p. 185.
5. Nasser in unity talks with Syrian and Iraqi leaders in Cairo, 19–21 March 1963. Minutes in *Al Ahram*, 5 July 1963. Translated in BBC SWB ME/1307/E/1–20.

Chapter 13. Developing Egypt: Five-Year Plan and Political System, 1962–7

1. Miles Copeland, *The Game of Nations* (London, 1969), p. 221.
2. M. H. Heykal, *Al Ahram*, 5 April 1968.
3. *Observer*, 3 July 1964.
4. Galil Amin, 'The Egyptian Economy and the Revolution' in *Egypt Since the Revolution*, ed. P. J. Vatikiotis (London, 1968), p. 45.
5. Vice-President Baghdadi in Cairo unity talks, *Al Ahram*, BBC SWB ME/1307/E/13.
6. O'Brien, *op. cit.*, p. 154.
7. Saab, *op. cit.*, p. 188.
8. See also M. Riad el Ghonemy, 'Egyptian Agriculture since 1952' in Vatikiotis (ed.), *op. cit.*, pp. 66ff., who gives a slightly different set of figures.
9. Saab, *op. cit.*, p. 186.
10. Beng Hansen, 'Planning and Economic Growth in the UAR' in Vatikiotis (ed.), *op. cit.*, p. 26.
11. *ibid.*, pp. 30–31.
12. Amin, *op. cit.*, pp. 43–4.
13. Doreen Warriner, *Land Reform and Development*, RIIA, pp. 201–2; also Saab, *op. cit.*, pp. 175ff. and Appendix I.
14. Riad el Ghonemy, *op. cit.*, p. 77.
15. Heykal, *op. cit.*
16. Malek, *op. cit.*
17. Peter Mansfield, *Nasser's Egypt* (Harmondsworth, 1969), rev. edn, p. 139.
18. *ibid.*, p. 141.

Chapter 14. The Yemen War, Arabia and Arab Unity Moves, 1962–3

1. Mohammed Said el Attar, *Le Sous-développement Économique et Sociale du Yémen. Perspective de la Révolution Yéménite* (Algiers, 1964), p. 256.
2. *ibid.*, p. 251.
3. *ibid.*, pp. 251–2.

4. Dana Adams Schmidt, *Yemen, The Unknown War* (London 1968), pp. 22–4.
5. Abdullah Mohammed Nomaan in interview with the author, March 1968.
6. Schmidt, *op. cit.*, p. 25.
7. *ibid.*, pp. 22–3.
8. *ibid.*, p. 33.
9. Attar, *op. cit.*, p. 278.
10. Quoted in *ibid.*, p. 275.
11. Interview with William Attwood, *Look*, 4 March 1968.
12. Schmidt, *op. cit.*, p. 51.
13. *Nasser's Speeches*, 1963, p. 34.
14. Private information to the author, October 1962.
15. Author's private information.
16. Schmidt, *op. cit.*, pp. 75–6.
17. *ibid.*, p. 76.
18. Attar, *op. cit.*, p. 266.
19. *Al Ahram*, 21 June–17 July 1963, BBC SWB ME/1283–1350.
20. *Al Ahram*, in BBC SWB ME/1297/E/3.
21. From private diplomatic sources.
22. Abu Jaber, *op. cit.*, p. 80.
23. *ibid.*, p. 84.

Chapter 15. Arab Conflict and Arab Coexistence: Yemen, Saudi Arabia, the Baathists and the Maghreb, 1964–9

1. Interview, *Observer*, 3 July 1964.
2. *The Times*, 14 May 1964
3. *ibid.*, 21 May 1964.
4. *ibid.*, 25 May 1964.
5. Interview with the author, 3 July 1964.
6. Schmidt, *op. cit.*, p. 225.
7. *ibid.*, p. 27.
8. Nomaan interview with the author, March 1968.
9. *ibid.*
10. Schmidt, *op. cit.*, p. 238.
11. For a detailed summary of the evidence of gas bombing – which the Egyptians denied – see Schmidt, *op. cit.*, pp. 257–73.
12. Most of the foregoing account of the Yemen at this time is taken from eye-witness reports by Schmidt, *op. cit.*, pp. 289–90 and David Holden, *Sunday Times*, 23 April 1967.
13. Mohammed Nasser, 'The Yemen Divided', *Observer Foreign News Service*, 3 May 1968.

Chapter 16. The Arabs, Israel and the Great Powers: The Breakdown of the Peace, 1957–67

1. For example, Theodore Draper, *Israel and World Politics* (New York, 1968).
2. Interview, *Sunday Times*, June 1962.
3. Karanjia, *op. cit.*; *Nasser's Speeches*, 1958, p. 402.
4. Nasser's speech in Damascus, 18 October 1960.
5. Interview with M. H. Heykal, *Al Ahram*, 30 June 1959; *Nasser's Speeches*, 1959, pp. 556–66.
6. *ibid.*
7. Dearden, *op. cit.*, p. 157ff.; see also Georgiana G. Stevens, *The Jordan River Partition* (Stanford, 1965); C. G. Smith, 'Diversion of the Jordan Waters', *The World Today*, November 1966, p. 491ff.: G. H. Jansen, 'The Problem of the Jordan Waters', *The World Today*, February 1964.
8. Smith, *op. cit.*, p. 498.
9. Author's information from French official sources.
10. Text published by UAR Information Department, Cairo, 1962.
11. Arthur M. Schlesinger Jr, *A Thousand Days: John F. Kennedy in the White House* (London, 1965), pp. 493–4.
12. *Middle East Mirror*, vol. 16, no. 4, 25 January 1964.
13. Al Fatah spokesman to the author, March 1968.
14. *Middle East Mirror*, vol. 17, no. 23.
15. *ibid.*, no. 38.
16. Nasser's speech of 23 July 1967, BBC SWB ME/2525/A/1–17.
17. *Middle East Mirror*, vol. 17, no. 48.
18. *ibid.*, vol. 18, no. 11.
19. *New York Times*, 28 May 1966.
20. Interview with Alastair Hetherington, *Guardian*, 18 July 1966.
21. Nasser's speeches of 23 and 26 July 1966 in *Middle East Mirror*, vol. 18, nos. 30 and 31.
22. *Middle East Mirror*, 15 October 1966, vol. 18, no. 42; UN Security Council, Provisional Verbatim Record, 14 October 1966, p. 13; quoted in Draper, *op. cit.*, p. 37 fn.
23. *US News and World Report*, 26 December 1966.
24. See speeches by Foreign Minister Eban on 24 January and 14 February 1967, quoted in Draper, *op. cit.*, p. 50.

Chapter 17. Over the Brink: Syria, UNEF and Aqaba, May–June 1967

1. Speech of 23 July 1967, UAR Information Department.
2. *Middle East Mirror*, vol. 19, no. 15.

3. BBC SWB ME/2473/A/1-6.
4. Nasser's speech, 23 July 1967.
5. *Israel Weekly News Bulletin*, 9-15 May 1967, p. 20.
6. See Michael Howard and Robert Hunter, 'Israel and the Arab World: The Crisis of 1967', Adelphi Papers, no. 41 (London, 1967).
7. For a detailed discussion of these reports, see Walter Lacqueur, *The Road to War* (Harmondsworth, 1969), pp. 87-9. Lacqueur discounts their importance.
8. Draper, *op. cit.*, p. 56.
9. Private information to the author from a reliable UN source.
10. Lacqueur, *op. cit.*, pp. 93-5.
11. James Reston, *New York Times*, 4 and 5 June 1967.
12. Special Report of the Secretary-General, 18 May 1967, UN doc. A/6669.
13. *ibid.*
14. UN press release, EMF/449.
15. General Rikhye to the author, June 1970.
16. Cairo Press Summary of the Egyptian Middle East News Agency, 20 February 1968.
17. Report of the Secretary-General to the Security Council, 26 May 1967, UN doc. S/7806.
18. Nasser's speech of 23 July 1967.
19. BBC SWB ME 2 477/A/3-5.
20. BBC SWB ME/2478/A 17.
21. *Al Ahram*, 6 October 1967.
22. *ibid.*, 21 June 1968.
23. Nasser's speech on 9 June 1967.
24. Lacqueur, *op. cit.*, p. 142.
25. Nasser's speech of 29 May 1967.
26. Private information to the author from French diplomatic sources.
27. Haaretz, 4 June 1967, quoted in Lacqueur, *op. cit.*, p. 176.
28. Charles Yost, *Foreign Affairs*, January 1968.
29. Nasser's speech of 23 July 1967.
30. Private information to the author, see *Observer*, 4 June 1967.
31. Heykal to the author, July 1969.
32. Nasser's speech of 23 July 1967.
33. *Middle East Mirror*, 2 March 1968.
34. Nasser's speech, 23 July 1967.
35. Draper, *op. cit.*, p. 111.
36. Lacqueur, *op. cit.*, p. 160.

Chapter 18. The Six-Day War: 'The Setback', 5–11 June 1967

1. Howard and Hunter, *op. cit.*, p. 30.
2. Heykal in *Al Ahram*, 28 June 1968. See BBC SWB ME/2809/A/1.
3. Heykal, *op. cit.*
4. Heykal, *Al Ahram*, 13 October 1967. BBC SWB ME/2595/A/3.
5. Rouleau, *op. cit.*, p. 120; also, Heykal to the author.
6. Report on trial of Shams ed-din Badran, *Egyptian Gazette*, 27 February 1968.
7. Heykal.
8. Nasser to the author, July 1969.
9. Figures issued to press on 6 and 7 June by David Wood of Institute of Strategic Studies in London.
10. Heykal.
11. *ibid.*
12. Howard and Hunter, *op. cit.*, p. 36.
13. Brigadier Peter Young, *The Israeli Campaign, 1967* (London, 1967), p. 109.
14. Heykal.
15. *Egyptian Mail*, 11 February 1968.
16. Young, *op. cit.*, pp. 110–11.
17. Nasser's speech of 23 November 1967.
18. Nasser's speech to Arab journalists, *Egyptian Gazette*, 16 February 1968.
19. Nasser's speech of 23 November 1967.
20. Rouleau, *op. cit.*, p. 135.
21. Nasser to the author.
22. *The Times*, 10 June 1967.
23. Rouleau, *op. cit.*, pp. 135–6.
24. *ibid.*, p. 136.

Chapter 19. The Aftermath: The Struggle to Recover, 1967–70

1. Nasser's speech at Cairo University, 25 April 1968. BBC SWB ME/2755/A/1–12.
2. Nasser's speech at Helwan, 1 May 1969. BBC SWB ME/3064/A/3.
3. Nasser's speech, 23 July 1967.
4. *Al Ahram*, 4 September 1967.
5. *The Times*, 16 September 1967.
6. *Daily Telegraph*, 22 September 1967.
7. Nasser's speech to the armed forces, 30 April 1968. BBC SWB ME/2738/A/1.
8. BBC SWB ME/3064/A/3.

9. Interview with the author, *Observer*, 20 July 1969.
10. BBC SWB ME/3134/A/1–20.
11. BBC SWB ME/3064/A/3.
12. Interview with the author, July 1969.
13. Gavin Young, 'Young Egypt Warns Nasser', *Observer Foreign News Service*, 10 December 1968.
14. *The Times*, September 1968.
15. To the author; see *The Observer*, 31 December 1967.
16. Private information in June 1969 from a senior Western diplomat who had talks with Nasser in Cairo.
17. The texts of the Soviet–UAR communiqué, the Rogers letter, the Israeli reply and relevant extracts from Nasser's speech are conveniently reprinted together in the October 1970 issue of *Survival*, journal of the Institute of Strategic Studies, London.
18. M. H. Heykal, *Al Ahram*, 16 October 1970. BBC SWB ME/3511/A/1–6.
19. M. H. Heykal, *Al Ahram*, 29 September 1970.
20. *Al Ahram*, 16 October 1970.
21. *ibid.*
22. *ibid.*
23. *Daily Telegraph*, 29 September 1970 and *Guardian*, 2 October 1970.

Chapter 20. Conclusions

1. M. H. Heykal, *Al Ahram*, 12 January 1969, BBC SWB ME/2669/A/1.
2. Warriner, *op. cit.*, p. 189.
3. James Baldwin, *The Fire Next Time* (Harmondsworth, 1964), p. 67.

Select Bibliography

Abbas, Mekki, *The Sudan Question. The Dispute over the Anglo-Egyptian Condominium 1884–1951* (London: Faber & Faber, 1952).

Abdullah, King, *Memoirs*, ed. P. P. Graves (London: Cape, 1950).

Abdul Malek, Anouar, *Egypt: Military Society* (New York: Random House, 1968).

—, *La Pensée Politique Arabe Contemporaine* (Paris: Éditions du Seuil, 1970).

Abdul Nasser, Gamal, *The Philosophy of the Revolution* (Cairo: Ministry of National Guidance, 1954).

—, *Toute la Vérité sur la Guerre de Palestine* (Cairo: Direction des Relations Publiques des Forces Armées, 1955).

—, *Speeches and Interviews*, 1958, 1959, 1960, 1963 (Cairo: Information Department).

Abul Fath, Ahmed, *L'Affaire Nasser* (Paris: Plon, 1962).

Abu Jaber, Kamel S., *The Ba'th Socialist Party* (Syracuse, N.Y.: Syracuse University Press, 1966).

Acheson, Dean, *Present at the Creation* (London: Hamish Hamilton, 1970).

Agwami, M. S., *The Lebanese Crisis. A Documentary Study* (Bombay: Asia Publishing House, 1965).

Ahmed, J. H., *The Intellectual Origins of Egyptian Nationalism* (Oxford: O.U.P., 1960).

Antonius, George, *The Arab Awakening* (London: Hamish Hamilton, 1938).

Amin, Galil, 'The Egyptian Economy and the Revolution' in *Egypt Since the Revolution*, ed. P. J. Vatikiotis (London: Allen & Unwin, 1968).

Attar, Mohammed Said el, *Le Sous-Développement Économique et Social du Yémen, Perspective de la Révolution Yéménite* (Algiers: Éditions Tiers Monde, 1964).

Ayrout, Henri, *Fellahs d'Égypte* (Cairo: Éditions du Sphinx, 1952).

Baer, Gabriel, *A History of Landownership in Modern Egypt, 1800–1950* (Oxford: O.U.P., 1962).

Baldwin, James, *The Fire Next Time* (Harmondsworth: Penguin, 1964).

Barawy, Rashid al, *The Military Coup in Egypt, 1952* (Cairo: Renaissance Bookshop, 1952).

Barbour, Nevill, *Nisi Dominus* (London: Harrap, 1946).

— (ed.), *A Survey of North-West Africa* (The Maghreb), 2nd edn (Oxford: O.U.P., 1962).

Bar Zohar, Michel, *Ben Gurion* (Paris: Fayard, 1966).

—, *Suez Ultra-Secret* (Paris: Fayard, 1964).

Beaufre, General, *L'Expédition de Suez* (Paris: Grasset, 1967).

Behr, Edward, *The Algerian Problem* (Harmondsworth: Penguin, 1961).

Ben Gurion, David, *Israel: Years of Challenge* (New York: Holt Rinehart & Winston, 1963).

Bentwich, Norman, *Israel* (London: Benn, 1952).

Berger, Morroe, *Bureaucracy and Society in Modern Egypt* (Princeton: Princeton University Press, 1957).

Bernadotte, Folke, *To Jerusalem* (London: Hodder & Stoughton, 1951).

Berque Jacques, *Histoire Sociale d'un Village Égyptien au XXme Siècle* (Paris: Mouton, 1957).

—, *L'Égypte, Impérialisme et Révolution* (Paris: Gallimard, 1967).

Birdwood, Lord, *Nuri Es-Said* (London: Cassell, 1959).

Breasted, James Henry, *A History of Egypt from the Earliest Times to the Persian Conquest* (London: Hodder & Stoughton, 1906).

Bromberger, Merry and Serge, *Les Secrets de l'Expédition de l'Égypte* (Paris: Éditions des Quatre Fils Aymon, 1957).

Bullard, Sir Reader, *Britain and the Middle East* (London: Hutchinson, 1951).

— (ed.), *The Middle East: A Political and Economic Survey*, 3rd edn (Oxford: Royal Institute of International Affairs/O.U.P., 1958).

Burns, Lieutenant-General E. L. M., *Between Arab and Israeli* (London: Harrap, 1962).

Burton, J. W. (ed.), *Nonalignment* (London: Deutsch, 1966).

Bustani, Emile, *March Arabesque* (London: Robert Hale, 1961).

Calvocoressi, Peter (ed.), *Suez Ten Years After* (London: BBC, 1966).

Caractacus (pseud.), *Revolution in Iraq* (London: Gollancz, 1959).

Chandos, Lord, *Memoirs* (London: The Bodley Head, 1962).

Childers, Erskine, *The Road to Suez* (London: MacGibbon & Kee, 1962).

Churchill, Winston S., *The Second World War*, Vol. II (London: Cassell, 1949).

Churchill, Winston and Randolph, *The Six-Day War* (London: Heinemann, 1967).

Colombe, Marcel, *L'Évolution de l'Égypte* (Paris: Maisonneuve, 1951).

Copeland, Miles, *The Game of Nations* (London: Weidenfeld & Nicolson, 1969).

Cremeans, Charles D., *The Arabs and the World: Nasser's Arab Nationalist Policy* (New York: Praeger, 1963).

Cromer, Lord, *Modern Egypt*, 2 vols. (London: Macmillan, 1908).

Daumal, J. and M. Leroy, *Gamal Abd-el-Nasser avec ses textes essentiels* (Paris: Seghers, 1967).

Davis, John H., *The Evasive Peace* (London; Murray, 1968).

Dayan, Major-General Moshe, *Diary of the Sinai Campaign* (New York: Schocken, 1967).

Dearden, Ann, *Jordan* (London: Robert Hale, 1958).

de Gaury, Gerald, *Faisal, King of Saudi Arabia* (London: Arthur Barker, 1966).

de Lacy, O'Leary, *A Short History of the Fatimid Khalifate* (London: Kegan Paul, Trench & Trubner, 1923).

Draper, Theodore, *Israel and World Politics* (New York: Viking Press, 1968).

Economic Development in the Middle East, 1945–54 (New York: UN, 1955).

Eden, Anthony, *Full Circle* (London: Cassell, 1960).

Egyptian Government, *Green Book, Records of Conversations, Notes and Papers exchanged March 1950–November 1951* (Cairo: Government Printing Press, 1951).

Eisenhower, Dwight D., *The White House Years*: Vol. I, *Mandate for Change*: Vol. II, *Waging Peace* (New York: Doubleday, 1963–5).

Eytan, Walter, *The First Ten Years, A Diplomatic History of Israel* (London: Weidenfeld & Nicolson, 1958).

Finer, Hermann, *Dulles Over Suez* (Chicago: Quadrangle, 1964).

Forster, E. M., *Alexandria, A History and a Guide* (New York: Doubleday, 1961).

Gardner, Brian, *Allenby* (London: Cassell, 1965).

Ghonemy, M. Riad el, 'Egyptian Agriculture since 1952' in *Egypt Since the Revolution*, ed. P. J. Vatikiotis (London: Allen & Unwin, 1968).

Gibb, H. A. R., *Modern Trends in Islam* (Chicago: Chicago University Press, 1947).

Glubb, Lieutenant-General Sir John Bagot, *A Soldier with the Arabs* (London: Hodder & Stoughton, 1957).

Hakim, Tewfik el, *L'Âme Retrouvée* (French translation from Arabic) (Paris: Bibliothèque Charpentier, Fasquelle, 1937).

Hansen, Bengt, 'Planning and Economic Growth in the UAR (Egypt)' in *Egypt Since the Revolution*, ed. P. J. Vatikiotis (London: Allen & Unwin, 1968).

Heyworth-Dunne, J., *Religious and Political Trends in Modern Egypt* (Washington, D.C.: by the author, 1950).

Hickinbotham, Sir Tom, *Aden* (London: Constable, 1958).

Higgins, Rosemary, *United Nations Peace-Keeping 1946–67* (Oxford: O.U.P., 1969).

Hitti, Philip K., *History of the Arabs* (London: Macmillan, 1956).

Holden, David, *Farewell to Arabia* (London: Faber & Faber, 1966).

Hopkins, Harry, *Egypt, the Crucible* (London: Secker & Warburg, 1969).

Horowitz, David, *State in the Making* (New York: Knopf, 1953).

Hoskyns, Catherine, *The Congo Since Independence* (Oxford: O.U.P., 1965).

Hourani, Albert, *Syria and Lebanon* (Oxford: O.U.P., 1946).

—, *Minorities in the Arab World* (Oxford: O.U.P., 1947).

—, *A Vision of History, Near Eastern and Other Essays* (Beirut: Khayats, 1961).

—, *Arabic Thought in the Liberal Age* (Oxford: O.U.P., 1962).

Howard, Michael, and Robert Hunter, *Israel and the Arab World, The Crisis of 1967*, Adelphi Papers No. 41 (London: Institute of Strategic Studies, 1967).

Hurewitz, J. C., *Diplomacy in the Near and Middle East*, Vol. II, *1914–56* (Princeton: Van Nost, 1956).

Husaini, Ishak Musa, *The Moslem Brethren* (Beirut: Khayats, 1956).

Husry, Khaldun S. al, *Three Reformers, A Study in Modern Arab Political Thought* (Beirut: Khayats, 1966).

Hussein, King, *Uneasy Lies the Head* (London: Heinemann, 1962).

Hutchinson, Commander E., *Violent Truce* (London: Calder, 1956).

Ingrams, Harold, *The Yemen* (London: Murray, 1963).

Ionides, Michael, *Divide and Lose: the Arab Revolt 1955–58* (London: Bles, 1960).

Issawi, Charles, *Egypt in Revolution: an Economic Analysis* (Oxford: O.U.P., 1963).

Jiryis, Sabri, *The Arabs in Israel, 1948–66* (Beirut: Institute for Palestine Studies, 1968).

Johnstone, Charles Hepburn, *The View from Steamer Point* (London: Collins, 1964).

Kedourie, Elie, *The Chatham House Version* (London: Weidenfeld & Nicolson, 1969).

Kerr, Malcolm, *The Arab Cold War, 1958–64*, Chatham House Essays Series (Oxford: O.U.P., 1965).

—, *Islamic Reform: The Political and Legal Theories of Mohammed Abduh and Rashid Rida* (Cambridge: C.U.P., 1967).

Khadduri, Majid, *Independent Iraq, 1932–58*, 2nd edn (Oxford: O.U.P., 1960).

—, *Republican Iraq* (Oxford: O.U.P., 1970).

Khalidi, Ahmed Samih el, *The Arab–Israeli War 1967* (Beirut: 1969).

Khouri, Fred J., *The Arab–Israeli Dilemma* (Syracuse, N.Y.: Syracuse University Press, 1968).

Kimche, Jon and David, *Both Sides of the Hill* (London: Secker & Warburg, 1960).

King, Gillian, *Imperial Outpost, Aden*, Chatham House Essays Series (Oxford: O.U.P., 1964).

Kirk, George, *The Middle East in the War, 1939–46* and *The Middle East, 1945–50* (Oxford: Royal Institute of International Affairs/ O.U.P., 1952–4).

Kirkbride, Alec Seath, *A Crackle of Thorns* (London: Murray, 1956).

Lacouture, Jean, *Cinq Hommes et la France* (Paris: Éditions du Seuil, 1961).

—, *Nasser* (Paris: Éditions du Seuil, 1971).

—, *Quatre Hommes et leurs Peuples* (Nasser, Bourguiba, Sihanouk, Nkrumah) (Paris: Éditions du Seuil, 1969).

—, and Simone Lacouture, *Egypt in Transition* (London: Methuen, 1958).

— and J. F. Held and Eric Rouleau, *Israel et les Arabes, Troisième Combat* (Paris: Éditions du Seuil, 1967).

Lacqueur, Walter Z., *Communism and Nationalism in the Middle East* (London: Routledge & Kegan Paul, 1956).

—, *The Road to War* (Harmondsworth: Penguin, 1969).

Landau, Jacob M., *The Arabs in Israel* (Oxford: O.U.P., 1969).

Lawrence, T. E., *The Seven Pillars of Wisdom* (London: Cape, 1935).

Le Groupe d'Études de l'Islam, *L'Égypte Indépendante* (Paris: Paul Hartman, 1937).

Legum, Colin, *Pan Africanism* (London: Pall Mall, 1962).

Lewis, Bernard, *The Arabs in History* (London: Hutchinson, 1950).

Little, Tom, *High Dam at Aswan* (London: Methuen, 1965).

—, *Modern Egypt* (London: Benn, 1968).

Little, Tom, *South Arabia* (London: Pall Mall, 1968).

Lloyd, Lord, *Egypt Since Cromer*, 2 vols. (London: Macmillan, 1934).

Longrigg, Stephen, *Oil in the Middle East*, 2nd edn (Oxford: O.U.P., 1961).

—, *Iraq, 1900–1950* (Oxford: O.U.P., 1953).

Love, Kennett, *Suez, the Twice-Fought War* (New York: McGraw-Hill, 1969).

Macmillan, Harold, *Tides of Fortune* (London: Macmillan, 1969).

—, *Riding the Storm, 1956–1959* (London: Macmillan, 1971).

Makarius, Raoul and Laura, *Anthologie de la Littérature Arabe Contemporaine*, Vol. I (Paris: Éditions du Seuil, 1964).

Mansfield, Peter, *Nasser's Egypt*, rev. edn (Harmondsworth: Penguin, 1969).

Marlowe, John, *Anglo-Egyptian Relations, 1800–1953* (London: Cass, 1954).

—, *Arab Nationalism and British Imperialism* (London: Cresset, 1961).

—, *The Seat of Pilate* (London: Cresset, 1959).

McBride, Barrie St Clair, *Farouk of Egypt* (London: Robert Hale, 1967).

Menzies, Sir Robert, *Afternoon Light* (London: Cassell, 1966).

Monroe, Elizabeth, *The Mediterranean in Politics* (Oxford: O.U.P., 1938).

—, *Britain's Moment in the Middle East, 1914–1956* (London: Chatto & Windus, 1963).

Morris, James, *Sultan in Oman* (London: Faber & Faber, 1957).

—, *The Hashemite Kings* (London: Faber & Faber, 1959).

Murphy, Robert, *Diplomat Among Warriors* (London: Collins, 1964).

Nasser, Gamal Abdul, see Abdul Nasser.

Neguib, Mohammed, *Egypt's Destiny* (London: Gollancz, 1955).

Nutting, Anthony, *No End of a Lesson* (London: Constable, 1967).

O'Ballance, Edgar, *The Sinai Campaign, 1956* (London: Faber & Faber, 1959).

—, *The War in the Yemen* (London: Faber & Faber, 1971).

O'Brien, Patrick, *The Revolution in Egypt's Economic System* (Oxford: O.U.P., 1966).

Pannikar, K. M., *Asia and Western Dominance*, 2nd edn (London: Allen & Unwin, 1959).

Peretz, Don, *Israel and the Palestine Arabs* (Washington, D.C.: Middle East Institute, 1958).

Perlmutter, Amos, *The Military and Politics in Israel* (New York: Praeger, 1969).

Polk, William R,. *A Decade of Discovery: America in the Middle East, 1944-58*, St Antony's Papers No. 11 (London: Chatto & Windus, 1961).

Reilly, Sir Bernard, *Aden and the Yemen* (London: H.M.S.O., 1960).

Rifaat, Bey M., *The Awakening of Modern Egypt* (London: Longmans, 1947).

Robertson, Terence, *Crisis* (London: Hutchinson 1964).

Rondot, Pierre, *The Changing Patterns of the Middle East, 1919-1958* (London: Chatto & Windus, 1962).

Rowlatt, Mary, *Founders of Modern Egypt* (Bombay: Asia Publishing House, 1962).

Royal Institute of International Affairs, *Great Britain and Egypt, 1914-1951*, Information Papers No. 19 (London, 1952).

—, *British Interests in the Mediterranean and Near East* (London, 1957).

—, *Surveys of International Affairs; Documents on International Affairs.*

Saab, Gabriel, *The Egyptian Agrarian Reform, 1952-62* (Oxford: O.U.P., 1967).

es- Sadat, Anwar *Revolt on the Nile* (London: Wingate, 1957).

St John, Robert, *The Boss* (London: Arthur Barker, 1961).

Schlesinger, Arthur M., Jr, *A Thousand Days: John F. Kennedy in the White House* (London: Deutsch, 1965).

Schmidt, Dana Adams, *Yemen, The Unknown War* (London: The Bodley Head, 1968).

Schwartz, Walter, *The Arabs in Israel* (London: Faber & Faber, 1959).

Scott, Hugh, *In the High Yemen* (London: Murray, 1942).

Seale, Patrick, *The Struggle for Syria* (Oxford: O.U.P., 1965).

Shah, Ikbal Ali, *Fuad, King of Egypt* (London: Herbert Jenkins, 1936).

Sorensen, Theodore C., *Kennedy* (London: Hodder & Stoughton, 1965).

Stevens, Georgiana G., *The Jordan River Partition* (Stanford, Calif.: Stanford University Press, 1965).

Stevens, Richard P., *American Zionism and U.S. Foreign Policy* (New York: Pageant Press, 1962).

Stewart, Desmond, *Young Egypt* (London: Wingate, 1958).

—, *Turmoil in Beirut* (London: Wingate, 1958).

Sykes, Christopher, *Cross Roads to Israel* (London: Collins, 1965).

Syrian Government Ministry of Information, *Syrie Deux Ans Après la Révolution* (Damascus, 1965).
—, *Programme du Parti Baas* (Damascus, 1965).

Thayer, Charles, *Diplomat* (London: Michael Joseph, 1960).
Thomas, Hugh, *The Suez Affair* (London: Weidenfeld & Nicolson, 1967).
Tibawi, A. C., *A Modern History of Syria, including Lebanon and Palestine* (London: Macmillan, 1969).
Torrey, Gordon H., *Syrian Politics and the Military, 1945–58* (Ohio State University Press, 1964).
Trevelyan, Humphrey, *The Middle East in Revolution* (London: Macmillan, 1970).
Twitchell, K. S., *Saudi Arabia*, 2nd edn (Princeton: Princeton University Press, 1953).

US State Department, *The Suez Canal Problem* (Washington, D.C., 1957).

Vatikiotis, P. J., *The Egyptian Army in Politics* (Indiana University Press, 1961).
—, *A Modern History of Egypt* (London: Weidenfeld & Nicolson, 1969).
—, *Politics and the Military in Jordan* (London: Cass, 1969).
— (ed.), *Egypt Since the Revolution* (London: Allen & Unwin, 1968).
Vaucher, Georges, *Gamal Abdul Nasser et Son Équipe*, 2 vols. (Paris: Juillard, 1959).

Warriner, Doreen, *Land Reform and Development in the Middle East* (Oxford: O.U.P., 1962).
Watt, D. C., *Britain and the Suez Canal* (London: Royal Institute of International Affairs, 1956).
—, *Documents on the Suez Crisis, 26 July to 6 November 1956* (London: Royal Institute of International Affairs, 1957).
Weizmann, Chaim, *Trial and Error* (London: Hamish Hamilton, 1949).
Wheelock, Keith, *Nasser's New Egypt* (London: Stevens, 1960).
Wilson, Henry Maitland (Lord), *Eight Years Overseas* (London: Hutchinson, 1950).
Wint, Guy, and Peter Calvocoressi, *Middle East Crisis* (Harmondsworth: Penguin, 1957).
Wynn, Wilton, *Nasser of Egypt* (Cambridge, Mass.: Arlington, 1959).

Young, Brigadier Peter, *The Israeli Campaign 1967* (London: Kimber, 1968).

Youssef Bey, Amine, *Independent Egypt* (London: Murray, 1940).

Zeine, Zeine N., *Arab–Turkish Relations and the Emergence of Arab Nationalism* (Beirut: Khayats, 1958).

—, *The Struggle for Arab Independence* (Beirut: Khayats, 1960).

Periodicals, Newspapers, etc.

The BBC Summary of World Broadcasts, Part IV, Middle East and Africa; *Chronology of Arab Politics* (Beirut, 1963); *The Mid-East Mirror* (Beirut); *Arab Report and Record* (London); *Middle East Forum* (Beirut); *Jewish Observer and Middle East Review* (London); *The New Middle East* (London); *The Middle East Journal* (Washington, D.C.); *Orient* (Paris); *Oriente Moderno* (Rome); *The Israel Weekly Digest* (Jerusalem); *The Arab Chronicle* (London); *The Arab Observer* and *The Scribe* (Cairo); *Al Fatah* (Beirut); *Egyptian Mail and Gazette*; *La Bourse Égyptienne*; *Al Ahram*; *Al Mussawar*; *Jerusalem Post*; *Iraq Times*; *Baghdad Observer*; *The Times*; *New York Times*; *Guardian*; *Observer*; *Sunday Times*; *Le Monde*.

Index

438; effect of Six-Day War on morale of, 511; Nasser holds balance between left and right in, 541–2; assessment of Nasser's role as leader of anti-colonial revolution in, 560–80

Arabi Pasha, Col, 13, 14, 15, 25, 41, 42, 116

Arafat, Yasir, 519, 553, 554, 555

Aref, Col Abdul Salam (of Iraq), as deputy premier, 289; pro-Nasser policy of, 294; arrested by Kassim, 295; leads army *coup* against Kassim, 301, 399; and becomes President, 401; heads all military revolutionary council, 409; overthrown by Hassan Baqr, 540; mentioned, 286, 291, 411, 413

Aref, Brigadier Abdul Rahman, 409

El Arish, Egyptian base at, 82, 225, 231, 232, 495, 496, 501

Arms Control, Tripartite Declaration on (1950), 93, 154, 157, 167

Army Officers' Club (Cairo), 98, 103, 104

'Army of National Liberation' (Egypt), 209

Asaly, Sabri el, 264, 333

Asnag, Abdullah al, 384, 424

Al Assifa ('Lightning': military arm of Al Fatah), 453

Assiut (Egypt), 21, 23, 26, 376

Aswan Dam, hydro-electric power station at, 187

Aswan High Dam, financial and political factors in building of, 170–73; Sudanese-Eyptian dispute over Nile waters and, 171, 172, 309; Soviet Union offer to finance and help build, 172, 296, 299–300, 307, 310, 569; Western doubts about financing, 189–90; and USA withdraws offer, 193, 196, 254, 325; inauguration of (1964), 412–13; mentioned, 129, 179, 188, 335, 356, 367, 368, 530, 531, 562, 567, 574, 580

A S U *see* Arab Socialist Union

Atassi, Dr Nureddin el, 459

El Attarin secondary school, Alexandria, 29

El Auja demilitarized zone, 82, 83, 166, 231

Al Azhar, Sheikh of, 46

Al Azhar university, Cairo, 30, 53, 376

Azhari, Ismail el, 131, 171–2

Aziz, Col Abdul, 74

Azm, Khaled el, 264

Baath movement, party (in Iraq), 294, 399, 401, 402–5, 408–9; in Jordan, 259; national command in Lebanon, 379

Baath movement, party (in Syria), conflict between Nasser and, 253, 322, 333–4, 337, 379, 407–8, 411, 443, 454,

563, 574; and alternative ideologies of Nasserism and, 270–71; favours union between Syria and Egypt, 271–6; growing tension between Sarraj and, 337–9; reaction to break-up of UAR by, 342; 'unity' talks between Nasser and, 402–5; rivalries within, 467–8, 411, 540; encourages Arab revolutionary movements, 451–2; neo-Marxist wing takes over government (1966), 459; mentioned, 135, 151, 178, 256, 264, 265, 269, 469

Baban, Ahmed Mukhtar, 265

Badr, Crown Prince Mohammed al (of Yemen), 383, 386, 387–8, 415, 419

Badran, Shams ed-din, 361, 483, 489, 514

Bagdash, Khaled, 264, 272

Baghdad, 144, 286, 290

Baghdad Pact, signing of, 144, 151; Nasser's opposition to, 148, 158, 169, 179, 181, 252, 270; and Israeli reaction to, 156, 162, 169; conflict over Jordan joining, 170, 173–6; effect in Arab world of, 177–8; Council meeting in Teheran of, 183; West abandons extension of, 188; French opposition to, 198; discussion of Lebanese civil war by, 285; Iraqi suspicions of, 287; and withdrawal from 291; mentioned, 152, 161, 168, 184, 255, 258, 262, 266, 571

Baghdadi, Wing-Commander Abdul Latif, 39, 74–5, 90, 104, 120, 123, 132, 323, 359, 360, 385

Bahrein, Arab Sheikhdom of, 421

Bakhoury, Sheikh Ahmed Hassan el, 119

Baldwin, Roger, 155

Balfour, Lord, 438

Balfour Declaration (1917), 14, 85

Bandung Conference (1955), 148, 158, 309, 310, 311

Banna, Sheikh Hassan el, 34, 52, 57, 89

Baqr, Hassan, 540

Barawy, Dr Rashid al, 114

Bat Galim (Israeli ship), incident over, 153–4, 155

Beidhani, Abdur-rahman al, 386, 388, 407

Beigin, Menahem, 486, 529, 548

Beirut, 16, 52, 288

Belgium, 308, 311, 312, 393

Belgrade conference of non-aligned nations (1961), 302, 303, 319–20, 357

Ben Barka, 406

Ben Bella, Ahmed, 318, 356, 378, 406, 411, 413, 454

Ben Gurion, David, 'Lavon affair' and, 154; authorizes attack on Gaza, 155, 156; importance of Negev to, 163–4;

614   Index

ideas on, 12–13; failure of Arabi revolt in, 13–14, 25, 41; effect of First World War on, 14; Zaghloul Pasha founds Wafd party in, 15; and 1919 Revolution, 15, 17, 25, 63, 350; development of Arab nationalism in, 15–16; political and social structure under British rule of, 24–5; conflicts over 1923 independence declaration and constitution for, 26–8, 34, 35; and clash of cultures and manners in, 30–31; Fuad I's dictatorship of, 31, 33; nationalistic groups in, 33–4; return to parliamentary government in (1935), 35–6; and Farouk succeeds to throne, 36, 45–6; 1936 military treaty between Britain and, 36–7, 39, 40, 51, 63, 64, 68, 69, 71, 87, 91; role of army in, 41–3, 66; economic and social conditions in. 44–5; and social hierarchy, 45–6; and new middle class in, 46–7; attitude to European imperialism in, 47–8; Farouk dismisses Wafd (1937), 50; and Aly Maher leads 'palace' government, 50–51; abortive army conspiracies in, 51–3, 57–8; pro-Axis sympathies in, 53, 54, 57; breaks off relations with Vichy France, 54; Abdin Palace coup of British, 54–6, 64; nationalists' demands, 58–9; and postwar wave of revolution in, 63–6; Nasser organizes secret army movement in, 66–8; negotiations fail for withdrawal of British troops, 68–73; anger over Palestine Partition, 73–4; and Palestine War (1948–9), 74–84; riots against Jews and Europeans in, 88–9; and government reprisals against Muslim Brothers, 89; Nasser reorganizes secret army network in, 89–90; Wafd party returned to power, 90–91; and Wafd corruption, 91–2; crisis over British military base in, 93–6; and abrogation of 1936 Treaty, 96–7; British seize control of Canal Zone, 97–8; struggle between Farouk and Free Officers in, 98–9; 'Black Saturday' riots in, 100–102, 109; Farouk's manoeuvres, 102–3; and Free Officers' coup (1952), 103–8; Farouk abdicates, 108; problems facing new regime in, 109–10; Free Officers emerge as ruling élite of, 110–11; and Nasser's political aims for, 111–14; agrarian reform in, 114–18, 137; Council of the Revolution replaces old party system in, 118–21; and power structure of new regime, 122–3; Nasser wins struggle for power against Neguib, 123–8; and eliminates Muslim Brothers' opposition, 123, 124, 125,

135–6, 155; settlement with Britain over Sudan, 129–31; and over Canal Zone military base, 131–5; foreign aid to, 135, 140, 142, 146, 188; regime's lack of economic ideology, 137–8; foreign policy of, 140–45; and arms expenditure, 140, 141, 142, 143, 157; role in Arab world of, 141–2, 144–5; opposing pressure of nationalists and Western Powers on, 142–3; neutralist policy of, 147–9, 158; conflicting foreign policies of Iraq v., 149–51; Israel raids Gaza strip, 151–2, 155–7; and blockade of Israeli ships by, 153–4; 'Lavon affair' in, 154–5; arms race between Israel and, 157–62, 169–70; and growing tension, 165–7; Anglo-American peace initiatives to, 162–5, 167–9; help to Algerian nationalists by, 169, 253; Aswan High Dam loan negotiations, 170–73, 179, 189–91; Sudan declares independence of, 171–2; opposition to Baghdad Pact by, 173–6, 177–8, 270; cease-fire between Israel and, 178, 189, 217; last British troops leave, 179, 184; Nasser prepares draft of new constitution for, 179; Glubb's dismissal and, 179–81; British tougher policy towards, 181–3; recognition of Communist China by, 183–4, 190; Nasser elected first President of Republic of (1956), 184, 185; new constitution for, 184–6; Nasser's relationship to public in, 187; and his achievements (by 1956), 178–8; and international position, 188–9; value of Suez Canal Co. to, 192–3; USA withdraws offer of loan for High Dam in, 193–4, 254; and nationalization of Canal Co. by, 194–7; and crisis over, 198–215, 217, 220–21; France, Israel and Britain plan attack on, 215–17, 218, 219, 220, 221–2, 223; disposition and strength of military forces of, 225, 246; outbreak and progress of Sinai War (1956), 226–8, 231–2, 233–4; rejects Franco-British ultimatum, 228–9; and Suez operation, 229–31, 233, 234–7; agrees to cease-fire by UNEF, 232, 234; problems of withdrawal of foreign troops and re-opening of Canal in, 237–45; policy of 'Egyptianization' in, 245–6, 326, 437; consequences of Suez-Sinai War in, 246–7; Nasser's engagement in Arab Revolution, 251–4; Eisenhower Doctrine and, 256–8, 268; and Jordan crisis (1957), 259, 261, 262, 267, 268; cold war between USA and, 261–3; Syria demands union with, 268–9; rivalry in Arab world between Baath and, 270; and advantages of